Lecture Notes in Computer Scienc

T0238184

Commenced Publication in 1973
Founding and Former Series Editors:
Gerhard Goos, Juris Hartmanis, and Jan van Leeuwen

Peter van den Besselaar   Satoshi Koizumi (Eds.)

Digital Cities III

Information Technologies for Social Capital:
Cross-cultural Perspectives

Third International Digital Cities Workshop
Amsterdam, The Netherlands, September 18-19, 2003
Revised Selected Papers

 Springer

Volume Editors

Peter van den Besselaar
Royal Netherlands Academy of Arts and Sciences
Department of Social Sciences, NIWI
P.O. Box 95110, 1090 HC Amsterdam, The Netherlands
and
University of Amsterdam
Amsterdam School of Communication Research ASCoR
The Netherlands
E-mail: p.a.a.vandenbesselaar@uva.nl

Satoshi Koizumi
Japan Science and Technology Agency
Digital City Research Center
Kyoto, Japan
E-mail: satoshi@digitalcity.jst.go.jp

Library of Congress Control Number: 2005902216

CR Subject Classification (1998): K.4, C.2, H.4, H.5.2-3, K.8, I.2, J.4

ISSN   0302-9743
ISBN-10   3-540-25331-9 Springer Berlin Heidelberg New York
ISBN-13   978-3-540-25331-0 Springer Berlin Heidelberg New York

Springer is a part of Springer Science+Business Media

springeronline.com

© Springer-Verlag Berlin Heidelberg 2005
Printed in Germany

Typesetting: Camera-ready by author, data conversion by Boller Mediendesign
Printed on acid-free paper   SPIN: 11407546   06/3142   5 4 3 2 1 0

Preface

Digital cities constitutes a multidisciplinary field of research and development, where researchers, designers and developers of communityware interact and collaborate with social scientists studying the use and effects of these kinds of infrastructures and systems in their local application context.

The field is rather young. After the diffusion of ICT in the world of organizations and companies, ICT entered everyday life. And this also influenced ICT research and development. The 1998 Workshop on Communityware and Social Interaction in Kyoto was an early meeting in which this emerging field was discussed. After that, two subsequent Digital Cities workshops were organized in Kyoto, and a third one in Amsterdam.

This book is the result of the 3rd Workshop on Digital Cities, which took place September 18–19, 2003 in Amsterdam, in conjunction with the 1st Communities and Technologies Conference. Most of the papers were presented at this workshop, and were revised thoroughly afterwards. Also the case studies of digital cities in Asia, the US, and Europe, included in Part I, were direct offsprings of the Digital Cities Workshops. Together the papers in this volume give an interesting state-of-the-art overview of the field.

In total 54 authors from the Americas, from Asia, and from Europe were contributed to this volume. The authors come from Brazil (two), the USA (eleven), China (three), Japan (fourteen), Finland (two), Germany (two), Italy (three), Portugal (two), the Netherlands (eight), and the UK (seven), indicating the international nature of the research field.

This volume is organized as follows: It starts with an introductory chapter which briefly describes the developments and challenges of digital cities research. The introduction also summarizes the papers included in this volume. The eight chapters in Part I present a series of in-depth case studies of digital cities and community networks, showing the commonalities and differences in experiments from all over the world. The last chapter in this part is an effort to compare the cases. Part II of the book consists of four chapters, each proposing a specific design of a platform for digital cities and virtual communities. Part III focuses on data and knowledge modeling approaches for community systems. In Part IV, issues of participation and design are discussed, as well as systems for monitoring the use of community systems. This part concludes with a chapter on the relations between real space and media space. Part V focuses on experiments with the use of information and communication technologies for improving local social capital in very different contexts. Four chapters discuss small and large experiments in different countries, urban as well as rural ones.

We are grateful to the members of the Program Committee, to the reviewers, and of course to the participants, who all contributed very much to the success of the workshop. Last but not least, we want to thank our sponsors who made the workshop possible, in particular the Social Sciences Department of NIWI, Royal Netherlands

Academy of Arts and Sciences, the Center of Excellence on the Knowledge Society at Kyoto University, and the Japan Science and Technology Corporation.

December 2004

Peter van den Besselaar
Satoshi Koizumi

Organization

Workshop Chairs

Peter van den Besselaar   Social Sciences Department, NIWI-KNAW,
Royal Netherlands Academy of Arts and Sciences,
&
Amsterdam School of Communications Research, ASCoR,
University of Amsterdam

Satoshi Koizumi   Digital City Research Center, Japan Science and
Technology Corp.

Program Committee

Jun-ichi Akahani   NTT Communication Science Laboratory, Japan
Allesandro Aurigi   University of Newcastle, UK
Fiorella De Cindio   University of Milan, Italy
Noshir Contractor   University of Illinois, USA
Vanessa Evers   University of Amsterdam, The Netherlands
Toru Ishida   Kyoto University, Japan
Satoshi Koizumi   Digital City Research Center, JST Corp, Japan
Peter Mambrey   Fraunhofer Gesellschaft and Duisburg University,
Germany
Carolien Metselaar   City of Amsterdam, The Netherlands
Douglas Schuler   Evergreen State College, USA
Sheng HuanYe   Shanghai Jiao Tong University, China
Peter van den Besselaar   Royal Netherlands Academy of Arts and Sciences,
The Netherlands

Sponsors

Social Sciences Department, NIWI-KNAW, Royal Netherlands Academy of Arts and
Sciences, The Netherlands
Center of Excellence on the Knowledge Society, Kyoto University, Japan
Japan Science and Technology Corporation, Japan

Table of Contents

Part III   Knowledge and Data Modeling for Digital Cities

Part IV   Participation, Design, Monitoring

Part V   ICT and Social Capital

Local Information and Communication Infrastructures: An Introduction

Peter van den Besselaar

Social Sciences Department, NIWI, Royal Netherlands Academy of Arts and Sciences
P.O. Box 95110, 1090 HC Amsterdam, the Netherlands
&
Amsterdam School of Communication Research, ASCoR, University of Amsterdam
p.a.a.vandenbesselaar@uva.nl

Abstract. The ICT revolution has had a considerable impact on the city: It has affected the urban economy, the global urban networks, various dimensions of urban life, and social divides within cities. In this introduction we discuss some of the effects of ICTs on the city, to put *Digital Cities* experiments into social context. Next, we describe the diversity of existing local ICT infrastructures, followed by a summary of this volume. The 26 chapters give a broad overview of some ten years of experimenting with and research on digital cities. We conclude with a few observations about the research field.

1 Information Technology and the City

The chapters in this book describe and analyze a large variety of digital city experiments that have been carried out during the last decade. This diversity reflects that technological systems are *socially shaped*: the technologies, methods and applications are all developed in local situations by specific actors with different aims [37]. In other words, local ICT infrastructures are socio-technical systems, and the development, use and effects are heavily influenced by *local* organizational and social factors [20, 21]. At the same time we are living in an increasingly *globalizing* world, and therefore share the same global environment. Before discussing the different perspectives on digital cities in the next section, we will first discuss some of these social developments, in order to put digital cities research and experiments into context.

Cities are depended on infrastructures: The larger the city, the stronger the dependence. Examples of this reliance include the water supply system, the sewer system, the electrical power system, and transport systems. The streetcar [42] and the automobile [32] have heavily influenced urban structures and processes. . Scholars have also recognized that information and communication are crucial in urban life, and some have conceptualized cities as information processing systems [9, 27]. Apart from transport, it is communication technologies that have enabled the growth of cities, and the differentiation of urban structure (the emergence of suburbs or functional zoning). More recently, the political and scholarly debates have extended from the quality and maintenance of existing urban infrastructures to the impacts of new ICTs on urban and regional change [11, 25, 47]. Five dimensions of the

P. van den Besselaar and S. Koizumi (Eds.): Digital Cities 2003, LNCS 3081, pp. 1-16, 2005.

relationship between ICTs and the city emerge from these debates: the geography of structural economic change; the changing meaning of distance; globalization and urban competition; the rise of local technology policies; and changes in social integration and inequality.

The geography of structural economic change. The economic crisis of the late 1970s and the early 1980s marked the transition of the industrial society to the information society. In terms of the neo-Schumpeterian *long waves theory* of economic development, the mature 'old' industries and technologies had lost much of their innovative capacity and therefore of their growth potential: e.g., car industry, chemical industry, electro-technical industry. New technologies, leading to new dynamic industries, were needed to get the economy in a new, extended 'upswing' [7]. The required structural changes in the economy did indeed occur around what was called in those days *micro-electronics* – a new set of technologies with pervasive effects throughout the economy and society. Since then, economic growth has been strongly related to the development of ICT. It has led to new economic activities, and at the same time it revolutionized existing industries. Companies producing or heavily using ICTs were indeed growing much faster than other companies [8]. Additionally, the geographical dimension of the changes in the economic structure were becoming an issue, as the new ICT producing industries were not always situated in the same region as the old ones [14].

The meaning of distance. An old theme in the discussion about the social effects of ICTs is the prediction of the end of geography. Modern telecommunication technologies with increasing bandwidth would enable us to work from any location, and at the same time would allow for other everyday activities such as e-shopping, e-learning, and e-healthcare. The role of proximity in physical space and face-to-face communication would decline and gradually be replaced by various forms of *telepresence* and *virtual organizations.* Dematerialization of production would reinforce this tendency. In the e-society, concentrations of resources and people in cities would lose its meaning, resulting in the dissolution of cities and the emergence of the global village. A further 'disurbanization' was expected to occur, deepening the already existing urban crisis.

This, however, did not happen. Around the mid 1980s, the negative spiral of the urban crisis reversed, and cities actually increased their roles as economic, cultural and knowledge centers. Since then, quite some observers have argued that face-to-face communication is indispensable for creativity and innovation, the main resources of the knowledge economy.

The geography of the Internet, and of telecommunication networks in general, point in the same direction. Network capacity is distributed very unequally on the global level, on the national level, and also on the level within cities [39, 47]. The new industries producing ICTs (for example, the content industry and the multimedia industry) are actually highly concentrated in specific metropolitan areas, and these areas have by far the highest density of advanced networks. The same holds for the heavy users of ICTs, such as the financial sector, and there is little indication that this trend is reversing in the network society [5]. Modern theory of network dynamics may explain why this concentration takes place [1, 3, 43]: Concentrations of companies, which heavily use network capacity, result in high investments in networks in those areas, which in turn attracts even more companies that require this infrastructure.

Globalization and competition between cities. If concentration instead of dispersion is the dominant trend, advanced urban telecommunication infrastructure becomes of utmost importance. Through investing in a high-tech telecommunication infrastructure, municipalities had hoped to improve their position in the new economic landscape. The goal was to attract new and growing high-tech and creative industries, mainly in hardware and software, communication, media, business and financial services – all of which are highly depend on the new information technologies.

ICT did not result in the disappearance of geography, but it did contribute to the globalization of the economy. Modern ICTs are reshaping the global economy and its geographical dimension, resulting in a network society that functions as a space of flows [4, 5]. ICTs make companies more 'footloose', and enable them to move globally between cities and regions. The choice of settlement, while remaining dynamic, is based on differences between local conditions. Depending on the local opportunities for making profits, parts of the world are connected to or disconnected from this space of flows [4, 5, 11, 31]. The network society differs from the earlier industrial society, in that the centers of the international system are less fixed, but are flexibly determined from the perspective of the global system. However, as path dependency with its positive feedback mechanisms plays an important role [1], cities have to compete more than ever for their position in the global network.

Local technology policies. It is generally accepted that the availability of an advanced ICT infrastructure is a necessary condition for 'being connected'. In the early 1980s, cities and towns started to formulate their local technology policies, and concepts such as *teleport* and *telecity* became increasingly popular. A central metropolitan teleport was needed to connect the urban business districts, through a high capacity network and dish aerials, to satellite systems. Over the years, the idea of what counts as an appropriate communication network evolved from a centralized glass fiber telecommunication network between business districts via the introduction of the Internet, to an up-to-date glass fiber broadband network to every single office, house and apartment in the city. As return on investments in the existing networks is still below the initial expectations, private companies are not very eager to invest in an even newer generation of networks. Consequently, and despite the dominant market ideology, municipalities increasingly take a leading role in the development of the local broadband infrastructure.

However, it is not only the infrastructure itself that counts, but also the deployment of the network. Here the local e-government agenda becomes relevant, as this is considered a main instrument for integrating ICTs in urban life. By stimulating e-government, citizens (in their role as consumer) get used to electronic service delivery. This also reduces computer illiteracy, and contributes to the required critical mass for markets of e-services. E-government is also expected to improve service delivery to companies, citizens and tourists, enhancing the quality of the local environment. Finally, e-government is expected to contribute to new and more flexible forms of governance, and this makes government more responsive to the demands of modern volatile economy and society.

Of course, ICTs alone are not enough, as the knowledge economy also needs high level transport systems, first-rate institutions for research and education, the availability of a high skilled labor force, and a computer literate population. In addition, an excellent quality of living is needed to attract high skilled professionals for the advanced parts of the economy; ICTs, by the way, are increasingly applied to improve these urban qualities [46].

Social integration and urban inequality. Not only does global competition result into an increasing inequality between world cities and regions, it also influences inequality *within* cities and regions. Technological development and innovation result in more economic growth, but at the same time in less social equality. This tendency of increasing inequality is visible everywhere in the world, and manifests itself in old and new (digital) divides. For example, low-income groups in booming cities not only suffer from the increasing costs of living, but also from computer illiteracy [30].

A related issue is the decline of the traditional mechanisms of social integration. Changes in the urban economic and social structures have resulted in a lessening of community and of social integration at the neighborhood level, and have influenced the distribution of social capital [29]. Some argue that community and neighborhood structures are no longer the relevant framework as people nowadays are not members of a community, but of a multiplicity of social networks. Social interaction and social integration now have other forms, sometimes described as networked individualism [44]. The Internet seems to support the maintenance of these social networks [15, 16, 45]. Nevertheless, people do live in neighborhoods, with different social characteristics. Neighborhood oriented social experiments with ICTs have taken place in recent years; examples include networks and websites supporting local communities, privileged [15, 16] and underprivileged [33], and community computer literacy projects, helping people to acquire skills and social capital [26, 33]. However, as various chapters in this book will show, these experiments often are small scale and of short duration, and produce mixed results.

2 A Variety of Digital Cities

The term digital city was first conceived in 1993 when the *De Digitale Stad* (DDS)[1] was founded. Using a city metaphor, the DDS combined characteristics of a community network, a local WWW, and a platform for virtual communities [40, 41]. The combination of these models may have been the strength, but also the weakness of the system. Since then, the term Digital City is used for a much wider set of local information and communication *infrastructures*, *systems*, and *projects*, all related to the issues described in the previous section. We distinguish several types of digital cities: grassroots community and civic networks, municipal information and communication networks, city oriented commercial websites, virtual communities, and social ICT experiments in neighborhoods. In practice, digital cities may combine characteristics of the different types.

---

1 Dutch for The Digital City

1. The oldest examples of local community networks or civic networks are the *community memory systems* and *freenets* that began in the mid-1970s in the USA and Canada, and spread over the world [35, 36, 6]. They aim at empowering the local community and generally offer free access, in order to enable community members to improve mutual communication, to access relevant local information and other resources, and to participate in local deliberation on important social, political and cultural issues (a virtual public sphere). Finally, they create an environment that facilitates learning how ICTs can be used for these aims, and increasingly are socio-technical test beds.

Community networks are grassroots initiatives. Generally, they are run by volunteers, and are dependent on subsidies to maintain their operations. University based researchers often play a crucial role in the sustainability of the systems, and sometimes linkages exist with public (libraries, municipality) and private (telecom operators, media, IT companies) organizations.

2. The second model shows the digital city as a municipal project [2]. Here a wide variety of initiatives can be discerned, ranging from a municipal website and local information systems, to urban programs for advanced networks, and e-government programs. An example is the EU *TeleCities* network, which consists of some 120 cities and towns in 20 countries, promoting the use of ICTs for improving the quality of local public services, and for economic and social development [10]. The focus is on the use of ICTs by the public sector itself (e-government). Although social inclusion is emphasized as a guiding principle, the TeleCities network mainly focuses on improving the efficiency of the administrative operations, improving the quality of services for citizens and companies through municipal information systems and through 'one-stop government', and promoting the city as an excellent location for economic activities. Citizens are perceived as *customers* and e-government seems mainly to consist of the application of e-commerce technologies within the public sector. In many cases, large-scale municipal digital cities experiments take the form of public-private collaborations.

3. The third use of the term digital city is for commercial websites with information about a city or town, such as the digital cities operated by America Online [18]. This type of system offers information about hotels, restaurants and retail stores, useful addresses, current weather, information about cinemas, theatres, concerts and other leisure activities. The intended audiences for these digital cities are local consumers and tourists.

4. The next type of digital city consists of virtual environments for virtual communities, often using a spatial metaphor in the design and the interface. These environments are used by geographically dispersed communities of interest, related to work, leisure, or other shared interests, such as specific diseases. In the network society, people take part in many social networks, which are to a large extent not local. In other words, virtual communities may have similar aims and effects as local community networks do, that is creating social capital, mutual support and empowerment. Incidentally, geographically dispersed communities of interest are not a very new phenomenon. For example, scientific communities ('invisible colleges' [28]) can be seen as virtual communities *avant la lettre*. Of course, the new media may affect the way they function [16a].

5. Since the 1980s, social experiments with ICTs have been carried out. Typical goals include improving social cohesion, learning computer skills, and increasing social capital of specific social groups, often in less privileged neighborhoods. Computer clubhouses, neighborhood email lists, and community memory systems for cultural minorities are examples. In some cases, these social experiments are part of governmental programs that support the social use of ICTs. More often these experiments are grassroots initiatives, and the work is generally done in collaboration with the researchers driving the project. Funding then comes from a research project or from other grants – and in both cases, this sets limits on the sustainability of the project.

3 Overview of This Volume

The 26 chapters in this volume are organized into five parts: case studies of digital cities and community networks, technical platforms for community networks and digital cities, information and knowledge modeling, participation and design, and social capital. Together, they provide an overview of the various dimensions of research and application in the field of local information and communication infrastructures. Most chapters are thoroughly revised versions of papers that were presented at the 3rd Digital Cities Workshop. We have also included a few in depth case studies, which examine several of the major experiments with digital cities in different continents.

3.1 Digital Cities Around the World: Case Studies

Without claiming that the first chapters provide a representative or even complete overview of digital cities, the selection does illustrate a variety of experiments from all over the world. They differ in terms of size and available resources, orientation (civic, governmental, or primary commercial experiments), focus (social experiments with ICTs versus high tech development projects), and age, but variation is also clear in terms of the types of participants and stakeholders, organizational forms, and social contexts. Two of the case studies are North American, three are European, and the other two are Asian digital cities.

Douglas Schuler describes and analyses Seattle Community Network (SCN). The project emerged from collaboration between computer professionals, local community groups and civic organizations. He discusses how SCN has functioned as a community resource, and how successful it has been in strengthening community relations. The main focus of the analysis is, however, the question of what actually counts as 'success'. Success should not be understood mainly in terms of the (individual) use of the system. According to Schuler, a community network is successful if it provokes discussions about community development, and about social inequality and exclusion, and when it contributes to social movements addressing these issues (including the international community networks movement). Based on this view, issues such as sustainability of community networks are addressed, and

Schuler emphasizes the importance of relations with local actors, mainly universities and the public library.

Blacksburg Electronic Village (BEV) was founded by very different actors than were present with SCN: BEV consisted of the regional telecom operator, the city council, and the local university – all of which held different goals. Although BEV emphasized community aspects, in the beginning the technical and economic aspects were dominant. Only after the initial core actors left the project, the community became involved, and the model behind BEV changed considerably. The community network was no longer seen as a local Internet, but rather as collaboration between researchers and local community organizations in social ICT projects. A variety of projects were carried out, such as the local school project described in this chapter. The intimate relationship between a community network and university based researchers is one of mutual interests, as researchers often bring with them resources for the community network, whereas the latter creates research opportunities for the researchers. Carroll emphasizes that BEV has been a very successful research environment.

In early 1994, the Amsterdam Digital City (DDS) started as an experiment conducted by media activists and computer hackers to improve communication between citizens and politicians, but soon it also became a portal for local (and other) information, a place for experimentation with the Internet, and a platform for supporting a variety of communities. Peter van den Besselaar and Dennis Beckers studied the DDS from its launch in 1994 as a 'local WorldWideWeb', through the golden years as a not-for-profit platform for communities of interests, to its halt as a commercial Internet provider in 2001. At least two lessons can be learned from this case. Firstly, local information and communication infrastructures face an inevitable fragmentation – as did the WWW and the Internet at large. Second, the lack of local and civic ownership of the DDS seems to be the crucial factor behind its ultimate failure.

Digital Bristol was highly inspired by the Amsterdam DDS model, but at the same time, it developed within a completely different context. Alessandro Aurigi analyzes the history of Digital Bristol using a 'science and technology studies' perspective. This leads to interesting insights about the social shaping of local ICT infrastructures within an arena of various actors with diverging needs and interests. According to Aurigi, the resulting system reflected the lowest common denominator of the various stakeholders: a lean portal for local information. At the same time, any local social group felt ownership of the system, which explains the rather modest use of Digital Bristol.

A completely different example is Virtual Helsinki. It aimed at stimulating the adoption and use of broadband by the local community, and looked at aspects such as technological advancement (GIS, VR, integrating of real and virtual space), social relevance (participation and social cohesion), and profitability (the economic point of view). Risto Linturi and Timo Simula argue that these three interests are not contradictory, as the transition to the knowledge society in their view presupposes a good local infrastructure and social equality. At the same time, they do stress that one needs to convince potential customers that adopting the new technology is important for themselves, and for society in general. Therefore, the project tried to develop use models for local content provision. As the authors argue, Virtual Helsinki was a high profile effort to advance the *memetical* spreading of the idea of the Digital City.

Like the Helsinki case, Digital City Shanghai is very much technology driven. But where in Helsinki (and in other cases), a 'translator' tried to convince other partners to participate and take their roles in the project, Digital City Shanghai is centrally steered by the local authorities wanting Shanghai to move economically forward into the knowledge society. The civic dimension is therefore much less developed. Ding Peng, Lin DongHui, and Sheng Huan Ye describe the various elements of this policy, especially the basic design of the networks and the efforts to stimulate the 'informatization' of Chinese society. A summary is provided of the intended applications and the main institutional constraints. According to the authors, the overregulation makes it difficult for companies to play their roles in the smooth transition to the information society.

Toru Ishida gives a concise overview of the Kyoto Digital City, a project in which researchers from universities and companies play a central role. The main aims were to design a local information and communication infrastructure for providing services to inhabitants and tourists, and to develop the technologies needed for this. As a research program, it was rather successful. One of the larger projects – together with a downtown shopping street – showed how the digital city might revitalize local communities. Another important finding is the application of three-layer architecture for digital cities. Additionally, many systems were developed that could be used for creating a digital city, such as applications for information integration and for social interaction. Various chapters in this book describe these results in more detail.[2] In order to strengthen the relation with the city, a 'forum' with 100 members from a large set of local organizations was established. Although the forum did formulate proposals, these generally failed. In other words, the integration of users in the design and development of the digital city technology remained difficult to realize.

What are the communalities and the differences between these (and other) digital cities? In the last chapter of this (first) section, Toru Ishida, Alessandro Aurigi and Mika Yasuoko compare digital cities, as they exist around the world. The differences between American, European and Asian digital cites are discussed in terms of the variation between the involved actors from companies, government and the local community. However, the authors stress that these contextual factors only explain part of the differences – the adopted technological and design perspectives are also crucial. In the end, the authors argue that digital cities research should be a multidisciplinary effort, which combines (social and technical) research with a participative approach for designing local information and communication infrastructures. This is not easy, as social scientists are generally ignorant about the advanced technological possibilities, whereas computer scientists' ignorance is generally about the complexities of adoption and use of the technology by citizens.

3.2 Platforms for Community Networks

The chapters in this section present various platforms for the development of digital cities and community networks. In the first chapter, Hideyuki Nikanishi, Satoshi Koizomi and Toru Ishida present an example of the integration of real and virtual spaces. The authors describe how digital city technologies can be used for supporting

---

[2] See chapters 1, 3 and 4 in part 2, and chapters 2 and 4 in part 3 of this volume.

emergency evacuation in real spaces. The developed system can be used as a learning environment for safety personnel, but also for real life guidance of crows in emergency situations. This second use of the system requires a further development of ubiquitous computing, and many privacy issues have to be solved. But the paper shows us how future space will be increasingly hybrid - that is integrating real and virtual spaces.

Marco Benini, Fiorella De Cindio and Leonarde Sonnante build on their experience of ten years managing Rete Civica de Milano (RCM). After having used BBS technology, RCM did not want to change to a WWW-based system, as the WWW lacked adequate communication facilities. The latter is a prerequisite for community networks, and therefore RCM selected the (proprietary) First Class system to replace the BBS. As availability is lacking for a good communication oriented open source technology, RMC recently decided to develop its own platform to replace First Class. In the paper, the authors describe their open source engine for civic networks. The developed platform is also suited for e-government and for electronic transactions, because the authors suggest that this is the direction in which civic networks are moving.

Another way of looking at the digital city is the 'local portal' model. However, a variety of systems providing local information may exist in parallel, as partially overlapping local portals. For the user, it is of course practical if these portals can be accessed using a single interface. In the third chapter, Tomoko Koda, Satoshi Nakazawa and Toru Ishida present such a universal portable interface for heterogeneous digital cities. They have experimented with a prototype, and expect that the usefulness of their approach will increase when semantic web technologies are applied in geographical information systems. It should be noted that in this chapter (as in several others) mobile telephones play a central role. This seems to be an important trend, as mobile phones together with WiFi and CCTV are the main technologies for integrating real and virtual space. These technologies will therefore influence the social construction and the social use of space, as well as our perception of and behavior in those hybrid spaces.

In the last chapter in this section, Satoshi Koizumi and Hiroshi Ishiguro describe their platform for quick production of 3D representations of real spaces, based on the use of omni-directional cameras. They describe the tools in some detail, and discuss a field test in an educational environment. The results show that the Town Digitizing platform does yield high quality digital spaces.

3.3 Knowledge and Data Modeling for Community Networks

Storytelling is seen as a fundamental to the sharing of experience, and therefore for reproduction of social cohesion in communities. What role can new media play in this mainly oral tradition? Can new media actively be used to open up new possibilities for sharing the communities' narratives? In the first chapter of this section, Ramesh Srinivasan describes a project with the Somali community in the Boston area. To preserve their cultural heritage, he developed a system (the Village Voice) with video pieces of narratives of the community. A participatory strategy was adopted to create an ontology for organizing the video pieces, and the authors of the pieces did annotation of the video pieces. In this way, the ontology reproduces the cognitive model and the value system of the community. A comparison with a key words based search system showed the appropriateness of the ontology. As communities develop over time, the ontology needs regularly updating. At the same time, the changes of the ontology itself embody a reflexive image of the changes in self-perception and values of the community.

Digital cities by nature include geographical information; the amount of such information on the WWW is exploding. Therefore, manually searching for the relevant information to include in a digital city is an inoperable task. Also, an automatic keyword search does not result in sufficiently good recall and precision, as for example, the same geographical name may refer to different geographical locations, and words that seem to have geographical references may in fact be unimportant. In the second chapter, Lee and his colleagues introduce an approach to optimize the search processes, and they evaluate the proposed algorithms in a series of experiments – with promising results.

Recent developments in wireless technologies and PDA's potentially offer new possibilities for integrating real space and virtual space. Above, we have already mentioned the use of the mobile phone as an interface to the digital city. In the third chapter, Wanji Mai, Chris Tweed and Gordon Dodds introduce a portable system for building-recognition to be used by travelers in a town. An important part of the work consists of the development, implementation, and testing of recognition methods for objects such as buildings.

In the final chapter, Yuseke Yokota, Shumian He and Yahiko Kambayashi describe their Retax system, a tool for making and annotating omni-directional videos with complete views of the activities in some place. The concept behind the system is to store everything and select later. The system aims to realize applications that are not possible with conventional video database systems, such as full registration of human behavior and communication.

3.4 Design and Participation of Local Information and Communication Systems

Part 4 of this volume includes papers that focus on the design process, the participation of users in the design, and the monitoring of systems in order to improve the design. An often-neglected issue is the diversity of users in ICT based systems. Different levels of education, but also different cultural backgrounds may influence the way a system is used, and the ways the interface is 'read' by the users. Niek Van Dam, Vanessa Evers, and Floor Arts experimentally tested this with an e-government site in Amsterdam, and with 30 participants from Moroccan, Surinamese and Dutch backgrounds. The findings of this paper support the hypothesis that users with different cultural backgrounds experience different use problems, in line with social theorizing about cultural differences.

Although a wide variety of virtual spaces are available, our understanding of how these technologies influence the way people access information and expertise, and the way they socialize, etc., is very limited. In the second chapter, Katy Börner and her colleagues present an advanced tool that generates visualizations of data about user interaction in virtual spaces. Understanding social navigation and interaction patterns in these spaces may inform designers to improve the design, content, layout, and selection of interaction possibilities. The tool, which automatically generates the data and the visualizations, is also useful for the social researcher interested in social interaction and behavior in virtual spaces.

In the next chapter, Ahmad Reeves and Patrick Healey argue that the technological infrastructure designed for sustainable digital communities influences and is influenced by human communicative organization. Using a theoretical framework based on work by Goffman, they compare communication in a text based virtual city with communication patterns typical for informal face-to-face conversations. Reeves and Healey find interesting differences between the two settings, and the effects are different for primary and peripheral participants in the conversation. These findings do have implications for the design of virtual spaces, and the authors highlight the limitations of the spatial metaphor as an organizing architecture for online communities. They conclude with five communication-oriented issues for design.

The section continues with a chapter by James Zappen and Teresa Harrison, who extensively describe the problems when one seriously wants to collect and interpret data about user needs for developing design specifications. Using methodologies such as focus group and participatory design meetings, and a conceptual framework based on activity theory, they develop an approach to decode users' (conscious and unconscious) intentions and motives from their activities. Further development of concepts to categorize user activities will be necessary, however, to fully operationalize the theory, and to make the approach useful for designers and system developers.

How should we understand the relationship between the 'real' space' and the 'media space'? Gary Gumpert and Susan Drucker address this question in the final chapter of this part. First of all, they sum up those salient characteristics of new media that produce the main social, political, and psychological effects of those media: interactivity, immediacy of response, privacy concerns, anonymity of interaction, increased sense of control, access regardless of distance, the eradication of time, simultaneous channels of communication, and the problem of controlling properties of digital objects. In the end, these characteristics change the way people live in their physical and virtual environment, and this implies that the new media are not simply added to the old structures. As they argue, 'the media-literate 21st century citizen has absorbed techniques, grammars and expectations into their media psyche'. In other words, 'the new media must be integrated into the bricks and mortar of the digital city, which is something between (tertium quid) the physical and the virtual city'.

3.5 Information Technology and Social Capital: Social Experiments

In part 5 we have collected a set of papers that illustrate the change within community computing from infrastructures (such some examples of digital cities in part 1) to local projects deploying ICTs for social capital, learning, and economic recovery of underprivileged regions and neighborhoods. The chapters presented here analyze local initiatives in very different environments, such as a metropolis (São Paulo), neighborhoods and youth centers in large cities (Amsterdam and Bremen), and in small towns, villages, and rural areas (in Portugal).

In the first chapter, Stefan Welling and Andreas Breiter analyze their experiences with a regional learning environment for teenagers. Sociological theorizing about learning and social capital suggests that learning (and overcoming the digital and other divides) requires an organic integration of the learning environment in the teenagers' life world. However, developing adequate learning environments (especially for deprived groups) requires the collaboration of many people and organizations (such as parents, schools, neighborhood centers), but this process often proves to be very difficult: Expectations and professional identities differ, and many institutional and legal barriers appear when organizing the learning environment. Nevertheless, the teenagers received a great deal from participating in the project, and they found the activities increasingly personally important. Interestingly, the success had nothing to do with provision of access, as most of the participating teenagers already had a PC and Internet access at home.

The next chapter discusses a study about the use and effects of a community email network on social capital and participation in a heterogeneous urban neighborhood. Also here, the concept of social capital is the starting point for the study. Dennis Beckers and his co-workers found that ICT based networks do not have an autonomous effect on social capital. The effects prove to be dependent on traditional social indicators, such as the level of education and income. The authors also found that the use of the new neighborhood network was low. Comparing this with other local ICT projects, they concluded that the neighborhood network was too much of a top-down initiative. As a consequence, inhabitants' identification with the system, the feeling of ownership, and consequently the use were all minimal. The authors discuss the implications for designing and organizing local information and communications systems that aim at improving social cohesion and social capital.

The third chapter holds interest as it describes similar activities in a huge metropolis (São Paulo) in a developing country, which adds two dimensions to the problem of using ICTs for social capital and development: the scale of the social context, and the level of economic development. Mariana Reis Balboni and Gilson Schwartz focus on their program of creating sustainable social networks by training the professionals that do the grassroots work in telecenters and in public access points all around the city. The program consisted of some 10 projects, in which 280 of these so-called 'digital inclusion agents' participated. Another important element of the program is the role of public universities in supporting the development of these networks. The support was on two levels, both institutionally and in supplying relevant knowledge.

The issue of social networks and learning for local development is also discussed in the last chapter. José Moutinho and Manuel Heiter describe a series of digital cities initiatives that aim at supporting the development of less favorable zones in Portugal – as part of the inclusive information society. The information society is, in this chapter, conceptualized as a knowledge society, or even better, a learning society. The comparison of the cases results in useful insights, and these are related to recent theorizing about regional networks, social learning, and innovation. Although the context is important and varies between the cases, the authors emphasize the distinct roles of the public sector and the private sector in the various phases of the projects. They stress the role of adequate institutional frameworks and infrastructures, and of incentives for the various actors involved. Basically, the digital cities experiments supported the emergence and development of networks among local and regional actors, and these networks proved to be crucial for local economic and social development.

4 Some Final Observations

ICT applications have moved from business to everyday life, and from the market and formal organizations to the community [19]. Digital cities are one of the manifestations of these changes. Can we discern a development of digital cities in terms of generations, based on the technologies available, and on the dominant actors and their aims [22]? This book suggests the contrary. Digital city experiments are characterized by very different aims, divergence in size and scope, different technologies used, varying organizational forms, ownership and business models, and dissimilarities in terms of actors involved. Of course, the development of local ICT infrastructures is heavily influenced by technological development, but a dominant socio-technical design has not emerged, and heterogeneity and local adaptation may remain dominant [37]. Having said this, we can still identify several patterns.

Firstly, the fragmentation of the WWW and the Internet is also visible in the digital cities experiments. Many digital cities started as a kind of local WorldWideWeb, with all functionality on a local level: Internet access, local portal, local public sphere, virtual communities, chat, and so on [41]. But over the years most of them fragmented into a variety of local projects, using the available Internet infrastructure, and focusing on specific niches. This development is visible in the grassroots community networks as well as in the municipal digital city initiatives. Increasingly, the relevant distinction is between large-scale infrastructural projects and smaller scale social experiments with ICTs. A variety of these social experiments are described in this book and elsewhere [17, 17a, 33, 38]. It would be interesting to conduct a meta analysis to improve our understanding of the factors influencing success and failure.

Secondly, in many projects academic researchers play an important role. Researchers bring with them resources from which the local projects profit. Additionally, the local networks and projects are perfect research and application sites for computer science researchers as well as for social science researchers. As clearly shown in the case studies, academic researchers may be essential for the sustainability of local ICT networks and local projects. More generally, this suggests that local universities are one of the most important resources in the local community.

Thirdly, from a social informatics perspective, community networks and digital cities are socio-technical systems. But if we look at the projects more carefully, they seem to be either high tech projects, in which computer scientists play a central role and have hardly any relationship with the intended users and the wider social context, or social experiments with ICT, focusing on users but often neglecting the possibilities and constraints of ICTs. Again, we see that a multidisciplinary approach is often propagated, but seldom realized. This is unfortunate, as a relationship does exist between the project aims on the one hand and the selected technical solutions on the other. The choice of specific technologies does constrain and enable the digital cities and community networks based on it. For example, the case studies show that the transition to WWW-based designs did improve the informational capabilities at the expense of communicational capabilities, and this affected both users and use. The interaction between user needs and technology development therefore remains important.

Fourthly, different kinds of users are addressed in digital city and community networking projects. Often the focus in on individual users, or on social groups or communities. But in other cases, social experimentation with ICTs aims at supporting social movements.

Finally, digital cities and community networks constitute virtual public spaces, which were often considered as a separate layer added to real cities, independently and with its own dynamics. However, the 'virtual' and the 'physical' do not constitute two separate urban spaces any more, as they are increasingly interwoven. Recent technological developments, such as ubiquitous computing, mobile phones, wireless connectivity, and digitalization of traditional media result in a virtualization of real public space. Hence, the concept of hybrid space (and related concepts) comes up in various chapters in this volume. Virtual (or media) spaces and real spaces have merged, and this requires a rethinking of the design of hybrid spaces in terms of their functioning, esthetics, and their social and behavioral implications [12, 13, 23, 24].

References

1. W.B. Arthur, "Competing technologies, increasing returns, and lock-in by historical events." Economic journal 99 (1989) pp. 116-131.
2. Aurigi, "Digital city or urban simulator?" T. Ishida, K. Isbister Eds., Digital cities, experiences, trends, and perspectives, Lecture Notes in Computer Science 1765, Springer Verlag, 2000.
3. A-L. Barabasi, Linked; the new science of networks, Cambridge, Perseus Publishing, 2002.
4. M. Castells, The Rise of the Network Society, Oxford, Blackwell, 1996.
5. M. Castells, The Internet Galaxy. Oxford, Oxford University Press, 2001.
6. Michael Cohill and A. Lee Kavanaugh (eds.), Community Networks, Lessons from Blacksburg, Virginia. Boston, Artec House, 1997.
7. Freeman, J. Clark and L. Soete, Unemployment and Technical Innovation. Pinter, London, 1982.
8. Freeman, L. Soete (eds.), Technical Change and Full Employment. Pinter, London, 1987.
9. J. Gottman, Megalopolis and Antipolis: The Telephone and the Structure of the City. In [27].
10. I Götzl, "Telecities: Digital Cities Network," M. Tanabe, P. van den Besselaar and T. Ishida, Digital Cities 2 Computational and sociological approaches. Lecture Notes in Computer Science 2362 (2002) pp. 98-106.
11. S. Graham and S. Marvin Telecommunications and the City, London, Routledge, 1996.
12. G. Gumpert and S. Drucker, "Privacy, Predictability or Serendipidy and Digital Cities," M. Tanabe, P. van den Besselaar and T. Ishida, Digital Cities 2 Computational and sociological approaches. Lecture Notes in Computer Science 2362 (2002) pp. 27-41.
13. G. Gumpert and S. Drucker, "The perfection of sustainability and imperfections in the digital community: paradoxes of connection and disconnection." In P. van den Besselaar, S. Koizumi (eds), Digital Cities 3. Lecture Notes in Computer Science, Vol. 3081. Springer-Verlag, Berlin Heidelberg New York (2005) pp. 363-373.
14. P. Hall and A. Markussen (eds) Silicon landscapes. Boston: Allen & Unwin, 1985.
15. K. Hampton and B., "Wellman Examining community in the digital neighborhood," T. Ishida, K. Isbister, eds., Digital cities, experiences, trends, and perspectives, Lecture Notes in Computer Science 1765, 2000.
16. K. Hampton, B. Wellman, "The Not So Global Village of Netville." B. Wellman and C. Haythornthwaite (Eds.) The Internet and Everyday Life. Oxford, UK: Blackwell 2002., pp. 345-371

16a. G. Heimeriks and P. Van den Besselaar, New media and communication networks in knowledge production, a case study. Forthcoming.

17. T. Ishida,(ed.), Community Computing and Support Systems, Lecture Notes in Computer Science, Vol. 1519, Springer-Verlag, 1998.

17a T. Ishida, K. Isbister (eds) Digital cities, technologies, experiences, and future perspectives. Lecture Notes in Computer Science 1765, Springer-Verlag, 2000.

18. T. Ishida, A. Aurigi, M. Yasuoka, "World digital cities: beyond heterogeneity", In P. van den Besselaar, S. Koizumi (eds), Digital Cities 3. Lecture Notes in Computer Science, Vol. 3081. Springer-Verlag, Berlin Heidelberg New York (2005) pp. 184-198.

19. T Ishida: Activities and Technologies in Digital City Kyoto. In P. van den Besselaar, S. Koizumi (eds), Digital Cities 3. Lecture Notes in Computer Science, Vol. 3081. Springer-Verlag, Berlin Heidelberg New York (2005) pp. 162-183.

20. R. Kling, "What is social informatics and why does it matter?" D-Lib Magazine 5 (1999) 1.

21. R. Kling, "Learning about Information Technologies and Social Change: The Contribution of Social Informatics. The Information Society 16 (2000) 3, pp. 217-232

22. H. Kubicek, R.M. Wagner, "Community networks in a generational perspectives." Information, Communication and Society, 5 (2002) pp. 291-319.

23. W.J. Mitchell, The City of Bits, Cambridge, MIT, 1995.

24. W.J. Mitchell, E-topia; It's Urban Life, Jim, But not as We Know It. Cambridge, MIT Press, 1999.

25. M.L Moss, "Technologies and cities". Cityscape 3 (1998) 3, pp. 107-127.

26. R.D. Pinkett, The Cramfield Estate-MIT creating communities connections project. M. Tanabe, P. van den Besselaar and T. Ishida, Digital Cities 2 Computational and sociological approaches. Lecture Notes in Computer Science 2362 (2002) pp. 110-124.

27. I de Sola Pool The Social Impact of the Telephone Cambridge, MA: MIT Press, 1977,

28. D.J. de Solla Price, Little Science, Big Science. New York, Columbia University Press, 1963.

29. R.D. Putnam, Bowling alone. New York, Simon & Schuster 2000.

30. J. Robinson. Special issues on the digital divide. IT and society 1 (2003) issues 4, 5, and 6.

31. S. Sassen (ed.), Global networks, linked cities. London: Routledge 2002 .

32. M. Sheller, J Urry, "The city and the car." International Journal of Urban and Regional Research 24 (2000) pp.737-757.

33. D. A. Schön, B. Sanyal, W.J. Mitchell, High Technology and Low-income Communities. Cambridge, MIT Press, 1999.

34. D. Schuler, P. Day (eds.) Shaping the networks society. Cambridge: MIT Press, 2004.

35. D. Schuler, New Community Networks, Wired for Change, New York, ACM Press, 1996.

36. D. Schuler, "Digital cities and digital citizens," M. Tanabe, P. Van den Besselaar and T. Ishida, Digital Cities 2. Lecture Notes in Computer Science, Berlin, Springer-Verlag, 2002. pp. 71-85.

37. K.H. Sorensen, R. Williams (eds.), Shaping technology, guiding policy. Cheltenham: Edward Elgar, 2002

38. M. Tanabe, P. van den Besselaar and T. Ishida, Digital Cities 2 Computational and sociological approaches. Lecture Notes in Computer Science 2362, Berlin, Springer-Verlag, 2002.

39. Townsend, "The internet and the rise of the new networked cities". In environment and Planning B 28 (2001) pp. 39-58.

40. P. Van den Besselaar, "E-community versus E-commerce: the rise and decline of the Amsterdam Digital City," AI & Society 15 (2001), pp. 280-288.

41. P. van den Besselaar, D. Beckers: The Life and Death of the Great Amsterdam Digital City. In P. van den Besselaar, S. Koizumi (eds), Digital Cities 3. Lecture Notes in Computer Science, Vol. 3081. Springer-Verlag, Berlin Heidelberg New York (2005) pp. 64-93.

42. S.B. Warner, Streetcar suburbs: the process of growth in Boston, 1870-1900, Cambridge, Mass.: Harvard University Press, 1978.

43. D.J. Watts, Six degrees. New York: W.W. Norton, 2003.
44. B. Wellman, "Little boxes, glocalization and networked individualism." M. Tanabe, P. van den Besselaar and T. Ishida, Digital Cities 2 Computational and sociological approaches. Lecture Notes in Computer Science 2362 (2002) pp. 10-25.
45. B. Wellman, A.Q. Haase, J. Witte, K. Hampton, " Does the Internet Increase, Decrease, or Supplement Social Capital? Social Networks, Participation, and Community Commitment". American Behavioral Scientist, November 2001, vol. 45, no. 3, pp. 436-455.
46. W. van Winden, Essays in urban ICT policies. PhD thesis, Erasmus University Rotterdam, 2003.
47. M. Zook, M. Dodge, Y. Aoyama, A. Townsend, "New digital geographies: information, communication and place". S.D. Brown et al. (eds.) Geography and technology. Kluwer Academic Publishers, 2004, pp. 155-176.

The Seattle Community Network: Anomaly or Replicable Model?

Douglas Schuler

The Evergreen State College
Public Sphere Project
douglas@scn.org

Abstract. The Seattle Community Network (SCN; http://www.scn.org) is a community owned and operated networked computer system that just marked its 10th anniversary. SCN now provides e-mail to thousands of people and web sites and distribution lists to scores of community groups. In the era of dot-coms and ubiquitous banner ads, SCN is somewhat of an anomaly. SCN focuses on local communication and information services but supports related efforts in places as far from Seattle as Nepal and Uganda. It is a free, public system that is built upon a set of socially responsible principles and policies and is maintained solely by people who volunteer their time without financial compensation. SCN has been emulated by community activists and studied by cyberspace researchers from all over the world. How might it evolve? Can it serve as a more universal model? This chapter will discuss SCN's history and the original motivation. It will also compare its socially ameliorative objectives with current realities. Theoretically, it will focus on the role of SCN and similar systems in an historical moment when major global forces are shifting dramatically and communication technology is affording new opportunities for social actors worldwide. Will public, non-commercial systems still have a place? What impacts have been observed in Seattle and what impacts might be expected in the future? Is SCN an anomaly or might some type of 'community network' model, possibly similar to SCN, become prevalent in the world? Is it possible to develop a 'digital city' that is inclusive and helps meet civic sector needs around the world?

"The associations in community are interdependent. To weaken one is to weaken all. If the local newspaper closes, the garden club and the township meeting will each diminish as they lose a voice. If the American Legion disbands, several community fundraising events and the maintenance of the ballpark will stop. If the Baptist Church closes, several self-help groups that meet in the basement will be without a home and folks in the old peoples' home will lose their weekly visitors. The interdependence of associations and the dependence of community upon their work is the vital center of an effective society."   - John McKnight (1987)

"At the core of network activity is the production, exchange, and strategic use of information. This ability may seem inconsequential in the face of the economic, political, or military might of other global actors. But by overcoming the deliberate suppression of information that sustains many abuses of power, networks can help reframe international and domestic debates, changing their terms, their sites, and the configuration of participants."
    - Margaret Keck and Kathryn Sikkink (1998)

"Networks of civic engagement embody past success at collaboration which can serve as a cultural template for future collaboration."   - Robert Putnam (1993)

P. van den Besselaar and S. Koizumi (Eds.): Digital Cities 2003, LNCS 3081, pp. 17-42, 2005.
© Springer-Verlag Berlin Heidelberg 2005

1 Community Networks

Before computers and digital networks became prominent, the term 'community network' was a sociological concept that described the pattern of communications and relationships in a geographical community [38]. This was the 'web of community' that helped us better understand how news traveled or how social problems were addressed in the community. New computer-based 'community networks' are a recent innovation that are intended  to help revitalize, strengthen, and expand existing *people-based* community networks much in the same way that previous civic innovations (such as the print-media inspired public library) have helped communities historically.

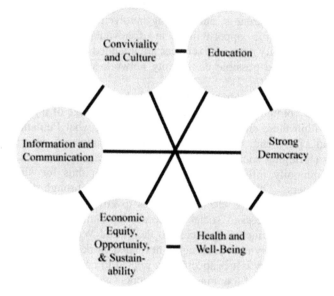

Fig. 1. Community Core Values

In my book *Community Networks* [26] I postulated that any community (inherently a civic sector body) has *systems* of *core values* that maintain its 'web of unity' [18]. These six core values – conviviality and culture, education, strong democracy, health and well-being, economic equity, opportunity, and sustainability, and information and communication (fig. 1) – are all strongly interrelated: Each system strongly influences each of the others, and any deficiency in one results in a deficiency of the whole [26]. It has long been known, to illustrate the interconnectedness of the core values with just one example, that the higher an individual's education and economic levels, the higher the amount of his or her political participation [10, 9]. Strengthening these community core values, therefore, is likely to result in stronger, more coherent communities.

For over a decade, community members and activists all over the world, often in conjunction with other local institutions including colleges and universities, K–12 schools, local governmental agencies, libraries, or nonprofit organizations, have been developing computer-based community networks. In fact, by the mid 1990s, there were nearly 300 operational systems with nearly 200 more in development [7] and the number of registered users exceeded 500,000 people worldwide. (Unfortunately user demographics for the aggregate are nearly impossible to obtain: the current worldwide explosion of efforts coupled with a lack of a universally shared concept of what a 'community network' is confound efforts in this direction.) Innovative examples can be found in Amsterdam (www.dds.nl) [36], Milan (wrcm.dsi.unimi.it), Barcelona (www.bcnet.upc.es/ravalnet), Japan (www.can.or.jp/index-e.html), and more recently, in Russia (www.friends-partners.org/civnet/index.html), where the development of civil society is an urgent matter after the abrupt breakup of the Soviet Union. These community networks (sometimes called civic networks, digital cities, Free-Nets, community computing-centers, or public access networks), some with user populations in the tens of thousands, are intended to advance social goals, such as building community awareness, encouraging involvement in local decision-making, or developing economic opportunities in disadvantaged communities. Broadly speaking, the community network's services are intended to support the core values of the community. Some possible community network services based on these core values are listed below (fig. 2).

A community network addresses these goals by supporting smaller communities within the larger community and by facilitating the exchange of information between individuals within these smaller communities (creating what Putnam calls 'bonding social capital' [22] and by encouraging the exchange of information among communities ('bridging social capital'). Another community network objective is to aggregate community information and communication thus focusing attention on community matters. This is done in a variety of ways: through discussion forums; question and answer forums; electronic access to government employees, services, and information and access to social services; electronic mail; and in most cases, basic Internet services, including access to the World Wide Web and Usenet news groups. Some community networks highlight related work - such as community radio development - and policy issues specifically related to communication systems. The most important aspect of community networks is probably their potential for increasing participation in community affairs. Since the Internet's original design makes little distinction between information consumers and producers, it helped spur idealism among community network developers that is not as pronounced among reformers of traditional media such as newspapers, radio, or television.

Community members interact with community networks in various ways. Community network terminals can be set up at public places like libraries, low-income housing, bus stations, schools, laundromats, community and senior centers, social service agencies, farmers' markets, and shopping malls. Community networks are generally accessible from home computers and from the Internet. In recent years, activists have also been establishing community computing centers or telecenters where people, often those in low-income neighborhoods, can become comfortable and adept with computer applications and network services (http://www.ctcnet.org for a listing of such sites in the U.S.). The telecenter movement is particularly active and important in Latin America and other less developed regions of the world where access to the telecommunications infrastructure is less common.

Conviviality and Culture
- Forums for ethnic, religious, neighborhood interest groups
- Recreation and parks information
- Arts, crafts, and music classes, events, and festivals
- Community calendar

Education
- On-line homework help
- Forums for educators, students
- Q&A on major topics
- Distributed experiments
- Pen pals
- Online tutorials

Strong Democracy
- Contact information for elected officials - 'Ask the Mayor'
- E-mail to elected officials and to government agencies
- Forums on major issues
- On-line versions of legislation, judicial decisions, regulations, and other government information
- Deliberative systems

Health and Well-Being
- Q&A on medical and dental information
- Alternative and traditional health care information
- Community clinics information
- Self-help forums
- Public safety bulletins
- Where to find help for substance abuse, etc.
- Resources for the homeless; shelter information and forums
- Pollution data

Economic Equity, Opportunity, and Sustainability
- Want ads and job listings
- Labor news
- Ethical investing information
- Job training and community-development projects
- Unemployed, laid-off, and striking worker discussion forums

Information and Communication
- Access to alternative news and opinion
- E-mail to all Internet addresses
- Cooperation with community radio, etc.
- Access to library information and services
- Access to on-line databases
- On-line 'Quick Information'
- Access to on-line periodicals, wire services
- Free web space and online publishing applications

Fig. 2. Example Services for a Community Network

1974	Community Memory (Berkeley) started; First community network
1981	Computer Professionals for Social Responsibility (CPSR) founded
1985	The Well BBS started (California)
1986	Cleveland Free-Net started
1988	Big Sky Telegraph launched in rural Montana
1989	Santa Monica (California) PEN; first local government community-wide network
	National Public Telecomputing Network (NPTN) started
1990	First community network presentation in Seattle
	First BBS established in the Soviet Union
1992	CPSR/Seattle begins SCN project. Editorial in Seattle Times
	Victoria (Canada) Free-Net opens
1993	The Digital City launched in the Netherlands
	Agenda for Action published by Clinton-Gore administration
1994	SCN goes online
	First Apple Ties That Bind conference
	Telecommunities Canada formed
1995	SCNA incorporated as a non-profit educational organization
1996	NPTN filed for bankruptcy.
	AFCN founded (at community networking conference in Taos, New Mexico)
	First discussion of global organization
1997	1st European Community Networking conference (Milano, Italy)
	1st Community Area Network (CAN) conference (Tokyo, Japan)
	Microsoft Sidewalk started
1999	Microsoft Sidewalk sold
2000	Cleveland Free-Net shut down.
	1st Global Community Networking (Barcelona, Spain).
2001	2nd Global Community Networking (Buenos Aires, Argentina)
2002	3rd Global Community Networking (Montreal, Canada)
2003	UN/ITU World Summit on the Information Society (Geneva, Switzerland)
2004	SCN 10 year anniversary; 'shut the doors?' question posed
2005	UN/ITU World Summit on the Information Society (Tunis, Tunisia)

Fig. 3. Selected Community Networking Milestones

Community networks are currently local and independent. Many were originally affiliated with the National Public Telecomputing Network (NPTN), a now-defunct organization that helped establish a large number of community networks — *Free-Nets* in NPTN's terminology [11]. New organizations, such as the Association For Community Networks (AFCN) in the U.S., the European Association of Community Networks (EACN) and the CAN (Community Area Networks) Forum in Japan have recently been launched but, until recently, community network developers hadn't explored deeply, in theory or in practice, the idea of stronger and closer relationships between them. Lately there have been hopeful signs that a community networking 'movement' will develop. Global community networking congresses were convened in Barcelona, Spain (2000), Buenos Aires, Argentina (2001), Montreal, Canada (2002) and elsewhere. A CPSR symposium on 'Shaping the Network Society' was hosted in Seattle in 2000 and another in 2002. Perhaps most significantly, the 'global community networks' proponents are planning to engage with the United Nations International Telecommunications Union as a potential civic sector advisee in their 2003 and 2005 'Information Society' summits.

Community networks have almost always had a difficult time financially. Increased public interest and some limited infusions from the government, businesses, and foundations have helped to alleviate some of the financial problems with some of the systems. For example, in Texas, a new initiative, the largest ever in the U.S., is devoting some thirty million dollars for community networking. This effort is a major exception, however: very few community networks - in Texas or elsewhere - have been adequately staffed or have had adequate office space, hardware, software, or telecommunications. Whether or not community networks in one form or another succeed hinges on the question of whether or not people and institutions can agree that democratic community communication is worthy of financial and other support.

2 Seattle Community Network: A Brief History

The first indication of strong interest in community networking in Seattle came at the October 16, 1990 meeting of the Seattle chapter of Computer Professionals for Social Responsibility (CPSR). Jon Jacky's living room was filled to capacity. Several people had even driven up from Portland, 180 miles south, for the event. At that meeting I presented my findings on the nascent community networking movement by reporting on the few systems that existed at the time: the Public Electronic Network (PEN) in Santa Monica California, the Big Sky Telegraph system in Dillon, Montana (spreading over much of rural Montana), the New York Youth Network, and the Cleveland Free-Net. Some milestones related to the use of cyberspace (and SCN specifically) by 'ordinary' citizens are shown below.

It took some time after the first meeting before CPSR/Seattle actually decided to launch SCN. After viewing the NPTN (National Public Telecomputing Network) videotape 'If it plays in Peoria...' [20] at the January, 1992 CPSR/Seattle meeting the members in attendance voted unanimously to make SCN an official project. (Those active in the early days included Ken Gillgren, Randy Groves, Phil Harrison, Heather Holmback, Phil Hughes, Aki Namioka, Sharma Oliver, Lorraine Pozzi, Doug Schuler, and others.) From the start there was a lot of excitement and participation. There was also a fair amount of confusion and disagreement. It became obvious that important decisions needed to be made--including how to make decisions--before we could make substantial progress on the project; decisions about how the project would be organized and what type of project SCN should be, for example. One of the earliest discussions centered on whether to affiliate with the NPTN. NPTN was the creation of Tom Grundner who intended it to be the umbrella organization for the Cleveland Free-Net and the other Free-Nets that he also engendered. Grundner's vision of 'Free-Nets' was based on that of a public library where access is free and universal and that everybody can be a contributor [12]. All Free-Nets at that time (pre-Web) used the Freeport menu-based software running on Unix systems.

At this early stage, Lorraine Pozzi suggested that we hold a meeting at Kay Bullit's house, which had been the launchpad for many civic projects in Seattle. Kay was amenable and invitations were sent to 50 or so community leaders in the region. At the meeting Aki Namioka and Doug Schuler presented the vision of a free, public access computer system that would help the Seattle community keep in touch with itself, a vision that was also reflected in an op-ed (July 16, 1992) that Doug had written for the Seattle Times. Although the presentation was undoubtedly somewhat naive and there was some skepticism, the general mood was optimistic and many attendees at that early meeting became enthusiastic SCN supporters. Yvonne Chen and Jim Taylor of the Seattle Public Library (SPL) were among the earliest advocates. We began a dialogue with them that night at Kay's and ultimately reached an important agreement with SPL. SPL allows SCN computers to be located at SPL facilities and provided some telephone lines to us. More importantly the library provided access to SCN from the downtown library and all its branch libraries, bringing us closer to our goals of universal access. The SCN relationship with SPL was an important strategic alliance that SCN would like to repeat with other civic organizations in the region.

Around this time we were trying to figure out how to organize the project. We originally convened five committees – outreach (Kevin Higgins), services (Ken Gillgren), hardware/software (Randy Groves and David Barts), policy (Aki Namioka), and staff and facilities (Sharma Oliver). A coordinating council (consisting of representatives from each committee and two at-large representatives (Doug Schuler and Joel Ware) was also formed at that time to act as a steering committee. An advisory board including Seattle civic leaders Michael Grant, Liz Stroup, George Zander, Andy Gordon, Sheryl Burgstahler, and Hazel Wolf was formed to help SCN developers think strategically about how to make an impact in the community.

We also developed several documents that we hoped would serve as guiding mechanisms during the design period but also into the future. Since SCN was originally a CPSR project and many of the founders came from a CPSR background, it was obviously very important to think of why we were doing the project and what policies would guide it. SCN's principles (fig. 4), hammered out at Sharma Oliver's house over the course of many Coordinating Council meetings, ultimately consisted of several public commitments: to access, to service, to democracy, to the world community, and to the future. The policy statement, shepherded by Aki Namioka, Karen Sy, and the rest of the Policy Committee, reflected important policy goals including freedom of speech and expression, privacy, and the right to a due process. Although these documents have been amended slightly they still form the intellectual foundation for the project. In January, 1994, SCN first came on-line. Hosted on a donated 386 running a donated copy of BSDI UNIX and using FreePort as the user interface software, we began running the system quietly as we looked for bugs and other problems. In June 1994, SCN was officially unveiled to approximately 100 people in a 'Community Introduction' at the main meeting room at the downtown Seattle Public Library. The introduction featured several brief speeches including those from Bob Mascott, Aki Namioka, Doug Schuler and then City Council president Jim Street and SPL City Librarian Liz Stroup. Randy Groves gave a live demonstration of SCN and three elementary school students, Barney, Isabel, and Reed, inaugurated the system by sending out a note to all the system's electronic well-wishers including people from all over the world, Washington State governor Mike Lowry, and several members of congress.

From the early days, it was recognized that SCN should not reside under the CPSR's organizational mantle indefinitely. The organizers felt that SCN needed a regional focus and that the issues facing SCN were different (though complementary) from those facing CPSR. After a one-day retreat on July 28, 1995 with about 15 attendees it was agreed that a new non-profit organization, the Seattle Community

The Seattle Community Network (SCN) is a free public-access computer network for exchanging and accessing information. Beyond that, however, it is a service conceived for community empowerment. Our principles are a series of commitments to help guide the ongoing development and management of the system for both the organizers and participating individuals and organizations.

Commitment to Access: *Access to the SCN will be free to all*
Commitment to Service: *The SCN will offer reliable and responsive service*
- We will provide information that is timely and useful to the community.
- We will provide access to databases and other services.

Commitment to Democracy: *SCN will promote participation in government and public dialogue*
- The community will be actively involved in the ongoing development of the SCN.
- We will place high value in freedom of speech and expression and in the free exchange of ideas.
- We will make every effort to ensure privacy of the system users.
- We will support democratic use of electronic technology.

Commitment to the World Community: *In addition to serving the local community, we will become part of the regional, national and international community*
- We will build a system that can serve as a model for other communities.

Commitment to the Future: *We will continue to evolve and improve the SCN*
- We will explore the use of innovative applications such as electronic town halls for community governance, or electronic encyclopedias for enhanced access to information.
- We will work with information providers and with groups involved in similar projects using other media.
- We will solicit feedback on the technology as it is used, and make it as accessible and humane as possible.

Fig. 4. Seattle Community Network Principles

Network Association (SCNA), should be formed. This association would oversee the administration of SCN but would also take part in other important activities relating to access to communication technology of all types. In addition it was decided that SCNA would be membership based (although dues could sometimes be waived) and SCNA members could run for the SCNA board and serve on the SCNA board. Having dues meant (we hoped!) that SCN would get some regular revenue stream. (Ensuring a reliable and enduring revenue stream for community networks has been a chronic problem afflicting nearly all community network enterprises). It is important to note that SCNA membership is not required for a person to use the SCN system, nor is residence in the Seattle region. Some time after these decisions were made, the articles of constitution and the by-laws were filed with the Washington State Secretary of State. In February, 1996, a letter was sent to all SCN users asking them if they'd like to become charter members of SCNA and about 10% of all SCN users joined SCNA. Currently SCNA has about 400 members (counting 50 non-paying volunteers) and clearly represents a potentially important force for democratic technology in the region.

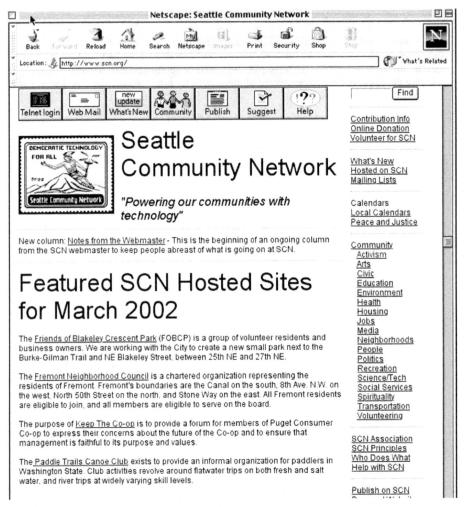

Fig. 5. Seattle Community Network homepage

3 Looking at SCN

Community networks take different forms in different communities, depending on who develops them and how they are used. Historical and demographic factors in the community, what types of services and institutions - computer based or not - already exist in the community, and availability of resources are also important factors. Changes in computer technology (new databases, graphical interfaces, plug ins, and distributed applications) also influence the evolution of community networks; the earlier text-based systems, for example, have been replaced for the most part with web-based systems. Although the Seattle Community Network (SCN) was launched with the text-based Freeport software pioneered in Cleveland, the system is now largely web-based. Registered SCN users log in 33,000 times a month and the SCN web site gets receives 1.5 million hits per month.

When a user encounters the Seattle Community Network (http://www.scn.org – fig 5) the first thing he or she sees is the SCN logo, blending communication metaphors and Seattle imagery; Hermes, the Greek messenger of the Gods, reclining on snowcapped Mount Rainier, beckons to future users, the Seattle Space Needle, an icon from the 1963 World's Fair, now retooled as a communications beacon, held tightly in his hands. (The uncropped version of the logo is framed with the perforated border found on postage stamps, referring to yet another communication artifact - the traditional letter.)

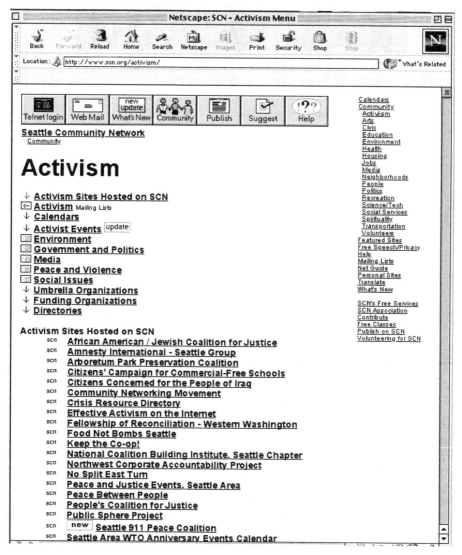

Fig. 6. Activism page

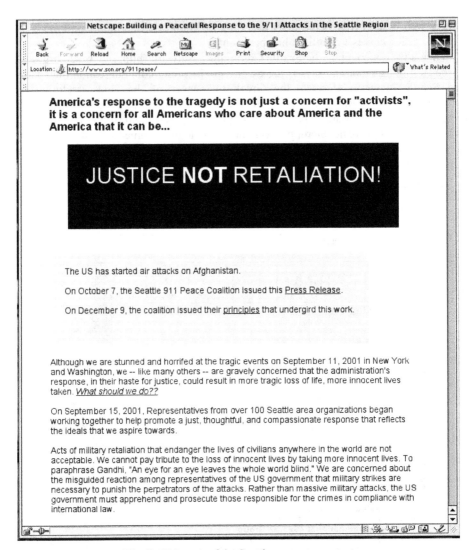

Fig. 7. Web page of the Seattle peace movement

In addition to providing free web space and e-mail, SCN also provides free support for electronic distribution lists via the *majordomo* program. Clicking the 'About SCN' link reveals information about SCN's policy (http://www.scn.org/policy.html) and principles. Basic information about contacting SCN, getting an account and publishing information on the SCN web site is found on the left side of the page, below the logo and the welcome message. Under that, the 'Seattle Site of the Week' is featured; the last time I looked it linked to 'Community Powered Radio' projects in Seattle. The SCN developers decided in an early design phase not to employ the building metaphor which was often used to organize information in Free-Net Systems ('Post Office', 'Public Square', 'Arts Building', 'School House', 'Sciences and Technology Center', 'Library', etc.). Instead they devised less concrete descriptors such as 'Acti-

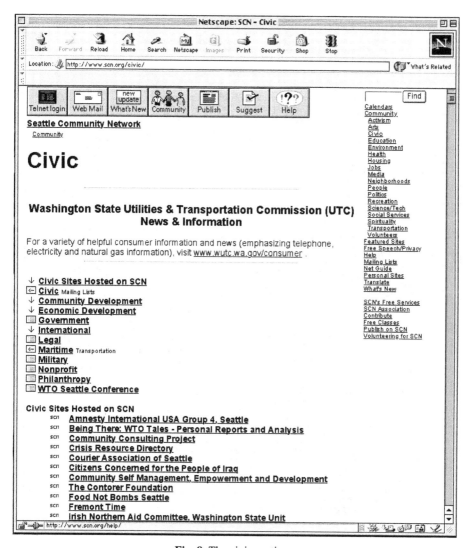

Fig. 8. The civic section

vism', 'Arts', etc. These major categories ('Activism', 'Arts', 'Civil', 'Earth', 'Education', 'Health', 'Marketplace', 'Neighborhoods', 'News', 'People', 'Recreation', 'Sci-
Tech' and 'Spiritual') are lined up alphabetically along the right edge of the page with
'activism' heading the list. While the placement is accidental, its prominent location
does help ensure prominence of 'Activism' to SCN web site users and of the idea in
general, a major part of the SCN project philosophy. Commercial search engines and
other major portals on the Web are, of course, unlikely to highlight this category at
all: selling things is the primary objective of those systems and social activism is
generally neutral or even hostile to the concerns and objectives of corporations.

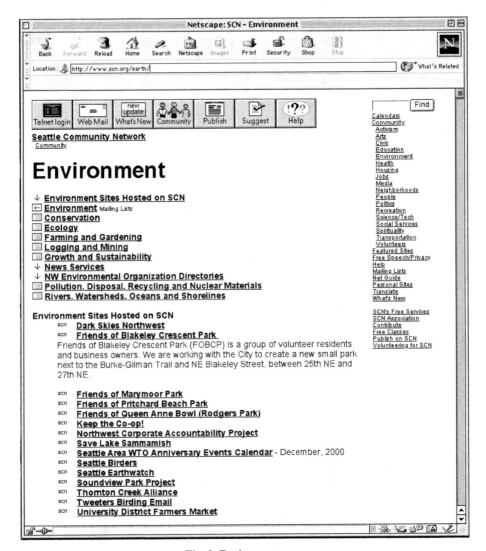

Fig. 9. Environment page

Clicking on the 'activism' link on SCN, brings up a wide range of information including links to 'Environmental,' 'Human Rights,' 'Hunger and Homelessness,' and 'Women' (fig. 6; http://www.scn.org/activism). Within days of the September 11 World Trade Center attack, Seattle's nascent peace movement had a web presence (fig. 7; http://www.scn.org/911peace) and email lists. All the information on this page relates to activism, generally in the Seattle area and generally on SCN, but not exclusively. The activism page, like all the other category pages on SCN, is coordinated and managed by a 'Section Area Editor,' one of the many volunteer roles at SCN.

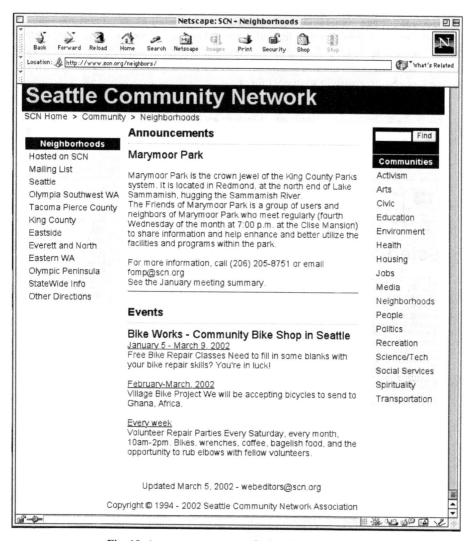

Fig. 10. Announcement page of a Seattle neighborhood

SCN, as of this writing, is run entirely by volunteers with all the advantages and disadvantages that this entails. Subject Area Editors, then, are basically free to organize their web page in the manner they prefer as long as they include the basic SCN header (which contains links to the other SCN subject pages) and are responsive to the information providers (IPs) who are adding information in that subject area.

The 'civic' section (fig. 8; http://www.scn.org/civic) has links to 'Social Services', 'Politics', 'Legal', 'Non-Profit', 'Philanthropy', 'Public Agencies' and 'International'. The Sustainable Seattle project deserves particular attention because of its potent model, which integrates community research, activism, and civic engagement. Sustainable Seattle has been developing a set of sustainability 'indicators' which – taken as a whole – provide a meaningful snapshot of the Seattle region's ability to provide long-range social and environmental health for all of its inhabitants – human and otherwise. Given Seattle's natural surroundings and strong environmental ethos, it's not surprising that SCN's 'Earth' section (fig. 9; http://www.scn.org/earth) is fairly rich. Links here point to 'University District Farmer's Market', 'Wannabe Farmers', 'Save Lake Sammamish' and many others.

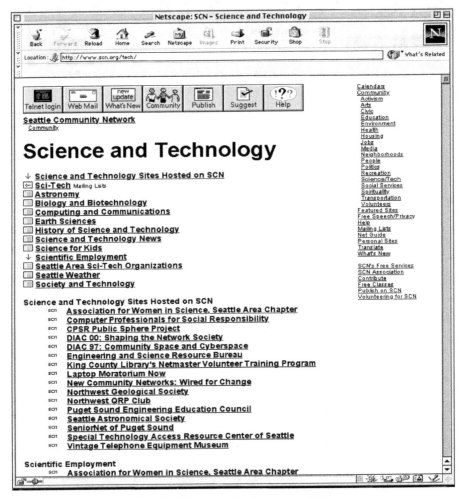

Fig. 11. Science and technology in SCN

The fact that the SCN 'Neighborhood' (fig. 10; http://www.scn.org/neighbors) section has been growing steadily over the years is important to the SCN organizers because supporting geographical communities has been a primary motivation from the project's onset. Although, ideally, a community network would exist for every community on the planet, it's clear that this is unlikely to happen in the near future. Although SCN places its main focus on the Seattle area, it is not intended to be its *exclusive* focus. Therefore other Washington state neighborhoods such as Kenmore,

Lakewood, and Bellingham use the SCN site as do such global neighbors as the 'Uganda Community Management Program' and the 'USTAWI: Promoting Self-Sufficiency in Africa' (sites which can be found on the 'Civic' section area). Neighborhood coalition groups such as the 'Seattle Neighborhood Coalition' and the 'Washington State Neighborhood Networks Consortium' also have links on SCN.

The 'Science and Technology' (fig. 11; http://www.scn.org/tech) section points to a large selection of important resources both on SCN and other locations. This page also lets users post a URL to science and technology resources or post information about upcoming meetings. There are links to several innovative projects such as the Community Technology Institute (which offers free voice mail to homeless and phoneless people around the US), and the volunteer-run Vintage Telephone Equipment Museum in Seattle. The 'Ask Mr. Science' service, currently not operational, allowed people to submit science questions to 'Mr. Science' who would then post the answers on-line. This feature, based on Cleveland Free-Net examples, was one of SCN's oldest features and had been used by many Seattle area classrooms.

4 The State of SCN

SCN, for much of its 10 year history, was a thriving computer system that has served as a model for many others throughout the world. SCN's future at this time is far from secure, however; after many years it still relies on volunteer labor and on financial donations, a reliance which dampens the technological modernization. The search for sustainability is not an issue for Seattle alone. Most, if not all, community networks throughout the world are finding it difficult to find the necessary support. For that reason many people suspect that community networks will need to rely on the government in the future for support, although this view is not universally shared. There is also apprehension that as billions of dollars are invested in commercial Internet ventures, community networks and other new civic institutions that employ digital technology may simply become more and more marginalized as time goes on. While relying on volunteers may be seen as virtuous by some, the drawbacks are numerous: volunteer labor is often unreliable and the available resources are generally inadequate for the wide-ranging tasks. 'Democratic self management' may also be considered an asset, yet in the absence of established chains of command, paralysis can set in. In January 2004, for example, one of the volunteer sysadmins posed the question of whether SCN should 'shut its doors' on the main SCN electronic distribution list. There was a brief flurry of messages from people who confirmed SCN's state of low-energy. Several years have passed since any significant program initiatives or proposal submissions have been initiated. The SCN board of directors has also been nearly invisible for the past few years in spite of one tepid letter of encouragement from a board member in response to the 'close the doors' suggestion. (Obtaining current usage statistics, for example, was not trivial; it took repeated messages to get any response to my queries for information.) On the other hand it must be noted that SCN has survived while other enterprises, both commercial and non-commercial have failed despite huge financial resources. Also, in fairness to SCN leadership, it should be noted that a frivolous lawsuit (ultimately thrown out of count) consumed a large amount of time that could otherwise have been devoted to SCN development.

4.1 SCN Users

The environment in which SCN exists has changed rapidly since its initial conceptualization. When SCN was first imagined in the early 1990s, the majority of Seattlites had no way of accessing the Internet: only those associated with military research and development, academia, or a hand-full of high-tech companies were provided with access - and individual users were not charged for their use. Now, a decade later, in early 2002, the Seattle region has changed considerably. The region has relatively high levels of income and education and has, thus, reached high levels of Internet penetration (city of Seattle, 2001). Also, due somewhat to the presence of Boeing, Microsoft, and a plethora of dot-com hopefuls (many now out of business), the region has a high level of technological sophistication and, therefore, a variety of ISPs to choose from. For those reasons, SCN has never enjoyed anything resembling a monopoly over Internet access in Seattle.

People use SCN for a variety of reasons. In 2002, over 14,000 people, for example, had an account on SCN in order to read and send email (from web or text-based interface) or to surf the web (using the text-based lynx browser). Over 12,000 of these had not logged into the system in the past six months. Because SCN is free and the accounts easily obtained and rarely purged the number of accounts greatly exceeds the number of active users. Many of these 'users' had never used their accounts! Presumably many of these former users (and non-users) had accounts elsewhere but only those who have their mail forwarded from SCN (nearly 3000) are definitely still users of networked digital services in general.

Local (and not-so-local) organizations are also SCN users. There are approximately 200 organizations represented on SCN although approximately 50 of them have not updated their web site within the last year. SCN also hosts a variety of email lists including several for the past September 11 Seattle Peace Movement. The web site enjoys the most attention; every week SCN receives approximately 300,000 hits, ranking it as one of Seattle's highest hit web sites.

In early 1997, Mark Herwick, then a doctoral candidate in Urban Planning, at Portland State University, put together the most comprehensive survey ever conducted of SCN users as part of his thesis on the development of a public computing infrastructure in Seattle. Herwick, with the assistance of Randy Groves reported on frequent SCN users. Some 20% of users accessed SCN from the public library while 71% accessed SCN from home. 76% of SCN users reported that they 'always' vote in local elections and nearly 75% of users have a bachelor, graduate or professional degree. Some 6% have not completed high school. Economically there was a wide distribution: 19% of users have household incomes under $15,000; 32% have incomes between $15,000 and $35,000; 23% have incomes between $35,000 and $50,000; and 19% have household incomes between $50,000 and $75,000. Herwick also learned that SCN is not as diverse as many of the developers would like. It turned out that nearly 75% of SCN's users are men and that 89% of all frequent users were white, 5% Asians and Pacific Islanders, while African Americans, Hispanics, and Multiracial people were about 2% each. Finally, 50% heard about SCN from the public library.

4.2 SCN's Effects

In the early days of SCN, newspaper reporters would often ask for 'success stories' that resulted from SCN use. Those stories weren't trivial to locate nor did they (or could they) accurately sum up either the potential or actuality of SCN. Any assessment of SCN (or any other community network) is necessarily going to be limited. For one thing, a community network user is generally not acting in an observable public way, nor is the user monitored or required to fill out monthly reports. Also, even if a snapshot of user effects could be obtained, there is no reason to believe that the snapshot represents a static unchanging situation. Conceivably a community network could cease operations yet a person or organization acting on ideas gleaned from community network ideas or from a relationship that the network helped foster could spring up years later--an event that an attempt to understand effects would almost unquestionably omit. Nor, of course, is it ever generally possible to precisely pinpoint the origin of any civic or community action. A variety of civic institutions and civic impulses is undoubtedly behind any complex or systemic civic or community amelioration.

But discussing the *difficulty* of evaluating, SCN doesn't obviate the need to seriously think about what it is, what its originators envisioned it to be, where it's heading, and what it could be. A community network, by definition, should probably claim community empowerment or other such community-oriented outcome as its major goal. But, computer use is often *individual* – not community-oriented. Thus community networks can address their objectives by helping individuals, who, presumably, go on to serve their community in some way. There are many instances of these although, as noted above, most go unnoticed. Also it should be mentioned that SCN serves as an educational venue in its own right. Chanh Ong, for example, the son of Vietnamese 'boat people' learned the rudiments of Unix and systems administration while volunteering as the educational editor on SCN. Although Chanh's motivation for volunteering was to 'give something back' to the community, his generosity in turn was rewarded: he has since found work using computers.

Hannah Levin [39] has written that the 'struggle to save community may create community.' In other words, a community network in and of itself can provide an occasion for shared work and, hence, help build community. Many of the SCN web pages are devoted to organizations, neighborhoods, and activism – which all rely on collective or *community* consciousness or action (as evidenced by the many non-profits with SCN addresses in Seattle independent newspapers). The continued growth of the number of those pages and the hits they receive is a testament (at least at this instant in time) to their usefulness to the community. Whether or not a community network is even used by many people in a community it can help (in conjunction with other efforts) to re-focus attention on the importance and legitimacy of community affairs. If a community network helps with economic development then it will probably alter the amount and effectiveness of democratic participation in that community. Contributing to the overall civic climate with a useful – and used – resource may be the most important (yet difficult to establish) community network goal, and one that SCN can justly claim credit for addressing.

SCN also has had effects that extend beyond the local Seattle environment. As we stated in our principles, we wanted SCN to serve as a model. In this respect the project has lived up to expectations. SCN's principles and policy statement have been adopted or adapted by other community networks around the world. SCN has been cited as a model or instance of civic innovation by many authors including Sirianni and Friedland [31] and Castells [4]. Within Seattle and outside SCN has helped build a civic culture. Beyond that SCN has helped promote and institutionalize the idea that computer networks can play a part in civil society worldwide -- if people are willing to put in the energy to make this happen.

5 Community Networks and Civil Society

Girded by basic democratic theory [5] and work by Habermas [34] and others, strengthening the civic sector, the sector of society which is neither governmental nor commercial (though intimately connected to both) could help ultimately, to address some of the staggeringly huge problems facing humanity and our natural environment. The civic sector contains educational institutions and millions of voluntary associations worldwide. Democracy, ideally, is a form of organized collective intelligence that could help society address major problems associated with social injustice and environmental degradation [30]. The major movements of the 20th Century, for human rights, civil liberties, sexual freedom, environmentalism, and women's liberation, were in fact, sparked by the civic sector.

The civic sector certainly has not allowed the implications of the network society and new communication technology (including the Internet) to escape them. A complete catalog of civic sector efforts, grounded and motivated by 'community core values' and the promise of richer communication is too large to be considered exhaustively here. Suffice it to say that NGOs and other civil society institutions are growing very rapidly [23] as are transnational advocacy networks organized along unified themes [16]. Community networks represent a complementary, principled impulse.

Community networks promote democracy in a number of different ways including (1) raising issues about control of technology and access; (2) supporting independent alternative media; (3) supporting civic associations; (4) supporting civic assets (e.g. non-profit organizations); (5) educating people about issues and about technology use; (6) sponsoring public forums on civic and other issues; (7) providing access to government, candidate, and referendum information and issues; (8) providing communication channels to government; (9) engaging in political work (organizing a rally in opposition to the US 'Communications Decency Act' for example); (10) providing access to relevant data and other pertinent information and knowledge; and (11) providing access to civic 'stories' [32] analogous to 'citizen schools' of the civil rights movement.

Although community networks are manifestations of democratic technology they are definitely works in progress. With little in the way of centralized administration or planning there are now hundreds of community network operational or planned projects in the U.S., Canada, and around the world. Many of these systems owe a debt to the now-defunct NPTN that popularized 'Free-Nets' and acted as an important broker for names of people that were interested in establishing community networks in specific locations. Currently no single 'community network' paradigm or sustainable model prevails and the corporate 'libertarian' rhetoric in the states has historically discouraged any consideration of public ownership or sponsorship of the networks. The idea of public ownership (at least in the U.S.) has few visible advocates and public institutions like libraries and public broadcasting affiliates have been relatively cautious in working with community networking projects.

6 New Directions for Community Networks

Because there is no paid staff or office space to rent, SCN's operating costs are very low; telephone lines and new equipment. Although their budgets are low and their obstacles nearly overwhelming, community networks offer compelling platforms for collaboration with computer professionals and other researchers. Some possibilities include usability studies, alternative user interfaces (including voice), new collaborative work environments [2], and communication spaces [24] and new collaborative and participatory design processes [26].

Civic applications are intended to be used by a wide variety of users and hence the design processes that are to be used are often more participatory. In some cases 'maximum feasible participation' of the citizenry is stipulated by law. There are various group processes that can be facilitated by computer technology [35]. GIS [14, 17] or simulation [37] systems can also be a key component in the participatory design of neighborhoods and public transportation. There are scores of possible civic applications awaiting exploration by community network developers. Search engines (Google being a notable exception), for example, are rapidly turning into 'TV Guides' for the Internet. What types of new search engines could support, public, non-profit, and educational uses? How would a public classification system, analogous to the Dewey Decimal system but geared towards network resources and without its strong English language and Western culture bias, help support a vast digital library to which everybody could contribute. What new on-line meeting tools for deliberation and decision-making are needed? A revised 'Robert's Rules of Order' [1] could extend into the electronic digital arena the same respect for process that Henry Robert19th century social technology for face-to-face meetings engendered. New tools are becoming available that help us understand large public conversations [24]. Web publishing kits (including those that use low-band width connections and older technology) could help grassroots organizations publish high-quality information electronically. What new user interfaces to these capabilities can be devised?

Many civic organizations are designing new systems for use by non-professionals. The RTKnet ('Right To Know' network) website (http://www.rtk.net) allows people to see what hazardous chemicals are being used in their communities. In Chicago, the Center for Neighborhood Technology established the Neighborhood Early Warning System (NEWS) that aggregates data from a variety of government agencies. Both systems provide consistent approaches to describe and present information from disparate sources. Complex situations demand data from various sources yet finding and assimilating the necessary constellation of interrelated information is one of the prime obstacles to effective data utilization [8].

Using computers and communications in developing countries provides additional challenges. Although these countries contain 75% of the world's population, they are home to only 3% of the web sites. How can these countries effectively reap the benefits that the Internet offers? (It is important to note that the idea of community networks is becoming more prevalent outside of Europe and North America. Early in 2002, for example, a book on community networks was published in India.) What tools can be devised that will help people in the developing countries preserve their own languages and cultures? Since money is scarce in the developing world, low cost approaches are particularly appropriate. For that reason, many developers in these countries are focusing on free software alternatives like Linux and older hardware; developing tools that could be used on those systems could also help leverage their development efforts. And newer technology such as wireless may also play important roles (see http://www.seattlewireless.net, e.g.) At a more fundamental level, the development of protocols for exchanging 'community work' information (such as task descriptions, schedules, etc.) could help spur work in inexpensive community 'groupware' systems. (This approach was suggested to me by Jakob Kaivo.)

History develops day-by-day, incrementally through an ongoing interplay of thoughts, discussions, decisions, actions, and events, many of which are irreversible. Communications technology presents a new spectrum of possibilities in terms of technology applications, policies, and use patterns. The Internet particularly can be thought of as a meta-medium, a medium that can serve as a host for other media. In recent years the Internet has been used as a substrate for analogs of a large number of familiar forms of communication including postal mail, bulletin boards, newspapers, radio, television, telephones, and video and audio conferencing. In addition, a host of hybrids and new forms such as MUDs and MOOs, avatars and virtual worlds, etc. are being postulated and developed all the time.

Clearly researchers will want to understand how these new forms affect people individually (who uses them, to do what, and for what reason), how they change the nature of small groups and organizations, and what effects the forms are having and could have at broader levels, across traditional boundaries, and at world-wide and transnational levels. But this paper suggests that a stronger, more engaged process is desired. *Researchers must actively participate in the development of democratic communication technology.* Community communication technologists offer researchers an opportunity to study first-hand communication systems that are grass-roots, spontaneous, community-oriented, and non-corporate. Researchers will want to learn how new communication technologies affect democratic practices within discrete geographic communities ('democracy-in-the-small') and, at the same time, how the spread of new technology affects democratic practices across geographic and human constructed boundaries ('democracy-in-the-large'). Researchers will also be interested in what peoples' expectations are for community networking in their jobs, homes, and communities.

Researchers can help make the community networking effort more effective while addressing important issues at the same time by concentrating on four areas: (1) informing the community networking community of relevant theory, history, policy and other issues in democracy and technology; (2) working with the community to establish and monitor conditions that facilitate learning, especially determining objectives, developing strategies, collecting data, measuring success, and evaluating and communicating results, and identifying future research; (3) offering other types of consulting and services related to educational programs, institutions, funding sources, and contacts in the community (including facilitating communication among and between the university community and the community networking community); and (4) integrating the community and the university [29].

7 The Community Networking Movement

Seattle Community Networks (and community networks generally) developed within a particular historical (social and technological) milieu. As such, its specific configuration can hardly be deemed to be a universal form. The context from which it emerged and the particular set of actors who elected to develop and use the system make it unique. Community networks such as SCN, nevertheless, may actually at a broader level represent – and support – universal needs, and may, in fact, be especially valuable at this moment in humankind's history. The need to communicate symmetrically and inexpensively is assuredly a given of the human condition. And in this era of migration and travel and dispersed communities, the people with whom other people communicate may not be in the local vicinity. The ability also to take part in local discourse without censorship or other control is certainly a prerequisite to a free society. Social change, of course, is unthinkable without communication.

But although communication is essential it is unlikely to help steer us towards more sustainable and humane ends by itself. Civic society historically has put forth social movements and other forms of social innovation to address concerns that were being neglected by extant organizations and institutions. Community networks can support these efforts by (1) giving voice to excluded people; (2) providing forums and venues for agenda-forming and deliberation; and (3) by helping to form bridges across various fracture points (economic, geographic, ethnic, etc.) can help that process.

The future of community networks and the future of the community network movement are strongly linked although individual community networks can thrive or languish somewhat independently of the other community networks and the movement as a whole. At the same time, much of the same discussion oriented around the future success of SCN or other community network systems can be re-used in relation to the success of a community network movement. A successful community network *movement* would necessarily include a network of individual community networks so strengthening individual networks is critical to any movement. Beyond that simple observation, however, lay numerous issues that need exploring as individual community networks and an emerging global movement continue to evolve and co-evolve. For one thing, in any community there will be a wide variety of related organizations and institutions that form the core of the civil society environment in a given community. It is within this environment that a community network must co-exist. How a community network collaborates with these other entities and how they mutually enhance (or detract from!) each other's efforts is a critical element of community networks everywhere and likely to be unique to each system. This situation applies to the community networking movement as well.

SCN's underlying objectives are to foster civic culture and to engender positive social change. How successful SCN is at achieving these objectives depends on SCN itself – its technological base and its organizational competence – and the community inside and outside of Seattle that uses SCN and becomes part of SCN's ongoing evolution. Note that an operational success, including lots of users, state-of-the-art technology, and an effective staff, does not guarantee that SCN's socially ameliorative goals will be met. Examining and exploring this presumed link between operational and social indicators is the crucial focus of any evaluation. It also is this link that will form the basis for ongoing development of operational goals (technological and organizational) and societally ameliorative goals (new programs and projects).

As might be expected, many potential critical issues arise at the boundaries between the local and the global. How much work in the developing 'network of networks' is done locally – within community networks that are intended to support specific geographical areas – and how much is done by umbrella groups that may or may not have substantial ties to local communities. Early 2002, the organizers ('secretariat') of the global community networking congresses in Barcelona and Buenos Aires had spirited discussions related to one of the most important issues in civil society – representation: who is entitled to speak, for whom, and on what issues? In addition to addressing the inherent conflicts between the local and the global, there are other important issues. What resources does the movement need? Can these be found locally or should an outside group that may have more experience in this area produce them? These issues also profound when considering the role of developed and developing countries. And, leaving the most important issue for last: What goals does the movement aspire towards and how are they identified? Related issues include how are internal conflicts handled and how does social learning occur in an equitable and effective manner so that the community networking movement as a movement can most advantageously maximize its potentials and opportunities while avoiding the numerous challenges. In short, how can the commu-nity networking movement manifest a 'civic intelligence' [30] that evolves as both its own potential and world dynamics shift?

Because there is little agreement on purpose or shared goals and little organized communication between efforts in different cities or regions, there is a diminished likelihood of widespread acceptance. Few organizers – in spite of occasional utopian rhetoric – have, for lack of time or inclination, even defined what they want to achieve or what their principles are. One community networker when pressed for a definition of community networking suggested that community networking was what community networkers did. SCN organizers formalized their objectives in a set of principles but that work was an exception. Moreover the NPTN founded by Free-Net pioneer Tom Grundner, the nominal umbrella group for Free-Nets, went out of business leaving the some two hundred Free-Nets and other community networks adrift with no single organization acting on their behalf. (Although an umbrella organization is not sufficient for success: the community radio effort in the U.S. in the early 20th century that failed in spite of a highly organized American Amateur Radio League presents an ominous and depressing precedent for community media at least in the states [15]). Although an 'Association For Community Networking' (http://www.afcn.org) was launched to fill the void in the US and there are compara-ble organizations in other countries (and a 'global' one as well), it is uncertain what ultimate impact these organizations will have and what success they will have linking and strengthening existing efforts.

The collapse of so many dot-coms may represent only a temporary setback for the 'new economy' based solely on digital networked transactions; all the old rules may indeed still be all rewritten and the new paradigm might still resume its inexorable rise to hegemony. Whether the setback is fleeting or evidence of a more fundamental barrier, this period offers a new window of opportunity for community networks and for the community network movement. The arrogant rhetoric of the digerati has, at least for the moment, has severely called into question several of the dominant myths of the 1990's. One of the myths is that ultimately by the sheer (and sole) force of the market every person in the world will have full (fast, reliable, inexpensive, uncensored) access to the Internet. Arguably, any path to that destination that relied solely on the market would result in a 'dumbed-down' Internet that looks more like commercial television than the new electronic agoras envisioned by social and technical meliorists.

At the core, the work of community networks (and a 'movement' of such) is intended to be socially ameliorative. While time may prove this objective to have been pathetically naïve, we must continue to keep these objectives central. On a local level this could mean helping to improve the quality of life for individuals in a community. While goals like this are laudable, it's not obvious that improving the lot of individuals – even the lot of *lots* of individuals – will stave off possible environmental and social disasters (such as nuclear annihilation). It's necessary, if regrettable, to point out that the problems facing the world today are in no way trivial, nor are they likely to go away on their own, by the 'free' market, or, even, through multiple reforms. This, of course, implies that radical changes may, in fact, be the *only* solution. This conclusion, however logical and inevitable it may be, is problematic. For one thing, there is no consensus (to say the least) on what these radical changes might be. No blueprint exists. Although we can – and *must* – envision a future and a roadmap for arriving there, a strategy of continual evaluation and re-evaluation – incremental change – is our only option. Incremental steps are necessary but hopefully – and against all odds – the incremental steps will not stop or be reversed after we attain 'modest' goals. A radical transformation, ultimately, will likely be necessary. In other words, civil society – through democratic discussion and action – must ultimately transform society and this will necessarily mean transforming – in a radical way – the dominant forces in our society. It should not surprise us that this work will almost certainly be resisted – and resisted in ways that may not abide by the niceties of civil society in spite of the claim that democratic societies have (or should have) the ability to radically transform themselves.

Acknowledgements

I'd like to thank Addison-Wesley for permission to adapt material from 'HCI Meets the 'Real World' Designing Technologies for Civic Sector Use published in Human-Computer Interaction in the New Millennium edited by John Carroll. Other material has been adapted from material that appeared in Technology and Democracy: User Involvement in Information Technology published by the Center for Technology and Culture, University of Oslo. Thanks also to Randy Groves who furnished the statistics for SCN and, along with a few others, has worked behind the scenes for years to ensure that SCN's technological platform functioned correctly.

References

1. Adams, J. and Powell, M.: Deliberation in the Digital Age. In (Day et al, 2000).
2. Arias, E., Eden, H., Fischer, G., Gorman, A. and Scharff, E. (2000). Transcending the Individual Human Mind: Creating Shared Understanding Through Collaborative Design. In (Carroll, 2001)
3. Carroll, J. (Ed.) (2002). Human-Computer Interaction in the New Millennium. Boston, MA: Addison-Wesley.
4. Castells, M. (2000). The Information Age: Economy, Society, and Culture, Three volumes). Oxford: Blackwell.
5. Dahl, R. (1989). Democracy and Its Critics. New Haven, CT: Yale University Press.
6. Day, P., Holbrooks, Z., Namioka, A. and Schuler, D. (2000). Proceedings of DIAC-00, 'Shaping the Network Society.' Palo Alto, CA: Computer Professionals for Social Responsibility. http://www.scn.org/cpsr/diac-00/
7. Doctor, R. and Ankem, K. (1995). A Directory of Computerized Community Information Systems. Unpublished report. Tuscaloosa, AL: School of Library and Information Studies, University of Alabama.
8. Durrance, J. (1984). Armed for Action: Library Response to Citizen Information Needs. New York, NY: Neal-Schuman.
9. Goel, M. (1980). Conventional political participation. In Smith et al. (1980).
10. Greider, W. (1993). Who Will Tell the People? New York, NY: Simon and Schuster.
11. Grundner, T. (1993a). Seizing the infosphere: an alternative vision for national computer networking. In Bishop (1993).\\\f
12. Grundner, T. (1993b). Organizing Committee Manual (The 'Blue Book'). Moreland Heights, OH: National Public Telecommunication Network.
13. Herwick, M. (2001). 'Shaping Public Access Technology: The Development and Use of a Metropolitan Community Information System. PhD thesis. Portland, OR: School of Urban Studies and Planning, Portland State University.
14. Lentz , B. (2000). Place Matters, Even in Cyberspace: Exploring Online Maps as Forms of Alternative Community Media. In (Day et al, 2000).
15. McChesney, Robert W. (1995). Telecommunications, Mass Media, and Democracy : The Battle for the Control of U.S. Broadcasting, 1928-1935. Oxford: Oxford University Press.
16. Keck, M. and Sikkink, K. (1998). Activists Beyond Borders: Advocacy Networks in International Politics. Ithaca, NY: Cornell University Press.
17. Krygier, J. (undated). Public Participation Visualization. http://www.owu.edu/~jbkrygie/ krygier_html/lws/lws_context.html
18. MacIver, R. (1970). On Community, Society and Power. Chicago, IL: University of Chicago Press.
19. McKnight, J. (1987). Regenerating community. Social Policy. Winter.
20. NPTN (1991). If it plays in Peoria Produced by National Public Telecomputing Network. Moreland, OH. 1991. Videocassette.
21. Putnam, R. (1993). The prosperous community—social capital and public life. The American Prospect. Spring.
22. Putnam, R. (2000). Bowling Alone. New York: Simon and Schuster.
23. Runyan, C. (1999). Action on the Frontlines. World Watch. November / December.
24. Sack, W. (2000). Navigating Very Large-Scale Conversations in (Day et al, 2000)
25. Schuler, D. (1996). New Community Networks: Wired for Change. Reading, MA: Addison-Wesley.
26. Schuler, D., and Namioka, A. (Eds.) (1993). Participatory Design: Principles and Practices. Hillsdale, NJ: Lawrence Erlbaum Assoc.

27. City of Seattle. Information Technology Indicators for a Healthy Community. Seattle, WA: City of Seattle Department of Information Technology. http://www.ci.seattle.wa.us/tech/indicators/indicators_report.pdf (2000)
28. Schuler, D. (1996). New Community Networks. Cambridge, MA: Addison-Wesley.
29. Schuler, D. (1997). Community Computer Networks: A Critical Opportunity for Collaboration Among Democratic Technology Researchers and Practitioners. Technology and Democracy: Comparative Perspectives. Oslo.
30. Schuler, D. (2001). Cultivating society's civic intelligence: patterns for a new 'world brain' Vol 4, Num 2, Summer 2001. Information, Communication and Society
31. Sirianni, C. and Friedland, L. (2001). Civic Innovation in America: Community Empowerment, Public Policy, and the Movement for Civic Renewal. Berkeley: University of California Press.
32. Sirianni, C., Friedland, L., and Schuler, D. (1995). The new citizenship and the Civic Practices Network (CPN). In Cisler, S. (1995) (Ed.) Ties that Bind: Converging Communities. Cupertino, CA: Apple Computer Corp. Library.
33. Smith, D., Macaulay, J., et al. (Eds.) (1980). Participation in Social and Political Activities. San Francisco, CA: Jossey-Bass.
34. Sparks, C. (1998). Is there a Global Public Sphere? In Electronic Empires: Global Media and Local Resistance edited by Thussu, D. (1998) New York: Oxford University Press.
35. Turner, N. and Pinkett, R. (2000). An Asset-Based Approach to Community Building and Technology in Day et al (2000).
36. Van den Besselaar, P., D. Beckers, The life and death of the great Amsterdam Digital City. In P. van den Besselaar, S. Koizumi (eds), Digital Cities 3. Information technologies for social capital. Lecture Notes in Computer Science, Vol. 3081. Springer-Verlag, Berlin Heidelberg New York (2005) pp. 64-93
37. Waddell, P. (forthcoming). UrbanSim: Modeling Urban Development for Land Use, Transportation and Environmental Planning, Journal of the American Planning Association.
38. Wellman, B. (1999). Networks in the Global Village. Boulder, CO: Westview Press.
39. Levin, H. (1980) The struggle for community can create community. In Gallagher, A. Jr., and Padfield, H. (Eds.) (1980). The Dying Community. Albuquerque, NM: University of New Mexico Press.

The Blacksburg Electronic Village: A Study in Community Computing

John M. Carroll

School of Information Sciences and Technology
Penn State University, University Park, PA.
jcarroll@ist.psu.edu

Abstract. This paper discusses the development of Blacksburg Electronic Village, and several of the ICT projects for local development. The stake-holders and their interests are analyzed, as well as the results, dilemmas and prospects.

1 Introduction

The Blacksburg Electronic Village[1] was an early example of a Web-based community network. The project achieved mass-media notoriety by projecting the image of an idyllic but isolated rural community pioneering the electronic frontier of totally wired life. Early high points were coverage of the project by the New York *Times* on January 16, 1994, and by NBC *Nightly News* on February 10, 1994. The incestuous nature of soft news, and the growing popular fascination with the Internet during this period led to a steady stream of derivative reports throughout the next two years.

The BEV project is interesting in many respects. It emerged from a tangle of visions about the future of telecommunications, notably the somewhat xenophobic fear of Japanese networking initiatives that pervaded the US in the early 1990s. It was always genuinely concerned with providing quality services to the people of Blacksburg, and yet it was planned and implemented almost entirely top-down, and without significant user participation in its early stages. Nevertheless, the project succeeded ultimately in attaining wide-spread community participation, in demonstrating many new applications and concepts for online community information and activity, and in transforming daily life in Blacksburg.

In my view, the BEV is a *transitional* example in the history of community networking. The first-generation of community network projects, chiefly from the 1980s, were strongly civic in their underlying motivations and core applications. Contemporary second-generation community network infrastructures are strongly commercial in their motivations and core applications. The BEV has always emphasized both.

The BEV incorporated the community development and social activism goals that were typical of the early community networks such as the Berkeley Community Memory [16], Big Sky Telegraph [32], and Cleveland Free Net [2], and still evident in projects like the Seattle Community Network [34]. It became a clearinghouse for

P. van den Besselaar and S. Koizumi (Eds.): Digital Cities 2003, LNCS 3081, pp. 43-65, 2005.
© Springer-Verlag Berlin Heidelberg 2005

community groups of all sorts — local chapters of mainstream service organizations, such as Kiwanis, the League of Women Voters, the Lions, the Rotary, and the Humane Society, as well as organizations more unique to the Blacksburg community, such as Beans and Rice[2] (a community development organization working with under-served populations of Central Appalachia), the Blacksburg Seniors[3], Citizens' Alliance for Sensible Gun Ownership and Legislation[4], Citizens Concerned about I-73[5], Friends of the Hand-in-Hand Park[6], the Montgomery County Christmas Store[7], and the New River Community Shelter[8]. The BEV Web site also provides links to 60 local churches, and too many local arts organizations and clubs (see figure 1).

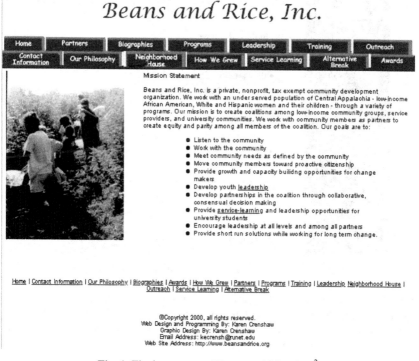

Fig. 1. The homepage of Beans and Rice, Inc.[2]

The Town of Blacksburg maintains an extensive Web-site for municipal information[9], including digital maps, dog licensing, parking, inspections and permits, road maintenance, parks and recreation, zoning and planning, and public transit schedules. The town provides some services directly online, for example, residents can request a vacation house check or participate in a government survey through a Web form, or have town announcements sent to them in email. For other services, forms can be downloaded from the Web-site[10].

However, the BEV also incorporated some of the commercial emphasis of contemporary digital city projects. The Village Mall portion of the BEV Web-site lists more than 550 businesses in 120 categories. Most of the listings are links to further Web-pages. This is quite an extensive yellow pages site, give that the town's population is less than 40,000. There is also a Visitor's Center link on the BEV homepage, providing Chamber-of-Commerce guidance to tourists and investors resources (fig. 2). A significant amount of the Town's online information also pertains to economic development. Indeed, one of the founding motivations of the project was to develop new products and services for home computing.

Fig. 2. The Blacksburg Electronic Village Visitor's Center[11]

I moved to Blacksburg in January 1994, joining Virginia Tech as head of the Computer Science Department and as a professor in computer science, education, and psychology. I was hired to help create a focus in human-computer interaction. When I arrived, the town and the campus were abuzz with excitement about the BEV project. I could hardly have not been drawn into it. Although I served as chair of the BEV Research Advisory Group for several years, I would characterize my main role in the project as a participant and observer. As for many of my neighbors, the BEV project has been an opportunity for me to learn and to try things out. I am fortunate to also be able to collect my reminiscences as part of my professional work!

2 Motivations for an Electronic Village

Technology develops in social, economic, political, and historical contexts. It is typical that groups of stakeholders must cooperate over spans of time, and that they bring slightly different visions and economic interests to the joint endeavor. Ultimately, the stakeholders create artifacts and techniques, but they also create interpretations and rationales. The Blacksburg Electronic Village is an interesting case study of how various conceptions of computer networking were constructed and reconstructed during the 1990s. Much of this history was archived as the project developed in the BEV HistoryBase, an archive of planning and policy documents, and announcements from the early years of the project that was available to the community through the BEV itself. (figure 3 [9])

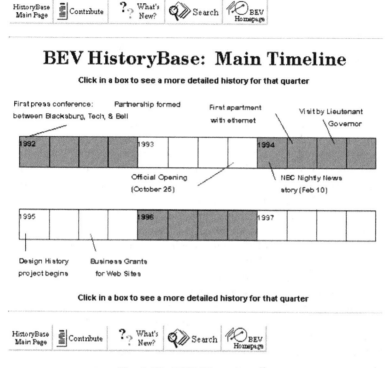

Fig. 3. The BEV HistoryBase[12]

The BEV project had its origins in a partnership among Virginia Tech (the primary research university in Virginia), Bell Atlantic (the regional telephone operating company), and the Town of Blacksburg. A further key supporter for the project was US Congressman Rick Boucher of Virginia's 9th District. In two major press conferences, one in January 1992, announcing a feasibility study for the Blacksburg Electronic Village, and another in January 1993, announcing that initial deployment would occur in fall 1993, representatives of the three organizations plus Congressman Boucher were the four principal speakers. In Fall of 1993, the BEV was operational, attracting about 1000 community members during its first year. In July 1994, Reed Hunt, Chairman of the US Federal Communications Commission (FCC) declared, "This private-public partnership sets an example for the rest of the nation" [1].

A variety of issues motivated the various stakeholders to participate in the project. Congressman Boucher was motivated in part by concerns about US competitiveness in telecommunications. This was a high-profile national concern in the early 1990s, often articulated as a need to respond to well-publicized Japanese initiatives. In a

1992 interview, Congressman Boucher stated that part of the urgency to develop the BEV was to help the United States compete with Japanese networking initiatives [30]. In early 1993, as the BEV project was preparing to launch, the new Clinton administration announced its intention to promote a National Information Infrastructure (NII). At the January 1993 press conference, Boucher characterized the BEV as one model for the implementation of the NII.

In the mid-1980s Virginia Tech was rethinking its strategy for campus telecommunications. There was frustration in the university with what was perceived as out-of-date and expensive telecommunications services. At this time, ambitious plans for a national research network were being developed through the NSFNET initiative. The university wished to play a leading role in such national research and development initiatives, and obtained state support to install a campus telephone switch and to build a high-bandwidth telecommunications network.

The campus network initiative of the mid-1980s motivated the university's participation in the BEV project in two rather distinct ways. First, better campus computing created a demand for better home computing. As early as 1989 the concept of what was referred to as a "community networking service" was discussed at Virginia Tech, and a 1990 university-internal white paper discussed how campus computing services could be extended to the community [27]. Narrowly, the community networking service concept was that faculty and students should be able to obtain the same level of computing support at home as they had in their offices and laboratories on campus [26]. More broadly, Virginia Tech saw the BEV project as an investigation of new ways of sharing knowledge. At the January 1993 deployment press conference, Virginia Tech President McComas envisioned networking as a means of bridging the gap between the university and the larger community, and of exploring new conceptions of literacy and citizenship.

The second way that the campus network development motivated the BEV project was that it provided a way of restoring relationships with the other stakeholders. When Virginia Tech established its own telephone switch and campus network, Bell Atlantic lost the revenues associated with providing these services, and the Town of Blacksburg lost the associated consumer utility taxes. The lost revenues were highly significant dimensions in the relationships among the three entities. For example, when my students interviewed Town Manager Ron Secrist ten years after these events, he quite fluently cited the exact amount of lost tax money [22]. The BEV project presented an opportunity for the three stakeholders to cooperate in exploring the future of telecommunications, and thereby also a means to better forget unpleasant aspects of their shared past.

Bell Atlantic (often acting through its subsidiary, Chesapeake and Pacific Telephone) was interested in the possibility that the BEV project could provide a model for future telecommunications services. Their vision was one of moving work, education, commerce, and leisure into the home. They saw their participation as investment in the development future products and services. They wanted to be the first of several corporate partners. Throughout the first two years of the project, 1992-1994, Bell Atlantic waited eagerly to confirm their vision through the participation of further corporate investors in the project. At the 1993 deployment press conference, they stated that further investments on their part would be made as new partners were identified. In 1995, it was discovered that Bell Atlantic had originally considered direct investments in the BEV project of as much as $5M, but had decided to proceed more cautiously, in the end spending only about $700,000 [27].

By 1995, Bell Atlantic was discouraged about the commercial possibilities of the BEV project, and looking elsewhere for new technology projects. In a November 1995 interview, at a point when Bell Atlantic had largely withdrawn from the project, David Webster of Bell Atlantic characterized their motivation for participating in the project as one of enhancing community and university relations [22]. This was indeed always a part of Bell Atlantic's motivation, but, based on statements made at the 1992 and 1993 press conferences, it was not originally their chief motivation, and was never their only motivation.

The Town of Blacksburg had two stated motivations (as summarized in a 1995 interview by Town Manager Ron Secrist [22]). One was to provide new ways for citizens to access local government services and to participate in local government. The second was to create new possibilities for local economic development, and thereby to also improve and promote the town's image. There are economic downsides to the romantic image of Blacksburg as an isolated place in the Appalachian Mountains. The vision of Blacksburg as a model for the future of telecommunications was very appealing in bringing the town from the national periphery into the national spotlight.

3 Tension Between Infrastructure and Community Participation

The early 1990s were a formative period in the history of the Internet. During this decade, computer networking was transformed from a rather arcane subculture into the center stage of popular culture. Citizens in general were not prepared for this; neither was government, especially local government. Research institutions and telecommunications companies also were scrambling to identify appropriate strategies. It was not clear to anyone exactly how the Internet would be useful or how that usefulness would be achieved. This uncertainty made exploratory development projects like the BEV even more exciting. But it also led to lack of coordination, and consequent tension between technology-driven initiative and user-driven initiative. This was true of Internet projects in general in the early 1990s, and it was true of the BEV in particular.

The early phases of the BEV project were absorbed with infrastructure. At the outset, the project committed itself to building upon existing network technologies, as opposed to pursuing fundamental innovations. However, it faced huge challenges in the integration and accessibility of network client software, in community content-development, and in user training and support. During the summer of 1992, a standard package of networking software, including ftp, gopher, a news reader and email was developed. The goal was to enable easy distribution and installation from floppy disk. Easy network access was by no means commonly available at the time; personal computers were not bundled with network client software as is now typical. Over the next two years, this software distribution was successively refined to improve both the tools and their ease of use. In early 1994, the BEV published its first Web page, and in the fall 1994, the World-Wide Web browser Mosaic was added to the BEV software package.

At the beginning of the BEV project, there was no community content to access. In November 1993, basic community information on schedules and activities was placed on a gopher server. However, this information was not updated for more than a year. Part of the problem was that few people in the community had the knowledge and skills to access Internet resources, let alone to publish and maintain such resources. Virginia Tech developed and provided training courses and documentation for community members to address these needs. However, a significant amount of the BEV group's effort went into individual user support. In the spring of 1994, Andrew Cohill, director of the BEV project for Virginia Tech, told me that building a community network was primarily a community education project.

Virginia Tech also initiated many hardware infrastructure improvements. In the summer of 1993, it established a high-speed modem pool for off-campus access, and began to install Ethernet in on-campus student housing.

Bell Atlantic accelerated the installation schedule for a digital switch [25], laid 42 miles of fiber optic cable, and announced an Integrated Services Digital Network (ISDN) trial. There is some uncertainty about the connection of some of this development to the BEV project. For example, in 1992, Bell Atlantic stated that the switch upgrade had nothing to do with the BEV project, but in 1993 they stated that the upgrade was a key part of their contribution to the project. The $6M cost of the switch was frequently cited in 1993-1994 to emphasize the magnitude of Bell Atlantic's contribution. Over the summer of 1993, Bell Atlantic installed Ethernet service in four off-campus apartment complexes, and a ten megabit per second connection to the Virginia Tech campus.

In spring of 1994, Bell Atlantic agreed to provide four T-1 Ethernet network connections to the Montgomery County Public Schools, free for one year. This modest donation had a significant effect in helping to engage the school system more fully in the BEV project. Later in 1994, the Montgomery County school system created the position of Technology Coordinator, and cooperated with Virginia Tech faculty on a successful proposal to the National Science Foundation for a $99,000 planning grant to develop concepts for a "virtual school". In spring 1995, the school system authorized $400,000 for school computing, and in fall of 1995, cooperated with Virginia Tech to win a $1.1M award from the National Science Foundation to create a virtual school within the BEV infrastructure.

Starting in February, 1992, the Town of Blacksburg expanded the scope of its cable television committee, the Blacksburg Telecommunications Advisory Committee (BTAC). After 1992, BTAC meetings were primarily concerned with the BEV project. The Town also coordinated the creation of BEV, Inc., a non-profit corporation created to handle grants. Unfortunately, and despite impressive and effusively positive national news coverage, no new partners joined the BEV project. The Town created a 3-year technology plan; it had never had such a plan before.

The people of the Blacksburg community were always an important element of the BEV vision. At the 1992 press conference, Joe Wiencko, director of the BEV project for Virginia Tech, said "This is a project about people, not technology." Robert Heterick, Vice President for Information Systems at Virginia Tech in 1992, called the project a "Field of Dreams scenario," a statement that conveys both the importance of local residents coming online, and a confidence that if the infrastructure were built, residents would come (see also [33]). At the 1993 press conference, Dr. Erving Blythe, Vice President for Information Systems at Virginia Tech in 1993, said "... in the end, the residents will define what the village is." Nevertheless, the involvement of community members in the planning phase was limited to reading about the BEV in the press.

The Blacksburg branch of the Montgomery-Floyd Regional Library played an important role in supporting the adoption of the BEV by the community. In January, 1994, the Blacksburg branch of the Montgomery-Floyd Regional Library, with the support of a federal Library Services Construction Act grant, installed seven networked computers, allowing access to the BEV and to the Internet on a walk-in basis. The January, 1994, NBC *Nightly News* story featured images of people using the BEV in the library. Libraries are now typical sites for community computing, but this role had not been developed in 1993. Indeed, the installation of computers in the Blacksburg branch was achieved over the objections of two members of its board of supervisors. Over the six months, the library trained about 500 community members, as well as providing one-on-one support for sessions in the library. (See figure 4)

Fig. 4. Community members accessing the Internet from the public library[13]

In February 1994, the library began acting as a receiving station for BEV applications. This was quite important as the BEV office was in a fairly remote campus location, whereas the library branch is in downtown Blacksburg, across the street from town hall. The library's role is especially interesting in that it was not included in any of the early planning process. It is the first example of a community group taking a share of control in the BEV project.

During the spring of 1994, the BEV developers began to actively solicit community participation. There was a note of anxiety in the invitation. After two years of planning and groundwork, the BEV was ready for the community, but it seemed that the community was sluggish in adopting it. For example, Andrea Kavanaugh, Director of Research for the BEV, said in an interview, "The community really has to take charge if it wants to get a lot out of it" [17]. With the perspective of time, the rate of adoption in the BEV was not slow. In 1994, home use of the Internet was almost non-existent. The early adopters of the BEV really were pioneers, something easy to forget as it has turned out that the whole rest of world followed them within the next five years. The early adopters included many community leaders and they brought great energy to the project of creating the BEV as an information and communication activities, as opposed to mere infrastructure. By the fall of 1994, after one year of operation, the BEV had about 1000 community members and 40 businesses. (See [24] for discussion of the technology diffusion process.)

In spring of 1994, Andrea Kavanaugh and Scott Patterson conducted the first of their BEV surveys[14]. Their 332 respondents indicated more interest in local content and services than in world-wide Internet content and services. Of course, it is important to recall how undeveloped the World-Wide Web was in 1994 with respect to entertainment, retailing, and other commercial services. The local content and services in the BEV were also far less developed in 1994 than they are now. But it is still notable that the residents initially came to the BEV for the local content and services.

The BEV's second year included many milestones. During 1995, one third of all businesses in Blacksburg had a listing in the BEV Village Mall Web page, many listings included links to Web pages maintained by these businesses. By the end of 1995, 14 Blacksburg companies provided Web design, server space, and Internet consulting; 12 of these companies were founded during that year. The Town of Blacksburg provided $15,000 to BEV, Inc., for 47 small grants to help local businesses establish or improve their World-Wide Web pages. Ken Anderson, a BEV, Inc, board member, explained that these grants were preferentially awarded to businesses that bring money into the town from outside, as opposed to businesses that "just circulate money inside the town" [22].

4 Reconstructing the Vision

After the excitement of 1994-1995, the BEV entered a relatively more steady state. It continued to grow, and in many ways to thrive. However, the original partnership dwindled, leaving the community in control, as had been originally envisioned. Bell Atlantic became more interested in video-on-demand, a more obviously commercialized technology vision. It became increasing less visible in the BEV partnership. Its current role is essentially that of the local telecommunications utility.

An interesting question about the BEV project is why, given the enormous national publicity of 1994-1995, no other corporate partners joined the project. Andrew Cohill, BEV Project Director, suggested one reason in a November 1995 interview, "Someone from IBM told us that nothing we're doing in Blacksburg has any relevance because we're not charging for the service" [22]. A related potential factor is the genesis and vision of control in the project. From the start, Virginia Tech provided most of the vision and energy for the BEV. Bell Atlantic and the Town provided supporting visions. Although there was a partnership framework, Virginia Tech operated the BEV and therefore made almost all the decisions in the early phases. Part of Virginia Tech's vision was that control of the network should ultimately be ceded to the community. Neither of these aspects of project control may have matched corporate expectations for a technology testbed.

Perhaps the original vision was flawed. In 1992, see above, Robert Heterick, Vice President for Information Systems at Virginia Tech, had called it "a Field of Dreams scenario" Many would argue that there should have been fuller participation of all stakeholders in the BEV project from the start — including community members. One response to this is that the town represented community interests in the original partnership. Another response is that the general lack of relevant knowledge throughout the non-Virginia Tech portion of the community would have led in any case to relatively poor participation. In this view, part of the BEV project had to be implemented — namely, the technology infrastructure and the training and educational outreach portion — *before* meaningful participation was possible. It is true that prior to the BEV project, community participation in telecommunications policy was limited almost entirely to Virginia Tech faculty and staff. Today, partly due to the BEV project, many non-Virginia Tech community members are informed and involved in local telecommunications discussions.

At the outset of the project, there also were competing visions about the future of telecommunications. For example, Herman Bartlett, superintendent on Montgomery County Public Schools, believed that interactive video would be a critical school technology. He initially resisted committing school resources to the BEV project. A liaison for the school system later commented: "We weren't talking to each other, and finally we started talking to each other, but we had different agendas" [27]. Some of the explanation for limited community participation in the early stages of the project derived from this unresolved conflict in visions.

There clearly were some negative consequences of the limited early involvement of the community. For example, during its first year, the project quickly assimilated the community's early adopters [24], but it struggled somewhat to make its case to the balance of the community. In 1994 the BEV project was perceived as a university initiative. The meeting minutes of the Blacksburg Telecommunications Advisory Committee show clearly that the Town saw the project as something outside that it was assessing and supporting, not as something it owned. As individuals, community groups, and the Town contributed to the project, publishing their information and carry out their activities, they gradually assumed more ownership for the BEV. This took many months and involved some significant crises.

In March 1996, Virginia Tech announced that it would cease providing Internet services to non-university BEV subscribers as of July 1. This decision was partly political: The state government of Virginia had been cutting university budgets for several years, and Virginia Tech felt it could not afford the appearance of squandering state resources. Along with the new policy on Internet services, the university reduced its funding for the BEV project; most of the staff were made part-time. Ironically, the decision was also due to the economic development success of the BEV: Local Internet companies were eager to assume roles as Internet Service Providers. Indeed, Bell Atlantic began offering ISDN services in August of 1996. The university wanted to support such private initiatives, and definitely not to compete, or to be seen to be competing with them.

The decision to transition non-university members to commercial providers clearly also follows from the original project vision of ceding control to the community. However, the fact that community members had been peripheral in the early planning, and were not involved in this specific decision, invited understandable misperceptions. There were outcries in the community that non-university residents had been "kicked off" the BEV. The issue persisted for months ([29]; notice that cancellation of university network accounts is the top story on the BEV homepage from June 1996, figure 5). The project that President McComas had envisioned as creating a new model for campus-community cooperation, had accidentally triggered a classic crisis of town/gown exclusion/inclusion.

Fig. 5. BEV Homepage in June 1996

Since this transition in networking services, the main role of the BEV group in Virginia Tech has been maintenance of the core Web pages, commercialization of the BEV model for other communities, and research on community computing. The university no longer leads the BEV project; most of the interesting initiatives since early 1996 have occurred elsewhere.

The transition to more distributed control was difficult even on the university's side. As the university withdrew direct support, the BEV group no longer had the resources or the responsibility to direct the project. In Fall 1995, I invited the BEV project director to visit my graduate seminar on "Community Networks, Network Communities." The class discussion suggested that the BEV might be enhanced with synchronous communication mechanisms like multi-user domains (MOOs) or chats. And I was surprised at how abruptly this idea was dismissed by the BEV director — on grounds that synchronous mechanisms consume too much network bandwidth. This dismissal motivated several of my students to create a community MOO, which proved to be practical and quite popular, and which helped to cause the BEV group to implement a chat a few months later [16]. In 1995, Mary Beth Rosson and I analyzed patterns of participation in the BEV, and concluded that a new topology of innovative activity was evident, one quite different from the historical organization of the project [7]. In our analysis, the BEV in late 1995 consisted of largely independent groups managing their own communication and activities through the Internet. Common local interests, and the loose integration provided by the BEV site, encourage and facilitate mutual awareness of the various groups. They use the network to present themselves to the larger community, to communicate, coordinate, and recruit. The main source of vitality in the BEV today is the innovative services, applications, and community activities of these groups.

5 Integrating Participation and Innovation

The more central role played by community groups in the BEV project after 1995 created many opportunities for research and development of innovative network services and methodologies. My group at Virginia Tech benefited from this. In 1994, we began a design collaboration with two public school teachers [21]. We wanted to investigate whether and how the teachers could contribute to the design of network tools for collaborative science learning. More generally, we wanted to investigate a broad-scope and long-term participatory design relationship in a domain in which users enjoy a high level of discretion regarding the use of technology.

This has proven to be a incredibly rich undertaking. The BEV is a genuine computer science research opportunity in collaborative software and in participatory design. It was also a research opportunity in educational technology, curriculum development, and school administration. Our research work in the BEV context has led us to develop and study new concepts, such as direct community mentoring in the schools, and community-oriented approaches to developing what the US federal government now calls an "information technology workforce."

Our project with the Montgomery County Public Schools continued through six years, during which we worked with six teachers, including two who collaborated with us through the entire period. The project involved regular observations of classroom practices, and demonstrations and discussions of new technology ideas and possibilities. We deployed, assessed and refined several versions of collaborative tools. Ultimately, we developed a virtual school environment, incorporating email, desktop video conferencing, chat, and a collaborative science notebook that allowed student groups to coordinate their projects at the level of typed sections (including a project planner, a collaborative whiteboard, a bibliography, and so forth; see figure 6 [19]). The virtual school allowed students in different local schools to work together on science projects.

Participatory design is a process of mutual learning, and thus of personal development for participants. But it is often exemplified by rather singular and ephemeral learning interactions. Much research on participatory design has focused on relatively short-term collaborative relationships. This is especially true in North America; for example, the well-known PICTIVE technique is directed at brief user interface design interactions of perhaps one hour [20]. Such methods are both effective and democratic, but it seems unlikely that the experience of manipulating a user interface mock-up during a brief participatory session can have a significant developmental effect on a person's knowledge, skills, self-confidence, or other professional capacities.

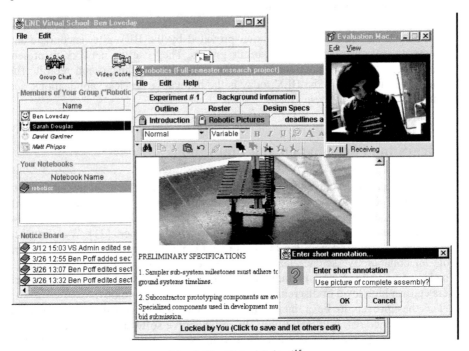

Fig. 6. The Virtual School[15]

Where participatory design investigations have focused on longer-term interactions, chiefly in Europe, these often involve extremely well-organized user groups with well-defined roles and prerogatives in the design process. In many cases, the users are represented by labor unions whose personnel provide legal representation of user interests in the design process. In these cases there is sometimes a clear demarcation, even conflict, between the user (union) interests and management's technology strategy. Indeed, this is an important element of the context for many of these studies. Because the user role in many of these studies is both specified a priori and representative (versus individual), the personal development of user-designers is not a central issue. These case studies also typically involve situations in which the development and deployment of new information technology is a given, and the challenge is to define appropriate technology for the users and their activities [3].

We felt we needed to create and study a broad framework for participatory design interactions. The US NSF program that sponsored our work was directed at producing models for how new computer networking infrastructures could facilitate systemic change in public education (as opposed producing specific curricular innovations). Thus, an important orienting goal was enhancing the autonomy of teachers with respect to our technology infrastructure. In other words, we assumed from the start that in order to succeed, we must someday fade from the project, and leave the teachers to maintain and develop its achievements. This meant that the teachers' involvement could not be limited to requirements interviews, or even to relatively active roles in conceptual design. We needed to think of them as collaborators in implementation, deployment, testing, and refinement, and as leaders in the development of courseware and classroom activities that would exploit the software.

Public education presents a rich challenge for participatory design. Teachers work in a complex and dynamic context in which measurable objectives and underlying values collide on a daily basis. Traditionally, teachers work in isolation from their peers; individual teachers have well-established personal practices and philosophies of education. Teachers have enormous discretion with respect to what goes on in their classrooms, yet are also routinely interrogated by supervisors, by parents and other community members, and by educational bureaucracies. This has led to an abiding tension in the culture of schools: Teachers' innovative practices are often not adequately acknowledged or valued, and at the same time, teachers often passively resist school reforms that are imposed top-down.

Technology is a particularly problematic element in the culture of schools. The isolation and discretion of the teacher's work environment requires that technology for classroom use be highly appropriate and reliable. Yet it is generally assumed that teachers are to be *trained* on new technologies, not asked to *define* what those technologies should be. From the teacher's standpoint classroom technology often is itself the problem, not the solution. This culture of technology development in the schools has been singularly ineffective — film and radio in the 1920s, television in the 1950s, computer-assisted instruction in the 1980s, among others, have been notable failures [13, 18, 31].

In part because our project was a long-term, community-oriented effort in which all the parties shared control, we were able to investigate the development of cooperative technology development relationships to a depth that had not been reached before [6, 14]. We developed a model of the developmental course of our long-term cooperative relationship that could be used to guide further such investigations.

The scope and depth of cooperation among stakeholders in this project directly enhanced the computer software we developed. For example, the school context presents strong requirements for integrating synchronous and asynchronous collaborative interactions: Students need to establish mutual trust and confidence, and assess overall project direction and progress in real-time. We observed a strong need and a great interest in desktop video conferencing, though we also identified many challenges in making it effective [15]. However, in our extensive experience, class schedules among two or more schools cannot be reliably coordinated; there are too many scheduling constraints in schools. Thus, asynchronous group work is crucially important to the success of collaborations. One concrete consequence of this is that chat logs must be persistent, and that collaborators must by provided with a persistent session log of some sort to help them remain aware of others' activity. These are not typical tools in education software packages, but they were central to the virtual school [19].

The virtual school project was an example of a community institution, the public schools, working cooperatively with faculty and students from Virginia Tech to create innovative educational technology. It is sharply different from the original genesis and organization of the BEV project, which flowed from the visions of top-level administrators in the town, the telephone operating company, and later the Town of Blacksburg. The vision in this case came from individual teachers, graduate students, and professors. The project was enabled by the BEV infrastructure broadly understood: the network, the community education, and the very notion that a community can undertake creative technology projects. But the specific innovation and execution in this case was delegated back to the individual level.

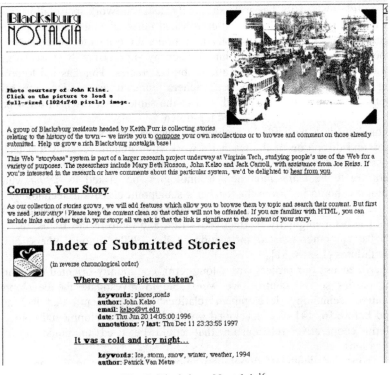

Fig. 7. Blacksburg Nostalgia[16]

Perhaps it is too much to suggest this pattern as a model case of community computing. But we have successfully carried out other projects essentially in this mold: We observed that senior citizens had organized a mailing list to exchange and develop stories about life in Blacksburg during the 1960s, a period when members of the group were young adults. The group was interested in preserving these stories and making them available to other community members. We worked with them to create a Web-based forum, Blacksburg Nostalgia, for posting and annotating stories ([12];

figure 7). We found that the forum was used not only by other seniors, but by younger people in the community, as well as by former members of the community — people who had moved away from Blacksburg, but who still felt connected to it. This is an example of a very traditional activity, namely community oral history, transformed by community networking.

In 2002, we were working with a variety of community groups to create a more innovative networking infrastructure for the entire BEV. Our MOOsburg environment is a place-based collaborative virtual environment that models the geography of Blacksburg: Users move around a virtual Blacksburg by pointing to locations in an interactive map. Each location presents distinctive tools, information, and activities; for example, pointing to the natural history museum presents various exhibits about the natural history of the Blacksburg area, discussions about exhibits and natural history, and whatever other users are currently visiting that location. This approach replaces the BEV view of Blacksburg as a hierarchical hypertext with a map-based view of the place itself. It utilizes knowledge and familiarity about the physical layout of the town, and more directly evokes feelings about places ([10,11]; figure 8).

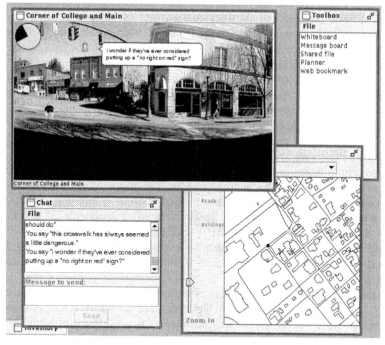

Fig. 8. MOOsburg[17]

Of course my view may not be fully objective, but I think these projects show great potential for community computing as a context for interdisciplinary research in social and computer science that is simultaneously practical community development. It is significant that these projects have brought over 2 million US dollars in funding from federal agencies and private foundations. This support is comparable to the total specific expenditures on the BEV project by Bell Atlantic and Virginia Tech.

6 Leveraging the Electronic Village

Community computing can be inspiring and fulfilling. It is a modern idiom for the romantic image of neighbors working together to create a safe haven and to prosper together. But community computing is socially and technologically important, both practically and from the standpoint of research throughout the social sciences and computer science [5,8]. It can be an engine and a tool for economic opportunity, education and training, self-expression and leisure, and social and political development. It can be a testbed and laboratory for studying issues ranging from the usability of computers and networks to the creation of social capital in participatory democracy.

The key challenge for community computing is that it is inherently a composition of somewhat contrasting agendas and interests. To succeed fully, community computing requires an ecumenical perspective, and the broadest possible participation across institutions and groups comprising the community. It must embrace several cross-cutting tensions. Understanding these tensions, and ways they interact and can be managed, forms the core of a research program for community computing.

One inherent tension is between community development and technology development. Early community networks were often implemented with relatively primitive computer networking technology — personal computer bulletin boards broadcast nightly via telephone modems. Such cumbersome infrastructure congers romantic images of electronic pioneers [23]. Perhaps living with information system hardships helps to emphasize that content is paramount. And it surely is true that control of community information is enhanced by lack of dependence on centrally-managed infrastructures. But this is also the logic that leads people to live in caves.

The BEV planners specifically rejected this axiom of primitive insularity in community networking, replacing it with an orientation that today is more typical, namely, a commitment to fully exploit the state-of-the-art. This orientation led them to integrate the BEV with the Internet, to adopt the World-Wide Web in early 1994, and to conceive of the BEV project as a testbed in home computing, including novel concepts in what became known as e-government and e-commerce. This strategy had its own downsides. Integrating the BEV with the Internet made it seem sometimes more a public relations experiment than an experiment in civic computing. It raised the question, which has become perennial, of exactly how the BEV is more than Internet access.

I believe that the BEV's orientation to technology was correct, and that it can be pressed further. Perhaps community networks are an ideal setting for prototype development and application of advanced networking infrastructures [5]. Communities are highly robust technology incubators; the diversity among users, applications, and hardware and software infrastructures that one finds in a community contrasts with the relative homogeneity of work organizations. Communities are also highly accessible technology incubators; they are easy to get to and inexpensive to use; we all live in one. Because the culture of community computing depends on intrinsic motivation, it is easy to get rich feedback, one only has to listen. Our work with the virtual school and MOOsburg shows how software ahead of the commercial state-of-the-art can be developed and applied in community contexts. In these projects, we found that rapid cycles of user feedback and prototyping were enabled by the accessibility of our community partners and the informality of our relationships with them.

Community development is facilitated when the technology supporting it is effective. Achieving this may involve employing advanced technology, as was the case when the Blacksburg community learned together about the World-Wide Web in 1994, and today is learning about Java enhancements to the Web. It may involve exploring and adapting new models for managing technology, as when commercial enterprises "host" community information. There is no inherent conflict between human values and technology. Technology is one of the salient creative forces and opportunities in contemporary culture. The challenge is not to merely rein in technology, but to push it toward effective applications for community development.

A second tension in community networking is that between the need for top-down initiative-taking in the creation of comprehensive and effective infrastructures, and the risk that top-down control can limit the adoption and creative development of community networking. One of the early ironies of the BEV project is that while all the visions pertained to new ways of empowering ordinary people with technology, those people were mostly left out of the discussions. They were represented by institutional proxies: university administrators and technicians, telephone company executives and planners, town government officials. "The community" — in the sense of groups like the League of Women Voters and Beans and Rice — was left out.

The community should have been involved earlier in the BEV project. However, it is not straightforward to describe just how community groups and individuals could have helped to direct the early stages of the BEV project. The university and the telephone operating company had computer scientists and technicians who could design and implement the BEV infrastructure and the first few examples of how that infrastructure could be brought to bear on community information and activities. The community, per se, did not have the relevant knowledge and skills, or the resources to create a comprehensive networking infrastructure. Knowledge and skill ineluctably engender control, and at the outset of the project, the university and telephone company had the knowledge and skill.

In our virtual school project we adopted a tenaciously participatory approach. We wanted to explore a methodological option *not taken* in the original BEV development. Although we showed how such a participatory approach can be used, and with what consequences, we still struggled in the initial years with the imbalance of knowledge and skill. We found that no matter how strongly and steadfastly the technical people ceded control to the teachers, the teachers still tended to defer to that knowledge and skill. However, we found that by including the teachers from the earliest stages, we also included *their* special knowledge and skill, that is, pertaining to classroom management, pedagogy, and learning [6]. Perhaps the best we can have is a symmetrical imbalance.

Community networks, because they are comprehensive information infrastructures, often utilizing innovative communication technology, require significant top-down direction. But this must be coordinated and balanced by grassroots initiatives originating throughout the community and from the outset of the project. The "Field of Dreams" model — build it and then they will come — is neither appropriate nor effective.

A third tension is between civic and economic motivations. The historically deepest root of community networking regards the networks as a sort of liberation technology — not as a panacea, but as a potentially significant tool for building social capital in local communities, and thereby re-energizing collective action. This vision has been clearly articulated by Doug Schuler [28]. A second, perhaps more contemporary vision sees the networks as a new sort of economic infrastructure, enabling commerce and tourism. This second vision is sometimes associated with the label "digital cities," though, as mentioned in the introduction to this chapter, the BEV project always incorporated this economic vision.

In principle, there is no conflict between the civic motivation and the economic motivation. The two ought to be mutually reinforcing; joint commitment and shared endeavor in one sphere should inspire commitment and endeavor in the other. Of course different individuals and groups working within a community network might be relatively more or less oriented toward one or the other. In practice, however, there is often a dissociation between the two. A good example is the set of digital cities hosted under America Online's Digital City, Inc. service[18]. One accesses the service by specifying a US postal (zip) code. Doing this, I found there is no service for Blacksburg, just a generic Central Virginia page. So I decided to explore the Richmond digital city, since it is pertains to a specific place, somewhat close to Blacksburg.

The Richmond digital city[19] was lopsided with respect to the dual motivations for community networking. There was a heavy emphasis on tourist information: attractions, hotels, restaurants, museums, amusement parks, day trips and itineraries, airport information, shopping, the gay scene, and so forth. There was a lot of "personals" information: email pen-pal listings, chat rooms, guy/girl of the month, forms for submitting one's photos, and so on. Interestingly, much of this "personals" information seemed to be aggregated over a larger geographical region than what one would think of as Richmond. Alas, the girl of the month was at least a 3-hour drive from Richmond.

Indeed, quite a bit of the content leveraged other AOL data and software. For example, the yellow page listing of Richmond businesses was apparently a filtered view of AOL's national yellow page database. In this listing, the names of companies were link anchors, but the links were not to individual business homepages, as might be the case in the BEV, they were links to Mapquest maps. The job listings were also presumably subsetted from a national database, and included generic links to relocation services. Of course, the digital city Web-pages included advertising banner applets, and from time to time spawned sub-browsers with advertisements and forms.

Although I have never been a Richmond resident, I felt that the proportion of generic information diluted the feeling that the site had much to do with Richmond. Clear cases of Richmond community information were scarce. There was an essay, Richmond 101, on the history and economy of Richmond. There was some information on neighborhoods, though it seemed to be mainly concerned with real estate purchase. There were no links to community groups or community activities. There was a link for family information, but it was limited to a list of a half-dozen swimming pools. And there is a small list of places to walk and bicycle. There was an interesting forum mechanism for posting comments on qualities of local businesses (and the comments were not all blandly positive!). Perhaps as this service develops, further community-specific and civic-oriented information and activities will be incorporated.

It must be acknowledged that the consequences, for people and for communities, of different approaches to community networking are not understood. Different motivations and models for the networks are now essentially matters of design philosophy. The state of the art in empirically evaluating community networks is a mere handful of survey studies of self-selected users [8]. One of the most important steps toward understanding how to reconcile civic and economic motivations — and a host of other issues — is better evaluation methods and more evaluation studies, including comparative studies, so that philosophical and apparent contrasts can be verified and elaborated. With the support of the US National Science Foundation, we have recently begun such a study of the current use and impacts of the BEV on the Blacksburg community. Our study includes two community surveys, remote session logging of home Internet computing, a series of ethnographic in-home interviews, and online participatory forums in which the entire BEV community will discuss both the BEV project and our evaluation of it (figure 9).

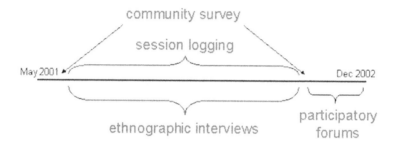

Fig. 9. Timeline for our BEV evaluation project[20]

The buzz of excitement that pervaded Blacksburg in 1993, and reached its peak in 1995, has long since subsided. Community Web pages today are too mundane for features in the New York *Times* or NBC *Nightly News*. What is not mundane is the possibility of focusing community energies on learning and using technology, and through that enhancing social capital, productivity, and other collective and individual goods. That was the original question and the original vision of the BEV project. Maybe it's not that the buzz of the BEV subsided, but just that the rest of world has started buzzing just as loudly.

Acknowledgements

I am grateful to many students and colleagues for drawing me into research interests concerning the BEV project. In particular, Stuart Laughton convinced me of the importance of a more serious approach to participatory design in the BEV. George Chin and Mary Beth Rosson developed these ideas and methods further in our long-term project with the Montgomery County Public Schools. Craig Struble, Marc Abrams, Philip Isenhour, Mary Beth Rosson, and Craig Ganoe guided our software projects. Dan Dunlap, Philip Isenhour, Dennis Neale, and Mary Beth Rosson have played big parts in designing novel community network activities. Dan Dunlap, Philip Isenhour, Andrea Kavanaugh, Mary Beth Rosson, Jennifer Thompson, and Lucinda Willis are currently helping to carry out an evaluation of the BEV. In this paper, I am particularly indebted to Carmen Sears, who produced an excellent course project in my Fall 1995 "Community Networks, Network Communities" course, a provocative Masters Thesis [29], and who collaborated with me in organizing a tutorial on community networking for the ACM Conference on Computer-Supported Cooperative Work in 1996. I am grateful to Mary Beth Rosson for comments on an earlier version of this paper. My research on community networking has been supported by the Hitachi Foundation and by the US National Science Foundation (CDA-9424506, REC-9554206, IIS-0080864, EIA 0081102, REC-0106552, IIS 0113264).

Notes

1. BEV http://www.bev.net
2. Beans and Rice http://www.beansandrice.org
3. The Blacksburg Seniors http://civic.bev.net/seniors/
4. Citizens' Alliance for Sensible Gun Ownership and Legislation
          http://www.civic.bev.net/casgoal
5. Citizens Concerned about I-73 http://www.civic.bev.net/cca73
6. Friends of the Hand-in-Hand Park http://www.civic.bev.net/handinhand
7. The Montgomery County Christmas Store http://civic.bev.net/christmas.store
8. The New River Community Shelter http://www.civic.bev.net/nrfs
9. The Town of Blacksburg for municipal information http://www.blacksburg.va.us
10. The Town of Blacksburg , forms http://www.blacksburg.va.us/forms.php
11. The BEV Visitor's Center http://www.bev.net/visitors/business.html
12. The BEV HistoryBase http://history.bev.net/bevhist/historyBase/mainTimeline.html
13. Image from a 1995 CNN videotape, retrieved from BEV HistoryBase.
14. BEV surveys http://www.bev.net/project/research
15. The Virtual School, Learning in a Networked Community http://linc.cs.vt.edu
16. Blacksburg Nostalgia   http://research.cs.vt.edu/storybase/nostalgia
17. MOOsburg   http://moosburg.cs.vt.edu
18. America Online's Digital City, Inc. service http://digitalcity.com
19. The Richmond digital city   http://digitalcity.com/richmond
20 "Interdisciplinary Views of the Blacksburg Electronic Village", NSF-IIS 0080864.

References

1. Ass. Press: FCC says network is model system for communities, *The Journal, July 19*, 1994.
2. A. Beamish. *Communities On-Line: Community-Based Computer Networks.* Masters Thesis, Department of Urban Studies and Planning, MIT, 1995.
3. S. Bødker, P. Ehn, J. Kammersgaard, M. Kyng, and Y. Sundblad. A utopian experience. G. Bjerknes, P. Ehn and M. Kyng, Eds., *Computers and democracy: A Scandinavian challenge*, Avebury, pp. 251-278, 1987.
4. P. Bowden, and J. Wiencko. *The Blacksburg Electronic Village partnership.* Oct. 1, 1993.
5. J.M. Carroll. Community computing as human-computer interaction, *Behaviour and Information Technology*, 20(5), pp. 307-314, 2001.

6. J.M. Carroll, G. Chin, M.B. Rosson, and D.C. Neale. The Development of Cooperation: Five years of participatory design in the virtual school, D. Boyarski and W. Kellogg Eds., *Designing Interactive Systems (DIS'2000)*, ACM, pp. 239-251. 2000.

7. J.M. Carroll, and M.B. Rosson. Developing the Blacksburg Electronic Village, *Communications of the ACM*, 39(12), pp. 69-74, 1996.

8. J.M. Carroll, and M.B. Rosson. Better home shopping or new democracy? Evaluating community network outcomes, *Proceedings of CHI 2001*, ACM, pp. 372-379, 2001.

9. J.M. Carroll, M.B. Rosson, A.M. Cohill, and J. Schorger. Building a history of the Blacksburg Electronic Village, *Proceedings of the ACM Symposium on Designing Interactive Systems*, ACM Press, pp. 1-6. 1995.

10. J.M. Carroll, M.B. Rosson, P.L. Isenhour, C. Van Metre, W.A. Schafer, and C.H. Ganoe. MOOsburg: Multi-user domain support for a community network, *Internet Research*, 11(1), pp. 65-73, 2001.

11. J.M Carroll, M.B. Rosson, P.L. Isenhour, C.H. Ganoe, D. Dunlap, J. Fogarty, W. Schafer, and C. Van Metre. Designing our town: MOOsburg, *International Journal of Human-Computer Studies*, 54, pp. 725-751, 2001.

12. J.M.Carroll, M.B.Rosson, C.A. VanMetre, R. Kengeri, J. Kelso, and M. Darshani. Blacksburg Nostalgia: A Community History Archive, M.A. Sasse and C. Johnson Eds., *Proceedings of Seventh IFIP Conference on Human-Computer Interaction INTERACT 99*, IOS Press/International Federation for Information Processing (IFIP), pp. 637-647, 1999.

13. L. Cuban, *Teachers and machines*, Teachers College Press, 1986.

14. D.R. Dunlap, D.C. Neale, and J.M. Carroll. Teacher collaboration in a networked community, *Educational Technology and Society*, 3(3), pp. 442-454, 2000.

15. R.T. Eales, D.C. Neale, and J.M. Carroll. Desktop video conferencing as a basis for computer supported collaborative learning in K-12 classrooms, B. Collis, and R. Oliver, Eds. *Proceedings of EdMedia 99 - World Conference on Educational Multimedia, Hype media & Telecommunications*, Association for the Advancement of Computing in Education, pp. 628-633, 1999.

16. C. Farrington, and E. Pine. Community memory: A case study in community communication, P. Agre, and D. Schuler, Eds., *Reinventing technology, rediscovering community*. Ablex, 1996.

17. S. Foster. Road still a bit rough to info-land, *The Roanoke Times and World News*. April 5, 1994.

18. S. Hodas. Technology refusal and the organizational culture of schools, *Educational Policy Analysis Archives*, 1 (10), September 14, 1993.

19. P.L. Isenhour, J.M. Carroll, D.C. Neale, M.B. Rosson, and D.R. Dunlap. The Virtual School: An integrated collaborative environment for the classroom, *Educational Technology and Society*, 3(3), pp. 74-86, 2000.

20. M.J. Muller. Retrospective on a year of participatory design using the PICTIVE technique, *Proceedings of CHI'92: Conference on Human Factors in Computing Systems*, ACM, pp. 455-462, 1992.

21. S. Laughton, *The design and use of Internet-mediated communication applications in education: An ethnographic study.* Ph.D. Dissertation, Computer Science Department, Virginia Tech, Blacksburg, VA, 1996.

22. J. Park, Interviews with Ken Anderson, Andrew Cohill, Ron Secrist, and David Webster. Community Networks, Network Communities, November, 1995.

23. H. Rheingold. *The Virtual Community: Homesteading on the electronic frontier*. Addison-Wesley, 1993.

24. E.M. Rogers. *The diffusion of innovations*. Free Press, 1983.

25. M. Rosenberg. Blacksburg users anticipate linking as "computer village.", *Roanoke Times and World News*, September 3, 1992.

26. J.R. Schorger. Interview with Bob Heterick. January 13, 1995.

27. J.R. Schorger. *A Qualitative Study of the Development and First Year of Implementation of the Blacksburg Electronic Village.* Ph.D. Dissertation, Curriculum and Instruction Department, Virginia Tech, 1997.

28. D. Schuler. *New community networks: Wired for change.* Addison-Wesley, 1996.

29. C. Sears. *(Re)visions of the village: Building and participating in the Blacksburg Electronic Village.* Masters Thesis, Science and Technology Studies, Virginia Tech, 1996.

30. D. Smith. Electronic village: Technology showcase, *Blue Ridge Business Journal,* February 15, 1992.

31. D. Tyack and L. Cuban. *Tinkering toward utopia: A century of public school reform.* Cambridge, Harvard University Press, 1995.

32. W. Uncapher. New communities/new communication: Big Sky Telegraph and its community, M. Smith and P. Kollock, Eds., *Communities in Cyberspac.* Routledge, 1999.

33. J.A. Weincko. The Blacksburg Electronic Village. *Internet Research, 3(2),* pp. 31-40, 1993.

34. D. Schuler, The Seattle Community Network: Anomaly or Replicable Model. In P. van den Besselaar, S. Koizumi (eds), Digital Cities 3. Information technologies for social capital. Lecture Notes in Computer Science, Vol. 3081. Springer-Verlag, Berlin Heidelberg New York (2005) pp. 16-41.

The Life and Death of the Great Amsterdam Digital City

Peter van den Besselaar[1], Dennis Beckers[2]

[1] Amsterdam School of Communication Research, ASCoR, University of Amsterdam &
Department of Social Sciences, NIWI, Royal Netherlands Academy of Arts and Sciences
P.O. Box 95110, 1090 HC Amsterdam, the Netherlands
p.a.a.vandenbesselaar@uva.nl
[2] Social Informatics, Department of Psychology, University of Amsterdam
D.Beckers@os.amsterdam.nl

Abstract. In this paper we describe the development of the Amsterdam Digital City DDS. We describe its content and functionality, its organizational form, and the context it operated in. We also describe the users and the ways they used the DDS. The paper explains why the DDS initially was a success, and why it in the end failed to become a sustainable local information and communication infrastructure.

1 History and Organization of the Digital City

In the summer of 1993, a few people met to establish an experimental virtual public domain in Amsterdam. Following the model of the freenets and community networks in the USA and Canada, *The Digital City* (DDS) was launched as a 10-week experiment early in 1994.[1] The success of this experiment caused the organizers to make it permanent. Now a very well known project, the DDS has attracted a great deal of attention from the popular press and from social researchers. By late 2001, the DDS ceased being a virtual public domain, however, and it is now a good time to evaluate what can be learned from the seven years of the DDS. These seven years were also a period which saw enormous growth in the Internet: it has changed from a public to a predominantly commercial domain. This chapter describes the development of the DDS, its organization, business model, functionality and content, users and the ways they used the Digital City. In the final section we evaluate the development of the DDS within the changing social, economic, and technological environment.[2]

---

[1] As far as we know, the term Digital City was invented in 1993 in Amsterdam. DDS is the abbreviation of De Digitale Stad, Dutch for The Digital City. The DDS was a virtual public domain, and the organization that maintained it. The URL of the DDS is: http://www.dds.nl
[2] This chapter is based on research using a variety of methods over an extended timeframe. We used data from three web surveys, content analysis of the DDS site, logfiles, interviews with users and with a variety of people involved in the DDS, and, of course, observation in the DDS (virtual ethnography). The data collection was done between 1996 and 2002. We reported some of the results in [26, 27, 28]. Finally, we used other studies on the DDS [3, 8,

P. van den Besselaar and S. Koizumi (Eds.): Digital Cities 2003, LNCS 3081, pp. 66-96, 2005.

The history of the Digital City can be seen as having undergone four phases: 1) from idea to successful experiment (mid 1993 – early 1994); 2) the period of institutionalization and growth (late 1994 – 1996); 3) from stabilization to increasing competition and decline (1997 – 1999); and 4) privatization, the struggle around ownership, emerging alternatives, and the end (2000 – 2001).

Analyzing the beginning and development of the DDS within Amsterdam's socio-cultural context is revealing because it will shed light on the changing aims and goals, as well as on the design and content of the DDS [3, 15, 25]. Moreover, the form of the initial phases also influenced development in the later phases, especially organizational structure and financial base. The history of the DDS is that of an 'experimental project' able to obtain government subsidies for a while, becoming transformed into a self-supporting non-profit organization, and finally into a commercial company. The goals changed accordingly: from an experiment in creating a public domain in cyberspace it emerged as an organization focused on profits from Internet projects that could be used to keep the Digital City alive. Finally, profitability became its main goal, and this resulted in closing down the Digital City because it was considered solely from the point of view of cost. As a commercial company the DDS image became merely a trademark.

1.1 From Idea to Experiment

The idea of building a digital city emerged in the context of the social and cultural movements in Amsterdam in the eighties and early nineties. Important factor in this was the fact that a local public media culture already existed: the city of Amsterdam had implemented a cable network for TV and radio around 1980, and almost all Amsterdam households were connected to this network. Using this network, several experiments with open access radio and TV were started, leading to an increasing use of public media. For example, the Amsterdam squatter's movement used local radio and TV for propaganda. The network was also used to involve citizens in local politics through the 'stadsgesprekken' (city conversations). These debates focused on specific local political issues among citizens and politicians were broadcast live on the cable network; they also offered the possibility for other citizens to comment and participate in the discussion using the telephone. Second, following examples of bulletin board systems that had emerged in the USA, such communication means were becoming widely diffused within the Netherlands. They were used mainly by computer hobbyists and hackers, since access to the Internet was not yet available to the general public. Later, the computer activist organization Hacktic was to become the first Internet access provider (XS4ALL: pronounce as "access for all") that would be affordable for a larger public. Third, cultural centers in Amsterdam such as De Balie and Paradiso were actively fostering programs about new media and its impact on society and culture. Various events were organized to increase awareness of the possibilities of the new media for progressive social and cultural movements. Several new organizations emerged in this context: for example, the Activist Press Service and Antenna, an organization aimed at supporting non-governmental organizations

---

22, 25, 29]. Interesting accounts about the DDS – focusing on the deviation from the initial ideas and ideals – by persons involved in its foundation and early developments: [14, 25, 21].

(NGOs) in using information and communication technologies (ICT).[3] Another organization that emerged in the early nineties was Press Now, established to support the democratic media in the former Yugoslavia, using e-mail and the Internet.[4]

With the North American freenets as examples, the DDS started as a project of the cultural center De Balie, in collaboration with leaders of the computer activist organization Hacktic and a few other people including some former squatters. The organizers wanted to introduce the Internet and its possibilities to a wider population by providing free access to the Internet, creating an electronic public domain for social and political debate and enabling free expression and social experimentation in cyberspace. The main inspiration was to develop a system for the general public to explore the possibilities of the Internet. The founders of the DDS were inspired by the idea that the Internet was would be a new cultural domain that would promote creative experimentation.

The name 'Digital City' was chosen to emphasize the idea of a digital public space where people would meet and communicate. The city metaphor was expected to promote easy access for people without any knowledge about modern media and the Internet. The name DDS was used without 'Amsterdam' to emphasize the global, geographically non-restricted nature of the DDS. The DDS was not intended to be limited to being a virtual representation of *real* Amsterdam.

The initiators of the project were able to link the digital city idea with upcoming local elections. Political participation in the Netherlands was declining in those years, as was (and is) the number of eligible people who voted – especially in local elections. This increasing gap between politicians and citizens was seen as a pressing issue, and various efforts were undertaken to decrease the gap. To fund the DDS project, the organizers convinced the municipal administration that a digital public space could be used to improve dissemination of political information and communication between citizens and politicians. The proposal would be funded on an experimental basis starting January 15, 1994, ending shortly after the local elections in March of that year. This proposal was successful, and the City of Amsterdam donated about € 45,000 as part of a larger program to use local media for improving communication with citizens. DDS obtained additional funding of about € 110,000 from the Ministry of Economic Affairs and the Home Office, which together was enough to pay for technical staff, equipment, and other operational costs.

Thus, the DDS started as an experiment to provide an electronic democratic forum to the citizens of Amsterdam to bridge the gap between the inhabitants and local politicians. To improve communication, the organizers linked the internal e-mail system of the City Hall with the DDS, and made all kinds of municipal and other local information available through the DDS. Electronic discussion groups on various topics were implemented, and informed specialists were asked to moderate these discussion groups.

As is usual with projects organized by the Balie, the Digital City was planned as a temporary activity, and the available budget only covered ten weeks. Thus it was clear from the beginning that new funding had to be found if the experiment were to become a success [30]. And it was! The number of registered users increased very fast: during the first ten weeks some 10,000 inhabitants were registered, who accessed

---

[3] Antenna was the Netherlands part of APC: Association for Progressive Communication.

[4] Interesting on early ICT grass root initiatives is [19]

the system more than 100,000 times. The DDS benefited from significant media attention, and it stimulated Dutch interest in the Internet enormously. While the Internet was not an issue in the Netherlands before the DDS, it suddenly became 'hot'. Most Dutch newspapers and TV channels paid considerable attention to the DDS, and to the Internet. DDS even appeared in the international news media.

1.2 Institutionalization and Growth

Immediately after the experiment began, the discussion started whether to maintain the DDS permanently. The impetus for this discussion was not only the success of the experiment, but also the fact that continuation of the DDS provided job opportunities for some of those involved. The debate about continuing the system took place within a small circle around the initiators of the DDS. While the original aim was to launch a temporary bottom-up experiment with a virtual public domain, continuation and institutionalization of this experiment would inevitably introduce stronger top-down elements, if only because of the financial issues involved. The people involved disagreed whether to continue it and institutionalize the DDS: the core dispute was whether a (virtual) public domain could be institutionalized at all [15].

After the decision was made to continue the system, the next important question was where to get the funds. Although the DDS tried to obtain governmental subsidies it was unable to. Neither local authorities nor the national government was willing to provide the DDS with structural funding. Instead, the DDS was able to get subsidies of € 300,000[5] from various bodies to continue its work during 1994. During this period the DDS had to find independent funding for the years to come.

In this first year there were several developments. First (to be discussed in more detail below), the number of users continued to expand rapidly. Furthermore, the DDS, at that moment still part of De Balie, was converted into an independent foundation, the Dutch legal format for non-profit organizations. Finally, a graphical interface was implemented for the DDS, based on the emerging World Wide Web protocol. This enabled inclusion of pictorial elements, as well as navigation through pointing and clicking. DDS 2.0 became operational in October 1994, but development of a full Web-based design had already started. While developing this interface may at the time have been somewhat risky because it was not at all clear that the Web and the recently launched Web browsers like Netscape would become a standard [29]. Nevertheless, the new Web interface (DDS 3.0) was launched on June 15, 1995 and was technologically advanced at that moment.

In the meantime the DDS developed a new business model which was based on earning revenues through Internet services to cross-subsidize the Digital City. The organizers offered consulting services about the Internet and the Web, disk space, website design, virtual 'office space', and possibilities for posting advertisements within the Digital City. Some revenue was generated through subsidies. Examples were development and hosting of the websites of the city of Amsterdam, and the production of a *Handbook Digital Cities*, funded by the Ministry of Economic Affairs. And, the Digital City itself functioned as the 'unique selling point'.

---

[5] The City of Amsterdam took part in this for 15%.

Goals: As a foundation the DDS had to formulate its goals explicitly in its bylaws, which can be summarized as follows.

1. Democratizing the electronic superhighway: Creating an electronic sphere that enables participation, discussion, and information exchange - that is, the creation of an electronic public domain, freely accessible, and with freedom of expression. The Digital City offers its inhabitants free e-mail, the possibility to create a 'digital house' in the city (a web page), facilities for chat and discussion, and access to a great deal of information about all aspects of life.
2. Innovation: Conducting research and dissemination of knowledge about information and communication infrastructures.
3. IT services: Developing applications for the Internet and the Web for small and medium sized companies and other organizations to strengthen regional economic structure.

The latter two goals clearly relate to the new business model. Although the main goal was to keep the Digital City alive, the need to earn revenue became an important – if not the most important – factor in everyday operations. It also strongly influenced the way the DDS was organized. The DDS started as a local activist project, but it never had a democratic structure. In contrast to the dominant idea of community networks as 'bottom-up' activities, owned by the users, and often based on public funds [23], the DDS was a foundation, and the digital citizens were 'users', without any formal, organized influence on the DDS-organization. Decisions about basic design of the DDS and development of new functionalities were exclusively made by the people within the DDS organization. The scope of what the users could do was relatively restricted: they were allowed to create a house (a home page) and apply for new newsgroups. Initially the plan called for establishing an 'advisory board' that included users of the system, but this never materialized. Some users of the Digital City did participate in various design activities, however: there was an advanced users group, for example, where new designs and tools were discussed and tried out. Despite the fact that the city metaphor suggested a democratic system in which digital citizens elect the administrators, the DDS became a project that maintained a traditional form of user involvement [4].

In the beginning the lack of formal influence by users resulted in several issues concerning legitimacy. One example of an important top-down decision, initially without support of the users, was the change in the design of the system. When the DDS moved from a text-based interface to a graphical Web interface, many of the more experienced 'digital citizens' opposed this change; they did not see the necessity. Nevertheless, the people in the DDS organization felt that they had to use the most advanced technology (in 1995: the Web) to remain attractive in the long-term, even if users initially opposed the change. Another reason to change the interface was that the Web interface was thought to be much easier to use for Internet novices.[6] The debate on these contested decisions was carried out in the very active discussion group dds.dds, but participation and activities in this discussion group declined sharply as the new top-down structure became clear to the digital citizens. Although there has not been much public debate about the policy of the DDS since

---

[6] However, Rommes [20] argues that the interface was difficult to use for some categories of users, and therefore de facto excluded these categories of users.

then, in the long run lack of ownership by the digital citizens led to a decline in their commitment and involvement.

The DDS as a non-profit organization, raising income from other activities to maintain the Digital City, seemed a sustainable solution. In this way it created independence from government, but competition from companies that provided similar services became more and more important, as we will see below.

1.3 Stabilization, Increasing Competition, and Decline

Between 1994 and 1996, the DDS became a successful digital city with a great deal of activity, innovation, and media attention. The DDS attracted 'whiz kids' who wanted to work there because of its innovative appeal, even if salaries were relatively low. Users were enthusiastic, helped to build the city, and participated in lively discussions about it. The design and the technological base of the DDS was considered quite advanced, as was its non-profit organization. The DDS was, in its early days, part of an emerging local *Internet culture.*

Despite this early enthusiasm and identification, the digital citizens were more consumers than owners of the DDS, which started to face competition from other initiatives. In this period, many alternatives for DDS users did become available. Free e-mail and Internet access were offered by many organizations, through schools and universities, and through new free Internet access providers such as *hotmail.com.* When more advanced forms of communication became available on the Internet (ICQ, Webcam), the DDS was not at the leading edge of these developments, and there were increasingly large delays in adopting the newer technologies.

As an early portal the DDS also faced competition from commercial and non-commercial search engines. The DDS was not able to increase the number of information suppliers, and quite a few former clients started their own Websites, leaving the DDS. For example, the city of Amsterdam started the *City of Glass* project (http://www.amsterdam.nl/glazenstad), because they did not want to remain be on the DDS, partly because that system was not very stable.

In the meantime, the Digital City itself did not change very much anymore. The overall design of the DDS was not updated or improved, and the interface remained the same. New technical possibilities were not implemented (or if they were, it was poorly done): these included the 3D interface and new tools for communication and awareness. In 1998, the DDS started providing 'content' and Web broadcasting about cultural, social, and political issues. The DDS began to see itself increasingly as a content provider, and less as an enabling platform for others, as it had been in the beginning. The DDS organization did experiment with real-time audio and video, but these were hardly integrated into the Digital City, or failed to become operational.

On the other hand, the commercial activities of the DDS organization were favorable, and the number of employees increased. Table 1 gives some estimates. In 1999, of the 30 staff, five were in management, five in programming, and five in systems design. Nevertheless, this growth was not enough to fund maintenance and further development of the Digital City, and innovation stagnated. The lack of sufficient funding created many problems. For example, the new interface was never implemented. DDS maintenance became increasingly problematic, and users complained about the declining service. DDS was often 'down', and the links to the private sites (the 'houses') regularly experienced problems. The awareness tool (pressing the 'who is here' button) never functioned properly, so it was not possible to determine who was *on line* in the DDS. These technical problems were mainly caused by failing systems management, resulting in 'spaghetti systems' which were impossible to maintain. Web cafés were often empty for days at a time, and the communication facilities were very limited. The free help desk was abolished and public terminals were closed. As we will see in a later section, despite the increasing number of digital citizens, the level of activity went down. Digital citizens were spending their time online elsewhere in cyberspace, and not anymore in the DDS. The Digital City lacked funding and strategies to compete successfully.

Table 1. Some figures on the DDS-organization

	1994	1996	1998	1999
Turn-over in €)	n.a.	500.000	n.a.	1.000.000
Costs of the Public Domain*	450.000**	n.a.	500.000#	n.a.
Number of staff	11	15	25##	30

*: Including social and political projects; **: Subsidies, excluding the contributions of De Balie and Hactick; #: 90% funded by DDS-organization [6]); ##: Source: [7]; n.a.: not available

1.4 From Privatization to the End

During 1999 the people of the DDS organization and the board of the foundation decided that the non-profit model was not working any more. In fact, since 1997 the DDS was largely dependent for its survival on one major client. To remain competitive and generate enough revenue to renew the DDS, additional external investments were seen as necessary. This was only possible by changing the DDS to a commercial enterprise that could use its large membership and well-known 'brand name' as assets to attract investors. The change to a commercial enterprise was announced on the sixth anniversary of the DDS, January 2000. It was split into DDS-venture Ltd, DDS-services Ltd., DDS-projects Ltd., and DDS-city Ltd, all under DDS-holding Ltd. owned by the DDS director Joost Flint and his business partner Chris Gobel. DDS-city Ltd. operated the Digital City. The new strategy never became successful, because of the decline of the dot.com sector, especially B2C (business to consumer) part. By the end of 2000 the DDS ceased its editorial activities and parts of DDS were sold, notably its popular portal for school-related information. Similarly, the ISP activities (DDS-City) and Web hosting activities (DDS-services) were sold.[7] The sale of these activities brought the DDS holding several millions guilders to alleviate debts, and to enable continuation of the remaining parts. Later on also DDS-projects failed, among others because of internal conflicts between the director and the staff.

By the end of 2000, the DDS director announced in an interview that he was planning to close the Digital City if no more external investments could be found. Digital citizens, former employees of the DDS, Internet activists, and others then started to join forces to save the DDS. *Save the DDS* was founded to take over and revive the DDS as a public domain owned by users. Unlike the DDS, this new association had a democratic structure that included members and an elected board.

---

[7] Source: press releases of October 5, 2000, October 27, 2000, and December 1, 2000.

But from the discussion list of the new association we see that there was intense debate about what the aims of the 'new' DDS would be, how it should be organized, and what the possibilities for funding were. Many problems had to be solved, as the DDS had become private property. The new association even had to adopt another name: Association for the Public Domain (Vereniging Open Domein VOD). Lack of a clear policy and slow decision-making by the new association, personal animosity, and the business interests of the owners of the DDS frustrated negotiations between the old and the new digital city.

The takeover failed, as did the other plans, such as mirroring the Digital City on other servers and starting it again, mainly because the VOD administrators could not agree on strategies and tactics. Within a year, various board changes took place, and before the VOD was stabilized, the DDS announced cancellation of the Digital City and with the free e-mail and Websites. On October 1, 2001 the DDS became an ordinary Internet access provider.[8]

Towards the end of 2001 the VOD announced it would start a new digital city: DeDS (www.deds.nl), which would apply an *open source model* to services as well as to software. It hoped to show how complex Web services could be set up and maintained by organizing expertise in workgroups and using a model based on trust and community. In its current form DeDS is closer to a small community than an infrastructure for a virtual public domain. Observers who were involved in the foundation of VOD report that the DeDS is moderately successful within its own – very modest – terms. It still exists (http://www.deds.nl).

2 Design and Functionality of the DDS

2.1 Access

In 1994 access to the DDS was mainly realized by dialing into the DDS modem bank, using modem and telephone. Users who already had access to the Internet could access the DDS directly through a Telnet session. In 1994 such access was restricted mainly to some students and university staff. There were also a few public terminals in several public places in Amsterdam. In the following years access to the Internet quickly expanded and became the main entrance to the DDS. The public terminals were no longer supported, became outdated and were not replaced. Yet it was still possible to call in directly to the modem bank of the DDS, which remained available.

The level of access to the DDS depended on the status of the user. DDS users could be occasional visitors (tourists) or registered users. Registered users were given a free e-mail address, could use the chat rooms, participate in the Metro (a Multi User Dungeon facility 'located' in the underground of the DDS), were allowed to vote in online referenda, and could build their own *house* in one of the neighborhoods of the

---

[8] The developments of DDS were not unique. In 1994, Hacktic, one of the founders of DDS, became the first Dutch Internet access provider XS4ALL, with similar ideas and ideals as the DDS had. However, also for XS4ALL economic pressure became dominant, as providing Internet access services was becoming increasingly capital intensive. The founders sold XS4ALL to Dutch Telecom in 1998. It is still and important ISP in the Netherlands.

DDS. To use these facilities it was necessary to log in to the system. Visitors traveled anonymously through the DDS, but could not participate in these activities. In the beginning the DDS provided full Internet access to its members free of charge. The free access was discontinued early on for two reasons: cost and because the DDS did not want to be an Internet access provider, but a platform for experimenting with cyberspace. DDS did not want members who only wanted free access to the Internet.

2.2 Interface

As we have seen, the DDS had three different interfaces. The first (figure1) was a traditional text based interface, similar to those used by the freenets and bulletin board systems (BBS). The city metaphor was implemented to a certain extent. The various functions had names of buildings and places.

To send e-mail, for example, it was necessary to access the virtual *post office* (3). The *public forum* (4) provided access to various discussion lists based on the Unix Usenet protocol. In the virtual *city hall* (7), a DDS user could access city information systems. The *elections center* (9) provided political information related to the upcoming local elections, as well as facilities to send e-mail to politicians. For accessing the Internet (in those days mainly for Telnet sessions, FTP, and Gopher) it was necessary to go to the virtual *central station* (13). It was also possible to access the *university* (12), the virtual *public library* (5), and the *house of arts and culture* (6). Of course, information about the DDS itself was also available (1, 2, 14).

```
                      De Digitale Stad


        1 BELANGRIJK: De Digitale Stad 2.0
        2 Helpdesk
        3 Het Postkantoor
        4 Openbaar Forum
        5 De Bibliotheek
        6 Gebouw voor Kunst en Cultuur
        7 Het Stadhuis
        8 Kantoorwijk
        9 Verkiezingscentrum
       10 De Kiosk
       11 Een Plein
       12 Universiteit van Amsterdam
       13 Centraal Station
       14 Configuratie-centrum
     -------------------------------------------------
     x=Exit h=Hoofdmenu v=Vorig Menu w=wie zijn er?


     Keuze ? : █
```

Fig. 1. First interface

Despite the simple interface, the advantage of DDS 1.0 was its integration of information and communication functions. It was easy to see which other users were online, and communication facilities were transparently available after logging in. Conversation through *talk sessions* was easy because the connection between the user's computer and the DDS remained open during the session. Switching to e-mail or to discussion groups was also possible within the interface. Good communication facilities were crucial to the success of the DDS, and one of the designers of the Web interface described his first visits to the DDS: "My visit to the DDS a few days after opening was not very impressive. Compared with other Bulletin Board systems, the Digital City was not advanced. The information available was not very interesting, waiting times were frustratingly long, and the DDS was still empty. The only good reason to use the DDS was the possibility to enter the Internet through the *Central Station*. However, then something happened, I had not experienced on any other BBS I knew. The DDS started to grow very fast and became very lively. The influence of the thousands of citizens became manifest. The amount and quality of the information increased fast, and interesting discussions took place in the newsgroups and in the web cafés." [29]

Very soon the first efforts were undertaken to extend the textual interface with the emerging Web technology, as the images and the point-and-click interface would make the DDS more attractive - but at the expense of the communication functions. These required an open connection between the user's PC and the DDS host, which is not the case for the Web interface. Consequently, to communicate with other digital citizens, it was necessary to switch to the textual interface. Although DDS 2.0 became operational in October 1994, development of the full Web interface with better communication possibilities was already under way. The fully functional Web interface was launched in June 1995. In this third interface the city metaphor was more literally implemented than in previous ones. The *Digital City* maintained both a text-based interface and a Web-based interface, but the large majority of users switched to the latter.

Fig. 2. Third interface DDS 3.0

The basic structure of DDS 3.0 consisted of topical squares, which formed a *city map* that provides an overview of the DDS (figure 2). The city consisted of more than 30 squares, with cultural, recreational, technological, civic, and political themes. A full list is given in table 3. The squares were locations where commercial, public, and non-profit information suppliers could rent virtual offices. For example, on *Europe Square* the Dutch Office of the European Commission and other organizations related to the European Union were located, all providing information to the public. The newsgroup for political debates on European issues was also located there. The topical organization of the squares was intended to help users find their way through the information spaces. Another example is *Travel Square*, where various travel organizations maintained an 'office' that is a home page or link to a home page hosted elsewhere. Figure 3 shows the map of Travel Square with the offices in the center. To increase availability of office space, every square also had an office building (verzamelgebouw) with nine smaller offices.

The office block of *TV Square* is shown in figure 4. All squares have the same design, except in the latest extension of the DDS: *Multicultural Square*. This was to enable the many organizations of cultural and ethnic minorities to all have a virtual office on this square.

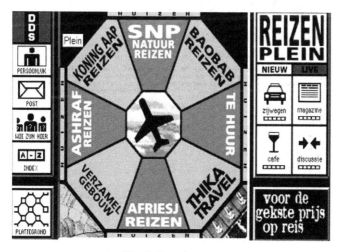

Fig. 3. Travel square

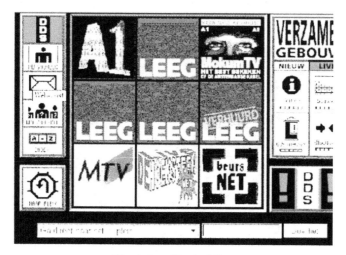

Fig. 4. An office building

At the left of every square were various navigation tools, including the 'who is here?' button and access to e-mail. Various navigation tools were available. If a user did not want to 'stroll' through the city, the alternative was to use the indexes for the squares, for the offices, or for the private houses. By clicking on the 'who is here?' button, a list was displayed of who was on the square and who was in the whole city (figure 5). Through this, additional information about active digital citizens could be obtained. Both features never functioned properly. At the right of every square were the communication tools: the DDS magazine, sometimes a Web café, the discussion lists related to the topic of the square, and more recently, the access to the *live* DDS broadcasting system. Also billboards for advertising and announcements were located on the squares of the DDS. Figure 6 shows a typical Web café, the *Gay Café*.

Fig. 5. Who is here?

Fig. 6. Gay Café

Neighborhoods were situated around the squares; and it was there that digital citizens could have a 'house'. Digital citizens used their houses for e-mail interaction with others and for presenting information they wanted to share. Some very interesting houses existed: for example, there was a house that provided links to the home pages of many media (journals, magazines, movies, etc.) throughout the world. Unlike the offices, the houses were free. There were, however some rules for building houses: they could not be used for commercial purposes, political content was allowed (some political parties used the free houses as their Website) but pornography was not (as this would attract too much Internet traffic). An example of a neighborhood can be seen in figure 7.

Fig. 7. A neighborhood

The size of the DDS interface limited the number of neighborhoods and houses that could be accommodated: a total of 1,500 houses could be built. Because of the large increase in the number of digital citizens, the demand for houses grew, resulting in a shortage of space for houses on the interface. Various measures were tried to solve this problem. One was to build 'apartments', thereby linking several Websites to a single main 'door'. Another was introducing a rule permitting users to 'squat' (take over) houses that were not maintained by their inhabitants. Still another way to expand the limited interface was to allow users to build Web pages in the Digital City that were not properly located in the 'city structure' but only linked to it through the index of houses. In 1996 some 3,300 users owned a house; this number doubled to 6,500 a year later.

In 1997 the DDS started to experiment with 3D virtual reality. Dam Square (figure 8) was built, and citizens were invited to extend the 3D virtual space with their own buildings, streets, and squares. This experiment with 3D was prompted by the need to attract users to the DDS and to remain competitive in the markets for Web consultancy. The switch to advanced technology, however, resulted in decreasing accessibility because users needed faster computers and better telecommunication connections to use the 3D interface. This dilemma stymied further development.

Renewal of the interface, however, remained an issue. When the DDS introduced its Web interface, it was quite advanced. Although three years later this interface was still satisfactory for the organizing the information, there was a clear need for much more sophisticated communication and awareness tools. In 1997/1998, several new communication possibilities were introduced such as the digital living room and DDS broadcasting. The purpose of the living room (Figure 9) was to create a space where digital citizens could jointly watch TV, using the virtual remote control as a mechanism for interaction. While this application worked for a while, it never became popular and eventually ceased to function.

Fig. 8. The 3D interface – Dam square

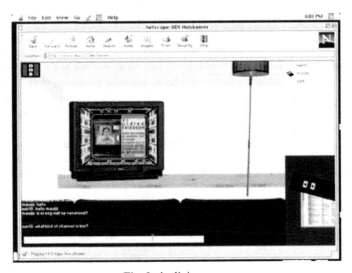

Fig. 9. the living room

The experiments with real-time audio and video started in 1998 as part of the new DDS strategy to focus on providing content. Pushing the *live button* (at the top right of every square) caused the TV/radio guide to appear; three programs were available (figure 10). Clicking on a specific program opened the TV screen. This DDS application is the only remaining one, and it allows many *De Balie* (one of the founding institutions of the DDS) lectures and discussions to be followed over the Internet.

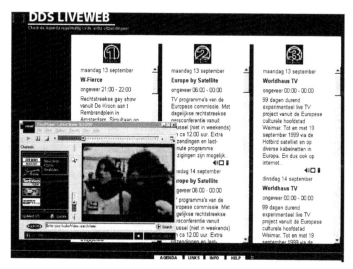

Fig. 10. DDS TV

It was in this period that the DDS announced a completely new and revolutionary interface (DDS 4) with sophisticated awareness and communication facilities, and in August 1999 the author of this paper got a demonstration of this new interface at the DDS office. Among others, the new interface enabled a global view of the city to see the locations of other digital citizens. A great deal of expensive programming time had been invested in the development, but it was never implemented, because of many technical problems. The system was impossible to manage, and the costs to develop it contributed to the rising financial problems of the DDS. Apart from that, the development came too late to save the effort. As we will see below, the DDS as a virtual community had ceased to function. In a city empty of people, awareness and communication tools are no longer relevant. In a much reduced version (DDS 3.5) the interface functioned for a while as portal for the DDS, but eventually it was dumped.

2.3 Information in the Digital City

What information could be found in the Digital City? In its experimental phase, it was possible to enter two large municipal information systems through the DDS. These included not only the public information system (PISA), but also the internal information system of the city hall (BISA), which received 9,000 'hits' [22]. While public access of these systems ended with the 10-week experiment, the DDS actively sought to attract information suppliers to the Digital City, and by mid 1996, some 200 virtual offices were rented to organizations and companies.[9] The number of rented spaces increased gradually to 300 offices in mid 2001 (table 2). Despite the fact that the DDS was an early provider of this type of service, a few years later, when Internet commerce really started, it did not succeed in positioning itself well in this growing market.

Table 2. Information suppliers in the DDS

	Rented offices	Offices available	Use rate
Mid-1996	200	496	40%
Mid-1998	263	560	47%
Mid-1999	291	560	52%
Mid-2001	302	560	54%

Source: Index DDS.

Table 3. Squares in the DDS

Squares / Topics	Number sites	Squares / Topics	Number sites
Art	8	Media news	5
Bar	1	Metro	1
Books	13	Movies	5
Computers	5	Multicultural	51
Culture	10	Music	7
Death	8	National authorities	6
Digital cities	1	Park	1
Drugs	9	Politics	6
Education	7	Regional authorities	5
Elections	2	Sport	6
Employment	4	Technology	5
Entrepreneurs	4	The Digital City	8
Environment	7	The world	8
Europe	8	Tourism	4
Health	8	Travel	9
Homo Lesbians	7	TV video	9
Internet	6	Women	8
Kids 13	11	Total 35 topics	263 suppliers

Source: [16]

The companies, shops, and organizations present in the DDS covered a wide variety of areas. [10] Nevertheless, transactions – other than asking for additional information – were not possible, and the experiment with digital money died before it really started. Table 3 shows how many companies and organizations were present (July 1998) on the various squares, indicating the type of information available in the DDS at that

---

[9] Renting virtual offices generated income for the DDS. Prices in 1996 were about the following [8]: An office generated about € 175 a month, and a small office in an office building about € 30 a month. The price of Web advertisements was between €200 and € 1750). Quite a few information providers, however, were subsidized by the DDS.

[10] We have not included the about 2500 personal sites in this analysis. Some of the more interesting houses changed into offices on the squares, as 'DDS projects'.

time. The table reflects the aims of the DDS, as all kinds of progressive social movements and interest groups are represented: from environmentalists and the gay movement to developmental organizations and the women's movement.

In the summer of 1998, as part of her MA thesis Isabel Melis did a content analysis of the DDS to map the available information in more detail [16, 28]. The Web pages were classified according to the type of information available (general versus practical information; local information or not) and the communication possibilities offered by the Websites (availability of e-mail, chat, discussion lists, electronic forms). The information was also classified in seven categories according to content: business, education, health, technology, media, leisure and politics. Table 4 shows the distribution for these categories, with leisure and politics being by far the largest. To find out how this developed, we compare the distribution of 1998 with the breakdown of the information providers for 1996. The categories used in the two studies are partly different, but we can still observe several remarkable changes. The size of the Computers & Internet category has declined considerably, and the share of sites devoted to political topics greatly increased. This was the second largest category (after Leisure) in 1998. Business, Education, and Health remained stable. The other content categories were not measured in 1996, and are therefore difficult to compare.

Table 4. Information providers by content categories

	1996	1998
Business	13%	13%
Education & Health	14%	13% (6+7)
Computers & Internet	11%	6%
Media	n.u.	12%
Leisure	n.u.	33%
Cultural	26%	n.u.
Life style	21%	n.u.
Politics	14%	22%

n.u.: not used for this year; source: [8, 16].

Table 5. Some characteristics of the sites in the DDS

Offices with:	
General information	95% *
Practical information	83%
General *local* information	33%
Practical *local* information	45%
The communication facilities	
E-mail	81%
Chat	12%
Newsgroups	19%
Electronic forms for reply	35%
No communication facilities	15%
Foreign languages (mostly English)	47%

*: percentage of sites with this characteristic; source: [16].

Since the DDS was not intended to be a 'virtual representation' of the city of Amsterdam, the information was not expected to be particularly local. Nevertheless, as table 5 shows, the share of sites with information about Amsterdam was fairly high: 45% of the sites contained practical information related to the city of Amsterdam. This is not less than systems with an intentionally local character, as we showed elsewhere [28]. [11]

Table 6. Distribution of newsgroups over topics (dds.newsgroups, end 1999)

Political and social issues (9)	Lifestyle and Leisure (2)	DDS (7)
1 Politics	14 Agenda (events)	25 DDS
2 Elections	15 City News	26 Help
3 Techno-polis		27 Metro.forum
4 Home Office Debate	**Social Groups (5)**	28 Metro builders
5 Multi-cultural	16 Femail	29 Metro
6 World news	17 Femail moderated	30 Nowmoo
7 Drugs	18 High school Students	31 Building houses
8 Crime	19 Elderly	
9 Reduce Consumption	20 Youth	**Culture and Media (3)**
		32 Poetry
Amsterdam (4)	**General (4)**	33 Fiction
10 Amsterdam	21 Commercial	34 Art
11 Building in Amsterdam	22 Miscellaneous	
12 Building and destroying	23 Market	
13 Car free city	24 Jobs	

2.4 Politics and Debate

One of the early aims of the DDS was to contribute to the revitalization of local democracy. As is well recognized in the literature, the quality of democracy depends on how the media function, because their role is to independently report on what politicians do and keep the public well informed [10]. Another important aspect is the quality of public debate that is supported by the availability of public places where people can meet to discuss (third places [18, 9]). Community networks and digital cities can play a role in both of these. First, they can provide new interactive media to improve the possibilities for informing the larger public, which may result in increased public debate and political participation. Second, they can provide new public places within cyberspace for people to meet and discuss, where public opinion can be shaped and expressed. In this way a *virtual public domain* may emerge.

The DDS implemented various functions to support this, especially through creation of Web cafés (as 'third places') and the Usenet newsgroups, which are interactive media where political, social, and other issues are discussed. The number of newsgroups fluctuated, and Francissen & Brants [8] report that there were about 100 in 1996, although they do not list them. Rustema [21] lists 53 newsgroups, of which 14 were related to the DDS itself, 14 to the city of Amsterdam, 17 to political topics, and another 8 to general topics. When we downloaded the DDS newsgroup archive in November 1999, there were 34 newsgroups (these are listed in various

---

[11] Concerning the local/non-local dimension of the digital city, the interviewees see the DDS clearly as an opening to the Internet, although some of them wished that it had a stronger local commitment.

categories in table 6). A relatively large number of these newsgroups were devoted to political and social issues, reflecting the aim of the DDS to stimulate public debate.

2.5 Projects

Part of the content of the DDS (neglected in most studies) are the projects involving non-commercial social and political groups and organizations. Three program tracks were defined: 'democracy', 'vulnerable groups', and 'diverse and high quality content'. One example of the last track is the *high school students site*, which contained excerpts of Dutch and foreign literature. This site was very popular, especially in spring during the examination periods.

A good example of a project aiming at 'vulnerable groups' was *Multicultural Square*. In the second half of the 1990s, ethnic and cultural minorities were largely absent from the Internet. To address this, the DDS started a project that included organizations representing these minorities: the Multicultural Square was developed to provide these organizations with Websites. As the number of ethnic minorities in Amsterdam is very large, the layout of the square had to be changed: the existing design only had space for some 18 organizations, but the new design enabled more organizations to be present. In addition, other social and cultural organizations sites were built in the DDS. We have not been able to evaluate the extent to which these sites did in fact functioned for the organizations involved. Our anecdotal impressions (and logfile analyses) are that this was not the case, and that the Websites were not very actively used.

The main project on democracy was probably *Election Square*, which was begun in 1998. For the local elections held in that year the DDS implemented a Website for every municipality in the Netherlands; there, local sections of the national political parties and local parties were able to put up information about their political program and candidates. The sites also included facilities to contact candidates. In total, 486 local sections of political parties from 223 (almost all) municipalities were represented. *Election Square* was rather successful, and also the debates on local political issues were lively, especially for discussions of such issues as parking policy in Amsterdam and local transport in Utrecht. A Website containing information, debate, and online think tanks for the national elections, was also developed.

3 Demography: The Digital Citizens

In the end the crucial issues are: who uses the DDS, in what ways, and what are the effects of this use. In this section we describe the users, and in the next we focus on ways of use. Both this and the following section are based on several data sources, including surveys among self-selected samples of digital citizens. The respondents were mainly registered users, so visitors who navigate through the Digital City or simply visit one site have not been included. The respondents were generally the most frequent and enthusiastic users. We also did some observation studies, and analyzed the logfile from a 2-week period. The logfiles cover every visit including occasional visitors, while the questionnaires reflect mainly the opinions of the more frequent users who consider themselves inhabitants of the Digital City. We also interviewed digital citizens to obtain more detailed information about their motivations for using the Digital City.[12] Finally, information was obtained from the DDS organization. Because their interest was favorable exposure, the figures they supplied may be overstated.

The DDS figures show that the digital citizenship developed considerably. Within 10 weeks, 10,000 people had registered, and by May 1998 the counter on the DDS home page showed 80,000 registered digital citizens. This trend continued, showing about 150,000 members at the end of the DDS in 2001. Since registration in the DDS was free, many of those registered may have been 'non-users', although the DDS claimed it removed members who had not used their account for 11 weeks.

The DDS also reported the number of daily visits, and these figures show increase and fluctuation. In the experimental period the DDS claimed to have about 1,500 visits per day, with figures on the period 1995-1998 varying between 10,000 and 16,000 per day. This includes visits by 'citizens' as well as (non registered) 'tourists'. Given the numbers presented in the next section, the reported statistics of daily visits are most probably overstated.

Table 7. Population of the DDS 1994-2001

	Early 1994	Late 1995	Mid 1996	Mid 1998	End 2001
Registered citizens*	10,000	33,000	48,000	80,000	150,000
Visits per day*	1,500	15,000	10,000	16,000	n.a.
Of which tourists	n.a.	n.a.	2,000	n.a.	n.a.
Working	60%	n.a.	39%	40%	n.a.
University & high school students	31%	n.a.	56%	48%	n.a.
Unemployed, old aged, & housewives	9%	n.a.	5%	12%	n.a.
Female users	9%	n.a.	16%	21%	n.a.
Local users	45%	n.a.	23%	22%	n.a.
Age distribution:					
under 19	6%		8%	20%	
19 – 25	29%		48%	38%	
26 – 30	23%	n.a.	15%	15%	n.a.
31 – 40	27%		16%	15%	
41 – 50	12%		9%	8%	
above 50	3%		3%	4%	

n.a.: not available. *: from DDS administrators - according to some informants, the real number of users has never been higher than 90,000. All other figures: [1, 22].

Initially, digital citizens were male, young, and highly educated (or students), a common phenomenon for the Internet population in the mid 1990s. Access was very unequally distributed, with only a small number of people having access from home or from the workplace. To overcome this, the DDS placed public terminals in Amsterdam that were intensively used. In the end, however, this means of public access did not function well: no human assistance was available for beginners, the terminals were frequently out of order, and when they did work, they were often used

---

[12] On the surveys: [27]; On log-file analysis and interviews: [28].

by schoolboys for hours on end. Something similar happened with a public terminal in an old people's home in the center of Amsterdam. The terminal was placed, but – because of lacking support – hardly used. The DDS considered it too expensive to maintain the terminals, and after a while they all became defective. Although access is less a of problem today, as recent US data show [11], this trend may be reversed if the free Internet access providers disappear from the market.

In the first weeks the population of the DDS was relatively well distributed in terms of age groups and main activity, but in the following couple of years the changes in the DDS population reflect the sequence various social groups were obtaining access to the Internet. In 1996 the first large group of new users entered the DDS: university students (and teachers), as they were the only ones with easy access to the Internet at that time. This is reflected in the age distribution: by far the largest group is between 19 and 25. In 1998 the youngest age group becomes much larger, for those are the years in which high schools obtain connection to the Internet; moreover, access (by teenagers) from home is becoming more normal. Of all DDS users, nearly 75% were under. For many digital citizens the DDS is their first acquaintance with the Internet, which reflected the aim of the DDS to be an instrument to democratize the use of the Internet and to provide possibilities to experiment with it.

Women were largely underrepresented, which was also in line with general Internet usage at that time. Employed DDS users mainly worked in the areas of education, culture, business services, and public administration. There were hardly any ethnic or cultural minorities that used the DDS, despite efforts to create a *Multicultural Square*. This may have been because the language used in the DDS was mainly Dutch, but it also reflects the ethnic minorities' unequal access to the Internet. Those who are poorly educated, as well as those who are neither employed nor students, such as the elderly, unemployed, and housewives, are all underrepresented, although their share in the DDS population did increase a bit. These groups also happen to have the lowest level of general Internet access.

Digital citizens were also distributed over the entire country: only 23% of the 1996 respondents were based in Amsterdam, and this share is even lower in the 1998 survey. This may be interpreted as the DDS losing its connection with 'real' Amsterdam. However, real cities attract many people from everywhere, so why shouldn't digital cities do the same? Those users who did not live in Amsterdam usually lived in other Dutch university cities.

Table 8. What do digital citizens do?

Functions	1994	1996	1998
Communication (E-mail)	52%	95%	87%
Searching information	54%	85%	50%
Building a house/homepage	n.a.	55%	67%
Political debate	16%	40%	45%
Web-café	22%	30%	35%

n.a.: did not exist in 1994; sources: [1, 22]

4 Digital City Life

What do people do in the Digital City? It is possible to *look for information* in the virtual offices or in the private houses, supply information in *one's own house*, take part in debate on political, social, and other issues in the *discussion groups*, communicate via *electronic mail*; and visit a virtual third place such as *Web cafés*. We asked the respondents how they valued these functions and how they used the functions for leisure and work-related activities. As table 8 shows, e-mail was the most important function, with many users using only this function. In 1996 searching for information was also fairly popular, although it became less prominent in 1998. In that year supplying information was more often mentioned as an important function, but we believe this may be true only for more frequent users. Debate and chatting were less important for the respondents, but were still mentioned by more than a third. Finally, most DDS use was for leisure - hardly ever work related. This was already true in 1996, and it became even more pronounced in 1998.

4.1 Navigating the Information Spaces

In the two-week period covered by the logfile, the DDS counted about 325,000 'hits', of which 13% were personal pages, 40% index pages (like the squares) or errors, and 47% visits to sites. Analyzing the logfile, we found that a few sites attracted many visits, while 78% of the sites in the Digital City were not visited at all in the period covered by the logfiles. The 10 most visited sites accounted for about 85% of all hits. Another finding was the great difference between the availability of content and its use. In table 9 we classify DDS content in seven categories, introduced in section 4. The distribution of visits over the categories is as follows: Business: 9%, Education: 3%, Health: 7%; ICT, including the DDS: 19%; Leisure: 12%, Media: 34%, Politics: 16%. This is quite different from the availability of information.

Table 9. Information supply and information use (summer 1998)

		Supply: DDS Sites	Users: All*	Users: Frequent**
Private sites (houses)		2500	13%	n.a.
Institutional sites (squares)		263	87%	n.a.
of which:	Business	13%	9%	1%
	Education	7%	3%	8%
	Health	7%	7%	2%
	ICT	6%	19%	25%
	Leisure	33%	12%	45%
	Media	12%	34%	5%
	Politics	22%	16%	9%

Source: log file (*); questionnaires (**); n.a. = not available

The popularity of three sites accounted for the high score for the 'media' category, and of these, Kidon (a site with links to many media around the world) was especially popular. This site attracted international attention and received 42,000 hits, 28% of all visits to the DDS. The 'ICT' category was also popular, reflecting the interests of the young male population of the DDS. It should also be noted that the 'politics' category scored high as well. The questionnaires may suggest a different picture, especially for the popularity of particular subject categories, but in our view they really reflect different use by the more frequent users who were focused more on the DDS itself, on computers, and especially on leisure and lifestyle, and much less on media and politics.

In section 3, we distinguished the sites according to the nature of the information they supplied (general or practical), the orientation of the information (local or non-local information), and the presence of communication facilities. The analysis of the logfiles (figure 11) shows that sites with non-local information were popular and were visited three times more often than sites with only local information. Finally, sites with e-mail facilities were more popular than sites without those facilities, although this not the case for 'chatting'. The questionnaires and the interviews with users suggest that *communication* became increasingly important. As this function became more important it would have required changes in the design, as Web-based systems tend to be strong in information but weak in communication facilities.

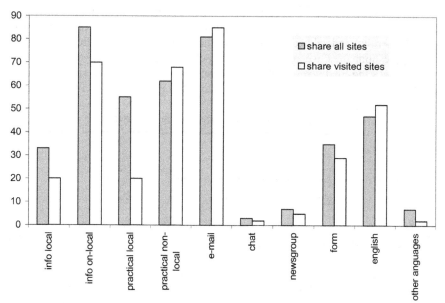

Fig. 11. Popularity of sites by characteristics Source: [16]

Table 10. Houses in the DDS (1996-2001)

Year	nr houses	Year	nr houses
1996, May	3300	1999, May	220
1997, May	6500	1999, October	118
1998, May	2500	2000, May	664
1998, October	1300	2000, October	795
		2001, March	782

Source: DDS index of houses

4.2 Building Virtual Houses

Although many people hosted their home page on a DDS server, the visibility of these home pages within the Digital City changed considerably over time. In the beginning, having a house on the DDS was very popular. More people wanted a house than there was space for, and this resulted in several creative solutions. In the DDS's *golden age*, many home pages were not real houses any more but were still accessible through the houses index of the DDS. In 1997/1998, there was a decline in the popularity of this function, and DDS users found it increasingly unnecessary to be visible within the Digital City (table 10). Thus, while many people kept their home pages on DDS servers, they generally did not find it important anymore to have it linked to the Digital City. There was no longer any identification with the Digital City as an environment for presenting oneself in cyberspace.

4.3 Conversations in Virtual Third Places

An important characteristic of public space is its role in enabling mutual interaction and unplanned conversations. To obtain information about this, the respondents were asked whether they indeed had contact with other digital citizens. As this was asked in the three questionnaires, we are able to record changes over time. Table 11 shows the results, suggesting that use of virtual public space is emerging over time. The intensity of contact and conversation clearly increased up to 1996 and then stabilized.

Table 11. Communication between digital citizens

	1994	1996	1998
Often	3%	19%	23%
Sometimes	18%	36%	29%
Seldom	33%	22%	20%
Never	46%	22%	29%

Examples of third places for conversation were the Web cafés. We observed activity in the cafés at various times. In the late summer of 1997 activity in some of the cafés was considerable, and the visitors talked about different types of issues. Some years later, however, the normal pattern was quite different. For example, when we visited Gay Café in November 2000, we found in a whole week only fifteen communications (of the size of a short sentence) from a few visitors. In other words, the café was hardly visited.

Table 12. Who are here?

Year	Average number of citizens present	Number of observations
1997, October, November	24	20
1999, January	11	10
2000, November	0	5
2001, March	0	5

The declining presence of digital citizens is also apparent when we compare the results of the 'who is here?' button over the years (table 12). As this tool never functioned properly, the emerging trend may be more significant than the absolute numbers. This counter only included the registered users that have properly logged in (required for the 'community functions' of the DDS) and who are somewhere in the public part of the DDS, not those who are visiting private houses or offices. In October 1997 we used this counter systematically over two weeks, both during the day and night. While the number of citizens fluctuated according to time of day, we observed the numbers to be generally between 20 and 40, with an average of 24 citizens present. If the average stay in the DDS was about 15 minutes, this suggests about 2,000 registered citizens per day may have visited the public part of the DDS (in 1997). In more recent periods the same method yielded very different results. The average number of citizens present decreased sharply and went down to zero in late 2000 and early 2001. Obviously, despite the increasing membership, the level of activity declined dramatically. Since only properly logged in members were (partially) counted, it is possible that many others visited the DDS unnoticed. But the data do show the decline of the DDS as a platform for virtual communities.

4.4 Emerging Virtual Communities

Several communities in the DDS organized themselves around the Gay Café, the Art Cinema, The Bicycle Path, and especially the Metro. The Metro is a complex text-based MUD (multi-user dungeon), and this popular Digital City facility was the only part of the DDS totally bottom-up and ruled by its users. It absorbed much of the participative energy that existed in the DDS community, and only the Metro remained active during the whole period. When the Digital City ceased functioning, the Metro migrated to another server. Kerckhofs [13], himself an active Metro builder for the past several years, reports that the number of active members of the Metro has been relatively stable. This is supported by the available statistics (table 13). As the Metro was and still is an active community, it deserves a separate study [13].

Table 13. the Metro Community

	1995	2001
Metro builders	1210	687
Of which female	n.a.	260
Registered Metro visitors	830	785

sources: [5, 13]

The digital citizens we interviewed emphasized that the main purpose of the effort was communication, and they especially liked computer mediated communication. How open were these communities to newcomers? In the early years the DDS maintained an open culture, but there were some interesting developments over the years. Some interviewees said they did not participate in chat conversations because they did not feel welcome. One interviewee stated: "I got in there and it did not feel right, as a newcomer." Another interviewee explained: "I wanted to go in the metro by myself and I got lost, and people were making fun out of me saying: look at the beginner! It's also like that a little bit in the chat rooms, you don't feel welcome. It is like the DDS belongs to *them* and not to anybody else." Such comments suggest that parts of the Digital City were 'taken over' by active users - the established ones - who behaved as a closed community and are perceived accordingly by the outsiders. These processes of norm building and tension among users are precisely what may indicate the rise of a virtual community [12, 24].

4.5 Debates in a Virtual Public Domain

There remains the newsgroups, which we will only discuss briefly here. We noticed several facts. First, *all* newsgroups have a highly skewed participation: a few participants were very dominant, while the large majority contributed only occasionally. The same holds true for the newsgroups as entities: a few were very big but most were small. This is very typical for many communication systems, for we also noted this type of distribution when describing the popularity of the sites within the DDS domain. Second, many (more than a third) of the newsgroups were focused on social and political issues, reflecting the initial aims of the DDS (table 6). The number of newsgroups on politics is not the decisive issue, but the activity within each newsgroup determined how popular it was. The number of megabits in the archives may be a good indicator for the level of activity, and, as figure 12 shows, the newsgroups on politics and social issues had the greatest participation.

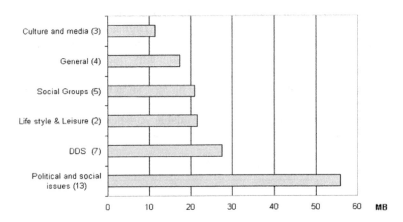

Fig. 12. Size of the newsgroups

We looked more in detail at the largest newsgroup more closely: dds.politiek (dds.politics). In this newsgroup some 12,000 contributions were posted between February 1996 and October 1999, which is an average of about 60 postings per week.[13] Does the activity in the newsgroups diminish over the years? In figure 13 we plotted the number of postings per month in this newsgroup, and it becomes clear that there was no downward trend. A strongly fluctuating level of activity can be

---

[13] We downloaded the newsgroup archives in October 1999, so our data stop there. The start date of the newsgroup is in February 1996. Older postings were lost (in all newsgroups) after the servers crashed early in 1996, and no backup system was available.

observed, which peaking every year around May. Strikingly, at the end of the period studied, the level of activity was actually higher than previously. A modest content analysis was enough to identify the background of the huge numbers of postings in May and June 1999: the war in Kosovo. Words that occurred very frequently in the 1,500 June postings are: NATO (1,760 times), Kosovo (1,166), Milosevic (429), fascism (324), ethnic (300), genocide (287), and terror (170).

The newsgroups formed an emerging virtual public domain. Open issues requiring further studies are the composition, changes, and size of the groups of people participating in the newsgroups, as well as the content of the newsgroups [2]. For example, in the first ten-week experiment the newsgroups were almost all moderated by specialists in the topic. Even then, doubts about the level of the discussions were expressed. And, although the DDS wanted to improve communication between citizens and politicians hardly any politicians participated in those early DDS discussions.

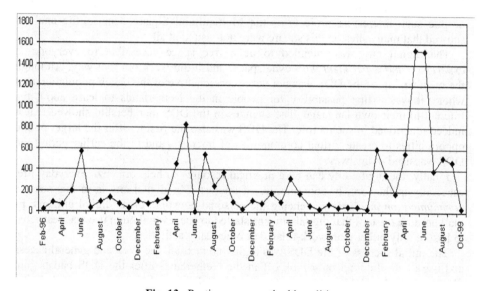

Fig. 13. Postings per month, dds.politics

5 What Can Be Learned from the Digital City Example?

Between early 1994 and early 1998 the DDS developed into a successful networked community with a high level of activities. In 1998 the decline started (except for the size of its membership) that ended with the demolition of the virtual public space. What can be learned from seven years DDS?

The DDS developed into a *social information infrastructure*, providing information about a real city. Following a good start, extension and maintenance of the information repository were neglected, which hampered the DDS from maintaining its position as a leading-edge portal. While the Internet exploded in size, the DDS grew only at a very modest rate.

The DDS also started early as a platform for *virtual third places* where digital citizens could meet and interact. These places were populated, and early observers noticed, "something was happening in the DDS." Also here the level of activity slowed, and digital citizens probably went elsewhere for their electronic conversations. An interesting development was the changing accessibility of the third places. As in the 'real' society, processes of norm building were apparent within the DDS that, resulted in similar patterns of established users versus outsiders. This suggests that new bonds were created, and users experienced an appropriation of the newly created virtual public space. Even if electronic networks foster interaction, that does not mean that such interactions will lead to a more democratic, participative, and inclusive society.

The DDS started partly as an experiment with a *virtual public domain* to improve local democracy and participation, but it did not function very well. Discussion took place, but the quality of the discussion was rather poor, and politicians and opinion leaders did not participate. Nor were civic organizations very active on the DDS, despite such interesting projects as the Multicultural Square. Our logfile analysis showed that many sites on this square were not visited at all.

The digital city was intended to be a free space accessible to everyone to *experience and experiment* with cyberspace, and it did work out that way. Although the membership of the DDS was not very representative of the Dutch population as a whole, it was a first possibility for people in the Netherlands to learn about the Internet in their own language. The changes in the DDS membership showed that it indeed functioned in such a role. The DDS was also the first to offer the larger public opportunities to create virtual communities of interests, and in the earlier period the DDS was used in this way.

Finally, the digital city can be a practical resource to help organize everyday life, especially in the form of communities of interest. The digital city is in this sense a *communication medium*, influencing the personal networks of its digital citizens. E-mail became *the* tool that digital citizens started to use, even though use was restricted to leisure only rather than work-related or other daily activities.

The initial success of the DDS was highly contextual: the Web and general access and use of the Internet only took off in the Netherlands after the DDS had begun. Shortly after the DDS began, many other digital cities, digital regions, and digital villages initiatives emerged within the Netherlands. Most of them failed, remained marginal, or became simply municipal information Websites than virtual public spaces.

During its decline the DDS still claimed many visitors per day. While that may be true, the visitors were mainly 'tourists' (in DDS terminology) who visited a website within the DDS domain that they may have bookmarked previously or found through a search engine. Hardly anybody logged in any more for the specific community functions the DDS offered. Thus, in its last years the DDS changed from a virtual public space to modest content provider. At the same time competition increased for all services the DDS offered to its members, and the DDS could not keep up with the competitors. Digital citizens disappeared from the DDS; they went elsewhere to find a better quality of virtual life. This is actually what happened: the goals of the DDS initiators were realized, but not within the DDS domain – they were realized on the whole Internet [21]. If the global village exists somewhere, it is in cyberspace.

Location is unimportant on the Web, and there is no need for people to stay within the DDS domain if better alternatives can be found elsewhere.

To turn the tide, the DDS wanted to become commercial, and take advantage of its large membership to attract private investors. Unfortunately for the new owners, the Internet bubble was over, and the strategy failed. Even if the DDS had done this earlier, however, success may have been difficult because going commercial requires a well-defined market, and it is questionable if a virtual public space is such a market.

Ultimately, we think that the main factor behind the decline of the DDS was the lack of ownership by the users. As soon as institutionalization took place, a different logic became dominant in the DDS. This logic can be summarized as *earning revenue to survive*. As a consequence the influence of digital citizens to shape and develop the initiative declined. Their lack of influence eventually resulted in declining participation and commitment, and in a radical change in the identity of the DDS itself. This is supported by the story of the *Metro*. The Metro remained the only part of the DDS which up to the end was completely owned by the digital citizens who built and used it. Strikingly, participation in the Metro remained stable over the seven-year period. In contrast to the DDS the Metro is an example of an initiative that was able to survive.

The DDS started as a grass roots initiative, became a non-profit organization, and was eventually transformed into a private company. Its vulnerability in a competitive market led to its demise. Although the experiment of the DDS as an institutionalized non-profit approach failed, the question is not so much how it could have avoided failure in the changed Internet climate, but rather what organizational forms and networks are needed to enable community networking, virtual social interaction, and non-commercial Internet culture. What does emerge from the DDS example is that a lively virtual public domain requires *active* collaboration among many individuals and organizations, without a hierarchical structure that discourages participation and creativity.

Acknowledgments

Isabel Melis is gratefully acknowledged for contributions to the research underlying this chapter. Patrice Riemens, Reinder Rustema, and Paul Vogel provided detailed inside information. The three of them, Teresa Mom, and Anne-Marie Oostveen suggested many improvements. The user surveys were a collaboration with the DDS. Discussions over the last years with Douglas Schuler, Toru Ishida, Fiorella de Cindio, Andrew Clement, Peter Day, Mike Gurstein and Peper Mambrey have been useful in the development of our thinking about digital cities. The first author gratefully acknowledges a sabbatical leave from the University of Amsterdam, Department of Psychology, the former Social Informatics Program.

References

1. D. Beckers: Use and users of the Amsterdam Digital City. MA thesis, University of Amsterdam, 1998.

2. D. Beckers: European Digital Cities – a comparative study, PhD thesis, University of Amsterdam, forthcoming.
3. M. Castells: The Internet Galaxy. Oxford, Oxford University Press, 2001.
4. A. Clement and Peter Van den Besselaar: Participatory design, a retrospective view. Communications of the ACM 26, 6, 83-91, 1993.
5. DDS Quarterly report, first quarter 1996. Amsterdam, DDS, 1996.
6. DDS Annual report 1998. Amsterdam, DDS, 1999 (a).
7. DDS Five years DDS – Conference Materials. Amsterdam, DDS, 15-01-1999 (b).
8. L. Francissen and K. Brants: Virtual Going Places, Square Hopping in Amsterdam's Digital City. In: R. Tsagarousianon, D. Bryan, C. Tambini, eds., Cyberdemocracy, Technology, Cities, and Civic Networks. London, Routledge, 1998.
9. G. Gumpert and S. Drucker: Privacy, Predictability or Serendipidy and Digital Cities. In: M. Tanabe, P. van den Besselaar and T. Ishida, Digital Cities 2, Computational and Sociological Approaches. Lecture Notes in Computer Science, Vol. 2362, Springer-Verlag, Berlin Heidelberg New York (2002) 27-41
10. J. Habermas: Structurwandlung der Öffentlichkeit. Frankfurt: Suhrkamp, (1963)
11. P.E.N. Howard, L. Rainie and S. Jones: Days and nights on the Internet: the impact of a diffusing technology. American Behavioral Scientist Vol.45, No.3 (2001) 363-382
12. S.G. Jones: Virtual Culture, London, Sage (1997)
13. S. M. Kerckhoffs: MUD – wrestling with identity. MA thesis Communication Studies, Catholic University Nijmegen, (2001) (in Dutch)
24. G. Lovink: Die Digitale Stadt Amsterdam, Medium wie alle anderen oder virtuelle Version des Speaker's Corner? In: Claus Leggewie and Christa Maar (Hrsg.), Internet & Politik, Bollmann Verlag, Koeln, (1998) 293-299
15. G. Lovink and P. Riemens: Amsterdam Public Digital Culture: Contradictions among User Profiles. In: RikVoice 002, Stiftung Risiko-Dialog, St. Gallen (2000) 1-8
16. I. Melis: The local electronic network society. MA thesis, University of Amsterdam (1998)
17. W.J. Mitchell: E-topia; It's Urban Life, Jim, But not as We Know It. Cambridge, MIT Press (1999)
18. R. Oldenburger: The Great Good Places, New York, Marlowe Co. (1999)
19. Michael Pollman and Peter Van der Pouw Kraan: Van bolwerken tot netwerken, datacommunicatie door maatschappelijke organisaties. Amsterdam, Ravijn (1995)
20. E. Rommes: Worlds apart, exclusion processed in the DDS. In: M. Tanabe, P. van den Besselaar and T. Ishida, Digital Cities 2, Computational and Sociological Approaches. Lecture Notes in Computer Science, Vol. 2362, Springer-Verlag, Berlin Heidelberg New York (2002) 219-233
21. R. Rustema: Rise and Fall of the DDS. MA thesis Communication Studies, University of Amsterdam (2001)
22. K. Schalken and P.W. Tops: Gemeenschap en democratie in de informatiemaatschappij, In: Jaarboek overheidscommunicatie (1995) 47-53
23. D. Schuler: Digital cities and digital citizens. In: M. Tanabe, P. van den Besselaar and T. Ishida, Digital Cities 2, Computational and Sociological Approaches. Lecture Notes in Computer Science, Vol. 2362, Springer-Verlag, Berlin Heidelberg New York (2002) 71-85
24. R Spears, M. Lea and T. Postmes: Social-psychological theories of computer-mediated communication: social pain or social gain. In: P. Robinson and H. Giles, eds., the Handbook of Language and Social Psychology. Chichester: Wiley, (2000)
25. B. Van Bastelaer and C. Lobet-Maris Eds.: Social learning regarding multimedia developments at a local level. The case of Digital Cities. SLIM project. Namur, University of Namur – CITA-FUNDP, (1998)
26. P. Van den Besselaar: E-community versus E-commerce: the rise and decline of the Amsterdam Digital City. AI & Society 15 (2001) 280-288

27. P. Van den Besselaar and D. Beckers: Demographics and sociographics of the Digital City. In: T. Ishida, ed., Community Computing and Support Systems, Lecture Notes in Computer Science, Vol. 1519, Springer-Verlag, Berlin Heidelberg New York (1998) 109-125.
28. P. Van den Besselaar, Isabel Melis and Dennis Beckers: Digital cities; organization, content and use. In: T. Ishida, K. Isbister, eds., Digital cities, experiences, trends, and perspectives, Lecture Notes in Computer Science, Vol. 1765, Springer-Verlag, Berlin Heidelberg New York (2000) 8-32
29. R. Van der Haar: Project report Digital City (1995) (In Dutch)
30. F. Van Jole: Start of the DDS. De Volkskrant, January 15 (1994) (in Dutch)

Urban Cyberspace as a Social Construction: Non-technological Factors in the Shaping of Digital Bristol

Alessandro Aurigi

School of Architecture, Planning and Landscape
Claremont Tower
University of Newcastle upon Tyne
Newcastle upon Tyne, UK NE1 7RU
a.aurigi@ncl.ac.uk

Abstract. This paper describes how an example of 'digital city' initiative in Europe was conceived and shaped in its early phases of development. The paper deals with Digital City Bristol, and looks at its deployment from a social constructivist perspective, focusing on the actors involved in the initiative, and the processes of interpretation and negotiation they went through in order to define a mutually agreeable configuration of the digital city. In particular the competing visions of a two-way, participative urban cyberspace, versus a more one-way, broadcasting facility, are highlighted. The case study describes how actors' needs and interpretations in the early stages of the digital city have influenced its future trajectory towards a 'portal'-like configuration.

1 Introduction

The 'digital city' phenomenon, with all its different experiments, has been widely observed and analysed in the past few years. This has been done mainly from the point of view of its technical development and innovations, or by trying to study the real, measurable 'impacts' or sometimes the forecast ones, of the several initiatives on the physical cities and the communities they are related with.

This paper is about a different way to look at the development of digital cities. It is the result of the analysis of a series of observations, interviews and documentary research carried out in the city of Bristol in the late 1997, and further observations in subsequent years. The aim of the study was to analyse the first steps of what looked like a promising digital city initiative in Britain, by focusing on the processes that underpinned the development of the initiative, rather than looking at its technological solutions or its contents.

There are precedents to this approach. A very influential piece of research was published at the beginning of the 1990s by Guthrie and Dutton, looking at early experiments of civic networking and information and communication technologies provision at the urban level in some US cities. In their study, Guthrie and Dutton noted that "Like policy, technology is a social construction. (...) However, in the case of technology, these policy choices too often are obscured or overlooked because

P. van den Besselaar and S. Koizumi (Eds.): Digital Cities 2003, LNCS 3081, pp. 97–112, 2005.

people focus only on decisions about the adoption or non adoption of a technology rather than also attending to decisions about design and implementation of the technology that influence its use and impact." [10. p575]

2 Technology as a Process of Social Construction

The sociological approach known as Social Construction of Technology (SCOT) provides a very effective framework that can be used to investigate processes of design, creation, deployment and stabilisation of technologies, and seems very suitable for multi-disciplinary studies. Wiebe Bijker explains that "In the SCOT descriptive model, relevant social groups are the key starting point. Technological artefacts do not exist without the social interactions within and among social groups. The design details of artefacts are described by focusing on the problems and solutions that those relevant social groups have with respect to the artefact. Thus, increasing and decreasing degrees of stabilisation of the artefact can be traced. A crucial concept in SCOT (as well as in the Empirical Program of Relativism, EPOR, in the sociology of scientific knowledge, to which SCOT is closely related) is interpretative flexibility. The interpretative flexibility of an artefact can be demonstrated by showing how, for different social groups, the artefact presents itself as essentially different artifacts." [3, p75-76]

So, in approaching the investigation of new technological implementations in cities, it can be beneficial to look not just at the system itself, but at what generates the need(s) for it, the problems it is supposed to solve, the solutions it is supposed to provide, and whom and what visions are promoting a certain setup, or a set of alternative ones.

Obviously these problems are – or can be – social and relational, not merely technological or functional. So, the social network or actors involved in the establishment of a technology, with the 'technological entrepreneurs' who promote certain 'solutions' in the first place, have to come to terms with their own roles and social, economic, political benefits they could derive from an initiative. The social dynamics behind the technological deployment are most important as "Technologies are born out of conflict, difference, or resistance. Thus most if not all the case studies describe technological controversies, disagreements, or difficulties. The pattern is that the protagonists – entrepreneurs, industrial or consumers, designers, inventors, or professional practitioners – seek to establish or maintain a particular technology or set of technological arrangements, and with this a set of social, scientific, economic, and organisational relations." [4, p9]

This concept of 'interpretative flexibility', and the social dynamics related to it, seems most important for approaching an investigation of Internet-based urban information systems, as their initially 'blurred' definition is likely to change during development.

2.1 Technology Contributes to Its Own Shaping: The Importance of 'Paradigms'

Interpretations and visions can also stem from technology itself, or better from the existence of previous or parallel technologies or working practices, that can affect the shaping and the establishment of a new system. As noted by Guthrie and Dutton: "Existing technology presents a variety of opportunities, problems and constraints that shape the future of technology. One way in which existing technology shapes new technology is by providing mental models of solutions. (…)" [10, p583]

This yet again reinforces the consideration that technology cannot be looked at as a self-standing fact, but as a development shaped by many different (f)actors. This involves the presence, and indeed the influence, of previous technologies, early experiments that have become 'exemplar', as well as accepted practices that can be 'projected' into the new artefact or system.

2.2 The Importance of the Early Stages: Change Versus Stabilization

All of these considerations are crucial especially for the early phases of design, development and deployment of technological innovation, as brilliantly explained by Langdon Winner: "By far the greatest latitude of choice exists the very first time a particular instrument, system, or technique is introduced. Because choices tend to become strongly fixed in material equipment, economic investment, and social habit, the original flexibility vanishes for all practical purposes once the initial commitments are made. In that sense technological innovations are similar to legislative acts or political foundings that establish a framework for public order that will endure over many generations." [19, p30-31]

So, the best time to study innovation in urban technologies, as indeed in any other technology, seems to be the early stages, as this is the time when characteristics and trajectories are particularly flexible, and tend later on to get 'stabilised' and fixed in an adopted, and much less changeable, form. It is then and there that meanings, specific visions and interpretations of society and reality, which come of course from specific social actors, are embedded into artefacts or initiatives, and influence their future configuration and use. The phenomenon of 'digital cities', especially in the second half of the 1990s, seemed to be therefore ideally positioned, in chronological terms, to be studied under this perspective.

3 Actors and Visions for Digital Bristol

3.1 HP Labs Kick It Off

All of these factors can be observed in the early development of Digital City Bristol. An arena was established in Bristol in the second half of the 1990s, where IT industry, academia, and local government were represented and ended up wanting to have a project in common. However, an initial set of ideas and a vision for a specific project such as Digital City Bristol was obviously going to come from a specific promoter, or 'technological entrepreneur'. In this case, this role was played by Erik Geelhoed, a

HP employee. As Linda Skinner, the project manager and research coordinator from UWE put it, "all of these projects have some idealist or ideologist promoting them, and we had Erik." [15]

The role of Geelhoed, especially in the first phase of conception and life of the initiative was indeed central. A psychologist engaged in studying behavioural aspects of people using high technologies, Geelhoed had been in talks about similar ideas with Joe Lambert, from San Francisco Digital Media Center. This contact was created as HP Labs – whose central offices are in Palo Alto – had started liasing with Lambert to gain a better understanding of issues concerning digital imagery on the Internet [9]. In the late 1990s, as the Internet seemed to be booming, as well as all sorts of business opportunities related to it, many IT giants had started to adjust their strategies towards the production and management of Internet content. It was quite natural for a company like HP to be proactive in considering how Internet content could be effectively delivered, and through which applications.

Following the contact between Geelhoed and Lambert, the first intention had been to work on some kind of digital 'twinning' between Bristol and San Francisco, through the creation of websites. However, other factors played a major role within this early phase of the conception of Digital Bristol. One factor was the fact that Geelhoed, probably facilitated by his Dutch origins, had in that same period got acquainted with the initiative that had established itself as a European paradigm for civic Internet: De Digitale Stad (DDS) in Amsterdam. [16] Geelhoed was fascinated by Amsterdam's digital city success, and managed to invite the 'mayor' of DDS, Marlene Stikker, to give a talk at HP Labs in Bristol convincing the top managers of the Laboratories that such an initiative would be "a good investment". [9]

DDS had a strong emphasis on interaction and participation, and this was being recognised as an important component of the research: "We saw the digital city as a possible research tool. The social aspects were interesting to us, those new ways for people to communicate. Our first thought was about facilitating communication in the digital city, rather than putting emphasis on information." [9]

Inspired by DDS, HP Labs funded two bursaries for a Masters degree at Delft University of Technology, Faculty of Industrial Design Engineering, in the Netherlands. These were meant to layout the basic concepts, ideas, and the interface itself for Digital Bristol. The results of the study and the design by Sierd Westerfield were summarised in a project report for HP Labs named 'Digital City Bristol Interactive', a title that also became the initial name of the initiative (DCBI). Coherently with HP's main interests, this piece of work was based on a case study on DDS, and aimed at envisaging optimal user interface and communication tools for Digital Bristol [17].

So it could be argued that the digital city in Bristol had been initially conceived as a minor R&D project initiated by a big multi-national company, whose main purpose was to study ways of creating highly interactive, grounded Internet sites. As Westerfield's report remarks: "The fundamental question addressed in the Digital City Bristol research is: What are the opportunities for HP in the Emerging Information Infrastructure (EII) consumer market?" [17, p11]. Technical issues of software implementation, as well as on human-computer interfaces, were very much at the centre of the project. Another student from Delft had also been involved to study the use of Java programming technology within the initiative [9].

However, the person in HP Labs who had started DCBI, Erik Geelhoed, had a wider vision for it, being strongly interested in the social aspects and implications of the establishment of an interactive digital city. In a short paper published at the time on the HP Labs Web site, in which different types of early digital cities were compared, Geelhoed kept remarking on the importance of people's presence: "What a digital city provides is people" (Geelhoed, 1996) and of their interaction and empowerment in an electronic equivalent of public space, as opposed to an electronic version of shopping malls. He quoted Geert Lovink, a Dutch philosopher and critic, endorsing his claims that: "A lot of people in government and in business think that if they are just offering information, it is enough. But this is not the case. It is very important that the people can find an identity themselves with the media and that they are part of the computer network. That they are not just treated as consumers who are just buying something" (Lovink, 1995; quoted in [7].

Fig. 1. One of the early versions of the interface of Digital City Bristol Interactive (DCBI)

This interest for letting the embryonic digital Bristol actually involve and empower real people, and go beyond the limited scope of a human-computer interface research project, was motivating Geelhoed to act as a central character and facilitator, trying to generate support within HP as well as enlarging the circle of the actors involved.

So, to a certain extent, Geelhoed and HP Labs could be seen as two distinct actors in the Digital Bristol arena, insofar as Geelhoed had been successful in enrolling HP – his own employer – in the initiative by highlighting those aspects that could interest the multi-national company's R&D division. He also presented DCBI as an inexpensive option, with the costs limited to a part of Geelhoed's time, the two studentships with Delft, and a small amount of equipment.

However, other important actors were to be involved in the management and shaping of Digital City Bristol, and their participation meant that different interpretations of the role and nature of the initiative were to be made, and these of course were going to have a deep influence over the actual way the digital city was going to develop. As we noted before, Geelhoed was looking for people to populate the forthcoming cybertown, and as Linda Skinner notes: "Erik claimed that he was going to have the digital city designed, but to bring it to life he needed people from the city and from the university." [15]

3.2 The University of West of England

Of the two universities in Bristol, it was the University of West of England (UWE) which became involved in the project. A couple of reasons seem to explain this: physical proximity – which in itself is a fascinating issue to have to consider when it comes to speaking of projects involving cyberspace – and the dynamism of the management. UWE's campus is located out of town, within walking distance from the HP buildings, which facilitated frequent contacts between researchers and managers, independently from this specific project.

Above all, however, it has to be noted that UWE is a second-generation university, one of the ex-polytechnics that had found themselves 'upgraded' in status in the 1980's, facing the new challenge of re-defining themselves from just teaching establishments to being research active institutions as well. Some of these universities were working very hard and proactively towards increasing their research output, and UWE was certainly considered to be a very positive example of this. As a consequence, UWE was bound to be very keen on innovative research or R&D projects that could boost its image, prospective funding, as well as its internal research culture. It was indeed an ideal potential partner for Digital City Bristol Interactive.

HP and the university had been in talks to organise some type of a 'media' event in Bristol that would "bring potentialities together" [15] in the city, generating new partnerships and new projects. Linda Skinner was an important player in this respect, as she had been appointed by UWE as a manager who was expected to create momentum for research projects and consultancies. After these first contacts, Geelhoed started working on the new digital city idea, and managed to involve UWE quickly, as the partnership with HP Labs was interesting and prestigious to them. Skinner defined the initiative as a "very good research about the city of Bristol itself, that would enable us to give design and organisational recommendations about this type of initiative" [15], possibly envisaging the university's ability to develop a know-how in innovative internet sites, that could be exploited on the consultancy side of academic business.

3.3 Bristol City Council Steps In

The other partner in DCBI had to be the 'city' itself, or rather the City Council. Linda Skinner contacted Bristol City Council shortly after Stuart Long, a new head of IT services had been appointed there. Bristol had become a Unitary Authority in Spring of 1996. This had lead to a process of re-organising and re-thinking about the ways the local authority should operate. Within this process, the idea of a specific initiative, or a cluster of initiatives involving information technology has started emerging, and was eventually named as 'IT in the Community'.

Stuart Long saw the proposal about the digital city as something that would fit well within this overall IT-based strategic vision for Bristol.

The interesting thing to notice about the Council's involvement in DCBI is that the digital city was going to be seen as just a complement to an existing and wider overall strategic plan for IT in the city. So, if on the one hand Bristol City Council was interested in participating in the initiative, this was being considered as a piece of a bigger jigsaw, and possibly not the central one. This was clear from the fact that the Council would keep developing and placing most of its information and service resources within its own Web site. Although this should not be seen as a necessarily negative aspect of the initial development of DCBI, as it was fairly normal that partners would retain their own separate identities, it suggests that in this Bristol case the fragmentation of agency could be mirrored in the Internet, rather than be moderated by it. And that this could easily lead to a wide fragmentation of interpretations of what the digital city was going to be there for. However, as long as a focus on common benefits and opportunities could be kept, the initiative could start and progress.

3.4 Why DCBI? Networking to Re-brand the City and Institutions

Bristol in the late 1990s was a city trying to re-define itself. We have seen how the local authority had assumed a new role, and the UWE too was working hard to re-launch itself as a proactive, research-based institution. Therefore a project like the 'digital city' could be seen as a great opportunity for helping to establish a strong and forward-looking image for the actors involved. Certainly it was also a good chance to network for some of these institutions, and experiment with closer partnerships. Linda Skinner was very explicit about this by saying that "this digital city is about getting the city's influential organisations together. There is a kind of new optimism in Bristol now, and what we are doing with the digital city is about right, using it to get key individuals and sections of the community to work together." [15]

It is interesting to notice the clear interpretation from Skinner of the specific digital city initiative as something to 'use', a good catalyst for collaboration among the 'key individuals' in Bristol. She clearly identified networking, together with the more obvious research, as the two main UWE's priorities.

Although from a quite different point of view, the City Council also had a clear re-branding agenda for the city, the council itself, and its activities. Quickly embedding the digital city into the wider set of projects and policies of 'IT in the Community', the Council was aiming to demonstrate "very explicitly the potential of the new Unitary Council to make a real impact in the city through the innovative application of IT." [2] Not surprisingly, the theme of efficiency was central among the reasons for the local authority to get involved, as could probably be observed in many other cases. Stuart Long confirmed this by describing the cybercity as a "new communication medium that allows the Council to do things in different ways and do new things. And above all do them more efficiently and spend less money to run certain types of services." [12]

The 'vision' from Erik Geelhoed of a participative, communication-intensive digital city can be seen as yet another interpretation converging towards the general expectation of a less provincial, more lively and proactive Bristol. It has to be said that Geelhoed's vision would go well beyond a simple place-marketing ethos. However, the will to provide a hi-tech space for facilitating collaboration and giving people and groups a certain degree of visibility could be easily seen – at least initially – by the other actors as a very coherent and desirable course of action towards the common goal of 'making things happen' in Bristol.

All major actors seemed to perceive the need to 'de-provincialise' the city and facilitate the emergence of a new image of forward-looking place. Image-making was paramount and was the real cohesive factor for the partnership, as the Council's 'IT in the Community' document stated openly: "A number of the specific areas of work completed have done much to transform the image of the City of Bristol towards a leading edge, high technology city. The profile established for the City Council through working with credible partners such as Hewlett Packard and the University of West of England on Digital City Bristol has been very positive." [2, p6]

However, the common goal of 'revitalising' Bristol provided a good reason to start the project at all, and to work in partnership, but it would not be able to address the main divergence of visions for the digital city for the long term. Beyond the re-branding of Bristol, the expectations about specific aspects of how the digital city should work could be simply opposite, within the managing group. This would eventually generate the need for a radical re-definition, and somehow scaling-down, of the initiative.

4 Public Space with Little to Do? The Gradual Demise of the 'Interactive' Character of Digital Bristol

Was Digital City Bristol an initiative aimed at creating a public 'cyberspace' in the city, a site where public discourse was going to be supported and have crucial importance? As we have mentioned before, the preliminary studies and plans made by Geelhoed and Westerfield seemed to claim that DCBI was a "people to people" project. Geelhoed had defined this aspect as the focus of the whole R&D project [8], and Westerfield had remarked that "The main theme is people to people communication (…) The DCBI will be the main site for Bristol. It will be the place where people can get information on the city, and a place where they can communicate with other people in the city." [17, p12]

Geelhoed had indeed based all his presentations about DCBI on the explicit link with the project of DDS Amsterdam. In a short study published as an internal HP Labs document and on the World Wide Web, he had compared different types of early digital city concluding that the most interesting was indeed the Amsterdam case, and arguing that: "DDS has also been a major source of inspiration for our thinking. We judged three aspects particularly attractive: novel ways of representing the information space, enhanced navigational clues and last but not least the social aspects of the city. Residents of the digital city can communicate with each other via the digital city computer interface as individuals or as groups, thereby energising the city." [7]

Clearly this vision was the course of action envisaged by the internal HP project report, and indeed by the initial design of Digital Bristol's interface and functionality. The digital city had been designed by HP Labs to look like a harbour, with an explicit reference to Bristol's past. The harbour was organised in 'piers' with virtual 'boats' moored to them. Piers and boats were there to host a wealth of different Web sites that could be owned and run by community organisations as well as private individuals. The several functions available through this interface were activated by Java routines, which would have supposedly allowed a very high degree of interactivity, such as real-time zooming and moving within the 2D virtual environment. Communication functions were planned as a crucial aspect of the digital city. The HP Labs project report claimed that: "DCBI will provide newsgroups as the basis for a discussion platform" [17, p36]. But one the main challenges that HP Labs were willing to face was working on the creation and implementation of a more intuitive and easy-to-use electronic environment to allow exchange of ideas among citizens. A whole chapter of the HP report was dedicated to the conception of what had been called the "multimedia notice board" for the digital city [17, p36-45].

However, neither the innovative notice board, nor the newsgroups would end up being available at all in Bristol. The 'vision gap' between Geelhoed's open, interactive, lively, and communicative conception of the digital city, and the way the other partners were expecting DCBI to be, was widening. In general, there was a strong concern for the problems that allowing free speech in the digital city could generate, and the majority of the actors involved shared this concern.

The City Council was declaring an interest in encouraging the development of an inclusive information society in Bristol, but mainly from the point of view of allowing the majority of citizens to use the new services and information. Communication-wise the municipality was only concentrating on providing councillors with email addresses.

Indeed, the Council's strategic document on 'IT in the Community' despite outlining a series of initiatives and prospective benefits on information provision, education, and economic development, had basically no significant mention of any governance-enhancing effects of the information society in Bristol, and no plans for increased public participation or consultation through the use of ICT.

Another important thing to notice is that Bristol City Council's policy had never been that of migrating council services or facilities – such as the councillors' email – into the digital city. The Council had its own well-established Web site, which was linked by DCBI, but nevertheless was completely independent from it, and its limited e-communication plans could well be carried forward outside the digital city.

On a similar 'line' was the attitude of the local press about the launch of DCBI. The local newspaper The Evening Post had been publicising the event with a positive review, but had been exclusively concentrating on the information 'broadcasting' benefits of the new medium, ignoring completely the two-way communication potential that the digital city could have embedded [13, p11].

So, despite the initial drive from Geelhoed towards a lively and participative digital city that could have been seen as an evolution of Amsterdam's DDS, the partnership behind DCBI was really not that keen on making it a cyber-Agora. Plans had been made to try and embed some debate facilities, but already with the clear awareness in mind that DCBI was not meant to be a place for debate and free speech.

If two-way, people to people communication was seen as a priority by Geelhoed, it was clear that the HP Labs researcher was isolated with his vision. Linda Skinner of UWE, when asked about public participation and public discourse issues, replied very uncompromisingly that "the digital city is not about that. Mostly, it is about other things" [15]. Skinner would also mention explicitly the Council as having a information broadcasting target: "The City Council is backing this specific initiative, among the several Bristol 'indexes' because of the involvement of local community groups and health care. Because it is about public information provision, it meets their public agenda. It is very different from the Amsterdam case." [15]

So, shaping the digital city was a task embedding conflict as well as convergence and partnership. Above all it seemed to embed a good degree of 'fragmentation' of vision, when it came to deal with developing specific aspects of a low-funded, resource-thirsty project. The result of this was that the notice board that the 'harbourmaster' Mark Day was expecting to see was never fully implemented, and that despite the claims from Geelhoed and Skinner herself that newsgroups would have been launched soon, none of these facilities was yet present in 1999, two years later, as noted by Annelies de Bruine: "At the moment the web site is a good information source for Bristol. It is not very dynamic; more interaction can energize the digital city and make users come back to communicate with others. The chat/forum on the music pier and in Erik's Café is a modest start, but more newsgroups are needed to make the web site a dynamic and more interesting place on the web." [6, p122]

It cannot be argued, however, that DCBI was denying completely all forms of 'grassroots' expression. Indeed, the 'piers' and 'boats' were there to be populated by community groups and individuals who were given space for self-representation on the World Wide Web, and under the Digital Bristol 'umbrella'. So, in a way the digital city was being shaped to become a highly diverse place. The problem, as far as encouraging public discourse was concerned, was that all the users – we could say the e-citizens – were able to become broadcasters and advertisers, but not to engage in debate within a public cyber-space. People were 'talking' to the world, but not necessarily together. Digital Bristol looked increasingly like a 'city' made of unconnected fragments.

The person who was still proactively trying to establish some communication within DCBI, Erik Geelhoed, ended up taking individual initiatives to make space for the exchange of ideas and interactivity. He was tolerated but not necessarily actively supported by the rest of the management committee. This meant that a new 'building' had quickly appeared in the virtual harbour, called 'Erik's Café'. This operation seemed to be again strongly inspired by DDS, even graphically. It was meant to be an interactive, multimedia-intensive meeting space. In its extremely short active life it had been equipped with a MP3 jukebox for digital music, a reading room, and video clips of Bristol-based events. Also, in 1999, following a conference on 'Music on the Web' held at HP Labs in February, a new 'music' pier was created and a chat/forum was implemented within it, targeted of course at music enthusiasts. Annelies de

Bruine was the researcher working on both the Café and the Music Pier, but HP Labs' commitment towards this was clearly very limited, as de Bruine was employed on a short-term contract and was soon going to move on to other occupations.

These sporadic attempts at actually establishing some form of public space within the digital city remained isolated within the wider context, and had a short life. Erik's Café had survived the first major modification of the interface, where 'version 2' of the digital city kept the harbour metaphor but dropped most of the Java contents to retreat to plain HTML. This also involved a symbolically very meaningful change of name, where the 'Interactive' was shed to redefine the initiative as 'Digital City Bristol'.

Erik's Café looked like the only resisting element supporting the original concept of DCB, trying to make the digital city truly communicative and interactive. But despite formally occupying a space on the main pier for quite a long time, the Café had rarely been active and accessible, and disappeared completely with the third re-design of the interface.

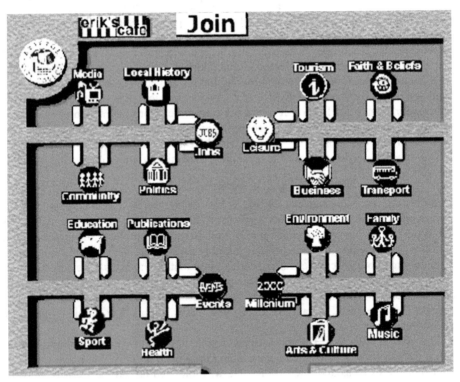

Fig. 2. The Java-free version of Digital City Bristol

5 Settling for the 'Lowest Common Denominator'

Shortly after it had been officially launched, Digital City Bristol was already in the need of a re-definition, as the power of novelty, together with the initial targets set by some of its shapers, had started wearing off. All of the main actors involved were recognising elements of success, which were of course related to their own expectations from the project. Obviously the shared goal of facilitating partnership, and linking some influential Bristolian organisations had been achieved.

As we have noted before, the City Council was certainly satisfied about the image return from the operation, its coherence with the wider 'IT in the Community' strategy, and interestingly the fact that the Council's own website, clearly linked and advertised on Digital Bristol, had increased its visibility [2, p6].

Hewlett Packard Labs had been able to do some 'live' experiments with Java-based community networking, and content distribution. UWE had started networking with the other two important actors involved, and had carried out some prominent research and development.

However, differences and divergent visions had soon become stronger than the good reasons to work together. The cohesion of the management team, and above all the trajectory of the project and its momentum, had suffered because of these different interpretations and expectations.

As a result, despite a certain amount of self-confidence manifested in talks by the interviewees as well as in their documents and papers, Digital City Bristol's role and character were not very clear at all towards the end of 1997. And indeed tensions and dualisms were going to last throughout the two or three years to follow, if we have to judge things from de Bruine's paper presented at the Digital City conference in Kyoto at the end of 1999. In her paper she still refers to the tensions existing between the DDS-based paradigm supported by Geelhoed, and the broadcasting model that was increasingly becoming dominant: "It is important to focus on communication in the web site to make it more than an information database." [6, p124]

Several similar tensions had been developing between different aspects of the project. The limited resources allocated to the digital city were appropriate for a research operation with a narrow scope, but definitely insufficient for a fully-fledged civic service, even if just one-way.

Another important issue that was creating problems was about the interface and functionality of the digital city. We have seen how strong the dualism between the participative paradigm and the broadcasting one had been. This was clearly reflected in the rejection by some partners of the initial concept design of DCBI, and its radical transformation that abandoned the DDS-like model.

Still connected to this, a 'browsing vs. searching' dualism had been developing, about what was best for the digital city's interface. This again was not just a matter of technological preference, but a dilemma deeply rooted in the different interpretations of the initiative. Geelhoed claimed that DCB had to be 'browsed' to make people do more than just retrieving the specific bit of information they needed [9]. At the same time Day, who was working for UWE, complained exactly about the fact that too much browsing was involved, and that people had to download pages they were not interested in, before reaching the relevant information [5]. This was of course a perfectly legitimate thing to argue, if the digital city had to be considered a 'civic database' [1, p495], but it was nevertheless totally opposite to Geelhoed's position, and his vision of a complex, bi-directional, 'social' environment.

What was DCB at the end of 1997 and in the following years? The interpretations that had contributed to start it, could also contribute to terminate it, and all of the actors could let the initiative go downhill without losing out significantly, having already enjoyed a series of benefits from it. Most of the envisaged trajectories that had motivated the partners had either reached their end or not progressed at all because of tensions in the different approaches.

If DCB had to die, this would not have too heavy a bearing on the Council's operations, and many of its initiatives were already hosted by its official Web site. UWE had reached its networking aims, and did not have the capacity for letting the project grow further and in a sustainable way. Skinner was "not going to be upset if [the digital city] dies" and was openly considering a change of ownership for the initiative [15].

HP had experimented with innovative interfaces and Java, and as the experiment was gradually diverging from the initial intentions and paradigm, Geelhoed himself was willing to hand the project over to someone else [9]. But the handing over process was not going to be an easy one, and in fact it would take a much longer time than expected. Beyond the agreement on the need to find new managers, clear tensions had been developing among the three partners. This looked like a consequence of several factors such as the loss of momentum and interest from the actors, the fulfillment of the initial, narrow common aims of the group, the emergence of the fragmentation of the paradigms and the shift towards a broadcasting one, and the crucial gradual withdrawal of the central technological entrepreneur, embodied by Geelhoed.

Stuart Long was explicit about these growing tensions, confirming much of what has been argued so far: "The taking over process is going to be much more difficult than I expected at the beginning, because there are some tensions. They are organisational tensions. For example, HP's vision about this is – I guess – that people would buy more computers etc. UWE are a research academic institution and this is from their point of view an interesting research project. It also publicises their courses and the university. In a way we could have a similar view, as we have developed quite a substantial Web site that will continue even if DCB does not (…). Each of the organisations has different objectives towards the site. Eric for instance is very keen on the Java side, for obvious reasons. But we are getting complaints about Java from most of the users. So, where do we go? Do we drop the Java? HP would not be very happy about it. UWE will have new research projects coming along that could be more exciting and innovative than this, and their interest may wane overtime." [12]

In order to discuss and plan the future of the digital city, an advisory group had been formed, including up to sixteen representatives from businesses and organisations based in Bristol. However, the effectiveness of the committee was doubtful, possibly because of the fact that the obvious fragmentation of ideas and possible trajectories was weakly managed by the core management team. Pete Wignall from Hub45, a member of the committee, in a letter sent to Linda Skinner lamented a lack of definition of strategy and direction for the initiative, arguing that such uncertainty would make it difficult for an external organisation like his to decide to get involved [18]. The advisory committee was not providing a real answer to the urgent problems of DCB, being itself encumbered by fragmentation and lack of direction, as shown by De Bruine's remarks a couple of years later: "An advisory committee, which represents a range of citywide community, business, and training organisations, exists to gain valuable grassroots feedback and advice. The advisory committee is a group of around sixteen organisations from all sectors with focus on voluntary sector involvement. The advisory committee meets in theory quarterly and is chaired by a

Councillor from Bristol City Council. In fact this group meets very infrequently and has not met for some time" [6, p113]

Eventually some new partners would emerge, one of them from the advisory group, to re-shape the digital city as an information service and a relatively smart 'portal' for the city and area of Bristol. In a way was adopted what had been left in terms of a trajectory by the previous management team: a broadcasting paradigm that seemed to be the lowest common denominator for DCB. This attracted two new partners: Kaliba Netgates (formerly City Netgates) a local software house and Internet Service Provider, able to provide infrastructure and hosting, and the Bristol arm of the BBC, a presence that confirms somehow that the broadcasting paradigm was becoming dominant in the digital city. This meant a yet more radical redefinition of the digital city. The changes made the 'spatial metaphor' interface ('harbour' concept) irrelevant, and a far more traditional 'portal' or newspaper-like look was preferred.

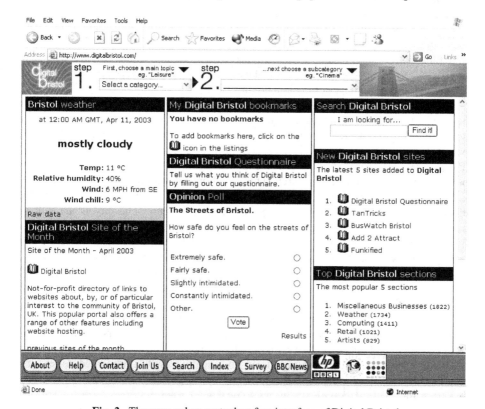

Fig. 3. The new, urban metaphor-free interface of Digital Bristol

This in a way was the sign that the initiative had completed a cycle to re-define itself as an information broadcasting facility about Bristol, dropping the emphasis on electronic public space altogether. Digital City Bristol yet lost another word in its name. 'City' was dropped to leave it as 'Digital Bristol', something very different – if not opposite – from the DDS-like environment initially envisaged by Geelhoed.

6 Conclusions

This case study is a 'history' of the early development of Digital Bristol. Things, obviously, change overtime and will keep doing so. But a few reflections can help practitioners involved in the shaping of urban ICT initiatives, as well as researchers looking at them.

The importance of the impact of paradigms and exemplar cases, such as DDS, should not be underestimated, as digital cities never start from 'scratch', and the symbolic power of previous successful and well-reputed initiatives can have a strong appeal with entrepreneurs trying to establish new cybercities.

Above all, it has to be noted how crucial the interpretations of different actors – and their interrelationship – are in the actual shaping of a digital urban project, and how these can influence the design as well as technological choices and results of the initiative. Technology can indeed impact over society, but the opposite is dramatically true – and sometimes overlooked by those who design and implement these experiments.

We have seen how, as a consequence of the previous issues, the winning paradigm in Bristol ended up being what could be seen as a 'lowest common denominator' among the interpretations of the main actors.

Being able to be aware of these social processes, and consider their influence can be crucial to understand where a project is going to, and is of paramount importance within the context of urban initiatives, which take place in an invariably socially and politically complex arena. This suggests how strongly needed is a solid cross-disciplinary collaboration between technological design and development, town planning practice and social research. This collaboration should generate a very broad knowledge and expertise base on which to build the winning strategies for the electronically augmented city. As Page and Phillips argue "The city is a result of many players and forces that operate through global, regional, and local spheres of influence, utilizing tools and techniques that are permanent, ephemeral, invisible and strategic. They are knitted together through both real and virtual networks of physical connection, telecommunications, social relationships, and political positioning." [14, p3] This indicates how unrealistic would be keeping 'pigeonholing' the roles of those who deal with making choices that will affect city form and functions, and limiting their ability to communicate and work together. However, this is exactly what happens in the majority of cases. Koolhaas and Mau have a few years ago highlighted how outdated and in some cases marginalised most of the current town planning practice, incapable of reinventing itself and dealing with fragmented cities and fragmented agency in the city [11]. No single social group or actor can successfully approach the extreme complexity it has to deal with when it comes to designing and deploying an urban technological initiative, and a knowledge and awareness base which is as wide as possible is crucial for the long-term success of a project. The social, economic, political and technological pieces of the urban jigsaw cannot be dealt with separately, and this paper seems to show that this applies to 'digital' cities as well as physical ones.

References

1. Aurigi A. and Graham S. (2000) "Cyberspace and the City: The Virtual City in Europe" in Bridge G. and Watson S. *A Companion to the City*, Oxford: Blackwell
2. Bristol City Council, Corporate Services Directorate, IT Division (1997) "IT in the Community", Mimeo
3. Bijker W.E. (1992) "The Social Construction of Flourescent Lighting, or How an Artifact Was Invented in Its Diffusion Stage", in Bijker W.E. and Law J. (Eds.) *Shaping Technology/Building Society: Studies in Sociotechnical Change*, Boston: MIT Press
4. Bijker W.E. and Law J. (1992) "General Introduction", in Bijker W.E. and Law J. (Eds.) *Shaping Technology/Building Society: Studies in Sociotechnical Change*, Boston: MIT Press
5. Day M (1997) Interview carried out by the author
6. De Bruine A (2000) "Digital City Bristol: A Case Study", in Ishida T and Isbister K *Digital Cities*, LNCS Berlin: Springer-Verlag
7. Geelhoed E (1996) "Comparing Digital Cities", mimeo, previously published on HP Labs website at http://www-hplb.hpl.hp.com/psl/itd/people/eg/webpubs/dcbi/comp.htm
8. Geelhoed E (1996-2) "Digital City Bristol Interactive: The Hewlett Packard Research Labs Angle", Mimeo
9. Geelhoed E (1997) Interview carried out by the author
10. Guthrie K. and Dutton W. (1992) "The Politics of Citizen Access Technology: The Development of Public Information Utilities in Four Cities", *Policy Studies Journal*, 20, 4.
11. Koolhaas R. and Mau B. (1995) *Small, Medium, Large, Extra-Large: Office for Metropolitan Architecture*, New York: Monacelli Press
12. Long S (1997) Interview carried out by the author
13. Onions I (1997) "Surfers ready to head for Bristol", *Evening Post*, 19/3/97
14. Page S. and Phillips B. (2003) "Urban Design as Editing", Mimeo
15. Skinner L (1997) Interview carried out by the author
16. Van den Besselaar, P, Beckers, D. (2005) The life and death of the great Amsterdam Digital City. In P. van den Besselaar, S. Koizumi (eds), Digital Cities 3. Information technologies for social capital. Lecture Notes in Computer Science, Vol. 3081. Springer-Verlag, Berlin Heidelberg New York (2005) pp. 64-93.
17. Westerfield S (1997) Digital Bristol Interactive – Final Project Report, HP Labs, Bristol
18. Wignall P (1997) letter to Linda Skinner, Mimeo
19. Winner L. (1985) "Do artifacts have politics?", in MacKenzie D. and Wajcman J. (Eds) *The Social Shaping of Technology*, Bristol, PA: Open University Press

Virtual Helsinki
Enabling the Citizen, Linking the Physical and Virtual

Risto Linturi[1], Timo Simula[2]

[1]Helsinki University of Technology
risto@linturi.fi
[2]Elisa Communications Corporation
timo.simula@kolumbus.fi

Abstract. Helsinki Arena 2000 was a catalyst project to quicken the adaptation of broadband usage and strengthen such usage models and technological capabilities that would increase local content provision in a way that would be beneficial commercially both to local community and local operator, which acted as the prime mover of the project. Many useful approaches were studied and advocated, and the project was the umbrella for these activities.

1 Introduction and Project History

In 1995, Helsinki experienced an early fast increase of Internet and mobile phone usage. Helsinki Telephone had at that time approximately 700 thousand local subscriber lines from the total population of 1 million in its operating area. Helsinki Telephone was also major owner of Finland's second largest mobile operator Radiolinja, long distance operator Kaukoverkko Ysi, and Datatie, which provided countrywide data communications services. One Helsinki Telephones division, Kolumbus also provided Internet services as the second largest countrywide ISP.

ISDN technology was available in the Helsinki Telephones network, but due to difficulties with PC adaptors and the lack of interesting services, ISDN access was not yet widely used in 1995 as data access. ADSL was not yet a commercial service. Due to fast growth, many Finnish decision makers became ready to leave their earlier role as fast adaptors and start ambitious pioneering projects.

Virtual Helsinki was initially suggested by Risto Linturi in late 1995 as the spearhead of Helsinki Telephone Corporation's multimedia strategy. Helsinki Telephone had by then conducted a technically successful Video on Demand field trial led by Timo Simula. Virtual Helsinki had clearly commercial goals. Helsinki Telephone Corporation wanted to catalyze fast technological development, widespread adoption, and rich content provision for local broadband, fixed, and mobile Internet usage. However, this difference may be only superficial. Just like Blacksburg Electronic Village [42], we wanted to activate local citizens and local content providers. Like Digital City Kyoto [43] and Shanghai [44], we wanted to develop futuristic visions and increase communal cohesion like the Amsterdam [45] and Seattle [46] experiments.

P. van den Besselaar and S. Koizumi (Eds.): Digital Cities 2003, LNCS 3081, pp. 113-140, 2005.
© Springer-Verlag Berlin Heidelberg 2005

During late 1995, after the initial publicity of the Virtual Helsinki goals [17], the CEO of Helsinki Telephone, Kurt Nordman decided to grant resources for the planning of the Helsinki Arena 2000 project. During late 1995 and early 1996, a detailed plan for the catalyst project was designed, a large consortium was gathered to support the project and initial goals were agreed upon. Members of the consortium included Nokia, The City of Helsinki, IBM, Finland's largest media house, largest bank, largest IT companies, and all local universities. Each party agreed to nominate two professionals to participate part-time in the project activities and a high level directorate was formed from the executives of the member organizations. The main reason for the consortium was twofold. The top management knew that if the consortium could be formed the project would be attractive to other large organizations. It also functioned as a door opener for various Helsinki Telephones business interests towards the other partners and got them to look favourably towards joint efforts within the project.

The consortium had a high-level board and an executive board consisting of the member organizations. These boards accepted the catalyst plan, on which all members agreed to act. The main catalyst was, however, Helsinki Telephone Corporation's internal Helsinki Arena 2000 –project office that was funded internally. The project office created and funded various plans and experiments and took an active part in Virtual Helsinki –related projects started by consortium member companies, other companies and organizations, and also Helsinki Telephone Corporation's various business divisions.

From the Helsinki Telephone Corporation's viewpoint, the Helsinki Arena 2000 – project was not to be a regular project with ample resources to fulfil its aims. The project office had funds to plan and conduct various trials and market strategically important initiatives to various interest groups. The funding required for the bold visions were hundreds of times larger and they were available only through business divisions' independent activities if the project could convince business divisions to invest in the project target areas.

As Helsinki Telephone Corporation was mainly interested in providing a platform and tools for access and content provisioning, it was quite satisfied to see everyone else taking active roles in supporting them in collaborative projects and creating added value by providing useful ideas and compatibility with other projects. This was also aligned with the Internet's character as a self-organising media with common protocols. Naturally, this is not the way to get a centralized and well-structured set of services. Success results in an increased number of local modern Internet services, which possibly are aligned with much of the original vision.

During its five year span the project did succeeded in producing many designs and trials that have already been followed by several commercial adaptations. A general awakening to various possibilities of telecommunications was accelerated by the Helsinki Arena 2000 –project's very high and long-lasting profile both in the local and international media including extensive coverage by dozens of the world's largest TV channels, magazines, and newspapers.

One of the initial goals was to achieve catalytic results similarly to Kennedy's plan to put a man on the moon; by focusing attention on one grand scheme of a full-fledged virtual and participatory city, which was fully bi-directionally linked to the real city [19, 20]. This functioned as planned as the high profile publicity and clear and far reaching visions got the several thousand employees of Helsinki Telephone and a large number of its customers and suppliers of technology to focus on similar issues and align their way of viewing the complex structures of the telecom market.

Some of the more concrete aims were promoting ISDN and ADSL accesses to 100.000 and 10.000 users respectively within Elisa Communications' (Helsinki Telephone changed its name to Elisa Communications in 2000) operating area by the end of 2000. These goals were achieved just a few months late during the spring 2001 and the strong exponential growth has continued, so far.

As Elisa Communications Corporation is a network operator the transformation of the basic telephone network into an efficient IP-based multimedia network and corresponding change in the user behavior with increased traffic was the most important business goal. Several technologies were tried and many successful features are now widely utilized by customers and competing ISPs alike. There were many design options, which greatly affected the characteristics of the network. Many of the preferred features support participatory and local usage models instead of massive content delivery from producers to consumers.

Many attempts were made to create multimedia content and to activate businesses and interest groups to supply content for the networks. Among these were avatar-based group meeting systems, easily adaptable virtual private network protocols, video telephony platforms, 3D city models, and other means utilizing geographical data for navigational and informational purposes. Cultural content was also promoted and civil and communal services were provisioned. A major attempt was to create value networks and user examples for fixed always-on lines by connecting building automation functions to public networks via DSL lines and multi-tenant Ethernet connections. Many of these functions have also been linked to cellular technology through WAP, SMS, and cellular positioning systems.

In the following chapters, we will discuss different aspects of the project and many of its spin-offs and businesses that have been affected by the Helsinki Arena 2000 project. The main emphasis however is on the design philosophy and the technological, social, and economic implications when trying to create a holistic digital city or a major movement towards such.

Helsinki Arena 2000 has been a successful project even though it has not lived up to its wildest visions. Some unrealized visions [21] are waiting for technologies that are more advanced or perhaps a more mature market. The single most important enabler, the participatory network design was adopted for commercial usage and a large part of the other initial ideas have also been commercialized or are still being processed in spin-off projects. After a rapid growth of IT utilization, Finland reached first position in the Technology achievement index [38] of the UNDP 2001 Human Development Report. This is a good foundation for further development and perhaps a sign that many things in Finland need to be well designed in order to succeed in the current competitive situation.

2 Philosophy of the Conceptual Models: Connectedness

There are many reasons why Digital Cities need to be considered as both mental and physical network building exercises. The earliest Digital City -projects were motivated by civil interests and very different designs have resulted from early commercial interests. We want to show in this chapter that societal interests may be advanced if commercial interests are well understood and that commercial actors also benefit from understanding the value structures of their user communities. This will lay a foundation to the underlying design principles and goals that connect all the various Virtual Helsinki activities.

Manuell Castells defines cities as information-based value production complexes [3]. Physical networks enable information sharing across distances, but Castells shows that information production still tends to concentrate in specific urban areas. Francis Fukuyama arrives at similar conclusions through slightly different logic, which is based on networks of trust benefiting from physical closeness [4] rather than accessibility of services and resources as Castells claims. William J. Mitchell [24] shows that new infrastructures, such as data communications networks, only assist in eliminating some needs for physical grouping while others still remain. All agree on varying degrees that communications networks increase dynamism and with it, both opportunities and threats to the cities are increased.

Pessimistically Sophie Body-Gendrot says in the conclusion of her study [2]: "In my research I have demonstrated that the market does not favor social cohesiveness but generates tensions: it reinforces economic polarization and inequalities in cities, the recomposition of space unveils power conflicts among major actors, and hundreds of thousands of marginalized people and their children may use their 'voice' as a threat to express their claims." As productivity in the information society is very much human resource related, this kind of alienation of people Body-Gendrot refers to cannot enhance productivity of the city any more than it can support social and economic trust that is also necessary for a stable and productive society. Social cohesion, the lessening of inequalities, and increasing of efficiency by enabling technologies are thus tasks that a digital city project should assist. As we aim to show, much positive development in these areas can be achieved motivated purely by business interests, but naturally a functioning society needs also rules for the market.

Castells introduces two important concepts for the analysis of the networked cities: the space of flows and the space of places. "The space of flows is the material organization of time-sharing social practices that work through flows. By flows I understand purposeful, repetitive, programmable sequences of exchange and interaction between physically disjointed positions held by social actors in the economic, political, and symbolic structures of society." The space of places he defines as follows: "Indeed, the overwhelming majority of people, in advanced and traditional societies alike, live in places, and so they perceive their space as place-based. A place is a locale whose form, function, and meaning are self-contained within the boundaries of physical contiguity."

Helsinki Telephone as a network operator clearly felt the space of flows –aspect appropriate. Increasing demand for communications services and bandwidth would, if well harnessed lead to a strong growth in spite of growing competition. All players were promoting the benefits and lowering the threshold of acquiring network content. A new viewpoint was that lowering the threshold of local content supply was an economically sound practice if this content would mainly be accessed within the local network of a single network operator. Due to the design of IP networks, it is cheaper for an operator to maintain a network where people favor local communication patterns and this composes a motivation to bridge Castell's two spaces, local users should be interested in local phenomena also within Internet. It was also felt that due to high computer literacy in Finland [29], a large number of people would be willing to create content for others both professionally and socially, if they only are given practical and easily available possibilities.

There was not a clear acceptance of this strategy within Helsinki Telephone, although the project itself shared this vision and was allowed to further it. This vision was well aligned with the Scandinavian egalitarian attitudes and created a strong missionary statement of enabling the citizen and pursuing a clear alignment of physical locality with network locality. It was also an easy decision to assist others to provide content, as the company itself did not have a strategy to become a strong content provider by itself.

It is very important to realize that there are valid rationalizations for network operators to promote local usage patterns. Results can be unexpected if local behavior patterns are not supported. David Ruelle [31] says that social and economic systems undoubtedly follow the laws of chaos and complexity. When you allow for greater flexibility and efficiency e.g. through lower transaction costs, you may get turbulence. Castells claims after talking about his two spaces of flows and places that "Unless cultural, political, and physical bridges are deliberately built between these two forms of space, we may be heading towards life in parallel universes whose times cannot meet because they are warped into different dimensions of a social hyperspace." The important conclusion here is that it seems to be in the best interest of a local operator to provide many of the enabling elements that combine the space of flows with the space of places in order to maximize its profits and in so doing, lessen the unwanted turbulences of the complex self-organizing systems. This is contradictory to the conclusions of Sophie Body-Gendrot, but the situation is also new. And in this new situation socially responsible and technologically aware actors can possibly get unexpected help from economically aware local network operators in pursuing their social and business interests respectively.

Paschal Preston criticizes optimistic visions that emphasize the democratizing effects of the Internet. He also shows how recent development has favored growing income differences. He holds possible that the power elite may "adapt and harness Internet in line with elite interests" [30]. He then wrongly sees various pressure groups as the only method out of this dilemma. Basically, an ill functioning city with growing income differences cannot be an optimal information production complex for all businesses. Moreover, the information economy does not benefit from masses of poor uneducated people as the resource dependant industrial economy of Marx's time did.

Naturally, not all possible ill effects of loosening the existing hierarchies and behavior patterns can be listed, but many of the cures have been pointed out. They seem to coincide well with many of Helsinki Arena 2000's aims. Fukuyama argues that "'Weak' ties remain to be important; networks need to overlap one another if ideas and innovation are to flow freely. On the other hand, it is hard to turn ideas into wealth in the absence of social connectedness, which in the age of the Internet still requires something more than bandwidth and high-speed connectivity." Mitchell discusses the topic of a digital city: "The result – if it is done well – can be an urban fabric of vigorous, pedestrian-scale neighborhoods that take advantage of the affordances of remote electronic connection to produce a high density of face to face interactions at the local level."

David Morley and Kevin Robins question the new media development's relation to communal identities [25]: "Postmodern culture must be elaborated out of differential and plural identities, rather than collapsing into some false cohesion and unity. It must be about positions and positioning in local and global space: about contexts of bodily existence and about existence in mediated space." This would seem to support the idea that a high international profile for both Helsinki and Virtual Helsinki would assist in creating such identities to inhabitants of Helsinki that also assist them towards greater social cohesion. Subsequently, this identity building became one of the project aims.

The fundamental aim of the Helsinki Arena 2000 project was to try to create or enhance and promote electronic communication routes between all inhabitants, services, and devices within the capital operating area and in a manner where place would not lose its meaning. The project intentionally encouraged those ideas that connected events and flow to recognizably local physical places. As an extreme symbol for this, the project promoted creation of a 3D virtual reality duplicate of Helsinki linking physical events to the model as well as virtual reality events to physical reality.

As this kind of an approach lowers transaction costs within the city and enhances services, it may simultaneously allow people to be more in control and aware of their surroundings. If this increases user penetration and local identity sufficiently, it can be shown also to directly increase the amount of social connections within each locality. This sort of increased social connectedness was clearly shown in the Netville project, where network penetration was extremely high [7].

Sophie Body-Gendrot concludes her book by saying: "It is at the core of the city of the new millennium that the future of democracy and of cohesive values will be played. Future generations will have to dream of the Third Age city before it actually takes shape." We hope that this important task of dreaming and shaping the future of cities will not be left to future generations. It is a task that needs constant attention. Moreover, it is a task where we need to make value judgements. Our world will be very different if we select the elitist values supported by Nietzsche and continue talking about the importance of high quality content instead of talking about the importance of participation and those egalitarian values supported by e.g. Karl Popper in a groundbreaking manner in his famous opus "The Open Society and Its Enemies".

Paul Lewinson says [18] that "We can start the digital age with an ethical imperative that control of information by disparate individuals is better than its control by central authorities." This basic belief in self-organizing systems and global freedom is shared by us, although it requires many safeguards in order to create a transparent and law-abiding society, which maintains social trust and individual freedom against informational abuse [20].

3 Network Issues

Practically all applications of a digital city utilize the telecommunications network. There are clear limitations in service implementations if certain specifics of the network design, even minor ones, are not taken into account in the original design. The most crucial network properties relate simply to the network's capacity and accessibility both in locally and globally, although there are other important resource considerations also.

In the Helsinki Arena 2000 project, the main benchmark applications were specified at an early phase. The practical implementation was then phased into several steps during the years 1997 - 2000. During the first rollout phase in 1997, many things were learned and plans for later steps were modified accordingly. Helsinki Telephone built the Helsinki Arena 2000 - network (later Arenanet) as an integrated part of its general local telecommunications network with many other requirements besides those defined by the project itself. This led to some uncomfortable compromises, but on the other hand made sufficient funding possible.

3.1 Social and Economic Implications of Symmetrical and Asymmetrical Designs

The telephone network is originally planned to offer symmetrical speech connection between two people and that it has been doing for over a century. Lately it has also been used for other services such as dial-up connections for accessing Internet services. In addition, telephone lines ('last mile') are used for high speed data connections equipped with ADSL modems.

ADSL-based symmetrical network structure supports two-way broadband connections, which allow such demanding services as remote working, video telephony services and, which is quite interesting, sending multimedia streams both ways, e.g. near VHS quality video multicasting from any home. Using the telephone network, it is economical to send video streams simultaneously from a large number of homes or businesses to a combination of small or larger audiences in a non-hierarchical manner. Conversely, TV broadcasting uses limited bandwidths and this leads to a limited number of channels. Due to a large amount of receivers and a limited number of possible channels, only hierarchical models are feasible and the content is most commonly defined by the smallest common denominator and financed by advertisements. A well-known TV critic George Gilder says that "Anyone with access to the information highway will be able to distribute a film at a tiny fraction of current costs. Moreover, webs of glass and light will free the producer from the burden of creating a product that can attract miscellaneous audiences to theaters. Instead producers will be able to reach equally large but more specialized audiences dispersed around the globe. Rather than making lowest-common-denominator appeals to the masses, film-makers will be able to appeal to the special interests, ambitions, and curiosities of individuals anywhere, anytime" [28]. However, this will not be possible unless the networks are designed to be symmetrical.

An important implication is that that a genuinely symmetrical network structure radically lowers the threshold to offer communities' or even private citizens' own broadband services to the rest of the community. Finally, this opens the possibility to form new value chains or rather value networks along with traditional centralized value chains, e.g. media industry. Evidently, it is quite impossible to supervise the content in this kind of network. The same problem has been encountered on the Internet earlier with low bandwidth content like text or audio.

3.2 Fixed Network and the Two-Layered Design Favoring Local Content

The Helsinki Arena 2000 network 'Arenanet' offers citizens different levels of access and bandwidth (figure 1). The minimum Arenanet bandwidth level is provided using ISDN access. It is enough for video telephony services, but does not suffice for delivering video with near VHS quality. ISDN is switched technology and it could theoretically provide always-on functionality, but due to the high implementation cost, it has not been implemented in Elisa's network [8]. In the beginning of the project, ISDN technology was already available everywhere in the local telephone network and during spring 2001 the number of ISDN lines had risen to 100 thousand from a total of 700 thousand telephone lines provided by Elisa Communications Corporation. Besides increasing the number of ISDN lines, one important goal was to optimize the switched telephone network for the continuously increasing IP traffic in order to make the network more cost effective.   This kind of network is generally cal-

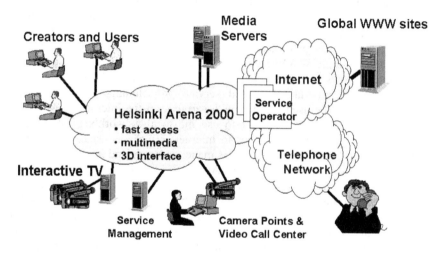

Fig. 1. Telephone Network Optimized for IP-Traffic.

led a next generation network amongst telecom operators. Optimization has been done by separating the IP traffic from telephone traffic as close to a customer as possible with distributed dial-up servers in central offices and then directing the IP traffic to a IP core network instead of capacity wasting switched connections. All ISP operators were offered a reasonably priced possibility to connect to the local network and provide Arenanet users with global Internet service. Efficient usage of network resources allowed a lower price for connections than local calls in the regular telephone network, the prices of which in the Elisa Communications network were already among the cheapest non-substituted prices in the world according to various studies. The customers have enjoyed a discounted calling price or flat rate when connecting to the multimedia network. However, these discounted and flat rates are currently under investigation by the Finnish Competition Authority. The delays caused by the operation of the competition authorities are something that especially ILEC should be prepared for when launching this type of optimized service and cost-based pricing.

ADSL access is an always-on connection. Commercial products usually offer several speeds ranging from 256 kbps to 4 Mbps downstream and up to 1 Mbps upstream. Elisa Communications' first rollout of ADSL connections was made in 1997 within the Arenanet framework. The user base of ADSL connections has started to grow exponentially. However, it is hard to say how large an influence the local broadband communications and services have had on the growth rate.

Most new apartment buildings in Finland are equipped with generic data wiring instead of the traditional telephone wiring. This allows for symmetrical 10 Mbps, or even 100 Mbps, multi-tenant Ethernet to be economically offered to apartments. Multi-tenant Ethernet is better than ADSL also in the sense that it is fully symmetrical as an access network. This can then be seen as the newest technological network model and the first to fully reach the goals of the project.

Arenanet can be considered a citywide intranet, which needs ISP services in order to be connected to the global Internet and its services. Due to competition requirements and various customer demands, the Arenanet was designed to allow a free selection of ISP services by access customers, if the ISP itself was directly connected to the Arenanet through a sufficient broadband access. Due to the very unorthodox Arenanet design, customers are able to select from several competing ISP operators using a simple WWW-based user interface. The new technology that this design required allows several service networks or ISPs to be selected at the same time. This is very important for local service provisioning, since it lets local broadband services to be used together with services on the Internet. Local services are favored by giving them the right to use the local network's greater capacity simultaneously to allowing connections to Internet services as usual. Connecting to the network as a local service provider was made very easy and inexpensive in order to support local services further. The local Arenanet portal included most of the local services implemented in the project. It was also a place to share plug-ins for using the Arena's services and information about new possibilities. The portal could be partially accessed also by any user of the Internet from outside Arenanet, even though they could not use the applications requiring the most bandwidth. This was done because the project wanted to spread knowledge of itself and usage of the services to spread to reach critical mass even before the broadband technology itself actually was widely available or affordable.

As the basic design philosophy was to support self-organizing, the users were supplied with tools that enabled them to build their own structures within the citywide intranet. These included e.g. open WINS and DNS services, which are normally used in all Local Area Networks (LAN) of an enterprise, but are not supported in a usual Internet environment. This offers the most economical way for a distributed enterprise or any other networked community to build a virtual LAN and use the same simple procedures that are available for LAN users across the whole of Arenanet. However, from the technology's point of view, this is not an easy task to do and it increases the complexity of the network and as well as its costs.

While a great deal of Internet traffic is global, it was believed within the project that as the Internet took over more and more functions, patterns of communication would start to follow more closely those of the telephone network, where about 80% of the traffic in Helsinki was local calls. Due to the nature of communications networks, it is much cheaper to achieve high data transmission speeds when a high percentage of the traffic remains among a logically defined group of commuters, for which the communication routes can be optimized. For Helsinki Arena 2000 purposes, the people and businesses of the Helsinki area were considered such a group. They also consisted of paying customers and in a way any effort to enhance the quality of the service was rewarded by customers who received higher value. Internal information on the distribution of telephone calls was used as proof that communication on the Internet will inevitably move towards more local patterns. This happens when Internet penetration grows and the quality and availability of Internet communication reaches the level of existing, locally available means of communication, i.e. telephone network, local newspapers etc. This tendency could be strengthened further by showing that within the Helsinki Arena 2000 network, the quality of broadband communication can be excellent and very cost efficient. In practice, due to bottleneck effects and cost structure, the capacity offered to a customer was clearly superior inside the local area and much lower for international Internet services.

There are still several other areas of development that have required extensive study and where equipment and software suppliers have only recently been able to provide satisfactory standard-based solutions, even though the project has required suitable solutions from all significant manufacturers since 1996 and simultaneously encouraged other network operators to require similar functionality. These features include open multicasting, quality of service concepts for guaranteeing bandwidth, multi-point Internet-based video conferencing platforms, and QoS and usage-based billing infrastructures [12, 32]. In addition, efficient customer connection and maintenance systems have been developed only lately for DSL accesses. These are all crucial issues for the community oriented business model that had been selected. In 1996, many of these technology ideas were quite new and did not exist in the manufacturers' roadmaps. Lobbying them was seen to be one of the tasks to be done several years in advance, since the development time from an idea to a commercial product is still quite long in network technology. Waiting was often very frustrating because manufacturers were unwilling to provide the technologies, even though they understood the needs, as their other customers had not yet started requiring similar functionality. After long periods of waiting, the first implementations were often disappointments in terms of capacity and cost problems. This slowness of development caused insecurity within the more short-term oriented business units and disagreements within the project, although not changing the long-term goals.

3.3 Mobile Wireless Networks: Implications for Digital Cities

The market penetration of mobile telephones in Finland is among the highest in the world. Increasing mobility seems to change user behavior and expectations to favoring features that are available in a mobile environment. The GSM telephone is already the most important terminal for communication. Call and SMS charges are reasonable, but the bandwidth is relatively low leaving out most multimedia services. This limitation is seen to hinder the use of multimedia also in the fixed networks as the users' focus has transferred to service types available in a mobile environment.

In the Helsinki Arena 2000 project, several services have had a link to mobile telephone services. Chat services have had a user interface for WAP. Building and home automation could be controlled with SMS and WAP. The mobile telephone's navigation features were connected to the 3D model of the city and location information was supplied via mobile phones. Some of the implementations are described in connection with Hewlett-Packard tram tracking –project.

Wireless Local Area Network (WLAN) technology offers sufficient capacity to carry multimedia information including video streams of near VHS quality if it is not shared with other customers. A good example is the wireless home network that could be built using WLAN, which is connected to ADSL network termination. The Arenanet's commercial ADSL offering includes the option to purchase WLAN that is integrated with an ADSL modem.

Inside the buildings of enterprises or public places such as libraries, schools, airports, and restaurants, hot spot coverage could be achieved with WLAN technology, but the bandwidth of an individual customer is not steady, since other users in same area share the bandwidth. The same problem applies to most other alternative wireless technologies. The key issue now, is the roaming between a wireless home network and public hot spot areas in order to provide a widely applicable mobility of services

4 HCI Experiments and Designs in Helsinki Arena 2000

Tens of applications and services were designed and demonstrated in the Helsinki Arena 2000 project in order to catalyze local content provisioning. The focus was to offer network and service infrastructure for various different purposes, e.g. remote work, community intranet, and a delivery channel for content providers. A service portal was created to link other consortium members' and third parties' novel content for easy retrieval. In designing new services, the usability and novelty of the services were always main concerns. Short-message-service (SMS) for mobile phones served as an example that success does not require easy user interfaces, if they meet adequately important user needs. However, in most cases user friendliness is crucial to the success of services. In the project, some of the services were quite complex both technically and in terms of features. A large amount of work went into hiding the internal complexities and enhancing usability.

4.1 Video Conferencing

Both ISDN and ADSL are capable of delivering real-time video and audio with reasonable quality. Several kinds of video telephony services were offered in Helsinki Arena 2000 with important supplementary services such as videoconference bridging, 3D virtual environments for meetings, chat, mobile telephone services, and tools for shared applications. The services were accessed from an HTML-based user interface.

Initial experiences of video meeting points were gathered during the annual office technology exhibition in 1996. The Helsinki fair centre was 3D modelled with several exhibition stands included. Several video cameras were connected through a videoconference bridge. The total number of hits on the www pages of this experiment was 22000, which was a good result as the total number of real visitors was about 70000. Only a part of the users was able to utilise the 3D model and the video chat or real-time video feeds. The fair centre had a number of workstations where these services could easily be accessed. In many senses, this was the first project trial to link the physical world with its virtual replica enabling participation both physically and virtually. The service did not require broadband connection as that was not available at the time and the service was fully available only during the duration of the few days of the fair.

Another service, which used videoconferencing, was a virtual language school, where traditional education was combined with distant learning assisted by the newest technology. The functionality was almost the same as that used in BEV's Virtual School. This subproject was a part of the National Multimedia Program funded by the Finnish Technology Fund. The National Multimedia Program's main outcome and continuation was the Helsinki Arena 2000 project. The pilot phase was started in 1996 and the service was offered commercially from 1999. A significant portion of the training sessions was performed through videoconferencing. The educational results of remote training were even better than in normal class work, but the quality of the video and audio were criticized to not be adequate, as the project was conducted too early to benefit from the multimedia network and was compelled to use public Internet. However, the possibility to gain from early experimenting was considered important enough to tolerate this lack in order to reach at least some results applicable for offering the concept of remote video telephony-based education in general [14].

In 1998, the public IP-based H.323 videoconference service was launched. The service included an online video telephony directory, several meeting "rooms", and a "video mirror" for testing. Several communities found the service useful, the most exotic or demanding perhaps being a jazz band, which used a MIDI connection between band members in addition to the video connection. In 1999, the service was selected one of the TOP20 videophone services in whole world by www.netmeet.net in the US.

In 1999, Vistacom's H.320 ISDN video telephony software was distributed to every new ISDN customer. Elisa was the first operator to adopt this business model, which was partially catalyzed by the project, where the operator bundles video telephony to an ISDN access product. After Elisa Communications' decision, about 30 Finnish and several international operators have adopted the same model. At the same time, a digital camera was offered at a very aggressive price. However, critical mass was not been reached. The initial conclusion is that there should be enough public services for using videophones from the beginning. Probably the change of human behavior towards using the video feature in telephone calls is relatively slow and further hindered by the main part of telephone calls transferring to mobile phones. As video features will be included in mobile telephones in the future, this could create suitable conditions for the wide acceptance of video telephony in both fixed and mobile environments.

One of the several attempts to lower the threshold of creating local content was a facility similar to a telephone booth where anyone could just walk into the booth and start talking to a camera. In 1999, this virtual "Speaker's Corner" was opened in the centre of Helsinki. This was realized by installing a web camera inside a telephone booth located in the Lasipalatsi media centre, which contained many other empowering-the-citizen-oriented information society-centric functions. It gave any citizen the possibility to influence others by giving a public speech as the speakers face and voice were published in real-time on the Arenanet portal's web pages.

4.2 Video Distribution

Video distribution is an important part of the total supply of services in a multimedia network. Currently the TV set is still the most important delivery platform at home with a dominating share of user time in comparison to other entertainment and telecommunications services [29]. TV broadcasting services are currently in the process of being digitalised in order to offer wider possibilities for interactive services. Using a telephone modem or other corresponding means as a back channel, a customer may interact with TV programs. This interaction is, however, very limited and the video content is sent as a broadcast with a limited number of centrally distributed channels. Connecting digital TV to a symmetrical broadband network enables personal video content as well as on-demand type services.

An early field trial for video on-demand services was made during the years 1994 - 1995 in Helsinki [39]. The results proved that video services alone were not economically viable and thus did not justify investments in broadband network technology. However, the trial encouraged Elisa to continue with new technologies and find more applications for broadband access.

Video streams use a lot of bandwidth and other resources of the network. People have been used to quite good quality in TV services, which require a complex integrated network design instead of commonly available technology. On the other hand, this type of network is not especially sensitive to how many separate channels there exist. However, the number of simultaneous users is significant. In cable TV and terrestrial TV, only some tens of channels can be sent. In the Helsinki Arena 2000 project, several small radio and TV channels have been providing content to the Arenanet. The ultimate long-term goal has been to aim for a theoretical network model, where the network load would be clearly lighter when, for example, several thousand sources transmitted near VHS quality content to a hundred thousand simultaneous viewers than when the same number of users had one-to-one communication. Connected with usage-based tariffs, this would allow cheaper tariffs for users supplying local content for a number of others than for those merely viewing content supplied by others. This would also give the possibility of paying for popular content without having to charge for or include advertisements. This would differ radically from the current media business models opening up and empowering anyone to start video content delivery without their own network investments.

4.3 Avatar Experiments and User Behavior: Real and Virtual Meeting Places

The Helsinki Arena 2000 project aims to support rich communication possibilities among all citizens. As people tend to organize around different interests, these types of self-organized networked communities should be supported. Some of these communities are formed totally virtually while others have very strong connections to the physical world. Different design dimensions for these communities are discussed in [26]. In the virtual Helsinki, it was not intended that one could meet other people in the street. To facilitate a high enough hit rate and in order to avoid design problems with the whole city potentially having tens of thousands of avatars, specific meeting points were designed. Some designs experimented with technology and others with surrounding content. Not all were related to existing places. There exists, for example,

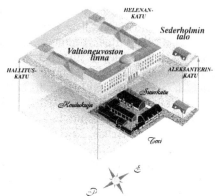

Fig. 2. : Lasipalatsi, a Virtual Meeting Point.   **Fig. 3.** Virtual Museum

an underground 3D meeting point, which gives the designers and the users more freedom to explore the imaginary worlds, participate and create something of their own.

The Lasipalatsi project connects the citizens both in the real as well as in the virtual world and offers citizens advanced web-based services. In the real city, Lasipalatsi is a building located in the middle of Helsinki. It has a digital library and freely available computers with Internet connections. It also offers the citizens a digital meeting point, which connects the real meeting point in Lasipalatsi building to meeting points in some other cities. In addition, there is a virtual version of Lasipalatsi. Virtual Lasipalatsi has been an experiment with several services with the intention of finding out the importance of things like background music and informational content as means of gathering a group of similarly oriented people in the meeting room. A user survey has been conducted at the 3D meeting place in the virtual Lasipalatsi (figure 2). Less than half of the users were able to function without any technical troubles with their viewers. The result was much better than with the earlier virtual fair experiment, which resulted in limiting users to those motivated enough to fill in an application, and in the generally more robust level of software and computers that were available to the users in this later experiment. The results show that the visual 3D layout was considered very good and the 3D meeting point was considered a very good service overall by 73% of the surveyed users. 79% of those that had visited several times intended to come again. 30% had used user-to-user communication, 29% had used 3D product presentations, and 25% had followed the live radio broadcasts or live disc jockey performances. Only 2% had used electronic shopping in the telco store and 4% had used other telco services provided in the virtual Lasipalatsi. When we studied frequent visitors, the picture was slightly different. Communication with other visitors amounted to 75% and live radio broadcasts to 54% and getting acquainted with other people to 54%. People generally wished for more cultural content. Overall, the results were considered encouraging at this early phase and clearly showing the connection between background content and user-to-user interaction, which is not surprising as a similar phenomenon happens in the physical city also. Some people come for the content and some others for the discussions and most of them end up conversing with each other.

In 2000, the virtual meeting point called Hotelli Kultakala (Hotel Goldfish) was commercially launched. It is an imaginary hotel-like space implemented in 2.5D format, which was selected instead 3D, because 3D did not seem to be of benefit to users in this kind of application. Its business model is based on electronic shopping of virtual goods that can currently be used only within the meeting point environment. Users can buy virtual furniture in order to decorate their rooms or to give as presents to other users. Purchases are paid with mobile phone messages (SMS). This service has already risen to the most popular chat places in Finland supporting complex interaction patterns between users, such as hotel room specific user-arranged prize winning quiz contests etc. The concept is currently being exported to other countries as well (http://www.habbohotel.com).

5 Local Services of City Authority and Other Communities

Naturally, the city of Helsinki has been one of the Elisa Communications' main content partners in the project. Elisa operates in the area of many cities in Finland, but Helsinki is the largest and has good resources and the will to carry out a continuing development of services for its citizens. This is true especially in the area of providing public services and cultural content in the network.

The main part of this work has been prepared within the framework of the Infocities project [11], which is a European Commission funded project in the TEN Telecom program. Digital services for citizens are developed in seven European cities, Helsinki being one of them. For Helsinki, the Infocities services are developed jointly with the Helsinki Arena 2000 project and the city of Helsinki. These services include public and civic services, Helsinki City Museum services, and cultural services. In addition, the Virtual Language School, developed in the National Multimedia Program has been tested by users (see section 4.1 for more information). Many public and civic services have traditionally been provided to the citizens by the various bureaus of a city. Within the subproject, these services were considered from the citizens' point of view, which lead to integrated public and civic services. The services were organized according to the different roles of the citizens, such as a tourist, a house builder, and an organizer of an event. Furthermore, we also wanted to find out all the new needs in citizens' every-day life. The expectation was that Helsinki could provide better services to the citizens with fewer burdens to the employees of the city. Finally, we considered how the multimedia network and the possibilities it offered could enhance these services. For instance, ip phone and video-based techniques have been experimented on. Libraries of the city have had an ip phone connection from their www pages and the service has been working with such good quality that the customers or call center's employees could not tell whether calls come from the telephone network or IP-network. The services of Helsinki City Museum (figure 3) were developed to increase the interest towards the history of Helsinki. Our aim was to make the historical places so interesting that many new citizens would study them by using multimedia and visualization. For instance, the 3D modeling offers the employees of the museum tools for showing already non-existent buildings, such as a model of the historical centre of Helsinki in 1700, before the current empire style centre was built.

6 Tools and Applications for 3D Mapping in Virtual Helsinki

The initial project aim for quick adoption of local networked multimedia was in many senses clear. Achieving this kind of a major change in technology and user behavior in a unified manner seemed, however, a task that would also require a unifying metaphor. That metaphor should be bold and fascinating enough as a far-reaching vision to inspire enthusiasm. It should also be able to make local people feel that this is their network and that there is a place here for themselves and their content. This vision came to be a virtual reality-like user interface that would be a recognizable and detailed 3D duplicate of the city, which was supposed to fulfill everyday functions similar to telephone catalogues containing city maps and yellow pages. However, both within the project and outside it, there were constant pressures to change this aim towards more modest and short-term goals.

There are many reasons besides navigational assistance for using a spatial metaphor for hypertext information [22]. The spatial environments can be extremely useful if natural mappings to the information are found from the point of view of the user tasks [33]. This connection to people's everyday needs was constantly encouraged when designing application trials for the 3D user interfaces.

As the virtual city is modeled to be recognizable, it is at least partially known to many of its inhabitants, which makes the virtual city itself meaningful even when it is seen for the first time. In addition, things learned when viewing the virtual city may prove to be meaningful when facing the physical world. This helps in navigation and in creating a cognitive map that structures the services both in the physical and virtual city. A sample view of the city with different types of links is shown in figure 4.

The first demonstrations of the city metaphor were completed by fall 1996. Simultaneously with the internal planning of Helsinki Arena 2000, a new company Arcus Software (Current name Fontus) had been formed independently from Elisa for modeling virtual cities. They could produce a very realistic and detailed 3D map of about one square kilometer of central Helsinki in three months time.

At the autumn 1996 IT fair, this and another realistic and functional model with real-time video feeds, video telephony links and a few realistically modeled stands within the detailed outside and inside model of the Fair centre building got very much local publicity. Earlier models of Helsinki had been small and intended only for professional city planning or traffic simulation usage.

However, after this initial effort, this part of the project did not get additional funding, as its usefulness was not widely accepted within Helsinki Telephone. It was only in early 1999, when the 3D mapping of Helsinki really started as Helsinki Telephone and several other companies invested in Arcus Software and committed to financing the 25 square kilometers of the 3D map of the city that were completed in late spring 2001 (figure 5).

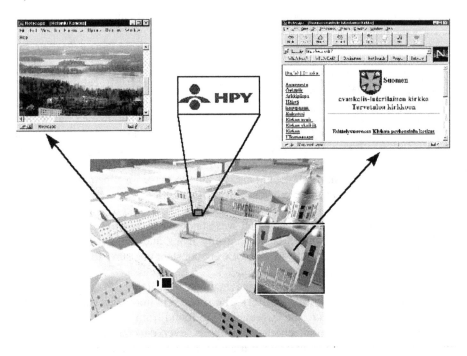

Fig. 4. A Sample View to the City and Its Services

Fig. 5. The 3D-Mapped 25 Square Kilometers of Helsinki

6.1 Fontus Modeling Process

The Fontus 3D city modeling process consists of creating a base model and a model with facades and object handles with various attributes attached to them. From the technical point of view, the virtual city itself is a large web information system, which will be connected to an information database of the actual services offered to the user [36]. Various geographical information systems (GIS) are important as well as other databases that contain addresses and position dependent information that is available from the users' mobile phones and various sensors in buildings and other places within the city. All these may need to be linked flexibly and efficiently to the 3D map, either dynamically or within fixed intervals with no manual effort, because of the massive number of the links.

The source material is modeled into hierarchical objects, which are stored in the database. The base model starts with aerial photos. This initial phase resembles other similar systems starting from a cartographic process [6]. The base model can also be incorporated from existing digital maps with 3D information. Arcus has combined both approaches through utilizing an object-oriented, vector based methodology, with which flexible multi-resolution models with a unified output format are achieved [13]. This is extremely important if the 3D map needs to be distributed over DSL lines, ISDN lines, and to mobile devices [27].

The following estimates give a fairly good approximation of 3D maps' sizes and of the required effort converted into commercial modeling prices of professional modelers. The Helsinki Centre 3D map currently consists of 25 square kilometers of urban area (http://www.stadi3d.com). The required storage or file size of the completed model is circa 400 MB. The cost estimate for a project of this size is between 1 and 1.5 million Euros. A completely different set of values is reached in Virtual Kainuu (http://www.virtualkainuu.net). Kainuu is a province of 24.000 sq kilometers and a population of 100.000. The 24.000 sq kilometers include both a rural model and models of all the rural villages (600 sq kilometers) and urban centre models (10 sq kilometers). The estimated modeling cost is less than 1 million Euros.

6.2 Applications of the City 3D Map

The first real application experiment was using these address links and co-ordinate the information to link Helsinki Telephones telephone directory information to each address link. This feature was patented in 1996 [37]. According to the design philosophy, the feature was implemented in a manner that the user can visually search for any location of the city and then place a call to that location by activating the link. Jointly with the Hewlett-Packard Bristol laboratories, the methods of providing dynamically changing data to the viewers of the Helsinki 3D model were researched. Mobile phone positioning schemes were studied as the source of positioning information. In addition, delivery schemes and display schemes were studied. Within the Hewlett-Packard Tram Tracking experiment, a method of communications was utilized that permitted viewers to express their interests. The originator of the positioning information would send the positioning and class information independently of the actual 3D model server to the browser of the interested viewer to be shown as an avatar. This solution has two advantages over many undistributed solutions such as the Alphaworld. Each provider of positioning information can start publishing positioning data following the guidelines, but independently of any central server. Only data that users have subscribed to is transmitted to them and so the extra data does not burden the servers or the user communications channels.

When one compares a regular 2D map with a 3D map, it is clear that a 2D map has clear disadvantages. The user needs to recognize symbols and street names and either have the 2D map available or street names memorized when searching for a place. After viewing the 3D map and having virtually walked through the path, it is much easier to find the way. Combining these both gives an even better result as can be seen from a demonstration (http:// www.perille.net).

Within this concept, the navigational 3D pictures from popular landmarks to the destination are generated in various formats suitable for viewing both in mobile phones and in web terminals (figure 6).

Fig. 6. 3D Map Utilized with a Mobile Phone

Arcus conducted a survey among potential users of the navigation services [40]. The survey consisted of 30 decision makers of small and medium sized businesses located in central areas of the city and other businesses slightly further from central landmarks. The target people were shown examples of the 3D navigational directions on a PC and a hand-held computer. According to the results, 80% considered the proposed product at least moderately useful. 90% of the interviewed persons considered 3d-enhanced directions at least somewhat better than 2D map-based directions, and 46.7% considered 3D directions to be much better. When the subjects were asked to evaluate the product from the viewpoint of usefulness for their own business locations, Arcus got mixed results. Subjects in districts with ample local well-known landmarks generally believed that their location is easy to find and did not believe the application to be useful in their particular case. Companies 1-2 miles away from the very best business location had, however, very positive expectations. A full 100 % of the interviewed persons in these districts thought that the demonstrated VisitGuide product would be at least moderately useful for their visitors, and 42.9 % believed that a VisitGuide would be very useful.

7 Connecting Sensors and Actuators in the City

Electronic communication removes distances and in so doing, allows for more immediate attention to various subjects with less need to use time and resources for travelling. In addition, as some of the major problems of cities are the congestion of streets and pollution due to excessive travelling as well as instability due to empty suburbs, there is variety of reasons for using electronic communications.

We must also remind ourselves of the concepts of space of flow and space of place. This is not just a question of creating communications networks between people. It is a question of linking our physical world to the virtual world and supporting the notion of telepresence. People who tend to orient towards space of flows should get a closer feeling of the space of places and vice versa allowing for greater cohesion between the two groups Castells saw separated. This intention is fulfilled only one-sidedly if our physical surroundings cannot be accessed through networks. This leaves insufficient motivation for space of place-oriented people to enter the networks.

One example of excess traveling is maintenance people who monitor and control the way different physical reality related functions work. This causes the need for other people to accompany them, for example, to open doors. As both the cities and the number of different gadgets that require monitoring and maintenance are growing [23], these problems will increase unless good solutions arise.

Within the Helsinki Arena 2000 project, many traveling related problems were addressed. In some subprojects fixed DSL-lines were piloted for remote work. Many businesses have rather strict security considerations, which mean that the network considerations for remote work connections are much more demanding than regular home leisure usage would require. These properties were developed and piloted jointly with Nokia and ICL.

Fixed connections to buildings allowed for connecting building automation sensors and actuators to the network and, consequently, the provision of a platform for remote maintenance, monitoring and control of building-related functions. Initiating activities in this sector became a part of the Helsinki Arena 2000 project in 1997. It noticed that these functions could be made available for mobile users and the mobile service personnel's position information could be utilized for optimizing their traveling.

Due to the cold climate, Finnish houses are well insulated and heated. Automated ventilation and central heating are required in urban buildings. Good automation systems, which are based on usage and need, save a great deal of energy, since the unnecessary ventilation and heating of incoming outside air are minimized. Savings could be as high as 30%.

In 1997, the project decided to take part in the Art and Design School's research activity that studied automated homes. Simultaneously, there was a private building project by Risto Linturi's family. This project was used as a design example for an automated home. The remotely controlled 'Linturi house' became one of the most famous results of the Helsinki Arena 2000 project [5, 35] and as a working example has motivated followers and industry projects both in Finland and abroad.

7.1 Home Automation Experiments and Human Behavior Research

The 'Linturi house' was one of the first occupant-aware intelligent homes around the world. There has been a great deal of study on the technologies that could be used, but no experiments where the residents' actual responses could have been surveyed. In the 'Linturi house', the owners of the home paid for all the equipment and services and made final decisions on the feature set. Equipment providers paid for automation design as part of their product development. Thus the feature set was needs based.

Many of the used technologies came from the office environment, where intelligent user-aware functions were already being built. Ideas were also taken from literature and earlier experiments, such as Bill Gates' house. During the planning, a number of original ideas arose. Architecturally the house was designed to support remote work in many ways [34].

Most of the ideas that came from Bill Gates' house were discarded. Interaction with the house through microphones in the walls and remotely readable personal identification tags (RFID) carried by the family members or visitors were strongly objected to by the family's children, who felt their privacy being threatened. As family members were to trust their home as their castle, this approach was rejected.

Infrared sensors were used for monitoring occupancy. Temperature sensors in each room measuring room air and floor temperatures, humidity sensors in the washing rooms and the garden, carbon dioxide sensors, luminance sensors gave additional information. Automation nodes were responsible for adjusting the actuators to provide suitable air and water circulation, floor and room temperature, and necessary lighting. This kind of automated environment means that each function of the house can also be controlled and monitored from remote devices if the control programs are connected to data networks. In the 'Linturi house', the basic remote control was the mobile phone. The most used remote control feature proved to be the front door where, if nobody was home, the doorbell connected a telephone call from the door microphone to a resident's mobile phone and the door could be opened remotely when necessary. Answering the doorbell for keyless people or unexpected parcel deliveries and giving instructions on whether the parcels could be left at the door or inside after remotely opening the door proved very practical. In a sense, it is no wonder that this novel feature became one of the icons of the project. It demonstrated many of the basic properties that an efficient digital city must incorporate. It did this in a way that carried a clear connection to people's everyday lives and the arising popularity of mobile society and the dream of being freed from the constraints of time and place; being able to remotely monitor and control any device.

The Finnish Consumer Behavior Group researched home automation and the intelligent home in 2000. They interviewed a group of families that had prepared by reading several scenarios of the intelligent home of the future. The members of the families also kept an exact diary about their daily routines.

The results supported Linturi's thoughts. Home was considered a place, over which residents wanted to have full control. Outside the home, it was impossible to control the environment and thus home was the only place where they expected to be able to do that. They did not want an excessively intelligent home, which would interrupt or manage daily life. In addition, they were rightly afraid of what would happen if the technology were not working for some reason. If this happened, people might be helpless even with traditional routines. Families took the technology very emotionally. Feelings and common sense competed and this is important in life. However, most families still supported the concept with some limitations and they accepted the fact that the development of technology is a natural phenomenon and it is not worth resisting. The project got many detailed results about using different types of home equipment and how the members of a family were communicating with each other [15].

7.2 COBA-Project

The COBA project (Connected Open Building Automation) was initially planned in 1999 and started in 2000. It was clearly catalyzed by the Helsinki Arena 2000 project. The ideology is a derivative of the Helsinki Arena 2000 project and the gathering of the project consortium was greatly assisted by the experiments and fame of the 'Linturi house'. Initiators of the COBA project were Risto Linturi and CEO Tuomas Koskenranta from Lonix, who had been chief automation designer in the 'Linturi house' experiment. Initial members of the COBA project included Nokia, ABB, Hewlett-Packard, Securitas, Elisa Communications, two of the largest Finnish construction companies YIT and NCC, the largest energy supplier Fortum, and several large or medium sized service, maintenance, and technology suppliers and large customers (http://www.coba-group.com). COBA defines and provides a common software solution for remotely and locally accessing and controlling building automation. COBA defines application software interfaces for various service providers operative software needs and also device interfaces for different device manufacturers' devices and field buses. COBA is based on a Linux environment in order to be distributable free of charge by the members of COBA.

Within the 'Linturi house' experiment, it was clearly identified that many of the advanced features would be difficult or impossible to be provided in a heterogeneous environment unless there was a horizontally unifying standard for controlling the various manufacturers' devices. This was also identified as a problem for service providers. They could not provide remote maintenance services for building-related functions if each equipment manufacturer had their own remote interfaces or totally lacked them. It was also a major problem that these manufacturer-dependent remote interfaces, when they existed, were too costly and difficult to operate and it was difficult for service providers to handle several different versions. Based on these types of needs, the consortium members agreed to fund the development of a cross-platform standard, the COBA white paper.

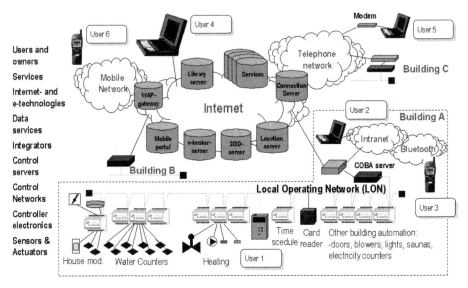

Fig. 7. Device Architecture of COBA

COBA maintains positioning information for both user devices and control network devices as well as other information useful for maintenance and remote control (figure 7). It also allows for connecting the user interface devices to the building servers via Bluetooth, WLAN, WAP, or a fixed Internet connection. COBA supports industry standards such as LON, OSGi (Open Systems Gateway initiative), HTTP, and XML, while being between the controllable resources and the user devices that translate the information both ways for monitoring, configuration, handling of alarms, data access, and other purposes. The server can support applications running from different locations, thus creating an open multiple third party service providers' environment. Automation projects that comply with the COBA specifications have already been commercially sold to major new office buildings and experiments are being carried out to provide them for residential areas also.

8 Creating a Movement Towards a Digital City

It is clear that within a liberal democratic society, people and organizations cannot be centrally ordered to build themselves a digital city. This kind of self-organizing system tends to follow the laws of complexity, as Andrew Ilachinski points out in his study [9]: "Self-organization is a fundamental characteristic of complex systems. It refers to the emergence of macroscopic non-equilibrium organized structures, and is due to the collective interactions of the constituents of a complex system as they adapt and react to their environment. There is no God-like 'oracle' dictating what each and every part ought to be doing; parts act locally on local information and global order emerges without any need for external control."

This does not mean that a complex or chaotic system cannot be controlled. Ilachinski continues [10]: "The extreme sensitivity of chaotic system to small perturbations to initial conditions can be exploited to stabilize regular dynamic behaviors and to effectively 'direct' chaotic trajectories to a desired state. Moreover, this can be done using only experimental data in which no model is available for the system."

In principle, there are many ways to persuade organizations and people to move towards the creation of a digital city. Authorities can give administrative orders, operators and others can build enabling platforms, and content providers can supply content. Ultimately however, there has to be a change in people's mindsets. This kind of influencing people's minds is a widely researched subject, but recently the theory of memes that was originally proposed by Richard Dawkings, has got wide recognition and was found useful when promoting the various ideas in the Helsinki Arena 2000 project. Dennett claims in his book "Consciousness Explained" that memes spread now in this networked era much faster than ever before. Susan Blackmore argues [1] that memes spread and influenced our decision making: "On this view, all human actions, whether conscious or not, come from complex interactions between memes, genes and all their products, in complicated environments". Anyone who succeeds in creating self-propagating memes has clearly found a cheap way to advocate ideas and change people's voluntary behavior.

City officials, universities or civil groups have originated many digital city projects. Helsinki Arena 2000 seems to be unique as the only large well known project originated and lead by a former local telecom monopoly. Even though it sounds strange that telecom operators have not been more actively promoting increased usage of networks in the form of digital cities, it is also understandable. Elisa Communications at that time was a city operator. In most other countries, telecom companies were countrywide and not targeted towards one urban area. From other starting points, digital city projects often end up as research experiments, digital "city hall" type of web sites, or networked virtual communities with an interest towards discussing common city-related interests. A telecom company might also have had a different viewpoint using the proprietary network control as a competitive edge for content provisioning. This is clearly a selection of business logic based on competitive capabilities as shown in section 3.

As Helsinki Telephone decided that the project would be a catalyst project, with a task of creating a movement towards a digital city, but not have the resources to do it alone it was a cautious, but in retrospect, a wise choice. A digital city is not a project or a platform. It is a way people and organizations within a city collaborate. Moreover, in the case of a digital city with myriads of details, where each individual is a decision maker of various investments of money or time, it becomes impossible to convince everybody unless the metaphorical ideas have such memetic properties that they propagate independently. Equally well, a telecom company with thousands of employees cannot commit to major investments and drop ongoing businesses to redirect its operations towards new visionary directions with executive orders only. The middle management of the business units needs to be convinced that the new directions are beneficial to their businesses for the company to operate efficiently and profitably. This propagation of ideas and designs and general goodwill towards a digital city was the task for the Helsinki Arena 2000 project.

As the Internet and mobile phones were making their advances independent of the Helsinki Arena 2000 project, the main emphasis of the project concentrated on those identified issues where the project could possibly influence the trajectories and speed of the development. Internally and among the consortium members, this meant the creation of numerous plans, joint experiments, and committee meetings. Since the member companies were large corporations and most of the people, whose mindset the project wanted to influence, were outsiders, this was naturally not adequate. Public opinion forming was emphasized as part of the project.

Public opinion can be said to consist of memes. The project intentionally created various such memes and combinatory memeplexes that were capable of easily copying themselves in the media and peoples minds to create a favorable atmosphere for the introduction of a wide variety of digital city applications and for the motivation and orientation for people to create such ideas. As it was generally accepted in 1995 in Finland that new ideas came from California, it seemed useful to gain also an international reputation in order to support a communal identity that would give people sufficient self-esteem to trust their capability of inventing and bringing forward new ideas. Before 1995, there were very few international articles about Finnish technology and when they were published, it was almost a national occasion. By 2001, Finland had become well known for its technology all over the world. This has happened partially due to Nokia, but very much of the initial growth of the publicity between 1996 and 1999 was related to Helsinki Arena 2000. Among the English-speaking international media that have covered various parts of the project are ABC, CNN, PBS, MSNBC, CBS, NPR, Granada, BBC, New York Times, Fortune, Time, Newsweek, Wired, Wall Street Journal, International Herald Tribune, Guardian, Business Week, and European. Dozens of German, French, Japanese, Chinese, and Italian articles have also been published.

Due to this publicity, there have been many international ministerial groups, government advisors, mayors, top executives of Fortune 50 companies, and numerous other study groups visiting to learn from the project or to discuss potential co-operation. This high profile was essential when discussing the needs of the project with equipment manufacturers, as existing products did not support all the requirements of the project designs. The high profile also assisted in getting good job applications, convincing business units of the importance of following joint objectives, and even in talking about the same things with the same words. The original intention of achieving aligning effects similar to Kennedy's "man on moon" project clearly proved to be successful.

9 Conclusions

We believe that we have shown the importance of a local network operator's role in the development of a digital city. The nature of communal interaction can vary greatly depending on the different implementation options that can be used in a physical communications network. The important conclusion here is also that it is in the best interest of a local operator to provide many of the enabling elements that combine the space of flows with the space of places in order to maximize its profits. This realisation, if it is widely understood by both the network operators and policy makers, can greatly ease the problems arising from the so-called digital divide within a technologically advanced city.

The market area of the Helsinki city and surroundings was proven large enough to be offered broadband network services for a reasonable price with the total service being commercially viable. As Helsinki and its surroundings have a population of only 1 million people, the same conclusions are applicable to a large number of cities. However, right timing and careful network optimisation is important in order to save many costs in the network.

In many phases of the project, the technology set the limits. The new technology, which was to be used, was so complicated and the limitations so strict that even details mattered. Knowing and understanding technology deeply enough demands very good human resources and this is only possible through networking with operators, manufacturers, research institutes, and service providers. We obviously had several hen & egg and small volume problems, which have now become much easier to solve as broadband technology is becoming more widely used and technologically more mature.

The 3D maps proved to be very successful in getting attention to the project. The same can be said about the experiments with building automation. These visions and demonstrations contained several memetic characteristics and succeeded in spreading the Helsinki Arena 2000 statements even much further than anticipated.

Some services suffer of the slow change in human behavior. The traditional way is being used even if new services exist, which could help them to be made easier and with smaller costs. New services should be introduced by somehow binding them to the old way. Naturally, young people are the easiest group to test new services on and they can affect the decisions of older people with their opinions, attitude, and assistance.

In many of the project's aims, it was clearly demonstrated that the visionary approach and strong belief of the fast paced technological advances have paid off. Approaches that are more conservative would have been old fashioned when they became ready for the roll out. The high profiled memetically spreading ideas also greatly assisted the aims of the project by creating a widespread mindset that favored the project aims. It seems that Helsinki as a city gained positive publicity both locally and globally due to the numerous international media's references to the project when Helsinki was not yet considered one of the high tech centers of the world. We estimated that this had a positive effect also on the citizens' local identity by adding one more reason for them to be proud of their city's achievements.

Finally, it is hard to estimate how things would have been without the Helsinki Arena 2000 project. Elisa Communications Corporation and many people in other companies and communities in the project consortium have worked several years towards projected goals, which were not uncontested, and in many cases, the effort to get acceptance from the business divisions for the project's goals took a long time and much effort. Inside a company, task sharing between different departments takes a great deal of communication anyway and usually the business division's reasons for reluctance are related to the timing of the investments. Basically, the catalytic approach worked surprisingly well, although there were many situations where the clearer commitment of the top management to the project goals would have saved much effort and resources. Besides a vision that was shared by many, the project clearly created a common conceptual framework of terminology and a way to handle problems and offered a suitable place for discussing and developing future business, which from the Elisa Communications' point of view relates to the technology and telecommunications operator's role in general in the current rapidly changing business environment. The project has catalyzed a high number of intended activities and the effects are still growing. When comparing the current situation with the original goals of Helsinki Arena 2000, the goals have been well met. The only major surprise has been the wide international recognition of the project.

References

1. S. Blackmore: The Meme Machine. Oxford (1999) 237
2. S. Body-Gendrot: Social Control of Cities. Blackwell (2000) 227-260
3. M. Castells: The Rise of the Networked Society, 2nd Edition. Blackwell (1996) 407-459
4. F. Fukuyama: The Great Disruption. Free Press, 197-211.
5. J. Geary: Digital Cities, Time June 29, Vol.151 No. 26 (1998)
6. E. Gülch: Extraction of 3D Objects from Aerial Photographs, Information Systems and Processes for Urban Civil Engineering Applications, Workshop Proceedings, Rome 21-22 November, 1996. European Commission (1998) 55-70
7. K Hampton, B. Wellman: Examining Community in the Digital Neighborhood, Early Results from Canada's Wired Suburb. In: T. Ishida (ed.): Digital Cities: Experiences, Technologies and Future Perspectives, Lecture Notes in Computer Science Vol. 2362. Berlin etc., Springer Verlag (2000) 194-208
8. P. Hietanen: IP-technology and multimedia in telephony network, Research Centre of Elisa Communications Corporation (1998)
9. A. Ilachinski: Land Warfare and Complexity I, Center for Naval Analyses (1996) 66
10. A. Ilachinski: Land Warfare and Complexity, Part II, Center for Naval Analyses (1996) 136
11. Infocities project: Final Report. http://www.infocities.eu.int (2000)
12. M. Isomäki: Quality and Billing in Integrated Services IP Networks, HPY Research Report No. 144 (1999)
13. J. Kukkonen, J. Myllärinen, A. Nissinen, M. Voipio: A dual approach for creating very large virtual models. In: International Symposium on Virtual and Augmented Architecture (VAA01), Dublin Ireland (2001)
14. KULTU consumer research group: Report of Virtual Language School. TEKES (1996)
15. KULTU consumer research group: Report of Intelligent Home. TEKES (2000)
16. P. Kyheröinen: Transition to Internet Protocol version 6: Teleoperator's view, HPY Research Report No 148 (1999)
17. H. J. Kyyrö: ISDN kantaa liikkuvan kuvan työasemiin. Kauppalehti, Dec. 1, (1995) 9
18. P. Levinson: Digital McLuhan: A Guide to The Information Millenium. Routledge (1999) 197-200
19. R. Linturi: Management of Urban Space and Services by VR Systems in Helsinki. Information Systems and Processes for Urban Civil Engineering Applications, Proceedings of Workshop Rome 21-22 November 1996. European Commission (1988) 51-54
20. R.Linturi: Virtual Environments in the World Ahead. IST 98 Summary Proceedings, European Comission (1998) 118-119
21. R. Linturi and I. Hannula: 100 Phenomena, http://www.linturi.fi/100_phenomena (1998)
22. R. Linturi, M. Koivunen, J. Sulkanen: Helsinki Arena 2000 – Augmenting a Real City to a Virtual One. In: T.Ishida (Ed.): Digital Cities: Experiences, Technologies and Future Perspectives, Lecture Notes in Computer Science Vol 2362. Springer Verlag (2000) 83-96
23. M. Mazarr: Global Trends 2005. The Center for Strategic and International Studies (1999) 35

24. W. Mitchell: Designing the Digital City. In: T. Ishida (Ed.), Digital Cities: Experiences, Technologies and Future Perspectives, Lecture Notes in Computer Science, Vol. 2362. Springer Verlag (2000) 1-6
25. D. Morley and K. Robins: Spaces of Identity. Routledge (1995) 40
26. E. Mynatt: Design for Networked Communities, CHI'97, (1997)
27. A. S. Nissinen, T.Kytönen, J. Kukkonen, J.Myllärinen, M. Voipio: Maps and virtual worlds - does History repeat itself? In: International Symposium on Virtual and Augmented Architecture (VAA01), Dublin (2001)
28. Norton: Life after Television. New York (1994) 204
29. J. Nurmela: Does modern information technology select its users, Reviews 1998/5, Statistics Finland (1998) 84
30. P. Preston: Reshaping Communications. Sage (2001) 209-273
31. D. Ruelle: Chance and Chaos. Princeton University Press (1991)
32. T. Simula: Helsinki Arena 2000 - a virtual meeting point. In: Telecommunication Development Asia-Pasific. International Clearing House Limited (1998) 86-88
33. S. Shum: Real and Virtual Spaces, Mapping from Spatial Cognition to Hypertext. Hypermedia 2 (1990) 133-158.
34. E. Selse: Fin de Siecle. The World of Interiors (2000) august, 88-97
35. S. Silberman: Just Say Nokia. Wired (1999) September, 144-145
36. K. Takahashi, S. Yokoji, N. Miura: Location Oriented Integration of Internet Information – Mobile Info Search. In: T. Ishida (Ed): Digital Cities, Experiences, Technologies and Future Perspectives. Lecture Notes in Computer Science Vol 2362, Springer Verlag (2000) 364-377
37. J.Tähtinen, K. Lehtinen, R. Linturi: Patenttijulkaisu FI 102867, National Board of Patents and Registration of Finland (1996)
38. UNDP: Human Development Report, United Nations Development Programme (2001) 48 http://www.undp.org/hdr2001/.
39. P.G. Van de Haar, A.F.Schoenmakers, E.S.Eilley, D.N. Tedd, S.A.Tickell, P.R Lloyd, M. Badham, S. O'Brien, R.Poole, P. Sampson, J. Harding, T.Simula, T. Varonen, S. Sauvala: DIAMOND Project; Video-on-Demand System and Trials. European Transactions on Telecommunications, 8 (1997) 337-344
40. A. Wiio: Customer Survey. Arcus internal report (2001)
41. COBA white paper: http://www.coba-group.com/files/COBA_WP_011119.pdf
42. J.M. Carrol: The Blacksburg Electronic Village, a Study in Community Computing. In P. van den Besselaar, S. Koizumi (eds), Digital Cities 3. Information technologies for social capital. Lecture Notes in Computer Science, Vol. 3081. Springer-Verlag, Berlin Heidelberg New York (2005) pp. 42-63
43. T Ishida: Activities and Technologies in Digital City Kyoto. In P. van den Besselaar, S. Koizumi (eds), Digital Cities 3. Lecture Notes in Computer Science, Vol. 3081. Springer-Verlag, Berlin Heidelberg New York (2005) pp. 162-183
44. D. Peng, D.H. Lin, H.Y. Sheng: Digital City Shanghai. In P. van den Besselaar, S. Koizumi (eds), Digital Cities 3. Lecture Notes in Computer Science, Vol. 3081. Springer-Verlag, Berlin Heidelberg New York (2005) pp. 138-161
45. P. van den Besselaar, D. Beckers: The Life and Death of the Great Amsterdam Digital City. In P. van den Besselaar, S. Koizumi (eds), Digital Cities 3. Lecture Notes in Computer Science, Vol. 3081. Springer-Verlag, Berlin Heidelberg New York (2005) pp. 64-93
46. D. Schuler: The Seattle Community Network, Anomaly or Replicable Model? In P. van den Besselaar, S. Koizumi (eds), Digital Cities 3. Lecture Notes in Computer Science, Vol. 3081. Springer-Verlag, Berlin Heidelberg New York (2005) pp. 16-41

Digital City Shanghai: Concepts, Foundations, and Current State

Peng Ding, DongHui Lin, HuanYe Sheng

ICHI Lab, CS Department of Shanghai Jiaotong University,
Huashan Road 1954, Shanghai, 200030, China
dingpeng@cs.sjtu.edu.cn, lindh@sjtu.edu.cn,
hysheng@mail.sjtu.edu.cn

Abstract. The fastest developing city in China is Shanghai; its annual growth rate (GDP) exceeded 11.9% average in every year from 1992 and GDP per person in 2003 reached 4909 USD. Economists, industries and the government have been considering how to keep Shanghai developing in a sustainable manner. In 1994, the Shanghai Municipal Government put forward the concept of "information harbor" and set the goal of establishing a series of information infrastructures in the following five years. The Shanghai city informatization project started in 1999, and by the end of 2001 it had spread across Shanghai. At the same time, some applications based on Internet technologies were designed and developed. In the beginning of 2002, based on the current information infrastructures and systems, Shanghai Municipal Government announced the "Digital City Shanghai" strategy. This chapter will introduce the background of the Digital City Shanghai project, the current state of the information infrastructure in Shanghai, and the concept of system design & user interface. The Digital City Shanghai project will be described in four parts: Spatial Data Infrastructure, City Informatization, Shanghai City Grid, and Shanghai Logistics Information Platform. We will also introduce some research projects. In addition to the strategy, we describe and discuss social perspective and problems.

1 Introduction

1.1 Basic Information of Shanghai

Shanghai, built in the Tang dynasty some 1500 years ago, is located on the east coast of China. It occupies 6340.5 km2, 0.06% of the total area in China (Fig.1, Fig.2). Shanghai is flat except for several small hills in the north, which makes it a pleasant place to live. It is made up of 18 districts and one county, and as of the end of 2003 was home to more than 13.418 million people (Table 1). Shanghai is famous for its richness of water because the Changjiang River flows through Shanghai on its way to the ocean. There are many historic sites in Shanghai that are of sightseeing importance. Shanghai is now the biggest industrial city; the economic and financial center of China after more than 1500 years of development. Over the last ten years, the city has changed greatly. The annual growth rate of GDP has exceeded 11.9% since 1992 and GDP per person reached 4909 USD in 2003.

P. van den Besselaar and S. Koizumi (Eds.): Digital Cities 2003, LNCS 3081, pp. 141-165, 2005.
© Springer-Verlag Berlin Heidelberg 2005

Table 1. Basic Information of Shanghai

Item	Value
Area	6340.5 km2
Population	13.418 million
Density of population	2014/ 1 km2

Fig. 1. Location of Shanghai in China   **Fig. 2.** Map of Shanghai

How to make the development of the city sustainable? How to catch up to the new economics of the world? How to connect with international business smoothly? How to make the daily life of residents and visitors in Shanghai more comfortable? Those questions have been considered by economists, industries, and the Municipal Governments. The project 'Shanghai InfoPort', a key component of the information infrastructure of Shanghai, was initiated in 1996; its is detected towards upgrading the infrastructure to secure the new global economics. So far, there are 7.33 million telephone lines, 3.67 million cable TVs, including an interactive cable TV network offering broadband access to 924.9 thousand users. The total revenue of the IT sector Shanghai became the first place. The economy of Shanghai is transiting to high value-added sectors. In order to meet international standards, the business plans and practices of Shanghai have started changing significantly. The services offered to people have become colorful and interesting [6] [27].

To make these changes more effective, the municipal governments set up the 'Bureau for Informatization'. There is also an informatization office in each district and county whose responsibility is to promote and coordinate the implementation of projects. The tasks of the government are as follows: 1. Announce the goals for each stage in city informatization. 2. Determine related standards and regulations. 3. Coordinate diverse sectors of the economy to implement certain projects. 4. Offering occasional financial support for common needs.

1.2 Design Guidelines of Digital City Shanghai

Digital City Shanghai is a large-scale, extendable, distributed system that will cover most aspects of peoples' daily life in Shanghai. Design guidance should be set in advance to decrease mistakes during implementation. The current guidelines fall into four areas: Services-Oriented, Intelligent, Participation-Encouragement, and Government-Guidance &Commercialization.

Services-Oriented means that Digital City Shanghai is not only an information platform, but also a services platform. There are already many ISPs and ICPs that offer information and Internet access to the public, such as Shanghai Online (http://www.online.sh.cn), Kali (http://www.kali.com.cn), Shanghai Yellow Page (http://www.yp.online.sh.cn), Internet Shanghai (http://www.sh.com), and Shanghai News (http://info-po.online.sh.cn). They provide information to the public, including news, financial, education, health care, sports, jobs, etc. With regard to service, Digital City Shanghai will be different from ISP, ICP, IDC which are general websites. It aims to integrate all information services, whether online or offline, to meet the requirements of residents and visitors by constructing an open, distributed, shareable platform.

An interesting challenge called "72 hour online survival," was run from September 4, 1999 to September 6, 1999. Its goal was to find out whether there were enough services for online living in China. 12 participants (half in Shanghai, half in Guangzhou in South China) were locked in flats with nothing but a PC connected to the networks. They had to find ways to survive for the 3 days using the PC connected to Internet. They had to search for appropriate servers and order all things and services needed for living via the network. Information providers offer information on restricted areas to the consumer, the user. However, what the users require is not only the information itself but also the service provided by the service providers. Therefore, services are regarded as exploring the potential value of information [21]. Intelligent technologies could be used in various aspects in digital cities.

1. *Intelligent Interface.* Users of Digital City Shanghai are quite diverse with different educational backgrounds, so the interface should be easy to learn and easy to use. Graphical icons on touch screens are already popular. Speech recognition and speech output will be adopted more widely. For security, some systems will need to be underpinned by finger-printer recognition. As Shanghai is an international city with many visitors from foreign countries, a multi-lingual interface is needed.

2. *Intelligent Agent.* To serve users better, Digital City Shanghai will apply agent technology to analyze their requirements, to locate the needed information on the Internet, to compare different sources and to select and display the most appropriate results. Many of the tasks in Digital City Shanghai will be conducted by intelligent agents.

3. *Intelligent System.* Natural language processing systems will be used for abstracting information from the Internet. They will also be used for intelligent conversation systems to explore human behavior in the environment of e-business. Multi-lingual issues will have to be solved if the system is to serve people from foreign counties.

4. *Intelligent Transportation.* Intelligent transportation is another attractive and potential field that deserves special attention. This is especially true in Shanghai whose transportation infrastructure is being rapidly developed only recently. Intelligent transportation is an important component of Digital City Shanghai.

Participation-Encouraged. Large-scale cooperation among governments, academies, industries, and individuals is needed. To solve the many technical challenges of this system, it is necessary to bring together researchers, engineers, and managers from different fields. As the most developed city in China, Shanghai has long established relations with Chinese cities as well as cities in other countries. The design and implementation of Digital City Shanghai provides an excellent opportunity to cooperate with partners to create new business and to exchange experiences. In the last two years, Asia-Pacific City Informatization Forum was held in Shanghai twice. Over 500 attendees took part in these events and great interest was evidenced in the promotion of digital cities. Many cities and provinces in China have initiated similar projects. Singapore and Kuala-Lumpur are cooperating with Shanghai in the area of digital libraries. An open, shareable lab that researchers and developers from different fields are welcome to join is being established at Shanghai Jiaotong University. Digital City Shanghai will not only serve the government, but also society. It should be oriented to residents rather than professionals. All citizens are welcome to offer their suggestions, comments, and energies for ensuring the success of implementation. All participants can benefit from this project. Investors can benefit from the new markets established while and researchers can gain from the access to topics and projects. The government will be enhanced by the social impact of this project. The common citizens are welcome to contribute to the implementation of the Digital City.

Government-Guided & Commercialized. It is not realistic for the governments anor for some special organizations to build a system of the scale of Digital City Shanghai on their own because of the huge investment needed. Digital City Shanghai has to be profitable and sustainable so that it gains the interest of industries and social organizations in contributing to the effort. At the beginning, companies such as banks and financial organizations, were encouraged to invest; they benefit in several ways including advertising, website operation, service providing, marketing, and cost effectiveness. However, it is obvious that such a large system should be centrally managed. In Shanghai, as well as other cities in China, only the municipal or provincial government has the wherewithal to undertake such a long-term task. Some of the critical functions can be undertaken only by the government: (1) systematically organizing the information; (2) making regulations for its operation; (3) keeping information open to the public and making policies to support the project.

It is hoped that its existence will stimulated new research topics. The government is organizing universities, institutes, and labs to work together in finding new ideas and new topics in the digital cities field [2, 14].

2 Current Information Infrastructures in Shanghai

In April 1990, the Chinese government announced the development of the PuDong area as one of the new economic zones. The Shanghai Municipal Government proposed to build the local Information Highway in Shanghai in 1994, and formally initialized the InfoPort Shanghai project in 1996. July 1998, the 'Bureau for Informatization' was founded to speed up the implementation of the InfoPort Shanghai project. Its goals, clarified in 2000, are: (1) to complete the infrastructure of InfoPort Shanghai, unify the standards; (2) to complete five backbone networks, build a set of commercial databases and public information databases and form the information market (3) to promote the IT sector as a new backbone branch of industry in Shanghai (GDP goal is 100 billion RMB) (4) to establish the Shanghai social information system.

Over the last few years, a lot of new IT service industries have been developed rapidly, such as network services, information contents services, and information management services, which promote the developments of E-commerce, E-government, information resources in Shanghai. Many of the systems needed for designing and implementing Digital City Shanghai have been finished.

The broad bandwidth network that provides a common communication platform for system integration and information exchange in Shanghai was completed in Oct 1999. The five backbone networks based on the municipal area network provide a service platform for city informatization. They are Shanghai Internet eXchange networks (SHIX), Shanghai Electronic Data Interchange network (SHEDI), Shanghai Community Services network (SHCS), Shanghai Social Security network (SHSS), and Shanghai Golden card and POS network (GC & POS) [7].

Shanghai Internet eXchange network (SHIX). SHIX aims to optimize the current network architecture and provide a better platform for information exchange. Therefore, various kinds of networks have been connected to it, such as Shanghai Online, Shanghai Tech Network (STN), Shanghai Education and Research Network (SHERNET), Shanghai Science Institute Network (SHSIN), Shanghai Golden Bridge Network (GBN), Shanghai Economical Information Network (EINET) and so on. SHIX is open to the groups and organizations who meet the following requirements: (1) be a legal ISP (2) provide network services to their users (3) to have their own international connection channel (4) have a self-governed network with connection rate under 10 Mbps [4].

Shanghai EDI network (SHEDI). The goal of SHEDI is to automate the electronic data exchange for international trading extends to some related authorities, divisions and banks. It was initiated by Shanghai Planning Committee, Foreign Trade Committee, Transportation Office, CIQ and Post Committee in late 1996. The complete system is composed of Shanghai EDI center, Shanghai CIQ EDI center, Shanghai Harbor EDI center, and Shanghai Foreign Trade EDI center. The functions of SHEDI are: (1) to interconnect Shanghai CIQ EDI center, Shanghai Harbor EDI center, and Shanghai Foreign Trade EDI center, (2) to realize and manage EDI data exchange among the EDI centers, and (3) to provide services for and management of the communication networks, devices, and user maintenance.

Shanghai Community Services network (SHCS). SHCS provides social information services to 15 million people in Shanghai. It is a community-based, services-oriented public information network that connects most communities in Shanghai. Various connection techniques are used, including telephone fixed line, wireless, and CATV. SHCS is responsible for serving a society that consists of 4.5 million families and 15 million citizens and emphasizes daily life. The backbone of SHCS is a 100M ATM network and it linked to the Internet via 2M DDN. The terminals connected to the backbone use 10Mbps lines with different protocols such as ISDN, Telephone line, and HFC of Cable TV. Several daily life related databases and web query operations have been built, for instance, supermarket service, online shopping, legal assistance, second-hand market, news, and lotteries. All web pages were designed base upon guidelines for 'services' and the essential purpose of SHCS is to improve the quality of daily life for residents [15].

Shanghai Social Security network (SHSS). SHSS aims to provide a platform for five types of insurance: endowment insurance, hospitalization insurance, unemployment insurance, transportation insurance, and work place insurance. SHSS is built based upon the Shanghai Insurance Management system. It provides a unique management and operation service to 4 million employees and 2 million retirees in Shanghai. The main functions are insurance account management, individual account management; balance declaration management, finance management, query system, analysis system and pension delivery system. The final goal of SHSS could be described using the term 'seven in one' which means one insurance number, one set of basic information, one insurance IC card, one unique interface, one backbone network, one central database and one data exchange center. Currently, several new SHSS projects have been proposed or been implemented whose goal is to make the social security information more convenient to residents. They are a large-scale information system based on databases and supported by the broad bandwidth network [12].

Golden Card and POS system (GC & POS). GC & POS was built to promote electronic finance and electronic commerce, and to quicken Shanghai informatization. The basic tasks of the GC & POS project are to build a network center based upon current X.25, DDN, and PSTN networks using a TAN-DEM mainframe for exchanging information of bankcards of different banks and to establish a complicated system that connects to the Bank Card Exchange Center and all member banks, ATMs, and POSs throughout Shanghai. The GC & POS consists of three subsystems: Multi-Bank Card exchange network, Multi-place Card exchange network, and Multi-national Card exchange network. Currently, satellites, optical fiber, telephone lines, and wireless networks have been integrated together to yield a unified information communication network that covers most areas in Shanghai and provides a platform for information exchange.

There are a lot of demands being placed on the communication infrastructures: (1) System integration. (2) Multimedia applications. (3) E-commerce. (4) Three networks (i.e. Telephone-network, Cable TV-network and Computer network) in one. In order to meet the needs described above, the Shanghai Municipal Government is speeding up the development of the communication infrastructure called Shanghai City Wide Broad Bandwidth Network. It consists of four subprojects: Shanghai ATM Network, Shanghai IP Test Network, Shanghai Cable TV HFC, and Shanghai ADSL Network [13]. The five backbone networks described represent the information platform of Info Port Shanghai. In order to promote applications, some typical systems were built upon the platform from 1996 to 2000. They covered most aspects of modern life in Shanghai, including economic, culture, life, law, entertainment, education, finance, career, and city management. These systems carry the majority of contents of Digital City Shanghai. To save space, table 2 merely summarizes them by providing just their names and key service.

3 System Architecture, User Interface, and Content Design

Many applications have been developed, are being developed and will be developed for Digital City Shanghai. From the application viewpoint, there are government applications, industrial applications, academic applications, and cultural applications. From the communication viewpoint, computer networks, telephone networks, broadcast and television networks cover all of Shanghai. From the technology viewpoint, network technologies, software technologies, communication technologies play important roles. It is important to make a concept design for the system architecture and user interface of Digital City Shanghai.

Table 2. Overview of the Content - Digital City Shanghai

Name	Style
Shanghai People Building OA system	City Management
Shanghai People Congress Information system	City Management
Shanghai Finance & Tax Information system	City Management
Shanghai Statistics Information project	City Management
Shanghai Industry and Trade Management system	Economic
Shanghai Court Information system	Law
Shanghai Human Resources Management Information system	Career
Shanghai High and Elementary school Education Information system	Education
Shanghai Commerce network	Economic
Shanghai City Remote Sensing Information system	City Management
Digital City Planning Information system	City Management
Shanghai Quality Supervising Information system	City Management
Shanghai Health Information system	Life
Shanghai Real Estate Information system	Life
Shanghai Audit Information project	Finance
Shanghai Medicine Trade network	Life
Shanghai Meteorological Information system	Life
Shanghai Public Culture Information network	Culture
Shanghai Public Information Service network	Life

3.1 System Architecture

The system architecture of Digital City Shanghai presented in Fig. 3 consists of six parts: 2D/3D & GIS/Graphics interface; Agents; Application systems; Local search engine; Databases and Distributed ICPs. 2D/3D & GIS/Graphics interface provides a user-friendly, map based and intuitive interactive environment for citizens who have no or just a little knowledge about information processing and digital cities. Agents retrieve and classify information from the "information pool" and submit them to users according to their preferences.

Current applications, for example, E-commerce, E-government, distance learning, tele-medicine, and city management are developing rapidly in Digital City Shanghai. Databases such as aviation remote sensing, GIS, multimedia databases, which store huge amounts of professional information, construct the "information pool". Distributed ICPs that offer Internet connections and contents to users, are now speeding up their services by changing from narrowband to broadband. Local search engines dispatch software robots to the Internet sites in Shanghai for retrieving information from distributed ICPs. These six parts are integrated with each other as shown in the system architecture. The description of each part is given below:

2D/3D & GIS/Graphics interface. Most Digital City Shanghai users are common citizens that are not familiar with computer systems, so a friendly, easy to use and convenient interface is essential in improving the quality of Digital City Shanghai services. The traditional 2D interface is the primary technology for computer human interaction in Digital City Shanghai while the 3D space is intended to be a real one since it is linked to the physical city rather than a virtual one. Geography information system (GIS) technology that provides a map-based interface, allows users to share digitalized data of the land's surface (sometimes also in depth) for management, cartography, building rules, environment assessments etc. Users can easily find solutions to many daily life related issues. GIS may become a key technology for digital cities [8, 9].

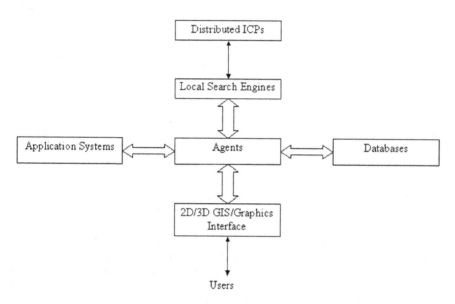

Fig. 3. System Architecture of Digital City Shanghai

Agents. Agent-based computing has been recognized as a new revolution in software and it has been predicted that agents will become pervasive in every market in the near future. Because of the huge amount of information created for digital cities, it is impractical, low efficiency and time-consuming, to expect users to manually search and organize information. Agents that can do the tasks entrusted to them by users, are the best way of solving this problem. Agent technology gives the common citizens who have little idea of computer science and software an opportunity to become involve in the social activities of digital cities.

Application Systems. Application systems, such as E-commerce, E-government, distance learning, tele-medicine, and city management are developing rapidly in Shanghai. Some typical applications are: Shanghai Finance & Revenue Information system; Shanghai Labor Force Market Information network; Shanghai Court Information system; Shanghai High school and Elementary school Education Information system; Shanghai City Remote Sensing Information system; Digital City

Planning Information system and so on. These systems cover most aspects of the economic, daily life, and cultural activities of Shanghai and are extending rapidly to cover other fields. It is unnecessary and impossible for the designer of Digital City Shanghai to rebuild these systems. These systems are currently linked only very weakly. Their goals, technologies, and data formats are also diverse. The lack of knowledge and information sharing among systems makes them 'isolated applications'. An urgent task is to find a way to integrate these systems and construct a platform for knowledge and information sharing.

Databases. Databases such as aviation remote sensing, GIS, MIS, multimedia databases, form the basis of the "information pool" of Digital City Shanghai. Aviation remote sensing data integrated with digital maps are the key contents of the basic databases of the city GIS. MIS and multimedia databases improve the quality of services that are becoming more popular with the public. The problems faced by the current Shanghai databases systems are how to share the data and how to improve the retrieval efficiency. Because of the huge amount of data, especially the aviation remote sensing and multimedia data, it is hard for most current database management systems such as Oracle, Sybase, DB2, and SQL Server, to locate the correct data and submit to users rapidly and efficiently. Data mining is expected to contribute the solution of this problem. Intelligent parallel database and distributed database technologies that can process huge amounts of data, are important in improving the efficiency of accessing the 'information pool' of Digital City Shanghai. Shanghai Jiaotong University is cooperating with other universities and research institutes in studying the database issues for Digital City Shanghai.

Distributed ICPs. Shanghai Online provides information and services covering daily news, commerce, entertainment, sports, education, real estate and games. Sina (http://www.sina.com), Netease (http://www.netease.com), and Sohu (http://www.sohu.com) also have branches in Shanghai, and offer services similar to Shanghai Online. Some other professional ICPs that focus on special domains such as tourism, commerce, banking, universities, and real estate, present more detailed information to the public. Shanghai super computing center, one of the grand projects of 'Info Port Shanghai', was finished in June 2001. This center provides a powerful tool for engineering computing, climate forecasting, production designing, gene technology, ocean engineering, city planning, and so forth. From the beginning of 2000, top IT companies, including China Telecom, Netcom, Unicom, invested in the establishment of broadband networks in Shanghai, upon which many new applications, such as VOD, Video meeting, virtual reality, will be run. The spectrum of ICPs will be extended in the next five years, and the services provided will continue to improve. The resources of Digital City Shanghai will also be significantly increased.

Local Search Engines. The importance of search engines to the utilization of the Internet and WWW needs no further explanation. The four ICPs introduced above have developed their own search engine that is able to search web pages within China, in the same way as other famous search engines in the world, such as Google, Yahoo, Infoseek, they are a kind of global search engine. The back end of this kind of search engine is a soft robot that traverses the global Internet and captures web pages for storage and later retrieval by users. Digital cities focus on providing local information and services so that local search engines are more useful for residents and visitors. The resources of local search engines are restricted to web pages in Shanghai, so their efficiency is much higher than those of global search engines. Local search engines are able to search not only web pages, but also some more advanced contents. Digital City Shanghai demands continual improvement in search technologies and the development of new paradigms.

The six parts of the system architecture cooperate with each other. Users provide their requirements via the 2D/ 3D and GIS/Graphic interface. Agents understand these requirements, divide them into sub-tasks and distribute them to application systems, databases, and local search engines according to task type. Enhancing the interface, agents and local search engines, are urgent tasks faced by Digital City Shanghai.

3.2 User Interface Design

A variety of interface technologies can be used in different applications. As Digital City Shanghai aims to be a distributed system that serves as many residents and visitors with different education levels as possible, the interface has to be designed to support the most unskilled users.

GIS interface. General speaking, GIS is a platform upon that will support many applications, so that 2D maps are the first choice as an interface for accessing Digital City Shanghai. The user can move the cursor everywhere on the screen and get the associated information from DB systems or websites.

3D interface. The 3D space derived from the real city offers an exciting model to users who can go forward, backward, turn left, turn right and fly in 3D space. Databases linked to the 3D space can be directly accessed by through the viewpoint.

Graphical icon. This is the traditional window style interface. Unskilled users can select the functions desired by mouse clicking (sometimes several clicks are needed). The desired functions are then performed and information is displayed on the screen.

Speech interface. Speech technology is a more natural way of communicating with a computer. Text to speech technology offers the possibility of outputting speech both in Chinese and certain other languages. Speech recognition has developed rapidly in the last few years. The key problems have been solved. IBM's Via Voice system is able to recognize speech input with error rates under 5%. Current software system is feasible if the interaction contents are restricted to special domains such as travel, weather, etc, [3].

Languages. Digital City Shanghai also serves visitors from foreign countries with languages such as English and Japanese; it is not difficult to support different languages using artificial translation. However, information in Digital City Shanghai is so huge that machine translation system should also be considered.

Fingerprint recognition. For security reasons, several applications must be protected by fingerprint recognition. The applications are closely related to sensitive information held by the government, banks, and special organizations. Moreover, information security technologies such as authentication, cryptography, and PKI also play important roles in Digital City Shanghai.

3.3 Content

Digital City Shanghai is made up of five parts: digital government, digital enterprise, distance shopping, distance education, and digital community.

Digital Government. Digital government is the organizer and manager of digital city Shanghai. It uses the IT and communication technology to reform the government's organization and the general workflow. Building a digital government promotes democracy, improves the efficiency, and enforces the administration's dictates. The basic functions of Shanghai digital government are: Internet information services, Internet office automation, mobile administration, computer aided decision making, and electronic capital management.

Digital Enterprises. Digital enterprises enable factories and companies to integrate their information in several key tasks, such as possibility studies, production design, material purchase, management, quality control, and sales. The core issues of digital enterprises are: B-to-B e-commerce in the production process, agile production, and intelligent management. Currently, most enterprises in Shanghai undertake their tasks in traditional ways; even worse, quite a large percentage is still not connected to the Internet. They represent a significant potential market both for enterprises and ISPs.

Online shopping. Online shopping makes it possible for people to purchase in supermarkets, multiple shops and stores. Online shopping needs effort to be spent on establishing online shopping malls, security certification, electronic payment, and distribution systems. In Shanghai, some ISPs already provide this kind of service, for instance, Shanghai Online and Kali. Top markets are advancing the construction of their own websites to provide online shopping services to the public. Implementing online shopping systems will change the publics' purchasing and consuming habits.

Distance Education. Education plays a more important role in the era of the knowledge economy, especially 'lifetime education', which enables people to improve their skills throughput their lifetime. Distance education is built based upon the national information infrastructure and it realizes the dynamic organization and management of education all over the world. In Shanghai, there are about 3 million students in schools, and 5 million employees need post-school education. There are far fewer schools in Shanghai than are needed. Many high school students have no chance to enter university, and many employees cannot receive post-school education. Distance education is a feasible and efficient way to solve this problem. Shanghai Jiaotong University built a distance education system and opened it to the public in 1998. The next step is to extend it to other universities, colleagues, high schools and elementary schools.

Digital Community. Digital community integrates the community information services and application functions together to promote community informatization based upon the space information infrastructure. Digital community realizes digital survival by applying IT and communication technologies to people's daily life, such as interaction, entertainment, traveling, health, education and broadcasting. It reduces the usage of energy and materials, and achieves sustainable development in Shanghai. Municipal government has invested much in building the backbone of the community networks, which connect the sub-networks of nearly 1000 communities. Services such as water supply, energy supply, food supply, emergency services, remote management, inter-community and communication are being changed and improved [10, 20].

4 Digital City Shanghai Project

The construction of Digital City Shanghai had already started when the concept of digital earth was first put forward in 1998. In fact, as early as 1994, Shanghai Municipal Government announced the concept of the information harbor and planned to establish series of information infrastructures in Shanghai before 1998. In 1999, preparing for the construction of Digital City Shanghai, the Municipal Government started the city informatization project. By the end of the year 2001, city informatization had rapidly spread throughout Shanghai. At the beginning of 2002, Shanghai Municipal Government announced the "Digital City Shanghai" strategy. The government expects to complete the architecture of Digital City Shanghai by 2007 and serve the 2010 Shanghai Expo effectively.

The projects in Digital City Shanghai can be divided into four main parts, Spatial Data Infrastructure, City Informatization, Shanghai City Grid and Shanghai Logistics Information Platform. In this section, we will also introduce some practical projects and research projects in Digital City Shanghai.

4.1 Spatial Data Infrastructure

Aviation Remote Sensing Data. A project for "obtaining and analyzing aerial earth surface observation data" supported by "Hi-Tech Research and Development Program of China" started March 2000. In half a year, 12 subprojects were completed; the data, in excess of 100GB, covers more than 4200 square kilometers. Table 3 shows the statistics.

An example is the DOM graph of the Pudong area in Shanghai. The 1:10000 DOM diagram of the PuDong area and one typical part area are shown in Fig.4 (a) and (b), respectively. Using the zoom-in button of IE, readers can see details of the elements in this diagram; the Orient Pearl Tower and the Jin Mao mansion are easy to discern.

The traditional map displays information mainly using lines and dots. This kind of map cannot give the information about the earth's actual surface. DOM uses real photos of the earth surface as its basic elements, so complete information of the district is shown in the photo itself. With the addition of some explanations, DOM can give users far more information than the traditional map. The process workflow of DOM consists of ten stages: (1) Air photo or satellite remote sensing; (2) Encryption; (3) Image scanning; (4) Data correction; (5) Automatic embedding; (6) Color adjustment; (7) Page assembly; (8) Spray checking; (9) Inspection before distribution; (10) Printing and issuing the final graph.

Spatial Information System For Digital City Shanghai The project of "Research on key technologies of Spatial Information Systems in Digital City" supported by Shanghai Science & Technology Committee was conducted through the cooperation of the Shanghai Institute of Technical Physics, Shanghai City Development Research and Information Center, Shanghai Jiaotong University, East China Normal University, China Aviation Radio Electronics Research Institute, and Shanghai Flysky Aerospace Remote-sensing Company. The project started in 2002 and will finish in June 2004. The objective of this project is to collect spatial information data of Shanghai by remote sensing flights and to build a comprehensive spatial information system.

Table 3. Aviation Remote Sensing Activities

Place	(area km2)	Purpose	Device used
Shijiazhuang city	(110)	Crop analysis	OMIS
Shijiazhuang city	(310)	Environment, traffic investigation	OMIS
Niaodong bay	(600)	Ocean water quality inspection	OMIS
NeimengguNaimanqi	(1150)	Desert elucidation	OMIS
Tun zhou	(29)	Characteristic recognition	OMIS
Tai lake	(300)	Water quality inspection	OMIS
Suzhou river	(30)		WHI
Heilong river	(360)	Mine detection	WHI
Zhongguan chun	(580|)	Earth surface analysis	OMIS, HHI, CCD camera

(a) 1:10000 DOM Graph   (b) One Typical Part of the DOM Graph

Fig. 4. Pudong Area

4.2 City Informatization

Shanghai Tourist Information and Services system (STIS) was commenced in March 1999 by the "Bureau for Tourism in Shanghai." Shanghai Jiaotong University implemented this system and provided further technical support. The website of STIS was opened to visitors on September 7th, 1999 and has received more than 23.5 thousand visitors since then. One of the goals of this project is to get some experience for the implementation of Digital City Shanghai.

Two navigation methods are offered in this system. Fig. 5(a) shows the menu-based method and (b) shows the map-based one. In menu-based services, users can select items from menus or input keywords to make a query. In map-based services, users can click on spots of the map and can navigate across all of Shanghai. The information in STIS (Fig. 6) includes tour news, landscapes, shopping malls, hotels, restaurants, recreations, cultural events, and exhibitions. Both tourists and residents need these kinds of information. STIS now offers three kinds of consultation services to the users in different ways: Face-face consultation requires the user to go to the agent center and talk to the staff, E-mail consultation is done by Q&A between users and staff, and the WWW advice service uses online forum technology. After describing two projects, 'remote sensing data' and 'Shanghai Tourist Information and Services network', we give a short explanation of four other pilot projects in the following paragraphs.

Shanghai Health Consultation network (SHC) uses WWW technology to bring doctors in hospitals together to cover more areas and provide more medicine services to the citizens. SHC wants to meet the needs of patients without any restriction on location, specialty, or doctor. SHC is divided into three parts: Health consultation, Experts recommendation and Hospital distribution.

Health consultation offers diagnoses and suggestions to remote users. Experts' recommendation provides information of medical experts in member hospitals. Each record of experts includes individual information, field, experience, position and so on. Hospital distribution provides information of member hospitals. Patients can query them by name, specialty and location. More than 100 hospitals in 30 provinces have joined the consultation center and now provide their information. After SHC was built, more than 1000 cases in different hospitals and experiments have been completed.

In 2003 when the Severe Acute Respiratory Syndrome (SARS) was spreading in many areas in China, Shanghai Municipal Government created special funds for the fight against SARS. A typical project, "SARS Remote Consultation System", involved Shanghai Jiaotong University. It is an effective multimedia cooperative consultation system, with narrow-band access, and based on net-meetings and digital cameras. A typical consultation takes just twenty minutes. The system was tried in several hospitals in Shanghai and achieved great success; the municipal government is now trying to spread similar remote systems throughput Digital City Shanghai.

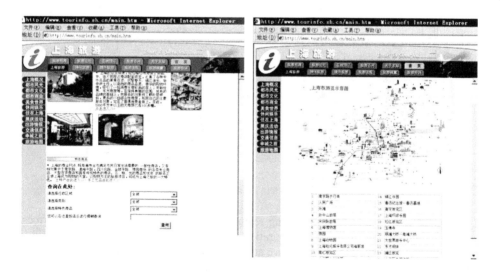

Fig. 5. (a) Menu-based Navigation in STIS   (b) Map-based Navigation in STIS

4.3 Shanghai City Grid

In July 2003, Shanghai Jiao Tong University and IBM China announced the 4.4 establishment of the SJTU-IBM Grid Computing Center. The Grid Computing Center is the first university grid research center in China and is based on IBM's high performance computing technologies. The center provides a research base for cross-discipline computing technology, and offers grid services to both in-campus and external customers. In November 2003, in the International Forum on Digital City and City Grid, which was a part of the 5th Forum of Shanghai International Industry Fair, the project of "Shanghai City Grid" was announced as one of the five most important projects on Grid Computing in China. The construction of Shanghai City Grid is an important and promising part of Digital City Shanghai. In fact, Shanghai Municipal Government is the first government in the world to establish Grid Computing as a part of the city's development strategy.

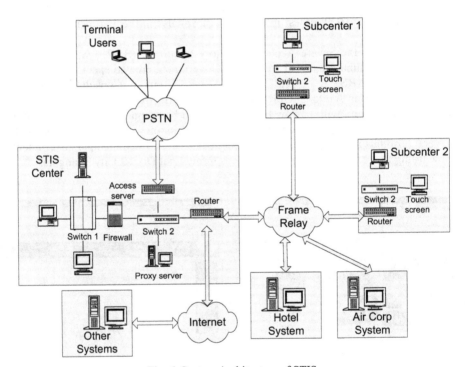

Fig. 6. System Architecture of STIS

Shanghai City Grid has the following features: (1) City wide. (2) Sharing resources. (3) Dynamic organization. (4) Cooperation. (5) Site autonomy. Shanghai City Grid is expected to strengthen the competitive advantage and innovation edge of Shanghai, to make government more effective, to enhance the competitiveness of enterprises, to improve academic institutes' ability to tackle key problems and to let citizens enjoy the achievements on informatization [28].

Shanghai City Grid is divided into two parts as shown in Fig.7: City Grid Infrastructure and City Grid Platform. City Grid Infrastructure consists of a series of vertical services and related services while City Grid Platform includes cross-organization services such as emergency response, intelligent traffic control, a research & education platform, and so on. The two parts will be integrated by setting up virtual organizations, business processes, security strategies, application adaptors and system implementation.

Currently, several grid application demonstrations are planned. There are three grid classifications: scientific computing grid, data grid, and service grid. Consensus forecast grid, E-government grid, remote medical service grid and city emergency response grid are four grid applications planned for Shanghai City Grid.

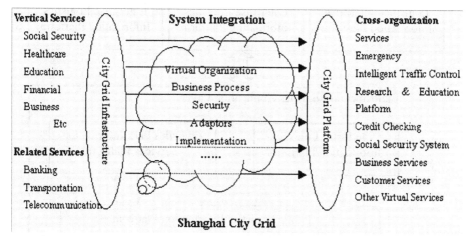

Fig. 7. Frame Draft of Shanghai City Grid

4.4 Shanghai City Logistics Information Platform

Shanghai is one of the most important harbors in North-east Asia and indeed the world. Therefore, modern logistics are regarded as an indispensable part of Digital City Shanghai. Shanghai Municipal Government has added the modern logistics project to the tenth five-year plan.

In 2002, aiming at achieving key technologies of modern logistics and build pilot logistics information system in Shanghai, the Modern Logistics Research Center was established in Shanghai Jiaotong University. In September 2003, the center started a project named 'Modern Logistics Information System Key Technologies Integration & Pilot Project' supported by Shanghai Science & Technology Committee in cooperation with Department of Computer Science & Engineering of Shanghai Jiaotong University, Department of Computer Science & Engineering of Tongji University, Shanghai Institute of Standardization and some logistics companies in Shanghai. The project will last two and a half years.

The objectives of the project include the following four parts: (1) Strategies of Shanghai logistics information platform technologies and business (2) Standards of modern logistics information technologies (3) Key Technologies of construction of modern logistics information systems, (4) Pilot System of Shanghai logistics information platform.

As shown in figure 8, the pilot system includes three layers: city logistics basic information layer, fundamental logistics application layer, and advanced logistics application layer. Shanghai public logistics infrastructures in the bottom layer include geographic-information-based services systems and city transportation services systems.

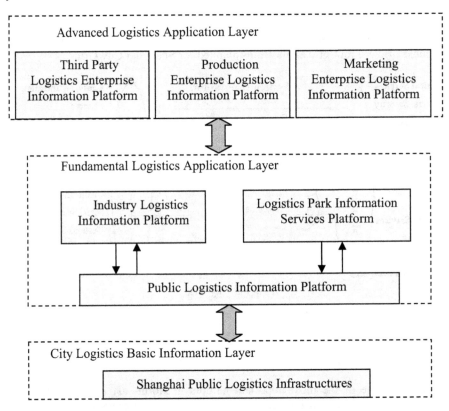

Fig. 8. Frame of Shanghai City Logistics Information System

4.5 Some Research Projects in Digital City Shanghai

The laboratory targeting Intelligent Computer Human Interaction (ICHI) in Department of Computer Science and Engineering in Shanghai Jiaotong University aims to promote research into Digital City Shanghai. The ICHI Lab is addressing the following research topics.

Demo 3D City Model. With the development of the Internet, visualization has become one of the important attributes of Digital City Shanghai. A demo 3D city model of the Pudong area based upon remote sensing data was built using Builder 1024, a modeling tool provided by TGNET Company. Builder 1024 is a tool uniquely designed for creating 3D city models, either on-line by connection to an analytical stereo plotter or off-line by means of inputting data files produced by stereo plotter, field survey, or commercial data products. Four typical modeling techniques in 3D graphics have been applied: extrude, lathe, skinning, and slicing. A general platform is provided to users for interactively editing the 3D city model.

This 3D model can be accessed via the dedicated view tool named Flight1024 offered by TGNET Company or via IE after installation of a plug-in component. Flight1024 helps users to fly and walk through any 3D model, 3D city, 3D Digital Earth, and 3D terrain at refresh rates above 24 frames per second. It supports seamless spatial databases of varying resolutions. The 3D model is a 'real' model derived from the physical world. The X, Y coordinates of each element, i.e. house or road, is the same with those of the entities location in the physical world.

Prototype Interactive Agent. Interaction between users and software has been studied by experts from all over the world. If software could chat with the user, answer user's questions, and generate plans for users, digital cities will become more interesting and attractive. Furthermore, the complexity of the current user-computer interface in Digital City Shanghai could be decreased allowing more users to access it. A prototype agent system named ICHI-Reply that can interact with users in natural language was created based upon an idea derived from earlier experiments [3]. The architecture of the system consists of two parts: The back-end control part consists of the administrator and the server in which the ICHI-Reply Agent resides; the user with terminal connects to the back-end part via the Internet.

The essential interaction process is as follows: the user talks to ICHI-Reply who tries to answer by itself. If no feasible answer can be found, ICHI-Reply asks the administrator for help. The administrator then gives an answer to ICHI-Reply, who forwards this answer to the user automatically. At the same time, ICHI-Reply learns by this exchange and stores the information in its database. ICHI-Reply can answer similar questions without the help of the administrator on subsequent occasions. It means that ICHI-Reply has the ability of learning and of becoming more and more powerful and clever over time.

Intercultural Collaboration Experiment. Shanghai is now an international city, which means that Digital City Shanghai should also supply information and services to foreigners. This necessitated the solution of we two problems: language barriers and cultural conflicts. Generally, a common language, English, is used to solve the language barrier problem. However, we found that it is really difficult for non-native English speakers to express their thoughts concisely. In 2002, researchers in ICHI Lab. took part in the Intercultural Collaboration Experiment [29] which started in 2002.

Initiated and controlled by ISHIDA Lab., Department of Social Informatics, Kyoto University, Japan, the Intercultural Collaboration Experiment (ICE) involves many Asian universities. The experiment is to support intercultural and multilingual collaborations using machine translation technologies. This experiment saw the participation of about 40 students majoring in computer science or informatics from Kyoto University, Japan, Shanghai Jiaotong University, China, Seoul National University and Handong University, Korea and the University of Malaya, Malaysia. The participants conducted an experiment in open source software development over the Internet. They were required to communicate using only their mother tongue. One of the objectives of the experiment was to see if the participants could overcome the language barrier by using machine translation tools. ICE2002 was carried out in two tracks, each of which took two months. Each track was divided into two four-week-phases: the Software Design Phase and the Software Implementation Phase. During the two phases, each sub team (one from each country) succeeded in designing and completing an intercultural collaboration tool. These tools included a search engine (China), a Web-based email system (Japan), SMS (Malaysia), and a Web-based chat system (Korea).

This experiment is still in progress. Current research issues include the design and development of a practical intercultural collaboration environment that supports multinational collaboration and communication.

5 Lessons Learned

5.1 Strategic View

Theory and practice basis. In theory, the digital city is a very important to the strategy of developing the national economy. It is a general-to-particular process and an approach to national informatization. Implementing digital city Shanghai should select some highly productive, well managed districts as the starting point and explore a suitable way for establishing the entire digital city [23]. Looking at the process of city informatization, Shanghai is now changing from the "material bazaar" to the "information bazaar". Region-wide informatization has become the basis of implementing digital city Shanghai [6].

The approach of digital city Shanghai. First, the rapid development of information industry, the popularity of computers, and the production of information devices construct the physical foundations of digital cities. This is followed by the construction of the information infrastructure and citywide network. Informatization then spreads to the whole economy a, including the government, business, management, production and so on. Last, digital city Shanghai covers the full-scale informatization of society, such as education, entertainment, consumers, health, traveling, interaction, culture, game etc [11] [23].

Evaluation of the system. Objective analyses depend on a good evaluation system. This involves a national informatization index. The index should be long-term, stable, comprehensive, and rational. The government is responsible for achieving some informatization level based upon the index and selecting the best development strategy [22].

Three relations. In order to avoid redundancy in creating digital city Shanghai, three relations must be considered. The first one is the relation between national informatization and city informatization. Some overall projects, such as the information backbone for tax matters, trade, and CIQ, should be planned and implemented based upon the national guidelines. Citywide informatization cannot ignore national informatization. The second one is the relation among different government departments. The last one is the relation between internationalization and localization. It is important for digital city Shanghai to consider its position in the future global economy [20, 24].

Hotpoint of digital cities. The public's wide acceptance of the informatization concept will increase information consumption, which will promote informatization in most economic fields and benefit other fields indirectly, such as energy, transportation, environment and so on. This kind of consumption-leading strategy yields significant benefits in digital cities.

Laws and ethics. The conflicts caused by digital cities include monopolization, illegal competition, cheating, privacy, knowledge right, technology security etc. Laws and ethics must be strengthened to protect legal activities and building a fair environment for digital cities [17, 19].

5.2 Sociological Perspective

The digital city is a new concept for future city living. Along with the spreading of IT technology and the establishment of a citywide space information infrastructure, digital city Shanghai will promote the switch of Shanghai's economy from industry dominated to information dominated. This change will impact the future of Shanghai enormously and will be far-reaching.

Citizens' ways of living and working will be changed. The development of a comprehensive network makes it possible to switch human-to-human interaction from face-to-face meetings to remote communication. People can accomplish tasks without leaving home, such as online shopping, online entertainment, distance education, and office work. The changes in the working environment will save time and energy, and reduce the problems of transportation. The remote management of big corporations and organizations will be possible. Dynamic alliances among enterprises will realize benefits in the processes of design, manufacture, and sale [5].

City industry structure will be reformed. The IT industry will become the dominant industry of Shanghai and the industrial economy will be replaced by the service economy. IT technology, communication technology and service industry will merge together, so that the competition, trade and service will become more and more dependent on the creation and application of information technology. This will make the service industry develop more rapidly and greatly elevate its status [16].

Social labor distribution will be remodeled. With the strengthening of the IT economy, white-collar workers will outnumber blue-collar workers. As the information industry is fundamentally different from the production industry, new industrial spaces will be formed and working space division will be changed. These trends could determine the direction and structure of Shanghai's development [18].

Government's function will be changed. Digital cities' function will be transformed from the administration type to administration-serving type. The government will emphasize the establishment of suitable policies, maximizing the potential of information technology, and coordinating all departments, for example, establishing a policy that promotes the standardization of communication technology, adding direct or indirect investment, providing public channels for users, and so on [25].

5.3 Problems

Digital Shanghai is encountering many of the problems experienced by other digital cities. Experts argued that implementing digital city Shanghai would need a large amount of venture capital, good management talents, and sophisticated technologies.

This is true, but its biggest problem, different from other digital cities, is the 'system problem' [26].

The first serious problem in China is that all companies have to be examined and approved by the governments before they start. In some important business areas, an examination and approval process is used to ensure public confidence. This reasonable, but China is unique in that all companies must be examined. Everybody has the right to manage their own career, but the rules in China effectively transfer this right to the government officials. You cannot decide whether to start a company or not. Even if you get permission, a lot of time and energy is needed to obtain the tens of, or hundreds of seals from different departments of the government. Sometimes, starting a company is harder than running it.

For example, in the USA, registering a company takes only a few minutes if the Internet is used. In Hong Kong, registering a company takes half a day. In Shenzhen, this task takes two weeks. In Shanghai, at least two months is needed. Why such a long time to register a company? It is because of the examination and approval rules. Table 4 is a comparison of registering a corporation in USA, Hong Kong and China.

Table 4. How to Register a Corporation

	USA	Hong Kong SAR	China Mainland
Who can register	Anyone	Anyone	Chinese citizen, one of applicants must be resident of the registering city
Verification of applicants	None	Passport/ID	Passport/ID
Minimum number of owners	1	2	3
Minimum capital	None	HK$ 1	RMB 100,000 – RMB 30,000,000 depending on the nature of the business and type of corporation
Methods of registration	Online	Telephone & mail	In person
Turn-round time	Few days	2 weeks	Several weeks
Restrictions on type of business	None	Little	Very stringent
Restrictions on naming the company	None	None	Many. Must follow vicinity & adjective & nature of business. No "China" is allowed, etc
Restriction on issuing shares	None	More shares higher tax	Very stringent
Feasibility study required	None	None	Required for certain businesses
Other requirements	None	None	Must have a physical office must pay for verifying the capital (RMB 3,000 for a RMB 300,000 company)
Economic development	High	Medium	Low

Digital city Shanghai is an example of city informatization in China. To promote digital cities, or city informatization, the Chinese government should respect everyone's right to manage their own career. If the current examine and approve rule is replaced by a more reasonable registration rule similar to that in the USA, we expect that the GDP of China would increase 30%, and corruption would decrease 50%.

The second serious problem is the legal system. The current Chinese law system is rather ad hoc, which blocks economic development. The biggest problem is that almost any government department can issue "legal interpretations" as means of expressing its "rights" without any limitation. Officials often release strange rules, all of which have serious repercussions. The officials often state that the reasons for the rule is to "protect the national advantage," "standardize the market," etc. but, after deep analysis, it seems that most rules are arbitrary. For example, the Chinese Information & Industry Department states that all network companies must obtain its permission before opening for business. This rule greatly hinders the development of city informatization and digital cities. Chinese informatization cannot be realized unless this legislative right of Information & Industry Dept is abolished. Why is this true? First, knowledge that the government can issue arbitrary rules at any time badly disturbs the people's expectations. Individuals and enterprises make decisions based upon their "expectations". The threat of arbitrary rules makes the investors and consumers hesitate to invest and consume. Current IT investors do not know what the rules are because the Chinese Information & Industry Dept they can change the rules quickly and irregularly. Of course, the market includes some form of uncertainty. The uncertainty in west countries is due to the "state of nature". The uncertainty in China comes from the government, so we call it the "state of government". A foreign businessman said that forecasting the behavior of the Chinese government is harder than forecasting the weather because the government changes its mind so rapidly.

Second, the rules that are issued tend to be rather vague since this reinforces the power of the government departments. Businesses must spend large amounts of time and energy on establishing relations with officials. If there are any problems, they could obtain a helpful ruling.

6 Conclusion

After more than 1500 years of growth, Shanghai is now China's biggest industrial city, the economic and financial center of China. Implementing Digital City Shanghai is an urgent task for ensuring the continued sustainable development of the city and matching the advances in new economies around the world. Shanghai municipal governments proposed to build the local Information Highway in Shanghai in 1994, and formally initialized the InfoPort Shanghai project in 1996. After several years', many systems and applications have been completed to offer innovative services to society. It might be the foundation on which Digital City Shanghai can be designed and implemented as the next step. The broadband network that connects all subsystems and provides a general communication platform for system integration and information exchange in Shanghai was completed in Oct. 1999.

There are five backbone-networks built based on the municipal area network and they represent a service platform for the digital city, namely, Shanghai Internet exchange networks (SHIX), Shanghai Electronic Data Exchange network (SHEDI), Shanghai Community Services network (SHCS), Shanghai Social Security network (SHSS), Shanghai Golden card and POS network (GC & POS). Digital City Shanghai is a large-scale, extendable, distributed system that will cover most aspects of the citizens' daily life.

Even though some design guidelines, system architecture and user interface technologies for Digital City Shanghai have been discussed, new ideas in these aspects must be continuously raised to keep pace with the development of the economy, expansion of the city, and improvements in the quality of people's life. The applications will cover more and more aspects of the economy, environment, city management, education, culture, law, health, entertainments and daily life. The technology used will be developed constantly. The data of those systems will increase explosively. Extendibility, compatibility and common access are essential features of every project in Digital City Shanghai, which may be pursued by different groups and companies.

Some typical projects of Digital City Shanghai have been started in recent years and they are expected to support Shanghai Expo in 2010. These systems, including spatial data infrastructure, city information applications, Shanghai city grid, city logistics information platform, will significantly impact almost every aspect of Shanghai.

From our many years of experience, we found that many hard problems remain to be solved in building digital city Shanghai, one of the hardest is that current regulation system is too complicated and unfair for information industry development. It set obstacles for starting, running, and developing new and small information companies, which will play important roles in building digital city Shanghai. We believe that this situation will improve greatly since China joined the WTO in Dec. 2001.

Acknowledgements

Dept. of Computer Science & Engineering, Shanghai Jiaotong University and Ishida Laboratory, Dept. of Informatics, Kyoto University signed an agreement for long-term cooperation in September 1998. The dispatch of exchange students and researches started in April 1999. This provides a chance to take part in both projects, Digital City Shanghai and Digital City Kyoto.

Many people have and are contributing to the Digital City Shanghai Project in Shanghai Municipal Government, Shanghai Jiaotong University and other organizations. They provided us with new ideas, useful discussions, and first-hand documents and systems.

We'd like to give special thanks to prof. Toru Ishida for his valuable suggestions in writing this paper. He also helped with polishing the sentences in this paper. We also want to thank prof. Peter van den Besselaar for his useful advice and encouragement in revising this paper.

References

1. Diao Wen Kui. Promoting EDI to realize no-paper trade. Shanghai Informatization Office Eds,. Info Port Shanghai Project, SanLian Press, pp.34-46, 1999.
2. Ding Peng, Mao Wei Liang, Rao Ruo Nan, Sheng Huan Ye, Ma Fan Yuan and T. Ishida. Digital City Shanghai: Towards Integrated Information & Services Enviroment. T. Ishida and K. Isbister, Eds., Digital Cities: Technologies, Experiences, and Future Perspectives. LNCS 1765, Springer-Verlag, pp.125-139, 2000.
3. Ding Peng. Research on agent society based interactive planning. Ph.D thesis, 2001.
4. Fan Xi Ping. Establishing Shanghai Infoport, Proceedings of CIARP'00, pp.V-21, 2000.
5. Fu Xiu Feng. WWW based interactive network component developing technology, Computer Engineer and Application, pp.21-22, 1998.
6. Guo Qiang. Thinking of knowledge economy, China Economy Press, 1999.
7. He Shou Chang. Promoting IT application and improve the level of city informatization, Proceedings of CIARP'00, pp. V-17, 2000.
8. T. Ishida, J. Akahani, K. Hiramatsu, K. Isbister, S. Lisowski, H. Nakanishi, M. Okamoto, Y. Miyazaki and K. Tsutsuguchi. Digital City Kyoto: Towards A Social Information Infrastructure. M. Klusch, O. Shehory and G. Weiss, Eds., Cooperative Information Agent III. LNCS 1652, Springer-Verlag, pp. 23-35, 1999.
9. T. Ishida. Understanding Digital Cities, T. Ishida and K. Isbister, Eds., Digital Cities: Technologies, Experiences, and Future Perspectives. LNCS 1765, Springer Verlag, pp7-17, 2000.
10. Li Qi. Digital cities: for 21st century living, Proceedings of CIARP'00, pp.V-4, 2000.
11. Lv Xin Kui. Establishing and developing informatization in China, Chinese Information Report, pp.86-91,1999.
12. Qian Xiao Qing. Establishing Shanghai social security network, Shanghai Informatization Office Ed., Info Port Shanghai Project, SanLian Press, pp.58-70, 1999.
13. Nao Cheng Xing. Shanghai GC & POS system: approaching era of electronic money, Shanghai Informatization Office Ed., Info Port Shanghai Project, SanLian Press, pp.71-85, 1999.
14. Sheng Huan Ye and Ding Peng. Infrastructure, Contents and Services in Digital Cities: Case studies of Info Port Shanghai, T. Ishida Ed., Bit, Kyoritsu Shuppan, Vol.33 No.4, pp.25-27, 2001 (In Japanese).
15. Shi De Rong. Improving the level of community services using information technologies, Proceedings of CIARP'00, pp.V-18, 2000.
16. Wang Xiao Ming. The role of government in city informatization from the viewpoint of system science, Proceedings of CIARP'00, pp.VI-3, 2000.
17. Wen Hai. Enhance the development of information laws, Policy and Law, 6, pp. 25-28, 1998
18. Wu Jia Pei. Network revolution and network economics, Economics Trend, pp. 18-23, 1996.
19. Wu Jia Pei. About information laws and policies, Information World, 4, pp. 6-7, 1998.
20. Wu Jing Wen. City informatization architecture in China, Proceedings of CIARP'00, pp. VI-4, 2000.
21. Xu Ru Jing. New century: Developing services industry, Technology Tide, pp. 76-81, 2000.
22. Yan Xiao Pei. The trend of city development, Foreign City Plan, pp. 75-81, 1998.
23. Yang Jia Wen. Thinking about the change of city architecture in the IT era, 21st Century City Development, pp. 15-18, 1999.
24. You Xian Sheng. Developing strategy of IT industry, Development Research, pp.34-39, 2000.
25. Zhang Yun Qing. The role of government in E-commerce development, Computer and Information, pp. V2-7, 2000.

26. Zhang Wei Ying. Study of system of economy informatization in China, Proceedings of CIARP'00, pp.VI-6, 2000.
27. Wang Gen Xiang. Survey of building Info Port Shanghai project, Shanghai Informatization Office Eds,. Info Port Shanghai Project, SanLian Press, pp.1-10, 1999.
28. Yadong Gui. City Grid & HPC, International Forum on Digital City and City Grid, Shanghai, Nov. 2003.
29. Saeko Nomura, Toru Ishida, Naomi Yamashita, Mika Yasuoka and Kaname Funakoshi. Open Source Software Development with Your Mother Language: Intercultural Collaboration Experiment 2002. International Conference on Human-Computer Interaction (HCI-03), Vol. 4, pp. 1163-1167, 2003.

Activities and Technologies in Digital City Kyoto

Toru Ishida

Department of Social Informatics, Kyoto University
NTT Communication Science Laboratories
ishida@i.kyoto-u.ac.jp

Abstract. We have developed a digital city for Kyoto, the old capital and cultural center of Japan, as a social information infrastructure for urban everyday life including shopping, business, transportation, education, social welfare and so on. The project was initiated by researchers in NTT and Kyoto University in 1998. In 1999, the Digital City Kyoto Experimentation Forum was launched. The forum includes several universities, local authorities, leading computer companies, local newspaper companies, historical temples, as well as photographers, programmers, students, volunteers and so on. Researchers and designers from overseas have also joined the project. One of the salient features of Digital City Kyoto is that computer scientists from universities and companies have continued to play a leading role in the organization. As a result, Digital City Kyoto is based on the newest technologies including GIS, VR, animation and social agents. The *three-layer architecture* for digital cities has been proposed: a) the *information layer* integrates both Web archives and real-time sensory information related to the city, b) the *interface layer* provides two and three dimensional views of the city, and c) the *interaction layer* assists social interaction among people who are living/visiting in/at the city. In this paper, the organization and activities of three year experiments, from 1998 to 2001, named Digital City Kyoto, and the technical/social lessons we have learned are described in detail.

1 Why Digital Cities?

Many of the problems created in the 20th century, such as crowding, environmental pollution, food and energy crises remain to be solved in the 21st century. Effective solutions require the existence of a global consensus mechanism based on the Internet. In addition to negotiation at the national level, cross-border collaboration among countries and communities will form an essential part of the consensus mechanism. Intercultural interactions in daily life equal the importance of formal discussions held at inter-governmental conferences.

The notion of digital cities can be defined as follows: *digital cities will collect and organize the digital information of the corresponding cities, and provide a public information space for people living in and visiting them to interact with each other.* Digital cities have been developed all over the world, and can be connected to each other via the Internet, just as physical cities are connected by surface and air transport systems.

P. van den Besselaar and S. Koizumi (Eds.): Digital Cities 2003, LNCS 3081, pp. 166-187, 2005.
© Springer-Verlag Berlin Heidelberg 2005

Why do regional information spaces attract people given that we are in the era of globalization? We realize that the Internet has fostered global businesses, but at the same time, it enables us to create rich information spaces for everyday life. While the Internet makes businesses global, life is inherently local. Business requires homogeneous settings to allow global and fair competition, while daily life can remain heterogeneous reflecting our different cultural backgrounds. If differences exist in business, standard protocols are needed to overcome them, but we do not need any standard for social interaction. If the differences are significant, we should develop support tools for intercultural communication.

Table 1. Two Extremes in Internet Use

Business	Everyday Life
Global	Local
Market (Competitive)	Community (Collaborative)
Homogeneous	Heterogeneous
Standard Protocol	Intercultural Communication

Table 1 shows two extremes of Internet use. The table does not mean that the two types of usages are always disjoint, various combinations are common in Internet use. The motivation for studying digital cities is to shift our view of Internet use from one side (business) to another (everyday life). Both perspectives should be combined to build a public information space in which people can participate and interact, and to create the consensus needed to tackle the various problems. The rest of this section discusses each of the aspects in Table 1 further to clarify our motivation with regard to digital city research.

1.1 From Global to Local

With the development of the Internet, economies of scale have made business activities more global. Even small companies can participate in the worldwide business network, since the Internet significantly reduces search and negotiation costs to find partners and markets. The Internet makes commercial transactions much easier in most business areas. On the other hand, globalization is not so frequent in everyday life. Although the Internet has widened the information channels available, it cannot physically move people. Statistics show that people still spend their income for housing, shopping dining and so on where they live. Everyday life substantially remains local even though the Internet offers international reach.

Digital cities should support our everyday life. It is natural for people living in a city to create a public information space that corresponds to the physical city. The question is, however, whether or not it represents an efficient usage of the Internet. The Internet is often viewed as a new continent. For example, the Internet yields the possibility of building a virtual mall comprising a huge number of shops that cannot exist in any physical city. The locality of digital cities might constrain the possibilities inherent in the Internet.

To discuss this issue, we examine the interesting example of a shopping street community in Kyoto. The community consists of 3,000 Kyoto shops. They jointly started a site that enables customers to make electronic account settlements by debit and credit cards. Purchasing requests from within or beyond the local community are processed electronically and goods are delivered by logistics companies. As a result, many Kyoto shopping streets now appear on the Internet. Thousands of shops are already offering services under this framework. At first glance, this seems to be just another form of global virtual mall like Yahoo. However, its business model is totally different.

Global virtual malls are often called platform businesses. Providers of the platform offer reliable and trustful sites, and invite suppliers as well as customers. It does not matter whether or not the suppliers have a presence in the physical world. The Kyoto shop alliance, on the other hand, represents real world entities. Credibility has been established through the long history of physical Kyoto. The question is how this local mall can compete with huge existing global virtual malls. The Internet naturally encourages economies of scale and it appears hard for small malls to achieve success because they offer fewer services. It seems that local malls, which are hard to scale up, cannot compete with global malls. This, however, is not the entire story if consumers are interested in the city as a whole, not just buying goods. In this case, a digital city, which creates a whole city in the Internet, can support local malls.

1.2 From Market to Community

According to Webster's Dictionary, the word *community* is defined as "a body of individuals organized into a unit or manifesting usually with awareness some unifying trait." More specifically, Hillery reported that there were at least 94 definitions for this word even in the early 1950s [4]. His summary of the factors of community showed that they include *locality*, *social interaction* and *common ties*. MacIver also pointed out that the concept of community is based on the locality of human life, and is the counter concept of *association*, where people share a common goal [15].

With the advance of global computer networks like the Internet and mobile computing, discussion of the virtual community has become more active. The term *community* is being used as a metaphor for the next stage of computing technologies, including the methodologies, mechanisms and tools for creating, maintaining, and evolving social interaction in human societies. We believe there will be a dramatic shift in computing metaphors: from *teams* and *markets* to *communities*.

We first address how to extend technology called *groupware* (designed for team work) to *communityware* for community support. In the 1980's, research on groupware was triggered by the advance of local area networks. Though there is no specific definition of the term *group*, previous research into groupware mainly addressed the collaborative work of already-organized people. Various tools have been developed for communication among users in different places. A typical example is where project members in the same company synchronously/ asynchronously work using workstations connected by local area networks.

The word *communityware* has been created for more diverse and amorphous groups of people [7,8]. The metaphor of community has become important given the advance of global computer networks such as the Internet and mobile computing. The goal of communityware is to support the process of organizing people who are willing to share knowledge and experience. In other words, compared to groupware studies, communityware focus on an earlier stage of collaboration: group formation from a wide variety of people.

Table 2. Teams, Communities and Markets

	Teams	Communities	Markets
Network	LAN	Internet	Internet
Agent number	10^1-10^3	10^2-10^4	10^3-10^5
Organization	Closed Collaborative	Open Collaborative	Open Competitive
Computational Model	Cooperative Problem Solving	NA	Market-based Computing
Example Application	Groupware Work Flow	Community Network Digital City	Network Auction

Every community has rules that can be represented logically. The rules may specify how to elect leaders, make decisions, to collect monthly fees, and so on. Groupware technologies can provide tools for supporting these formal procedures. In the case of communities, however, people require more than logical support. For communities, it is essential for members to share feelings such as *we-feeling, role-feeling,* and *dependency-feeling* [15]. The obvious question is whether community feelings can be established and maintained within a virtual space like digital cities. The challenge is to enrich the human community in physical cities through the use of digital cities. Therefore, communityware should become a key technology for digital cities.

While the Internet has created worldwide competitive markets, daily life is more collaborative. A concept that counters the global market is the local community. Compared to the computational study of markets, however, studies on communities are still immature. Given that the team and market metaphors have created research fields like groupware and network auctions, however, it is quite possible that the community metaphor will generate new fields in both research and practice. Table 2 compares the three different metaphors.

1.3 From Homogeneous to Heterogeneous

When we search for "digital cities" in the US, we find many instances created by America Online (AOL). AOL provides locally focused online network services for several hundred cities and the number is still growing. Each AOL digital city collects tourist and shopping information of the corresponding city. Besides those information services, AOL provides local advertising opportunities for vertical markets including auto, real estate, employment and health. The AOL digital cities form the largest and most popular local information service in the US. The success of AOL digital cities shows that people need regional information services for their everyday life.

The feature of AOL digital cities is that, as with other commercial portals, the efficiency of site creation is paramount since it is aimed at business. As a result, the hundreds of AOL digital cities have almost the same face. Though the information sources are different, the tools they use are standard and the way of organizing information is homogeneous. It is inevitable that commercial sites will be constructed in such a way, since even if hundreds of physical cities were to be built, the same tools and design methodologies would be employed by the same company.

European digital cities represent a more bottom-up approach. The organization named TeleCities promotes information and technology sharing in Europe. Each city develops its digital equivalent following its own direction. Consequently, digital cities in Europe have different faces [17]. Similarly, Digital City Kyoto has a unique organizational structure because of the historical background of physical Kyoto. Cost efficiency should not the main goal for creating this digital city. What we look for is not the efficiency of accumulating information but the differentiation of public information spaces to reflect the cultural backgrounds of Kyoto.

1.4 From Standard Protocol to Intercultural Communication

There are two reasons for discussing intercultural communication in the context of digital cities. The first is that, in any city in the world, the citizens are becoming more diverse. A public information space can play a major part in bridging the cultures. The second reason is that a digital city will represent a real city on the Internet. We have 40 million visitor-day annually in Kyoto, but we expect more people will visit Kyoto via the Internet. Therefore, intercultural communication must be supported, even though the main purpose of digital cities is to support the everyday life of local residents. A local information space and a platform for intercultural communication are two sides of the same coin.

Kraut reported that the Internet impacts both cosmopolitanism and domestication. In the HomeNet project [12], he observed that the number of long distance e-mails increased as people became more familiar with the Internet. At the same time, the Internet strengthens family ties: e-mails are also used as a communication tool within the family. Digital cities will have the same effect. A site with local everyday life eventually becomes a nexus linking residents to visitors from overseas.

We should be aware that the ratio of English Web pages worldwide has been decreasing rapidly. As the Internet will be applied to everyday life more and more, the ratio of English Web pages will keep on decreasing. It is obvious that the need for intercultural communication will increase significantly. Without linguistic and cultural support tools, it is not possible for people to create productive interaction. The latest machine translation technologies can increase the opportunity to participate in intercultural communication.

2 Activities in Digital City Kyoto

2.1 Design Policy

There are several policy options in building a digital city. Kyoto was the capital of Japan for more than a thousand years, and has been the cultural center of Japan for even longer. To begin a digital city project for Kyoto, we started with its design policies.

The first option is to select either a top down (centralized design) or bottom up (self organizing) approach to build the digital city. As mentioned earlier, city portal services provided by companies apply the same tools and systems to different cities mainly to maximize cost efficiency. Though the information accumulated differs, all commercial digital cities have a homogeneous structure. On the other hand, the US community networks and most European digital cities are heterogeneous, having different architectures and interfaces [17].

We tried to respect the long history of Kyoto when building Digital City Kyoto. We did not specify tools for its creation. We allowed our colleagues to use any technology, any software and any content. We tried to build a public information space from the bottom up. The unique aspects of Kyoto, which were not noticed at the beginning of the project but discovered through building Digital City Kyoto, include historical and cultural accumulation, closed and self-reliant communities, and plenty of rich personal Web pages. A single Web building package is not enough to describe all of the aspects of Kyoto.

The second option is how closely the physical and digital cities should correspond. We adopted the policy of making Digital City Kyoto *real* by establishing a strong connection to physical Kyoto. Unlike GeoCities, our digital city is not an imaginary city existing only in cyberspace. Instead, our digital city complements the corresponding physical city, and provides an information center for everyday life for actual urban communities. Digital activities will become an essential part of the real city in the near future. We think "digital" and "physical" make things "real." We are thus working on a digital version of the real city.

How strongly are other digital cities connected their physical origins? Helsinki [13,14] was planning to build a high-speed metropolitan network. Under this plan, to fully utilize the new network, the digital city must be tightly connected to the physical Helsinki. This is why the 3D virtual city is the core of the project. Amsterdam seems quite different [2,3]. This digital city is not directly connected to physical Amsterdam. The inhabitants of large metropolitan areas, like Amsterdam, mostly come from other cities. Their interests are not necessarily focused on Amsterdam. Though Digital City Amsterdam succeeded in introducing a city metaphor into regional information services, since there is no direct mapping between digital and physical Amsterdam, the ratio of Amsterdam-based digital citizens decreased from 45% in 1994 to 22% in 1998.

This fact highlights the design issue of how much reality we should put into digital cities. If we make digital cities without strong connections to the corresponding physical cities, the connection may gradually disappear. The Amsterdam organizers thought of this as a good sign. This is probably because of the size of the country and a role of the city in the country. In the Netherlands, there are 14 million people living in a small area. Amsterdam is the capital and 1.5 million people live in the greater Amsterdam area. The political power of Amsterdam makes it possible for the digital city to keep centripetal force beyond the physical boarder of the city. There exists a reason why the project welcomed the growth of the digital city beyond its boarder.

In the case of Digital City Kyoto, since its goal is to create a social information infrastructure for Kyoto, we set very strong links between the digital and physical cities. As the level of real-time sensory data continues to be increased, the linkage becomes strengthened even further. There is no reason to restrict communication within the city. However, when we started the project, only 10% or so of the population in Japan were Internet users, and most were young "office workers familiar with technology." Accordingly, the Internet has had a very limited influence on daily life. Due on this fact, the goal of the digital city project (to create a social information infrastructure of Kyoto) may become vague without the strong connection. While Amsterdam is the capital of Netherlands, Kyoto is not. Netherlands can be the border of Digital City Amsterdam, but Japan is probably too large to act as the border for Digital City Kyoto. The strong connection between digital and physical Kyoto was designed by assessing the Amsterdam experience.

The third option is the communication media used. It is well known that selecting media influences not only communication bandwidth but also the semantics of messages. It has been only ten years since the Internet began to influence the world. We are just beginning to see the impact of Internet use on everyday life. The current Internet technology can efficiently handle logical information like research and business documents. However, the information necessary for everyday life is more informal. While Web mainly provides texts and pictures, peer-to-peer communication with videos or sounds will soon be feasible. The issue is to select the appropriate media for services in digital cities. Though new technologies are not always useful for current services, we believe it is worth trying them for new services. Since many research organizations are gathered in Kyoto, e.g. Kyoto University, NTT Communication Science Laboratories, ATR, CRL (NICT fron 2004) etc., we decided to pursue new technologies for designing our digital city.

As a summary, the design policy of Digital City Kyoto is to create a public information space in a bottom up fashion, to directly connect it to the physical Kyoto, and to develop it around the latest technology.

2.2 Services

Figures 1(a)(b) show screen shots of the top page of the Digital City Kyoto prototype. They were designed by Ben Benjamin, a graphics designer in Los Angeles. Four-season shots overlay the Daimonnji (mountain) in a GIF animation. Benjamin joined this project during a one-year stay in Kyoto. He also designed a link list that is static but offers simple and impressive color combinations. Japanese, English (Figure 7.1(c)), and Chinese link lists are available from the top page. The Chinese link list was created by Chinese students in Kyoto triggered by a call from Jouin Teramae, the chief priest of Kodaiji (temple). Like the English page, the link list is the only page that is translated into Chinese, and almost all linked pages are written in Japanese. Though an active discussion was held on translating every Japanese page into English or Chinese, it did not work because of open issues such as a copyright policy and the responsibility for mistranslations. Services provided are divided into four categories, "Information," "Community," "Showroom" and "Laboratory." This classification is quite different from those of other digital cities and community networks. However, this is the result of dividing the services of Digital City Kyoto into groups of about the same size. The four classes show the current Internet activities in Kyoto. In particular, "Showroom" and "Laboratory" reflect Kyoto's features, where many cultural heritages and advanced research institutes coexist. The number of services totals 34.

The site also provides links to world digital cities and statistical data on service access frequency.

"Information" is linked to service sites, and contains dedicated regional information sites such as Kyoto Shinbun (newspaper), and Kyoto Municipal Transportation Bureau. Kaoru Hiramatsu devoted himself to setting links to public spaces in the map. This system is called GeoLink [5]. There are more than 5000 linked pages of restaurants, shops, schools, sightseeing spots, shrines, temples, etc. It does not include private Web pages. GeoLink has become the most popular site among the services accessed through the top page. We obtained the permission of all site authors for linking, because it was not clear whether or not a third party could legally link those sites to the map and open them to the public. Most of the sites agreed, however, some of them (for example, kindergarten sites) declined to be linked to the map. Some site authors had a hard time deciding whether they should agree or not. It was not clear for people what would be the impact of linking their sites.

(a)   Top Page for Summer   (b) Top Page for Winter   (c) Link List in English

Fig. 1. Top Page of Digital City Kyoto

"Community" is a category for interaction among participants. Ben Benjamin and Shoko Toda developed a site (Figure 2(b)) for vegetarian visitors from overseas. This site became a precious source of information and a place for interaction because there are not many vegetarians in Kyoto. In the category of "Community," there is a page that cannot be seen in other digital cities. Koichi Yamada and Satoshi Oyama, one of the volunteers who participated in the Experiment Forum, gathered personal Web pages provided by residents of Kyoto, and established the site called PersonalPages. The page was designed by Taeko Ariga (Figure 2(a)). Each personal site offers remarkably high quality and plentiful information. The number of sites exceeds 25. Every individual site shows the creators' enthusiasm and attachment to Kyoto.

A story of the birth of this site is as follows. One day, I was seated in a taxi going to Kyoto University. The conversation with the taxi driver became lively over a 15 minute period and occasionally we talked about the Internet. The driver told me that he was maintaining his own site as a sightseeing guide. He spent two to three hours per day updating his site, and carefully answering questions from students planning school trips to Kyoto. I explained to him our activities on Digital City Kyoto and got off the taxi. When I accessed his site from my laboratory, I was amazed. "All about Kyoto (Kiwameru-Kyo)" provides plenty of information together with the atmosphere of the ancient capital as it changed from season to season. Even the municipal tourist section does not offer the same atmosphere. It seems that only a volunteer who loves his city and who directly contacts people in the city can create such a site.

(a) Personal Pages   (b) Vegetarian Restaurant

Fig. 2. Volunteer Sites in the Category "Community"

"Showroom" is a category peculiar to Kyoto. Cultural heritages are being accumulated electronically through the leadership of Koichi Shimizu, Kyoto Digital Archive Initiative. Many archives such as designs of Nishijin (cloth) and digitized cultural assets are linked.

"Laboratory" shows the technological advances of Digital City Kyoto. Interesting but not yet practical systems are displayed. "3D Kyoto" is a system that is attracting the greatest attention. Stefan Lisowski, the primary developer of 3D Kyoto, came from San Francisco to stay in Kyoto for one year to work with this project. We developed a 1.6km long modern shopping street and historical Nijo Castle in the 3D virtual space. At the same time, we started discussing various problems with the shopping street community: since we are using photos, information in the photos becomes old; the advertisements in the photos quickly become out-of-date. We also received shopkeepers' requests such as: the photos of their shops were not bright enough; they want the photos to change; and they wanted us to take another photo. Furthermore, some photos had a potential legal problem about registered trademarks. It is important for engineers, researchers and shop owners to start thinking of these issues. It seems to be necessary to develop tools that can support people in the participatory design process. One solution we are working to implement is a Web and FTP interface to allow individual shopkeepers to update the advertisement photos on their 3D buildings by themselves.

The virtual space building tool "3DML" was adopted for this project. Since 3DML is easy to use, college students in Kyoto have started to join us in cooperatively developing the 3D Kyoto. Students of Kyoto Computer Gakuin (school) recreated the area around their buildings using 3DML. This movement has spread to schools like Kansai University and Makino High School in Osaka. This follows the "bazaar approach" to software development. We hope that having contributors from all over Kyoto will keep the project from becoming a small handful of stagnant areas, and make this a vast and dynamic city.

Besides 3D Kyoto, links are available to systems developed by universities or corporation researchers, such as a digital bus tour. We believe that digital cities will be forever changing the technologies used; a dynamic living space cannot be founded on static technology. The name "Laboratory" contributes to establishing a more dynamic view. This category is also important in strengthening the users' image of the future digital city and directing their attention to the future.

2.3 Organization

Digital City Kyoto was established in October 1998. The project is an initiative sponsored by NTT and housed in the new NTT Open Laboratory [1]. The aims of the project are to create next-generation systems for digital communities and to explore basic research issues. The project consists primarily of researchers from NTT and Kyoto University, but also includes a wide variety of people from other organizations. The project has a cross-cultural research team: it includes a social scientist, computer scientists, programmers and designers from U.S. and staff from Japanese industries and universities.

NTT pursued the possibility of cooperating with outside organizations in a social information study, and so invited a research project leader to organize an open laboratory. At the same time, Kyoto University launched a department of social informatics to pursue the inter-disciplinary study in computer science for human society. The reason why a telecommunication enterprise NTT supported empirical study is not same to the Helsinki situation. The open laboratory was set up within the enterprise sections but in basic research laboratories. NTT is trying to open up a new application field together with researchers of outside organizations to find future research issues.

The challenge from NTT was attractive enough for university researchers to take it up. Activities of Digital City Kyoto started in the open laboratory in consultation with Fumio Hattori, the director of NTT Laboratories. The project has conducted fieldwork on digital cities in cooperation with the city government and shopping street communities. The open lab produced all sorts of prototypes over an eighteen-month period: A map-based Web search system, a three dimensional virtual Kyoto, a city guide by the social agent, and so on. The result was as if an accumulation of computer science technologies met a different field of study and unexpected needs, and energy was generated without restraint.

The key to the success of the open laboratory was that NTT did not stick to the established approaches to computer science, but tried to promote research without restraint. GeoLink, described later, and 3D Kyoto are outcomes of this policy, and it is more suitable to call the project an initiative than a study. In GeoLink, public Web sites are linked to the map, and photos of each building on the Shijo (shopping street) were taken to build 3D Kyoto. This came as a surprise since there was no research schedule or proposal describing this activity when this initiative started. Since the initiative was carried out by basic researchers, the research topics were discovered while 'doing it', the research papers were published afterwards. The open laboratory's norm was "move then think."

The problem of the open laboratory was that ownership of the research results was not well thought through. Once Digital City Kyoto was appeared in newspapers and TV, NTT made use of it in various advertisements. The number of press reports exceeded 20. The extensive coverage, most of which used expressions like 'NTT Digital City Kyoto', raised a paradox in digital city studies. At that time, project members finally realized that there was a dualism about the word "open." For researchers, NTT was offering an open study place for society. For NTT, however, the place was intended to attract the knowledge and energy of researchers outside the company.

The experiences from the open laboratory show the importance of contacting people in the city. For example, the permission of residents is required to link their Web pages from Digital City Kyoto. Legal problems such as handling trademarks could not be resolved by the research group. To increase the level of interaction among researchers, local authorities, people and communities in Kyoto, an open meeting was held at Kyoto University in September 1999. Subsequently, Digital City Kyoto Experiment Forum started activities in October 1999. The period was set to two years on the basis of the open laboratory experience. It was risky to set a longer period in such a rapidly changing field.

At the same time, the Digital Archives Initiative was established in Kyoto to accumulate cultural heritages. Moreover, Kyoto Shinbun (newspaper) started work on Web news. As a result, the Forum gathered over 100 members from more than 30 organizations, who joined on a personal basis: local authorities such as Kyoto prefecture, Kyoto city, fire stations, transportation departments, local town paper, companies such as NTT and NEC, researchers, photographers, resident, priests and volunteers came together. Although the Forum is a collection of individuals, many participants can represent their organizations. Unlike the situation in Europe and the United States, the border between individual and organizational activities is not so rigid in Japan. Companies (participants' bosses) are also conscious of two aims, profit seeking and contributing to society. What the gathered people have in common is a desire for an attractive public information space for Kyoto.

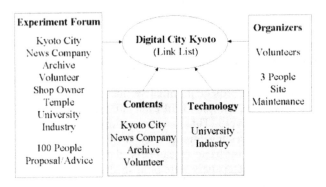

Fig. 3. Organization of Digital City Kyoto Experiment Forum

Site management of Digital City Kyoto moved from the open laboratory to the Experiment Forum at this point. A site created by the Forum was named the "Digital City Kyoto Prototype." The term "prototype" was used to make room for the real Digital City Kyoto, which is hoped to emerge after the experiments, and to achieve the freedom needed to challenge various issues. Figure 3 shows the organizational structure of the Forum. Digital City Kyoto Prototype was essentially a link list consisting of various regional information sites and individual sites. It was not a full-fledged information service site like AOL. There was no permanent staff for information services. The site was maintained by three volunteers who renewed the link list as needed. The policy of linking was simple: "link all interesting trials." When receiving a request for linking, the three volunteers consulted the Forum on the renewed link list. If there was no problem, the new list was released to the public within a few days. The Experiment Forum closed in September 2001 after completion of the two-year period.

2.4 Use and Users

The top page (Japanese) of Digital City Kyoto Prototype was accessed more than 170,000 times in two years. There were more accesses to the link list than the top page. Moreover, the total number of accesses to the linked sites far exceeds those of the link lists. The reason for this is that the linked sites are directly bookmarked by users and search engines. Access to the English link list was about 7% of the total, while access to the Chinese link list was about 2%.

Contents that used new technologies such as Geolink and 3D Kyoto won high ranking in terms of access frequency. Another tendency noted was that real time information such as headline news of Kyoto Shinbun (newspaper company) and Web cameras at Kyoto Gozan (hills) and City Hall were often accessed. Community oriented contents such as Personal Pages and Kyoto Fun Guide were also accessed frequently. According to a time-based observation of access frequency, access number strongly increased right after a press release, but then returned its average value. At the beginning of the Digital City Kyoto Prototype, 3D Kyoto saw more accesses than Geolink, however, they traded places afterward. Given the current bandwidths available, Internet users in Kyoto have difficulty in using 3D. Although many people accessed it once, not many came back. There was no killer application that made a convincing argument for the 3D interface.

Our survey shows that 69% of users accessing to Digital City Kyoto are from the *jp* (Japan) domain, followed by domains such as *com* and *net*. In the *jp* domain, *ne.jp* was the most common. This means that most users were accessing via commercial providers. We checked the accesses to Chinese and English top pages to investigate the distribution of access by languages. It is found that *tw* (Taiwan) was the main user of Chinese pages, while the English page was accessed by *de* (Germany), *uk* (England), *ca* (Canada), and *au* (Australia).

It is also interesting to know how people access information using a map. According to the access log, *search by address or location*, such as specifying street numbers or station names, accounted for 33.7%, *search by organization*, such as schools or companies, accounted for 24.2%, *search by building* accounted for 11.7%. In total, *search by physical objects* accounted for 69.6% of all accesses. Search by other expressions, e.g. general terms such as "hotel" or "noodle," accounted for 30.4%. There is a clear tendency to use names of physical objects in the city, when using a map interface. It appears that the search behaviors seen in digital cities closely match those in physical cities.

2.5 Lessons Learned

The excitement we experienced over the three years far outstripped our initial expectations. 3D virtual Kyoto has revitalized the local shopping street community. Shijo is the main shopping street in Kyoto, and many stores have histories stretching back hundreds of years. It became the first street in Japan to offer an Internet café, the first street to use the debit card, and the first street to have ISDN lines installed in every shop for Internet connection. The community created a committee called the *informatization initiative*. The members of this committee deeply understand computers and networks. The day we visited the Shijo community with the first prototype of 3D Shijo was unforgettable. The 3D virtual Shijo was supported right away by the committee members. They quickly got permission for building the 3D virtual Shijo from the community. In the century-old community, elderly people never fought against proposals from young reformers saying "Stop, because I don't understand." Instead, they gave encouragement saying "Get on with it, because I don't understand." In a few days, we got their approval, and in a few weeks, the project was introduced to ten other shopping street communities in Kyoto. Requests for another 3D virtual street came from the neighboring community called Gion. It appears that traditional groups contain far more energy for innovation that could be predicted.

In the Experiment Forum, a meeting was held once every few months in which 30 to 50 participants discussed a wide range of topics. The idea of the Digital City Kyoto prototype was widely accepted. The prototype was created in the Forum by a combination of local authorities, companies, universities, and volunteers. Risky but innovative ideas were created in the Forum, some of which were stimulated by the use of the term "experimentation." Photos of shopping streets were published in 3D Kyoto without permission. Translation projects were planned in detail before resolving the problem of infringement of intellectual property. It turns out that the Forum was extremely useful in promoting new challenges to social problems, and developing understanding gradually in an open community.

Though the Forum attracted a variety of people in Kyoto, the organizational goals of the Forum were vague. The motivations of the participants varied. Many people were interested in the movement and activities in the Forum, but only a few people took initiative. The Forum tried to have its own projects, each of which involved more than two organizations. However, most of these projects ended in failure. The successful projects were created by small groups of confident people, not by large groups created from discussions within the Forum. We experienced two extremes, enthusiasm and stagnation, at the same time. Compared to the participants' expectations, the organizational power of the Forum was very poor.

The greatest success achieved by the Forum was PersonalPages. Our eyes were opened by the many individuals who created rich and personal Web sites. Many qualified volunteers have been playing an active but quiet role in the Internet. PersonalPages succeeded in making those volunteer sites stand out.

To develop a fully-fledged Digital City Kyoto, it was necessary to slim down the Forum to speed up its decision-making process and empower the working groups to create new contents daily. However, it appeared that there are several difficulties hindering Digital City Kyoto. The city municipal government does not like the idea of being involved in a local portal business. They believe the role of authorities is to be restricted to provide basic infrastructures for information services. NTT is worried about the competition between digital cities and its own portals. Although the shopping street communities and newspaper publishers are cooperative, they think they cannot become a primary player. Volunteers and universities are not qualified to manage digital cities. The key to making Digital City Kyoto a success seems whether or not different organizations with different goals can see the common benefits of creating a digital version of Kyoto.

3 Technologies in Digital City Kyoto

3.1 Three-Layer Architecture

To design Digital City Kyoto, we started with a discussion of its system architecture. We proposed the three-layer model illustrated in Figure 4 [7].

1. The first layer, called the *information layer,* integrates and reorganizes Web archives and realtime sensory data using the city metaphor. A geographical database was used to integrate different types of information. We created a tool for viewing and reorganizing digital activities created by people in the city.
2. The second layer, called the *interface layer,* uses 2D maps and 3D virtual spaces to provide intuitive views of digital cities. The animation of moving objects such as avatars, agents, cars, buses, trains, and helicopters demonstrate some of the dynamic activities in the cities. If an animation reflects a real activity, the moving object can become an interesting tool for social interaction: users may want to click on the object to communicate with it.

3. The third layer, called the *interaction layer,* is where residents and tourists interact with each other. Communityware technologies are applied to encourage interactions in digital cities.

The above three-layer architecture is very effective in integrating various technologies. Only a small guideline was required to determine where each technology should be positioned. Some of the technologies developed in Digital City Kyoto are introduced below.

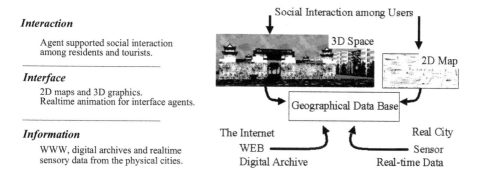

Interaction

Agent supported social interaction among residents and tourists.

Interface

2D maps and 3D graphics. Realtime animation for interface agents.

Information

WWW, digital archives and realtime sensory data from the physical cities.

Fig. 4. Three-layer Architecture for Digital City Kyoto

3.2 Information Layer

Let us start with the first layer, the *information layer*. Operations on current Web sites mainly involve text: users search information by keywords and software robots retrieve information. This search-and-retrieve metaphor works well, especially if the needed information is distributed worldwide. If the Internet is to be used for everyday life, however, the geographic interface will become more important. As shown in Figure 4, the core of our digital city is GIS. The geographic database connects 2D/3D interfaces to Web/sensor-sourced information. From the viewpoint of system architecture, introducing the geographic database allows us to test various interface/ information technologies independently.

GeoLink currently holds 5400 pages that we collected on public spaces including restaurants, shopping centers, hospitals, temples, schools and bus stops. Figure 5 (a) shows the results of locating pages on the map. We can see how Web pages (restaurants, schools, temples, shopping centers, etc.) are distributed throughout the city. After digital cities become popular, people will directly register their pages in geographic databases, but until then, we need some technology to automatically determine the X-Y coordinates of each Web page. Kyoto is, however 1200 years old, and there are various ways to express the same address; this makes the process very complicated.

GeoLink uses a new data model called *augmented WEB space.* As shown in Figure 5 (b), the augmented Web space is composed of conventional hyper links and *geographical links.* A typical example of a geographical generic link is "within 100 meters." The link is called *generic*, because it is created according to each query issued by users. Suppose the query "restaurants within 100 meters from the bus stop" is posed. The links are virtually created from a Web page for the bus stop to those of restaurants located within 100 meters. Efficient query processing methods for the augmented Web space have been developed.

Real-time sensory information includes bus schedules, traffic status, weather condition, and live video from the fire department. In Kyoto, more than three hundred sensors have already been installed and they are gathering the traffic data of more than six hundred city buses. Each bus sends its location and route data every few minutes. Such dynamic information really makes our digital city live. The first trial collects real-time bus data and displays them on the digital city.

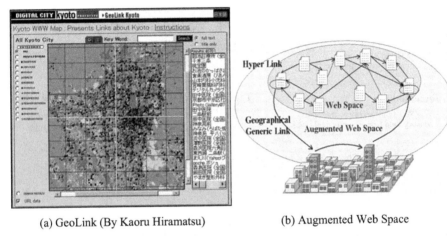

(a) GeoLink (By Kaoru Hiramatsu)   (b) Augmented Web Space

Fig. 5. GIS to Integrate Information

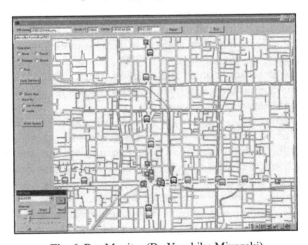

Fig. 6. Bus Monitor (By Yasuhiko Miyazaki)

Figure 6 shows a bus monitor developed by NTT Cyber Solutions Laboratories. Buses in the city run on the Web in the same manner as in the physical city. Real-time city information is more important for people who are acting in the physical city than for those who are sitting in front of desktop computers. For example, people would like to know when the next bus is coming, where the nearest vacant parking lot is, whether they can reserve a table at a restaurant, and what is on sale at the department store close to them. We can provide live information to mobile users through wireless phones.

3.3 Interface Layer

An enormous amount of information can be accessed through the Internet. Humans have never before experienced any similar expansion in terms of scale and speed. People's various activities are being recorded in the semi-structured database called the Web over time. Consequently, it might be possible to visualize human activities and social interaction, which cannot be directly measured, by investigating the information collecting on the Internet.

In GeoLink, the latitude and longitude of a shop are determined from its Web page address and a link is placed on the map accordingly. As information in the Internet increases, downtown areas will be gradually visualized on the map. We can "feel" the activities in the town from the map showing restaurants, schools, hospitals, etc. Observing this map over several years will enable us to understand the growth of the town. It is important that this observation can be carried out by anyone. A map of a digital city is not just a database to measure distances or to check addresses. A map will become a new interface that helps us understand the activities of the city.

Similarly, the three dimensional (3D) graphic technology will become a key component of the *interface layer*, when used in parallel with 2D maps. Providing 3D views of a digital city allows non-residents to get a good feel for what the city looks like, and to plan actual tours. Residents of the city can use the 3D interface to pinpoint places or stores they would like to visit, and to test walking routes. Fig. 7(b) shows a 3D implementation of Shijo Shopping Street (Kyoto's most popular shopping street).

(a) Sample View of 3D Kyoto   (b) 3D Shopping Street with GeoLink

Fig. 7. 3D Kyoto (By Stefan Lisowski)

We use 3DML (http://www.flatland.com), which is not well suited to reproducing gardens and grounds, but has no problem with modern rectilinear buildings. 3DML was originally used to make it easy to construct games. We applied this tool to the development of 3D cities, since it makes us easy to build a town. A 3DML city can be basically understood as a city made of building blocks. For a start, we use a digital camera to take photos of the city. Some correction is needed in Photoshop, since it is inevitable that the upper parts of buildings appear smaller due to perspective. The next step is to pile blocks up to create the buildings and paste the appropriate photos. Although this requires patience, technical knowledge of virtual reality is not necessary. However, we cannot expect a precise 3D space like those produced by virtual reality professionals; it is more a tool for non-professionals.

Fig. 8. Kobe City after the 1995 Earthquake (By Stefan Lisowski)

Figure 8 shows a reproduction of Kobe right after the earthquake in 1995 created using existing photos. This work was requested by the Kyoto University Disaster Prevention Research Institute, which houses 15,000 photos taken of the Kobe area. The organization tried to display the photos on the Web, but the result was not easy to look through. By rearranging the photos in a 3D space, the data could be used in various ways. It was not easy to reproduce buildings from the photos, but we were able to reproduce one part of the city. In performing this, we realized that reproducing a 3D virtual city from photos or videos is an attractive approach. We currently have two approaches to building a 3D space: modeling it with CAD and reproducing it from photos or videos. 3DML can be seen as a tool that combines the two approaches while giving us the pleasure of personal creation.

3.4 Interaction Layer

Social interaction is an important goal in digital cities. Even if we build a beautiful 3D virtual space, if no one lives in the city, the city cannot be very attractive. We plan to use cutting-edge technologies to encourage social interaction in Digital City Kyoto. Katherine Isbister, a social psychologist from Stanford University, hit on an interesting idea. To encourage intercultural interaction in digital cities, she implemented a digital bus tour for foreign visitors. The tour will be an entry point for foreigners to the digital city, as well as to Kyoto itself. The tour has been implemented within the Web environment using I-Chat and Microsoft's agent technology (see Figure 9). The tour guide agent will lead the visitors, who can interact in many ways, through the Nijo Castle in Kyoto simulated using 3DML.

Kyoto city, as the owner of Nijo castle, allowed us to take photos of the inside of the castle. The 3DML world created from those photos is so beautiful that nobody would believe the work was done by non-professional photographers. To prepare for creating the tour guide agent, Isbister participated in several guided tours of Kyoto. She noticed that the tour guides often told stories to supplement the rich visual environment of Kyoto and provided explanations of what Japanese people, both past and present, did in each place [6].

This system includes two new ideas. One is a service that integrates information search and social interaction. Unlike Web searches, which are solitary tasks, the digital bus tour creates an opportunity for strangers to meet. Another is to embody social agents that perform tasks for more than one person. Unfortunately, this agent cannot understand the contents of conversations at this stage. After this experience, however, we have developed a virtual city platform FreeWalk [18,19] and a scenario description language Q [10]. In the near future, agents will participate in the conversation of tourists on the bus and become famous as bus guides in the Internet world. Guide agents will stimulate various ideas about future digital cities.

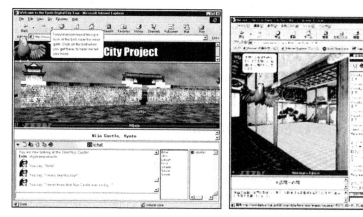

Fig. 9. Digital Bus Tour with Agent Guide (By Katherine Isbister)

3.5 Lessons Learned

We have learned important technologies for digital cities and future research directions from the experience of Digital City Kyoto.

1. *Technology for information integration* is essential to accumulate and reorganize urban information. Digital cities typically handle Web information and real-time sensor-based data from physical cities. Voluminous high quality digital archives can also be accessed through digital cities. The idea of "using a map" is commonly observed in digital cities. In this case, technologies are needed to integrate different kinds of urban information via geographical information systems (GIS). It is also necessary to introduce a technology to handle photos and videos of the city so as to

understand its activities. Great numbers of sensors embedded in the city will collect visual information automatically. These infrastructures will make 'sending and receiving information' in everyday life much easier.

2. *Technology for public participation* is unique to digital cities. To allow various individuals and organizations to participate in building digital cities, the entire system should be flexible and adaptive. For designing a human interface that supports content creation and social interaction, a new technology is required that encourages people with different backgrounds to join in. *Social agents* can be a key to encouraging people to participate in the development and life of digital cities. So far, most digital cities adopt the direct manipulation approach to realize friendly human-computer interactions. Social agents are used to support human-human interaction. The direct manipulation approach allows users to explicitly operate information objects. Since social agents (human-like dog-like, bird-like and whatever) will have the ability to communicate with humans in natural languages; users can enjoy interacting with the agents and access information without explicit operation. This allows a digital city to keep its human interface simple and independent of the volume of stored information [14].

3. *Technology for information security* becomes more important as more people connect to the digital city. For example, it is not always appropriate to make links from digital cities to individual homepages. We found that several kindergartens declined our request to link them to the digital city. This differs from the security problem often discussed for business applications, where cryptography, authentication and fire-walls are major technologies. Just as we have social laws in physical cities such as peeping-tom laws, digital cities should introduce social guidelines that provide the security people need to feel comfortable about joining the information space.

4 Collaboration with Other Digital Cities

The concept of digital cities is to build an arena in which people in regional communities can interact and share knowledge, experience, and mutual interests [11]. Digital cities integrate urban information (both achievable and real-time) and create public spaces in the Internet for people living/visiting in/at the cities. Each digital city has its own goal. Digital City Amsterdam [2, 3] is intended to provide a public communication space to people living in the city. Helsinki [13, 14] plans the next generation metropolitan network. In Kyoto, various new technologies are being developed for a social information infrastructure. Urban planning in which community members can directly participate in the design process is another motivation behind digital cities.

Unlike the conventional telephone network, there is no centralized control mechanism in the Internet. Even the power of governments cannot stop the flow of information. Anyone such as a politician, scholar, businessperson and student has equal access to the enormous store of information. Instead of huge hierarchical organizations, a knowledge network of small organizations or individuals covers the world. Unlike conventional mass media, the Internet allows us to directly contact thousands of vivid instances. While mass media filters collected information, refines and edits them, the Internet is a huge depository; it simply accumulates original instances. For example, children who want to be music conductors can find plenty of information not only about famous conductors but also about other children in foreign countries with the same dreams.

To gain a better understanding of the big picture of digital cities on the Internet, we held international meetings on digital cities in 1999, 2001, and 2003. We invited people and papers representing their activities from cities including Amsterdam, Antwerp, Bristol, Helsinki, Seattle, Shanghai, Oulu, Turin and Vienna. We learned that each digital city has developed or is developing an information space that reflects its own cultural background. Since it is not realistic to standardize those activities, collaboration among digital cities becomes interesting. For example, a tool to traverse related cities is useful. Machine translation and conversational agents will be a great help in traversing digital cities. With such tools, cities that are geographically remote and that have different cultures will be brought closer together.

During this project, we found that digital cities have many directions including tourism, commerce, transportation, urban planning, social welfare, health control, education, disaster management, and politics. Digital cities attract people because different types of expertise contribute to building a richer city, and provide people with opportunities to create a new public space for their everyday life.

Acknowledgements

This work would not have been possible without the contributions of a great many people. The author wishes to thank Jun-ichi Akahani, Taeko Ariga, Shinji Awa, Ben Benjamin, Fumio Hattori, Tamotsu Hizume, Kaoru Hiramatsu, Katherine Isbister, Hiroshi Ishiguro, Kenji Ishikawa, Kenji Kobayashi, Kanako Koide, Satoshi Koizumi, Yoko Kubota, Stefan Lisowski, Yasuhiko Miyazaki, Ichiro Morihara, Hideyuki Nakanishi, Clifford Nass, Satoshi Oyama, Koichi Shimizu, Katsumi Tanaka, Jouin Teramae, Shoko Toda, Ken Tsutsuguchi, Koichi Yamada, Hirofumi Yamaki, Mika Yasuoka and Yuko Ohara for their collaborative work, and many other colleagues for helpful discussions.

References

1. J. Akahani, K. Isbister and T. Ishida. Digital City Project: NTT Open Laboratory. *CHI-00*, pp. 227-228, 2000.
2. P. van den Besselaar and D. Beckers. Demographics and Sociographics of the Digital City. T. Ishida Ed. *Community Computing and Support Systems*, Lecture Notes in Computer Science, State-of-the-Art Survey, 1519, Springer-Verlag, pp. 109-125, 1998.
3. P. van den Besselaar, Dennis Beckers. The Life and Death of the Great Amsterdam Digital City. In P. van den Besselaar, S. Koizumi (eds), *Digital Cities 3. Information technologies for social capital*. Lecture Notes in Computer Science, Vol. 3081. Springer-Verlag, Berlin Heidelberg New York (2005) pp. 64-93
4. G. A. Hillery. Definitions of Community: Areas of Agreement. *Rural Sociology*, Vol. 20. pp. 111-123, 1955.
5. K. Hiramatsu, K. Kobayashi, B. Benjamin, T. Ishida and J. Akahani. Map-based User Interface for Digital City Kyoto. *The Internet Global Summit (INET2000)*, 2000.

6. K. Isbister. A Warm Cyber-Welcome: Using an Agent-led Group Tour to Introduce Visitors to Kyoto. T. Ishida and K. Isbister Eds. *Digital Cities: Experiences, Technologies and Future Perspectives*, Lecture Notes in Computer Science, State-of-the-Art Survey, 1765, Springer-Verlag, pp. 391-400, 2000.

7. T. Ishida Ed. *Community Computing and Support Systems*. Lecture Notes in Computer Science, State-of-the-Art Survey, 1519, Springer-Verlag, 1998.

8. T. Ishida Ed. *Community Computing: Collaboration over Global Information Networks*. John Wiley and Sons, 1998.

9. T. Ishida. Digital City Kyoto: Social Information Infrastructure for Everyday Life. *Communications of the ACM (CACM)*, Vol. 45, No. 7, pp. 76-81, 2002.

10. T. Ishida. *Q*: A Scenario Description Language for Interactive Agents. *IEEE Computer*, Vol. 35, No. 11, pp. 54-59, 2002.

11. T. Ishida, A. Aurigi and M. Yasuoka. World Digital Cities: Beyond Heterogeneity. In P. van den Besselaar, S. Koizumi (eds), *Digital Cities 3. Information technologies for social capital*. Lecture Notes in Computer Science, Vol. 3081. Springer-Verlag, Berlin Heidelberg New York (2005) pp.184-198.

12. R. E. Kraut, W. Scherlis, T. Mukhopadhyay, J. Manning and S. Kiesler. HomeNet: A Field Trial of Residential Internet Services. *CHI -96*, pp. 284-291, 1996.

13. R. Linturi, M. Koivunen and J. Sulkanen. Helsinki Arena 2000 – Augmenting a Real City to a Virtual One. T. Ishida and K. Isbister Eds. *Digital Cities: Experiences, Technologies and Future Perspectives*, Lecture Notes in Computer Science, State-of-the-Art Survey, 1765, Springer-Verlag, pp. 83-96, 2000.

14. R. Linturi and T. Simula. Virtual Helsinki: Enabling the Citizen: Linking the Physical and Virtual. P. Besselaar and S. Koizumi Eds. *Digital Cities III, Information Technologies for Social Capital*, Lecture Notes in Computer Science, 3081, Springer-Verlag, 2005. pp 110-137.

15. R. M. MacIver. *Community*. Macmillan, 1917.

16. P. Maes. Agents that Reduce Work and Information Overload. *Communications of the ACM*, Vol. 37, No. 7, pp. 30-40, 1994.

17. E. Mino. Experiences of European Digital Cities. T. Ishida and K. Isbister Eds. *Digital Cities: Experiences, Technologies and Future Perspectives*, Lecture Notes in Computer Science, State-of-the-Art Survey, 1765, Springer-Verlag, pp. 58-72, 2000.

18. H. Nakanishi, C. Yoshida, T. Nishimura and T. Ishida. FreeWalk: A 3D Virtual Space for Casual Meetings. *IEEE Multimedia*, Vol. 6, No. 2, pp. 20-28, 1999.

19. H. Nakanishi. FreeWalk: A Social Interaction Platform for Group Behavior in a Virtual Space. *International Journal of Human Computer Studies (IJHCS)*, Vol. 60, No. 4, pp. 421-454, 2004.

World Digital Cities: Beyond Heterogeneity

Toru Ishida[1], Alessandro Aurigi[2], Mika Yasuoka[3]

[1] Department of Social Informatics, Kyoto University & Japan Science and Technology
Agency
ishida@i.kyoto-u.ac.jp
[2] School of Architecture, Planning and Landscape, Newcastle University
A.Aurigi@newcastle.ac.uk
[3] KID Laboratory, RCAST, University of Tokyo
mika@kuis.kyoto-u.ac.jp

Abstract. This paper reviews worldwide activities on regional information spaces. In the US and Canada, a large number of community networks appeared in the early 1990s. As a platform for community networks, information spaces using the city metaphor are being developed worldwide. In Europe, more than one hundred digital cities have been tried. Asian countries are actively adopting the latest information technologies for city informatization. All of the above are independent activities, and thus their goals, services, and organizations differ. In parallel, local commercial portals provided by global companies are becoming very common in major cities. Unlike regional community networks and digital cities, to increase the efficiency of gathering and maintaining local information in a large number of cities, the companies often provide uniform platforms to develop local sites. As a result, local portals look homogeneous though the information is always particular to each city. Regional community networks and digital cities must accept that they are in competition with global companies. However, it does not mean that the homogeneous platforms will govern the heterogeneous activities. We observe that heterogeneity of the regional information spaces is also increasing just as local commercial portals.

1 Introduction

Since the early 1990s, and particularly with the popularization of the Internet and the World Wide Web, a wave of experiments and initiatives has emerged, aimed at using Information and Communication Technologies to – broadly speaking – regenerate and enhance communities and local economies. This paper reviews worldwide activities focused on the creation of regional information spaces. In the US and Canada, a large number of community networks appeared in the early 1990s. Since then, as a platform for community networks, information spaces using the city metaphor have been developed worldwide. In Europe, well more than one hundred similar initiatives have been tried out. Asian countries are rapidly adopting the latest information and communication technologies for actively presenting city information and creating civic communication channels.

P. van den Besselaar and S. Koizumi (Eds.): Digital Cities 2003, LNCS 3081, pp. 188-203, 2005.
© Springer-Verlag Berlin Heidelberg 2005

All of the above are related but independent activities, and thus their goals, services, and organizations differ. Many denominations and buzzwords have been employed for labeling localized information and communication networks, depending on the fashion of the moment and the popularity of certain paradigmatic examples: 'cybercities', 'virtual cities' and 'civic networks' are examples of names that have been attached to all sorts of projects. However vague – and therefore disputed – such a definition could be, we will then refer to these regional information spaces as 'digital cities' throughout this paper, following up the 'digital city' conferences and research activities that we have been involved in, during the past few years.

The digital city, as a regional information space, has been initiated by two distinct phenomena: the development by private companies of local portals, which are very common in major cities, and the birth of non-profit, 'grassroots' community-generated electronic forums, such as the 'freenet' movement in the US. If the cities are large enough, commercial sites are a cost-effective way of providing fresh and accurate information including events, transportation, and weather forecasts. Unlike non-profit digital cities, however, these local portals are cost sensitive. One trend has been to increase the efficiency of gathering and maintaining the information by adopting uniform platforms. As a result, the structures and interfaces of local portals tend to be homogeneous even through the information is customized for each city. At the opposite end of the spectrum, other regional Web sites are being constructed by small communities. Individual volunteers are also creating an enormous number of personal local sites. Their sites are completely heterogeneous reflecting the cultural backgrounds of the corresponding cities.

Digital cities commonly provide both profit and non-profit services and face a dilemma in trying to balance these two different ways of relating with their users. As their physical counterparts, they need to find ways to articulate both profit and non-profit dimensions. Cities do not exist without commerce, and without commercial services, digital cities can lose attractiveness and fail to relate successfully with the real city. Without non-profit services, the digital city becomes too commercialized as a result of pursuing economic benefit, and it utilization is bound to get highly socially polarized, and scarcely beneficial for the wider community. Technology is also shifting the border between profit and non-profit services. For example, free e-mail and free desk space services have often been provided to guarantee an equal opportunity to anyone who wants to access the Internet. However, since free e-mail services are now also provided commercially, it is no longer clear whether the provision of this service should still be seen as a challenge or a mission for the non-profit sector.

This paper overviews American, European and Asian perspectives towards digital cities. It observes the heterogeneity of models and experiments in the field, and tries to reflect on the wider, cross-continental issues of the articulation of agency, governance and economic sustainability within the electronic city. It concludes stressing on the need for wider, cross-disciplinary research and development efforts for constructing the digital city of tomorrow.

2 American Community Networks

2.1 Brief History of American Community Networks

In the early days of the Internet, somewhat avant-garde attempts were made in many places to explore concepts for developing the future of the network. It seems, however, that at that time no clear vision had been formed on the structure of the information space for regional communities. President Clinton's administration announced the National Information Infrastructure Initiative (NII) in March 1993, and the NII agenda was proposed in September. Both efforts contributed to establish the foundations of information networks in the United States. NII was proposed as one of the key scientific and technical policies directed towards satisfying the High Performance Computing Act. It specified concrete target values for six items like universal access and scientific and technological research. Research areas included the impacts on the economy, medicine, life-long education, and administrative services. As a consequence, it promoted and catalyzed a wide range of network studies.

However, the United States is so vast that it is impractical to depend on the state-sponsored information superhighway to construct an information network that can cover all regions. This, coupled with a political tradition of community-centered, privately inspired grassroots engagement and the ever strong emphasis on freedom of speech and expression, made possible from the beginning that leading community activists recognized the necessity for local, independent networks structured to support the everyday life of citizens. Such activities gained quickly a high profile in the United Stated, and a great deal of worldwide visibility because of their innovative potential.

The Cleveland Free-Net, born in 1986, was the world's first citizen-led community network. It started from a free electronic help line that connected doctors and patients, and provided a communication channel for everyone with a modem and computer. It promoted the exchange of ideas and opinions of inhabitants in Cleveland region, and their encounters within the region. At the same time, the WELL (Whole Earth 'Lectronic Link), a pioneer 'virtual community' that would become famous worldwide, was born in 1985 [17]. Stemming from a series of various electronic "conferences," it formed a great virtual community where people of all generations and occupations could gather from all over the world. They ruled out anonymity and emphasized 'exchange with a human face.' The WELL was a network-based virtual community but it was not bound to locality. Though some of its 'conferences' extended from the virtual into the physical world and promoted face-to-face meetings and offline exchanges, the WELL was not designed to support regional communities. The early years of networked communities were characterized by a strong emphasis – to the point of being an almost blind faith – towards the myth of the inevitability of the global village and what had been hailed as the 'death of distance' [5]. However, a distinction between globally-oriented displaced 'non-grounded' projects and 'grounded' virtual cities with a clear relationship with geographical communities had to be drawn as place-based digital spaces were rapidly emerging [1].

More typical examples of region-oriented community networks started being constructed at the beginning of the 1990s [8]. The Blacksburg Electronic Village [6] was born in 1991, and the Seattle Community Network [18,19] appeared in 1992.

They differ in that the former was started by a consortium consisting of regional companies and universities, while the latter emerged from civil activities. In the case of Blacksburg, Virginia Polytechnic Institute and State University worked with Bell Atlantic and local authorities. They built a consortium to create a virtual information space close to the region. The first two years were spent in preparing computers and communication equipment, and dial up services started in 1993. Blacksburg Electronic Village gradually grew large enough to attract regional inhabitants. In Blacksburg's case, the leading role was taken not by the citizens who used the network, but by the university, companies and administration. The network was constructed from the technological viewpoint of companies and universities: a sort of research into telecommunication. In the same way, many of the early community networks were promoted by 'technical' leaders. The citizens lacked technology and experience and could not take the lead. Most community networks require the guidance provided by technical leaders in constructing network infrastructure. However, once the technical infrastructure is in place, users rapidly acquire skills to manage the equipment. In 1995, the activity of Blacksburg Electronic Village decreased. This was the result of a fundamental disagreement that was discovered between technology providers and users in terms of goals and expectations of community networks.

The Seattle Community Network (SCN) emerged from civil activities. In 1990, SCN was started as a part of the CPSR initiative (Computer Professional for Social Responsibility) with the goal of creating a cyber space accessible to the public. In 1992, the project was launched in Seattle and started to work on its ideals, vision, and strategy. Services started in 1994. Though SCN was faced with financial problems and competition with commercial portals, it grew in size by cooperating with regional libraries, seen as a key entry platform, and offering a network accessible by everyone. The noteworthy characteristic of SCN was that the project was led not by universities or city administration, but by citizens, and its purpose was to provide a sustainable information space for the region's inhabitants. Its services included e-mail provision, homepage creation, and support for regional activities rooted in everyday life. SCN lead the way for grassroots locally relevant networking, and just after it started operation, similar attempts were raised in many places in the US. In 1993, the Greater Detroit Free Net started services, and in 1995, Genesee Free Net commenced operation. In 1998, the number of community networks exceeded 300 but most were found to be plagued by many problems. For example, volunteer-based activities often suffered chronic fund shortages, highlighting the problem of the economic viability of community-driven electronic networking.

After the birth of pioneering community networks like Blacksburg and Seattle, commercial sites like AOL Digital City, and Microsoft Sidewalk came into being. A detailed explanation of these projects will be provided in Section 5 "Commercial Local Portals." These are profit-oriented portals that provide local information. Their outstanding usability and rapid growth has raised the warning that "the pursuit of profit will destroy grass-roots community networks." On the other hand, small ventures have also started to construct local portals. Though these sites are not run by the citizens, unlike the commercial portals offered by global companies, they are offering community sites dedicated to specific regions [18]. Their future is noteworthy as a medium intermediate between community networks and commercial portals.

2.2 Issues in American Community Networks

American society traditionally has a strong attachment to the values of local community, and said it has been noted that "the township comes first followed by the county, and lastly the state" [20]. The basic idea is that "Activities related to everybody should be executed by everybody. Moreover, everybody should use it by his or her own volition" [15]. American community networks tend to be independent from administration and companies. The participation and the self-motivating efforts of the citizens have been seen as essential for the success of the electronic community. Maintenance and operation tasks have been performed by volunteers who tended also to be the main users of the system. The activity is based on the American interpretation of philanthropy. Rather than a private charity-like virtue, the concept is emphasized as the offer of services to enrich the community. Philanthropy has been recently shifting to social enterprise: relatively strong institutions are supporting the various NPO activities undertaken by the citizens, and this is providing a significant boost to their success. Though the activities are voluntary-based, they conceptualize ideals, set targets, and explicitly give direction to the community.

The proactive ness of both grassroots community, the state, and commercial institutions, coupled with the fact that these tend to operate independently from each other, makes finding the right balance between local and public interests and economic viability a source of concern. Fragmentation of agency means that it is likely that different, competing projects will operate in the same arena, stemming from different actors and institutions. If an initiative is administration/technology oriented, the challenge is to how to bring in social activities. If the activity is socially oriented, shortfalls can appear in technical/financial support, and the competition with commercial portals can become a problem. Citizens can end up participating in both sets of activities. They may work for companies during the day, and work within the community as volunteers in their off hours. This life model, which is common in the US, can be seen as a result of the functional differentiation of society. The polarization of commercial portals and community networks, and the dual involvement in office and home activities can be an unusual and unlikely perspective to people whose societies are less functionally differentiated, as the section on Asian digital cities will show.

A more recent trend is the gradual demise of the technology-oriented, non grounded community networks which were popular in the early days whilst community sites rooted in regions are increasing in popularity. At the same time, commercial portals acquire a large number of users and are establishing themselves as useful tools for everyday life. It will be interesting to see how the relationship between commercial sites and local community networks develops. The commercial sites by global companies may subsume the small community networks and wipe them out. Smaller-scale commercial local portals may boost their connections to regional communities. The main concern of American community networks is finding how to coexist and create synergies with their commercial counterparts.

3 European Digital Cities

3.1 Brief History of European Digital Cities

The European conceptualization of the 'digital city' started with the experience of Amsterdam's *De Digitale Stad* [2,3] in 1994. The Amsterdam case was the first to use the word 'digital city,' but this project quickly got so well known and admired for the scope of its aims and its openness, to literally become a paradigm, and start a sort of 'digital city' movement within Europe. The Dutch digital city started its activities as a grass-roots and non-profit organization, but the crucial difference respect to earlier American experiment was that government was directly involved, and supportive of the project. DDS' functionality ranged from the support of community activities to the encouragement of political discourse and engagement, like linking the citizens to the administration. Digital City Amsterdam was initially funded by the regional administration, but later it had to become financially independent. To stand on its own feet, the digital city acquired a company-like character. To cope with the radical technological changes, top-down decisions are often required.

The beginning of Digital City Amsterdam was slanted towards the aspects of democracy, administration, politics and economy. Its 'urban' character was also strongly metaphorically emphasized by its interface, graphically presenting and structuring the system like a city with thematic squares, cafes and 'residential' sections hosting individuals' websites, hence the 'digital city' idea. But several accounts on DDS indicate that its character tended to become more like that of a non-grounded, virtual community, able to offer web space, email, and social virtual places to users not necessarily interested in Amsterdam as a city. Commercial pressure eventually made DDS change into something rather different from its initial 'vision.' It lost its urban metaphorical character and had to compete with a much more varied and articulated offer of free internet services and connectivity becoming available from many other companies. This has eventually made it lose much of its attractiveness and its 'cutting edge' status as a digital city [13].

At the end of 1995, Finland decided to commemorate the 450th anniversary of Helsinki, and as one part of its celebrations initiated construction of a high-speed metropolitan network. The consortium was established by Elisa Communications (former Helsinki Telecom) and Helsinki city. The members included companies like IBM and Nokia, and universities in Helsinki. They jointly developed virtual tours as well as public/civic services. For example, Helsinki City Museum provided a cultural service for the citizens and visitors interested in the history of Helsinki [11,12]. A three-dimensional virtual space was set up where the visitors could wander around the Helsinki city hall of 1805. Even though the actual hall did not exist anymore, they built it on the Web and re-created the atmosphere of that age. The three-dimensional virtual city model of Helsinki was meant to allow visitors to make a call just by clicking the screen.

The notable point here is that Europe has many digital city initiatives born through the cooperation of public administrations, companies, and social activists. Frameworks similar to Helsinki have been introduced in other European cities. In Ireland, for instance, the Eircom telecommunications company constructed the 'Ennis

Information Age Town' with the assistance of the administration and with public and voluntary partnerships [7].

Trying to integrate and coordinate the efforts of the private, public and voluntary sectors towards better regional and local information systems has been an important theme in Europe. We need to mention TeleCities, an alliance of EU cities that started the European Digital City Project in 1993 [16]. This was originally characterized as a program to support telematics applications and services for urban areas. The TeleCities consortium characterizes itself as "an open network of local authorities dedicated to the development of urban areas through the use of information and telecommunications technologies." Its target is to share the ideas and technologies born from various city projects, and to strengthen the partnerships between EU cities through this sharing. In this model, each city sets the targets of (1) to utilize information and communication technologies to resolve social/economic/regional development issues, and (2) to improve the quality of social services through the use of information.

The TeleCities support program allows each city to take its own course of actions while facilitating the formation of partnerships and the successful bidding for European Community funds. However, while this approach seemed to have a good potential in bringing together local authorities and the industrial/commercial sector, grassroots community and voluntary projects tended to be left out, and many initiatives appeared to be 'pushed' to their potential users in a top-down fashion. Especially in the early stages of projects' conception and construction, the top down management failed to stimulate the citizens' participation, even though it ensured good levels of support. However, in some cases management became aware of this operational gap, and started to emphasize the need to "base the informatization on society" or the importance of informatization in resolving "social issues."

Along with this direction, Vienna city, one of the longest-standing members of TeleCities, created the informatization plan called "The Strategy Plan for Vienna 2000." In Vienna, both the city and the citizens shared the responsibilities for informatization: the city was responsible for the civil services and the citizens were responsible for the projects executed by individual communities. The digital city was run by this cooperative structure. For example, if the city wanted to resolve the issue of digital signatures, the citizens would willing participate in a trial project and enable its speedy introduction. Such collaboration was realized based on this cooperative structure. Moreover, their plans, processes, results and lessons learned are reported to the EU for use by the other cities, so that effective information sharing is being realized. Similarly, in the Italian city of Bologna the 'Iperbole' – Internet for Bologna and the Emilia Romagna region – initiative was started and run by the local municipality with the intention of being fairly open to grassroots contributions. The city council would provide information and civic services, but would leave an open door to voluntary organizations and citizens group, allowed to become information providers and publishers, as well as engage in debate, within the official digital city.

About 100 cities from 20 countries have been taking part in TeleCities. EU support of city informatization is strengthening, and each city is developing its own digital counterpart taking advantage of the sharing of best practices, project plans, and success stories. While increasing its members base and facilitating the projects, however, TeleCities found that their activities still largely lacked the commercial viewpoint and so tried to steer to accommodate this need. In 2001, three of the main urban informatization organizations, eris@, ELANET and TeleCities, moved towards cooperation; they also support Global Cities Dialogue which aims to construct a worldwide urban network.

3.2 Issues in European Digital Cities

Since Europe consists of various nations with different cultures, histories, economies and socio-political traditions, it is an obvious consequence that digital city approaches are heterogeneous and diverse. Within this perspective it is easy to see why European coordination has proved important. The 'digitization' of European cities has at some notable characteristics. One is that networks are generally generated within, and restricted to regions. The other is the increased sensitivity towards inclusionary themes and the governance of the digital city. Attempts have been made at collaborating from different social groups like citizens, companies, universities and administration. The top-down activities by administrations and public-private partnerships have in some cases tried to meet the bottom-up activities by small-to-medium businesses and universities, and so have been more rooted in the region and its inhabitants. There tends to be less dualism and confrontation between grassroots community activities and commercialism than in the US. We analyze these two characteristics in detail below.

The region-centered networking might well be an obvious consequence of the traditional fragmentation, regionalism and municipalism that have characterized the spatial and institutional organization of most countries in Europe throughout the centuries. In some cases this goes to down to the neighborhood scale. Instead of one overarching network that covers the whole city, many small networks that were constructed to serve micro-regions could be combined. For example, the networks in Barcelona were created to serve the barrios, the inhabitants' life units; they were connected to create a communication network for the whole city. This method yields networking at the daily life unit level, thus seems more suitable to facilitate the participation of citizens. In Europe, cities and towns of all sizes, including rather small ones, have been active trying to develop some electronic information system, possibly because this is coherent with their micro-region networking traditions.

The second characteristic is the relative openness towards trying to form partnerships of different social groups and institutions. In Europe, citizens, universities, city administration and companies often cooperate to form complex communities. In the U.K., for example, nation-wide regional network development was started in London by a public-private partnership supported by IBM in 1999. In Milan, the community network, started by a university, has involved for a certain period direct participation of profit-making companies and the local public administration. This collaboration style is common in Europe: companies contribute to civic networks not necessarily on a purely commercial basis. The coordination and potential for exchange between administration and citizens seems stronger in Europe than other areas.

The above characteristics are reflected in the activities of groups like TeleCities, and the European community itself. The EU's vision of the information society has been linked to the movement of European digital cities, and digital cities have greatly benefited from the flow of funds from the EU towards a variety of projects and clusters, usually awarded within the EU's Framework Programmes for research and development The assumption is that various models of the information society (where information can be stored and transferred at low cost and in real time) will emerge and lead to the knowledge society followed by the wise society. However, it doesn't mean that the EU is planning to integrate all cities into a one huge pan-European city. While being supported by the EU, each city is constructing its own community that reflects its cultural background. Cultural differences might trigger problems when connecting independent communities, but such problems can be eased by information sharing and communication among cities such as the ones fostered by TeleCities. This two-tier situation of independent networks and voluntary adherence to some wider alliance within consortia, encouraged by an easier access to funding opportunities, can produce innovation stemmed from international cooperation, and encourage its dissemination. It remains to be seen how strong is many initiatives' dependence on EU or national funding, and how able these can or cannot be to become self-sustained, viable services in the longer term.

In the future, how will digital communities develop in Europe? As explained above, Europe seems keen at balancing administrative and civil activities. Even if companies have been providing significant contributions from the point of view of technology and development, most European digital cities have been keeping commercialization at arm's length. But the imperative of economic sustainability implies that most projects, especially large ones, will have to deal with profit issues, and possible commercialization of services and information. Will the rise of commercialism stimulate community activities or create new conflicts? Will European digital cities find ways to retain their original traditions even if they strengthen their coordination with the private sector?

4 Asian City Informatization

4.1 Brief History of Asian City Informatization

The most significant trend in Asia was the emergence of city informatization as a governmental national project. Though the momentum generated by American grass-roots activities had a great influence, digital cities in Asia were created as a part of governmental initiatives. The first country in Asia to implement an informatization project was Singapore. The administration started the Singapore IT2000 Master Plan in 1992. In 1996, it launched the plan called "Singapore One: One Network for Everyone" to develop a broadband communication infrastructure and multimedia application services. Korea proposed the KII (Korea Information Infrastructure) in 1995 in response to the American NII. In 1996, the Malaysia administration announced the plan called the Multimedia Super Corridor. Their new high-tech cities, Putrajaya and Cyberjaya, are part of the Malaysian e-Government; the surrounding regions are designated as multimedia zones. One organization similar to the Western community network is the research project called MINOS (Malaysian Institute of Microelectronic Systems). MINOS, which also acts as an Internet provider, broke away from the Malaysian government in 1996. Three different sectors: public administration, business and citizens, cooperate with each other to improve everyday life and promote social interaction. They realize technical innovations with the aim of contributing to the development of the country.

In Japan, the regional network Koala was born with the assistance of a prefecture government. In 1985, it set up an information center, in 1994 it connected to the Web, and in 2000 it was reorganized as a business corporation that promoted community networks. After that, many regional community networks have been developed in Japan with assistance of administration and telephone companies.

The originator of informatization in Asia is the administration. It is rare to see leadership exerted by civil activities or grassroots organizations. The reaction from commercial sites has also been slow. As for Koala, though it appears to be a community activity, it started as a part of the informatization policies set by the administration. The policy of introducing IT proactively and implementing coast-to-coast informatization was originally proposed by the government. What tended to happen were the emergence of a precise and relatively rigid government-oriented information strategy, rather than the clarification of rules and purposes for community networks in order to prepare the ground for bottom-up initiatives. As a result, the promoters often aimed at large-scale investment such as laying optical fiber lines or equipping all schools with PCs. The activities of Asian digital cities can be seen as mainly governmental initiatives often named city informatization.

An interesting example of rural networking can be seen in Yamada village, Japan. This project started in 1996 with the aim of reversing the depopulation trend in rural areas, and can be defined as a regional informatization project to stimulate village life. The community site, which is mainly for village inhabitants, was developed with the support of the administration. In 1998, the ratio of connected villagers reached 60%, and the interaction within the village and with the outside increased. The Yamada project greatly contributed to our understanding of the potential of civil participation in rural areas. However it is worth noting that the Yamada village project was mainly driven by the administration, and despite its success it cannot be described as a citizen-led activity.

More recently, however, due to a better understanding of the limitations of the top-down approach, many countries have started, since the late 90's, to preach the importance of civil initiative. This movement seems to have been fostered by the influence of American community networks. People who have experienced the grass-roots activities in the US have played important roles in introducing the concept to Asia. In Japan, organizations like the Community Area Network (CAN) Forum have emerged. CAN was inspired by American community networks and its goal is to promote human communication in actual communities by utilizing the Internet and to create a rich information space. CAN itself is not a digital city but a promotion organization to build regional networks in Japan.

4.2 Issues in Asian City Informatization

As described above, Asian regional informatization is mainly based on administrative activity. The grassroots activities and university driven projects such as Digital City Kyoto [9,10] have strengthened, but they have not entered the mainstream, remaining standalone exercises.

The challenge is to predict the future of the Asian digital cities. In Japan, Internet access from the wireless phone system called i-mode has sprang into wide use in the past several years. Individuals are quite active on the Web, and their homepages are often richer than those created by the administrations. In Korea, broadband access via ADSL is rapidly spreading and various utilization trends like IP telephony have emerged. China has organized large scale digital city symposiums several times concentrated on the emerging information industry. In Asia, the functional differentiation of society is less pronounced than in the US. Regional informatization has started to take a more complicated aspect with mixed initiatives. Participants of digital cities can be representatives of some companies and at the very same time act as volunteers, as work and private life is less separated. The multilateral motivation of individuals might lead activities complex. However, this fuzziness could also be exploited in a beneficial way to facilitate the creation of consensus and the convergence between administration, business and civil activities. The forthcoming of Asian digital cities can be shaped differently from what we have seen in Western countries.

5 Advances in Commercial Local Portals

Urban commercial portals have become most noticeable in the US. There are many local commercial portals run by telephone companies, Web companies, airline companies, and so on. As companies are trying to create portals for the same city, the competition between them is getting strong. The companies hammer out their own ideas and go head-to-head to gain the upper hand over their competitors. The best-of-breed commercial portals place all key information on one page, which enables an overview of the digital city features to be instantly grasped. The general orientation of these initiatives tends to be towards providing easy to find and search information, with good maintenance of the system and frequent updates. Many of these commercial portal sites consistently set the benchmark in terms of update frequency and information volume etc.

Commercial portals might soon cover cities all over the world. Even if no regional company is available to run a commercial portal in a country, some global company will find a way to cross the border and gain access. For example, AOL's 'digital city' family of portals has the highest user number among the regional information sites of major US cities. AOL's digital city provides entertainment, shopping, people and more. It also provides regional information based on the concept of "the nation's largest locally-focused online network." Another regional portal is Citysearch. In May 1996, the site started to provide latest information from the viewpoint of local inhabitants to major American cities. The information provided includes not only hotel vacancies, events, and sightseeing information for tourists, but also museums, movies, and restaurant information for the benefit of the local inhabitants. Sites like this aim at eliminating the need to reference the yellow pages, maps, and guidebooks, and provide some value-added information, but all of this comes at the price of a top-down, heavily controlled, selected and edited set of contents, and very little – if any – two-way interaction and communication.

It has been noted that the development of a field in technology consists of three phases: the *technology driven phase*, the *productivity driven phase*, and the *appeal driven phase* [21]. Considering this transition pattern, the current status might be regarded as the second phase, a phase however wherein the commercial viewpoint is emphasized. The emergence of commercial sites run by large companies tends to be regarded as threatening to regional information communities. Both in North America and Europe, community-based sites tend to repel commercial activities for the understandable fear of the 'commodification' of the concept of community networking. They warn that commercialism will prove detrimental to the future growth of community networks. The prime purpose of commercial sites is advertising, and their approach to community information and activity has to be coherent with their commercial strategy. Someone said that the bud of community activity will be nipped before it is noticed and so will be lost forever: the competition with commercial sites might bury community activity before it starts.

However, commercial portals often effectively provide access to up to date public event information, a function that might not be easy to be provided by community voluntary sites. Especially in Asia, which does not have a long history of community activity, the provision of public event information is highly appreciated, even if it comes from a for-profit organization. There might well be a role for commercial portals serving community purposes, and this might spell synergies as well as a degree of competition between commercial sector and voluntary projects. Therefore, the dualism between the two types of initiatives seen in North America may not appear in Asia.

6 Advances in Information and Communication Technologies

In the previous sections we have mainly concentrated on contextual issues for urban digital initiatives in North America, Europe and Asia. Obviously we need to keep in mind that we cannot overlook technological innovation as another important factor influencing the construction of the digital city. How do we look, however, at this relationship between technology and urban societies? Traditionally there has been a split between social scientists' approaches and how computer scientists would look at the problem. We would like to argue that filling the interdisciplinary gap is becoming vital for the future design of digital cities. Traditional social sciences tend to downplay technological issues and put weight on issues related to the socio-economic context or impacts of cybercities, and on participation of the citizens. Computer scientists on the other hand concentrate on technical development and declare that technology is ultimately what creates the online community.

The words of Alan Key well represent the mood of computer scientists: "the best way to predict the future is to invent it." Moore's Law "chip densities double every eighteen months" was expounded in 1965, and still holds valid today. In the last 15 years, computer speed has increased by a factor of 1000 while railway speed has increased only 1.5 times. Computer scientists, who believe they can create the future, can fail to acknowledge the social complexity their designs have to face. This inadequacy is often justified by the belief that time is what is needed, and the new systems will gradually become more accepted and used by the population. This can be true only to an extent. The recent history of digital city projects is constellated of failures and allegedly brilliant ideas that have not withstood the test of time. Acceptance, above all, can imply a future level of usage, but does not imply at all that a certain system was indeed what was needed, or the best possible solution to certain urban problems.

On the other hand, it is not easy for social scientists to analyze and give direction to a continuously evolving technology. This is coupled with the fact that social sciences have been used too often in isolation from the technology they were supposed to deal with. Technological objects and systems have been often been treated by social scientists as mysterious 'black boxes,' penetrable only by those technically-gifted people who had designed them. By doing so, social scientists might tend to remove or ignore vital technological and design-based issues that themselves embed social constraints and opportunities, those possible 'futures' that computer scientists try and embed into their projects.

It is therefore clear that the digital city lies at the border between computer and social sciences. On the one hand it is true that technology creates a number of possibilities as well as constraints. It is also true that technology does not happen – and is not deployed – in a void, and that socio-political influences and policy-making have a direct bearing over the final 'shape' of the technological 'solution.' Finally, it is the citizen, the participant of the digital city, who actively interacts with these embedded possibilities, selects from among them and creates a future that can sometimes be very different from the one initially envisaged by the scientists who had designed the new technological system.

We also need to acknowledge that the speed of technical innovation is such that what is crucial for scientific studies in computing is often not suitable for encouraging social activity. A reasonable approach for digital cities is to adopt legacy technology so that the citizens can easily participate in parallel with exploring the technological frontier to outline bold futures. The digital city should be designed as a space for everyday life and at the same time, embed the experiments that will allow it to be a space for the future.

Information technology, which impacts the future of digital cities, has two strands. One is the continuous improvement of computing speed and storage capacity represented by Moore's rule, coupled with the sharp increase in communication bandwidth, that allow us to move from text to images or video. Another strand is the importance of the social value of networking. Computer science is familiar with the first strand of computing and transmission capacities, and knows how to deal with it in quantitative terms. The 'bit' unit of information has been defined and used to measure the improvement of computing speed and storage capacity. The history of computer science is the process of optimizing technologies to deal with bits, reducing redundancies, optimizing their usage, increasing capacity to handle them. On the other hand, the second strand cannot be reduced to 'bits.'

Some approaches that are eminently social but that try and bring into the equation the technological components and their design, exist. The perspective of the so-called Social Construction of Technology (SCOT), or Social Shaping of Technology [4,14] for instance, can provide a good basis for starting considering the relations between social actors and technical artifacts, and understanding better the intertwined potentials of design, policy-making, and use-adoption of technological systems like digital cities can be. There also seems to be a very strong need for envisaging methods to measure the impacts, and possibly the benefits of digital cities over urban societies. It is urgent and essential to establish methodologies that can be used to forecast/validate the social value of networking.

7 Conclusions

The purpose of this paper has been to elucidate the activity on digital cities after 1990, providing some reflections on some overarching issues that seem crucial at this stage in the development of 'digital cities' around the world. We have mentioned how digital cities have been developed by various organizations and thus have different characteristics problems. Those started from a grass-roots activity depend on volunteers and often face financial and management problems. The non-profit associations yield regional information spaces at relatively low cost, but there is difficulty in maintaining adequate leadership and social responsibility. On the other hand, digital cities assisted by public administrations can utilize their funds and facilities, but a strong bias toward regional economic development or bureaucratic improvement, can hinder more active social participation. In the case of Private Finance Initiative, the initial investment can be effectively reduced. In the case of Public-Private Partnership, fund raising is rather easy in the initial stages, but difficulty exists in establishing a sustainable budget structure. In any case, it is not easy to design and maintain digital cities that benefit all participants.

For-profit and non-profit community sites compete and coexist in North America. Characteristic of European initiatives is the attempt at coordinating administrations, companies and citizens, while that of Asia is government-directed growth. Obviously the digital city is a mirror of society, and there is no assurance that the model that succeeds in America will succeed in Asia. We need to create models that suit each region.

However, some basic issues, common to most initiatives, have been identified and merit further scrutiny and improvement efforts. First, the arena of actors involved in shaping the digital city. Synergies help making the projects effective, sustainable, and holistic, and therefore efforts to find ways to coordinate actors and create pluralist, complex projects should be welcome. Cities – the 'physical' ones – are complex entities. They have been successful for centuries, and keep their prominence despite all sorts of past predictions about their dissolution, just because of their ability to concentrate and somehow articulate the co-existence of community, voluntary movements, politics, commerce, tourism, culture etc. Digital cities need to deal with the same complex mix of things in order to attract and retain usage, and function as entities that 'augment' their physical counterparts. A city famous for its tourist attractions will not develop its digital city without an eye on tourism, because the commercial aspect is a part of the basic structure of everyday life. Physical squares would not be used as much as they are without the presence of shops. The same, we expect, should apply to virtual squares and places.

Complexity calls for pluralism and participation. Combined, multi-disciplinary research has been identified in this paper as the way forward to think the present and the future of digital cities. Participatory design and development is similarly needed to sum up the activities in the three elements of cities, namely administration, companies and citizens.

References

1. A. Aurigi and S. Graham. The 'Crisis' in the Urban Public Realm. Loader B. Ed. *Cyberspace Divide*, London: Routledge, 1998.
2. P. van den Besselaar and D. Beckers. Demographics and Sociographics of the Digital City. T. Ishida Ed. *Community Computing and Support Systems*, Lecture Notes in Computer Science, State-of-the-Art Survey, 1519. Springer-Verlag, pp. 109-125, 1998.
3. P. van den Besselaar. The Life and Death of the Great Amsterdam Digital City. P. van den Besselaar and S. Koizumi Eds. *Digital Cities III, Information Technologies for Social Capital.* Lecture Notes in Computer Science, State-of-the-Art Survey, 3081, Springer-Verlag, 2005. pp. 64-93
4. W. E. Bijker and J. Law Eds. *Shaping Technology / Building Society: Studies in Sociotechnical Change.* MIT Press, 1992.
5. F. Cairncross. *The Death of Distance: How the Communication Revolution Will Change Our Lives.* Texere Publishing, 1998.
6. J. M. Carroll. The Blacksburg Electronic Village: A Study in Community Computing. P. van den Besselaar and S. Koizumi Eds. *Digital Cities III, Information Technologies for Social Capital*, Lecture Notes in Computer Science, State-of-the-Art Survey, 3081, Springer-Verlag, 2005. pp. 42-63
7. I. Gotzl. TeleCities: Digital Cities Network. M. Tanabe, P. van den Besselaar and T. Ishida Eds. *Digital Cities II: Computational and Sociological Approaches.* Lecture Notes in Computer Science, State-of-the-Art Survey, 2362, Springer-Verlag, pp. 98-106, 2002.
8. K. Guthrie and W. Dutton. The Politics of Citizen Access Technology: The Development of Public Information Utilities in Four Cities. *Policy Studies Journal*, Vol. 20, No. 4, 1992.
9. T. Ishida. Digital City Kyoto: Social Information Infrastructure for Everyday Life. *Communications of the ACM*, Vol. 45, No. 7, pp. 76-81, 2002.
10. T. Ishida. Activities and Technologies in Digital City Kyoto. P. van den Besselaar and S. Koizumi Eds. *Digital Cities III, Information Technologies for Social Capital*, Lecture Notes in Computer Science, State-of-the-Art Survey, 3081, Springer-Verlag, 2005. pp 162-183.
11. R. Linturi, M. Koivunen and J. Sulkanen. Helsinki Arena 2000 – Augmenting a Real City to a Virtual One. T. Ishida and K. Isbister Eds. *Digital Cities: Experiences, Technologies and Future Perspectives*, Lecture Notes in Computer Science, State-of-the-Art Survey, 1765, Springer-Verlag, pp. 83-96, 2000.
12. R. Linturi and T. Simula. Virtual Helsinki: Enabling the Citizen; Linking the Physical and Virtual. P. van den Besselaar and S. Koizumi Eds. *Digital Cities III, Information Technologies for Social Capital*, Lecture Notes in Computer Science, State-of-the-Art Survey, 3081, Springer-Verlag, 2005. pp. 110-137.
13. G. Lovink. The Rise and the Fall of the Digital City Metaphor and Community in 1990s Amsterdam. Graham S (Ed) *The Cybercities Reader*, Routledge: London, 2004.
14. D. MacKenzie and J. Wajcman Eds. *The Social Shaping of Technology.* Open University Press: Bristol, PA, 1985.
15. M. Mead and M. Brown. The Wagon and the Star: A Study of American Community Initiative. Chicago, Rand McNally, 1966.
16. E. Mino. Experiences of European Digital Cities. T. Ishida and K. Isbister Eds. *Digital Cities: Experiences, Technologies and Future Perspectives*, Lecture Notes in Computer Science, State-of-the-Art Survey, 1765, Springer-Verlag, pp. 58-72, 2000.
17. H. Rheingold. *The Virtual Community.* Secker & Warburg, 1994.

18. D. Schuler. Digital Cities and Digital Citizens. M. Tanabe, P. van den Besselaar and T. Ishida Eds. *Digital Cities II: Computational and Sociological Approaches.* Lecture Notes in Computer Science, State-of-the-Art Survey, 2362, Springer-Verlag, pp. 72-82, 2002.

19. D. Schuler. The Seattle Community Network, Anomaly or Replicable Model? P. van den Besselaar and S. Koizumi Eds. *Digital Cities III, Information Technologies for Social Capital,* Lecture Notes in Computer Science, State-of-the-Art Survey, 3081, Springer-Verlag, 2005. pp. 16-41.

20. A. Tocqueville. *Democracy in America.* University of Chicago Press, 2000.

21. T. Winograd. From Programming Environments to Environments for Designing. *Communications of the ACM*, Vol. 38, No. 6, pp. 65-74, 1995.

Virtual Cities for Real-World Crisis Management

Hideyuki Nakanishi[1], Satoshi Koizumi[2], Toru Ishida[1,2]

[1] Department of Social Informatics, Kyoto University
`nakanishi@i.kyoto-u.ac.jp, ishida@i.kyoto-u.ac.jp`
[2] JST CREST Digital City Project
Kyoto 606-8501, JAPAN
`satoshi@digitalcity.jst.go.jp`

Abstract. In this paper, we present the evacuation simulation system that is the combination of a virtual city and a crisis management simulation. The system allows users to become virtual evacuees in an evacuation simulation to learn about crowd behavior. In the experimental use of the system, we found that the synergic effects between a bird's-eye and a first-person views in learning emergency escaping behaviors. Based on this result, we designed a novel communication system that allows a remote leader to guide escaping crowds in an emergency situation. We deployed our prototype in the Kyoto Station.

1 Introduction

The increased graphical performance of PCs and the proliferation of broadband networks have accelerated R&D on virtual cities [10, 10a]. Typical applications include route guidance in an urban area, link collection of regional Web sites, and graphical chat environments. On the other hand, it has become popular to represent crisis management simulations through 3D graphics. For example, an emergency situation is simulated in the realistic 3D model of a building [1]. If we could find a way to use virtual cities for visualizing crisis management simulations, we would be able to build more useful simulations at lower development cost.

In the Digital City project [4], we are pursuing a new method to construct crisis management simulations. In this paper, we propose a way to connect virtual cities with crisis management simulations. If it works, we can extend crisis management simulations beyond the 3D animated representation of emergency situations. First, a virtual city can become an evacuation simulation system for education and training. Users become avatars escaping in the virtual city. Second, a virtual city can become an evacuation guidance system. A remote leader and on-site escaping people can communicate with one another through the virtual city.

2 The Evacuation Simulation System

Multi-agent simulation is a typical method of evacuation simulations [3]. Virtual cities are basically multi-user environments but few of them support the function of

P. van den Besselaar and S. Koizumi (Eds.): Digital Cities 2003, LNCS 3081, pp. 204-216, 2005.

multi-agent simulation. To develop evacuation simulation systems, we need a technique to combine multi-user and multi-agent functions. *FreeWalk* is a good example of such a technique. We originally developed FreeWalk for supporting communication [12], and for the current application, we added a function to support multi-agent simulation [5, 5a]. In the next section, we describe the system architecture, which can handle both multi-user and multi-agent functions.

2.1 Multi-user Multi-agent Architecture

To allow users to participate in a multi-agent simulation of a virtual crowd, they can be an 'avatar' or an 'agent'. 'Avatar' stands for an element of a virtual crowd that is manipulated by a user through keyboard, mouse, and other devices. An 'agent' is an element of a virtual crowd controlled by an external program connected to the command interface of FreeWalk. We use the term 'character' for either of them.

Figure 1 illustrates our multi-user multi-agent architecture and the relations among FreeWalk, users, and programs. The figure illustrates that FreeWalk only administers the external states of the characters. The external state is a set of visually and acoustically observable parameters as position, posture, and utterances. The internal state is a set of such invisible and causal elements as intention, belief, knowledge, emotion, and characteristics. The internal state of each character is administered by either the user who manipulates it or the program that controls it. From the users and programs, FreeWalk accepts requests to change the external states.

The exclusion of internal mechanisms is an important design choice for FreeWalk. If agents and avatars can be defined separately in the simulation beforehand, it is possible to incorporate such internal mechanisms as a planning engine into the simulator [15]. However, in the case of FreeWalk, it must be easy to switch an agent to an avatar and vice versa. Since avatars are manipulated by humans who have their own internal mechanism, we designed FreeWalk to exclude any internal mechanism. In Figure 1, you can see that the boundary between FreeWalk and a program is the same as that between FreeWalk and a user. There has already been a successful example of applying the same design principle to a single-user single-agent simulation [9].

Another important design choice is the distributed architecture of FreeWalk. If a multi-agent simulation does not require very heavy calculation, a single computer is sufficient to run it. However, the multi-agent simulation of FreeWalk is executed in a distributed style since the simulation must be compatible with the multi-user function of FreeWalk. Figure 1 illustrates this compatibility. Each agent can be assigned to any machine that may be used by a user. An avatar and multiple agents can run simultaneously on the same machine. Their external states are changed by FreeWalk running on the machine. The changes are transmitted between machines so that the external states of all characters can be shared by them.

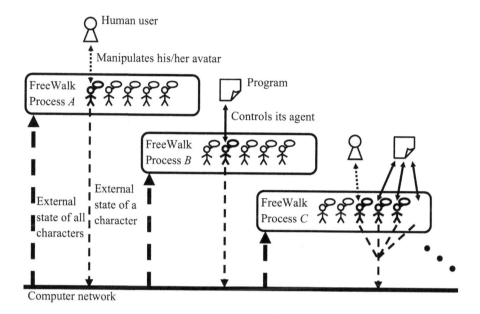

Fig. 1. Multi-user multi-agent architecture

2.2   Unified Control Mechanism of Avatars and Agents

In the multi-user multi-agent architecture, the difference between the control mechanisms of avatars and agents may result in unequal behavioral abilities. To make an evacuation simulation fair to both human and computer participants, the control mechanisms should be designed in the same way as much as possible. For example, in FreeWalk, the calculation process to determine the next position is equally designed for avatars and agents.

To move avatars, users manipulate input devices to indicate the direction to proceed. To move agents, programs call the command to begin walking toward the indicated coordinates. The subsequent process to determine the exact next position is equally designed for avatars and agents. This process includes collision avoidance [13] and gait animation generation [16]. Furthermore, movements are automatically adjusted to such social manners as forming a line to go through a doorway and forming a circle to have a conversation [8]. Figure 2 shows the data flow of this unified control mechanism.

The control mechanism of the gestures is also unified. Since deictic gestures play an important role in crowd behavior, characters have the ability to use facing and pointing gestures. Both avatars and agents can equally control the angles of their faces and arms. Users indicate the angles through input devices. Programs indicate the angles as the argument of the facing and pointing commands.

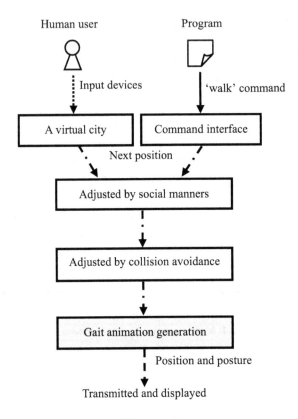

Fig. 2. Unified control mechanism

2.3 Command Interface

The multi-user multi-agent architecture provides a command interface for outside programs to control agents. The command interface was designed to simulate social interaction. Some of the action and perception commands are listed below.

walk: walk to the coordinates.
face: face to the direction.
point: point to the direction.
speak: speak the sentence.
see: perceive seeing the character.
hear: perceive hearing the sentence.

When programs call commands, the commands are stored and listed in the memory shared by the FreeWalk and the outside programs. FreeWalk repeats the cycle of changing the external states of characters and drawing them based on the changes. Before beginning the next cycle, FreeWalk loads the commands listed in the shared memory and begins running them. The detailed mechanism of command execution is as follows. If the loaded command is an action command that takes some period of time to complete, FreeWalk continues to change the external state across the cycles. The degree of change in each cycle is determined by the period of the time passed from the previous cycle. For example, in the case of the 'walk' command, it is repeated to draw a character that goes forward a little more than in the previous frame until it reaches the coordinates indicated by the caller program. For the convenience of caller programs, the command interface has the two modes to call. One is a blocking mode and the other is a non-blocking mode. In the blocking mode, an agent can begin the next command after finishing the ongoing one, while in the non-blocking mode, an agent can begin the next command immediately.

Through the command interface, FreeWalk is currently connected with the scenario description language Q [6]. This language represents behavioral rules of each agent as a scenario. In the scenario, the simulation is divided into several scenes. Each scene has a set of rules like "if the agent perceives event A, then the agent executes action B."

3   Evacuation Simulation Experiment

3.1   Hypothesis

Our evacuation simulation system enables people to experience crowd behavior and observe it from their first-person views (Figure 3(b)). Such experience should be valuable to people for learning the crowd behavior. However, the bird's-eye view (Figure 3(a)) may be more effective in understanding crowd behavior as well as navigation [2] than a first-person view. Probably, both views have different efficacies. To compare them and also derive their synergic effects, we tested each view and a combination of them in both orders. We compared four groups: experiencing a first-person view (FP group); observing a bird's-eye view (BE group); experiencing a first-person view before observing a bird's-eye view (FP-BE group); and observing a bird's-eye view before experiencing a first-person view (BE-FP group). The subjects are 96 college students. They are divided into the four groups. Six subjects participated in the simulation at once (Figure 3(c)). So, four simulations were conducted in each group.

3.2   Measure

The previous experiment [14] gave us a gauge to measure subjects' understandings of crowd behavior. This study demonstrated how the following two group leading methods cause different crowd behaviors.

Follow-direction method: The leaders point their arms at the exit and shout out, "the exit is over there!" to indicate the direction. They begin escaping after all evacuees go out.

Follow-me method: To a few of the nearest evacuees, the leaders whisper, "follow me" and proceed to the exit. This behavior forms a flow toward the exit.

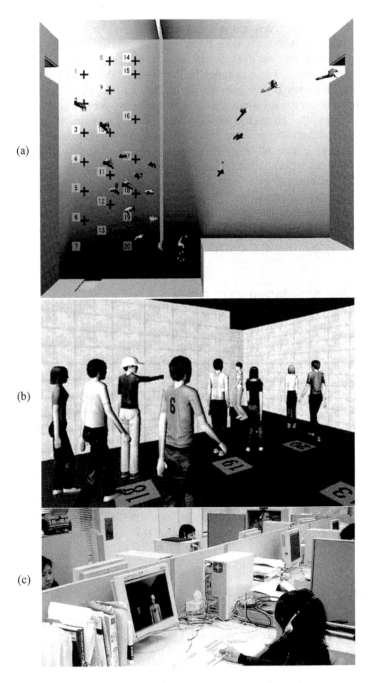

Fig. 3. Evacuation simulation experiment

The simulation is based on this study [11]. At the beginning of the simulation, everyone was in the left part of the room, which was divided into left and right parts by the center wall as shown in figure 3a. The four leaders had to guide the sixteen evacuees to the correct exit at the right part, and prevent them from going out through the incorrect exit at the left part. In the FP simulations, six evacuees were subjects and the others were agents. In the BE simulations, all evacuees and leaders were agents.

In the experiment, subjects observed and experienced the two different crowd behaviors caused by the two methods. Subjects were asked which of the two methods did cause the specific crowd behavior. In a questionnaire with 17 questions, the subjects read the descriptions of crowd behavior and had to select one of the two methods. The questionnaire was completed before as well as after the experiment. A t-test was used to find significant differences between the scores of the pre-test and the post-test. A significant difference means that the subjects do learn the nature of crowd behavior through his or her observation and experience.

3.3 Results

Table 1 summarizes the results of the t-test for nine questions. Since no group could correctly answer the other eight questions, they are omitted here. The results seems to indicate that a bird's-eye observation was necessary to grasp the crowd behavior. The FP group could not answer correctly questions 3 to 9 about the evacuees' behavior. However, a first-person experience is not worthless. It is interesting that the BE-FP group did learn to understand the behavior described in questions 6 and 7, but that the BE and FP-BE groups didn't. These questions seem to be related to the dense nature of crowd behavior. This result implies that the background knowledge of overall behavior enables subjects interpret gathering behavior, based on their first-person experiences of density.

We conclude that a bird's-eye view is effective in understanding the spatial movements of crowds, and that this understanding can be increased by first-person experiences.

Table 1. Summary of the results of the questionnaire (one-sided paired t-test)

No.	Question (the correct answer is the follow-me method.)	FP	BE	FP-BE	BE-FP
1	Leaders are the first to escape.	***	*	*	***
2	Leaders do not observe evacuees.	**	***	***	***
3	Leaders escape like evacuees.		*	*	**
4	One's escape behavior is caused by others' escape behavior.		*	**	**
5	Nobody prevents evacuees from going to the incorrect exit.		***	***	***
6	Evacuees follow other evacuees.				*
7	Evacuees form a group.				*
8	Leaders and evacuees escape together.		*		**
9	Evacuees try to behave the same as other evacuees.		*		

*$p<.05$, **$p<.01$, ***$p<.001$ (df=23)

4   The Evacuation Guidance System

The result described above showed that communication between a person who can observe the bird's-eye view of an emergency situation and another person who is inside the situation is meaningful for grasping the situation. Thus, we designed a communication interface that allows a remote leader to lead escaping crowds in an emergency situation.

Recent advances in wireless communication and sensor devices will allow virtual cities to simulate the current state of real cities synchronously. These synchronous virtual cities can be used to observe what is happening in a real-world emergency situation. We developed an evacuation guidance system that is a synchronous virtual Kyoto Station to connect the staff and the passengers. The staff can watch the behavior of the real passengers represented in the virtual station and guide them.

4.1   The Transcendent Communication Interface

The evacuation guidance system provides a bird's-eye view that is appropriate for observational tasks. To explain our system, we propose a new communication style called transcendent communication. First-person view is immanent since it is supposed that the user exists inside the virtual city as an avatar. Conversely, a bird's-eye view is transcendent since it is supposed that the user is looking at the virtual city from outside. The evacuation guidance system is a user interface for transcendent communication. The transcendent communication interface is a seamless combination of a visualization interface to observe the real world and a pointing interface to choose people to talk to.

A sensor for determining the locations of people is necessary to implement transcendent communication interfaces. For those purposes, the most generally used tools currently include a map, a mouse, and GPS. A transcendent communication interface that combines them can work as follows. The telephone numbers of people and their locations are transmitted to the interface. Then, they are represented as the icons shown on the map. When the user clicks one of the icons, the interface establishes a vocal connection between the user's microphone and the mobile phone of the clicked person. To implement the evacuation guidance system, we used a virtual city instead of a map, and a vision sensor network instead of GPS [7].

Figure 4 is a photo of the evacuation guidance system. In this figure, a remote leader looks over the virtual Kyoto Station and freely chooses people to talk to. In the virtual station, virtual crowds try to walk along the trajectory data continuously transmitted from the vision sensor network of Kyoto Station. The bird's-eye view of the virtual station is displayed on a large-scale touch screen so that the leader can grasp the entire situation of the crowd behavior. When the leader touches people displayed on the screen, the system establishes voice channels between the leader's microphone and the mobile phones of these people.

The evacuation guidance system enables the leader to guide several groups of crowds separately. This ability is nearly impossible with conventional announcement facilities. Our system brings a distributed fashion to evacuation guidance announcements.

Fig. 4. Evacuation guidance system

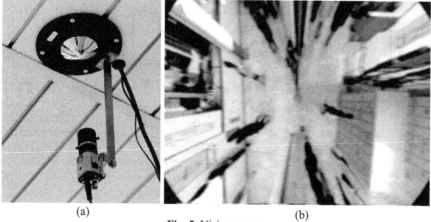

(a)   (b)

Fig. 5. Vision sensor

4.2   The Vision Sensor Network

To synchronize the virtual Kyoto Station with the real Kyoto Station, we installed a vision sensor network. Figure 5(a) is a picture of the vision sensor installed in the station. In this picture, you can see a CCD camera and a reflector with a special shape. This reflector is necessary to cover a wide range with a small number of sensors. If we could expand the field of view of each camera, we could reduce the number of cameras. However, a widened field of view causes minus (barrel) distortion in the images taken by conventional cameras. The reflector of our vision sensor can eliminate such distortion. The shape of the reflector can tailor a plane that perpendicularly intersects the optical axis of the camera to be projected perspectively

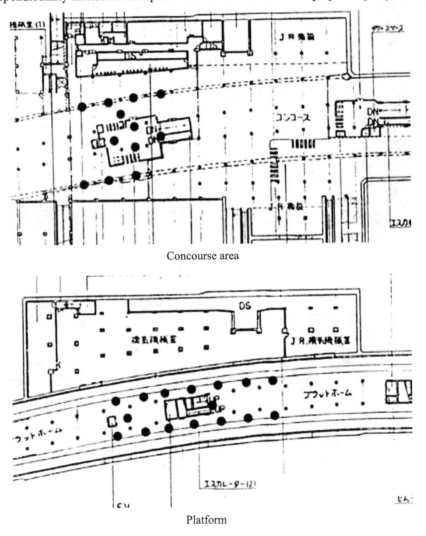

Concourse area

Platform

Fig. 6. Installed positions

to the camera plane. This optical device makes it possible to have a large field of view without distortion. Figure 5(b) is an image taken by our vision sensors attached to the ceiling of the station platform.

We installed 12 sensors in the concourse area and 16 sensors on the platform. The small black circles in figure 6 show the positions of the sensors. In figure 7, one sees

Concourse area

Platform

Fig. 7. Installation of vision sensors

how these sensors are installed at the station. The vision sensor network can track the passengers between the platform and the ticket gate.

The facilities installed at the station include 28 vision sensors, 7 quad processors, 7 PCs for image processing, and a PC for trajectory detection. The method of processing images is as follows. First, a quad processor assembles the images taken by four sensors into one video image and sends it to the image-processing PC. Next, the PC extracts the regions of moving objects by the background subtraction technique and sends the results to the trajectory-detection PC. Finally, the PC detects the positions of the moving objects based on geographical knowledge such as the positions of the cameras, the occlusion edges in the cameras' views, and the boundaries of the areas.

5 Conclusions

In this paper, we presented the multi-user multi-agent architecture. The architecture enabled a virtual city to function as a participatory crisis management simulation. We found that the bird's-eye view of the simulation provided an overall understanding of crowd behavior, whereas the first-person view provided more in-depth understanding. This result showed the valuable of the transcendent communication interface. The interface enabled a virtual city to be an evacuation guidance system. It is a future work to explore the potential of our approach of using virtual cities for crisis management in real-world cities.

Acknowledgements

We express our thanks to the cooperation of Municipal Transportation Bureau and General Planning Bureau of Kyoto city. Hiroshi Ishiguro advised us on the deployment of the vision sensor network. We received a lot of support in the construction of the simulation from Toshio Sugiman, Shigeyuki Okazaki, and Ken Tsutsuguchi. Thanks to Reiko Hishiyama, Hideaki Ito, Tomoyuki Kawasoe, Toyokazu Itakura, CRC solutions, Mathematical system, and CAD center for their efforts in the development of the evacuation simulation and guidance systems.

References

1. CAD center. Virtual Reality Simulation Program for Architectural Performances (VR-SPAP). http://www.cadcenter.co.jp/en/webgallery/webgallery_vr5.html
2. S. Fukatsu, Y. Kitamura, T. Masaki, and F. Kishino. Intuitive Control of "Bird's Eye" Overview Images for Navigation in an Enormous Virtual Environment. ACM Symposium on Virtual Reality Software and Technology (VRST98), 67-76, 1998.
3. D. Helbing, I.J. Farkas, and T. Vicsek. Simulating Dynamical Features of Escape Panic. Nature, Vol. 407, No. 6803, pp. 487-490, 2000.
4. T. Ishida, H. Ishiguro, and H. Nakanishi. Connecting Digital and Physical Cities. M. Tanabe, P. van den Besselaar, and T. Ishida Ed., Digital Cities II. Lecture Notes in Computer Science 2362, Springer-Verlag, pp. 246-256, 2002.

5. T. Ishida. Digital City Kyoto: Social Information Infrastructure for Everyday Life. Communications of the ACM (CACM), Vol. 45, No. 7, pp. 76-81, 2002.

5a. T. Ishida, Activities and technologies in Digital City Kyoto. In P. van den Besselaar, S. Koizumi (eds), Digital Cities 3. Information technologies for social capital. Lecture Notes in Computer Science, Vol. 3081. Springer-Verlag, Berlin Heidelberg New York (2005) pp. 162-183.

6. T. Ishida. *Q*: A Scenario Description Language for Interactive Agents. IEEE Computer, Vol. 35, No. 11, pp. 54-59, 2002.

7. P.H. Kelly, A. Katkere, D.Y. Kuramura, S. Moezzi, and S. Chatterjee. An Architecture for Multiple Perspective Interactive Video, International Conference on Multimedia, (Multimedia95), pp. 201-212, 1995.

8. A. Kendon. Spatial Organization in Social Encounters: the F-formation System. A. Kendon, Ed., Conducting Interaction: Patterns of Behavior in Focused Encounters, Cambridge University Press, pp. 209-237, 1990.

9. J.E. Laird. It Knows What You're Going To Do: Adding Anticipation to a Quakebot. International Conference on Autonomous Agents (AAMAS2001), pp. 385-392, 2001.

10. R. Linturi, M. Koivunen, and J. Sulkanen. Helsinki Arena 2000 - Augmenting a Real City to a Virtual One. T. Ishida, K. Isbister Ed., Digital Cities, Technologies, Experiences, and Future Perspectives. Lecture Notes in Computer Science 1765, Springer-Verlag, New York, pp. 83-96. 2000.

10a R. Linturi & T. Simula, Virtual Helsinki. In P. van den Besselaar, S. Koizumi (eds), Digital Cities 3. Information technologies for social capital. Lecture Notes in Computer Science, Vol. 3081. Springer-Verlag, Berlin Heidelberg New York (2005) pp. 110-137.

11. Y. Murakami, T. Ishida, T. Kawasoe, and R. Hishiyama. Scenario Description for Multi-Agent Simulation. International Joint Conference on Autonomous Agents and Multiagent Systems (AAMAS2003), pp. 369-376, 2003.

12. H. Nakanishi, C. Yoshida, T. Nishimura and T. Ishida. FreeWalk: A 3D Virtual Space for Casual Meetings. IEEE Multimedia, Vol.6, No.2, pp. 20-28, 1999.

13. S. Okazaki and S. Matsushita. A Study of Simulation Model for Pedestrian Movement with Evacuation and Queuing. International Conference on Engineering for Crowd Safety, pp. 271-280, 1993.

14. T. Sugiman and J. Misumi. Development of a New Evacuation Method for Emergencies: Control of Collective Behavior by Emergent Small Groups. Journal of Applied Psychology, Vol. 73, No. 1, pp. 3-10, 1988.

15. W. Swartout, R. Hill, J. Gratch, W.L. Johnson, C. Kyriakakis, K. Labore, R. Lindheim, S. Marsella, D. Miraglia, B. Moore, J. Morie, J. Rickel, M. Thiebaux, L. Tuch, R. Whitney and J. Douglas. Toward the Holodeck: Integrating Graphics, Sound, Character and Story. International Conference on Autonomous Agents (AAMAS2001), pp. 409-416, 2001.

16. K. Tsutsuguchi, S. Shimada, Y. Suenaga, N. Sonehara, and S. Ohtsuka. Human Walking Animation based on Foot Reaction Force in the Three-dimensional Virtual World. Journal of Visualization and Computer Animation, Vol. 11, No. 1, pp. 3-16, 2000.

Virtuose, a VIRTual CommUnity Open Source Engine for Integrating Civic Networks and Digital Cities

Marco Benini[1], Fiorella De Cindio[2], Leonardo Sonnante[3]

[1]Dipartimento di Informatica e Comunicazione, Università degli Studi dell'Insubria, Italy
marco.benini@uninsubria.it

[2]Dipartimento di Informatica e Comunicazione, Università degli Studi di Milano, Italy
fiorella.decindio@unimi.it

[3]Fondazione RCM - Rete Civica di Milano, Italy
leonardo.sonnante@rcm.inet.it

Abstract. This paper outlines the development of digital cities in Italy from 1994 to the present and then shows how this became the basis for the design principles of *Virtuose*. *Virtuose* may be termed *communityware*. It was conceived specifically for managing (local) virtual communities and drew inspiration from social as well as technological design concepts, using an open-environment philosophy. *Virtuose's* basic requirements and its essential design and implementation choices are presented, and a pragmatic example of its application is given. The paper also provides a specific description of how the messaging structure supports both publication and dialog.

1 Introduction

Digital cities emerged in Europe in 1994-95: The Amsterdam Digital City (DDS, *De Digitale Stad*) [36] started in Spring 1994, the Milan Community Network (RCM, *Rete Civica di Milano*) in Autumn of the same year. The Bologna Iperbole experience became operational at the beginning of 1995. Several other digital cities then followed these early initiatives.

In Italy the phenomenon was rather explosive mainly because of its interplay with the political situation, which led to the transition from the First to the Second Republic and to the adoption of new election laws for mayors and city councils. The Internet was seen as a way for promoting citizen participation in public affairs [31] – now called *e-participation* – and for reinventing citizenship and democracy [13] – now called *e-democracy*.

Inspired by these principles, several municipalities (in Italy and elsewhere in Europe) followed Bologna's example, which became well known after winning the Bangemann award. In other cases, the Milan experience, promoted by the university, provided the inspiration for civic networks that were started as grassroots initiatives by civil society. The distinction between institutional and grassroots initiatives in most cases led to a technological difference: Richer experiences directly promoted by the municipality adopted the Web as their network infrastructure, while grassroots initiatives with lower budgets often adopted cheaper BBS technology. However,

P. van den Besselaar and S. Koizumi (Eds.): Digital Cities 2003, LNCS 3081, pp. 217-232, 2005.

despite these differences, all these early experiences were called *civic networks*: As [25] describes, "the primary aim of early civic networks was promoting the publication of official documents and promoting citizen participation in the life of the municipality". It is important to point out that publishing official documents was seen as a means of assuring transparency: Allowing citizens to access official documents is a prerequisite for their active participation.

In the same year, 1995, another significant digital city was started in Italy by the municipality of Turin. It was named differently – the Public Telematic Service – to stress the fact that, unlike other digital-city initiatives, its main emphasis was on providing online services to the local community: Citizens, as well as professionals and enterprises, could benefit from reducing interaction time with local government (for getting a certificate or a map, for paying taxes, etc.). An argument could be made that, in Italy, the Turin initiative started what we now call *e-government*. It is important to note that the promoters of the Turin Public Telematic Service insisted from the outset, as subsequent research confirmed, that e-democracy and e-government are not mutual exclusive, but rather complement and enrich each other. As a result, one phenomenon we now observe is that the use of the Net for publishing information and delivering online services overrode the role of the Net as an environment for participation. Over the course of the years from 1996-7 to the present, digital cities increasingly turned into the official websites of local government, providing information and transactional services. In most cases, the pioneering spirit of civic networks was lost. In Italy, this change is consistent with a corresponding mutation in the political climate wherein the participation issues of the second half of the nineties nearly disappeared. People were increasingly seen as *users* of ICT applications or as *consumers* of online services, although it ought to be borne in mind that citizens own *a sovereignty right* that should allow them to contribute to shaping the information society [15].

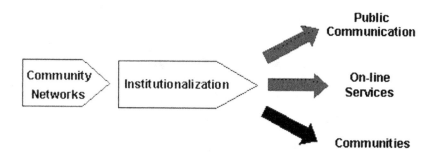

Fig. 1. The specialization of Digital Cities (source: Censis)

Censis, an outstanding Italian national research institute that has been tracking the evolution of digital cities in Italy since 1997 and publishing annual reports, depicts the increasing institutionalization of digital cities in its last two reports (also [25]). Censis shows that this process has now led to the specialization of digital cities, as shown in figure 1 [14, 9]. Different kinds of digital cities can actually be observed:

- digital cities that focus primarily on delivering public information, where the communication pattern is broadcasting from the public sector (which tends increasingly to be not a single entity but a consortium of local authorities in the same area) to the citizens (and in general to the local community);
- digital cities (often called *city portals*) that focus mainly on delivering e-government services, where the communication pattern is two-way interaction according to a predetermined information flow;
- digital cities (often called *civic networks*) that aim to provide the local community with a communication environment for free dialog, where the communication pattern is the peer-to-peer conversation typical of virtual communities.

Censis selects paradigmatic examples for each of these types of community networks[1]; what is relevant for our purposes is that the most recent report [9] strongly emphasizes the need to integrate the three approaches: a good digital city should provide well-integrated information and online services, both for residents and for those with occasional business or tourist interests in the city, and a good digital city should also provide a dialog-oriented communication environment (figure 2). Because the present scenario is e-government, i.e., the integration of information and on-line services, it is interesting to consider the reason Censis gives for expanding a city website to include community facilities: "To create online communities among the users of the local-government website means offering a chance to interact with local government in a different way, to recover and develop a sense of belonging and trust in the local and institutional context.".

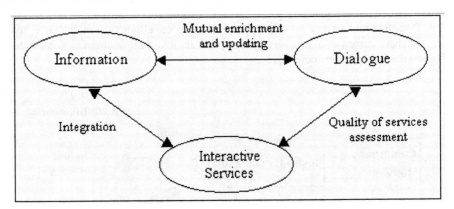

Fig. 2. The interplay between dialog, publication, and services

Because of the cumulative experience of having designed RCM in 1994 and managed it since then, we came to the same conclusion. Our perspective has always been that of a civic network trying to keep its original emphasis on citizens' and civil society's direct involvement. Indeed, in the framework described above, a civic network cannot merely offer an environment for dialog, but needs ways to extract information

---

[1] In the Censis slides, the Milan Community Network (RCM) is presented as the paradigmatic case of the third kind.

and knowledge from people's small talk. This is what spurred us to work on the technology that could be used for digital cities.

2   Software for Community Networks

When we decided to start RCM in 1994, we had several design alternatives to consider, including the choice of software platform. The first natural option we entertained was *FreePort* software [17], which was developed at the Case Western University to run the Cleveland Free Net and then became a sort of standard available very cheaply anyone wishing to start a community network. Unfortunately, *FreePort* adopted an outdated text-based interface, whereas the standard was already the window, icon-based graphical user interface.

The other option considered was to develop RCM on the Web, then in its early stages of development. However, we were forced to discard this option for two reasons. On the one hand, a large majority of people and policy makers in Italy and Europe considered e-mail rather than full Internet access the universal network service to be provided to everybody, see, e.g., [1]. On the other hand, the Web had been conceived for enhancing the publishing capabilities of the Internet – which was initially confined to the protocol known as FTP – and poorly supported the kind of peer-to-peer communication that, in contrast, typically takes place through email, mailing lists, forums, and chats. We feared that the shift from a communication platform such as that offered by BBSs to a publishing platform, as the Web was at the beginning (and long remained), might radically change the community network from being a local virtual community where everybody is considered an information provider to a rather standard medium for information broadcasting where the website owner is responsible for providing information to its customers.

Hence, our need was for software that was very easy to learn and to use, while providing standard BBS features. The choice thus fell to *FirstClass* (originally produced by SoftArc Inc., now by OpenText), which we knew as the platform used by the Open University. Unfortunately, *FirstClass* is proprietary software, and, over the years, we encountered the problems typical of using proprietary software, namely: cost, a closed data format, and a fixed, non-modifiable set of features.

As noted, RCM was a reference model for other, mainly grassroots, civic networks, mostly in the Lombardy region. Thanks to the support of the regional government, in 1996 Lombardy's civic networks joined to form the Association for Informatics and Civic Networking (AIReC Lombardia)[2]. The various members of AIReC made different choices for running the civic network. Some community networks adopted *Lotus Notes* because it was the intranet/extranet platform used by the host municipality. Others chose proprietary software quite similar to *FirstClass* called *Worldgroup*. A couple of them opted for Web-based, free software environments. But none of them was truly satisfied with its choice.

---

[2] AIReC [3] groups the community networks located in Lombardy. It was established under the auspices of the Region of Lombardy and the Department of Computer Science of the University of Milano.

Therefore, after considering the *CSuite* software [23, 12] – an open-source platform adopted by several community networks in Canada – which did not meet our needs because of its character-based user interface, we started some preliminary analysis developed as part of a few masters theses. In 2000, AIReC obtained funding from the Region of Lombardy to undertake the development of a civic network software platform whose distinguishing feature was the homogeneous coupling of both *information* publishing and *dialog* facilities. These facilities enrich information with community-generated knowledge (an expression we deem more expressive than the more common "content generated by users"). Moreover, the platform was to be open to integration with interactive services.

The rationale behind this basic design choice can be illustrated through the following example. Let's suppose Fiorella, a citizen, wants to know the list of movies showing in Milan this evening. She can look at the city website, which usually provides this information. However, by accessing the "Cinema" forum on the community network, she enriches this information with community knowledge that was created through discussion. For instance, about a couple of movies, her favorite opinion-maker in the community says: "Beautiful plot". At this point, she makes her choice and books a place in the nearest theater showing the selected movie. After viewing the movie, she comes back and comments on the movie or the state of the theater in the local forum, e.g., in terms of the fairness of the automatic booking procedure.

The same pattern can be applied to many situations, from the choice of a restaurant to the need for a clinical-analysis laboratory. In the latter case, comments following use of the service provide a powerful way for assessing *Quality of Service*[3]. Figure 2 illustrates the interplay between these elements: the positive cross-fertilization between the discussion facilities of a community network and the information and interactive-service facilities of the municipal website. This cross-fertilization can help overcome the increasing institutionalization of digital cities mentioned above, while enhancing the impact of the discussions carried on within the community.

The present paper, which significantly extends [5], discusses the result of the project: the *Virtuose* software, a *VIRTual CommUnity Open Source Engine*. In the framework of the technologies for digital cities envisaged in [20], *Virtuose* can be seen as a "technology for public participation that supports both content creation and social interaction." Pursuing our driving idea, mentioned in [33], that *"Les maison font la ville, mais les citoyens font la cité,"* (J.J. Rousseau, *Du Contract Social*) *Virtuose* focuses on the basics of integrating information and communication, so that digital citizens [32] can be information providers (rather than merely passive consumers of information provided by public- and private-sector organizations) and can actively discuss any issue related to city life.

Advanced graphics facilities such as the presentation of information based on interactive maps [8] are, of course, useful and effective for enhancing user interfaces. In the above examples, for instance, they might help indicate where, in town, movie theaters, restaurants or clinical-analysis laboratories are located. We actually

---

[3] The need to assess the quality of public services and their acceptance through citizen feedback is explicitly referred to in Republic of Italy Law No. 150/2000, "Discipline of government information and communication activities."

experimented with such user interfaces in one of the pre-studies for *Virtuose* [2], although the version we present here concentrates on the kernel engine.

3   Our Solution: *Virtuose*

This section is devoted to illustrating and discussing *Virtuose's* basic system requirements, its fundamental design choices, and how these choices have been translated into software architecture. Finally, this section analyzes an example of practical application.

3.1   Requirements

As discussed above, the requirements of *Virtuose* are both an abstraction and a synthesis of the needs that emerged from experience managing community networks in the Italian context. Such experience, where AIReC and its members (RCM, RecSando, RCL, etc.) played the leading role, came both from the citizen side and the administration side. Comments, suggestions, requests for improvements, and criticism were collected and evaluated. Thus, albeit indirectly, every category of community users, i.e., normal citizens, moderators, administrators, directors, etc., contributed to developing the specifications for *Virtuose* through experience accumulated over the years. Consequently, *Virtuose* was designed on the basis of a social rather than technological perspective. This centered around two main activities: publications and dialog.

Both activities were modeled from the outset on a small and general set of simple concepts. The key idea, borrowed from most community-oriented applications [12, 24, 37, 23] is that the information unit is a *message*. Formally, a message is divided into a *header* and a *body*. Both are composed of *fields*, i.e. named and categorized pieces of data. The header contains information that identifies the originator, the destination, the type of content, and the subject, i.e., a textual description of the content. The body consists of the message content.

Every field has a name and a type. The whole message has a type which completely defines the types and names of the fields of its body. In a word, the message type identifies the *structure* of the message.

Unlike from most other applications, *Virtuose* allows message types to be dynamically defined. The community administrator, who maintains the community service, may define new message types at any time, without interrupting service.

Messages are grouped into *conferences*, which are structures defined by a name, and a list of messages, which may be threaded. Conferences can group messages by any criterion an administrator wishes to adopt. They might hold a set of messages on the same topic (e.g., a discussion list on football), messages from an institutional organization (e.g., the book records of a library), or more subtle groupings, like messages to a single community member (e.g., a mailbox). It is very important to note that limiting the conference to accept only messages of a fixed set of types enables the use of the conference concept to model most of the important tools employed in building community software. As a matter of fact, the personal website of a community member is nothing other than a named set of HTML pages, i.e., a set of messages of type "HTML page." Moreover, a calendar can be modeled as a conference where messages are appointments and notes. All these examples have been implemented in *Virtuose*, which supports discussion lists, as well as publication conferences, mailboxes, calendars, and user websites by means of the unified framework just described.

A fundamental aspect of social relations is the *role* of a person. Typically, the concept of role has been confused with the technical concept of *permission*, i.e., the ability to do something. This is only the half of a good technical rendering. Actually, permissions determine what a community member can or cannot do on the information units, i.e., permissions define a community member's ability to manipulate messages, or, in a social view, to create publications or to take part in a discussion. But, equally fundamental in defining a role is how information is viewed. Depending on the role s/he plays, a community member may or may not view certain types of messages, and the way they are presented graphically may change. For example, in a discussion, the role of moderators is important. They filter messages by avoiding publishing those that may be offensive or irrelevant. When a community member plays the role of moderator, s/he should be able to view all the messages posted to a conference, and s/he may approve some of them and delete others. When the same community member wants to post a message, s/he assumes a different role, one that allows posting but excludes approving. Moreover, in the second role, only approved messages may be viewed.

Therefore, a strong requirement of *Virtuose's* specifications is to model roles in the way just explained. Every community member has an identity, and, thus, can assume a role that defines her or his degree of control when viewing a conference and determines the way messages in the conference are displayed.

A social role is more than just permissions and visual presentation. It may be interpreted as a way to group people, or, conversely, to group conferences. For example, community members interested in music may wear the role "music" to access thematic conferences, which are uninteresting for other members at that moment.

The main requirement of *Virtuose* is to implement conferences and roles as described above, that is, it must allow dynamic manipulation of message types. Every conference has to have a set of admissible message types, every user must have an identity, and every user may assume a role, both in the sense of group membership and in the sense of manipulation power. These requirements are referred to as *flexibility* in the management of the virtual community. The flexibility requirement calls for a non-traditional programming technique: having a small set of basic concepts, the message, its type, the conference, the user, and his or her roles, that can combine dynamically in any way possible. This requires an approach to development that is closer to an artificial intelligence product than to a traditional Web application.

Moreover, *Virtuose* had to be concept software, that is, a system developed specifically to test our ideas of what a virtual community should be and to check that our concepts, as stated above, can be effectively used for a faithful rendering of community life. For these reasons, *Virtuose* had to be compact and easy to modify and to manage, even at the expense of performance or range of features.

Nevertheless, many other features were included in the specifications for *Virtuose*, such as multilingual support, graphical themes, strict adherence to the open source paradigm, etc. Although these features are important, and their analysis might be of interest, we believe a discussion of them is beyond the scope of this article, because the core of *Virtuose* lies in the flexibility requirement, which represents the real novelty of this piece of software and, we hope, a significant contribution to the designers and developers of virtual communities.

3.2   Design and Implementation

Virtuose is a Web application written using PHP [27, 22, 29] as the server-side development language, PostgreSQL [28, 26, 34] as the supporting database management system, Apache [4] as the Web-server engine, Javascript [16] as the client-side scripting language, and HTML [18, 10] as the presentation-markup language.

From an architectural point of view, *Virtuose* is fairly standard, adopting a variant of the classical three-layer structure [29] that divides an application's logic, presentation, and data. The architecture of *Virtuose* is depicted in Figure 3.

The main difference between *Virtuose* and similar applications [12, 37, 23] lays in the flexibility required by design and the compactness of coding techniques. Both requirements were discussed in the previous section, but not from the point of view of technical implications.

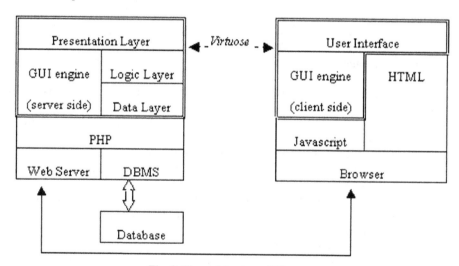

Fig. 3. The architecture of *Virtuose*

In fact, the GUI engine plays the role of an application server [21], although it is really an application framework [30], developed from scratch for the purposes of *Virtuose*.

The flexible nature of message types, which can be defined by the community administrator at any time, requires a dynamic approach in defining the database. Indeed, because messages are subject to searching, they should be represented as the rows of one or more interrelated tables in the database, the columns being message fields. However, fields depend on message types, which are stored in the database as well. Thus the database schema must change dynamically whenever a message type is added or deleted. Hence the data layer of *Virtuose* provides both an interface to the DBMS and the functions assigned to tracking the evolution of the database schema over time.

The flexibility requirement has its strong point in the concept of role, interpreted both as ability to manipulate and grouping. In order to implement this concept, two new entities were introduced in the design: *views* and *profiles*. The former renders the first meaning of the notion of role, while the latter is used for grouping. Their interaction defines what we call flexibility.

A profile is nothing other than a named set of users. A single user may appear in many profiles, that is, a single user may act as a member of many different groups. A view is, as the name suggests, a way to look at and to interact with a conference. It is defined by a set of message types that are allowed to appear in the conference, and, for each message type, a set of permissions and a set of graphical templates[4]. The only way to inspect a conference is through a view. The list of messages in the conference is thus filtered by the view, so to display only messages whose type appears in the view. Moreover, when a given individual message is to be displayed, the view permits display of its content only if the read permission for that type is true. Likewise, creating, deleting or modifying a message is allowed only if the view contains the appropriate permission for the message type involved in the operation.

When a message is to be displayed for a user, either as an element of the list of messages or as a single, complete message, the GUI engine selects the right template to use according to the message type. Moreover, the whole message list has its own template in the view structure. Therefore, the community administrator, by creating her or his own templates, may control the way information is presented with no constraints.

In figure 4, a piece of the database schema is shown: It represents the main entities involved in rendering the concept of role, along with their relations.

A user may be associated with a potentially large set of profiles through the group relation. A profile provides access to a number of views by means of the access relation. A view displays the content of the associated conference by means of the show relation. Thus, a user may look at a conference by choosing a profile that provides access to a view for that conference. Consequently, the user may look at the same conference through many different views, depending on the profile he chooses. A virtual-community administrator may set access to conferences by defining views and by distributing their access to different profiles so as to partition groups of users based on their interests, their responsibilities, and so forth.

A view refers to a conference by means of the show relation. The message types it manipulates are the ones related to permissions by means of the visible relations. The logic layer assures that each visible relation is a subset of the admissible relations. A

---

[4] Although, in principle, graphical templates in a view are grouped according to the message type they apply to, there are default templates for all messages, independent from their type, but specific to the view, and there are templates, associated with conferences, that are used as defaults for views that do not provide more specific templates. This template hierarchy is quite involved to describe, although it has been designed to be natural to work with. In the following, we adopt the simplified assumption that every message type has its own templates.

message has a type and is a member of a conference and is divided into two tables, the header and the body. The body table is dynamic, i.e., there is a distinct table for every message type, whose columns are exactly the records of the field table related to the type.

The logic layer defines the procedures to manipulate the concepts defined in the previous section, mapping them to the database schema, and assuring integrity of data semantics. The presentation layer provides the primitives to capture events from the client side of the application, and to generate presentation of the virtual community by means of HTML templates.

Actually, the picture of the insides of *Virtuose* presented so far is partial. Many entities in the database schema have been omitted for the sake of simplicity and a series of important functions the logic layer provides have not been included in our description. The most complex piece of code in *Virtuose* is the GUI engine, which introduces many abstractions the need for which is apparent when the details of implementation are considered. As noted, although these considerations may be interesting, we believe that the important part of *Virtuose's* implementation lies in its dynamic-database message management and in the structure of views. For this reason we are limiting our discussion of the internal workings of *Virtuose* to this and must refer readers interested in other topics to the technical documentation [38].

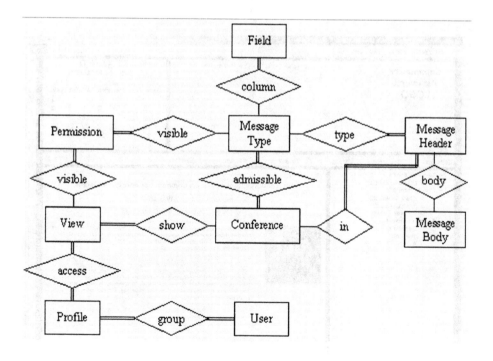

Fig. 4. The relevant part of the database schema

3.3   A Pragmatic Example

The goal of this section is to offer an example of how the described model of conference management is an effective way to represent publication and dialog around a specific topic, while preserving the separation between the two activities without losing their underlying relationship.

One topic commonly found on community networks consists of the cultural, social, and sporting events and the like taking place in the community network's geographic area. Let's see how the community manager can arrange a conference around this topic using the *Virtuose* platform.

S/he can create a suitable type of message named *event* whose fields are *title, date and place, description,* and *image* with the obvious meanings. This will be the "publication part" of the conference. S/he also wants to allow people to send comments to the published events as text or as related web links. Therefore, s/he creates a conference named *events* that accepts messages of type *event,* but also *comment* and *weblinks*. The latter is a message type with a structure suitable for inserting a list of URLs with their descriptions, while the former is a message type with a body that consists of a text field. This is the "dialog part" of the service. For each message type, the community manager may also write an HTML template for formatting field content for publication. For example, figure 5 shows an event message, as it appears in the *Virtuose* interface.

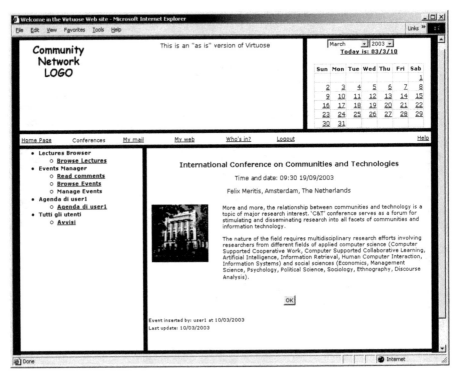

Fig. 5. A message of type *event.*

As already explained, a conference can be accessed only through a view, so the next step is to create some views to allow users to insert events and comments. If the community manager decides to allow all community members to insert their events, s/he may want to choose some of them as moderators, i.e. those users who make events readable by others. No matter what s/he decides, s/he needs a view that grants every user who can access the conference the right to write events in it. If the same view also gives the right to write comments, we might have a configuration like the one shown in Figure 6. On the left side of the page is the list of views, grouped by the profiles the user belongs to. Clicking on a view brings up the list of messages filtered by that view on the right side of the page.

In the list of messages, we can emphasize the differences among message types thanks to different background colors or other visualization clues. We are also able to display different fields of the message: date and place for event messages, author for comments and weblinks. When a community member wants to write a message, s/he has to choose the type of the message s/he is going to create, thus providing implicit information about the semantics of what s/he is going to write. This information can be very useful for search features: If someone is interested in related web sites, he can focus his search on weblinks messages, ignoring all comments and events.

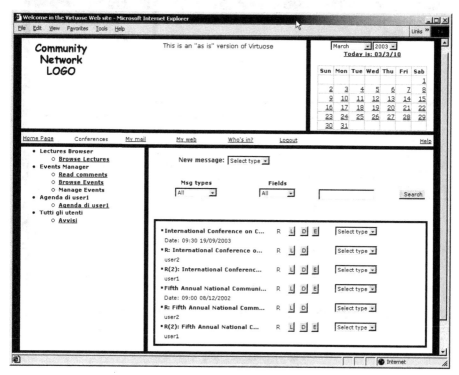

Fig. 6. The list of messages of the Events conference

It will now be readily apparent to the reader that in order to allow distinct access to events and to comments, the community manager need only create two views, with their appropriate permissions, one for events and one for the comment and weblink message types, see, e.g., Figure 7. These two views enable the reader to focus either on matters of information (the list of events) or on discussion, with a tight correlation between them made possible by belonging to the same conference and, therefore, to the same topic. Of course, given the flexible nature of *Virtuose*, any other policy for defining views may be implemented in similar fashion.

4   Conclusions and Discussion

As we said in the introduction, the idea and the development of *Virtuose* was basically driven by the need of software for managing online communities, homogeneously coupling the publishing of *information*, and facilities for *dialog*, which enriches information with community-generated knowledge. More in general, this can be seen as the kernel of a software platform for virtual communities. The need for *communityware* was confirmed after we started to develop *Virtuose*.

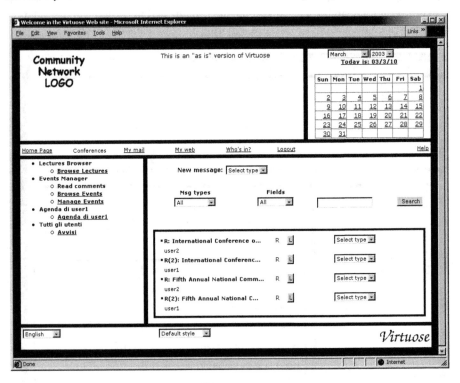

Fig. 7. The read comments view

In March 2001, Etienne Wenger, published on the Web a detailed report surveying community-oriented technologies for supporting communities of practice [39]. He considered and classified a large number of applications from different fields (knowledge management, online conversations, community-oriented e-learning spaces, website communities, and others). None of them, save one, falls into the intersection that represents software providing to a satisfactory extent the features needed to manage a community of practice. According to Wenger's survey, the only software that approximates the requirements is *Communispace* [11], which is, however, more a service than a software product, as it is available only on an ASP basis at relatively expensive rates. Although the emphasis of Wenger's survey is slightly different from ours, since he focuses on "a technological platform to support communities of practice across a large organization," the result of his survey confirms that "the ideal system for a general platform for communities of practice still does not really exist."

In Spring 2002, the American Association For Community Networking raised a call for software to manage community networks, promising an award of $2,000 to the winner. Most of the required features were included in *Virtuose*, although the general architecture was quite different. Indeed, the call required collecting in a common framework the standard open-source applications that support the required features (e.g., *PHORUM* for managing forums or *Mailman* for mailing lists). Nevertheless, we decided to submit the first version of *Virtuose* and its associated documentation [6]. It was surprising to find that *Virtuose* was the only submission, and gratifying to receive, from the promoters of the award, after they had tested the software, a $500 premium to encourage its further development.

Finally, it is worth mentioning that, while we were developing *Virtuose*, a somewhat similar technology appeared, i.e., Internet weblogs, which have now become quite popular. The similarity lies in the fact that weblogs allow generic users to easily publish their own content and to enrich it through readers' comments in threads of discussion. In this respect, weblogs share *Virtuose's* purpose of integrating publishing and discussion. We are experimentally testing a couple of weblog environments as satellites of RCM. This early experience points at the main differences between web-logs and *Virtuose*, namely:

1. Each weblog contains one specific pattern of publishing and discussing ("news" and "forum" sections), while *Virtuose* gives its administrators the flexibility to design their own patterns of integration between information and discussion;
2. Weblogs are much more individual tools, while *Virtuose* is conceived to support communities.

From a more technical point of view, *Virtuose* has been the occasion to develop a solution for managing dynamic databases by significantly extending standard database technology. Although this feature is one of the reasons why the present prototypical implementation suffers from inefficiency, it also proves that *Virtuose* provides much more flexibility than the other similar applications. This is to say that *Virtuose*, in its present state of development, as it will be for the near future as well, is an open framework where ideas and techniques involving communities can be tested. For this reason it can be freely downloaded (www.virtuose.it).

We are developing an XML-based implementation that keeps this flexibility while improving performance. This technological solution was discarded in the current version because of the lack of tools available at that moment in the design phase. Because some apparently mature tools, e.g., the Tamino XML database management system [35], have since been brought to market, we are now able to reconsider the choice. This opens up the opportunity to relate *Virtuose's* open architecture more deeply to the concepts of Semantic Web [7].

Acknowledgments

Virtuose was mainly developed in the framework of the project 'Development of services and technologies to turn local communities to account in the Information Society' funded by the Region of Lombardy and carried out by AIReC (the Association for Informatics and Community Networks) and its members. Subsequent improvements were partially supported by the Italian MIUR (FIRB "Web-Minds" project).

References

1. Anderson R.H., Bikson T.K., Law S.A., Mitchell B.M, *Universal Access to E-mail: Feasibility and Social Implications*, Rand, Santa Monica, CA, 1995.
2. Aletti M., De Cindio F., Rossi G., Sonnante L., *A Web-based platform for third generation community networks*, presented at the ECSCW'99 Workshop on "Broadening Our Understanding", Copenhagen, September, 1999.
3. AIReC Web site: http://www.airec.it.
4. Apache Web site: http://www.apache.org.
5. Benini M., De Cindio F., Sonnante L., *VIRTUOSE: a VIRTual CommUnity Open Source Engine*, Proc. DIAC-02 Symposium "Shaping the Network Society: Patterns for Participation, Action and Change", Carveth R., Kretchmer S., Schuler D. (eds.), CPSR, pp. 40-43, Seattle, WA, May 2002.
6. De Cindio F., Benini M., Sonnante L., *VIRTUOSE White Paper*, A.I.Re.C. Report, February 2002.
7. Berners-Lee T., Hendler J., Lassila O., *The Semantic Web*, Scientific American, May 2001.
8. Bolatto G., Sozza A., Gauna I., Rusconi M., *The Geographic Information Systems (GIS) of Turin Municipality*, in [19]
9. Censis ed., *7th Report on Digital Cities in Italy*, February 2003. A summary is available at http://www.censis.it/censis/ricerc.html. (italian)
10. Connolly D., Masinter L., *The 'text/html' Media Type*, RFC2854, June 2000.
11. Communispace Web site: http://www.communispace.com.
12. CSuite Web site: http://csuite.ns.ca.
13. De Cindio F., *Community Networks for Reinventing Citizenship and Democracy*, in M. Gurstein (ed.), *Community Informatics: Enabling Communities with Information and Communications Technologies*, Idea Publ. Group, Hershey (USA), 2000.
14. Dominici G., *Città digitali: quale limite alla partecipazione?*, presented at the Fifth National Meeting of Civic Networks, COMPA Exhibition, Bologna, September 2002. (in italian)
15. P. Day and D. Schuler (eds.), *Shaping the Network Society*, The MIT Press (forthcoming).
16. Flanagan D., *Javascript: The Definitive Guide*, 4th edition, O'Reilly & Associates, 2001.
17. Case Western Reserve University, Free Port Version 2.3: product overview, freeport-info@po.cwru.edu.
18. World Wide Web Consortium, *HTML 4.01 Specification*, 1999, available at http://www.w3.org/TR/1999/REC-html401-19991224.
19. Ishida T., Isbister K. (eds.), *Digital Cities: Experiences , Technologies and Future Perspectives*, Lect.Notes in Comp.Sc. 1765, Springer-Verlag, 2000.
20. Ishida T., *Understanding Digital Cities*, in [19].
21. Leander R., *Building Application Servers*, Cambridge University Press, June 2000.
22. Lerdorf R., Tatroe K., *Programming PHP*, O'Reilly & Associates, 2002.

23. McMahon S., *Open Source Tools for Community Networks*, Cisler S. (ed.), "Technology Issue", Community Networking, Quarterly of Association For Community Networking, December, 1998.
24. Midgard Project Web site: http://www.midgard-project.org.
25. Miani M., *The Institutionalization of Civic Networks: the Case of Italian Digital Cities*, presented at the Second Euricom Colloquium *Electronic Networks & Democracy*, University of Nijmegen, October 2002.
26. Momjian B., *PostreSQL, Introduction and Concepts*, Addison-Wesley, 2000.
27. PHP Web site: http//www.php.net.
28. PostgreSQL Web site: http://www.postgresql.org.
29. Ratschiller T., Gerken T., *Web Application Development with PHP 4.0*, New Riders Publishing, 2000.
30. Rumbaugh J., Jacobson I., Booch G., *The Unified Modelling Language Reference Manual*, Addison-Wesley, 1998.
31. Schuler D., *New Communities and New Community Networks*, in M. Gurstein (ed.), *Community Informatics: Enabling Communities with Information and Communications Technologies*, Idea Publ. Group, Hershey (USA), 2000.
32. Schuler D., Digital Cities and Digital Citizens, in M. Tanabe, P. van den Besselaar and T. Ishida (eds.), Digital Cities II: Computational and Sociological Approaches, Lecture Notes in Computer Science 2362, Springer-Verlag, 2002.
33. Serra A., *Next Generation Community Networking: Futures for Digital Cities*, in [19].
34. Stinson B., *PostgreSQL Essential Reference*, New Riders Publishing, 2001.
35. Tamino Web Site: http://www.softwareag.com/tamino/.
36. Van den Besselaar, P., D. Beckers, The life and death of the great Amsterdam Digital City. In P. van den Besselaar, S. Koizumi (eds), Digital Cities 3. Information technologies for social capital. Lecture Notes in Computer Science, Vol. 3081. Springer-Verlag, Berlin Heidelberg New York (2005) pp. 64-93.
37. Vignette Corporation Web site: http://www.vignette.com.
38. *Virtuose* Web Site: http://www.virtuose.it.
39. Wenger E., *Supporting Communities of Practice: a Survey of Community-Oriented Technologies*, version 1.3, March 2001. Available at http://www.ewenger.com/ewbooks.html.

Talking Digital Cities: Connecting Heterogeneous Digital Cities Via the Universal Mobile Interface

Tomoko Koda[1], Satoshi Nakazawa[2], Toru Ishida[3]

[1]JST CREST Digital City Project/Kyoto University, Kyoto Japan
koda@digitalcity.jst.go.jp
[2]Fuji Research Institute Corporation, Tokyo Japan
satoshi_nakazawa@fuji-ric.co.jp
[3] Department of Social Informatics, Kyoto University, Kyoto Japan
ishida@i.kyoto-u.ac.jp

Abstract. Digital Cities have been developed all over the world to provide regional city information. This paper proposes a new approach to integrate existing digital city systems via a universal mobile interface. The universal mobile interface integrates various media representations in connected digital city systems representing the same real city with audio semantic annotations. It is also applicable for a mobile use without developing a specific mobile interface. The demo system that connects three heterogeneous digital cities, namely, a 3D modeled virtual space, image-based virtual space, and map-based information space, successfully showed the connectivity of the universal interface. The current system provides the following functions: 1) a single and simple interface to navigate users into multiple digital cities, 2) a simultaneous walk-though into the connected digital cities, 3) audio descriptions of scenes using semantic annotation of objects in the connected digital cities, 4) prioritizing semantic annotation according to users' needs.

1 Introduction

Digital cities have been developed all over the world. Among them are efforts to make a virtual city where users can walkthrough, such as a 3D model of a real city, 2D map of a city, digital photo albums of a city, and so on [3]. As computers are becoming more powerful and cheaper, more digital representations of real cities will be developed. Moreover, the recent rapid growth of the digital camera market would increase the motivation of creating new digital cities.

However, digital cities that aim to provide a 'walkthrough' are developed in different ways, as no common design approach exists. At the same time, there is no common interface for users to walkthrough and manipulate those digital cities. An interface that would integrate heterogeneous digital cities representing the same city would be very helpful for users.

Digital cities are developed to provide regional information [3]. However, users also need information when not sitting in front of their computer. However, a precise 3D model of a real city cannot be displayed on a small PDA or a mobile phone. In

P. van den Besselaar and S. Koizumi (Eds.): Digital Cities 2003, LNCS 3081, pp. 233-246, 2005.

order to make full use of the existing digital cities, there is a need for a portable interface to information provided by digital cities.

The aim of creating the universal mobile interface is to connect various heterogeneous digital cities representing the same area. The universal mobile interface should enable a user to navigate through multiple digital cities by means of a single interface. The universal mobile interface has the following goals:

1. Single and simple interface: The universal mobile interface provides a single interface to multiple digital city systems so that a user can navigate oneself without learning specific commands to operate each system. The manipulation or movements within the city spaces should be intuitive and simple. Thus the universal mobile interface supports three input devices, namely, arrow keys, a joystick, and voice commands to move around the virtual spaces connected to the universal mobile interface.

2. Shared location: The universal mobile interface provides a simultaneous walkthrough experience of multiple digital cities. The universal mobile interface has its own coordinate system. The user's current location (coordinates) is converted to other coordinates that correspond to other virtual spaces. A mobile user with GPS can move around virtual spaces via the universal mobile interface. Detail description of the system is made in the later chapter.

3. Text based information: The universal mobile interface provides text-based information based on the user's current location by using text annotations attached to objects in the virtual spaces. The texts are converted to audio descriptions using text-to-speech. Users with vision problems or mobile users who do not have a display can in this way receive textual information from multiple virtual spaces.

4. Prioritizing location based text information: The universal mobile interface works as a filter to provide most useful text information for the user. Each virtual space has an initial priority value for giving text information to the user. The user can change each priority value according to his preferences.

2   Existing Digital City Systems

This section describes examples of existing digital cities that the universal mobile interface can integrate. Applicable digital cities should be organized in a spatial-geographical way, such as 3D model-based and 2D map-based cities.

2.1   3D Geometrical Models of a Real City

3D representations of a real city provide the most realistic model. One example is the Helsinki Arena 2000 developed by Helsinki Telephone Corporation. Helsinki Arena 2000 provides users an advanced web platform and services through a real 3D model of the city of Helsinki via broadband networks [9, 10]. Another example of a 3D model is FreeWalk, which was developed within the Universal Design of Digital City project [4]. Users enter into the FreeWalk virtual space via computer networks as avatars to navigate through the space and communicate with other avatars. Figure 1 shows a 3D VRML model of downtown Kyoto using FreeWalk.

Fig. 1. A 3D VRML model of Kyoto city using FreeWalk

Fig. 2. Image based virtual city of Kyoto using TownDigitizing

2.2 Image-Based Virtual Cities

Developing a 3D model of a real city requires time, money and expertise. Researchers have been investigating easier ways to build a digital city. One of those efforts is the use of digital photographs or digital photo realistic images for building a pseudo 3D digital city. One example of the above technologies is "3-D Photo Collage System" developed by the University of Tokyo [11]. The Photo Collage System provides non-experts a way to create a 3D space by associating 2D digital photos. Another example is "TownDigitizing" that uses omni-directional images instead of normal 2D images [7, 8]. Images are captured by an omni-directional camera that takes 360-degree images of the real city. The images are automatically fused based on the visitor's virtual location to reproduce what the user would see in a corresponding physical city. Figure 2 shows a TownDigitized version of downtown Kyoto. A next version of Town-Digitizing is currently under development in the Universal Design of the Digital City project. This version will capture life images with omni-directional cameras installed inside a city, in order to create automatically an image based virtual space.

2.3 Map-Based Geographical Information Systems

Whereas 3D models and image-based digital cities try to represent a real city, map-based geographical information systems on the web put together various types of local information and organize it by spatial or geographic coordinates [13]. Numerous local GIS's have already been developed [12]. Among them are the Geographic Information System of Turin municipality [1], and KyotoSEARCH [6]. KyotoSEARCH extracts city related events and elements by analyzing web data. It calculates relations between these elements and events and describes them. Figure 3 shows a map of downtown Kyoto using KyotoSEARCH.

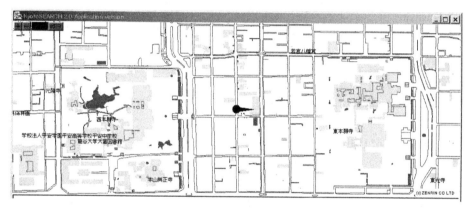

Fig. 3. Map of Kyoto city by KyotoSEARCH

2.4 Characteristics of Information from Digital Cities

The three types of virtual cities mentioned above provide specific information according to the nature of the technology used. The 3D model with FreeWalk is suitable for providing static and detailed information about buildings and shops, such as their size and color. However, developing a detailed 3D model is costly and time-consuming, and requires technical knowledge. Avoiding obstacles while walking through a 3D city with a joystick or cursor keys may be difficult for a novice user.

The image-based virtual city created with TownDigitizing can provide lively scenes of the real city at relatively low cost and in a short development period, and without high technical skills. Live cameras are useful for providing information on mobile entities of the real city, such as pedestrians and traffic on the road. However, walkable routes are limited to the places where photos of the real city are available. Users of an image-based virtual city cannot walk freely into the space.

The 3D model of a real city and the image-based virtual city are useful to provide detailed micro view of a user's location, while the map-based KyotoSEARCH tool can provide geographical and directional information through a macro view of the user's location. However, a map-based system lacks visual images of the real city. Table 1 compares the characteristics of the three digital cities, and in section 3, we will discuss this in more detail. The universal mobile interface aims to provide combined city information by strengthening and complementing the characteristics of those virtual spaces each other.

Table 1. Comparison of characteristics of digital cities that use different spaces.

	3D virtual spaces	Image-based city spaces	Map-based city information spaces
Feature	Detailed 3D model	Photo-realistic images	Scalable 2D map
World Dimension	3D	2-2.5D	2D
User space dimension	2D	2D	2D
Movable space	Anywhere except obstacles (walls etc.)	Along pre-defined routes	Anywhere
Interactivity	Very high	High	Low
Macro view	High	Not provided	Very high
Micro view	Very high	High	N/A
Real-time information	Possible but expensive	Possible with live camera, relatively easy	Possible (GIS)
Development Cost	Very high	Relatively low	Low

2.5 Scenario of Using the Universal Mobile Interface

Typical scenarios of using the universal mobile interface are as follows:

Scenario for an immobile user: A senior person or computer novice is accessing a virtual city of Kyoto via the universal mobile interface. He does not know how to use a mouse or keyboard. He selects the location where he wants to start exploring the city by telling the system "Shijo-kawaramachi." He uses voice commands to move forward, turn right, stop and so on to navigate himself into the space. The system presents the 3D model, images and map of his current location, while explaining shop names, their specialties, etc. The 3D virtual space tells the user: "The brown-colored shop on your left sells tea utensils." The image-based system shows a live image of the shop. The map system adds: "The shop is located at 50m south from the Shijo-kawaramachi intersection." The universal mobile interface provides three different views and audio descriptions of the same place.

Scenario for a mobile user: A first-time visitor of downtown Kyoto is walking around in the city with a mobile phone. The mobile phone is equipped with GPS and can run Java applications on it. The mobile phone is connected to multiple digital cities of Kyoto via the universal mobile interface. As the user moves forward along a street, the universal mobile interface gives audio information on landmarks ahead, shops to be visited, which way the street is leading, etc. The 3D virtual space gives the user detailed information on each landmark, such as "The brown building on your right is a famous bakery." The map system gives directional information such as "If you keep going along this street to the west for 1.6 kilometers, there is another bakery on your right." The image-based virtual space gives lively information to the user, such as "There is a long line in front of the bakery ahead of you." The user can change priority values that are set to each virtual space by giving feedback to each virtual space while it is giving audio description to the user, such as "That sounds interesting." (while the 3D virtual space is giving information on the bakery). Then the priority value of the 3D virtual space increases so that it can give information more often than other virtual spaces. The mechanism of achieving the above scenario is described in the following section.

3   System Description

This section gives detailed system description of each component that realizes the goals of the universal mobile interface described in the section 1.

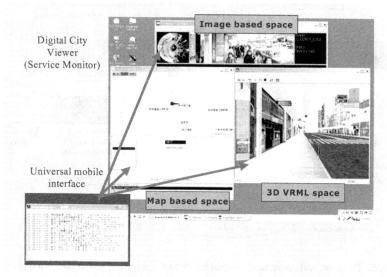

Fig. 4. The mobile interface window and service monitor, displaying 3 connected digital cities.

3.1   Single and Simple Interface

The universal mobile interface is a windows-based application that communicates with various digital city systems via TCP/IP. A user can connect to digital cities via the universal mobile interface by selecting a specific geographical point (i.e., an intersection, a department store, etc.), or by using a longitude and latitude of a geographical point. A user can move around the connected digital cities with arrow keys, joystick, or voice commands. Figure 4 shows the universal mobile interface window and service monitor that displays three connected digital cities, namely, an image-based virtual space, 3D VRML model, and 2D map of downtown Kyoto. All three digital cities display the same location.

3.2 Location and Movement Control – Shared Location

To achieve synchronous location and movement control among various digital cities, the universal mobile interface has its own coordinate system. When a user moves around the connected digital cities, the user actually moves within the coordinate system of the universal mobile interface. Figure 5 shows the diagram of location and movement control provided by the universal mobile interface.

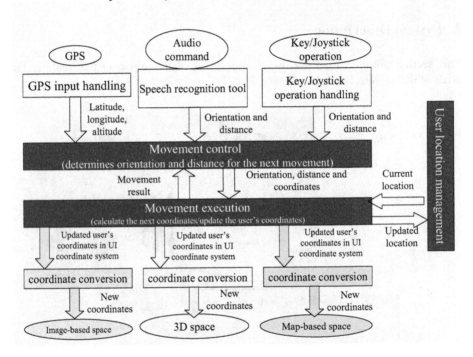

Fig. 5. Location and movement control between the interface and connected digital cities.

The three connected systems have their own coordinate systems. For example, the image-based system has a two dimensional coordinate system that uses relative position of each photographic image, while the map-based system has a two dimensional one (Table 1). Thus, a user's position is represented differently in each system. The universal mobile interface solves this technical problem in the following two ways.

Synchronizing Location and Orientation

The universal mobile interface has its own 3 dimensional coordinate system based on longitude, latitude, and altitude to achieve synchronous location and orientation control. The user's current location is represented by the universal mobile interface's coordinates and maintained by the universal mobile interface system. To each of the connected system we added a function that converts coordinates between these systems and the universal mobile interface. This function enables synchronization of the user's location and orientation by just sending the location and orientation data from the universal mobile interface to each connected system (Figure 5). Advantages of having a standard and independent coordinate system in the universal mobile interface are:

- To be able to move into any location when a user is outside the area of either of the connected systems. It is rare that the connected systems have exactly the same area as a movable space.
- To be able to maintain the user's current location when one of the connected systems is not operating.

Synchronizing Movements

It is important for synchronizing movements to adjust a timing to send the user's location from the universal mobile interface to the connected systems. In the concrete, each connected system receives the user's location data, calculates the user's location based on its own coordinate system, changes the coordinates of user's location to the new ones, then sends a notification of a completion of the movement operation to the universal mobile interface. The universal mobile interface waits until it receives the notifications from all the connected systems.

The connected systems need to have a function that changes the user's location, orientation and movement in their own coordinate systems. There is a case that the connected system does not allow a user to move to any location. For example, the image-based system has fixed routes (Table 1) and the relative position of photo images are represented as points on a map. The universal mobile interface calculates the points on the map and selects the closest image from the user's location. In this way, the universal mobile interface provides a transparent interface in terms of movement and location control both for users and connected systems that have their own virtual spaces.

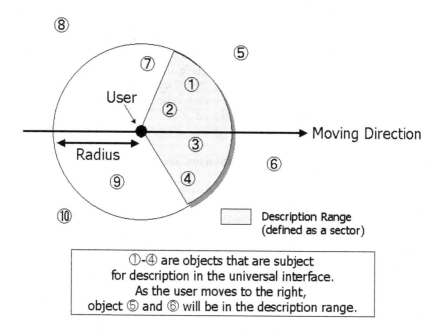

Fig. 6. The scope of objects described in the universal mobile interface

3.3   Semantic Annotation – Text-Based Information

The universal mobile interface provides text-based information based on the user's current location. This text-based description of the scenes uses semantic annotations attached to visual objects (i.e., streets, buildings, signs) in the connected virtual spaces.   The semantic annotations are converted to audio descriptions using text-to-speech. Users with vision problems or mobile users who do not have a display can in this way receive audio descriptions from multiple virtual spaces.

As the user moves around the connected digital cities, the universal mobile interface receives semantic annotations of each object seen in front of the user's point of view from the connected digital cities. As shown in figure 6, a description range is a sector where the user's location is in the center. A definition file defines the sector's radius and center angle. The closer objects are to the user, the higher priority they have to be described. Objects in the description range change as the user moves around the digital cities. The text description of the scene is provided as follows:

- Objects are classified with ontology-based definitions. Figure 7 shows the "buildings" class tree used in the universal mobile interface.
- Each class has its own attributes defined in an annotation definition file and inherits its upper classes' attributes. For example, a MacDonald's shop has attributes such as "color: yellow, category: hamburgers, number of seats: 65, seasonal menu: chicken, etc."
- The Universal mobile interface uses a template definition to generate textual descriptions of an object using its attributes. For example, the above MacDonald's can be described as "The Macdonald's shop has 65 seats. Its seasonal menu is chicken."

Using characteristics of connected virtual spaces: As described in 2.4, each connected virtual space has characteristic information. The universal mobile interface can generate various annotations by using a semantic annotation mechanism. For example, the 3D virtual space can have attributes of shop objects, such as the shape and color. The image-based virtual space can have attributes such as the popularity of the shop by using live images. And the map-based space can have attributes such as the exact location of the shop, its address and direction. In this way, the annotations described in the scenario in 2.5 can be achieved.

3.4   Prioritizing Location-Based Text Information

The connected digital city systems have their own semantic annotations to describe the same object, i.e., an 3D model based digital city would describe the object as a brown square building, while a map based system would describe it with its actual address. Each connected digital city system has its own priority value. A priority value controls a priority of each system to "speak", (in other words, its audio description of an object is presented to a user) about an object within the pre-defined scope. A user can change each system's priority value by using an audio command "No interest." or "Tell me more." while an audio description is made. Figure 8 shows a system component that generates descriptions of objects and priority control. As shown in the mobile user's scenario in 2.5, this prioritizing mechanism is especially necessary in a mobile scene. A mobile user may not want to listen to architectural

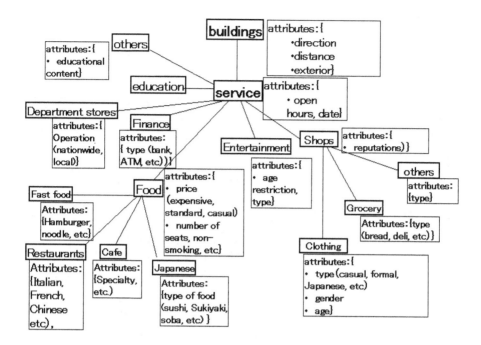

Fig. 7. Ontology of "Buildings" used in the Universal Mobile Interface

information of a department store when looking for other information. If her interest is on "finding other bakeries", then she may want to change the priority value set to the map-based system higher. If she wants to know how crowded another bakery is, she can set the priority value of the image-based system higher.

The universal mobile interface provides on-demand city information by allowing mobile users to select what they want to know most and skip unnecessary information.

4   Evaluations of the Current System and Future Development

4.1 Current System Implementation

The current universal mobile interface system connects three heterogeneous digital cities with a spatial/geographical organization, namely, a 3D modeled virtual space, image-based virtual space, and map-based information space successfully. Although some digital cities have a more topical architecture and lack a spatial/geographical organization, the current system does not include those cities as connectable cities.

The universal mobile interface is designed to use GPS in the future as it uses longitude/latitude for its coordinate system. We will be able to use the universal mobile interface on a mobile phone in a real city when high capacity mobile phones are available in the market.

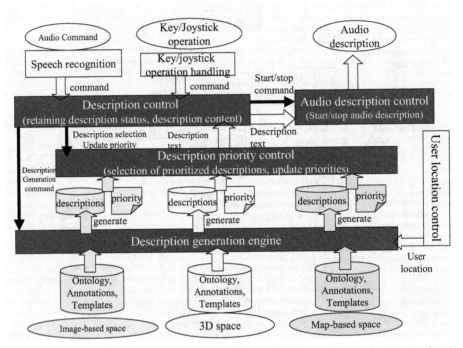

Fig. 8. System components that generate descriptions of objects and controls priority of each digital city to "speak."

4.2   Is the Information Up to Date?

The universal mobile interface is connected to three existing digital city systems. Each connected system was developed in a different time period. There are some shops that don't exist any more, and some that exist in one system don't exist in other systems. This inconsistency of digital cities is inevitable, since cities are alive and change constantly. In order to complement the lack of up-to-date city images, semantic annotation can add recent information on changed objects. For example, "This bank's name has been changed to ... after a merger." can be generated by adding attributes to the ontology definition file.

4.3   Semantic Annotation Generation

The current implementation requires creation of annotations of each object. Such content creation is a labor-intensive and costly task.

One solution to the problem is to make use of existing geographical information systems. As in [3], GISs will be one of the key technologies for digital cities that provide regional information. Kyoto city already has a GIS of Kyoto called InfoMap [2] in addition to Kyoto SEARCH. InfoMap provides an extended image map interface system that enables users to browse a lot of information using 2600 homepages located in the Kyoto metropolitan area. The universal mobile interface can be developed to use such GISs for creating object annotations.

Another solution is to develop an annotation-authoring tool. As the semantic web plays a major role in the current WWW, especially with respect to city information spaces and GISs, semantic annotations of objects in digital cities can be automatically gathered and converted to semantic annotations by a new authoring tool.

4.4 Autonomous Prioritizing

The current description priority setting is initiated by a user. In order to make this priority control mechanism to fully work in a mobile situation, the mechanism should include pre-set user preferences (i.e., user A wants to know directional descriptions; user B wants to get detailed information about restaurants). A general priority setting can be done by a user preference file, while adapting the user's situation can be initiated by the user.

5 Conclusion

The universal mobile interface integrates various existing media representations (digital city systems) representing the same real city. This approach is different from existing approaches that would develop a specific mobile interface for each digital city system, such as a scalable interface for a 3D city information system for mobile services [14]. The universal mobile interface has the following distinct characteristics.

- **Connect**: The universal mobile interface connects heterogeneous digital cities with a single interface.

  Three different virtual spaces are currently connected to the universal mobile interface, and if other virtual representations of downtown Kyoto would become available, they can be connected to the universal mobile interface too. In other words, the universal mobile interface provides a "universal" system interface to connect heterogeneous digital cities.

- **Carry**: The universal mobile interface makes digital cities portable with audio semantic annotation.

  The main goal of the universal mobile interface is to provide on-site, on-demand city information for a mobile user. The current efforts to develop digital cities are divided into two groups: one is to create realistic digital cities with 3D model or digital photo's, the other is to develop a mobile city information system specially dedicated to mobile users. The former systems aim to provide "virtual space walkthrough experience" to a user. We may be able to enjoy visually represented digital cities via a mobile phone or PDA in the near future. However, the universal mobile interface assumes different use. Mobile users cannot always look at a display when they are busy doing other things. The universal mobile interface provides audio information of a city like background music. Thus, the universal mobile interface is "portable" and can be used by city walkers independently of the situation they are in. The universal mobile interface does not require specifically developed mobile systems.

- **Extract**: The universal mobile interface extracts the required information.
  The universal mobile interface extracts information required by the user, following a prioritizing mechanism. This function is especially important for mobile use, and it also solves the problem that audio annotation is slow, and still busy explaining a scene whereas the user already moves on to the next situation.

Our current demo system connects three heterogeneous digital cities of Kyoto and successfully showed the connectivity of the universal interface. We believe our approach of integrating digital cities will be more useful when semantic web technologies are widely used for GISs.

Acknowledgements

This work would not have been possible without the people who have previously developed digital cities of Kyoto. Satoshi Koizumi of JST/CREST Digital City Project developed TownDigitizing system and contributed to the early design of the universal mobile interface. Hideyuki Nakanishi of Kyoto University developed FreeWalk and the 3D model of Kyoto together with his students. Yusuke Yokota gave us advice on the map-based information system. Professor Arai and Cho Heeryon designed the digital city ontology. This work has been supported by CREST of JST (Japan Science Technology Agency).

References

1. Bolatto, G., Sozza, A., Gauna, I., and Rusconi, M.: The Geographic Information System (GIS) of Turin Municipality, In: Ishida, T., Isbister, K. (eds.): Digital Cities: Experiences, Technologies, and Further Perspectives. Lecture Notes in Computer Science 1765, Berlin Heidelberg New York, Springer-Verlag (2000) 97-109
2. Hiramatsu, K.: Log Analysis of Map-Based Web Page Search on Digital City Kyoto, In: Tanabe, M, van den Besselaar, P., Ishida, T. (eds.): Digital Cities II: Computational and Sociological Approaches. Lecture Notes in Computer Science 2362, Berlin Heidelberg New York. Springer-Verlag (2002) 233-245
3. Ishida, T.: Understanding Digital Cities. In: Ishida, T., Isbister, K. (eds.): Digital Cities: Technologies, Experiences, and Future Perspectives. Lecture Notes in Computer Science 1765, Berlin Heidelberg New York, Springer-Verlag (2000) 7-17
4. Ishida, T.: Digital City Kyoto: Social Information Infrastructure for Everyday Life, Communications of the ACM, Vol. 45, No. 7 (2002)
5. T Ishida: Activities and Technologies in Digital City Kyoto. In P. van den Besselaar, S. Koizumi (eds), Digital Cities 3. Lecture Notes in Computer Science, Vol. 3081. Springer-Verlag, Berlin Heidelberg New York (2005) pp. 162-183
6. Kambayashi, Y., Cheng, k., Lee, A.: Database Approach for Improving Web Efficiency and Enhancing Geographic Information Systems, 2001 IRC International Conference on Internet Information Retrieval. (2001) 159-176

7. Koizumi, S, Dai, G., Ishiguro, H.: Town Digitizing for Building an Image-Based Cyber Space. In: Tanabe, M, van den Besselaar, P., Ishida, T. (eds.): Digital Cities II: Computational and Sociological Approaches. Lecture Notes in Computer Science 2362, Berlin Heidelberg New York, Springer-Verlag (2002) 357-370
8. Koizumi, S. and Ishiguro, H.: Town Digitizing, Omnidirectional Image-based Virtual Space. In P. van den Besselaar, S. Koizumi (eds), Digital Cities 3. Lecture Notes in Computer Science, Vol. 3081. Springer-Verlag, Berlin Heidelberg New York (2005) pp. 242-253.
9. Rinturi, R., Koivunen, M., and Sulkanen, J. Helsinki Arena 2000-Augmenting a real city to a virtual one. In: Ishida, T., Isbister, K. (eds.): Digital Cities: Experiences, Technologies, and Further Perspectives. Lecture Notes in Computer Science 1765, Berlin Heidelberg New York, Springer-Verlag (2000) 83-96
10. Rinturi R. and Simula, T.: Virtual Helsinki . In P. van den Besselaar, S. Koizumi (eds), Digital Cities 3. Lecture Notes in Computer Science, Vol. 3081. Springer-Verlag, Berlin Heidelberg New York (2005) pp. 110-137.
11. Tanaka, H., Arikawa, M., and Shibasaki R. A 3-D Photo Collage System for Spatial Navigations, In: Tanabe, M, van den Besselaar, P., Ishida, T. (eds.): Digital Cities II: Computational and Sociological Approaches. Lecture Notes in Computer Science 2362, Berlin Heidelberg New York, Springer-Verlag (2002) 305-316
12. The University of Edinburgh GIS WWW Resource List
http://www.geo.ed.ac.uk/home/giswww.html
13. U.S Census Bureau The Geographic Information Systems FAQ!
http://www.census.gov/geo/www/faq-index.html
14. Vainio, T., Kotala, O., Rakkolainen, I., and Kupila, H.: Towards Scalable User Interfaces in 3D City Information Systems. In: Paterno, F. (ed.) Mobile Human Computer Interaction. Lecture Notes in Computer Science 2411, Berlin Heidelberg New York, Springer-Verlag (2002) 354-358

Town Digitizing: Omnidirectional Image-Based Virtual Space

Satoshi Koizumi[1], Hiroshi Ishiguro[2]

1 Digital City Research Center, JST CREST,
Kawaramachi Nijo bldg. 2F, 366 Ichino Funairi-cho, Nakagyo-ku, Kyoto, 604-0924 Japan
satoshi@digitalcity.jst.go.jp
2 Graduate School of Engineering, Osaka University,
2-1 Yamada-oka Suita, Osaka, 565-0871 Japan
ishiguro@ams.eng.osaka-u.ac.jp

Abstract. This paper proposes a new method for building a walk-through virtual space that uses the Town Digitizing tools we have developed. The virtual space is built by smoothly interpolating a large number of omnidirectional images captured from the real world. This paper discusses how to build the virtual space and describes three of our software tools. We call them TDEditor, TAG-Editor, and TDViewer. Town Digitizing is divided into four steps: omnidirectional image acquisition, parameter estimation among omnidirectional images, registration of information, and smooth interpolation among the images. A system based on Town Digitizing allows users to explore a unique virtual space that is similar to earlier 3-D graphics system. It works better than existing methods especially for complex environments that include natural objects like trees. For adding tag information to the walk-through virtual space, we introduce a new method that sets rectangular areas with information, written in HTML language, in the panoramic view. The user is presented with information associated with the object of interest on his web browser. We believe that the techniques and approach described here represent a powerful modeling method with which to build virtual cities.

1 Introduction

How can we rapidly build high quality 3-D models of a town within a couple of days? Town Digitizing solves this problem and provides a new method of building photo-realistic virtual spaces. Previous modeling methods based on 3-D geometrical models can be used to reconstruct an urban space. The methods, however, are expensive since we need to measure the geometric parameters of the environment and have great difficulty in modeling natural objects like trees. Moreover, using a number of models leads to high physical storage costs. On the other hand, Town Digitizing is simply since we are just taking images with a regular intervals by an omnidirectional camera [1]. These omnidirectional images provide sufficient visual information to build a highly realistic virtual space. Unlike the images obtained from conventional cameras with their restricted views, the omnidirectional camera offers the significant ability of

P. van den Besselaar and S. Koizumi (Eds.): Digital Cities 2003, LNCS 3081, pp. 247–258, 2005.
© Springer-Verlag Berlin Heidelberg 2005

capturing a single image that contains almost all the visual information needed to recreate the environment seen from that point.

We developed three software tools for Town Digitizing. The first software tool, TDEditor, automatically computes various parameters of the omnidirectional images, based on routes drawn on a map. This software tool not only computes parameters automatically, but also adjusts parameters by manual operation. The second software tool, TAGEditor, pastes information written in HTML language onto the omnidirectional image and edits it. Based on the parameters output by TDEditor, the third software tool transforms omnidirectional images into perspective views and smoothly interpolates them. This is used to realize a virtual walk-through in the town. We call this software tool TDViewer. These three software tools allow anyone to easily build photo-realistic virtual spaces.

A lot of research has directed towards constructing image-based virtual spaces. The 3-D photo collage system developed by Tanaka et al.[2] provides users with a walk-through virtual space by using rectangular areas, similar to signboards, that display pictures. Based on globe images regenerated using 45 or 71 pictures, Teller et al.[3] have made a system for calibrated, terrestrial image acquisition in urban areas. In their research, the relation among globe images is based on GPS data. Similarly, by compounding multiple images, QuickTime-VR[4][5] provides a virtual space from a static viewpoint. In the following sections, we describe Town Digitizing, the three developed pieces of software tools, and some applications of Town Digitizing.

2   Town Digitizing

A simple idea, which does not incur expensive memory or computational costs, is to estimate the changes of visual appearance along lines that connect two arbitrary omnidirectional images. A zooming ratio between a pair of omnidirectional images, is used as a parameter to represent the changes. Figure 1 illustrates zooming stereo using a pair of omnidirectional images(C_i & C_j). A view range parameter ψ_{ji} is estimated by a simple template matching method between a fixed view that is transformed by an initial view range at C_i and a view which is transformed by a view range at C_j. Here, zooming ratio Z_{ji} is represented by $Z_{ji} = \tan(\psi_0/2)/\tan\psi_{ji}$.

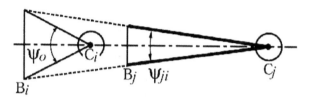

Fig. 1. Zooming stereo

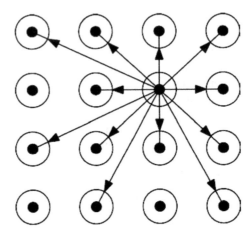

Fig. 2. Plenoptic representation using zooming stereo

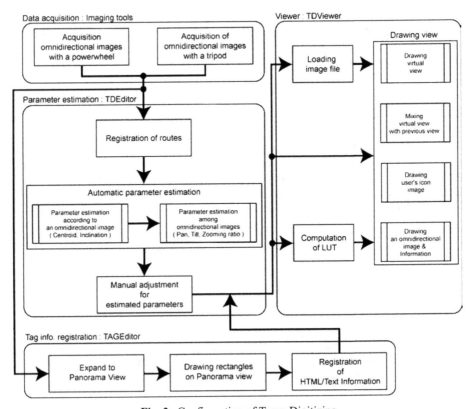

Fig. 3. Configuration of Town Digitizing

For transforming [6, 7] into a perspective view, pan angle and tilt angle are needed. To estimate these parameters between a pair of omnidirectional images, we use FOE (Focus Of Expansion) [8]. No disparity is apparent on a line connecting them, even if we observe from two different points. Since the omnidirectional image includes omnidirectional visual information, the two FOE points surely appear on each image. The two FOE points on each omnidirectional image always must keep the interval of π radians. Therefore, if two feature points at intervals of π radians on the omnidirectional image are chosen, two feature points on another omnidirectional image must keep the interval relation of π radians between them. We call this condition the FOE constraint. Based on the FOE constraint, Town Digitizing precisely estimates these parameters by using simple template matching.

This method cannot be applied if there are obstacles between the pair of omnidirectional images. If several omnidirectional images are located along a line as shown in figure 2, zooming stereo can be established between all pairs of omnidirectional images along the line. Town Digitizing, which uses zooming stereo, mainly consists of four steps, image acquiring, parameter estimation, and model reconstruction, as shown in figure 3. To quickly and smoothly perform those steps, we developed a photographic head with power wheel, TDEditor, that automatically computes the parameters among the omnidirectional images. TAGEditor registers tag information on the omnidirectional images, while TDViewer reconstructs modeled environments.

Fig. 4. View sequences based on zooming stereo

First, users take omnidirectional images using the power wheel or the monopod with omnidirectional camera at some spatial interval along a line. They register the captured omnidirectional images and route information into a map of the photographed locations using TDEditor. Based on the registered information,

TDEditor performs automatic parameter estimation. Here, this software the center and gradient of each omnidirectional image and estimates pan angles, tilt angles, and zooming ratios of a pair of omnidirectional images for zooming stereo. If the estimation is invalid, which may be due to weather-based changes and the existence of obstacles, these parameters are edited manually. TAGEditor overlays tag information, written in HTML, on the omnidirectional panoramic view and edits them. TDViewer provides continuous view sequences, as shown in figure 4, to the user by using zooming stereo based on the estimated parameters. The continuous viewer, TDViewer, allows users to explore in an entirely natural space similar to those created by 3-D graphics systems. To suppress gaps caused by the difference in focal position when the omnidirectional image changes, TDViewer performs a mixing process the pixel level.

3 Developed Software Tools

3.1 TDEditor

TDEditor (Town Digitizing Editor) software can automatically compute the parameters for pairs of omnidirectional images by registering the route and omnidirectional images on a map. The system window we developed is shown in figure 5. Figure 6 shows a block diagram of TDEditor. The process flow for building a walk-through virtual space with TDEditor is as follows:

1. Load a map image showing where omnidirectional images were taken.
2. Draw routes on the map image. Acquire locations of start node and end node for the route.
3. Add new routes on the loaded map image. Set a number of omnidirectional images for each new route and their ID numbers.
4. Mediate between the new nodes and pre-registered nodes.
5. Convert data structure to route data format.
6. Estimate a center and a gradient of omnidirectional images for the new routes.
7. Calibrate the omnidirectional images.
8. Estimate parameters of a pair of omnidirectional images.
9. Manually adjust parameters if necessary. Conduct trial walk-throughs.
10. Go to 8., for while pairs of omnidirectional images.
11. Save parameters based on the registered data.
12. Save calibrated omnidirectional images.

To perform all these processes smoothly, TDEditor uses a data structure to manage route data and ID numbers for omnidirectional images. Since the structure is based on the routes formed by the connection of node pairs, the software greatly simplifies the representation of complex routes consisting of several nodes.

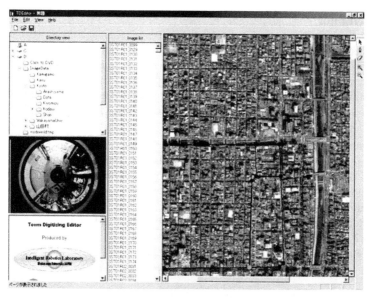

Fig. 5. System window of TDEditor

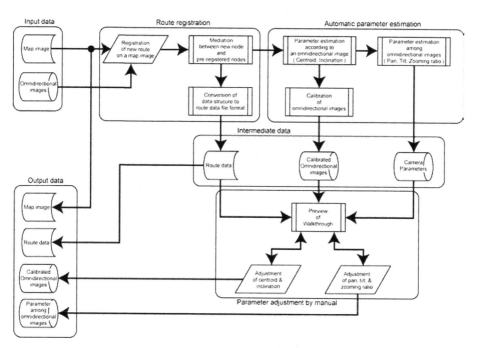

Fig. 6. Block diagram of TDEditor

3.2 TAGEditor

To register HTML or text information on an omnidirectional image, we developed TAGEditor software (figure 7). Figure 8 shows the concept of TAGEditor. TAGEditor consists of three routines for expansion, management, and parameter computation. Using TAGEditor, a user draws rectangles with a pointer device and registers HTML/text information. The process flow for registering HTML/text information with TAGEditor is as follows:

1. Expanding an omnidirectional image to a panoramic view (the expansion routine).
2. Drawing a rectangle with a pointer device (the management routine).
3. Based on equations (1) and (2), compute four parameters; two azimuths and two elevations, from the rectangle drawn on the panoramic view (the parameter computing routine).
4. Registering a URL or a text file's name (the management routine).
5. Go to 2. while rectangles remain unlabelled.
6. Saving parameters based on the registered data.

$$Azimuth = 2\pi x/W \tag{1}$$

$$Elevation = \tan^{-1}\left(2\pi(H_c - y)/W\right) \tag{2}$$

Where W is the width of the panoramic view, H_c is the location of the horizontal line on the panoramic view, and (x,y) are the coordinates of the upper left (or the lower right) corner of the rectangle on the panoramic view.

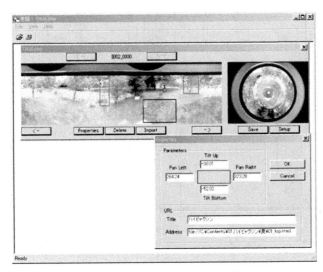

Fig. 7. System window of TAGEditor

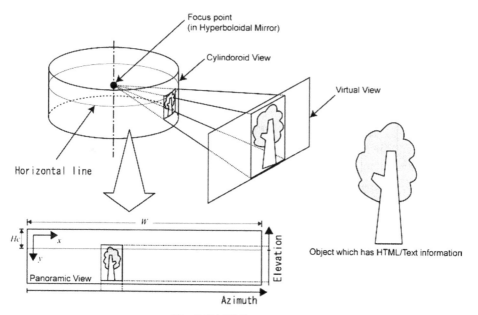

Fig. 8. TAGEditor concept

3.3 TDViewer

To view the walk-through virtual space, we developed TDViewer (Town Digitizing Viewer) software (figure 9). As shown in figure 10, TDViewer consists of three routines for file loading, look-up-table (LUT) computation, and drawing. Since the cost

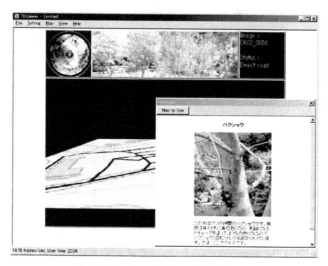

Fig. 9. System window of TDViewer

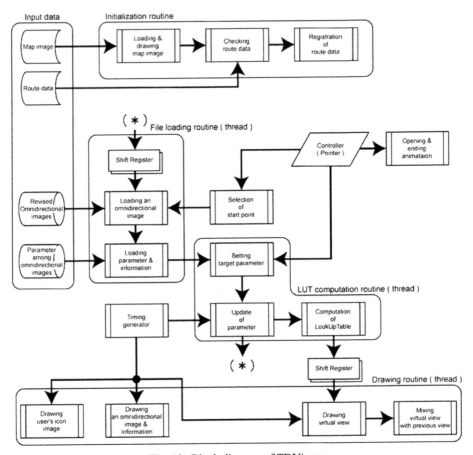

Fig. 10. Block diagram of TDViewer

of storing digital images is increasing because of the increase in resolution, we must consider file loading time. By loading the omnidirectional image files which are connected to the current omnidirectional image via a multi-thread program, the user is not presented with unnatural delays. Based on the parameters estimated by TDEditor and route data, the second routine computes a LUT for the perspective image to be provided to the user. This LUT is generated by the perspective projection using the geometry between the hyperboloidal mirror and the digital camera. Using zooming stereo, TDViewer generates a view in which the zooming ratio changes. When the zooming ratio equals the estimated ratio, the current omnidirectional image changes to the next omnidirectional image. By continuously changing the omnidirectional image, TDViewer allows users walk-through the virtual space. To retain the natural feel in the presence of gaps in the views, we apply a mixing process to the drawing routine. This mixes the current perspective view with the last one at the pixel level.

TDViewer also displays HTML/text information via an Internet browser (Internet Explorer in the current version). To browse that information, the user clicks an area of interest in the virtual view.

4 Applications Using Town Digitizing

In this section, we introduce two applications that use Town Digitizing. The first one focuses the environmental learning in which importance is attached to experience. The other one provides information about remote facilities or places that are normally inaccessible.

4.1 Environmental Learning

Indirect environmental learning tends to be poorly received since it lacks the impact of "actually being there". It does, however, have several benefits one of which is the ability to access reference material easily; safety and low cost are other advantages.

Yasukawa [9] proposed an indirect learning system using Town Digitizing. Using 326 omnidirectional images, they built the walk-through virtual space of Kamigamo Experimental Forest, Kyoto University. In this virtual forest, they inserted 14 educational materials; three plants and eleven trees. TAGEditor was used to lay these materials over the virtual forest. Figure 11 shows a system view of indirect learning. The materials are displayed in the information window at the upper-right of figure 11.

An experiment was conducted to evaluate an acceptability of the proposed system and learning effectiveness. The participants in this experimentation were 60 individuals - 30 males and 30 females. Questionnaire results indicated that system stability was very high. It appeared that all participants received an excellent learning experience in the virtual walk-through forest.

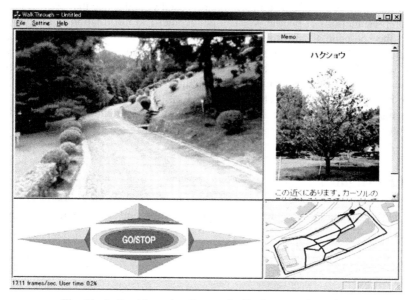

Fig. 11. Indirect Learning System for Environment Learning

4.2 Information Discovery

It will be possible to use the real-time images captured by omnidirectional cameras connected to the Internet to generate walk-through spaces for surveillance and information discovery. This ensures the user's personal safety since many industrial sites (e.g. a nuclear plant, a dump-site, and a chemical plant) can be dangerous. Town Digitizing can reconstruct these facilities and sites, easily. In the future, Town Digitizing will provide peoples with a state of the production line in the facilities and activity of these places.

5 Conclusions

In this paper, we have proposed Town Digitizing, which uses omnidirectional images for building virtual walk-through spaces. We described our three software tools, TDEditor, TAGEditor, and TDViewer, created to support the implementation of Town Digitizing. By using the three software tools, anyone can easily build photo-realistic virtual walk-through spaces.

In Section 4, we introduced two applications based on Town Digitizing. The first application has already been developed and the tested. In the trial, a virtual forest was constructed into which educational materials, based on HTML tags, were inserted. If they use 3-D geometrical modeling method, they could not apply to the environmental learning. Because, complex objects, like plants and trees, represented by 3-D models are indistinguishable for participants. The trial results show that Town Digitizing yields high quality virtual spaces.

Our next step is to build a complete image-based virtual space that provides image-based representations of people. We can get geometrical information of the people by using the perceptual information infrastructure (PII) that consists of many omnidirectional cameras set in the real world [10]. Our idea is to combine the virtual space with PII. Further, to view the real world, the image-based virtual space is connected to those cameras with Town Digitizing.

We believe that the complete image-based virtual space made possible by Town Digitizing will be a next-generation information infrastructure that connects the computer network to the real world.

Acknowledgments

This work was partly supported by Japan Science and Technology Corporation (CREST).

References

1. H. Ishiguro.: Development of low-cost compact omnidirectional vision sensors and their applications, Proc. Int. Conf. Information Systems, Analysis and Synthesis, 433–439, 1998.

2. Hiroya Tanaka, Masatoshi Arikawa, and Ryosuke Shibasaki.: A 3D photo collage system for spatial navigations. Proc. The Second Kyoto Meeting on Digital Cities, 305–316, 2001.
3. Seth Teller, Matthew Antone, and Zachary Bodnar.: Calibrated, registered images of an extended urban area. Proc. IEEE Computer Vision and Pattern Recognition, Vol. 1, 813–820, 2001.
4. S. E. Chen.: QuickTime VR - an image-based approach to virtual environment navigation. SIGGRAPH '95, 29–38, 1995.
5. http://www.apple.com/quicktime
6. K. Yamazawa, Y. Yagi, and M. Yachida.: Omnidirectional imaging with hyperboloidal projection. Proc. Int. Conf. Intelligent Robots and Systems, 2(7):1029–1034, 1993.
7. Y. Onoe, K. Yamazawa, H. Takemura, and N. Yokoya.: Telepresence by real-time view-dependent image generation from omnidirectional video streams. Computer Vision and Image Understanding, 71(2):154–165, 1998.
8. Takushi Sogo.: Localization of sensors and objects in distributed omnidirectional vision. Ph.D. Thesis, Kyoto University, 2001.
9. N. Yasukawa, S. Koizumi, T. Sakai, et al.: Environmental learning system using an image-based virtual space(in Japanese). IPSJ Symposium Series, 2003(7):215–216, 2003.
10.Hiroshi Ishiguro.: Distributed vision system: A perceptual information infrastructure for robot navigation. IJCAI (1), 36–43, 1997.

Articulating the Digital Environment Via Community-Generated Ontologies

Ramesh Srinivasan

Doctoral Candidate - Harvard University, Graduate School of Design
rsriniva@gsd.harvard.edu

Abstract. In this paper, I introduce my graduate research focused on the design of digital environments for community expression. I introduce the specific project, Village Voice, which originates from my MSc work at the MIT Media Laboratory. This project involved the design of a digital environment that could make possible the sharing of knowledge, story, and cultural tradition as documented through video and audio across a physically bounded Somali refugee community located within the Boston-area. I point to the unique architecture around which the system is designed, and where it stands relative to important issues of public space and urbanism. Finally, I discuss how this new type of ICT-space evaluates (based on an empirical study) as a mechanism of engaging community.

1 Introduction

A combination of social, economic, and political dynamics have created an environment that has called for a new understanding of community that exceeds neighborhood. The individual has become a member of multiple social groups today, many of which need not be defined by local boundaries. While this phenomenon is not unprecedented, the level to which it has expanded is notable. The field of social networks has appropriately surfaced as a useful means of analyzing these dynamics. Social networks measure the actor's position in a network of connections, some of which may be interconnected themselves. As the quantity of information has been exploded [1], the network metaphor emerged to describe the new social condition of the individual who receives and gives resources from/to multiple directions. Social networks are a useful contemporary methodology because they allow for the visualization and understanding of the complexity that characterizes the individual's relationships with multiple communities. Enabling these new dynamics are new networked technologies, which serve as "mediators" of new social networks that are being consummated and upheld.

Communities have begun to re-orient themselves as the virtual has enabled interaction to occur independent of spatial proximity. Today, communities tend to be "far-flung, loosely-bounded, sparsely-knit, and fragmentary" [2].

The hot term in the literature today is "virtual community" [3]. I define the virtual community as a space of association or interaction that is mediated by digital technology. In general, the discussions of how new media affects communities has

P. van den Besselaar and S. Koizumi (Eds.): Digital Cities 2003, LNCS 3081, pp. 259-273, 2005.
© Springer-Verlag Berlin Heidelberg 2005

been fraught with disagreement. Some pundits have argued that networked media is ill-suited for the expressive, emotional actions that are fundamental to the sustenance of community [4], while others have seen it as integrative and rich as a mechanism of connecting people [2]. My belief is that new media can strengthen already strong connections, open up new previously "latent" connections [2], and make possible rich communities that only meet across the online space [5].

1.1 Urbanism, Neighborhood, and Community Media Systems

Because there is such a significant amount of research done on communities that are formed or sustained with new media, this paper will focus on my research related to communities that maintain a relative level of physical proximity. My interest is in how virtual environments can add to these communities, and strengthen their conjugate social capital.

Only a few studies have examined the impact of Information and Communication Technologies (ICTs) on local neighborhoods, but there are a few relevant benchmarks in this research. Hampton et al.'s study of four Boston-area neighborhoods (E-neighbors) has shown that internet use can have both positive and negative effects on local communities depending on how interactive the type of usage is (e.g.; chatting or emailing vs. watching videos) [6]. Regardless, the finding that community does not have to be physically bounded does not mean that local communities are necessarily disenfranchised. In fact, several studies in underprivileged neighborhoods [7] have demonstrated that ICTs can empower local neighborhoods to share assets, communicate about issues, and feel more of a sense of community. Finally, the now famous Netville study has shown that residents of a wired suburb can expand their social networks to include those that are in the neighborhood and far away [2].

What is the relevance of community and how do I define it? I define community as a set of individuals with a shared set of interests, values, or ideals. One's community can be characterized as the set of interpersonal networks that provide sociability, social support and social capital to its members [2]. The key aspect to community is one of solidarity, and traditional notions of community have identified solidarity around the notion of neighborhood, which imposes the bounds of spatial proximity. Communities are integral in the maintenance of an individual's social capital, which describes an individual's ability to access needed resources, whether they be material, physical, or emotional/psychological. Social capital has begun to flow to the individual from numerous sources, as he or she has become a member of multiple communities, and a significant amount of research has surfaced to show what are advantageous vs. disadvantageous configurations of the individual's social networks that maximize this property [8].

Critics have lamented the loss of public space and fragmentation of urban environments [9] that have accompanied recent urban dynamics (economic, sociological, and political) and pointed to a recombination of social networks that are greater in number yet fluid in the sense that they no longer depend as inherently on spatial proximity.

Because the phenomenon of the virtual community is relatively recent, and its epistemological foundations are still in their development, I believe this is a debate without a clear outcome. Instead, it points to exciting opportunities in the design in the largely unexplored world of ICT and digital community design. Possibilities remain for the virtual place to embody the goals of the public space as being a sphere of interaction and communication [10].

1.2 Village Voice, Ontology, Narrative Systems, and Social Agents

My specific case will center on Village Voice, a narrative-based community multimedia system I have designed, developed, and evaluated. I will present the methodology by which Village Voice builds upon the growing movement in community publishing and storytelling. A number of studies have demonstrated that empowering communities to create their own stories stimulates a process of reflection, which in turn facilitates the sharing of values, knowledge, structure and dreams.

There is a purpose behind my naming this project Village Voice. A village is a set of people who have a shared history, co-dependence, and present-day connections with those who are living in proximity to them. These links are not merely passive ties, but allow the villager to actively occupy a role within the larger community.

I have modeled Village Voice after the work of Murtaugh [11], who pioneered content-driven, decentralized navigation of narrative. In such systems, narrative unfolds based upon both what the viewer is watching and an overarching model of story. I expand on Murtaugh's work both by incorporating content generated by the community and by utilizing the Concept Maps techniques developed by Novak and Cañas. Concept Maps are learner-created knowledge models [12].

Village Voice has shown potential as a system that can archive content generated by community members through its departure from traditional methods of using the web to represent museum exhibits. Instead of basing content and their interrelations around ad-hoc indices, Village Voice allows the user to interact with material based on how the community itself articulates the relationships within its different pieces. The interface is based around a dynamic collage, which is able to reveal the complexity of the artifacts of a community because of how it can adapt to a user's browsing history and the intricate relationships within the different materials in the exhibit.

This paper is a study of my hypothesis that a knowledge model, or ontology, created by community members, better facilitates the sharing of knowledge across a community as compared to keyword indexing. My contribution is a demonstration that a community-built ontology is more than a static structure with which to represent community knowledge: When continuously populated with their stories, ontology becomes a dynamic structure that is used by members to model the evolution of their community. Additionally, this paper also will incorporate my ongoing research related to software agents that can potentially add a deeper level of social facilitation to already rich digital community systems.

2 Methodology and Community Design

This section will begin by explaining the rationale behind the system design by explaining why narrative and community ontology are important topics to design for. It will then discuss the introduction of this project into a community of Somali refugees located in the Jamaica Plain neighborhood of the Boston Metropolitan Area.

2.1 Narrative and Community

Village Voice is built upon the premise that storytelling is fundamental to the sharing of experience. In cultures throughout the world, story exists to serve a range of purposes from teaching a moral, contemplating divinity, or preserving history. Stories are clearly one of the many ways in which we, as humans, present who we are to others [13].

Human beings are storytellers by nature. In many guises as folktale legend, myth, epic, history, motion picture and television program, the story appears in every known human culture. The story is a natural package for organizing many different kinds of information. Storytelling appears to be a fundamental way of expressing ourselves and our world to others [14, p.27].

Alfred Lord, whose work on oral storytelling focused on the singing bards who narrated stories to their respective cultures, explains that the oral tradition has persevered because "the picture that emerges is not really one of conflict between preserver of tradition and the creative artist; it is rather one of the preservation of tradition by the constant re-creation of it." [15]. The oral tradition has persevered through its adaptation to the change that is inevitable to all cultures.

In a number of cultures worldwide, the oral process of storytelling is embraced. Historically, the esteemed storytelling bards of each clan transmitted this culture through poetry. Do computer networking and digital storytelling have a role in such a tradition, particularly related to the process of preserving and sharing issues of cultural heritage?

The possibilities computation offers changes the dynamic. Hypermedia is a paradigm that allows content to be related using pre-defined links. The interaction is discontinuous, however, because the user has to click on one of a set of choices to allow the story to continue. However, stories could take advantage of computer systems to empower the user the power to grasp linkages within the content in a more personal way. This can enable the multimedia systems of cultural heritage to preserve and share the community material in a way that allows the visitor to take his or her own journey through the material that is presented. I believe that the methodology I point to below provides an interesting set of issues that all media designers must consider when working with communities and matters of cultural heritage.

2.2 Somali Community Introduction

As the focus of my hypothesis was to test whether a community-created model could be a strong foundation for the design of such a multimedia narrative system, I realized that I needed to work with a local community that I could visit repeatedly, teach a number of video story classes with, and work iteratively to elicit an evolving ontology that could structure the communications within the digital space. With this in mind, I sought out the Somali Development Center (SDC) in Jamaica Plain, Massachusetts. In the next two sections, I briefly introduce Somalis and their ancestral culture, and the community in Jamaica Plain. In the meantime, the project in India continues to proceed, but to really establish this project, I focused on this local community.

The Somali refugee community in the Boston area is concentrated amongst a few pockets in Jamaica Plain, Roxbury, Revere, and Charlestown. The population of this group has expanded over the last five years, from about 3000 to 5000 [16]. Refugees span a variety of ages, however, because of the mercurial nature of some of the programs that brought Somalis to Boston, a number of families have been broken up in the process. Refugees today are victims of a civil war that has torn apart these families and decimated a once thriving culture. This community has dramatically expanded over the last five years due to the civil war in Somalia. According to community members with whom I have spoken, there is a desire to archive their experiences as they face new challenges in the United States. They wish to find a means to tell stories to their community, as well as to incoming refugees and others outside of the community. Traditionally, story has been orally transmitted in Somali culture, so the use of a medium that records and retells story is new to them.

There are only a few major hubs around which Somalis traditionally gather. Most important seems to be the Somali Development Center (SDC), on 205 Green St. in Jamaica Plain. Since 1996, the SDC has been a hub for educational and social services for the growing Somali community in Boston. SDC was established and funded by a small group of Somali-Americans who originally came to the United States to obtain higher education.

I introduced myself to the community as a graduate student interested in using video to document the experiences of people in the community with the purpose of creating an exhibit that could serve as a growing archive of their shared issues, challenges, and experiences as recent immigrants to Boston.

The project was well received from the start. There were obvious needs that this project could fill for the SDC. One of the priorities of the SDC is to work to integrate incoming refugees with the existing Somali community, and ultimately with the basics of living in Boston. A technology that could introduce new members to issues and associated stories of the community would help the process of acclimation. In addition, building a tool that could document the unique culture of Somali-Americans could help future generations be connected to their traditions, and reflect on how they have changed over time. Finally, the SDC was interested in using the different video stories gathered by project to present thematic programs on their weekly cable access television show in the area.

A variety of SDC members had indicated to me that the center faced some significant problems. For example, the clan heritage with which many Somalis identify has been a significant stumbling block in the center's efforts to try to build a unified community that can benefit from the programs it offers. Is it possible to use technology to remind Somalis of this heritage yet still show that these refugees are one clan, together living in Boston? How can the designer of community-centered media help the community yet powerfully represent its stories to the outside world?

I became involved with the community first as a tutor and mentor for teenagers. This involved bi-weekly visits to the community center and other Somali institutions, where I would work on different subjects with these kids. After two introductory months, it became clear that I needed to involve members of the community to lead the project. This would allow the project and its purpose to be better communicated to the entire community, while facilitating the search for potential story creators. I began to introduce the project to the kids I was tutoring, elders in the citizenship classes, at the local high school (English High School) where the Somali teenagers of the area went to school, and via the weekly cable-access television show.

It took a short while, but the efforts paid off. I soon met many prospective story creators. After an introductory workshop to the basics of creating video, I gave very few instructions to participants except to focus their stories on issues that are relevant to them as Somali immigrants in Boston. Over a month, 50 stories were collected from the seven story creators.

I wished to use these stories to stimulate the design of a representation, or ontology, that could illustrate the intersecting issues of the community. My goal was to engage the community in the reflective process of creating an ontology that could articulate the relationships between relevant community issues. As issues in the community would change, the community could redesign this representation through future ontology design meetings.

In this research, my hypothesis was that a knowledge model, or ontology, created by community members, is more than a static structure with which to represent community knowledge: When continuously populated with their stories, ontology becomes a dynamic structure that is used by members to model the evolution of their community. Thus, ontology becomes a mechanism by which the stories and artifacts of a community can be represented and exhibited in the landscape of a multimedia system. It allows for the access and understanding of community-centered exhibits to occur through the community's own semantics. Values, discourse, and dreams are all framed in an architecture that allows for the museum to faithfully represent the evolution and experiences of communities worldwide. Before I continue with my discussion of the methodology of this project, I introduce some background material on ontologies.

2.3 Ontology

Ontology was found to be the missing representation, the architecture that could organize and interrelate the stories of a community in a way that was responsive and faithful to the existing social fabric.

I use Uschold's definition of ontology as an explicit representation or structure of knowledge [17]. Ontologies can be used to describe physical processes, educational fields, or in the case of Village Voice, the discourse of a community.

Ontology can also be seen as a conceptual map where the links between individual pieces of knowledge are delineated. An assumption researchers in this field make is that knowledge is without meaning unless it is contextualized. The specific nodes in the structure need to be understood along with the links that tie them together.

Roger Schank explains that through ontology, we make sense of the world. Information that we encounter is understood through our own internal "data structures", which he calls scripts. Scripts, to Schank, are our own implicit organizations of knowledge retrieved from the world we inhabit [18].

Joseph Novak and Albert Cañas have been responsible for some of the advances in the field of learner-created knowledge models. Their projects focus on Concept Maps (CMAP). Concept Maps are based on the idea that true learning involves the learner to construct relationships between the new information he or she acquires and which is already possessed [19]. The focus is to instruct the subject to explicitly map out the relationships within a certain process or object that is being studied.

Subjects were found to have a deeper understanding of the concept of "plant" after following these steps, particularly when subjects were involved in critiquing each other's work. The experimenters argue that there are two reasons why Concept Maps augment knowledge: first, because learning is structurally organized, and second, because a general understanding of epistemology is realized by the subjects [19]. It is this process that I have used in the development of an architecture that can represent the stories of a community. The next section of this paper reveals how.

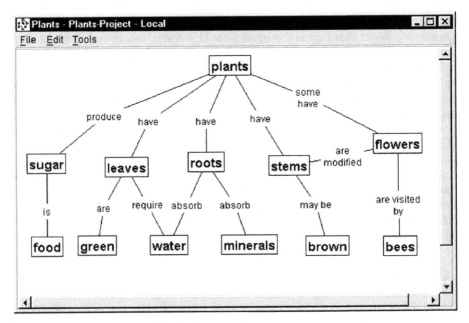

Fig. 1. An example concept map

2.4 Community Ontology Design

Here I present the methodology and result of our initial community ontology design:

Date of workshop: Thursday, April 11, 2002

Background: 50 stories created by community members were collected, and uploaded to the Village Voice system in Quicktime 5.0 Format. I converted these stories to a VHS tape for the meeting because the SDC lacks the computer resources to access the Village Voice site. The story creators had created approximately two hours of video footage by this point.

Presentation: We had divided up the workshop into two sessions, both of which were attended by many of the same participants. The first presentation took place in the morning after the citizenship class, and the second took place during the traditional tutoring sessions, after school for some of the younger participants. The two sessions went from 11 AM – 1 PM and 2:15 – 5:00 PM. Each session had about 20-30 participants.

Setup: Approximately 80% of the videos were in Somali, and had only been roughly translated for me. Many of the participants, particularly older members, did not speak any English as well. For these reasons, two leaders of the SDC helped me lead the workshop. They are Abdi Yussuf, current director of the SDC, and Abdul Hussein, the founder of the SDC and owner of Sagal Café and Enterprises.

Goal Explanation: Abdi and Abdul asked me to give them some examples of ontology so they could explain it to the community. I concluded on an approach of explanation through example. I showed them a variety of different ontology projects. Abdi and Abdul concluded that they would explain the ontology to the participants by asking them to discuss community priorities and the relationship between these.

Stories, reflection, and decision-making: Each session began with an explanation in Somali to remind participants about the purpose of the project. The movies were then shown on the VHS tape, and participants were encouraged to pause, stop, or repeat the video at any time. They were instructed to do this whenever they felt an issue that was relevant for their community was revealed in a story. During the pauses, the community would discuss the videos they were watching and craft a part of the ontology diagram on the white board in the front of the classroom.

The question of following tradition versus adaptation to being in America dominated the discussions participants had during the workshop. Elders would express consternation over the direction their kids had taken. One elder woman implored, "These kids don't have the respect for authority we did at their age. Look at the language they use. What has happened to what the Koran has taught them?" Some teenagers, on the other hand, while remaining quiet when elders were in the room, would tell me that while they had great pride in their heritage and religion, felt a need to fit in with their peers at school, and to follow the opportunities being in America has allowed them.

Particularly spirited arguments came up when movies related to women and sexuality, and generational issues were viewed. Even the older and deeply religious participants, were very divided on the question of female circumcision, which is performed on approximately 98% of Somali girls. Some participants argued that their move to a more democratic and diverse country should force them to reconsider such practices, which cause health problems and are invasive to women. Others, however, said that rejecting these traditions were insulting to their Somali Islamic heritage.

During these discussions, the community would come to a consensus on whether an issue that had come up should be included in the ontology. For example, one story was set at a Somali youth party. It showed teenage men and women dancing together dancing to hip hop music. The idea of a youth dance party without Somali music was disagreeable to some of the participants because of its disrespect to the Islamic taboo of pre-marital relationships, while most of the youth at the meeting argued that one could have a pre-marital relationship without being disrespectful to Muslim culture. During this discussion, the participants decided that issues of religious tradition, sexuality, and generational differences were relevant to the ontology. These topics were then added to the ontology and linked to each other on the white board.

The process of using these stories to allow the viewers to articulate their opinions ended up being the key to the design of the ontology that emerged. The fact that certain issues raised such discussion brought to light how relevant they were to the overall community, and allowed community members to flag them as relevant to include in the ontology. Over the course of the meeting, we went through several iterations, as different participants would offer input and sketch the consensus of issues on the whiteboard. The drawn structure changed multiple times in the process, as the community members reflected further on the issues that united them.

Every community issue listed in the above diagram is called a "node" in this thesis. The above ontology is a tree-like structure, where all nodes are considered a "part-of" the parent to which they are directly linked. Every video piece that was submitted was annotated according by the author according to its level of correspondence with the different topics within the community ontology.

Village Voice has been made publicly available on the web (http://village-voice.media.mit.edu). As stories are submitted from the upload page they are included in the database.

I found great value in the process of engaging villagers to create their own stories. It was clear that building a representation in community-terms for these stories could be the key to building a system that could share narratives across the community.

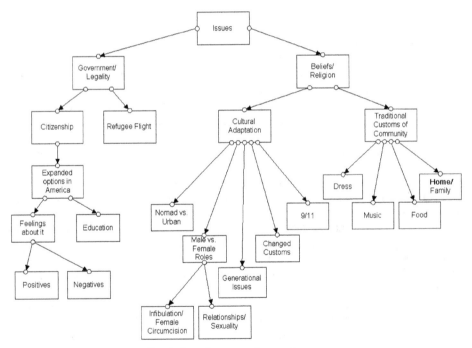

Fig. 2. Somali community ontology

3 Design, Implementation, and Ongoing Research

In this section, I will introduce the multimedia system and its features. This is followed by an evaluation of this system relative to other multimedia community systems organized by ad hoc indices. Finally, I will point to the potential to extend a system such as Village Voice further by empowering it with a greater capability for community facilitation.

3.1 System and Interface Design

The interface of Village Voice is suited for the representation of a community or a culture because it is designed to illuminate complex interrelationships between different topics visually. I will discuss the interface and system use as well as my ongoing in research in the design of systems that can have a level of agency and intelligence that can communicate cultural topics more proactively and independently.

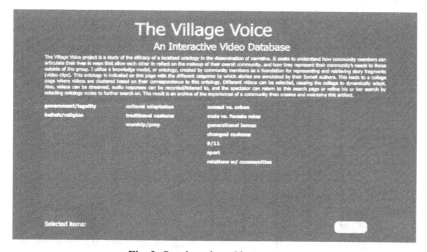

Fig. 3. Ontology-based browse page

Village Voice is entered via a "search" page. This page is organized hierarchically, according to the tree-based design of the ontology. The user can select multiple nodes from the tree that he or she is interested in watching stories about.

There are two colors of text on this page: white and yellow. The yellow text (at the bottom of the page) reflects the nodes that the user has selected to browse stories on. Above, these are citizenship, refugee flight, and sexuality/relationships. The white text (in the center of the page) reflects the ontology tree, from which can select an additional node to browse on by clicking on it. Finally, the user needs to click on the search button to reach the browsing page, which expresses the relevance of stories in the system to the topics chosen by the user. The browsing page is designed to give the user a wide range of information about the different video stories by displaying each story's thumbnails, while conveying their relationships to each other.

As seen in Figure 5 below, the thumbnails are illuminated to varying levels. This is reflective of how closely each thumbnail corresponds to the terms the user decided to search on in the search page. A brighter illumination indicates a closer match with the search query.

The story that best matches the query is known is the focus story, whose thumbnail has a pink-colored border. Once the browser is loaded a user can change the focus story by clicking on any other thumbnail in the collage. This changes the illumination of all the other thumbnails in the interface based on how closely their annotations match those of the new focus story.

As the above image shows, community members are given three options with which they can work on any given submission. The story can be played by selecting the play button, which is the leftmost of the three buttons below the thumbnail. This will stream the video in a frame to the right of the collage.

Users can also record their reactions to any story that they view. These reactions can be uploaded as audio file to Village Voice by selecting the Talk button below the thumbnail. This will open a page. Finally, the user can listen to the audio annotations associated with any story. These can be loaded by clicking on the middle of the three buttons under the thumbnail.

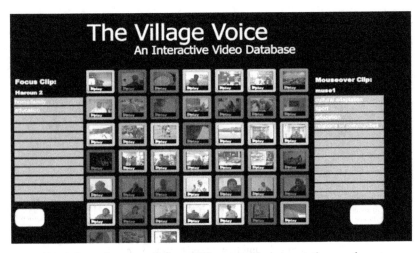

Fig. 4. Browsing page: Collage, Video streaming, Annotations, and more

Fig. 5. Collage showing relative similarities of different community submissions

Fig. 6. Submission icon and 3 buttons

Village Voice finds stories that "best" match a user's search queries or browsing choices based on its clustering algorithm. The level to which a story matches the browsing choices is revealed in its level of illumination, or alpha value. Alpha values range between 0 and 1, and are directly proportional to the score calculated below.

In this algorithm, I introduce the terms "branch nodes" and "end nodes". A story's end nodes are the ontology nodes with which it is explicitly annotated. A story's branch nodes, however, are not only the nodes with which it is annotated, but all the nodes on that story's branch of the ontology tree. For example, if a story is annotated with the nodes "Nomad vs. Urban" and "9/11", its end nodes would be the two nodes, but its branch nodes would also include their mutual parent, "Cultural Adaptation".

4 Evaluation and Ongoing Research

Now that both the methodology and interface for this community-centered story archive have been discussed, I wanted to study the effectiveness of village voice as a mechanism to engage the Somali community relative to a traditional technique of organizing content.

I designed an experiment to test Village Voice's use of ontology versus a keyword-based representation [20]. In the keyword version, I selected the five most frequently spoken words in each story, and annotated each of the stories in the system with these. The keywords were identified by the story-creators, who kept a histogram of the words that were spoken in their stories and gave me a list for each story. This list did not include "noise" words such as "is" or "and", which are without significant meaning. Because most of the stories were in Somali, the community's input was critical in creating the control for this experiment. We also translated Village Voice into Somali so all the conditions would be replicated.

As in Village Voice, in the keyword version, words can be selected as the basis for story search. Browsing is also possible in the same way. The only difference is that this version groups stories based on whether the story is annotated with the same keywords. No clustering is done based on relationships within the ontology, which is the key difference.

Over one week of testing, 30 subjects were tested, all of whom were Somali immigrants living in the Boston area. I asked each subject to sign an informed consent form, which assured them that the study was anonymous.

Each subject was asked to browse Village Voice and the keyword version for as much time as they wished, with a minimum of three minutes. Before using either version, the subject would log in to the system with an anonymous name so that I could monitor which sequences of stories the subject browsed, how long he or she stayed logged on, and how many stories were played. The audio annotation feature of the system was not completed when testing was conducted, so this was not measured. My results were as follows:

This data shows the mean and standard deviation values (across the 30 subjects) of the number of stories browsed, number of stories played, and time online for the keyword (KW) and Village Voice (VV) versions. The values for time online are expressed in terms of seconds.

This data shows a higher engagement for subjects across-the-board with Village Voice. In general, subjects spent a lot of time studying the interface and not interacting with it heavily, as can be seen by the rather small number of clips played or browsed on in either version. Many subjects mentioned to me that they would have browsed in more detail if they were more used to the system and technology, in general.

I present the story of one subject who browsed the system for 10 minutes. This subject was first exposed to the keyword version, where he spent his time selecting words from its search page viewing the browsing collage and then going back to the search page. In the approximately 3 minutes that the subject used the keyword version, only once was a clip played, and no browsing was done from the browsing collage itself. The ontology version shows a different behavior. Seven stories were played, and the data show that the subject clicked on multiple thumbnails on the browsing collage. Overall, the subject was measured as being more engaged over the three data variables of the study. It appears that the ontology version inspires more browsing activity from the browsing collage page, and that the clustering of stories in Village Voice enables subjects to perceive more connections between stories. This points to ontology based organization as a more powerful mechanism of communicating important issues across a community.

Table 1. Mean and Standard of Deviation values of Village Voice versus control

	Mean value	standard deviation
KW time online	263	205.36
VV time online	967	891.39
KW # clips browsed	2	0.697
VV # clips browsed	7	2.719
KW # clips played	1	0.433
VV # clips played	3	0.788

5 Concluding Thoughts

I have observed that ontology can become a dynamic structure that can model a community and the cultural material that it can produce. Thus, ontology-based design can enable community media systems to articulate the important issues across a community. I have demonstrated this idea through the introduction of a methodology that can allow a designer to work with communities, solicit and archive important community information and frame these experiences in terms of relevant community themes that have been articulated by members themselves. In Section 2, I point to dynamic collage and ontology based search as powerful forms of organization and interface to present to community members. Section 3 reveals that testing has shown the model I introduce as allowing for stories to be disseminated more effectively than the traditional index of keywords that are spoken. As the community changes over time, it can use ontology to contemplate where it has been, and where it is moving. I also point to the intriguing possibility of embedding an unprecedented level of power and autonomy in the system itself, through the development of bots of social facilitation. This points to the potential of the Village Voice model as a means to dynamically exhibit the experiences of a community. Basing the unfolding of these narratives around the community ontology opens up the possibility for them to be disseminated more effectively than the traditional index of keywords that are spoken.

Significant amounts of research remain to be done to better understand how to maintain dynamic models of communities and how to further empower community media systems. However, this approach has allowed a community to take control over the means by which it is exhibited to the public, yet use the exhibition as a means of reflection. I believe that continuing to push the design issues that this paper points to can allow for more deeply communicative digital cities to emerge.

References

1. Borges, Jorge Luis: Ficciones, New York, NY. Penguin Books
2. Wellman, Barry: Physical Place and Cyber Place: The Rise of Personalized Networking. International Journal of Urban and Regional Research 25(2) (2001) 227-52
3. Rheingold, Howard: The Virtual Community: Homesteading on the Electronic Frontier. Reading, MA. Addison & Wesley Co. (1993)
4. Kraut, R., Miller, M., Siegal, J.: Collaboration in Performance of Physical Tasks: Effects on Outcomes and Communication: In Proceedings of CSCW '96. New York, NY: ACM Press (1996)
5. Haythornwaite, Caroline: Strong, Weak and Latent Ties and the Impact of New Media. The Information Society 18(5) (2002) 385-401.
6. Smith, M.A and Kollock, P., eds.: Communities in Cyberspace. London: Routledge (1999)
7. Hampton, Keith: The Diversity of Personal and Neighborhood Networks in the Informational City. (2003)
8. Pinkett, Randal D.: The Creating Community Connections (C3) System Project. Submitted to the US Department of Commerce, Ars Portalis Final Report, June 18. (2001)
9. Putnam, Robert: Bowling Alone. New York, NY. Simon & Schuster Inc. (2000)
10. Sorkin, Michael: Traffic In Democracy, In Giving Ground: The politics of propinquity, New York, NY. Verso Press (1999)
11. Deutsche, Rosalyn: Reasonable Urbanism, In Giving Ground: The Politics of Propinquity, New York, NY. (1999)
12. Murtaugh, Michael: The Automatist Storytelling System. Massachusetts Institute of Technology. Department of Architecture. Program in Media Arts and Sciences. (1994)
13. Novak, Joseph: The Theory Underlying Concept Maps and How To Construct Them, http://cmap.coginst.uwf.edu/info/ (1998)
14. Campbell, J.: The Power Of Myth. New York, NY. Doubleday (1988)
15. McAdams, Dan: The Stories We Live By. New York, NY. William Morrow And Company. Inc. (1993)
16. Lord, Alfred: The singer of tales. New York, NY. Atheneum Press (1960)

17. Yussuf, Abdi: The Somali Development Center of Jamaica Plan, MA (self-published). (2000)
18. Uschold, Mike: Building Ontologies: Towards a Unified Methodology. Proceedings; Expert Systems Conference (1996)
19. Schank, Roger: Agents in the Story Archive. Institute for Learning Sciences, Northwestern University (1992)
20. Canas, Alberto J., Kenneth M. Ford, Joseph D. Novak, Patrick Hayes, Thomas R. Reichherzer, Nirajan Suri: Online Concept Maps – Enhancing Collaborative Learning by Using Technology with Concept Maps. In: The Science Teacher 68 (2001) 49-51.

Map-Based Range Query Processing for Geographic Web Search Systems

R. Lee[1], H. Shiina[1], T. Tezuka[1], Y. Yokota[1], H. Takakura[2], Y.J. Kwon[3], and
Y. Kambayashi[1]

[1] Department of Social Informatics, Kyoto University,
Yoshida-Honmachi, Sakyo-ku, Kyoto 606-8501, Japan
{ryong, shiina, yahiko}@db.soc.i.kyoto-u.ac.jp
2 Academic Center for Computing and Media Studies, Kyoto University,
Yoshida-Honmachi, Sakyo-ku, Kyoto 606-8501, Japan
takakura@media.kyoto-u.ac.jp
3 Department of Telecommunication and Information Engineering,
Hankuk Aviation University, Dukyang, Kyounggi-Do, Korea
yjkwon@tikwon.hangkong.ac.kr

Abstract. In order to utilize geographic web information for digital city applications, we have been developing a geographic web search system, KyotoSEARCH. When users retrieve geographic information on the web, specifying geographic location is an essential function. However, most current web search systems do not utilize location information sufficiently well to identify the user's intentions; available methods employ just keywords (for location names) and limited map functions. Furthermore, most map interfaces are used to select a determined geographic-hierarchy level or point to a specific location (sometimes specifying a radius). In this paper, we introduce two-dimensional range query processing for geographic web search, where users are able to specify a geographic area freely on a map interface. In order to handle such range queries more rapidly and efficiently, we adopt geometric operations to retrieve proper web pages. Without optimization techniques, however, the recall and precision of the search results become very low. Major problems come from erroneous extension of the computed geographic area due to i) same names for different geographic objects/locations (geowords), ii) redundant geographic hierarchy information, and iii) existence of non-important geowords. By resolving these problems, we can improve range query processing for geographic data. To that end, we propose an effective geographic scope optimization method for that supports geometric operations in geographic web search; experiments conducted on an implemented system are described.

1 Introduction

With the explosive adoption of the Web throughout the globe, we should be able to get useful and practical geographic information over the Web. This demands the ability to search for useful geographic information and locate it on a map. In order to make this rather complex job easier, we have been developing the geographic web search system called KyotoSEARCH [6, 7]. The major purpose of the system is to

P. van den Besselaar and S. Koizumi (Eds.): Digital Cities 2003, LNCS 3081, pp. 274-283, 2005.
© Springer-Verlag Berlin Heidelberg 2005

help users find comprehensive geographic web information through a user interface integrated with a map (its name came from the targeted area, Kyoto City in Japan).

In the system, a map interface is used for specifying a geographic area for localizing web searches. For a practical system, it is important to construct i) easy location specification methods that can express the search intentions of the user and ii) geographic web index methods that find the proper pages given the geographic query. Most users want to get the best results with the least effort; this shows the need for servers that provide effective light indices, which are better than keyword indices, and clever search methods whose computation costs are reasonable. In order to satisfy these requirements, we introduce a two-dimensional range query processing method based on geographically-indexed web pages. For geographic web indexing, we use MBR (Minimum Bounding Rectangle) to represent the 'geographic scope' of a page, using geo-referential words appearing in the content. Geographically-indexed web pages can be managed with any of the well-known two-dimensional index methods such as R-Tree [1].

We have actually implemented the above system in a server-client model; the server system hosts the geographic web index function, while the client provides a map-based search interface to the users. With the proposed index and map-based interface, the user can make and restrict a query by specifying a geographic area; the answer is returned by the server. Furthermore, search results can be manipulated by geometric operations (such as the 'Contain' relationship) between the user-drawn rectangular query and a MBR corresponding to a web page.

Assuming that the geographic scope of a web page is calculated from location names in the page content as an MBR, we have to identify the geographic scope of a web page to the smallest possible region. It is clear that recall is greatly degraded if unwarranted areas are assigned to a page when the 'Contain' operation is used. This problem can be solved by using the 'Intersection' operation or query correction. Unfortunately, this will degrade the precision of search results. When a user makes a rectangle query, in most cases they are assuming 'Contain' operation. Therefore, we focused on reducing the geographic scope of pages to support the use of the 'Contain' operation.

The major contribution of the paper is how to optimize the MBR for a given web page. For accurate computation of a page's MBR, we suggest some strategies and evaluate them in an experiment. Section 2 discusses related work. Section 3 describes the basic problems that arise when web pages are used as geographic information sources, focusing on the characteristics of geographic location names. We also give an overview of our approach. Optimization strategies are introduced in Section 4 and the experiment in Section 5.

2   Related Work

In order to search web pages with map interface, we should consider how to associate the pages with a location of map and what efficient and accurate methods are possible to answer geographic search queries.

Some related studies have attempted to compute the geographic scope of web pages or sites. The intrinsic problem comes from the deficiency of the geography of the web: that is the web page location itself is independent of real world locations. In order to resolve this and similar problems, there are two approaches for indexing the pages as follows:

- **Using Internal Information** [2, 9, 8]: A web page or a site has its own geographic area information, like addresses, phone number, etc. While using internal information yields relatively accurate results, few pages include such information. In order to apply this approach, we must prepare lists of geo-words and find all location names in each page.
- **Using External Information** [3, 4]: Another approach utilizes web-links. Internal information can be inaccurate such as the example of the 'NY Times' site introduced by [4]. The geographic scope of 'NY Times' should be larger than just the New York area, if we consider the geographic distribution of users assessing the site. However, limiting the extent to which the external links are followed is a major problem. A rather impractical solution is to depend on manual tagging such as is seen in Yahoo!'s Geographic Category and the registered pages.

With above techniques for computing geographic scope, its representation method is an important issue, since the selected method greatly affects the search costs and the accuracy of search results. Actually, representation methods of geographic scopes of web pages and user queries should be considered together. Each one can have two representation methods; one is geometric and the other is keyword-based. Geometric representation usually used in GIS research fields can effectively reduce search costs better than keyword matching, which is adopted in most web search systems.

If indexing and query methods are different, we need to convert one to the other; when there is the index of web pages associating certain pages with a corresponding position on the map of Kyoto, a keyword like 'Kyoto Station' issued by a user specifying a location needs to be converted into appropriate points/polygons/rectangles utilizing a lookup table transforming keywords into geometric figures. Then, geometric comparison of the query and index is realized and generates suitable search results.

Table 1. Comparison of Approaches to Computing Geographic Scope

Comparison	Our Method	Kokono[10]	GeoLink[5]	Localness[11]
Query	Rectangle	Circle	Point/Keywords	Keywords
Index	MBR	Polygon	Point	MBR
Index Cost	Low	High	Middle	Low
Used Info.	Internal	Internal	External	Internal
Search Operation	Geometric	Distance only	Keywords Matching	
Search Cost	Low	Middle	High	Middle
Search Results	Logical		Semantic	

As shown in Table 1, there are several types of geometric representation of web pages; point/polygon/MBR. Each of them has the different management and search costs of databases. When we use MBRs for indexing, the search costs will be lower than polygons or points. There are also various types of geometric search operations; distance, include, overlap, and so on. Though we do not discuss use cases of the specific geometric operations, these are useful tools on maps comparing to the conventional keyword-based search operation.

In this paper, we focus on the geometric comparison of users' queries and web pages indexed geometrically. This approach will ensure logical search results in the respect of map semantics with very fast comparison.

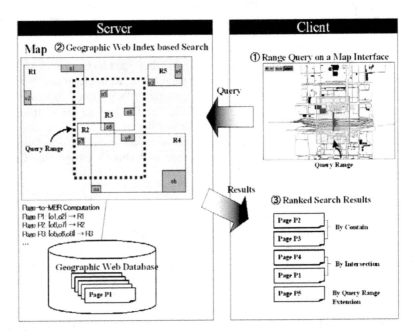

Fig. 1.   Range Query Processing based on Geographic Web Index

3   Our Approach and Contribution

We adopted the approach of using 'Internal Information', since our geographic area of interest is a local area (Kyoto City, Japan). That is, we determine the geographic scope of a web page from the geographic location names in the page's contents [2, 9, 8]. We first show all the process performed between a user client and the server system in fig. 1.

1.   First, the user makes a query by drawing a rectangular region on a map interface and selects the desired geometric operation, either from 'Contain' or 'Intersection' (left-side buttons in the interface). The client system then submits the query to the server system.

2.   Next, the range query which has its own coordinates for the user interface is then translated into the coordinate format used in the geographic web index (Latitude/Longitude in this case).

3.   Finally, the selected geometric operation is applied to retrieve web pages; In 'Contain' search, sometimes there is no search result; it occurs when actually related web pages are corresponding to an area larger than the user query. In

order to get such partially overlapped pages on maps, alternative methods like 'Intersection' or 'Extension of User Query Range' can be used.

To address the problems created by the characteristics of geowords, we represent each page as an MBR region in the server side of Fig. 1 and manage these MBRs by using an R-Tree [1] index (other two-dimensional index methods are also possible). This geographic web index can be used to retrieve web pages with geometric operations as follows:

Contain (Qa, Pa) : the query area (Qa) specified by user covers the area (Pa) of a web page geometrically.

Intersection (Qa, Pa) : the query area (Qa) has non-empty common area with the area (Pa) of a web page.

Geometric operations on web searches are discussed in other studies. There are several types; i) zoom-based range specification (available in most popular portal sites such as Yahoo!), and ii) a circle based on a center point with a diameter [10]. In addition, we propose a two-dimensional rectangular type query, which provides significant flexibility to the user.

Problems: As already noted, using geowords (names of geographic locations/objects) raises several serious problems:

Object name wrongly identified as geoword: A tough problem is that many objects have names that are possible geowords. In the Internal Information based geographic scope computation, there is a serious problem that the corresponding geographic area can erroneously be huge if all the homonymic locations were included. We must select one of the candidate locations that have the same name. This problem must be solved in order to get an appropriate geographic area corresponding to a page. Our solution is based on a heuristic that a homonym can be specified by geographic distances from other location names included in the same page. A homonymic geoword can be mapped to one unique location which minimizes the sum of the distances from other co-occurring geowords in the same page.

Redundant geographic information: A page can have geographic information of different levels. For example, if a postal address is provided, the page will contain 'city', 'ward', and 'town' names; town names are the most informative in determine geographic scope so 'city' and 'ward' names are unnecessary except when needed to differentiate towns with the same name.

Unimportant geowords: A web page can contain many valid geowords that are unimportant with regard to the user's search goal. Examples are the pages of tour guides and the branch offices of companies. Given that the title and anchor text parts are much more important than the others, we should focus on the level of the HTML tags in selecting the true geoword.

Figure 2 shows one example of how shared names can degrade search performance. In this case, adjacent wards have temples with the same name of 'Daijiin'. A web page that contains 'Daijiin' as a geoword can trigger unwarranted expansion of the MBR. The true MBR is defined by 'Hokyoji' and 'Daijiin' (Sakyo ward). Resolving this problem would yield the true MBR region as the small rectangle shown in the center of fig. 2.

We implemented a testbed system utilizing 2 million web pages crawled by us and the R-Tree function of PostgreSQL DB. In tests of the developed system, we found that most users drew a rectangle with the intention to express the 'Contain' operation.

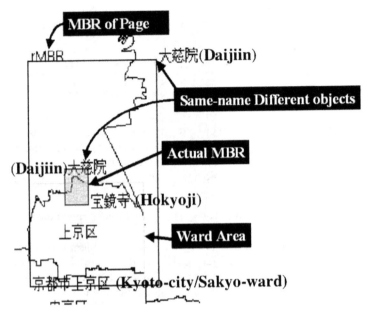

Fig. 2. Example of MBR for a Geographic Web Page

4   Optimizing Geographic Scope

In this section, we will describe the problems of geographic scope optimization in detail and propose a comprehensive solution.

To compute effective MBRs, we need to consider two types of geowords for Addresses from Geographic Objects' Names such as buildings, since there are many partially written Addresses. In that case, we need to guess full address from partial information. As the source data, we used map data for Kyoto City from (c)ZENRIN[6].

- **Addresses:** In order to extract addresses from a page, we must consider a convention to write an address in various types for geographic hierarchy. For example, a full address 'Kyoto-prefecture/Kyoto-city/Sakyo-ward/Yoshida-Honmachi' is used to specify the 'YoshidaHonmachi' (a town). However, there are other forms ignoring city name as 'Sakyo-ward/YoshidaHonmachi', 'YoshidaHonmachi', etc. These various forms should be normalized into the 'YoshidaHonmachi' location. To solve these problems also for the other levels of 'ward' and 'city', we made an address index as the below three types, and use

---

[6] (c)Zenrin-TOWNII: a map data set by a Japanese company.

them to recognize geographic hierarchy of each address by the maximum text matching in page contents. For these matching process, such overlapped 141,379 addresses are made from 4,966 towns names and 11 wards of Kyoto City. In our data, there are 30,063 MBRs in town-level addresses, but there are 3,658 distinct names. The average ambiguity of these distinct addresses is about 8.21. (This is relatively high, since we simply find other addresses including a town name. However, we are facing to such an ambiguity for addresses in Kyoto City).

- **Geographic Objects:** Other geowords such as buildings also have corresponding MBRs. Actually, we have 120,286 geographic objects (except for personal names), where 4,916 names are corresponding to 12,273 objects. The average ambiguity is about 2.49. These data are also managed to have all corresponding MBRs as choice candidates.

4.1 Heuristic Optimization Strategies

We now propose the following heuristic optimization strategies to deal with the geoword problems:

S1) Focus on Title+Anchor: Title and/or anchor texts are assigned significant importance in web page processing. Accordingly, geowords in these parts are taken as candidates. We will distinguish geowords appearing in titles of pages from geowords appearing in page contents. It is better to give more attention to title part, as discussed in our previous work [11].

S2) Reduction of Ambiguity: Often a web page will have one or more ambiguous geowords. Since accurate selection is difficult in practice, our heuristic method is to utilize the unique geowords, if any, on same web page to resolve this ambiguity.

S3) Reduction of Redundant Hierarchy Info: Generally, there is redundant geographic hierarchy information, which should be excluded in computing an MBR to a page. As described, if there are two geowords, one is a town name and the other is a ward name, and the town is included in the ward. In these cases, the ward name is redundant, and should be removed in the consideration. However, there are other cases where the ward name could not be removed. For example, we assume that:

1. A town name $T1$ is included only in a ward $W1$ ($T1$ is unique).
2. A town name $T2$ is included in both of wards, $W1$ and $W2$ ($T2$ is ambiguous).

A web page can have following cases (Gp is a set of geowords appeared in a page):
Case 1. $Gp = \{T1, W1\}$: T1 is not ambiguous and $W1$ is redundancy. Thus, $W1$ is removed.
Case 2. $Gp = \{T2, W1, W2\}$: T2 is ambiguous, and $W1/W2$ are not redundancy. Thus, $W1/W2$ cannot be removed without other information.
Case 3. $Gp = \{T2, W1\}$: T2 is not ambiguous and $W1$ is redundancy, since $T2$ becomes to be unique when $W1$ only appears. Thus, $W1$ can be removed.
Case 4. $Gp = \{T1, T2, W1, W2\}$: W1 and W2 cannot be removed as like above case 2. However, we can resolve this problem logically by selecting one near $T1$ by minimum

distance. *T2*'s ambiguity, then, is resolved. *T1* and *T2* are together uniquely included in *W1*. Finally, *W1* and *W2* are removed.

5   Experiments

This section describes the experiments conducted on actual web pages to show the effectiveness of the proposed algorithm. We created a set of web pages by following the links shown on a local information site[7] about Kyoto City. For web data targeting Kyoto City area (in Japan), we crawled 6,754 web pages that had the string 'kyoto' in their URLs. From the crawled pages, we used only 3,075 (about 45%) of them that included town and ward names (inside Kyoto City) as the experimental data set.

In order to show the relative effect of proposed algorithm, we compared PureMBR(representing the unoptimized geographic scope) size to the results gained by applying the Optimization Strategies described in Sect. 4.1.

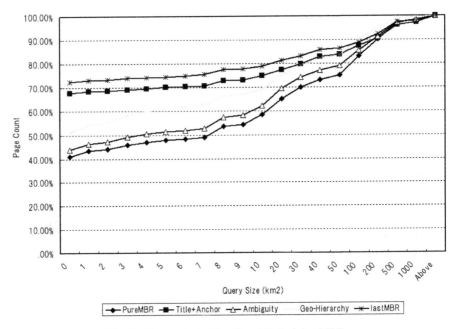

Fig. 3.   Experimental Results of Optimizing MBRs

Distribution of PureMBR Area Size: Each page in the experiment data set was parsed to find geowords and their locations; (i)Title+Anchor and (ii) all page contents. For (ii) of all page contents, PureMBR was computed by referencing a lookup table that transforms geowords into MBRs without any optimization method. The cumulative distribution of MBR size is shown in Fig. 3; less than 40% of the pages

---

[7] Kyoto City Information: http://www.city.kyoto.jp/koho/ind_h.htm

were within an area of $1km^2$, and more than 50% of the areas were larger than $8km^2$. It means that a half of experiment data set will not appear in search results to a range query smaller than $8km^2$.

We also tested the combination of all optimization methods in the LastMBR algorithm. As shown in Fig. 3, more than 70% pages are smaller than $1km^2$. By the proposed area reduction strategies, at least hidden 30% pages appear in results. Without these reductions, we need to perform 'Intersection' operation or extend the query size to about $50km^2$ in order to get those hidden 30% data, while these alternative query operations will result in low precision.

6 Conclusion

This paper described the problems raised by using geowords for extracting geographic information from web pages and proposed the utilization of conventional spatial indexing methods for geographic web searches. We also showed an implemented system that allows users to perform geometric operations to retrieve geographic web pages. Three heuristics were presented to overcome the problems and the results of experiments were shown to demonstrate the effectiveness of the heuristics.

Acknowledgements

This research is supported by Informatics Research Center for Development of Knowledge Society Infrastructure (COE program of the Ministry of Education, Culture, Sports, Science and Technology, Japan) and by 'Universal Design in Digital City' Project in CREST of JST (Japan Science and Technology Corporation). We also thank one of our international collaborative members, Internet Information Retrieval Center of Hankuk Aviation University for their cooperation.

References

1. G. Antonin, R-TREE: A Dynamic Index Structure for Spatial Searching, In Proceeding of ACM SIGMOD, pages 47-57, 1984.
2. M. Arikawa, K. Okamura, "Spatial Media Fusion Project," In Proceeding of Kyoto International Conference on Digital Libraries: Research and Practice, pp.75-82, Nov. 2000.
3. O. Buyukkokten, J. Cho, H. Garcia-Molina, L. Gravano, and N. Shivakumar, "Exploiting geographical location information of web pages," In Proceeding of the ACM SIGMOD Workshop on the Web and Databases, WebDB, 1999.
4. J. Ding, L. Gravano, and N. Shivakumar, "Computing Geographical Scopes of Web Resources," VLDB2000, pp.545-556, 2000.
5. K. Hiramatsu and T. Ishida, "An Augmented Web Space for Digital Cities," IEEE/IPSJ Symposium on Applications and the Internet (SAINT-01), pp.105-112, 2001.
6. R. Lee, H. Takakura, and Y. Kambayashi, "Visual Query Processing for GIS with Web Contents," The 6th IF Working Conference on Visual Database Systems, pp.171-185, May 29-31, 2002.

7. R. Lee, Y. Tezuka, N. Yamada, H. Takakura, and Y. Kambayashi, "KyotoSEARCH: A Concept-based Geographic Web Search Engine," In Proceedings of 2002 IRC International Conference on Internet Information Retrieval, pp. 119-126, Koyang, Korea, Nov. 2002.

8. C. Matsumoto, Q. Ma, and K. Tanaka, "Web Information Retrieval Based on the Localness Degree," In Proceeding of the 13th International Conference on Database and Expert System Applications 2002 (DEXA '02), pages 172-181, 2002.

9. K.S. McCurley, "Geospatial Mapping and Navigation of the Web," WWW10, 2000.

10. S. Yokoji, K. Takahashi, N. Miura, and K. Shima, "Location Oriented Information Collection, Structuring and Retrieval," IPSJ Journal Vol.41, No.7, pp. 1987-1998, July 2000.

11. N. Yamada, R. Lee, H. Takakura, and Y. Kambayashi, "Classification of Web Pages with Geographic Scope and Level of Details for Mobile Cache Management," The 2nd Int. Workshop on Web Geographical Information Systems, IEEE CS Press, Singapore, Dec. 2002.

Recognizing Buildings Using a Mobile System and a Reference City Model

Wanji Mai[1], Chris Tweed[2] and Gordon Dodds[1]

[1] Virtual Engineering Centre, Queen's University Belfast, Cloreen Park, Malone Road,
Belfast, BT9 5HN, Northern Ireland, UK
{w.mai, g.dodds}@ee.qub.ac.uk
[2] School of Architecture, Queen's University Belfast
2 Lennoxvale, Belfast BT9 5BY
c.tweed@qub.ac.uk

Abstract. Recent advances in the development of personal digital assistants (PDAs) and wireless communication networks enable a new generation of sophisticated mobile applications. PDAs can now support a range of add-on devices, such as digital cameras, and communicate using a variety of networking protocols, such as GPS, WiFi, and Bluetooth. This paper reports on research into and development of portable hardware that will enable users in the field to send images, and associated positional data from a PDA to a server for further image processing. The central aim is to provide navigational and informational services to an urban mobile user based on building recognition. The paper begins by describing the hardware system before presenting research into server-side building recognition methods that operate by comparing user-supplied images of similar images generated by an existing 3D digital model. This method uses a combination with segmentation and Hough Transform. Results of image capture and matching are given.

1 Introduction

With the increased availability and advanced features of low-cost, portable and mobile system devices, there is potential to develop a wide range of applications [9, 2]. The combination of mobile computational, imaging and positioning capabilities and network access opens the door to a variety of novel applications, such as pedestrian navigation aids, mobile information systems and other applications usually referred to as 'location services' [3]. Böhm et al project improves the GPS accuracy using the GPS data, orientation data, image, and also the Hough Transform method. The hardware system is similar with the one described in this paper except that this new system is mobile and portable, and the processing is carried out in real-time. Moreover, this research seeks to exploit the capabilities of the Personal Digital Assistant (PDA). It also applies different networks to realise the automation of data transfer between different devices and real-time information support within a city.

Several digital city projects [1, 6, 21, 7, 19, 16] concerned with cityscape and city model have been carried out. Most are designed to be an integrated information and service environment for everyday life and tourism [1, 6, 21, 7, 19, 8, 20]. Some of

P. van den Besselaar and S. Koizumi (Eds.): Digital Cities 2003, LNCS 3081, pp. 284–298, 2005.
© Springer-Verlag Berlin Heidelberg 2005

them also put much effort into the 3D models for city promotion application [16]. However this project sets up a system to help tourists identify buildings as they travel within the city and also provide immediate information in real-time with the help of the digital city model.

Visitors to a city sometimes find problems in understanding maps or guidebooks, even guidebooks with symbols. In another project, surveys of pedestrians in University Square, Belfast found that a significant proportion (12% of males, 24% of females) had difficulty in locating themselves on a printed map [14]. The developed system can increase location-awareness for visitors by identifying their location and getting information about urban objects using user-captured object images from a proprietary PDA.

This system is much more flexible and dynamic than kiosks, or any other fixed information displays. People can stop at any interesting object, take a picture of it and send the image with the corresponding GPS and orientation sensor data from the the PDA to the web server. The server can identify the object using reference online images generated from a 3D city model. These model images are linked to the GPS and orientation data sent by the PDA user. Positional data alone are not always accurate enough for the building recognition, and it is possible for server to identify the wrong building. This is especially the case for the common encountered urban-canyon situation or even in tree-lined streets, where spurious GPS position fixes can occur. Image processing with buildings can provide the location and orientation information where the GPS has failed. The model software generates several similar images based on the available GPS and orientation data. If the building is found to be the same as a model images, the building is identified and the server can provide the user with relevant information about the object.

To detect object reliably, a candidate model of the object is needed. Thus, one of the key components of our approach is a 3D city model. The system described in this paper uses a relatively small 3D model of a university precinct. The model was constructed from a manual survey and the texture maps were derived from photographs. At the same time, a Geographical Information System (GIS) has been used to provide location information and to enable the transformation of the coordination between the GPS and city model components.

The overall plan for this project is described below. Users are equipped with some hardware devices and a PDA to obtain different data, like the GPS data, orientation data and the image. Then users need to send the data and image to server for further processing. On the server side, this project is designed to do image processing for building recognition. If the image is confirmed to be part of the model, the image has been identified. In this way, users are able to identify their location and also the objects they are interested in. the position from the GPS receiver will never change if a user reports from the same location. However the building located there may possibly be changed with time. This system not only provides a way for tourists to travel around the city, especially as this system is very handy and low cost, but also a method to keep the model updated. A more detailed flow chart for the user operation sequence is shown in section 2.4.

The novel idea for this project is to integrate many different hardware devices, to use image for navigation and to apply the combinational method of segmentation and Hough Transform. All these devices are portable and relatively low-cost. Most of the previous research in this area has been concerned with the location-based services.

This paper presents a 'location and image-based service', which delivers information about a specific building of interest in real-time to a mobile user through the Internet by identifying the building from an image supplied by the user. Similar idea has been mentioned in [10, 11]. They use still video cameras along with image interpretation and extract object from the image to locate the position and enable the user to navigate indoor. However, in our project, object recognition is applied for outdoor city navigation. To realize the image-based service, requires not only the location data (GPS data) of the user but also the direction and tilt data (from the sensor attached on the PDA) of the image as well, as city objects are much more than the objects inside a building, and also more difficult to recognize. With these data, image processing for building recognition becomes possible. This project also shows some good result for roof shape detection and the line parameters for the roof by HT. Buildings are possible to be distinguished by its roof shape (see section 4.4).

Section 2 describes the system design, including each component of the hardware devices, software application and networks. Methods for object recognition are described in section 3 and results are presented in section 4. Section 5 summarises the main points of the paper and discusses the limitation and further research.

2 System Design

The system consists of three main parts: the client side, server side and the connecting networks. Fig. 1 shows the relationships between these different parts.

2.1 Client Side

The client side is a portable PDA system. It is composed of an *iPAQ 3870*, *NexiCam* PDA camera with resolution 600x800, orientation sensor and GPS receiver. Because of a limitation of the PDA development when this project started, it is not able to provide enough interfaces for all the devices we wish to use-for example, the *iPAQ 3870* provides one expansion connector for its expansion pack and one universal connector, which can be converted to a serial port and is integrated with *Bluetooth* and GPRS. For this reason, the USB roll-pitch-yaw sensor cannot be connected the Pocket PC. A laptop is used to receive the data from the sensor and Bluetooth supports communication between the PDA and laptop. However, this problem is being resolved by the next generation of PDAs. The GPS receiver and camera are connected to the PDA respectively using the universal connector and expansion connector. A WLAN card allows the PDA to access Internet through WLAN.

2.2 Server Side

3D City Model: A 3D model is constructed from the point clouds provided by a Cyrax2500 scanner and is imported into *3DMax* for visualization. With this 3D model, it is possible to generate images from any position and direction, such as the data from the clients. This model image provides the reference for building recognition.

Fig. 2 shows the building model of a university, which has been implemented as a pilot study. However, as the GPS and orientation is not very accurate, the image from the exact position and orientation is probably not the same with the user image. The server need to generate several different images based on the incoming GPS and orientation data for the building recognition, shown in Fig. 5. There are four windows shown in Fig. 2. Model views are on the left and a rendered image is shown bottom right. The server saves this image as a JPEG for further image processing (in Fig. 11).

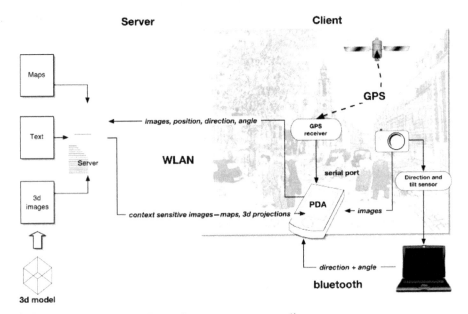

Fig. 1. System components diagram

GIS System With the GPS data from the receiver, users are able to identify their locations in the GIS. The GIS is also used to set up the correspondence between the GPS coordination and the model coordination.

Applications Three applications will be available on the server.

- 'Public space'. This space is for users to save their travelling pictures temporarily. As the size of memory cards for PDA cameras is limited, it will be helpful if the server can provide this public space for users, who can later download the pictures to a desktop computer. Normal security will be provided.
- Buildings identification. Provide user information in real-time from user-supplied images, e.g. transportation, accommodation, history and events.
- Position display. With the GPS data from the PDA user, server is able to display his location in a 2D GIS map in real-time.

2.3 Network Components

Bluetooth: A Bluetooth SDK from WIDCOMM has been used to develop applications for communication between the PDA and laptop. The SDK was compiled with Microsoft Visual C++. Before any communication, this application must synchronize the time between the two devices, as all the data are time-ordered. GPS data are received every 2 seconds and the PDA transfers the data to the laptop through Bluetooth. This data is synchronized with the orientation sensor data. Sensor data is also sampled when the GPS data arrive. When the user takes a picture and sends it to the server for processing, Bluetooth will instruct the laptop to send a corresponding GPS and orientation sensor data. The Bluetooth interface can also be used for locations where Bluetooth is used for access points.

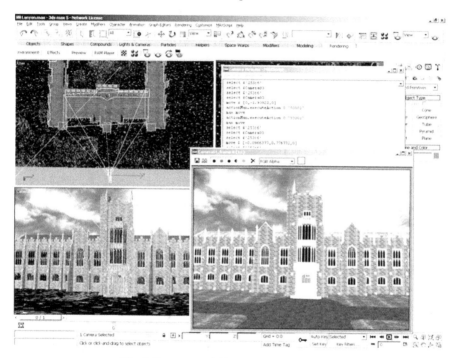

Fig. 2. Lanyon model in 3DMax environment

WLAN: Several WLAN access points have been set up in city so that PDA user can access Internet through WLAN with higher network quality and greater speed in that area, which is always crowded and with bad network. A WLAN card is used on the PDA to access the Internet in this way.

GPRS: GPRS (General Packet Radio Service) is integrated with the *iPAQ 3870*. This is the normal way to access the Internet when WLAN is not available. The system is being designed to switch between these communications services when they are available.

2.4 Flowchart of User Operation Sequence

Firstly, the user must run the custom-built program at the background before they start to take pictures. This program is mainly designed to read the serial port data from the GPS receiver, and send them to the laptop via Bluetooth every 2 seconds along with its PDA system time. The most recent (about 5 minutes) data will be saved on the laptop. When the laptop receives the GPS data, it also gets the orientation data from the sensor and saves all of these data together into a file. The file is managed according to the system time from the PDA. This enables the user to get the corresponding position when they take a picture. The program also keeps polling on the PDA if it takes any picture. Process starts as depicted in flowchart, shown in Fig. 3.

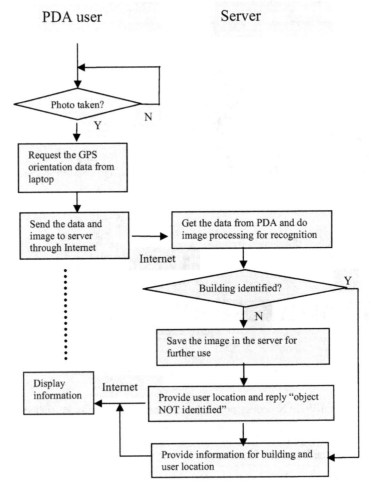

Fig. 3. Flowchart for users

The user opens the camera application on the PDA. When the user presses the button to take a picture, the background program mentioned above records the time of this action. After the user is satisfied with the picture and tries to send it to the server, background program will request the corresponding GPS and orientation data from the laptop to the PDA and send them to the server. When the data arrive, the server runs *3DMax* to generate pictures from the recorded user-position as the incoming data in the 3D model and also some adjacent positions and angles (as shown in Fig. 5). The server then processes these images for identification. If a building match is obtained, the server will provide information for the building together with the user location. Otherwise, a notice "object unidentified" will be sent to PDA user. But user location in a 2D map is still available to the user.

3 Object Recognition Methods

3.1 Hough Transform

There are two methods applied for object identification, line detection and colour-based segmentation.. The first method for object recognition relies on line detection. Several methods of line detection have been developed in the past decade. Hough Transform (HT) [17, 18, 13] and Radon Transform (RT) [15] are the two most important. These two methods can transform two-dimensional images with lines (original coordinate plane) into a domain (Hough space) of possible line parameters, in which each line in the image will produce a peak positioned at the corresponding line parameters. In the original coordinate space (image coordination), lines are represented using the form $y = ax + b$. However, in the Hough space (parameter coordination), lines are described in other forms. The most popular form expresses lines among them in the form $rho = x*cos(theta) + y*sin(theta)$ [4], where *theta* is the angle and *rho* the smallest distance to the origin of the coordinate system, also known as a polar coordinate system. In the image space, a line is made up of dots. However, a dot is displayed as a sine wave in the parameter space. The intersection of different sine waves represents the line, which is made of all these points, as shown in Fig. 4. The intersection with more waves going through means there are more points located on this line. We call this intersection a "peak". After sampling the image, we are able to find peaks in the parameter coordination that represent the main lines in the image.

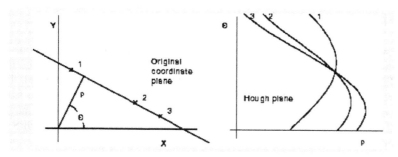

Fig. 4. Hough/Radon Transform

In this experiment, RT is applied with some modifications. For building identification, the sample angle *theta* was set to sample more points in the vertical and horizontal areas and fewer in the other directions, as lines in buildings tend to be found in these areas. Pre-processing of the lines included using different filtering and colour space conversions. For post-processing, the minimum difference between the parameters of the lines is set, e.g. the theta must be more than 20° and *rho* to be more than 30 pixels. If parameters are within these bounds, it means these two lines are too close, then they are considered as the same lines (see Fig. 7).

3.2 Segmentation

The segmentation of images based on colour and texture cues is formulated as a clustering problem. Small image patches are grouped together on the basis of local colour space statistics, which is captured by Gaussian models. Clustering is one of the fundamental methods for image segmentation [5, 12]. It follows these steps [5]:

- Data representation: The data types represent the objects in the best way to stress relations between the objects, e.g. similarity.
  There are three major types of data representation, vectorial data, distributional data and proximity data. Here, the data are represented in distributional format, which is described by an empirical probability distribution or histogram
- Modelling: How to formally characterize interesting and relevant cluster structures in data sets. The goal of modelling is to assign objects with similar properties to the same clusters and dissimilar objects to different clusters.
  For histogram data, distribution clustering objects are grouped according to the similarity of their histograms with a cluster specific prototypical distribution of features. The natural distortion measure between two histograms is defined by the Kullback-Leibler divergence.
- Optimisation: How to efficiently search for cluster structures.
  Here K-Means clustering is applied. It is a least squares partitioning method that divide a collection of objects into K groups.

4 Results of Building Recognition

4.1 City Model Image

Fig. 5 shows the images generated from a *3DMax* script for different positions and angles, which are very close to each other. Fig. 5 (a) is the original PDA image from the user. Fig. (b), (c), (d), (e) and (f) are generated from *3DMax*. The sizes of all these images are 600x800 pixels. Fig. 5 (b) is from the same position and angle as the incoming data in virtual model. However it is obvious that the most similar image is not (a) but (f). Result is discussed in Fig. 11. In another words, the incoming GPS and orientation data are not very accurate.

4.2 Radon Transform Results of Matching

Fig. 7 shows the lines found for Fig. 5 (a) before and after the post-processing, which was mentioned in Section 3. Fig. 7(a) contains more errors in vertical line detection (inside the oval in the long dash). This is because around those edge areas, the dots are very dense and noisy (caused by the pattern in the real image), and the computer will misinterpret a single line as several lines. The parameters (*rho* and *theta*) of these lines are very close to each other (see Table 1). Based on this knowledge, we can apply some post-processing from Section 3.1, to eliminate this error. After the modification, lines in Fig. 7(b) are more reasonable.

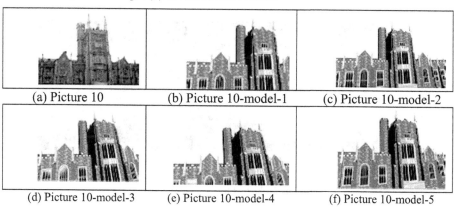

| (a) Picture 10 | (b) Picture 10-model-1 | (c) Picture 10-model-2 |
| (d) Picture 10-model-3 | (e) Picture 10-model-4 | (f) Picture 10-model-5 |

Fig. 5. Image generation from city model

Table 1. Line parameters

	Lines in Fig. 7(a)		Lines in Fig. 7(b)	
	rho	*theta*	*rho*	*theta*
Line 01	-398	0	-398	0
Line 02	-110	87	-110	87
Line 03	-94	1	-94	1
Line 04	-109	87	15	4
Line 05	15	4	152	7
Line 06	14	4	47	14
Line 07	14	3	-196	118
Line 08	-94	0	185	33
Line 09	152	7	264	179
Line 10	-95	1	354	178

Table 1 displays the line parameters for the user image before and after post-processing. In this table, each pair of *rho* and *theta* defines a peak in Hough space (shown as the starts in Fig. 6. In image space, this peak represents a line as shown in Fig. 7. In the parameter data for Fig. 7(a), Line 02 (-110, 87) and Line 04 (-109, 87) should be the same line. This error is caused by the dense and noisy dots in those areas. Also, line05 and line06, and line03 and line10 have the same problem. However, in the second set of data, represents the lines in Fig. 7(b), Line 04, Line 06 and Line 10 have been effectively filtered out.

4.3 Segmentation Matching Results

In this experiment, the image is represented in HSV space (Hue, Saturation and Intensity), which provides a separate channel for Hue, Saturation and Intensity information, from which colour features can be extracted. Clustering data are represented as probability data, which means each block of 3x4 pixels is grouped together and used to generate a Gaussian model based on its Intensity. Each block is represented as the vector of the mean value and standard deviation as one input data. KMeans is then applied to divide the picture into three groups.

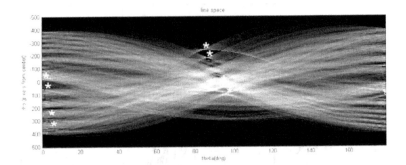

Fig. 6. Peaks of Fig.7 in Hough space

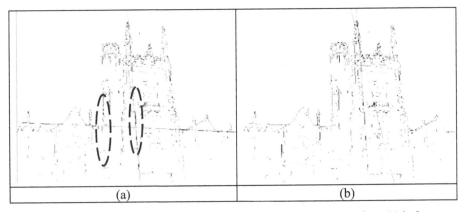

Fig. 7. Lines detected in the user-supplied images using the Radon Transform (a) before post-processing and (b) after post-processing

1. To arrive at an initial estimate of the underlying Gaussian alphabet for the later stages of clustering, a conventional Gaussian mixture model estimation step is carried out with the colour values of the image pixels as input data (this experiment use Intensity). In other words, the total input data is 200x200 (as the image size is 600x800). The following work is to cluster this 40,000 data set into 3 groups, which means, this experiment is going to segment the picture into 3 groups according to the Intensity values. The following results show the segmentation for

each picture and get the shape of the roof. The first step is to detect the sky. From Fig. 8, it is clear that, the sky is grouped into one in all the cases, even in Picture 12 (the building is quite dark and the sky is quite bright). After the sky pixels are set to be the same value, it becomes very easy to detect the shape of the skyline, as shown in Fig. 9. Figure 8 shows pictures of different buildings taken at different times. The problem of extracting a good roof shape (Fig. 9) from different buildings, taking different views, is clearly evident. This also allows the robustness of the building identification to be tested.

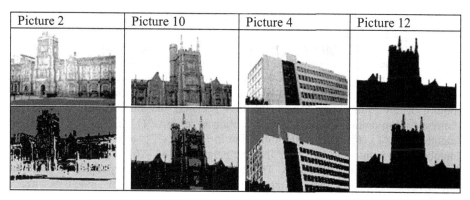

Fig. 8. Segmentation for 4 different pictures

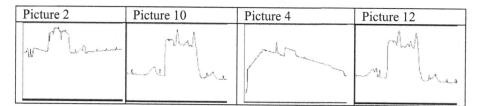

Fig. 9. Roof detection for pictures in Fig. 8

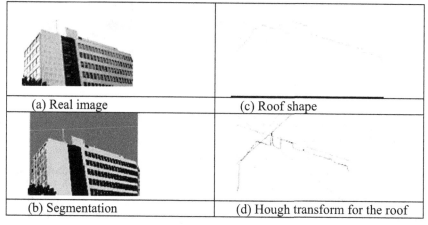

Fig. 10. Detection process for roof shape

4. 4 Segmentation and Hough Transform for Building Recognition

The process to detect the shape of the roof using the combination method of segmentation and HT is implemented as:

1. Segment the image into three groups as shown in Fig. 10 (b). This step is to group the sky pixels together and set them into the same value.
2. Get the shape of the roof. The points for the roof are displayed in Fig. 10 (c).
3. Apply the Hough Transform to get 10 line parameters for the roof (as shown in Fig. 10 (d)).

Once the above has been completed, the server uses the line parameters obtained from step 3 to recognize the building. Fig. 11 shows 10 images and each image has its 10 most important lines of the roof. Fig. 11(a) is the user image from the PDA camera. 10 line parameters have been listed right beside the picture. The line at the top has the most points. In another word, it is the most significant line in the image, so its weight is set to 10 points. For the same reason, the bottom line has least weight (set to 1 point). If any line from Fig. 11(b) to (j) match the line in (a), it gains the corresponding points. The matching condition is set to be (1), e.g. in Fig. 11 (b), the eighth line [84 -76] matches the third line in (a) [81 -77], so it gains 8 points. The number of 8 point is shown after the line parameter [84 -76] in parenthesis. And in total, this picture gains 23 points. The Italicised and underlined parameters stand for the matched line. The total points of each image represent how much this image matches the user image.

$$\Delta theta <= |3°| \ \& \ \Delta Rho <= |100| \tag{1}$$

The condition threshold for matching two pictures is set to be above 30 points. Whenever two images match more than 30 points, they are considered to be the same object. Otherwise, it is not recognized and may be saved in the database for model updating.

Fig. 11 (b) is generated from the exact GPS and angle data from the user. However, it is clear to show that, it gains only 23 points. And Fig. 11 (f) gets 39 points. Fig. 11 (f) is generated from a similar orientation data with 2 meters position and 10 degree angular differences. These are the expected values of GPS and orientation errors. Also it is clear to see the points for other images of different buildings are far less then the model images. For the space limitation, we only show line parameters of 4 pictures, and for others we only show the total scores of the image.

5 Conclusion

In this paper, a system to help people acquire urban information, including the building and geographical information is presented. It is implemented with different hardware devices, software applications and networks.

With this system, the city model is not only for the use of city promotion, indoor, environment planning or architectural design, but it also offers a useful database for tourists and travelers. We believe our system provides a good demonstration of a PDA application and is especially useful for tourists due to its mobility. Its main con tribution is that people can travel around without having to refer to maps and guidebooks. The city model is fully used to provide information to people at any time and anywhere, in contrast to fixed kiosks and indoor presentations. Some public space on the server is available for user to keep their pictures temporarily to overcome the limitation of the memory card. Two methods for object recognition have been described and improvements have been discussed.

Pictures	[theta,Rho] Weights		
	87 -112 (10) 119 -205 (9) 81 -77 (8) 93 -150 (7) 34 180 (6) 53 91 (5) 72 -5 (4) 7 153 (3) 74 -35 (2) 29 101 (1)		_89 ,-37 (10)_ _42 191_ 135 148 41 -115 _84, -68 (8)_ _94 -2 (7)_ _56 145 (5)_ _9 186 (3)_ _37 223 (6)_ 61 -80 **Points = 39**
(a) Picture 10		(f) Picture 10-model-5	
	_89 -46 (10)_ 135 157 41 213 41 -123 95 -14 11 214 _51 178 (5)_ _84 -76 (8)_ 33 257 63 -82 **Points = 23**		_74, 59 (4)_ 141 262 _72, 27 (2)_ 73 93 57 133 132 226 _53, 57 (5)_ 116 194 52 -18 48 170 **Points = 11**
(b) Picture 10-model-1		(g) Picture A4	
	**Points = 37**		**Points = 8**
(c) Picture 10-model-2		(h) Picture W1	
	**Points = 17**		**Points = 4**
(d) Picture 10-model-3		(i) Picture S2	
	**Points = 25**		**Points = 0**
(e) Picture 10-model-4		(j) Picture L7	

Fig. 11. Lines comparison for different roofs

Further works will include:

- Continue the custom-built program, e.g. the management between orientation data and GPS data and how to catch the "take picture" action
- Improvements in the system to direct the user to take further pictures or assist them in taking better pictures.
- Continue the building recognition research
- Automating of the whole system

Acknowledgements

The authors wish to acknowledge the financial support of the Virtual Engineering Centre, Queen's University of Belfast, (www.vec.qub.ac.uk).

References

1   American Online's Digital City, available at http://www.digitalcity.com
2   Banerjee S. et al, Rover Scalable Location-Aware Computing, Computer Science IEEE, Oct 2002.
3   Böhm, J., Haala, N., Kapusy, P., 2002. Automated appearance-based building detection in terrestrial images. International Archives on Photogrammetry and Remote Sensing IAPRS, Volume XXXIV, Part 5, pages 491-495, ISPRS Commission V Symposium, Corfu, September 2002
4   Bock, R. K., Krischer W. Data Analysis BriefBook, Springer-Verlag New York, In corporated, Version 16, 1998. ISBN: 354064119X.
5   Buhmann, J. Data clustering and learning in Handbook of Brain Theory and Neural Networks, Bradfort Books/MIT Press, 1995
6   Digital City Amsterdam, available at http://www.dds.nl
7   Digital City Kyoto, available at http://www.digital.city.gr.jp
8   Ding, P., Mao, W. L et al. Digital City Shanghai: Towards Integrated Information & Service Environment. Digital Cities: Experiences, Technologies and Future Perspectives, Lecture Notes in Computer Science, 1765, Springer-Verlag, pp. 125-139, 2000.
9   Donham, J., Fitterman, B. et al, 2002. Mobile Computing technology at Vindigo. IEEE Wireless Communications, pp. 50-58, Feb 2002.
10   Fritsch, D., Klinec, D., Volz, S. 2000. NEXUS - Positioning and Data Management Concepts for Location Aware Applications. Proc. of the 2nd International Symposium on Telegeoprocessing, Nice-Sophia-Antipolis, France, pp. 171-184.
11   Klinec, D., Volz, S.: NEXUS - Positioning and Communication Environment for Spatially Aware Applications, ISPRS Congress 2000, IAPRS, Amsterdam, Netherlands, pp.324-330. 2000.
12   Puzicha, J., Hogmannm, T., Buhmann, J. M., 1999. Histogram clustering for unsupervised segmentation and image retrieval, Pattern Recognition Letters, pp. 899-909, 1999.
13   Richard, O. Duda and Peter E. Hard, 1972. Use of the Hough Transformation to detect lines and curves in pictures. Pictures Communications of the ACM. Vol. 15, No. 1, pp. 11-15, 1972
14   Sutherland, M. Tweed, C. Teller, J. and O. Wedebrunn, (2002) Identifying the relations between historical areas and perceived values: Field tested methodology to measure perceived quality of historical areas. Unpublished report, School of Architecture, Queens University Belfast.

15   Toft, P. The Radon Transform - Theory and Implementation, Ph.D. thesis. Department of Mathematical Modelling, Technical University of Denmark, 1996

16   Virtual Los Angeles, available at http://www.ust.ucla.edu/ustweb/ust.html

17   Walsh, D., Raftery, A. E., 2001. Accurate and efficient curve detection in images: the Importance sampling Hough Transform. Pattern Recognition, volume 35, 2002

18   Xu, L., OJA, E. and Kultanen, P., 1989. A new curve detection method: Radomized Hough Transform (RHT)

19   Ishida, T. Actvities and technologies in Digital City Kyoto. In Peter van den Besselaar, Satoshi Koizumi (eds), Digital Cities 3. Lecture Notes in Computer Science, Vol. 3081. Springer-Verlag, Berlin Heidelberg New York (2005) pp. 162-183

20   Sheng, H, & P. Ding, Digital City Shanghai. In Peter van den Besselaar, Satoshi Koizumi (eds), Digital Cities 3. Lecture Notes in Computer Science, Vol. 3081. Springer-Verlag, Berlin Heidelberg New York (2005) pp. 138-161.

21   Van den Besselaar, P., D. Beckers, The life and death of the great Amsterdam Digital City. In Peter van den Besselaar, Satoshi Koizumi (eds), Digital Cities 3. Lecture Notes in Computer Science, Vol. 3081. Springer-Verlag, Berlin Heidelberg New York (2005) pp. 64-93.

Querying Multiple Video Streams and Hypermedia Objects of a Video-Based Virtual Space System

Yusuke Yokota, Shumian He, Yahiko Kambayashi

Graduate School of Informatics, Kyoto University,
Yoshida-Honmachi, Sakyo, Kyoto, 606-8501 Japan
yyokota@i.kyoto-u.ac.jp, shumian@db.soc.i.kyoto-u.ac.jp,
yahiko@i.kyoto-u.ac.jp

Abstract. By using several digital video cameras with omni-directional sensors, complete views of the activities at some place can be recorded as omni-directional videos. We utilize this technique for developing the Retrax System, which provides video-based virtual space environments as part of the Digital City infrastructure. The system aims to realize applications that are not possible with conventional video database systems, such as human activities and communications on computer networks based on recorded video data. This system archives the activities at some place in the real world and provides a virtual space based on the archived data for collaboration among users, such as walking, annotating, and communication. The user interface of the system bridges the real and virtual spaces or past and current human activities. This paper describes the purpose and usage of the system, and then introduces its architecture, data models, and the query language. Because both video data and hypermedia data are essential to the system, a query mechanism dealing with both types of data is required. The proposed query language is designed as an extension of SQL and realizes flexible management of both types of data.

1 Introduction

Due to the progress in technology including the increased capacity of storage devices and data compression techniques, it is becoming easier to store and retrieve various very large data sets of different types. It is becoming possible to store everything that happened at one location and access the data required to meet specific goals afterwards. What will be possible if we store everything in a database? We call this concept the *store-everything and select-later principle*. On the basis of this principle, we have been developing a distributed video database system by which users can experience a past meeting and interact with participants as a part of Digital City infrastructure. We call this system ``Retrax''. By using several digital video cameras with omni-directional sensors, complete sequences of activities, such as meetings, parties, events, or workshops, can be captured and stored. This data can be used to create video-based virtual spaces, to generate personalized video, and communicate with people shown in the images. Users also can annotate the virtual space with text comments, voice messages, and video data as hypermedia objects.

P. van den Besselaar and S. Koizumi (Eds.): Digital Cities 2003, LNCS 3081, pp. 299-309, 2005.
© Springer-Verlag Berlin Heidelberg 2005

This system records various past events that happened at some place in the real world and recreates the events for users on the computer network. The user interface of the system bridges the real-world and virtual space or past and current human activities. Users of the system can attend, annotate, and edit past events or meetings. It adds new value to past events or meetings as activities in Digital Cities.

In order to realize such functions, we defined a language called RSQL (Retrax SQL) for querying multiple video streams held in distributed video databases. RSQL is designed as a common API for the Retrax system; thus various applications will be developed without modification of the server-side architecture. RSQL is defined as an extension of SQL. The system consists of database servers, a control server, and client hosts. The client hosts translate GUI operations of the users into sentences in RSQL and sends them to the control server. The control server processes the query sentences and returns the data from each appropriate database server.

The remainder of the paper is organized as follows: Section 2 summarizes related work. Section 3 discusses the model and main concepts of the Retrax system. Section 4 shows definitions and usages of RSQL. Section 5 concludes the paper with a summary of the contributions of this research and issues impacting future work.

2   Related Work

The literature on designing querying spatio-temporal databases or temporal databases is voluminous. Santini et al. [1] proposed a spatio-temporal data model that queries interesting events in video sequences. A characteristic of their model is that it is divided into two layers: non-summarized and summarized data. The focus on the paper is the summarization mechanism which utilizes computer vision technologies. No specific query language is provided. In the Retrax system, our focus when designing the spatio-temporal data model is not the collection and summarization of event and object information from raw video data stream, but rather the simple and flexible representation of spatio-temporal information that enables the definition of a simple and plain query language and addition of instances to the database by users at run time.

SQL^{ST} [2] defines a spatio-temporal data model and query language as an extension of the SQL3 standard. This data model can depict the details of time-changing objects but it requires a very detailed data modeling procedure. The Retrax system uses its own simple spatio-temporal data model based on a hypermedia data model because complex spatio-temporal data models incur high authoring costs and so do not suit our application requirements.

Nelken and Francez [3] proposed a natural language interface to temporal databases, based on translating natural language questions into SQL/Temporal, a temporal database query language. As writing sentences in SQL or SQL-related languages is not simple task, it is important to provide users with simpler methods of querying databases. We have been developing, in contrast to their approach, a method of translating direct GUI input into SQL-based language sentences. This makes it easy to develop real-time applications on spatio-temporal databases, such as virtual reality systems. The translated sentences are stored as histories of users' operations and used for generating personalized video data.

To realize practical applications that deal with video data, high level functions of searching and retrieving video data must be developed. This demands appropriate designs and techniques for generating of video data metadata. MPEG-7 [4], called "Multimedia content description interface", is a standard metadata description of various types of multimedia data. Libsie and Kosch [5] have developed a framework for MPEG-4 video adaptation utilizing a generation mechanism of MPEG-7 documents corresponding to the MPEG-4 video data. We have chosen an original hypermedia data model as the metadata format of our system so as to capture the spatio-temporal nature of the contents of the system. Spatio-temporal information generated from video data or other sensing data will be merged into the hypermedia data. The hypermedia data model also supports standard hypermedia functions, such as various types of links, annotation, handling multimedia data, and so forth.

3   Retrax System

The Retrax system utilizes the omni-directional sensors developed by Prof. Ishiguro of Osaka University to realize video-based virtual spaces. *Retrax* is a coined word based on ``Re-tracks'', means tracking the past. This system is based on the store-everything and select-later principle. With this approach, the system enables users to experience past events, enrich the past contents, and communicate with the people who attended the events. This section describes the goals, architecture, and usages of this system.

3.1   Requirements of the System

We have been developing the system as a new type of application for Digital Cities; the application supports the activities and collaboration of participants in the virtual space composed of past real world video data. In preliminary experiments, the following events were recorded by a Retrax system.

A computer workshop at a primary school. Students of a primary school studied the usage of a novel educational platform called SqueakToys [9]. Each student studied at her/his own seat. Instructors walked around the classroom to teach each student. This workshop was part of the ALAN-K project [10] of Kyoto City.

A workshop at CAMP(Children's Art Museum Park) [11]. 7 to 17 year-old children studied and experienced novel technologies and arts in this workshop. The children and instructors walked around the classroom during the workshop. Figure 3 shows a scene of the workshop.

Characteristics of these events are summarized as follows:
– There are two or more roles, such as teachers, instructors, students and observers, in these events. Each user will assign a different level of importance to the different contents. It means that different playback requirements exist according to role.
– There are several simultaneous conversations. This is one difference between a workshop and a lecture. Because the importance of each conversation can not be

defined at the time of recording, all conversations should be recorded. It also means no one participant can follow the whole event (all conversations).
- Two or more moving objects may exist in the space. Typical moving objects are the participants. It may be necessary to generate views that track different moving objects.

Conventional video camera systems are able to capture only parts of the event. This limits the potential reuse of the recorded contents. The following requirements reflect the characteristics of the events.
- It must be possible to set arbitrary viewpoints after the event. Though conventional video conference systems need these viewpoints to be defined before recording, our system does not.
- It must be possible to track specific people. This permits personalized videos that track individual people or objects to be created from stored data. Instructors and students can use her/his own video for self-examination. Instructors also can use a student's video for later analysis.
- Functions for bookmarking and annotations are required. Users may find an important place and time during playback. Such a point should be recorded as a bookmark or annotated with video, audio or text for reuse of the contents.
- Data modeling loads placed on the system operator should be minimized. Some conventional video database systems require manual indexing for efficient retrieval. Spatio-temporal database systems that use detailed spatio-temporal data model also require an accurate data modeling process. The Retrax system captures a vast amount of video data, which cannot be analyzed and indexed by hand.

The Retrax system is designed to meet these requirements.

3.2 System Architecture

The Retrax system consists of two sub systems: a recording system and a playback system. The recording system consists of DV cameras with omni-directional sensors and additional wireless devices for tracking moving objects. Figure 1 shows a typical camera arrangement. Each camera records video data with a 360-degree view angle. Metadata of video data for retrieval is generated from the video data and the logs of wireless devices (see section 3.3).

The playback system consists of servers and clients. Figure 2 overviews the system. The database servers store video data and hypermedia data. The data is distributed among these servers to achieve load balancing. The control server receives and parses queries from clients and sends requests for the data desired to the appropriate database servers. The selection of database servers is defined by index data, which are collected from each database server and stored at the control server. Clients have a GUI for walking around a video-based virtual space (Figure 3). Each client manages user position and orientation in the space. User inputs are translated into sentences in the query language and sent to the control server. Clients receive the results of the queries from database servers, compose video data, sound data, and hypermedia objects, and then display them to the user. Clients support both spatio-temporal hypermedia functions such as walking around, annotation, and bookmarking, and video functions such as fast-forward, rewinding, back, and stop.

3.3   Construction of Virtual Space

As discussed above, the data model of the Retrax system should have following characteristics:
- Simplified 3D-space model for video data. A complex spatio-temporal data model is not needed to achieve the requirements of the system. To support the ease of

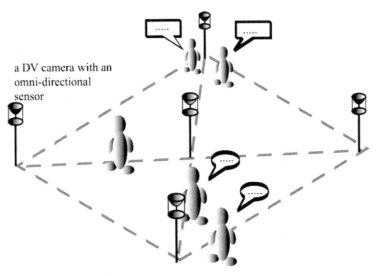

a DV camera with an
omni-directional
sensor

Fig. 1. A typical camera arrangement.

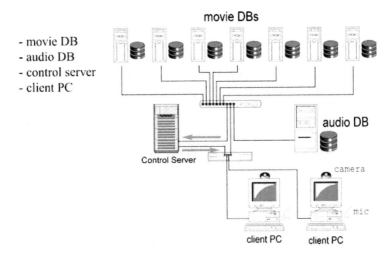

movie DBs

- movie DB
- audio DB
- control server
- client PC

audio DB

Control Server

camera

mic

client PC   client PC

Fig. 2. Overview of playback system.

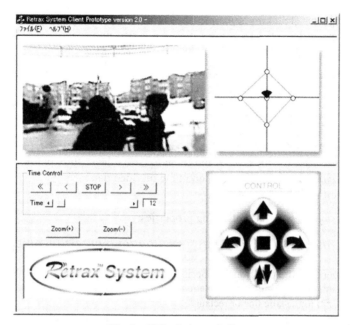

Fig. 3. GUI window of client.

authoring tasks of users, the data model should be simple and minimize the spatio-temporal aspect.

- Support hypermedia functions. To make more effective use of the video contents, hypermedia functions such as links, bookmarks and annotations should be supported. Such functions promote reuse of the contents.

To satisfy these characteristics, the data model of the Retrax system is divided into two types of data: video data and hypermedia data. Video data is raw data from the omni-directional sensors with minimum metadata such as position and time. Hypermedia data has two purposes: data for hypermedia functions and metadata of the video data for retrieval. Spatio-temporal aspect is covered by hypermedia data. For example, location information generated from the logs of wireless devices (see section 3.2) are integrated into the hypermedia data. The size of video data is very large and sparse: most of the data will not be 'interesting' to users. Thus the video retrieval function plays an important role in this system. Video data and hypermedia data will be merged and displayed at runtime.

This system uses the stored video data to build the virtual space. Objects are roughly divided into static objects like chairs, desks, and white boards, and dynamic objects like participants of the recorded events. These objects are modeled as hypermedia data by the following methods:

Specifying anchors by users. Users can specify an object as an anchor of hypermedia data. Anchors act ends of hyperlinks, targets of annotations or bookmarks. Registered anchors are shown to all users.

Tracking objects. Tracking dynamic objects in the capture phase utilizing wireless location sensor devices. Tracking data is converted into sequences of location data and stored in the hypermedia database.

Video data of each camera have the following properties. These properties are treated as metadata for retrieving appropriate data.

$$v_i = (camera, position, start, end, event)$$

- *camera* specifies the camera's ID;
- *position* specifies the location of the camera during the capture phase;
- *start* and *end* specify the start and end time of video data;
- *event* specifies the event recorded.

Hypermedia objects have the following properties:

$$h_i = (anchor, type, contents\_destination, authority, object)$$

- *anchor* specifies the position and period of the target object; for example: (x, y, z) for a static point, (x, y, z, start_time, duration) for a point that exists in a period, and (x1, y1, z1; x2, y2, z2) for a static line or rectangle;
- *type* specifies the link type (spatio-temporal link, annotation, WWW link); *contents_destination* indicates the contents or destination of a link; a destination anchor (spatio-temporal link), video, audio or text data (annotation), or URL (WWW link) are possible.
- *authority* describes access control information. It specifies which users or groups can access this link. This feature offers private, public and group annotation for the same object.
- *object* specifies the type of object (static or dynamic).

Hypermedia objects are indexed, and the index data are treated as metadata. All kinds of metadata are stored on the control server.

4   RSQL: A Query Language for Video-Based Virtual Space

RSQL (Retrax SQL), the query language used for acquiring video data and hypermedia objects from the distributed databases, is designed as an extension of the syntax of SQL. RSQL is a common API for the Retrax system; therefore applications on the system are required to use RSQL when they communicate with servers. It isolates the development processes of applications and servers and enhances system modularity.

4.1   RSQL Definitions

RSQL is defined as follows:

```
SELECT *|AUDIO|VIDEO|ANNOTATION|
       FROM space_references
```

```
          WHERE CAMNO, TIME [, X, Y, ANGLE, UID]
          [ORDER BY TIME [ASC | DESC]]
          [SPEED_definition]
          WHERE CAMNO, TIME [, X, Y, ANGLE]

INSERT INTO  space_references
       VALUES (expression,...),(...),...
       WHERE CAMNO, TIME [, X, Y, ANGLE]

UPDATE space_references
       SET col_name1=expr1, [col_name2=expr2, ...]
       WHERE CAMNO, TIME [, X, Y, ANGLE]

DELETE space_references
       WHERE CAMNO, TIME [, X, Y, ANGLE]
```

The following identifiers are unique to RSQL:

AUDIO: Only audio data is required
VIDEO: Only video data is required
ANNOTATION: Only annotation data is required
ANGLE: Present orientation of the user
X: X Present coordinate of the user
Y: Y Present coordinate of the user
TIME: Period of video or audio data
CAMNO: ID of camera that captured video and audio data
SPEED: Speed of replay
UID: Unique user ID

In SELECT statements, * means that AUDIO and VIDEO are acquired simultaneously. An element of FROM specifies the contents required. TIME and CAMNO are essential elements of the WHERE component. These elements will be used as parameters of a buffering mechanism of the system. ORDER BY has only the element of TIME. ASC (ascending order) specifies normal playback and DESC (descending order) specifies playback in reverse. SPEED specifies playback speed. The default value of SPEED is 1; if SPEED>1, playback or reverse playback is faster than normal, if 0<SPEED<1, the speed is slower than normal.

4.2   Translating Users' Operations into RSQL Sentences

User inputs collected by the client's GUI are dynamically translated into RSQL sentences with status information of the user such as coordinates, orientation, and elapsed time in the virtual space, and sent to the control server.

This section describes several translation examples on the assumption that the user enters the virtual space named VS1, her/his position is (100,200), is near camera No.2, and orientation is 45 degrees.

SAMPLE 1: Playback audio and video from time 15.5 second

```
SELECT * FROM VS1
  WHERE X = 100
    AND Y = 200
    AND ANGLE = 45
    AND CAMNO = 2
    AND TIME >= 15.5
```

SAMPLE 2: User U1 inserts her/his comment at time 18 second and the video data file has been saved as "video1.mpg"

```
INSERT VS1
    VALUES ANNOTATION_TYPE=video,
ANNOTATION="video1.mpg", UID=U1
  WHERE X = 100
    AND Y = 200
    AND ANGLE = 45
    AND CAMNO = 2
    AND TIME = 18
```

SAMPLE 3: User U1 has just inserted her/his comment in video at time 18 second, but s/he would like to replace the comment with a new audio file named "sound1.wav"

```
UPDATE VS1
    SET ANNOTATION_TYPE=audio, ANNOTATION="sound1.wav"
  WHERE X = 100
    AND Y = 200
    AND ANGLE = 45
    AND CAMNO = 2
    AND TIME = 18
    AND ANNOTATION_TYPE=video
    AND UID = U1
```

As demonstrated by these three simple examples, RSQL is defined as an extension of SQL and can queries video data and hypermedia data efficiently.

4.3   Discussion

Introducing a high level query mechanism like RSQL into a virtual space system brings the following advantages.

Retrieval and authoring functions. Users can search and edit objects in the virtual space using high level queries based on a minimal spatio-temporal data model. These functions will be the basis of collaboration via the system.

Reuse of queries.   All activities of users will be stored as histories of RSQL sentences yielding human-readable descriptions of the actions of users. By editing these histories, customized actions of users can be generated.

Separation of components. The RSQL mechanism separates client and server side components. It enables application developers to design various client applications using RSQL as a common API independent of the server-side architecture.

The high level query mechanism is one overhead of this system and may increase the response time to a user's operation.

RSQL supports two types of user interactions: real-time and non real-time interaction. The following scenario describes the usage of these two types of interaction. The primary application of the Retrax system is to support real-time walkthrough in the virtual space. The walkthrough function requires direct GUI inputs such as ``turn left'' and ``go forward''. When RSQL is introduced into the application, a translation mechanism that converts these inputs into a sequence of RSQL sentences is needed. Though the translation mechanism increases the response time of the application to some extent, generated RSQL sentences are valuable in reusing the contents. The RSQL sentences are stored on the database as a history of operations, which provides high level description of retrieval. It enables users to edit the history data for making their own personalized video contents. The editing tool is another application of the Retrax system. Tracking information of moving objects also assists in the generation of personalized video data. When a moving object can successfully identified and tracked, a unique ID will be assigned to the object. A user can issue a query to retrieve the moving object by specifying the ID as a RSQL sentence. The query will result in the generation of a video data that tracks the specified object.

5   Conclusion

This paper introduces a model of a video-based virtual space. Users can annotate the virtual space with their voice/video messages and make hyperlinks in the virtual space. RSQL is defined to realize a common interface for querying video and hypermedia databases simultaneously. Client applications translate user inputs into RSQL sentences and send them to a control server. The realization of RSQL requires several components: a direct manipulation conversion module, a parser module, a video data access module, and a hypermedia data access module. These modules are being developed.

There are several issues in the current system. One is the load balancing problem since the access frequency of each database server depends on the positions and contents of the recorded video data. If the contents in a server are accessed frequently, the performance of the whole system may fall. A method that can arrange the distribution of contents according to access frequency should be developed. Another issue is interaction with multiple users. When several users enter the same virtual space at the same time, interaction between them should be supported. These issues remain as future work.

Acknowledgments

This work was partly supported by Japan Science and Technology Corporation (CREST).

References

1. Santini, S., Gupta, A. and Jain, R., Querying multiple perspective video, Proc. of SPIE Vol. 3656, Storage and Retrieval for Image and Video Databases VII, January 1999.
2. Chen, C.X., Zaniolo, C., SQL ST : A Spatio-Temporal Data Model and Query Language, Proc. of International Conference on Conceptual Modeling (ER2000), pp. 96-111, Oct. 2000.
3. Nelken, R. and Francez, N., Querying Temporal Databases Using Controlled Natural Language, The 18th International Conference on Computational Linguistics (COLING 2000), Jul. 2000.
4. MPEG-7 Main Page, http://ipsi.fraunhofer.de/delite/Projects/MPEG7/.
5. Libsie, M. and Kosch, H., Content adaptation of multimedia delivery and indexing using MPEG-7, Proc. of the 10th ACM international conference on Multimedia,Dec. 2002, pp.644-646.
6. Jensen, C.S., Clifford, J., Gadia, S.K., Segev, A., Snodgrass, R.T., A Glossary of Temporal Database Concepts, ACM SIGMOD Record, Vol.21, No.3, pp.35-43, Sep. 1992.
7. Bohlen, M.H., Jensen, C.S., Snodgrass, R.T., Temporal Statement Modifiers, ACM Transactions on Database Systems (TODS), Vol.25, No.4, pp.407-456, Dec. 2000.
8. Chomicki, J., Toman, D., Bohlen, M.H., Querying ATSQL databases with temporal logic, ACM Transactions on Database Systems (TODS), Vol.26, No.2, pp.145-178, Jun. 2001.
9. Squeak Etoys, http://www.squeakland.org/author/etoys.html.
10. Konomi, S. and Karuno, H., Initial Experiences of ALAN-K: An Advanced LeArning Network in Kyoto, Proc. of 1st Conference on Creating, Connecting and Collaborating through Computing (C5 '03), pp. 96-103, Jan. 2003.
11. CAMP, http://www.camp-k.com/.

Cultural User Experience Issues in E-government: Designing for a Multi-cultural Society

Nik van Dam, Vanessa Evers, Florann A. Arts

Universiteit van Amsterdam, Roetersstraat 15, 1018 WB, Amsterdam, the Netherlands
nvdam@dds.nl; evers@swi.psy.uva.nl; arts@swi.psy.uva.nl

Abstract. This paper examines the influences of culture on the user experience of local e-government services. It investigates the hypothesis that citizens with different cultural backgrounds experience different problems when using e-government applications. Thirty participants with Moroccan, Surinamese and Dutch cultural backgrounds completed a short questionnaire for demographic purposes. Then, they were observed while using a local e-government website. After tasks were completed, a short interview investigated user experience issues in more depth. By referring to existing literature on cross-cultural values and norms, the possible origins of differences in user experience problems for the cultural groups were explored. The findings suggest that differences in user problems coincide with expectations about cultural characteristics derived from previous literature. The findings of this paper support the notion that users with different cultural backgrounds experience different user problems.

1 Introduction

In recent decades, computer and communication technologies have influenced society in a spectacular way, particularly with the development of the Internet. In recent years, the dependence on information technology has grown far beyond our expectations. Many institutions of society have recognized the advantages of this development and entered the digital highway. Governments worldwide have begun to recognize the potential of the Internet and, have started in introducing information and transactions online in what is now called e-government.

In providing services to citizens online, many aspects of computer mediated communication need to be considered. Issues such as access to technology and the e-government services, the type of information, services, interaction and functionality which is required and the goals the government and citizens have concerning e-government applications are but a few. In the multi-cultural society of today, cultural values and preferences may also play a role in the domain of e-government. In order to maximize the efficiency of government services from both the citizen and government perspective, the different cultural backgrounds of the population may need to be taken into consideration.

In a multi-cultural society such as the Netherlands, in which the percentage of the population with a foreign background and culture increases every year, it is important for the development of Internet and technology to focus on this multi-cultural aspect

P. van den Besselaar and S. Koizumi (Eds.): Digital Cities 2003, LNCS 3081, pp. 310-324, 2005.

of society. An interesting question is to what extent the government needs to take the cultural backgrounds of the non-native population into account when designing an e-government website. These groups may have different needs for information, functionality and interaction. In order to ensure that citizens from various cultural backgrounds can benefit equally from e-government services, it will be important to gain insight in the needs of the different user groups.

An initiative called Cyburg, subsidized by the city of Amsterdam (specifically for the city district of Zeeburg), offered a project in which the cross-cultural influences on user experience of e-government services could be analysed. This work is therefore based on the observation of participants from Dutch, Moroccan and Surinamese backgrounds using the Dutch local e-government site of Zeeburg. The remainder of this paper consists of a review of relevant literature. Afterwards, the methodology of the study will be explained followed by a discussion of the results.

2 Theoretical Background

This research is based on the premise that culture is an influential factor in user experience. The three main constructs on which this study is based are *e-government*, *culture* and *user experience*. Each of these constructs will now shortly be explored by reviewing some of the relevant literature on these topics. A more detailed review of the literature can be found in van Dam [1].

2.1 E-government

The spectrum of definitions available for e-government will be assessed in the framework of three perspectives, derived from Wilson et al. [2]: *Technological perspective, citizen perspective* and *government perspective*. Each perspective defines e-government from a different angle, focusing on different values.

The technological perspective focuses on the technological benefits of digitalizing the government services and applications as argued by Tambouris et al. [3] and Margretts and Dunleavy [4]. These definitions focus on the evolution of the government to the digital medium, but limit themselves to the actual process of digitalization, and not objectives, benefits or consequences.

From a citizen perspective, e-government is the use of technology to enhance the relationship between the government and the citizen. The convenience of the user is an essential argument for e-government. Ma [5] defines e-government as a citizen-oriented transformation evolving the role of the government in society. Another benefit, from the citizen perspective, is the transparency that stimulates the dialogue and participation between the citizens and government as stated by van Engers et al [6] and Atkinson and Ulevich [7].

Elaborating on these perspectives, e-government is a development, which benefits the government, promoting efficiency and effectiveness. Heeks [8] even calls it 'government re-invention'. The government perspective focuses on the improvement of the internal processes, facilitating more government services, and simplifying the link between government and citizen.

Combining the three perspectives, one could define e-government as the application of Internet and computer technology to make government applications and information accessible to the population twenty-four hours a day, in order to maximize the effectiveness and efficiency of the services, allowing the government to come closer to their citizens and adapt these services according to their needs. Dawes et al [9] describe the objectives of e-government as including the following:

- Enabling citizens to effectively participate in the knowledge society/economy
- Integrating, streamlining and customizing the delivery of services
- Improving the quality of policy and decision-making processes
- Reducing the compliance costs of government
- Improving the bottom-line effectiveness and efficiency of government
- Providing greater flexibility in the design and management of government
- Enhancing relationships between citizens and the state, and strengthening democratic processes and institutions

These citizen oriented objectives such as enabling citizens and improving effectiveness, may be interpreted and measured differently by citizens from different cultural backgrounds. What is thought of as efficient in one culture may be perceived differently in another. Culture is thought to affect peoples behaviour and thoughts in many and persistent ways, many of which are beyond an individual's awareness. There are many aspects of using e-government applications that may be culturally influenced. The study described in this paper will focus on differences between culturally diverse users when using e-government applications.

2.2 Culture

Definitions of culture are diverse, encompassing many aspects of human behaviour. Culture can be defined as a set of definitions of reality held in common by people who share a distinctive way of life. Definitions of reality include language, values and the norms that set the limits for behaviour[10]. Hofstede [11] defines culture as the collective programming of the mind, which distinguishes one group from the other. Lotman [12] agrees, but limits the influences to the totality of non-hereditary sources. One can also define culture in terms of results rather than influences. Schein [13] defines culture as the manner in which groups solve problems and reconcile dilemmas. The idea of feelings is elaborated by Kakabadse et al [14] who see culture as the feelings and decisions certain groups share in particular situations and settings.

As a consequence of such diverse and inconsistent definitions, it is difficult to base one's theory around culture, without a clear-cut description of culture. Most definitions tend to agree that culture is something which is shared by a group of people and influences many aspects of their lives. Not only the way people communicate and the habits that are developed in a group but also the way the social and physical world is perceived, the norms and values shared by the group and behaviour. For the purpose of this paper, we will use an elaboration of a definition used in previous research by Evers [15]: *Culture shapes the way people behave, view the world, express themselves and think. It is formed by historical experiences and values, traditions and surrounding, and affects the way people act and react to situations.*

Just as difficult as it is to define culture, measuring culture and the effects of culture is. Diverse cross-cultural models have been developed to compare and classify different cultures using value associations to organize cultural data (also termed cultural variables). Examples of researchers who identified such variables are Edward Hall [16], Fons Trompenaars [17] and Geert Hofstede [11]. Trompenaars introduces three variables with which cultures can be compared to each other: 1) The *significant others* variable, which indicates the importance for individuals to perform well in front of others, directing behaviour towards the expectations of others. 2) *Particularism* vs. *universalism*, which contrasts the extent to which individuals are willing to interpret socially formed rules in favour of friends or relatives. In universalist cultures rules apply to everybody without exception, while in particularists cultures rules are considered 'flexible' for the good of relationships. 3) The *neutral* vs. *affective relationships* variable, which defines culture in terms of the extent to which emotion is involved in the relationship of individuals with others. Affective cultures (as opposed to neutral cultures) are typified by a more expressive style of communication.

Hofstede describes four cultural variables. 1) *Masculinity* vs. *femininity* focuses on the acceptance of role-based behaviours and the desirability of assertive/modest behaviour. The masculine cultures are achievement-oriented and clearly distinguish social gender roles, while feminist cultures focus on good relationships and social balance and cohesion. 2) The *power distance* variable discusses the extent to which less powerful members of a culture expect and accept that power is distributed unevenly. The higher the power distance score, the greater the dependency of subordinates on their bosses. 3) The *uncertainty avoidance* variable, which describes the degree to which members of society feel comfortable with uncertainty and ambiguity. These cultures search for a certain structure, which makes events clearly interpretable and predictable. Members of the low uncertainty avoidance cultures, on the other hand, tend to have fewer problems with taking risks, and exploring the unknown. 4) The *individualism* vs. *collectivism* variable describes the way in which cultures perceive the role of the individual in a group. In collectivistic cultures, the interest of the group comes before that of the individual. In individualistic cultures, people focus more on the interests of the individual.

Cross-cultural variables are useful in categorizing cultures and explaining similarities as well as differences in behaviour between them. This information can then be utilized in intercultural communication, or when analyzing cross-cultural behaviour. The applicability of these cultural variables in measuring the effects of culture is not clear-cut. Hofstede and Trompenaars carried out the studies through which cultural value association scores were established in the late seventies and eighties. As culture is thought to be constantly evolving it is important to reconsider which cultural norms and values are relevant at any point in time. For the purpose of this study we will attempt to use cultural norms and value associations as a means to explain differences in behaviour of culturally diverse users. As such, it is a first step in investigating cultural differences.

2.3 User Experience

User experience is often confused with usability. While usability concerns the system itself, addressing concerns of productivity and efficiency, user experience is less clearly defined. It focuses on the subjective reactions of the users (motivation, fear, enjoyability etc.). Moeslinger [18] argues that the needs of the home user are significantly different from the needs of the professional user. In the home, emotional aspects are of greater importance, and efficiency and productivity matter less. Moeslinger includes practical experience, sensory experience and emotional experience as part of user experience.

Therefore, user experience may be seen as a different angle of looking at the use of computer systems, focusing on the use for personal purposes. It adds new aspects to the evaluation like aesthetics, excitement and pleasure, placing a strong emphasis on the subjective experiences of the user when using the system, and taking into account the elements of chance and the emotional state of the user as described by Boivie [19]. As found by Evers [20] experiences of the real world affect users' understanding of the virtual world presented to them by information systems. The expectations that users have of an interface and the way they understand information provided by the interface was found to differ between users of different cultural and national backgrounds. For E-government applications, it may be the case that differences in expectations and understanding of the information provided will affect the user's experience when using e-government applications.

2.4 Previous Cross-Cultural User Experience Research

Interestingly, many previous cross-cultural studies are based on inquiry, using self-reported data obtained through interviews and questionnaires rather than actual user observation.

Vöhringer-Kuhnt [21] investigates the influence of culture on usability in a recent study grounded on the belief that culture is a discerning variable concerning the attitude towards usability. Using Hofstede's cultural specific variables, and Davis' technology acceptance model, a survey was developed. 145 HCI students and professionals from 30 different countries were asked to explore the IBM website and answer the questionnaire. He found that the Individualism/Collectivism variable discussed by Hofstede is significantly connected towards satisfaction and the attitude towards product usability. Unfortunately, the survey was not combined with an observation study, a method that might have lead to more insight in influences of cultures on actual user behaviour.

Evers [15] investigated cultural applicability of user evaluation methods, evaluating cultural differences in the understanding of a virtual campus website across four culturally different user groups by using the same methods for each group. After analysing previous cross-cultural research, Evers concluded that many studies on cross-cultural user behaviour were based on self-reported data. Consequently, the study involved observation of user behaviour. It was found that shared experiences shaped users' perceptions and expectations of the interface. Evers also argues that one-on-one observation methods as commonly applied in usability testing may not be as appropriate for international users as it is for North-American users.

Bourgess-Waldegg and Scrivener [22] introduce a new approach to design for culturally diverse user groups called MIMA (Meaning in Mediated Action). This method involves the observation of users interacting with an application, followed by an interview focused on the problems encountered in order to record their understanding of meaning. MIMA is an attempt to help designers resolve these kinds of problems, based on including rather than excluding potential users on the basis of cultural differences.

A more elaborate review of the literature can be found in van Dam [1]. It was found that a limited number of studies focused on cultural differences in user experiences. Previous literature seemed to primarily investigate differences between users in different countries; the study reported in this paper aims to assess cultural differences of user experience within one nation.

3 Research Methodology

3.1 Problem Statement

When citizens use the Zeeburg e-government site, there are elements that hinder the successful completion of the users' goals. The aim of this study is to highlight user experience problems users from different cultural backgrounds encounter when using e-government sites, and identify what causes these problems. The study is part of a larger study, which aims to develop guidelines for e-government services for multi-cultural use. This study therefore focuses on identifying differences in user experience between culturally diverse users when using current e-government applications.
This leads to the main hypothesis of this paper:

Hypothesis: Citizens from different cultural backgrounds encounter different problems when using e-government applications.

In order to investigate this hypothesis, four research questions were posed.
Question 1. What are the user experience problems that users encounter when using local e-government applications?
Question 2. Are these problems different for users from different cultural backgrounds?
Question 3. What are the causes of these user experience problems?
Question 4. Are these causes different for users from different cultural backgrounds?

To address the aim of the study, it will be important to gain an understanding of the usability problems that users encounter when using the system. This shapes the first research question.

Insight in these problems across different cultural user groups will make it possible to evaluate whether users from different cultural backgrounds encounter different usability problems. Therefore, the differences between usability problems for the different cultural groups needs to be further investigated – this shapes the second research question.

In order to gain a detailed understanding of the cultural differences in using e-government applications, it will be important to evaluate what the causes are of the user experience problems encountered in research question one. These causes could for instance be due to a mismatch in user expectations and the actual functionality, misunderstanding of terms or language used, or apprehensive attitude towards the site. This shapes research question 3.

A final goal will be to find out whether the causes of the user experience problems differ between the cultural groups. This is the final step in understanding the influence of the cultural difference in the use of e-government application.

To answer these questions, a user experience study is carried out for an existing e-government application. The methods and sample will be described in the next section.

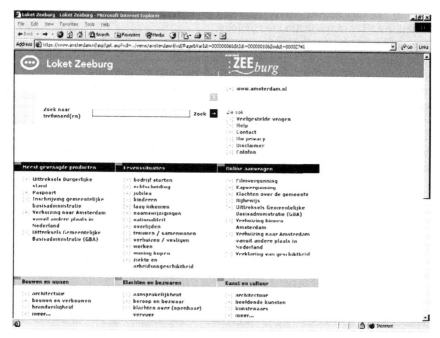

Fig. 1. First page of the Zeeburg e-loket (can be found on www.zeeburg.nl)

3.2 Methodology

Zeeburg E-loket. In the Netherlands in 1998, a program was initiated stimulating the development of an e-government portal (www.ol2000.nl), in an attempt to digitalize 25 percent of government services. This plan was an attempt by the Dutch government to digitalize the services in such a way that citizens would be encouraged to make use of e-government facilities. For this purpose, a portal referred to as 'e-loket' was developed (www.zeeburg.nl). The e-loket is the equivalent of a government official's counter at which communication between the government and citizens is achieved through electronic channels (see Figure 1). The goal is to optimize the local governmental services in line with the demands of the citizens. The Dutch e-loket combines static and transactional services, providing citizens with the possibility of exploiting the services of public sectors in a more efficient and effective manner.

Sample. In evaluating the diversity of the population of Amsterdam, it turned out that 54 percent of the population is native Dutch. When one analyses the local non-native populations, the Surinamese account for 9.8 percent and the Moroccans for 7.5 percent of the Amsterdam population. Being the groups with the largest representation in Amsterdam, the focus of the study was on people with Dutch, Moroccan and Surinamese backgrounds.

The data collection was carried out at two locations. The first location was a local Internet training facility called Cybersoek. This is a Zeeburg initiative, supported mostly by volunteers, to bring the average citizen of Zeeburg in contact with information and communication technology.

The study involved 10 Moroccans, 10 Surinamese, and 10 Dutch participants (N=30). The cultural background of participants was determined by establishing the country of birth of the participants and both parents. Participants were selected to have similar educational backgrounds and Internet experience as well as similar knowledge of the Dutch language

We used available empirical data to culturally classify participants in the present study, based on cross-cultural research by Hall, Trompenaars, and Hofstede. The variables shown in table 1 are the typical profiles used to describe the three cultures participating in the study reported in this paper.

Table 1. Cross-cultural variable scores, as found in [16, 17, 11]

Cultural Variable	Moroccan	Surinamese	Dutch
Significant Others	High	Low	Low
Particularism vs. Universalism	Particularist	Universalist	Universalist
Neutral vs. Affective	Affective	Neutral	Neutral
Masculinity vs. Femininity	Masculine	Feminine	Feminine
Power Distance	High	Low	Low
Uncertainty Avoidance	High	High	Low
Individualism vs. Collectivism	Collectivist	Collectivist	Individualist

Cultural Variables. When one compares the seven cross-cultural variables as in Table 1, it can be seen that the Moroccan culture diverges in many aspects from the Dutch culture. Consequently, it is expected that user experiences will vary most for users from these two cultures. At the same time, the value scores for the Surinamese and Dutch culture are similar. Only the high scores on uncertainty avoidance and collectivist nature of the Surinamese culture are different from the Dutch culture. Consequently, it is expected that user experiences for these two cultures will be more similar, with the exception of the influences of the last two variables.

The variables describe the Moroccan culture as sensitive to the thoughts of its environment (a high average on the significant others variable). Hence, the observer will need to remember this when considering the actions and reactions of participants. Moroccan participants might tend to provide answers to suit the observer's wishes. This is especially relevant since the Moroccan culture also is thought to have high power distance: the distance between the citizen and the government will be perceived as high, so the user may not be openly critical of the system to respect the hierarchy. These considerations will probably not play such an important role when observing Dutch and Surinamese participants.

The high uncertainty avoidance of the Moroccan and Surinamese cultures could also influence participants' approach to the e-loket website. Empirical evidence (e.g., [11]) suggests that people from these cultures will find it important to avoid making mistakes. Participants are thus likely to approach the research activities with caution.

3.3 Cross-Cultural Testing of User Experience

A Multi-method Approach. The study adopted a multi-method approach: combining several research methods into one study in order to extract a variety of information about the participant and the context as suggested by Kaplan and Duchon [23]. Each session consisted of three parts in order to retrieve different types of information.

First, participants completed a questionnaire with demographic questions and questions measuring their Internet and language skills. This was necessary to collect information on participants' Internet capabilities, knowledge of the Dutch language, age and cultural background.

Participants were then asked to perform three tasks on the Zeeburg website, each increasing in complexity:

Task 1: Find out at what age a child is of mandatory school age.

Task 2: Register your new home address, assuming that you have moved to Zeeburg from another address in Amsterdam. (False personal information was provided).

Task 3: Apply for a driver's license, assuming that you have lost your existing license, and need a new one. (False personal information was provided).

The goal was to investigate the users' experiences when using the e-loket. Evaluated was whether participants were able to carry out the tasks, which user experience problems occurred, and attitudes towards the system. The user was asked to think out loud while performing each task. During each of the three tasks, the observer noted the experiences and difficulties encountered. The scorecard that was developed served to collect standardised information on specific aspects of the user process, for example the problems users encountered, the navigation patterns (the route users took in completing the task), and problems in understanding.

After the participant completed (or at least attempted) the three tasks, a short five to ten minute interview was carried out in order to check the observer's findings. The user was given the chance to express his/her opinion of the site and discuss the problems that were encountered. The goal of this part of the study was to find out which difficulties the user found most frustrating, to gain an understanding of the causes of the difficulties, and to understand what the users' experiences were of using the Zeeburg e-loket.

4 Results

After the observation and interview sessions were completed, the results for the thirty participants were analysed. For each of the cultural groups 5 men and 5 women were involved, ages ranged from 18 to 50 and most participants had average Internet experience. This section will report the main findings.

First, the Moroccan and Surinam participants seemed to put more effort into reading all the information presented to them than the Dutch. This was first observed at the start of the first task, where Moroccans (9) and Surinamese participants (8) read all the options on the e-loket index page, before clicking on the correct link. The second and third tasks also started on this same index page. Even so, the Moroccans and to a lesser extent the Surinamese participants repeated their detailed reading to "*make sure I click on the correct link*" as some participants explained. The majority of Dutch participants tended to scan quicker and in a more general fashion, reading the column titles instead of all the sub-titles. In the later stages of the second task, the users arrived at a page offering information on how to register a house move. In this case too, the majority of Moroccans (7) and Surinamese (6) read the entire the text, while the majority of Dutch participants (8) simply scanned it. The result was that the Moroccans and Surinamese took much longer to complete the tasks than the Dutch.

Taking into account the previous literature, an explanation might be found in value associations for uncertainty avoidance. Members of cultures with high uncertainty avoidance do not feel comfortable with uncertainty and ambiguity. This description is consistent with the Moroccan and Surinamese value scores from the literature, and could explain the observed cautious approach towards the website and detailed reading of the content. The notion that the transactions involved government applications seemed to make participants even more cautious. One participant said: "*I am always careful with government things because it takes a long time to trace and correct mistakes*". The Dutch participants showed a lesser degree of uncertainty avoidance in their scanning behaviour, which corresponds to their cultural score as found by Hofstede.

However, in the third task, the number of Dutch participants who carefully read the explanation text for applying to a driver's license increased. This did not support the previously described interpretation. When these participants were asked about this, they explained that they were careful because a driver's license is an official document. An error in such a document results in it not being valid. They explained that they felt cautious about applying for an official document on the Internet. According to Hofstede [11], the uncertainty avoidance and power distance variables for the Dutch culture are low. Four out of five Dutch participants who showed caution explained that they considered the application for a driver's license a task that was directly linked to the government, whereas registering a move was thought of as more removed from government office. As such, even for members of cultures with low uncertainty avoidance scores, such as the Dutch, applying for official documents via e-government sites seems to cause some insecurity or caution.

The second finding relates to the manner in which the different groups approached the content of the site. Where the Dutch and Surinamese groups started out by reading the titles and other information on the left side of the page, most of the Moroccan participants started looking at every page in the top right-hand corner. A simple explanation for this could be that Moroccan is an Arabic language, which is read from right to left. This could explain the start of the scanning pattern in the top right-hand corner. As a result of their scanning behaviour, the Dutch and Surinamese participants initially missed a crucial link to an online application form that was situated in the top right hand corner on certain pages. Another link to the form was also provided at the bottom of the page, but consequently took longer to find.

Interestingly enough, the results also indicate that Moroccans saw items that were green or red, faster than the Dutch and Surinamese participants. Eight out of ten Moroccans were specifically attracted to those elements on the site that were green and red. When mistakes were made during the process of filling out forms, a red text would appear under the mistake. The Moroccans seemed to notice this text much quicker than the Dutch and Surinamese participants.

During each session, the observer attempted to evaluate the attitude of the user towards the website. A remarkable difference in reactions was noted between the Moroccan group and the Dutch and Surinamese groups. During the task observations, the Moroccan users voiced feelings of insecurity and regularly asked for confirmation that they were on the right track. The Dutch and Surinamese participants did not show this need for confirmation until after completion of the task. A possible explanation for this could be the high significant others score for Moroccans as described by Trompenaars [17]. It may have been perceived as important for the Moroccan participants that the observer was not made to lose face by openly criticising the website. Comments such as "*I hope I am doing well*" were frequently uttered among the Moroccan participants during the observation sessions. The need for significant others in combination with high uncertainty avoidance may have resulted in the participants' need for confirmation that they were performing in accordance with the expectations of the observer. Dutch and Surinamese culture both have a low score on the need for significant others, which may have been reflected in participants' emotional reactions to the e-government site.

Another finding that suggests the influence of the high need for significant others for the Moroccan users was their behaviour at the end of each task. After completion of the task they would ask the observer if they did well. They seemed very relieved when they completed a task, often reflected by a sigh or a moment of sitting back in the chair for an instant of relaxation between the tasks. The Moroccan culture is also a masculine culture, in which the recognition of achievement is important to the participants [11]. The observer found that Moroccan participants commenced the next task with more confidence after a previous confirmation of successfully completing a task.

In contrast, the Dutch and Surinamese reactions did not seem emotional, despite the high uncertainty avoidance score for the Surinamese. Surinamese people however, score low on the need for significant others and are thought to be a more feminine culture.

It is possible, however, that Dutch and Surinamese participants felt equally relieved after completing the tasks as the Moroccans were, but did not show this emotion to the observer. The Dutch and Surinamese cultures score high on neutrality, meaning that emotions are usually held in check. The Moroccan culture is though to be an affective culture, in which emotions are openly expressed.

Finally, the user's attitude towards mistakes should be discussed. In the post observation interviews, the users were asked to explain what caused the problems they had encountered while using the e-loket. The reactions varied. Moroccan participants mostly blamed themselves for the problems they had experienced. Dutch participants, on the other hand, blamed the system for the mistakes, listing discrepancies in the system to support their claim. The Moroccan high power distance and resulting respect for authority could perhaps play a role here. The reactions in the post-observation interview indicated that the Moroccans felt that websites made by the government must be well made. Therefore, if any problems occurred, they themselves must have made a mistake. The Surinamese participants, like the Dutch, blamed the system for encountered difficulties and mistakes. The Surinamese culture also scores low on power distance, which could mean that they do not feel the need to be as openly respectful towards the government as may have been the case for the Moroccans.

5 Discussion and Conclusion

The goal of the current study was to evaluate the hypothesis that people from different cultural backgrounds experience different problems in using e-government applications. The study described in this paper adopted observation methods to evaluate cross-cultural user experience of an e-government website. The findings show that a combination of observation and interview methods offers interesting insights into user's behaviour. By relating observations back to cultural variable scores as determined by previous literature, explanations for differences in behaviour were sought. In order to investigate the hypothesis, four research questions were investigated. These four research questions will now be answered in pairs.

- *Question 1: What are the user experience problems that users encounter?*
- *Question 2: Are these user experience problems different for users from different cultural backgrounds?*

The findings suggest that the user experience problems encountered were quite different for the different cultural groups involved. The differences in user behaviour found could be divided into four categories: Concern for detail, scanning behaviour, attitude towards the website, and perception of who is to blame for user experience problems.

Where the Moroccan and Surinamese participants were very concerned with the details of the web pages, the Dutch did not put much effort into reading the details - erratically clicking on links without concern for error. As a result, Moroccan and Surinamese participants needed more time to complete the tasks than the Dutch.

The scanning behaviour of the participants differed considerably. Where Dutch and Surinamese participants started scanning in the top left-hand corner, the Moroccans commenced in the top right-hand corner, each therefore missing elements of the site at first glance.

The attitude with which the website was approached also differed between the participants from the different cultural backgrounds: the Dutch approached the tasks in a casual manner and with confidence, whereas the Moroccans seemed more careful and uncertain. The latter were relieved after completing the task. The Dutch users encountered problems in finding the correct link, as they did not take the time to read details and instructions, while the meticulous Moroccan users found the long texts cumbersome.

Finally, a noteworthy aspect of the user experience was the participants' approach to mistakes. The Moroccans mostly blamed themselves for their problems and often ended up in an impasse, resulting in lengthy task completion times. The Dutch and Surinamese blamed the website and were therefore often hesitant to continue. This was either because they did not trust a flawed system with sensitive information, or they simply preferred not to deal with such a flawed system at all.

As such, it can be concluded that the findings of this study offer support for the notion that user problems encountered when using an e-government website are different for users from different cultural backgrounds.

- *Question 3: What are the causes of these user experience problems?*
- *Question 4: Are these causes different for users from different cultural backgrounds?*

An explanation for the different user experience problems was sought by relating cross-cultural variable scores as presented in section 2.2.2. The findings show that observed behaviour was in line with expectations derived from available literature on cross cultural differences.

Findings suggest that users from different cultures encountered different user experience problems. Cultural variable scores derived from previous literature offered some possible explanations for these differences. However, as can be seen in Section 4, it is not possible to identify a clear one-on-one match between cultural value scores and observed behaviour. Sometimes, behaviour corresponds with more than one cultural variable score. It could even be argued that for each observed action, a suitable explanation can always be found because of the overlap in definition and the various possibilities of interpretation that exist for the variables available to us. Future research is hoped to show to what extent socio-psychological variables such as those addressed in this study, actually are the cause for differences in behaviour and user experience. Such studies should preferably determine participants' actual cultural backgrounds, by measuring cultural value associations instead of inferring those from available general evidence on national cultures. However, culture is difficult to measure. Therefore, existing, original measurement instruments should preferably be available for such purposes to compare results. Even so, this study shows that there are reasons to believe that cultural backgrounds influence the user experience and that consideration of culturally based preferences and needs is important for the development of effective e-government services for a multi-cultural user population.

This study tried to explain differences in user experience with the help of cultural value scores. The study also assessed the applicability of individual observation as a method to evaluate cross-cultural user experience. For the purpose of this study the methods were found sufficient. However, for a more detailed evaluation of user experience issues, other methods may be needed to ensure valid data is collected.

Generalization of the results of this study should be made with caution. The sample includes 10 participants from each cultural background involved in the study. Future research will need to involve larger culturally diverse user populations to gain an understanding in the way cultural background influences user behaviour and experience. Even so, this study offers some interesting findings to support the notion that e-government development will need to take into consideration the needs of a multi-cultural society.

Acknowledgements

This research was supported by funding from the European Union EFRO fund, the Province of North-Holland, the City of Amsterdam and the University of Amsterdam. Acknowledgements also go to the organisation Cybersoek.

References

1. Van Dam, N. Cultural User Experience Issues in E-government: Designing for a Multi-Cultural Society. Master's Thesis, Faculty of Mathematics, Computer Science, Physics and Astronomy, University of Amsterdam (2003).
2. Wilson, R. T., Akselsen, S., Evjemo, B., Aarsaether, N. (1999) Teledemocracy in Local Government. Communications of the ACM, 42 (1999) 12. pp 58-63.
3. Tambouris, E., Gorilas, S., Boukis, G. Investigation of Electronic Government. In: Proceedings of the 8th Pan Hellenic Conference on Informatics, Vol. 2. Livanis, Athens (2001) 367-376.
4. Dunleavy, P., Margetts, H. Government on the web. Report by the controller and auditor general. UK Stationary Office, London (1999)
5. Hoi-Yan Ma, T., Zaphiris, P. The Usability and Content Accessibility of E-government in the UK. In: C. Stephanidis (Ed.): Universal Access in HCI. Lawrence Erlbaum, Mehwah, USA. (2003) 760-764
6 Van Engers, T., Kordelaar, P.J.M., Ter Horst, S.A., POWER to the e-Government. Report of the E-POWER project: European Program for an Ontology based Working Environment for Regulations and Legislation (2000) http://www.lri.jur.uva.nl/~epower/
7. Atkinson, R. D., Ulevich, J. Digital Government: The Next Step to Reengineering the Federal Government, Technology & New Economy Project. Democratic Leadership Council & Progressive Policy Institute, Washington (2000)
8. Heeks, R Reinventing government in the information age. Routledge, London, UK (1999)
9. Dawes, S., Bloniarz, P., Kelly, K., Fletcher, P. Some Assembly Required: Building a Digital Government for the 21st Century. Center for Technology in Government, SUNY, Albany (2000) http://www.ctg.albany.edu/resources/abstract/abdgfinalreport.html
10. Kluckhohn, C. Culture and behavior. University of Arizona Press, Tuscon (1962)
11. Hofstede, G. Cultures and Organizations: Software of the Mind. McGraw-Hill, New York (1991)
12. Lotman, Y. 'Gogol' and the Correlation of 'The Culture of Humor' with the Comic and Serious in the Russian National Traditional. In Baran, H. (ed): Semiotics and Structuralism: Readings from the Soviet Union. International Arts and Sciences Press, White Plains, New York (1976) 297-300.
13. Schein, E. H. Organizational Culture and Leadership. Jossey-Bass, California (1985)
14. Kakabadse, A. Ludlow, R. Vinnicombe, S. Working in Organizations, Penguin Business, Harmonsworth (1987)
15. Evers, V. Cultural Aspects of User Interface Understanding: An Empirical Evaluation of an E-Learning Website by International User Groups. PhD Dissertation. The Open University, Milton Keynes (2001)
16. Hall, E. Beyond Culture, Doubleday, New York (1976)

17. Trompenaars, F. Riding the Waves of Culture, Nicholas Brealey Publishing, London (1993)
18. Moeslinger, S. Technology at Home: A Digital Personal Scale. In: Pemberton, S (ed.): CHI 97 Electronic Publications, Formal Video Program, The Association of Computing Machinery, New York (1997) http://www.acm.org/sigchi/chi97/proceedings/video/sgm.htm
19. Boivie, I. Usability and Users' Health Issues in Systems Development. PhD Dissertation. Uppsala University (2003).
20. Evers, V. Cross-Cultural aspects of using a virtual learning environment. In: Proceedings of the International Symposium on E-learning beyond Cultural and Linguistic Barriers: Co-existence and Collaboration. Chiba, Japan (2002)
21. Vohringer-Kuhnt, Th. The influence of culture on usability. Master's Thesis, Freie Universitat, Berlin (2002)
22. Bourges-Waldegg, P., Scrivener, S. A. R. Applying and testing an approach to design for culturally diverse user groups. Interacting with Computers 13 (2000) 2. pp 111-126.
23. Kaplan, B., Duchon, D. Combining qualitative and quantitative research methods in information: A case study. MIS Quarterly 12 (1988) 4. pp. 571-587.

Visualizing Social Patterns in Virtual Environments on a Local and Global Scale

Katy Börner[1], Shashikant Penumarthy[2], Bonnie Jean DeVarco[3], Carol Kerney[4]

[1] School of Library and Information Science, Indiana University
10th Street & Jordan Avenue, Bloomington, IN 47405, USA
http://ella.slis.indiana.edu/~katy
[2] Computer Science, Indiana University, Bloomington, IN 47405, USA
[3] MediaTertia, 821 Walnut Ave., Santa Cruz, CA. 95060, USA
[4] San Diego County Office of Education, 6401 Linda Vista Road, San Diego, CA 92111, USA

Abstract. Today a wide variety of virtual worlds, cities, and gaming environments exist and become part of life of their human inhabitants. However, our understanding of how technology influences the way people can use these virtual places to access information, expertise, to socialize, etc. is very limited. Previous work [1-4] introduced a tool set that generates visualizations of user interaction data to support social navigation, aid designers of virtual worlds in the evaluation and optimization of world content and layout as well as the selection of interaction possibilities, and enables researchers to monitor, study, and research virtual worlds and their evolving communities. This paper applies an advanced version of this tool set to visualize and analyze local and global usage patterns in a virtual learning environment called LinkWorld. Resulting social visualizations have been used to inform a set of netiquette and reporting procedures, to fine tune training material and moderation guidelines, to analyze and report the progress of the LinkWorld project, and to create a "social compass" for teachers, moderators and students who collaborate in this unique environment.

1 Introduction

Multi-user 3D collaborative environments, or virtual worlds, are a mature technology to design online 'learning places' that foster community experiences for geographically distributed students. As part of a growing genre of Collaborative Virtual Environments (CVE's), virtual worlds offer diverse opportunities for community centered learning [5] and are encouraging a redefinition of teacher and student roles as well as of the relationships between school and society [6]. Because participants in 3D virtual worlds have a 'social body' or 'avatar,' identity construction and community building can be much richer than in text-based collaborative environments [7]. To use virtual worlds effectively, novel ways of facilitating online social interactions are needed [6, 8, 9]. Social 'design principles' become key to designing and sustaining successful virtual worlds for learning [9-11].

This paper reports first results from a collaboration of the BorderLink Project of Southern California with the Information Visualization lab at Indiana University on

P. van den Besselaar and S. Koizumi (Eds.): Digital Cities 2003, LNCS 3081, pp. 325-340, 2005.

the utilization of social visualizations [1-3]. The tools have been applied to map the 'social landscape' of a virtual world named LinkWorld that provides the user population with navigation maps and a level of self-reflexivity that allows a group to see the effectiveness of the virtual environment and their own collaborative patterns over time. The remainder of the paper is organized as follows: Section 2 introduces the BorderLink Project and its 3D virtual LinkWorld; Section 3 presents world evaluation and visualization objectives; Section 4 introduces the visualization toolset and provides sample visualizations of LinkWorld events; The paper concludes with a discussion and outlook.

2 The BorderLink Project and LinkWorld

The BorderLink Project (www.BorderLink.org/) is funded by a Technology Innovation Challenge Grant from by the U.S. Department of Education. The project is directed by the Imperial County Office of Education in partnership with the San Diego County Office of Education. It endeavors to impact the lives of high school students of Imperial and rural San Diego Counties through the use of technology in education. It utilizes video conferencing and distance classes to deliver advanced placement (AP) courses and provides a support infrastructure for online college prep and career counseling. Its goals are to (1) increase the number of students who qualify for universities and highly skilled careers, (2) provide college and career success skills, (3) prepare students to select a college, (4) provide comprehensive staff development, (5) reduce student/teacher isolation, and (6) provide equitable access to technologies.

LinkWorld (www.BorderLink.org/LinkWorld.html) is a 3D multi-user virtual world designed using ActiveWorlds technology (www.activeworlds.com/). It is spear-headed by Carol Kerney and Bonnie Devarco and is an integral part of the BorderLink Project. LinkWorld provides a low-cost way to provide regular learning, counseling, and collaboration opportunities to students, teachers, and counselors in the BorderLink Project who are geographically distributed across 6704.2 square miles of rural South California. Most schools are miles and hours away from the other schools (see also Fig. 1).

In addition to one-to-one and one-to-many video conferencing and online course delivery, LinkWorld supports many-to-many synchronous communication and offers a collaborative social space with access to realtime resources for student mentoring, guidance and support activities. The students can get to know each other as mentors, colleagues and friends in a BorderLink community in cyberspace.

Many participants in the BorderLink Project represent the first generation in their family who are able to attend college. Hence, they do not grow up in a community that emphasizes the importance of college or exhibit a background and experience with early college preparation during their high school years. LinkWorld aims to immerse students in a "college culture" in a virtual social setting that offers them regular opportunities to communicate and think about college options with college recruitment officers, university student mentors, counselors and other college-bound students. LinkWorld is also used to augment course delivery with collaborative learning activities that extend regular coursework in the arts, sciences, and humanities. Students learn by cooperating with their peers in problem-solving, idea exchange and skill sharing experiences [12, 13].

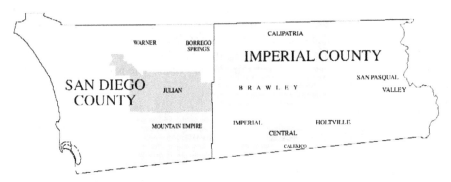

Fig. 1. Map showing the geographic spread of BorderLink schools

To ease acceptance, the areas in LinkWorld correspond to the natural biomes of the areas in Southern California covered by the BorderLink Project. The project serves twelve high schools in eleven districts in Imperial and San Diego Counties, the two counties that comprise the entire southern border of California with Mexico. BorderLink territory stretches from the east Arizona border for 170 miles westward. It includes the sand dunes in east Imperial County that are frequently seen in movies such as "Star Wars," "The Scorpion King," and "Lawrence of Arabia." The Anza Borrego Desert, Salton Sea, Cuyamaca and Laguna Mountains, an old gold mining town, and the Warner Ranch are all parts of BorderLink country. These areas are replicated in the nine regions of the virtual world using custom-made modular landscape components reflecting the mountain, meadow, desert and salton sea areas of San Diego and Imperial Counties.[1]

A sketch of the 1-kilometer by 1-kilometer virtual world is shown in Fig. 2, left. The right hand side of Fig. 2 shows the spatial layout of the world compiled from aerial views of the "satellite areas" of LinkWorld. Clearly visible are the nine discrete areas providing spaces for private meetings and events. Each satellite area features a different biome of Imperial and San Diego Counties.

Subsequently, we describe the diverse activities that have been carried out in LinkWorld during the first four years of the BorderLink Project. The first year was devoted to the plan, design, and development of the LinkWorld biomes. In year two, a number of leadership committee meetings and content development meetings were held and support resources were gathered. Drop-in tutoring and scheduled SAT (an important college entrance exam for US high school students) preparation began. The third year featured special outreach sessions for teachers and the design of new customized content to serve a range of user groups in the BorderLink Project. A special subject-area event series introduced veteran AWedu[2] community members

---

[1] Descriptions and comparison screenshots of the virtual and real world locations can be found at http://www.BorderLink.org/history/biomes.html.

[2] The AWedu is a special "Education Universe", a private universe that uses the ActiveWorlds platform. AWedu was initiated by ActiveWorlds in 1999 due to educators requesting a pri-

and their projects in the arts, humanities, and sciences to LinkWorld teachers, counselors and leadership committee members.

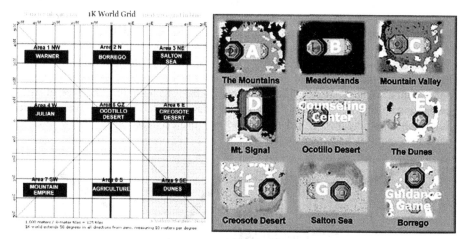

Fig. 2. Spatial layout map of LinkWorld (left) and its biomes (right)

In year four, eight subject-specific areas featured resources based on the California A-G subject area requirements (http://pathstat1.ucop.edu/ag/a-g/). The CollegeQuest guidance game area was designed and deployed for counselors to take students through college prep activities using a highly interactive gaming approach. Focus groups of counselors and teachers tested CollegeQuest and the subject area materials in all satellite areas. A vigorous activity schedule for students was launched in many areas of LinkWorld including:

1. College recruitment question/answer sessions for AVID (Advancement Via Individual Determination) students to meet with recruitment officers from six different California colleges and universities.
2. Art gallery opening for students in the Julian High School Modern Art course to show their Cubist artwork and discuss their motivations and understanding of Cubism with students from other high schools. AWedu guests from around the world joined this event (see Figure 3).
3. CollegeQuest counseling sessions and games in which counselors lead students through college prep resources linked to tokens in a scavenger hunt game (similar to the Super Mario Nintendo game) with four separate areas underground, on land, and in a sky "castle" (http://www.BorderLink.org/history/quest.html for a description).
4. "Treasure Hunt" language games for students in beginning Spanish and "Cinco de Mayo" historical role-play for advanced Spanish students (see Figure 4).

As LinkWorld evolves to serve a broad range of uses, it becomes crucial to create a "social compass" for teachers, moderators and students who collaborate in this unique

---

vate and safe location for teachers and students to design and use virtual worlds in educational settings. The AWedu universe resides online and consists of a cluster of 70 to 130 virtual worlds created, hosted and regularly used by educational institutions around the world.

environment. Planning and conducting one-to-many, one-to-one and many-to-many collaborative activities involving minors and 10-100 simultaneous participants (and sometimes a larger number of participants when simultaneous sessions occur in different areas of LinkWorld) requires answering questions such as: How do we initiate, moderate, and support chat-based discussions? How do we implement safeguards for appropriate behavior through netiquette and automated functions? What activities can most successfully use a "natural" environment in which students have a representative self and have a sense of social space as they meet with virtual participants? What design features are most useful for facilitating the ease of use and navigation in this environment? In order to answer these questions, evaluative tools that enable participants, world designers, and project leaders to analyze and view participant activity become essential.

Fig. 3. Art Gallery event screenshot (user names removed to preserve anonymity)

In addition, the BorderLink Project places a strong emphasis on evaluation using multiple methodologies. The BorderLink Project's external evaluator used the following methodologies: 1) teacher interviews, 2) student focus groups, 3) student interviews, 4) assessment and disaggregation of end-of-workshop surveys and questionnaires, 5) site visits, and 6) classroom observations. At the end of the 2002/2003 school year, the BorderLink evaluator acquired, evaluated and reported these data to the Technology Innovation Challenge Grant stakeholders. However, the BorderLink Project's standard evaluation methodologies used for other technologies were not completely sufficient to analyze the unique qualities of learning experiences utilizing LinkWorld. These qualities include a high level of virtual social space and embodied participants. Thus, evaluations that include spatiotemporal visualizations can be more useful than standard interviews and classroom observations. This provided an additional incentive to adopt the new social pattern and chat visualizations provided by the Indiana University team. These visualizations were then included, in narrative form, in the larger BorderLink year-end evaluation report that was made available to the BorderLink Project stakeholders as well as the funding source.

Fig. 4. Cinco de Mayo screenshot (user names are removed to preserve anonymity)

3 Evaluation and Visualization Objectives

This section first describes LinkWorld's user groups and their information needs. We then discuss how data analysis techniques and social visualizations can help to support these user groups. LinkWorld was designed to serve three distinct user groups:

1. Teachers/counselors/mentors, including selected teachers from all BorderLink high schools, counselors in San Diego and Imperial Schools, mentors from universities, colleges and the local communities, college counselors, college recruitment officers and SAT test preparation advisors;
2. BorderLink administrators, including members of the leadership committee, administrators of the project, special evaluators for the project, LinkWorld designers and in-world content and activity developers (so refinement of the world can follow user needs); and
3. BorderLink high school students ranging in age from 14-18 years.

Teachers/counselors need a way to assess student engagement, needs and learning styles. Moderators need to effectively guide participants through activities both temporally and spatially. Virtual world designers need to know what works to support in-world activities. Administrators need to report project results. Students need to have a way to gauge their performance in relationship to others in a task-based activity.

The needs of the BorderLink participants above were established via communication between the designers of LinkWorld and each group of users. All high schools that are part of the BorderLink Project are characteristically in rural settings with limited access to other student populations and resources for college preparation. For example, Julian High School, one of the case-studies presented below, is a very remote school district with only 226 students in the entire high school. Working with LinkWorld managers, the art teacher from Julian wanted her students to be able to share their work with an audience of peers that would include high school students from other BorderLink schools as well as other invited guests. In addition to offering a wider audience not bound by local geography, it was clear that a virtual world setting would offer her students the opportunity to reflect on their works of art, to summarize their methods and motivations, and to receive valuable feedback from others.

In the Spanish language case-studies presented below, the teachers established that their beginning Spanish language students needed to have the opportunity to rehearse and use this second language through the guided use of vocabulary words in conversation. The LinkWorld designers attempted to create a practical way in which to engage students in a kinesthetic activity (such as a treasure hunt) that could take place in a virtual 3D environment. BorderLink managers also established the need to understand the moderation styles that best suited student success in learning activities that take place in virtual settings. Understanding successful approaches to online moderation would enable future BorderLink teachers to better prepare by drawing from the best practices of the original teachers who led students in these new environments.

Because BorderLink serves high school students, an even more important challenge in LinkWorld is to ensure continuous appropriate behavior in all activities and events. Real time chat environments have rarely been used and scaled by K-12 community without many rules and regulations for limited use and solid moderation practices already in place. This is a result of the accelerated experience of off-task behavior and conversation that has initiated the standard netiquette rules to be put in place by all schools before each 1st grader is introduced to the WWW. Moderation of real time chat is difficult because the amount of time needed to monitor behavior is extensive and the self-regulation of behavior by K12 minors is not an option. The user groups of LinkWorld are in the critical age group between 14 and 18; because of this, safeguards for appropriate behavior were rigorously put into place before a scaling up of the user base in LinkWorld could be undertaken.

Mapping social activities such as movement and interactions with the world (web page access or teleport usage) and with other participants (via chat) can help to:

- automatically identify inappropriate words in chat in real time, their originators, as well as major areas and times in which inappropriate speech is typically observed;
- visualize and regulate appropriate behavior (including polite listening behaviors, following directions and staying on task);

- better determine the ideal conditions in the design of the virtual environment (including easy navigation, orienting materials in an aesthetically and spatially compelling way, ensuring presentations can be engaged in by all participants);
- understand and model successful moderation strategies (including setting expectations, adequate explanation, student learning style assessment, engaging students in the material through guiding activities, regular encouragement and completing lessons in a reasonable amount of time);
- present content in compelling and easy-to-use ways (including adequately complex materials, simple and engaging layout, and easy access to and comparison of varied materials);
- assist a teacher to better plan lessons beforehand or have a better "bird's-eye-view" of their content (types of objects, when objects were created, what they are linked to) in the spatial environment;
- enable students to effectively navigate through the world and the content of the lesson in it, assess their own progress in meeting the milestones of the activity, engage in peer-to-peer learning and mentoring and compare their personal performance to other students doing the same activity; and
- identify social networks based on physical closeness of participants.

4 Visualization Toolkit and Application

Research on social visualizations aims to analyze and visualize data about a person, to illuminate relationships among people, or to visualize user group activity. For a detailed review of lifeline visualizations, the visualization of very large-scale conversations, visualization of Web activity and user trails, representation of people by avatars, visualizations that support social interactions of participants, or visualization of MUDs or 3-D virtual, please consult [2].

To our knowledge, nobody has yet attempted to analyze and visualize spatially-referenced user interaction data such as navigation, object manipulation, Web access, or chatting in 3-D virtual environments. This may be due to the fact that most 3-D online browser systems provide an exclusive chat log (oftentimes restricted to a fixed number of spatially close avatars) of a 3-D world experience. Information about when and where a certain utterance was made, user positions, object movements, teleports/warp usage, or Web accesses is lost. However, the spatial reference is vital to identify places in which people typically speak, to find teleport designs that work, etc.

The social visualization tool set developed at Indiana University comprises algorithms for visualizing the evolution of 3D virtual worlds, for mapping dynamic user trails and chat activity in space and time, and to analyze and visualize chat activity [1-4]. The subsequent section demonstrates the application of those tools to provide guidance for the three major LinkWorld user groups. The tools are demonstrated using data that was recorded in LinkWorld in spring of 2003. There are two main types of activities in LinkWorld:

1. Highly mobile game-style treasure hunts, interactive galleries or student presentations.

2.   Highly conversant historical role-plays, guidance or recruitment question and answer sessions.

For the first types of activities, maps for guiding movement are very useful. For the second kinds of activities, it is valuable to analyze the number of utterances of each participant, to identify dominant chatters, and to review specific words used in chat.

As mentioned before, LinkWorld consists of eight different areas for private chat and activities and a commons area in Ground Zero. Frequently, separate events occur simultaneously in more than one area. A typical event includes up to 35 participants and up to five moderators/presenters. Subsequently, we explain how a map of a virtual world such as LinkWorld is generated and how it can be used to represent user interactivity over space and time.

To generate a map of the world, information on the location, orientation, and the size of virtual objects is needed. A so-called *propdump* file contains details about the time an object was created, its location in 3D space and orientation, and the type of object (e.g., a teleport) plus the action that the object will provide when clicked upon by the user (e.g., teleport to location 12N 45W). The *registry* file contains location-independent information about the size and shape of the bounding box of each object. The polygonal information about the objects is not available in the registry file and hence the exact shape of the object cannot be reproduced.

The actions performed by users in virtual worlds are tracked through a 'log bot', a computer program that continuously monitors all movement, chat, and interaction activity in the virtual world. Actions are recorded in an ASCII encoded log file. The header of this log file includes information about when the recording began the name and dimensions of the world, the name of the universe within which this world is located and the type of event that is being recorded. There is one entry per action performed in the virtual world. Each record comprises a timestamp of when the action occurred, the user, his/her coordinates and, if the action is other than movement, it records the type of action and content of the action (e.g., for a chat action it records the chat text string).

The visualization toolkit first reads the *registry* file and then the *propdump* file. Based on these files and the extent of the world, a grid with coordinate values is drawn to facilitate easy identification of regions in the virtual world. For each object entry in the *propdump* file, the location, size and orientation is determined and transformed based on the scaling used to draw the 2D map. The time of creation of an object is used to color-code the objects based on their age. Depending on the type of object, a different icon is used to represent it in the world. Objects that are simply structures, but are not of a special type, are drawn simply as polygons. Objects that act as teleports are represented by a purple plus sign; objects that provide access to web resources are represented by a green square.

Subsequently, the user activity log file is read, and the coordinates of the users are transformed into map coordinates using the selected scaling factor. A polyline is computed that connects the successive positions of each user. The timestamp of the user position determines the color-coding of the user trail. Idle times are denoted by cycles, the size of which represents the amount of time during which no movement took place. The color of lines and circles corresponds to the time at which the data was logged. If the user performs an action different from motion such as talking, teleporting, or accessing web pages, the location of the action is displayed as an icon on the map. These icons are defined in the legend drawn below the map of the world.

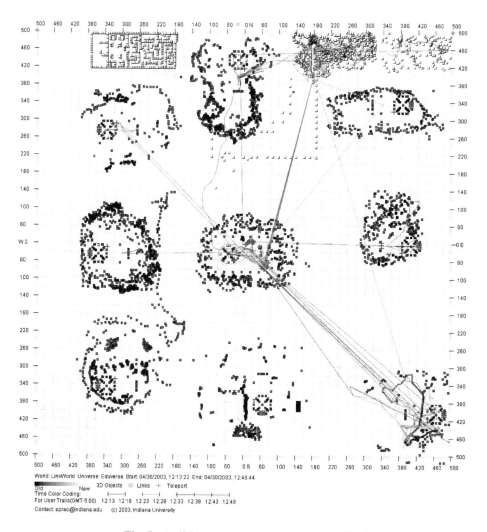

Fig. 5. April 30 treasure hunt movement visualization

Figure 5 shows a map of LinkWorld. Overlaid is all user movement activity that was recorded on April 30. Three separate activities can be identified. For beginning Spanish language students, two separate leaders conducted "treasure hunt" activities. These consisted of theme-based questions and answers on web pages linked to "tokens" distributed throughout two separate areas of LinkWorld. The El Juego del Tesoro treasure hunt, led by MatthewC, took place in the Foreign Language satellite area of LinkWorld (see Figure 5, lower right corner). The other treasure hunt, named Comida!!, was conducted in the Palm Oasis area (a small part of the Mountain Valley and Meadowlands, see Figure 5, upper right). It was led by Profesora Lima and concentrated on the food theme. The path of Profesora Lima is illustrated as a gray polyline. Figure 7 provides a close up of the upper right area.

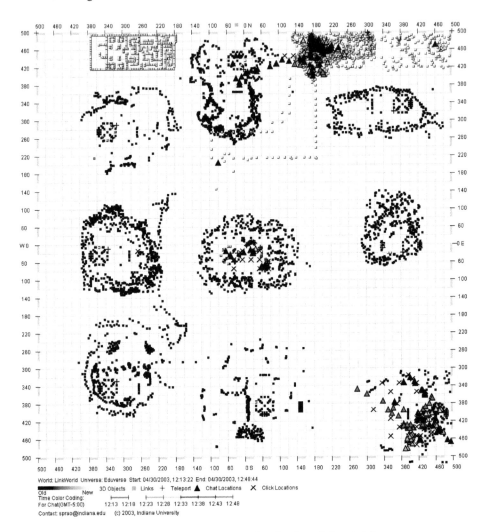

Fig. 6. April 30 treasure hunt visualization of chat activity

Participants in the treasure hunt activities were from Holtville and Brawley high schools. A college recruitment session also occurred during this day. It was led by Carolk and participants were from Rancho Bernardo and Carlsbad high schools. All classes entered at ground zero and teleported to the activity locations. Many participants actively took part in Profesora Lima's treasure hunt. The visualization immediately reveals areas of high activity, enables reviewers to correlate the trails of the main organizer with those of the participants, and points out areas that were used for talking while 'idling'.

A chat visualization of the same event time and place is shown in Figure 6. Here, color coded triangles indicate the places where the treasure hunt participants chatted. El Juego del Tesoro and Comida!! treasure hunt event participants can be compared based on the amount of utterances. The most active chat was by moderator Carolk, who led the recruitment session, MatthewC who led El Juego del Tesoro and Profesora Lima who directed Comida!! Profesora Lima, who gave regular feedback to her students, shows the most dominant chat behavior. It is also clear from the chat visualization how verbal various students were in the activities. A close-up of the upper right area of both maps is shown in Figure 7. It reveals the time sequence of movement and chat patterns during Profesora Lima's treasure hunt.

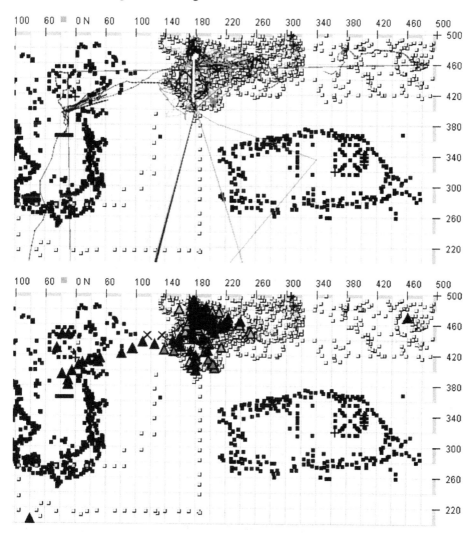

Fig. 7. April 30 treasure hunt visualization enlarged

Figure 8 shows the sorted number of chat utterances per user for the second treasure hunt that involved 19 participants. Profesora Lima (right most bar #19) holds the record with about 170 separate chat utterances. User names have been replaced by numbers to preserve anonymity.

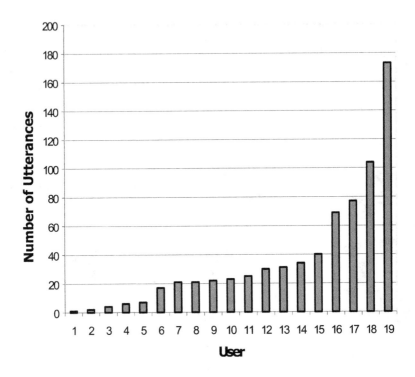

Fig. 8. Number of chat utterances per user during the Treasure Hunt Comida!!

5 Discussion & Outlook

In 2003, a large number of LinkWorld Spring events were logged, analyzed, and visualized. The movement and chat visualizations helped the coordinators of the project to picture how effective directions given at the start of each event were. If students were wandering all over the map, then students clearly did not understand or follow directions. This in turn lead to increased efforts to present clear instructions for students and helped BorderLink managers initiate management techniques to keep the students together in the right area. Subsequently, the visualizations were used to 'test' to what degree the new instructions and techniques improved students' engagement.

The maps and graphs that show participation through chat provided an objective way to evaluate the importance of verbal encouragement for students. Interestingly, the most effective teachers in a virtual environment talk unceasingly with the students, giving feedback, encouraging them, etc. With this knowledge,

Through a combination of after-event debriefs and formative evaluations, reports from chat logs, chat and social pattern visualizations and assessment of the spring 2003 events, the BorderLink Project has established a new set of resources for LinkWorld. These include:

1. a new set of netiquette and reporting procedures suited for a 3D multi-user environment serving high school students (http://www.BorderLink.org/history/teacher/moderation.html);
2. training materials (see http://www.BorderLink.org/history/teacher/#training) and moderation guidelines for teachers, moderators and presenters;
3. lesson plans and teacher templates for selected lessons and activities (see http://www.BorderLink.org/history/teacher/#templates); and
4. a new pre- and post-event profiling and documentation procedure for each activity (see: http://www.BorderLink.org/history/teacher/#eval).

Starting this year, the social visualizations will be included in the evaluation report for the project. They will also be used to report the success of LinkWorld events to potential adopters and partners in the next phase. Objectives for the 2003/2004 school year will include the further refinement of the event cycle and a wider distribution of social visualizations to BorderLink teachers, counselors, moderators, evaluators, and the LinkWorld development team. Through the adoption of a new coding procedure similar to one being pioneered by Janssen et al. with nine distinctive categories of chat (orientating, instructing, grounding, monitoring, testing, evaluating, rest, cognitive and off-task) [14], we are planning to visualize more qualitative conversational behaviors in LinkWorld. The visualization will help BorderLink managers to design larger event areas where the density of movement seems more contained as well as design richer experiences for larger student groups.

A close collaboration with the visualization team will be necessary to further optimize visualizations. Pre-event profiles, event locations, exact times, age groups, number of students, type of activity and information on preferred visualizations will be shared in advance. The focus will be on visualizations for specific time durations (e.g., specific classes rather than all activities in a day) in order to carry out side-by-side comparisons. Moderated events such as treasure hunts will show a more directed, homogeneous series of trails and patterns by each group (similar to color-coded "theme-based" tour paths in the Vatican Library in Rome). The self-directed paths of single-player CollegeQuest journeys will show a broader range of individual trails over a larger period of time.

Taken together, the visualizations provide a reliable, automated methodology for collecting meaningful assessment data. They assist a new group of teachers and activity leaders in developing better content, lesson plans, events and moderation methodologies. We believe they will also help us to identify moderator strategies that will enable student groups to perform successfully in the LinkWorld environment and to provide a "social compass" for a wide range of learning activities by enabling teachers to assess student group behavior and collaborative engagement as well as student self-assessment through visualizing their own experience from a different point of view.

Acknowledgements

BorderLink Partners include the Imperial County Office of Education that serves as the Local Educational Agent, San Diego County Office of Education, the University of California Prep Initiative, San Diego State University-Imperial Valley Campus, Imperial Valley College, Imperial Irrigation District, Digital High School Project, and the twelve target high schools. The BorderLink Project operates under the auspices of Mr. John Anderson, Superintendent of the Imperial County Office of Education and Dr. Rudy Castruita, Superintendent of the San Diego County Office of Education. Project directors are Todd Finnell and Harry Bloom.

We would like to thank Penny Twining, Craig Twining and Chad Rooney for their developmental and reporting assistance in the LinkWorld Project and Mitja Hmeljak,, Alan Lin, Gyeongja Jun Lee, William R. Hazelwood, Sy-Miaw Lin, and Min Xiao who have been involved in the implementation and evaluation of the social visualization tool kit.

This research is supported by Indiana University's High Performance Network Applications Program and an academic equipment grant by Sun Microsystems. The BorderLink project is a five-year project (1999-2004) funded through a Technology Innovation Challenge Grant from the United States Department of Education. Support comes also from a grant no. EIA-0124012 from the National Science Foundation to SRI International under subcontract to Indiana University.

The views and opinions of authors expressed herein do not necessarily state or reflect those of the United States Government or any agency thereof or SRI International and shall not be used for advertising or product endorsement purposes.

References

1. Börner, K., Twin Worlds: Augmenting, Evaluating, and Studying Three-Dimensional Digital Cities and Their Evolving Communities, In Digital Cities II: Computational and Sociological Approaches, M. Tanabe, P. van den Besselaar, and T. Ishida, Editors. 2002, Springer Verlag. p. 256-269.

2. Börner, K. and Y.-C. Lin. *Visualizing Chat Log Data Collected in 3-D Virtual Worlds*. In *International Information Visualisation Conference*. 2001. London, England. p. 141-146.

3. Börner, K., R. Hazlewood, and S.-M. Lin. *Visualizing the Spatial and Temporal Distribution of User Interaction Data Collected in Three-Dimensional Virtual Worlds*. In *Sixth International Conference on Information Visualization*. 2002. London, England: IEEE Press. p. 25-31.

4. Börner, K. and S. Penumarthy, *Social Diffusion Patterns in Three-Dimensional Virtual Worlds*. Information Visualization, 2003. **2**(3): p. 182-198.

5. Bransford, J., A. Brown, and R. Cocking, *How People Learn: Brain, Mind, Experience and School*. Washington, DC: National Academy Press, 1999. p 119-125.

6. Riel, M., *New Designs for Connected Teaching and Learning*. White Paper for the U.S. Department of Education Secretary's Conference on Educational Technology, 2000 (http://www.gse.uci.edu/mriel/whitepaper/).

7. Talamo, A. and B. Ligorio. *Identity in Cyberspace: The Social Construction of Identity through On-line Virtual Interactions*. In *First Dialogical Self Conference*. 2000. p. 8-16.

8. Berge, Z.L., *Facilitating Computer Conferencing: Recommendations from the Field*. Educational Technology, 1995. **35**(1): p. 22-30.

9. Jo Kim, A., *Community Building on the Web: Secret Strategies for Successful Online Communities*. 2000, Berkeley, CA: Peachpit Press.

10. Börner, K., M. Corbit, and B. DeVarco, *Building Blocks for Virtual Worlds*. 2003: p. Final Project Report. Available at http://vw.indiana.edu/building-blocks/report.pdf.

11. Preece, J., *Empathic communities: Reaching out across the Web.* Interactions, 1998. **5**(2): p. 32-43.
12. Vygotsky, L.S., *Mind in Society: The Development of Higher Psychological Processes.* 1978, Cambridge, MA: Harvard University Press.
13. Hogan, D.M. and J.R.H. Tudge, *Implications of Vygotsky's Theory for Peer Learning*, In *Cognitive Perspectives on Peer Learning*, A.M. O'Donnell and A. King, Editors. 1999, Lawrence Erlbaum Associates: Mahwah, NJ. p. 39-65.
14. Janssen, J., H.v.d. Meijden, and M. Winkelmolen. *Collaborating in a 3D Virtual Environment for Culture and the Arts: Metacognitive Regulation in a 3D CSCL Environment.* In *Proceedings of EARLI 2003 - European Association for Research in Learning and Instruction.* 2003. Padova, Italy

Participation in Community Systems: Indications for Design

Ahmad J. Reeves, Patrick G.T. Healey

Interaction, Media, and Communication Research Group
Dept of Computer Science, Queen Mary, University of London, E1 4NS
ahmad@dcs.qmul.ac.uk, ph@dcs.qmul.ac.uk

Abstract. We argue that design for sustainable digital communities must attend to the ways that the technological infrastructure is transformed by, and in turn transforms, human communicative organisation. We present evidence from a user-contributed 'talker' environment, TCZ, whose infrastructure and community of users have evolved over a ten-year period. TCZ is a text-based environment built on a spatial metaphor that is incorporated both into the structure of the environment and into the operation of commands. We describe a comparison of the communicative organisation of the virtual interactions in TCZ with those typical of informal face-to-face conversations. The results show that users exploit the flexibility of the online environment to overcome the constraints that spatial organisation normally place on the configuration of their communicative interactions. We highlight the limitations of the spatial metaphor as an organising architecture for online communities and identify five communication-oriented issues for design.

1 Introduction

Digital Cities are places where individuals, groups and companies are inter-connected and the 'City' is connected with the outside world [15, 16, 17]. They aim at effective communication, with information, commodities and services available via multiple technologies such as the personal computer, television or even the mobile phone. The 'City' is designed to support both recreational and commercial collaboration and communication.

As well as providing connectivity, such virtual communities can also create novel social spaces for interaction [12, 11]. Design for such community systems has had varying emphases. Kollock [7] describes some factors in the creation of successful and ongoing social interactions through design; moving the emphasis away from just technology and interface issues, and more towards supporting interaction and sustainability. Brown et al. [1] discuss issues relating to support for multi-user, multi-lingual community systems. Mynatt et al. [10] describe design issues that are central to supporting collaboration in network communities, such as the relationship between space and organisation, identity and representation and flexible coupling between technical and social elements.

Design could also benefit from a clearer understanding of the differences between the communicative organisation of face-to-face and virtual communication. Building

P. van den Besselaar and S. Koizumi (Eds.): Digital Cities 2003, LNCS 3081, pp. 341-353, 2005.
© Springer-Verlag Berlin Heidelberg 2005

systems that are both sustainable and support communicative practises is a real challenge. Therefore understanding how communication changes when moving from the actual to the virtual, and what this indicates for design will, we believe, help to meet this challenge.

We describe an empirical study of communicative behaviour and participation in a virtual environment called 'TCZ' or 'The Chatting Zone' [13]. TCZ is a user contributed, text-based virtual environment that has been in use for over ten years. It provides a unique example of an evolving corpus of technology and practices and illustrates how a group of geographically distributed people have adapted technology to form and sustain an online social community. Here we provide a broad overview of communicative practises in the environment, followed by a more detailed comparison of patterns of participation in TCZ and a corpus of real-life interactions. First we describe the framework used to model user participation.

2 Participatory Status

The concept of Participatory Status, developed by Goffman [5] provides a framework in which the relationship between the participants in an interaction can be captured. The notion of Participatory Status was introduced in order to move from a binary classification of interlocutors as either speaker or hearer to a richer characterisation. It recognises a variety of speaker roles, distinguishing between the author and originator of an utterance, the animator/relayer of the utterance, and a variety of kinds of hearer such as overhearer, bystander, and eavesdropper. Participant status is the relation of any participant in an interaction to a particular utterance (or other communicative event). The participant framework is the combined analysis of all participants' statuses with respect to a given utterance. Goffman proposed that "For a given speech act taken at a cross sectional instantaneous view, it is possible to describe the role or function of all of the members of that gathering (whether they be ratified participants or not)" ([5], p.137).

Clark [2] has adapted this concept to define a simple set of participant roles. Given this definition we can consider the roles and levels of participation within such a participation framework, moving from the main interlocutors (the speaker and addressee) to a side-participant, then to a bystander and finally an unknown eavesdropper. This framework is illustrated in Figure 1.

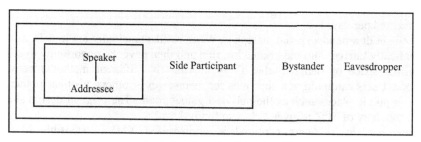

Fig. 1. Levels of Participation [2]

A side participant is described as a 'ratified participant' in the sense of Goffman [4]; i.e. a participant recognised by both addressee and speaker as a party to the conversation. A bystander is not a ratified participant, but the primary participants are aware that he or she can overhear. An eavesdropper is an overhearer that the primary participants are unaware of. Clark distinguishes between these different forms of participation by reference to differences in the obligations of the parties to a conversation to the maintenance of mutual understanding. For example the speaker is obliged to monitor the addressee for understanding, look for evidence of trouble and initiate repair as appropriate. The addressee also has reciprocal obligations to try to understand and signal when they are encountering problems with interpretation (cf. Garfinkel, [3]). The speaker's obligations towards the side participant are weaker in that, although they must understand in order to join the conversation at a later stage, their obligations and rights are less than those of the addressee. A speaker's obligations to a bystander are further reduced, and speakers have no obligations to an eavesdropper since, by definition, they are unaware of their presence. Not all possible participant types are covered by this approach and finer distinctions are made by other authors [8].

Jikorta, Luff and Gilbert [6] propose, but don't elaborate, an approach to requirements analysis and design based on analysis of participatory roles within interactions. Monk [9] applies a participation-based framework to the analysis of video-mediated medical consultations. He uses the proportion of time that each participant has a particular conversational status, as an index of their overall level of participation. For a primary participant in some work, it is natural to expect them to be speaker, addressee or side participant in roughly equal proportions during that interaction. In contrast, a peripheral participant would mostly be a side participant, bystander or eavesdropper. Monk uses this intuition to motivate an operational distinction between primary and peripheral participants. In this study we investigate how the participant roles of interactants, and the patterns of change in roles that unfold during interaction, contrast between face-to-face and virtual communication.

3 Data and Methods

TCZ is hosted at Queen Mary, University of London. All users agree, as a condition of use, that the system logs, with names and locations anonymised, may be used for the purposes of research. As of January 2004 there were 1028 residents occupying 3428 unique rooms. The average daily connection rate is 354 residents, with 5 new users created per day.

TCZ is built around a spatial metaphor. When residents initially log into TCZ, they automatically 'arrive' into their home location and then have the opportunity to utilise the virtual space or 'neighbourhood' by moving (by different methods) between locations. Users can build new locations for themselves or others, visit each other, or gather in public places such as the pub or a games room. The original design sketch for the topology of TCZ is given below in figure 2.

Interactions in TCZ are captured in anonymised XML (Extensible Markup Language) logs. These can then be parsed using XSLT (Extensible Stylesheet Language Transformation) stylesheets according to specific information requirements. An example message in XML format is given in figure 3. For the purposes of the study, 140Mb of logs covering a period of approximately one-week were analyzed. These logs contained a total of 219,355 messages from an average of 158 unique users each day.

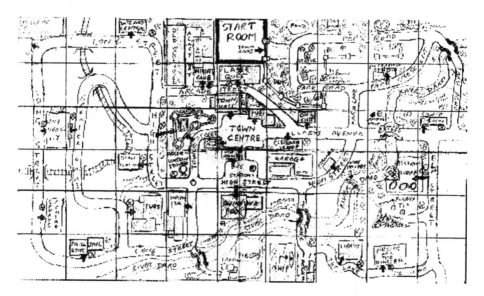

Fig. 2. Design sketch of locations in TCZ

```
<DIRECT>
 <COMMUNICATION_TYPE> PAGETELL </COMMUNICATION_TYPE>
 <Serial> 3087908 </Serial>
 <USAGE> TELL </USAGE>
 <MESSAGE_TYPE> EMOTE </MESSAGE_TYPE>
 <CHARACTER_ID> 67000 </CHARACTER_ID>
 <CHARACTER_STATUS> 3 </CHARACTER_STATUS>
 <LOCATION_ID> 45049 </LOCATION_ID>
 <TARGET_CHARACTER_ID> 23478 </TARGET_CHARACTER_ID>
 <TARGET_CHARACTER_STATUS> 6 </TARGET_CHARACTER_STATUS>
 <TARGET_CHARACTER_LOCATION_ID> 23244 </TARGET_CHARACTER_LO
                                           CATION_ID>
 <MESSAGE> Are you going to the party tonight? </MESSAGE>
 <TIME> 'Mon, 26 Nov 2001 15:40:29 +0000' </TIME>
</DIRECT>
```

Fig. 3. Example: message sent from user 67000 in location 45049 to user 23478 in loc. 23244.

3.1 Overview of Communicative Practises

The first part of the study involved analysing the log files to get an overview of the basic patterns of communication in TCZ. This entailed answering three main questions:

- Were the recipient(s) of messages in the same location as the sender?
- For each message, how many recipients did it go to?
- How much do users utilize the 'space' of TCZ?

These questions were aimed at firstly seeing if 'space' is a factor in organising users interactions, and secondly if interactions were mainly dyadic (two-person) or multiparty. This was then supplemented by a questionnaire, which was placed online, and a notification of it posted in TCZ's bulletin board (BBS News). The questionnaire itself covered:

- Locations used and movement
- Command usage
- Occurrences and control of multiple concurrent interactions
- Control of user availability

This information was useful not only in cross checking findings from the log analysis but also in providing some context for interpreting the XML logs of command use and other behaviours. In total, 56 questionnaires were returned.

3.2 Comparison of Participation Between TCZ and BNC

In order to provide baseline data from face-to-face conversation a parallel analysis of the British National Corpus (BNC) [14] was carried out. The spoken part of the BNC consists of over 4 million words of unscripted informal English conversation. Our sample was taken from the demographic portion of the corpus. This consists of volunteers, selected from different age groups, regions and social classes, who recorded all their conversations over a sample period. Portable tape recorders were used to record their own and others' speech over a period of up to a week. Individuals were selected from various age groups (age 15 plus), equal numbers of males and females, and equal numbers from four social classes. Individuals were able to record their conversations on a variety of days including weekends in order to get a variety of interactions in various locations. All conversations were recorded as unobtrusively as possible, so that the material gathered approximated closely to natural, spontaneous speech. Usually, the only person aware that the conversation was being taped was the person with the recorder. The guarantee of confidentiality and complete anonymity was given with all references to full names and addresses removed from the corpus and the log. For each conversational exchange the person carrying the recorder told all participants they had been recorded and explained why. Whenever possible this happened after the conversation had taken place. If any participant was unhappy about being recorded the recording was erased.

Selection of the samples from TCZ and the BNC was constrained to be as comparable as possible. The characteristics of the two samples are summarised in Table1. 25 subjects were randomly selected from both BNC and TCZ and all their interactions over the sample period traced. These subjects were taken from an even spread of the logs to ensure that either the time of day or the day itself could not bias the results. Transcripts of their interactions were then analysed over 50 conversational turns against the following criteria:

- Distribution of participatory statuses
- Occurrence of multiple, concurrent, statuses
- Levels of group messaging

- Numbers of 'conversations'
- Mobility of participatory status
- Number of words received by users in each participatory status

Table 1. Sample Characteristics: BNC and TCZ

	BNC	TCZ
Number in Sample	70	132
Duration	2-7 days	7 days (weekdays & weekends)
Anonymous	Yes	Yes
Age Range	15-60+	10-40
Demographic Area	UK	UK & North America
Male Vs Female	50% (M), 50% (F)	64% (M), 36% (F)

4 Results

4.1 Overview

With regard to message destinations, 70% of messages went to a location different to that of the sender. 67% of messages went to more than one recipient. Only a third of residents moved from their home location during a session, and there was an average of two moves per session. This suggests that the spatial metaphor has a relatively weak influence on the organisation of communication in TCZ. It also suggests that multiparty (non-dyadic) messaging is common. The typical pattern of use in TCZ is that people remain alone in a location and interact with individuals who are in several other locations.

The questionnaire also asked users: "where on TCZ do you spend most of your time?". 52% of respondents said they spent most of their time in their own room. 26% stated the Pub; with only four other locations being mentioned namely: friends' rooms, game rooms, the awards room and the bank. Importantly, for game rooms (scrabble, chess etc), the awards room (where users vote for each other) and the bank (where users can withdraw TCZ 'currency' from their account) the commands for these activities only work when the user is in that room, and cannot be utilised remotely.

This suggests that overall, movement is rare and where it does occur it is prompted as much by practical as by communicative considerations. Additional evidence for this comes from the responses to the question: "where else might you visit?". 90% of the 108 locations nominated were from only five possibilities: the awards room, the pub, friend's rooms, game rooms and the Bulletin Board.

The questionnaire also asked "how do you normally move about TCZ?". Amongst those who move 28% used the method of typing the room name to automatically go to that location, 22% 'teleported' and only 7% actually used the exits from each room. This again indicates that residents frequently violate the TCZ 'spatial' metaphor, rarely using doors and exits.

Users were asked to list the commands they use most frequently. This gave rise to a list of 491 commands. For exposition, we divide these into six generic areas:

- Communication: used to talk and interact with other users, e.g. 'say', 'tell', 'page', 'whisper'.
- Availability: used to see who else is online, e.g. 'who', 'lastseen', 'fwho' (friends who).
- Identity: used to check another users' details, e.g. 'scan', 'profile', 'title', and 'examine'.
- Movement: used to traverse TCZ, e.g. 'go', 'visit', 'warp'.
- Location: used to locate other users, e.g. 'where', 'finger', 'fwhere' (friends where).
- Other: general non-specific commands, e.g. 'help', 'repeat' (last action), 'cls' (clear screen).

The frequency with which commands in each category were cited is given in Table 2.

Table 2. Division of Commands

	Total
Communication	156
Availability	131
Identity	83
Movement	65
Location	14
Other	42

The questionnaire also addressed occurrences and control of multiple concurrent interactions. 97% of sessions involved the maintenance of distinct, concurrent interactions. There are two aspects to this, namely how these interactions were controlled and managed, and secondly why they were controlled and managed in that way.

36% of respondents said they used purely mental agility and typing skills to control these conversations. This 'cognitive time sharing' was utilised so that other messages were sent whilst utilising the delay for a reply being typed by another user. Residents mentioned the ability to scroll back as being important, as they had a permanent record of ongoing conversations to refer back to. Some residents commented that you "had to get used to it", or "it was a skill soon picked up". The use of colour to differentiate messages along with prefixes to denote resident's statuses probably aided this mental process. 54% of respondents used single or a combination of commands to control their concurrent conversations. One example would be combining the 'say' and 'page' commands concurrently. Users would have one interaction via 'say' (visible to all co-located users) and a second concurrent interaction as a form of collusive by-play with one of the same users via 'page' (which is only visible to explicit addressees). Another example would be the same two interactions as before, but with the addition of a third interaction on the administrators chat channel, and a fourth interaction via the 'tell' command with a user in a separate location.

Finally the questionnaire looked at control of user availability. When asked if they ever deliberately avoided communicating with other people on TCZ, 91% said they did. With regard to how they did this, the most popular reply was 'just ignoring their messages'. This was followed by 'resetting their friends flag' (which ensures that they do not receive messages from them, as they were no longer on their friend's list), and finally by avoiding a location they were in.

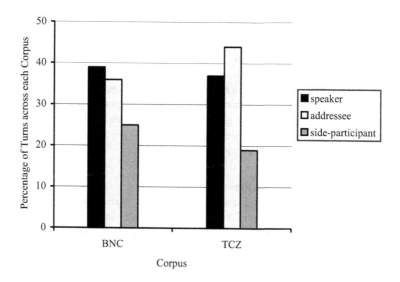

Fig. 4. Frequencies of Participatory Statuses in BNC and TCZ.

4.2 Comparison of Participation Between TCZ and BNC

4.2.1 Distribution of Participatory Statuses

Figure 4 shows the frequencies of participatory status between BNC and TCZ. The categories of speaker, addressee and side-participant all have the same definition as previously outlined in Clark's model. The bystander and eavesdropper categories are undetectable in the BNC corpus, and hence are not included on the graph. The findings indicate that face-to-face interactions have an even level of speaking and being addressed, with a smaller portion of time being a side-participant in an interaction. Although virtual users have the same level of speaker status as face-to-face, they have a higher level as addressee and a lower level as side-participant. The high level of multiparty messaging previously noted could explain this contrast. They also indicate that the TCZ environment does not provide sufficient support for these activities. Participants maintain the coherence of different conversational threads by adapting their use of commands, colors, channels and flags in ways that amount to strategic compromises.

Table 3. Instances of Multiple Participatory Statuses

	BNC	TCZ
Two Statuses	2	20
Three Statuses	0	5
Four Statuses	0	5

4.2.2 Multiple Status

As Table 3 indicates, the TCZ environment also makes possible to hold multiple conversational statuses. However, it also shows that even though holding two concurrent exchanges is common, it is also not uncommon to be involved in three or even four simultaneous exchanges.

4.2.3 Messages Sent to a Group

In the log samples used, 43.3% of messages in TCZ were sent to a group, that is, specifically addressed to more than one person. No messages in the sample of BNC that we analysed fulfilled the same definition of a group message. An example in face-to-face might be "You two get upstairs this minute" It is of course possible for more than one person to hear a message in BNC but the message was not specifically addressed to a defined group as was the case in TCZ.

4.2.4 Numbers of Conversations

An initial suggestion is that a change in primary participants denotes a change in conversation. So for example if A is telling B what C said (conversation 1); and A's mobile phone rings it changes from conversation 1 to conversation 2 as A has changed from 'relayer' i.e. relaying what C said to B, to 'addressee' from the caller, who has become the speaker. (Although conversation 1 can still persist - unless the other primary participant leaves). In TCZ, the average number of 'conversations' per subject (according to the previous definition) was 6.8. In BNC the average was only 2.8. This highlighted that virtual interactions are shorter than in face-to-face.

4.2.5 Mobility of Participatory Status

Mobility of participatory status is the process of moving between the two forms of participation. Table 4 shows although BNC had a higher number of moves than TCZ, the difference was not found to be significant (Mann-Whitney, U= 281, p=0.55).

Table 4. Total number of moves between primary and peripheral participation and vice-versa.

BNC	TCZ
75	46

4.2.6 Words Received per Status

The results shown in Table 5 highlight no significant difference between average number of words produced and received in primary statuses between TCZ and BNC (Speaker TCZ & Speaker BNC (Mann-Whitney, U=280, p=0.55, Addressee TCZ & Addressee BNC Mann-Whitney, U=245.5, p=0.19). Also, there was no significant difference across the same subjects in both primary statuses (Speaker BNC & Addressee BNC Wilcoxon, W= 80, z=1.07, p=0.28; Speaker TCZ & Addressee TCZ Wicoxon, W= 1, z=0.01, p=0.99), and across the same subjects between primary and peripheral (Addressee BNC & Side-Participant BNC Wilcoxon, W= 114, z=1.53, p=0.12; Addressee TCZ & Side-Participant TCZ Wilcoxon, W=46, z=0.61, p=0.54).

However, there was a significant difference between the average number of words received per turn in peripheral status (Side-Participant TCZ & Side-Participant BNC Mann-Whitney, U=102 p > .005). This suggests that although side-participants in face-to-face are not different from addressees, they are different from side-participants in online interactions.

Table 5. Average number of words received per status

	BNC	TCZ
Speaker	7.8	6.4
Addressee	6.1	6.4
Side-Participant	3.9	5.9
Primary	7.0	6.4
Peripheral	3.9	5.9

5 Conclusions and Discussion

TCZ incorporates a strong spatial metaphor into the structure and organisation of the online environment. However, the TCZ command language is sufficiently flexible to allow users to deviate from the underlying spatial model. The data presented in this paper show that in practice users routinely take advantage of this possibility. Normal face-to-face interaction is, by definition, located in physical space. This imposes constraints on participation i.e., it limits who can talk to whom and when. Users of TCZ exploit the fact that these constraints need not apply to online interactions. They conduct multiple, concurrent conversations with people who are typically in a variety of different locations. This additional flexibility in the ways that users can configure their patterns of participation in interaction leads to the development of different kinds of participant status.

Table 6. Participatory distinctions between BNC and TCZ

	BNC	TCZ
1. Status distribution	Even distribution between speaker and hearer	Higher level as addressee, lower level as side-participant
2. Number of interactions	Single interaction at a time	Many concurrent interactions
3. Length of interaction	Same in primary, shorter in peripheral	Same in primary, longer in peripheral
4. Mobility of status	No significant difference	No significant difference

Relative to face-to-face conversation, interaction in TCZ can be glossed as having 'flatter' participant structure than face-to-face interaction. There is more group-based interaction and peripheral participation is less common. These differences seem to be the result of strategic adaptations of the technology to re-configure the communicative organization of their interactions. Users take advantage of the ability to control who can overhear their conversations. They also take advantage of their ability to selectively bar some individuals from contacting them. This kind of control is difficult to achieve in face-to-face interaction. The main means of control available in the physical world is to move in and out of earshot; control of participation through displacement in space. Although users in TCZ could also use location in 'virtual' space to manage the participant structure of their interactions they prefer to exploit the possibilities the technology offers for more direct and flexible means of control. The use of the Participatory Status Model provided a view of some of the distinctions between face-to-face and virtual interactions. This is summarized in table 6. These findings suggest five candidate areas for designers to consider; space, group support, management of interactions, mobility of status and participation rights.

5.1 Space

A Digital City is based on a physical set of objects, a real city, and the intuitive step in moving this into a virtual setting is to incorporate locations, or rooms for users to inhabit. Mynatt et al [10] also note that although spatial metaphors provide a good foundation, virtual users exploit the ways technology breaks the properties of the physical world by communicating with spatially dispersed friends and 'teleporting' around an environment. They also note that designers should also support extensions to and breakage of the spatial metaphor. The findings of the present paper show that in this situation users develop new forms of conversational interaction and, correspondingly, new forms of participation. Users have to be somewhere in a virtual setting and the design solution lies in the balance between what is necessary for the individual to conceptualise where they 'are' in relation to others, and the communicative possibilities that such technologies provide.

5.2 Group Support

In TCZ, two thirds of all messages were multiparty. Community users are bound to have and make new friends based on social, interest or even business ties. Members of these 'sub-communities' may also be members of other 'sub-communities' and participate in multiple activities. Such interactions rely on awareness of the presence of others, and managing types of communication possible with others based on criteria such as privacy and scope (related to participation rights below).

5.3 Management of Interactions

Virtual conversations (according to the participatory definition of a conversation) are more frequent than in face-to-face. In environments that allow it, users maintain simultaneous concurrent interactions and supporting the management and control of these interactions is also an important design issue. Text based systems often offer better persistence of conversational history but do not provide support for segregating or tracking multiple conversations. For example, TCZ does not support multiple conversations, and users have to find unique ways such as message colouring and name prefixing to aid the management and control of this process.

5.4 Mobility of Status

Although there was no significant difference between the two corpora, mobility of status is still an important issue when 'competing' with other participants. One possibility is that systems can be designed to make it simple for users to signal that they wish to speak. Another possibility is that users could 'reserve' the next utterance in a discussion prior to a transitional point. Such ideas however depend upon the nature of the conversation taking place. In face-to-face there is normally only one speaker at a time, and where 'overlap' occurs (two people start speaking at the same time) one of them normally drops out immediately. In virtual interactions many people can speak at once, with the interlacing of messages guided by the time it takes to type and for the message to be distributed by the server. In face-to-face interaction, conditional relevance (the link between, say, an answer and the question it is a response to) is maintained almost always by temporal sequence. In a virtual environment these relationships can be supported in a variety of other ways. For example, allowing people to reorganise the text in a chat window, or the addition of graphical cues that indicate exactly what they are responding to.

5.5 Participation Rights

Having control over which, and by what method, others can participate with a user provides privacy when necessary and the scope, i.e. the number of available users, to participate with. This gives users a sense of control over their communications, with the ability to filter in or out messages from other users according to the 'participation rights'.

Online communities foster, both intentionally and unintentionally, new forms of communicative organisation. Designers need to be sensitive to this in both the design and evaluation of these environments. For example, the data in this paper underlines the point that making interaction in an environment more like face-to-face may inadvertently re-introduce some of the limitations of interaction in the physical world. Designing sustainable community systems can benefit from a clear understanding of the participatory and communicative differences between face-to-face and virtual interactions.

Acknowledgements

Reeves gratefully acknowledges the support of EPSRC through award number 00309527. Both authors wish to expresses their gratitude to the architects and residents of TCZ for their help in the development of this research.

References

1. Brown, J., van Dam, A., Earnshaw, R., Encarnacao, J., Guedj, R., Preece, J., Shneiderman, B., & Vince, J. Special Report on Human-Centered computing, online communities, and virtual environments. ACM SIGGRAPH Computer Graphics, 33(3), 42-62 (1999b).
2. Clark, H. Using Language. Cambridge: Cambridge University Press. 1996.
3. Garfinkel, H Studies of the Routine Grounds of Everyday Activities. Studies of Social Interaction. Sudnow, D (ed.). Free Press, New York. 1972
4. Goffman, E. Replies and Responses. Language in Society 5: 257-313. 1976
5. Goffman, E. Forms of Talk. Philadelphia: University of Pennsylvania Press. Ch 3. 1981.
6. Jikorta, M., Luff   P., Gilbert N. Participation frameworks for computer mediated communication. Proceedings of CSCW '91. Amsterdam. 1991
7. Kollock, P. Design principles in online communities. PC Update, 15, 58-60. (1998b).
8. Levinson S. Putting Linguistics on a Proper Footing. Exploring the Interaction Order, Erving Goffman pp. 170. 1988
9. Monk A. Participatory status in electronically mediated collaborative work. American Association for Artificial Intelligence. 1999
10. Mynatt, E. D.; Adler, A.;Ito, M.; O'Day, V. L. Design for network communities. Pemberton, S., editor, Human Factors in Computing Systems: CHI 97 Conference Proceedings; 1997 March 22-27; Atlanta, GA. New York, NY: ACM; 1997; 210-217 [MUD]
11. Preece, J. Online Communities: Designing Usability, Supporting Sociability. Wiley: New York. (2000)
12. Rheingold, H. The Virtual Community: Homestead on the Electronic Frontier, revised edition. MIT Press. (2000)
13. TCZ – http://www.tcz.net
14. BNC - http://www.hcu.ox.ac.uk/BNC/
15. http://www.dds.nl/
16. http://www.digitalcity.gr.jp/index-final.html
17. http://www.linturi.fi/HelsinkiArena2000/

Intention and Motive in Information-System Design: Toward a Theory and Method for Assessing Users' Needs

James P. Zappen[1] and Teresa M. Harrison[2]

[1] Rensselaer Polytechnic Institute, Troy, New York, U.S.A.
zappenj@rpi.edu
[2] University at Albany, SUNY, Albany, New York, U.S.A.
harrison@albany.edu

Abstract: Design of communication technologies such as our own effort to develop a youth-services information system for a local community, present practical problems in the collection and interpretation of data on users' needs and the development of design specifications responsive to these needs. Activity theory provides a conceptual framework for such a design effort by explaining how users' conscious intentions and unconscious or partially conscious motives can be inferred from their activities. Methodologies such as focus-group and participatory-design meetings provide appropriate means of collecting data on users' activities. Further development of conceptual categories for users' activities and for the development of design specifications will be necessary, however, to fully operationalize the theory.

1 Introduction

In its narrow sense, design is simply a model, representing a solution to a problem, as in *a design*. Mansell [21, p23-27], however, argues that design also encompasses an intention or purpose that guides the development of a model. This notion of design as intention or purpose is especially important for studies of communication technologies that encompass the creation as well as the use of these technologies, situated in their organizational and social settings and emerging and changing in space and time [20, p195; 25, p159-160]. Studies of communication technologies currently in use or after they have been in use for some time — including many studies of the Internet and the World Wide Web — focus their attention, quite reasonably, upon how users have *actually* used these technologies [11, 16, 22, 24, 26]. Research of this kind employs data-collection methods such as content analysis, surveys, questionnaires, and interviews, which provide direct reports of users' experiences [11, p353-356; 16, p333; 22, p411-415; 24, p297-299; 26, p20]. In addition, this research also employs focus-group or ethnographic methods to elicit more detailed accounts of these experiences [11, p 353; 22, p411-413].

In contrast, study of a communication technology still in process of development necessarily focuses upon how users expect or *intend* to use the technology. Such research will employ data-collection methods that seek to elicit users' expectations or

P. van den Besselaar and S. Koizumi (Eds.): Digital Cities 2003, LNCS 3081, pp. 354-368, 2005.
© Springer-Verlag Berlin Heidelberg 2005

intentions for a technology that they have never actually used and in some cases may not even have envisioned.

Activity theory provides a theoretical framework for such a study by distinguishing intentional actions from motivated activities, experienced at varying levels of consciousness and evident in the rules and conventions and the divisions of labor upheld within particular communities of users [3, 4, 5, 6, 7, 8, 9, 18, 19]. In addition, data-collection methods such as contextual inquiries, participatory-design sessions, focus-group meetings, and ethnographies permit more or less direct access to users' activities and experiences [1, 2, 10, 15, 17]. Guided by these theoretical and methodological perspectives, researchers may find that users' needs are more readily evident in their activities or in their accounts of their activities than in their explicit statements, especially with respect to a technology that the users have never actually encountered or even envisioned. However, even from these perspectives, users' needs will not be immediately intuitive or self-evident to researchers but will have to be inferred from users' accounts of their activities — thus adding to the challenge of data collection the further challenge of data analysis and interpretation.

We have drawn upon these perspectives in our efforts to develop a youth-services information system — called Connected Kids — for our own community of Troy, New York. We hope that our study of this system-in-use will contribute to the development of both a more fully functional system and a set of theoretical and methodological tools to support the *design* (as well as the *use*) of information systems and other communication technologies currently in process of development.

2 The Connected Kids Youth-Services Information System

The Connected Kids youth-services information system emerged from our efforts to develop an online community for the City of Troy, including both the technical and social infrastructures that we believed would be necessary to sustain such a community [13, p257-266; 14, p204-212]. A growing and increasingly sophisticated body of literature has established the close connection between online and offline communities as a correlative relationship that enhances both [11, p346-351, 365-368; 16, pp327-330, 339-342; 22, p410-411, 420-422; 23, p148-180; 24, p297-320; 26, p18-19, 26-31; 27, p2031-2033]. Putnam [23, p148, 166] traces a general decline of "social connectedness and civic engagement" in the United States in the last quarter of the twentieth century but views telecommunication as the most important counterbalance to this trend. But observable increases in social ties seem to depend upon a reciprocal relationship between online and offline communities rather than any characteristics of the medium as such. Wellman [27, p2032] observes that the development of online communities is not destroying but extending and transforming other types of communal association. Quan-Haase and others [24, p320] state simply: "Rather than weakening other forms of community, those who are more active offline are more active online — and vice versa." The result appears to be a net increase in social ties. Matei and Ball-Rokeach [22, p406, 420] claim a "the more, the more" relationship between online and offline social ties, and they find, moreover, that this relationship holds across differences in gender, income, age, education, and ethnicity. But the direction of this relationship is not yet clear. Kavanaugh and Patter-son [16, p340] refer to it as a "basic chicken or egg problem": Are social ties a prerequisite to or a consequence of the development of online communities? Or do they depend upon "a latent capacity for civic engagement in every community" [16, p340]?

Our work on Connected Kids does not attempt to answer these questions. Rather, it assumes a reciprocal relationship between online and offline communities, now well documented in the literature, and explores this relationship through an activist research agenda that seeks to design and implement and at the same time also to study both the technical and social components of an online/offline community. Our work began with our efforts to develop a World Wide Web presence for the City of Troy, called TroyNet (http://troynet.net/) [13, p257-258, 262-264; 14, p204-212] and became more focused and specialized as we became more aware of the special needs of particular segments of our community. Troy is a relatively small community with three colleges but also with relatively low levels of income and education within the general population. We initially envisioned TroyNet as a general-purpose information system serving this general population, including City and County government, City residents, tourists, students and their families, and not-for-profit organizations, among others. Thus we developed online resources such as planning and zoning ordinances, a directory of tourist information, accounts of local history, displays of local architecture, and the like. Largely as a result of an increasingly close partnership with the City of Troy, however, we soon became aware of special problems and needs such as the need to market tax-foreclosed properties and the City's new Historic Artist District (a revenue-generation issue) and the need to serve underserved and underprivileged segments of our population (revenue- and resource-allocation issues). TroyNet is helping to address the first of these needs, Connected Kids the second.

The Connected Kids information system (http://troynet.net/connectedkids/ and http://www.troyny.org/, under Other Community Resources) was initially proposed by the Mayor of Troy as a computer-based information resource for youth-services organizations, parents, and children [12]. It is currently being developed as a multipurpose database and World Wide Web interface by computer-science and communication faculty and graduate students at Rensselaer Polytechnic Institute and the University at Albany, SUNY, with funding from the 3Com Urban Challenge Program and the National Science Foundation and with support from the City of Troy, Rensselaer County, Rensselaer Polytechnic Institute, and numerous youth-services organizations. The information system will serve City, County, and public and private youth-services administrators, school officials, teachers and counselors, parents and children within this community and beyond. Our challenge is to design, develop, implement, and maintain a system that meets the needs of these diverse user groups, including the government sponsors who will administer the system, the youth-services managers and staff (sometimes the same person) who share decision-making responsibility for system components and contents and who will be responsible for entering their own and retrieving others' data from the system, and the various constituencies they serve.

3 Activity Theory as a Framework for Assessing Users' Needs

Activity theory provides a conceptual framework for situating the design of communication technologies — such as our Connected Kids information system — in time and space [3, 4, 5, 6, 7, 8, 9, 18, 19]. In its temporal dimension, design is a collaborative process in which participants from a diversity of perspectives question and analyze a problematic current practice; construct, examine, and implement a model solution to the problem; and evaluate and consolidate the outcomes of the process in new and stable forms of practice [5, p383-384; 8, p64-65]. This process is necessarily iterative and cyclical [3, p11-21] and encompasses a wide range of activities, from relatively simple purchasing decisions and procedural changes [5, pp. 385-402] to the most complex design activities [7, p327-370; 8, p67-77; 9, p139-147]. Engeström and Escalante [7, p338-370] demonstrate, however, that such processes can fail if designers are insufficiently attentive to the perspectives of both organizational service providers and the people who use their services.

In its spatial dimension, design is a complex set of technical and social components and relationships that together constitute "an activity system" [3, p22-42; 4, p29-32; 6, p73-91; 7, p365-370; 8, p61-64; 18, p34-37]. This activity system situates individual participants or subjects in relation to the objects of their activity, the artifacts that mediate that activity, and the communities, the rules and conventions, and the divisions of labor that both constrain and enable that activity. Within such as system, a design is complex, elusive, and constantly changing. Nonetheless, for our Connected Kids work this design is crucially important since it is precisely this design — this object — that we seek to identify and describe in our research. Activity theory tells us, however, that we should seek this object not in our users' conscious and articulate *intentions* but in their unconscious or partially conscious *motives* [4, p22-25; 6, p65-70; 7, p360-362; 8, p60-61; 9, p134-139; 18, p30-34; 19, p22-28], which are best reflected in their activities rather than their explicit expressions of goals.

In one of the founding texts on activity theory, Leont'ev [19, p22-28] distinguishes human activities, which are oriented toward objects and energized by motives; from actions, which are directed toward goals and guided by conscious intentions; and from operations, which are dependent upon specific conditions. According to Leont'ev [19, p22], the object of an activity may be either material or ideal but in either case is motivated by an unconscious desire or need. The goal of an action, in contrast, is guided by a conscious intention — "a conscious motive that is converted into a *motive-goal* precisely because it is conscious" [19, p25]. This conscious goal is the "intentional aspect" of an action [19, p26].

In activity theory, a design is not a conscious goal or aim, not even a singular object, but an ensemble of elusive and constantly changing objects, both material and ideal [7, p360-362; 9, p137-139). Engeström and Escalante [7, p. 360) explain that design objects, and especially those related to trade, administration, or scientific research, are "slippery and multi-faceted," "constantly in transition and under construction," and thus always potentially different for different participants. Their study of the design of an electronic kiosk for the delivery of postal services shows how such a design object may become very different ideal objects for different participants, at once both a mundane tool and an object of affection [7, p325, 365-370]. Similarly, Foot's [8, p68-69; 9, p139-141] studies of the development of a post-

Soviet ethnic-conflict-monitoring network show how another such design object may at once embody two different motivating ideals: the ideal of monitoring ethnic relations and providing early warning of potential conflicts and the ideal of building a community of expertise on post-Soviet ethnic relations. Engeström [6, p65-70, 73-82] finds the source of such differences in the larger social context of participants' activities and in the development of communities, each with its own rules or conventions and divisions of labor and each replete with contradictions, usually as a result of these divisions of labor. Despite such difficulties, participants' motives are nonetheless evident in their activities and in the larger social system in which these activities are embedded.

4 Methodologies for Collecting Data on Users' Activities

Methods of collecting data on users' needs—their expectations, intentions, and motives—thus focus upon their experiences and activities rather than their explicit statements and especially upon their collective experiences and articulations of these experiences. Proponents of data-collection methods such as contextual inquiries, participatory-design meetings, and focus-group meetings reaffirm these basic principles [1, 2, 10, 15, 17]. Holtzblatt and Jones [15, p182] maintain that data-collection methods such as surveys, interviews, and focus groups have limited utility for designers because they seem to depend upon what people say they want and need rather than what their work activities reveal about what they really want and need. In their work processes and in their use of computer tools, in particular, "people are engaged in doing work; they are not simultaneously reflecting upon their experience of doing work" [15, p182]. Holtzblatt and Jones [15, p181-199] therefore recommend their method of "contextual inquiry" — direct observations of workplace practices and structured interviews based upon these observations — as the best means of determining what users really want and need. Proponents of participatory-design methods likewise advocate direct observation of users' real-life or simulated work situations as the best means of determining users' needs [1, 2, 10]. Bødker and Grønbæck [1, p199-200] recommend their method of "cooperative prototyping" by which both designers and users participate actively and creatively in design processes by engaging users in fluent work-like activities with possible future computer applications, in either simulated or real-use situations, as a means of revealing otherwise unarticulated aspects of their work.

Proponents of these data-collection methods recognize also that both users' experiences and activities and their articulations of these experiences are often collective and collaborative [2, 10, 17]. Drawing upon Engeström's model of the activity system, Bødker and Grønbæck [2, p140-151] develop variations on the method of cooperative prototyping that engage designers and users in collaborative activities in both simulations of future work situations and explorations and investigations of future technological possibilities and current workplace practices in which users articulate their work tasks rather than actually doing them. Grønbæck, Grudin, and others [10, p80] note, furthermore, that these design activities always occur within particular socioeconomic systems, each with its own practices and rules and its own structures and processes for distributing labor and negotiating differences.

Krueger [17, p19-20, 34-36, 45] likewise notes the collaborative nature of focus-group discussions, which he claims can produce more useful information than individual interviews because they place participants in natural, life-like situations in which they both influence and are influenced by others. Krueger [17, p100-103] notes, however, that these group discussions depend for their success upon the guidance of a skillful and sensitive moderator.

5 Methodologies for Collecting Data in the Connected Kids Project

Based upon these theoretical and methodological perspectives, we developed a series of activities to involve our various users in the design of our proposed Connected Kids information system. These activities included focus-group meetings, participatory-design meetings, and user tests with representatives from youth-services organizations, parents, and children. For organizational users, we conducted focus-group meetings to develop system specifications, participatory-design meetings to elicit organizational users' perspectives on the design and operation of the system, and on-site user tests to check the WWW interface. For parents and children, we conducted focus-group meetings with different socioeconomic groups — including both low- and middle-income groups — to further refine the system specifications and to explore design possibilities for the WWW interface. We developed a protocol for each of these meetings, with a different set of "prompts" or illustrations and different kinds of questions for each group.

We suspected that many of our users would not fully understand the potential of an information system of the kind that we envisioned, and we therefore included prompts such as working illustrations of system capabilities and solicited responses to these illustrations from our users. For the focus-group meetings with organizational users, we developed a mock-up of our proposed information system. For the participatory-design meetings, we developed both a paper-based model of the system as a whole, based upon our users' responses to the initial focus-group meetings, and a functional online model of the data-input functions to permit hands-on experimentation with the system. For the focus-group meetings with parents and children, we presented a variety of working illustrations, including both search and browse operations for parents and dynamic and interactive WWW interfaces for children, selected by the children themselves.

We also developed different kinds of questions for each of these meetings. For most of the meetings, we asked questions designed to elicit users' responses to the prompts or illustrations that we had developed for each meeting. We expected that these responses would take the form of descriptive accounts or scenarios of our users' experiences or activities. At the initial focus-group meetings with organizational users, to elicit response to our mock-up of the proposed system, we asked, for example:

> So now, in looking at this, think about, say, the end product of what RPI would develop and that you would go to a terminal somewhere, and the organizations have already input their data, and you would come to something like this. How can you see something like this benefiting—two-part question—benefiting the different

organizations that are involved, and what concerns might your organization or other organizations have about this project?

For the participatory-design meetings with organizational users, however, we also asked some more direct questions to determine whether we had correctly understood our users' responses to the system mock-up presented at the initial focus-group meetings [12]. We asked, for example:

How do you see these database operations supporting the needs of your organization? Based upon what we heard you tell us in the focus groups, we are planning to provide information about your organization, its programs, and its events. Does this work for you?

At the focus-group meetings with parents and children, we presented a variety of working illustrations and asked questions designed to elicit users' accounts of their activities as information seekers and as computer users. We asked parents, for example:

What are the kinds of organizations, services, and activities in the Troy and Rensselaer County area that your children or other children you know are involved with now? How do you find out about the organizations, services, and activities that the Troy and Rensselaer County community has to offer for your children? Where do you get your information? How do you decide on the kinds of organizations, activities, or services your children will get involved with?

As expected, we received response in the form of descriptive accounts or scenarios of our users' activities. Even at the participatory-design meetings for organizational users, although we expected, and in fact received, direct answers to our direct questions, we also received descriptive accounts of the same kind that we received at the other meetings. We have previously presented a summary of our findings from the participatory-design meetings with organizational users [12]. Currently, we are transcribing the focus-group meetings with parents and children and developing descriptive categories for our analysis of the transcripts, based upon the theoretical and methodological considerations presented above. In the process, we have recognized that our analysis of these transcripts may not be as direct and straightforward as we had initially supposed since it will depend not only upon our categorization of certain kinds of activities but also upon our analysis and interpretation of the meanings and implications of these activities for the development of our information system. We have recognized, that is, that we will have to draw inferences that permit us to translate our users' descriptions of their activities into specifications for our design team, that our task is complicated by our users' sometimes conflicting accounts of their activities, and by differences in our own interpretations of these accounts. Below we present examples illustrating the difficulties of categorizing and analyzing the responses of each of two user groups: organizational users and parents.

6 Assessing Intentions and Motives in the Connected Kids Project

The responses of our organizational users focused largely upon the structure of relationships both between and within organizational units — reflections of their divisions of labor — and upon the representation of these structures of relationships to the organizations' constituents, in their roles as information seekers. The responses of parents focused upon their sense of responsibility as parents to provide positive activities for their children, with discernable differences, however, in the rules of behavior that operate within different socioeconomic groups. In both instances, users' accounts of their activities suggest a need to develop both online and offline communities of users, both the technical and the social dimensions of our information system. But these accounts do not convey our users' needs in the form of explicit design specifications. Rather, we need to infer these specifications from our users' descriptive accounts of their activities.

6.1 Example 1: Assessing Organizational Users' Intentions and Motives

On the basis of our meetings with organizational users, we developed the initial specifications for the Connected Kids information system and then confirmed and revised them as necessary. We had at the outset envisioned a system that would provide information about organizations' events and activities, with the capability to search for these events [12]. In our initial focus-group meetings with organizational users, however, we learned — and we believe that many of them also learned in the course of their discussions — that their more pressing expectations and needs were not so much to present information about events but to communicate their organizational identities and information about their programs and services, both among themselves and among their constituents. One participant presents a descriptive scenario in which the traditional structure of relationships among youth-services organizations has broken down since representatives from separate organizations, each with its own mission and purpose, no longer communicate with or even see each other:

> You would know more, about all of this, but it seems to me that when we did—and I used to be a part of it—but I used to see a lot of you a lot more frequently, and everybody would know what's going on, and everybody would be given [a word or two inaudible] money from the City to deal with youth. Now, I don't know how any of the [a word inaudible] here feel, but I mean we're dealing with youth, but yet we're the City of Troy and, and there isn't anybody to deal with youth, except separate organizations. There is no . . . we never have a meeting, I mean, I mean altogether, except for this, in years—at least eight to ten years. You're the County Youth Bureau, but I don't, I don't see you. Maybe you see my superior, but . . . on that level the people, the youth, the organizations—recreation especially—we deal with youth all year round. You [gesturing to another participant] deal with youth all year round. You [gesturing to a different participant] deal with youth all year round. But I never see any of you. You never see me.

This scenario suggests a need for more face-to-face communication among youth-services organizations. Another participant maintains, however, that the more immediate goal of these organizations should be to help us to define the information system. This participant suggests that goal of such a system should be to provide information not about organizations but about their programs and services:

> We wish that we could do that, but . . . so I don't actually think we need to know each other's missions, and I'd just as soon that we focus on the specifics of this task, which is really *defining* what it [the information system] needs to be because I don't think it's organizational as much as it is programmatic, you know, information about programs and activities, and that's what I think we should agree upon, and then perhaps, perhaps, this can be a catalyst for a forum, but I don't think we should mish mash one project from an ongoing . . . collaborative or group.

If we recall Leont'ev's [19] distinction between goal-oriented actions and object-oriented motives, then we might suppose that in this case the explicit goal of providing information about organizational programs and services does not seem to correspond (and the second participant suggests that it may actually conflict) with the underlying motive of helping organizations to communicate more frequently and more effectively among themselves — an apparent contradiction. These organizational users recognize their divisions of labor, their competition for funding, and their occasional "turf" battles, but they also recognize that they share a common mission of serving our area's young people, and they recognize as well a need to communicate more frequently among themselves. They do not seem to recognize, however, that the immediate goal of developing a youth-services information system and the underlying motive of improving communication among themselves complement rather than compete with each other. As we now know from the literature on online/offline communities cited above [11, 16, 22, 23, 24, 26, 27], the more people communicate online, the more likely they are to communicate offline, and vice versa. Such, at least, is the inference that we are inclined to draw from our organizational users' somewhat conflicted and uncertain discussion and from the results of numerous studies on the development of online/offline communities. But how should we translate such an inference into a set of design specifications? Should we build into our technical/social information system an email function? a bulletin board? a forum for face-to-face communication? all or some combination of the above?

In these same focus-group meetings, we also learned of our organizational users' need for a customizable WWW presence for their organizations, including a stand-alone presence for smaller organizations and an integrated presence with links to existing webs for larger organizations. In subsequent participatory-design meetings, we emphasized that we had heard our users' expressions of their need for an information system that provides information about their organizational identities, programs, and services, as well as their events, and that also provides a customizable WWW presence for their organizations. At these meetings, we provided both a paper-based model and an online prototype illustrating various components of the system, with emphasis upon the data-input functions. We then asked our organizational users whether we had understood correctly what they had told us at our earlier meetings. In response, they typically offered direct and explicit confirmations that we had correctly understood their initial descriptions of basic system contents and functions. But they almost immediately began to create descriptive scenarios depicting how the system might work for them. These scenarios apparently helped them — and also helped us — to understand how the various components of the information system mapped onto the complex structures of relationships — the divisions of labor — within their organizations. One participant from a large organization, for example, confirms that we share the same understanding of system contents and functions and then immediately attempts to envision how the system would represent the structure of relationships between his organization and his individual unit:[1]

> I think it will work well because I think in terms of an agency like [My Organization] where it is so large, and a lot of times, well just in terms of [My Unit] and some of the services that we offer, people just think [My Organization] and have to surf through a number of different links just to get to [My Unit], so it would be nice if we could have a direct link, as well as link back to the whole agency-wide site where you know they can gain more information and stuff like that, but it would be nice if we could have that link just so they could know what we're doing in terms of youth programming.

A participant from a small organization similarly confirms our shared understanding of the system and then immediately creates a descriptive scenario depicting the structure of relationships within her own organization and between her organization and the information system as a whole:

> I would say yes. I mean I don't have a website, I don't have the means to you know make a web page, I don't have the computer or staff to do that, to be my own person employed under this, so if there was one and you could connect it and then I could get up my own web page eventually, you could click on here so to speak and then get to my site as well, I mean you might get dual information though, I mean, you could stay with Connected Kids and work within [My Organization] it could have a site there, then if you want to go over to another one, out of it, could click over, you could click over, and then open up a whole, uh, [My Organization] itself.

In both instances, the participants attempt to depict the interrelationships of the various units within their organizations and to imagine how the information system will represent these interrelationships to their constituents. Their representations do not conflict and in fact appear to be complementary since the information system will include a WWW interface suitable for both large and small organizations. But how should it represent these organizations and the complex interrelationships of their respective organizational units? The two descriptive scenarios present a problem and a challenge rather than a solution, in the form of a set of design specifications. How should we translate these scenarios into a set of specifications that our designers can actually use to build the interface?

---

[1] In the following selection from one of the transcripts, we delete the names of the participant organizations and replace them with "My Organization" and "My Unit" [in brackets] to protect the identities of the organizations and to preserve the distinction between the larger organization and the smaller unit, which in this case actually has its own organizational identity. In subsequent selections, we similarly delete the names of participant organizations.

6.2 Example 2: Assessing Parents' Intentions and Motives

In our focus-group meetings with low- and middle-income parents, we sought to further refine the system specifications, especially the specifications for the search functions, and to explore design possibilities for the WWW interface. Like our organizational users, parents in both low- and middle-income groups typically responded with descriptive scenarios — but scenarios depicting not structures of relationships — divisions of labor — but rather parental responsibilities as defined and constrained by the rules or expected patterns of behavior that operate within each group. One parent from a low-income group, for example, describes the challenge of finding and accessing positive activities for her daughter, due to difficulties with transportation:

> Moderator: Are there other activities outside of Troy or Rensselaer County that your kids participate in?
> Female Parent 1: The Girl Scouts.
> Moderator: Where are they?
> Female Parent 1: They're in Albany . . .
> Moderator: Oh, They're in Albany.
> Female Parent 1: . . . on western Avenue [several words inaudible] . . . I use bus after bus after bus . . . four buses. But it's only one day out of the week, you know . . .

Later, she describes other kinds of activities and then—with encouragement from the moderator and another parent—reveals the unspoken rule or pattern of behavior that explains why she is willing to make such an effort to help her daughter to find appropriate activities:

> Moderator: What do you want to happen? What are the activities that you want . . ?
> Female Parent 1: Well, ah, you know, regular . . . baseball, basketball, some girls things, jump roping, ah, the girls like to, ah, . . . volleyball . . . I loved volleyball . . . you know, ahm, anything for the kids to do, like have plays and stuff like that . . .
> Moderator: OK.
> Female Parent 1: . . . that they could sign up for . . . talent shows . . . give them something they want to do with themselves, you know . . . maybe if they have a play to get ready for, you know . . . they'll practice . . . or have something to look forward to . . .
> Female Parent 2: Your daughter's very talented.
> Female Parent 1: . . . because, and I know, my daughter's one, she needed things to do . . . she was having really bad problems in school . . . her days wasn't going too good . . . she had too much energy for the little bit of time she had . . . and she's still bubbling with energy [a few words inaudible] . . . OK, let's color or, you know, let's go to the park [a few words inaudible] . . . she don't even want to go outside because there's nowhere to take her . . . she rides her bike . . .

Once again, if we recall Leont'ev's [19] distinction between goal-oriented actions and object-oriented motives, we can observe some dissonance between this parent's goal of getting her daughter to Girl Scouts and her underlying motive of keeping her troubled daughter busy with positive and constructive activities — again, an apparent contradiction. This parent's descriptive account of her activities does not help us to resolve the dissonance. Would she, in one possible interpretation, simply like to find a Girl Scout troop closer to home? Or might she, in another possible interpretation, be receptive to a variety of activities suitable for young girls? In this case, we do not necessarily need to resolve the dissonance and the potential differences in interpretation. Rather, we need to build into our information system a search mechanism that will find *both* Girls Scouts and other appropriate activities. But such a solution to the problem is, of course, quite complex both technically and socially. On the one hand, we will need to develop a *smart* search function that will find a range of activities suited to a user-entered profile, in this case, for a young girl. On the other hand, we will need to develop the social network sufficiently to ensure that we do in fact find — and enter into the system — both the local Girl Scout troop and a range of other activities — for the information system, however technically sophisticated, will be only as good as the social system that supports it.

Parents from a middle-income (and more computer-literate) group apparently have a similar sense of responsibility for their children, defined and constrained, however, by rules or patterns of behavior that require not only that they find and access appropriate activities for their children but also that they carefully assess the *quality* of these activities. Some of these parents describe a word-of-mouth sharing of information that they seem to assume as common practice. Parents looking for information about summer camps for their children informed us, for example, that they were interested not only in what an information system could tell them about the camps but also in what other parents could and would be willing to tell them:

> Female Parent 1: I would think that, uhm, comments from other parents would be helpful . . . some sort of reflection on the quality of the program, from their experience . . . because what, I think what parents do is . . . they ask each other . . . [several words inaudible, as several people talk at once] Then you find out. Was it a good experience? There's so many issues related to children being exposed to things that are inappropriate for their developmental level . . . uhm, you know, society is so much edgier, they have so much more access to information . . . a stimulus that really is not acceptable for them to be having access to . . . and so, uhm [several words inaudible] . . . but I think not sometimes, ah, but I think that that's important. What is, what, what is appropriate for what age group might be a good way to screen general [Inter]net, uhm, quality.
>
> Moderator: Uh, huh.
>
> Male Parent 1: I would, I would add to that . . . I agree that, you know, word of mouth seems to be or asking other parents about . . . seems to be important, but I think so much of that is sort of, uhm, is hard to, to sort of qualify because it's sort of like, you, you know, you sort of ask parents who you know maybe have shared the same sort of parenting skills or, or goals that you have, ah, you know, like if you like that camp, then I think it will be good for my daughter because, I know how, you know, I know how you raise your children, so therefore . . .
>
> Moderator: It's pretty subjective . . .
>
> Male Parent 1: Right. It's very subjective, but, I mean, it's sort of like, or, or you, uhm, maybe filter it like if so and so says this about it and, and this one says that about it well, you know, you know, there's issues with this child and parent, there's issues, you know, not issues, but you know, you know what people are like so you

sort of gauge your, your, your responses, so I guess it's difficult to, to maybe quantify that as a sort of hard fact.

These parents seem to be unusually sensitive to issues related to the quality of information accessible via the Internet and also cautious about the quality of information gathered from other parents. They recognize that different parents will have different perspectives on children's pursuits, and they also recognize that some perspectives may be better — for them — than others. In this case, the parents' goal of assessing the quality of the camps from the perspectives of other parents who share the same views of parenting as their own seems to accord with their underlying motive of finding quality activities for their children. But their motives may or may not accord with the motives of camp administrators. In either case, their description of their parenting activities does not translate directly into a design specification for our information system. Would these parents like to have access to a bulletin board or chat space where they could exchange information about summer camps and related activities? Can we build such a capability into our system? Assuming that we can, what will camp administrators think of such a capability? Will they appreciate such a free and open exchange of information about their camps? Will the motives of parents who want the best possible camp experience for their children accord or conflict with the motives of camp administrators to fill their camps and pay their bills — motives that they might not be willing to acknowledge, even to themselves? How should we attempt to resolve these contradictions?

7 Conclusion

We believe that activity theory and the methodologies for collecting and interpreting data that we have described above provide promising approaches to engaging users in the design process and making sense of their activities. But activity theory remains abstract, enriched by numerous case studies but difficult to operationalize in terms that are practically useful for designers. To render the theory operational, we will need to develop a set of conceptual categories for describing users' activities — more detailed and specific than the simple distinction between motives and goals and the broad concepts of divisions of labor and community rules and practices — and probably also a parallel set of categories for translating these categories of users' activities into specifications meaningful to designers. We anticipate that such a development will provide both a useful contribution to the theory and a practical guide for system developers.

Acknowledgements

This material is based upon work supported by the National Science Foundation under Grant No. 0091505. Any opinions, findings, and conclusions or recommendations expressed in this material are those of the authors and do not necessarily reflect the views of the National Science Foundation. The authors are grateful to Kirsten A. Foot for her comments on an earlier draft of this paper.

References

1. Bødker, S., Grønbæck, K.: Design in Action: From Prototyping by Demonstration to Cooperative Prototyping. In: Greenbaum, J., Kyng, M. (eds.): Design at Work: Cooperative Design of Computer Systems. Lawrence Erlbaum Associates, Hillsdale Hove London (1991) 197-218
2. Bødker, S., Grønbæck, K.: Users and Designers in Mutual Activity: An Analysis of Cooperative Activities in Systems Design. In: Engeström, Y., Middleton, D. (eds.): Cognition and Communication at Work. Cambridge University Press, Cambridge New York Melbourne (1996) 130-158
3. Cole, M., Engeström, Y.: A Cultural-Historical Approach to Distributed Cognition. In: Salomon, G. (ed.): Distributed Cognitions: Psychological and Educational Considerations. Learning in Doing: Social, Cognitive, and Computational Perspectives. Cambridge University Press, Cambridge New York Oakleigh Madrid Cape Town (1993) 1-46
4. Engeström, Y.: Activity Theory and Individual and Social Transformation. In: Engeström, Y., Miettinen, R., Punamäki, R.-L. (eds.): Perspectives on Activity Theory. Learning in Doing: Social, Cognitive, and Computational Perspectives. Cambridge University Press, Cambridge New York Melbourne (1999) 19-38
5. Engeström, Y.: Innovative Learning in Work Teams: Analyzing Cycles of Knowledge Creation in Practice. In: Engeström, Y., Miettinen, R., Punamäki, R.-L. (eds.): Perspectives on Activity Theory. Learning in Doing: Social, Cognitive, and Computational Perspectives. Cambridge University Press, Cambridge New York Melbourne (1999) 377-404
6. Engeström, Y.: Learning by Expanding: An Activity-Theoretical Approach to Developmental Research. Orienta-Konsultit, Helsinki (1987)
7. Engeström, Y., Escalante, V.: Mundane Tool or Object of Affection? The Rise and Fall of the Postal Buddy. In: Nardi, B. A. (ed.): Context and Consciousness: Activity Theory and Human-Computer Interaction. MIT Press, Cambridge London (1996) 325-373
8. Foot, K. A.: Cultural-Historical Activity Theory as Practice Theory: Illuminating the Development of a Conflict-Monitoring Network. Communication Theory 11: 1 (2001) 56-83.
9. Foot, K. A.: Pursuing an Evolving Object: A Case Study in Object Formation and Identification. Mind, Culture, and Activity 9: 2 (2002) 132-149
10. Grønbæck, K., Grudin, J., Bødker, S., Bannon, L.: Achieving Cooperative System Design: Shifting from a Product to a Process Focus. In: Schuler, D., Namioka, A. (eds.): Participatory Design: Principles and Practices. Lawrence Erlbaum Associates, Hillsdale Hove London (1993) 79-97
11. Hampton, K. N., Wellman, B.: The Not So Global Village of Netville. In: Wellman, B., Haythornthwaite, C. (eds.): The Internet in Everyday Life. The Information Age Series. Blackwell Publishing, Malden Oxford Melbourne Berlin (2002) 345-371
12. Harrison, T. M., Zappen, J.P.: Methodological and Theoretical Frameworks for the Design of Community Information Systems. Journal of Computer-Mediated Communication 8: 3 (2003)
13. Harrison, T. M., Zappen, J. P., Prell, C.: Transforming New Communication Technologies into Community Media. In: Jankowski, N. W., with Prehn, O. (eds.): Community Media in the Information Age: Perspectives and Prospects. Hampton Press, Cresskill (2002) 249-269
14. Harrison, T. M., Zappen, J. P., Stephen, T., Garfield, P., Prell, C.: Building an Electronic Community: A Town-Gown Collaboration. In: Shepherd, G. J., Rothenbuhler, E. W. (eds.): Communication and Community. Lawrence Erlbaum Associates, Mahwah London (2001) 201-216
15. Holtzblatt, K., Jones, S.: Contextual Inquiry: A Participatory Technique for System Design. In: Schuler, D., Namioka, A. (eds.): Participatory Design: Principles and Practices. Lawrence Erlbaum Associates, Hillsdale Hove London (1993) 177-210

16. Kavanaugh, A. L., Patterson, S. J.: The Impact of Community Computer Networks on Social Capital and Community Involvement in Blacksburg. In: Wellman, B., Haythornthwaite, C. (eds.): The Internet in Everyday Life. The Information Age Series. Blackwell Publishing, Malden Oxford Melbourne Berlin (2002) 325-344

17. Krueger, R. A.: Focus Groups: A Practical Guide for Applied Research. 2nd ed. Sage Publications, Thousand Oaks London New Delhi (1994)

18. Kuutti, K.: Activity Theory as a Potential Framework for Human-Computer Interaction Research. In: Nardi, B. A. (ed.): Context and Consciousness: Activity Theory and Human-Computer Interaction. MIT Press, Cambridge London (1996) 17-44

19. Leont'ev, A. N.: The Problem of Activity in Psychology. Soviet Psychology 13: 2 (1974-1975) 4-33.

20. Lievrouw, L. A.: Determination and Contingency in New Media Development: Diffusion of Innovations and Social Shaping of Technology Perspectives. In: Lievrouw, L. A., Livingstone, S. (eds.): Handbook of New Media: Social Shaping and Consequences of ICTs. Sage Publications, London Thousand Oaks New Delhi (2002) 183-199

21. Mansell, R.: Communication by Design? In: Mansell, R., Silverstone, R. (eds.): Communication by Design: The Politics of Information and Communication Technologies. Oxford University Press, Oxford New York (1996) 15-43

22. Matei, S., Ball-Rokeach, S. J.: Belonging in Geographic, Ethic, and Internet Spaces. In: Wellman, B., Haythornthwaite, C. (eds.): The Internet in Everyday Life. The Information Age Series. Blackwell Publishing, Malden Oxford Melbourne Berlin (2002) 404-427

23. Putnam, R. D.: Bowling Alone: The Collapse and Revival of American Community. Simon and Schuster, New York London Toronto Sydney Singapore (2000)

24. Quan-Haase, A., Wellman, B., with Witte, J. C., Hampton, K. N.: Capitalizing on the Net: Social Contact, Civic Engagement, and Sense of Community. In: Wellman, B., Haythornthwaite, C. (eds.): The Internet in Everyday Life. The Information Age Series. Blackwell Publishing, Malden Oxford Melbourne Berlin (2002) 291-324

25. Star, S. L., Bowker, G. C. How to Infrastructure. In: Lievrouw, L. A., Livingstone, S. (eds.): Handbook of New Media: Social Shaping and Consequences of ICTs. Sage Publications, London Thousand Oaks New Delhi (2002) 151-162

26. Van den Besselaar, P., Melis, I., Beckers, D.: Digital Cities: Organization, Content, and Use. In: Ishida, T., Isbister, K. (eds.): Digital Cities: Technologies, Experiences, and Future Perspectives. Lecture Notes in Computer Science, Vol. 1765. Springer-Verlag, Berlin Heidelberg New York (2000) 18-32

27. Wellman, B.: Computer Networks as Social Networks. Science 293 (14 September 2001) 2031-2034

The Perfections of Sustainability and Imperfections in the Digital Community:
Paradoxes of Connection and Disconnection

Gary Gumpert[1], Susan Drucker[2]

[1] Communication Landscapers,
6 Fourth Road, Great Neck, New York 11021, USA
listra@optonline.net
[2] School of Communication, Hofstra University
Hempstead, New York 11549, USA
sujie@optonline.net

> "The world is in chaos – struggling to master its own inventions. We are in danger of being annihilated by forces which we ourselves set up. The world calls for an answer to this problem of mastering our own inventions. And we propose, in 1939, to contribute to that answer." (Michael Hare, Secretary of the 1939 World's Fair)

1 Preface

In a world threatened by the inevitability of World War II the 1939 World's Fair featured the "Communication Zone." With the reshaping of the world through technological innovation the initiators of the fair understood that "in no field has the transformation been more come complete, more revolutionary than in that of communications." Television had just been introduced and was highlighted at the fair, but the public had yet to experience the impact of audio tape recorders, long playing records, Polaroid cameras, digital photography, facsimile, mobile telephony, cordless telephones, computers, the internet, satellite radio and television, cable television, xerography, CD (compact disk), DVD (digital versatile disk), hand-held communication devices or personal digital assistants and Walkman devices. The 1939 fair was dedicated to the 150th anniversary of George Washington's inauguration as President of the United States in New York City and highlighted the "new technological images of tomorrow." Michael Hare's prophetic double-edged description of the "world in chaos" and the "need to master our own inventions" seems particularly appropriate to an assessment of the impact of communication technology upon our urban environments 64 years later.

The phrase "the need to master our own inventions" causes one to pause and ponder what is meant. One implication is clear. Communication technologies are not neutral. They do not simply serve as conduits of distribution, as means of transferring information from place to place. But what exactly such technologies do to us is neither simple nor straightforward. In the foreground, communication technologies

P. van den Besselaar and S. Koizumi (Eds.): Digital Cities 2003, LNCS 3081, pp. 369-379, 2005.

connect one site with another. In the background, communication technology alters our expectations and our sense of self. Rebecca Solnits, in her fascinating biography of the early photographer Eadweard Muybridge, ponders over those great moments of technological gusts.

One way to describe this transformation of the world whose great accelerations came in the 1830s, the 1870s, and the age of the computer is as increasing abstraction. Those carried along on technology's currents were less connected to local places, to the earth itself, to the limitations of the body and biology, to the malleability of memory and imagination. They were moving into a world where places were being homogenized, where a network of machines and the corporations behind them were dispelling the independence of wilderness, of remoteness, of local culture, a world that was experienced more and more as information and images. It was as though they sacrificed the near to gain the far [23, p.22].

In a 1985 article entitled 'Media Grammars, Generations, and Media Gaps" Gumpert and Cathcart noted: 1) that each medium has a unique set of codes and conventions; 2) that these codes and conventions constitute a media grammar which become a part of our media consciousness; 3) that our personal perceptions and values are altered by such media grammars; and 4) that the order in which such grammars are acquired produces a generational world perspective uniquely defined by those available and inherited technologies [10].

It is the essence of the medium, the grammar that defines one medium from the other that also is built into the expectations and attitudes of a public that has inherited a set of communication technologies that characterize the temporal and spatial relationship of individual to place. Thus, for example, multiple perspectives juxtaposed in real time initially defined the medium of live television. In order to process the medium of television, the individual viewer had to accept the convention of multiple points of view and the relocation of self in relationship to place. The image of an object taken from a distance and than immediately followed by a close-up of that object is not perceived as discontinuous, but continuous. Every medium of communication imposes a similar set of such conventions determined by the technological features of that medium. Every individual inherits and is defined by the existing media available and operating. They are expected to be literate in film, radio, television, and the Internet. Media generations focus on the micro level with emphasis on the individual and interpersonal. *Medium theory,* particularly helpful in considering the large scale impact of media, examines "such variables as the senses that are required to attend to the medium, whether the communication is bi-directional or uni-directional, how quickly messages can be disseminated, whether learning to encode and decode in the medium is difficult or simple, how many people can attend to the same message at the same moment, and so forth." [17, p.50]. Media theorists taking this approach ask the question: "What are the relatively fixed features of each means of communicating and how do these features make the medium physically, psychologically and socially different from other media and face-to-face interaction?" According to Meyrowitz, medium theory represents a perspective through which to understand how a medium is appropriated by a culture and tries to account for its social, psychological, and political impact. While the focus is on the medium, this is not to suggest that medium theory looks at the technology alone. Rather, it is the interaction between the media technology and humans that is significant. Taken together, these two media theory perspectives provide an approach through which to examine the individual, interpersonal and societal impact of media.

The media literate 21st century citizen has absorbed techniques, grammars and expectations into their media psyche. These fixed features include:

1. *Interactivity/Interaction:* Action of the user generates a response either from another human being or computer program at the other end of the media connection. Interactivity is associated with action-reaction or command-response exchanges. Interactivity allows a user to make choices that will result in a variety of responses. Interaction and interactivity is associated with person-to-person contact and interactivity is associated with person-computer exchanges.

2. *Immediacy of Response:* The relative ease with which a sender receives a response to a specific message. Swift feedback becomes a norm. The expectation of immediate connection and prompt response results in willing interaction with either a constructed artificial r response system or a human being – sometimes they are indistinguishable.

3. *Privacy:* Control of personal contact and information. We have witnessed the ascendancy of privacy as a value in tandem with new opportunities for privately accessed interaction. While "private social space" is an important constituent of the media environment, surveillance technology suggests that privacy of information does not exist. Concern for privacy has stimulated a great deal of media coverage and commentary where repeatedly the message was that "legal, technological and cultural changes have undermined our ability to control" our personal information [21]. In the face of an ever-increasing awareness of the diminution of privacy, the illusion of privacy is fostered by the increased control of contact and content afforded by digital media.

4. *Anonymity of Interaction:* The nature of the medium makes it possible to hide or fabricate identity. Anonymity is extremely effective in promoting freedom of expression but anonymity hinders some methods of controlling the actions of other people. Alternatively, digital environments offer opportunities for pseudonymity. A pseudonymous user may be more responsible for his or her actions than the completely anonymous user but is still liberated to a degree from accountability. In reality, what is experienced is more aptly described an illusion of anonymity.

5. *Increased Sense of Control:* Choice of contact, channels and time is an essential component of the media environment. Digital media offer "bi-directionality". Data can flow in both directions. The increased ability to "block" or "pull" in data or programming on demand promotes a sense of control.

6. *Access Regardless of Distance:* Space and location are less significant if not irrelevant with connection a primary goal of a digital environment. Local does potentially become global and global local.

7. *The Eradication of Time:* The global standardization of time was a development of the late19th century. Before that, all time was local time. "Before the railroads, each city and region kept its own time by the sun" [23 p.59]. At 9:00 a.m. in New York it is 7:45 p.m. in Bangalore.[1] The "outsourced" service force of Bangalore is synchronized and coordinated to serve the United States work force. The relative immediacy of transmission juxtaposes time zones.[2]

---

[1] In his essay on Cybertime Lance Strate suggested, "we can look forward to the integration of computers and computer networks into one great global clock" [24 p.368].

[2] This aspect of time with regard to etiquette and effectiveness is media dependent. Each medium has conventions linked to fixed features. While one is able to make phone connections across multiple time zones, there remains sensitivity to the location based nature of time when determining how and when to use the medium. Some media appear appropriate

8. *Simultaneous Channels of Communication:* Simultaneous or concurrent activity via multiple channels of communication is promoted through media convergence. Multi-tasking facilitated by a transparent interface promotes gliding from medium to medium.
9. *Control of Digital Properties:* The transition from analog to digital brings with it the ability to control and reconstruct discrete binary elements that constitute any given content. This feature introduces all sorts of questions regarding authenticity, authorship and property rights.

2 Digital Presence

Identifying the features of digital media helps shed light on experience in both physical and media environments. The notion of "presence" is helpful in locating the relationship of individual to place. "Presence" refers to "a psychological state of subjective perception in which even through part of an individual's current experience is generated by and/or filtered through human-made technology, part or all of the individuals perceptions fails to accurately acknowledge the role of technology in the experience" [13]. The individual functioning in a digital environment operates in a unique environment that has been described as being convergent. Convergent technology refers to media environments in which discrete media, once considered unique, operate and function concurrently on the same digital platform. The person who enters the urban environment of the 21st century becomes part of a *"generation of convergence"* in which simultaneity, multiple processing, and compound perspectives are commonplace, necessary and expected. We keyboard the computer, listen to radio, and converse with a colleagues next us, while watching television and the news bulletins being scrolled along the bottom of the screen. It is disconcerting and distracting for some, but for others it is an accepted and understood convention. William Mitchell notes: "Over the course of a hundred years – particularly in the last couple of decades – the convergence of increasingly capable wireless technology with expanding network infrastructure, miniaturized electronics and proliferating digital information has radically refashioned the relationships of individuals to the their constructed environments and to one another." [18 p.2]

3 The Paradox of Communication Technology

There is an inherent sense of paradox in how communication technology functions. It is never a simple sensory extension. Elsewhere we have said: "The more we extend our connection, the more insular we become. The more we control our communication environment, the less is surprise or chance a daily expectation. The more we connect, the more we seek to control the connection. The more we detach from our immediate surroundings, the more we rely upon surveillance of the environment. The more communication choice offered, the less we trust the information we receive. The more information and data available, the more we need.

---

irrespective of time when asynchronous communication meets the needs of the communicator.

The more individuality we achieve, the more communities we seek. The more we extend our senses, the less we depend upon our sensorium." [9]

It is this sense of contraction that permeates the relationship of person and place when a medium of communication is interposed.

1. Every medium *connects* two or more locations.
2. Every medium involves some degree of *disconnection* between person and one of those locations.
3. Every medium functions either *centrifugally* or *centripedally* – that is moves information inward or outward.
4. The media of sound and photography rest upon the *'isomorphic fallacy'* – the assumption that a medium reproduces an image or sound that is, to some degree, faithful to the original.

4 The Changing Nature of Community

Communication technology is changing the means and ways that people relate to each other. As the organizers of this workshop have pointed out, the "role of place" is of crucial importance. Quite clearly the nature of "community" is at the heart of the matter. The concept of "digital cities" makes a number of assumptions.

1. That the contemporary city requires a technological infrastructure that supports economic and social development. John Eger, president of the World Foundation for Smart Communities has said, "Cities have no choice, to aggressively embrace information technology as a catalyst for transforming life and work...or be cut-off from the mainstream of economic development." [5].
2. That networking (the electronic connection of distant sites) plays an integral role in the reshaping of the city. The contemporary network refers not only implicitly to relationships, but also explicitly to the configuration and description of community grounded upon wires, fiber optics, nodes, routers, and strange blinking lights.

It is in this context that cities and community need to be assessed. Much has been written about the demise of American cities and the nature of community, much tends to romanticize a state of existence that probably never existed. What is self-evident is that American cities have suffered under the tyranny of suburbanization. The reasons for this state of disintegration are complex and outside the time and scope of this paper, but certainly the rise of an automobile society, restrictive zoning policies, relatively low-cost suburban housing, the incorporation of air-conditioning (with its accompanying disconnection of outside from inside) and the acceleration of communication technology have contributed to the current situation. The city in which obligation and responsibility to the immediate community was a requirement gave way to different social structures facilitated by newer modes of communication. Communities of "connection" rather than "obligation" have become the focus of much attention - from Melvin N. Webber's consideration of "community without propinquity" or "non-place communities" back in 1964 [26 p.116] to Howard Rheingold's seminal "Virtual Community" [20] onward there has been a growing literature examining online community construction, community networks, and the fabrication of digital communities [2, 22]. A shift in values and civic responsibility has occurred. In his book on "Great Streets" Allan B. Jacobs wrote: "...Streets are what constitute the outside for many urbanites; places to be when they are not indoors. And streets are places of social and commercial encounter and exchange.

They are where you met people - which is a basic reason to have cities in any case. People who really do not like other people, not even to see them in any numbers, have good reason not to live in cities or to live isolated form city streets." [14 p.4]

The invigorating street has given way to the quite street. The very nature of public has been privatized. It is the strange bizarre behavior of the public use of mobile telephones in which private conversations occur on the street, in buses, trains and planes, in cafes and restaurants as if there were no one else around. It is what Solnit describes as "disembodied private space in public. A space they share with those who are not there and that shuts out those we are [23 p.256]." The exciting socially bound community has given way to the rise to the mentality of the "Suburban Nation" [4].

The traditional neighborhood was the fundamental form of European settlement on this continent... It continues to be the dominant pattern of habitation outside the United States, as it has been throughout recorded history. The traditional neighborhood – represented by mixed-use, pedestrian-friendly communities or varied population, either standing free as villages or grouped into towns and cities – has proved to be a sustainable form of growth. It allowed us to settle the continent without bankrupting the country or destroying the countryside in the process.

Suburban sprawl, now the standard North American pattern of growth, ignores historical precedent and human experience. It is an invention, conceived by architects, engineers, and planners, and promoted by developers in the great sweeping aside of the old that occurred after the Second World War. [4 p.4]

Somewhere in the transition from the tradition of "neighborhoods" to "scatteredhoods" the accelerated contribution of the computer comes into play perhaps even to the rescue. The computer, in tandem with a host of other communication technologies, in all of their digital magic, began not only to facilitate communication, but also to rescue or liberate the user from the dictates of the fixed place and dedicated points of communication. The city as we knew it began to stimulate and compete with its newer variations:

1. *The virtual city*, based on the paradigm of the old, but residing in the structured assembly of a city.
2. *The edge city*; the imitation of the corporate inner city located somewhere between the edge of the old city and suburbia.
3. *The teleport*, the newly created hi-tech computer oriented city generally placed in a developing nation.
4. *The digital city*, the older city revitalized, seldom by plan, by a newer electronic infrastructure.
5. *The online or smart city*, an existing physical city with services and structure represented and available on the Internet.

All of the variations on a theme of city assume that the old romanticized notion of dynamic "metropolis" with its stress on face-to-face interaction, civic engagement, social obligation, and entertainment needs to be adjusted, at least modernized. All of the variations require a degree of modifying the notion of "presence" – the location and relationship of individual to the city of place.

5 Displacement Revisited

When we presented some of our ideas at the Digital Cities II conference in Kyoto we introduced the idea of "displacement" - the "reciprocal and defining interdependence of place modified by communication technology." [7 p.30] We approached that concept primarily from a temporal perspective – that is, the amount of time spent in media activity fundamentally alters the amount of time available for other traditional events. It is thus self evident that the contemporary individual spends an increasing amount of time electronically connected with others in lieu of physical interaction on a face-to-face basis. But it also occurs to us that process of connection brings with it a degree of "replacement" as well. By "replacement" we mean the substitution and or alteration of one or more locations for another." Digital connection reconstitutes the paradigm of place and location.

6 The New City – The "Tertium Quid" City

The reconstituted city, altered in any degree by communication technology represents the *tertium quid* - an organization and structure linked to two or more locations and times, but distinct and unique. This new city is related to and yet distinct from the other types of cities and is a *tertium quid*, since it is unknown but related in some way to known things [3]. The city is greater than the sum of its electronic and physical parts. Let us assume the following about the individual functioning in the 21st century city:

1. That such an individual will spend some proportion of his/her time in mediated communication activities.
2. That some elements of daily life will have been transformed from a primary locus of operation (in which location and presence coincide) to an extended and secondary one.
3. That it is not only media content but also the form of the medium that must be considered. The media of the digital city consist of both discrete and convergent technology – from voice mail to e-mail, from radio and television broadcasts to data transfer, from DVD to digital photography.

The *tertium quid city* represents a conceptual compromise between the city that was and the city that has been electronically created. Digitalization alters and irrevocably modifies the nature of relationships between individuals and their environment [6].

The physical environment and the media environment have come to define each other. Another way of stating that premise is that the relationship of non-mediated and mediated communication activity is recombinant in the sense that William Mitchell has used the term to describe the phenomenon of digital technology recomposing homes, office, communities, and cities. In the preface to Thomas A. Horan's *Digital Places: Building Our City of Bits* William Mitchell discussed the publication of his 1994 volume, *City of Bits* explaining the significance of digital revolution upon cities: "I suggested that digital telecommunications networks would transform urban form and function as radically as piped water supply and sewer networks, mechanized transportation networks, telegraph and telephone networks, and electrical grids had done in the past. By supporting remote and asynchronous interaction, these networks would loosen many of the spatial and temporal linkages that have traditional bound human activities together in dense clusters, and they would allow new patterns to emerge. We would see the fragmentation and recombination of familiar building types and urban patterns." [12 p.xi]

Much has been made of "Recombinant Architecture" focusing on computer mediated collaboration and the changing conditions of architecture in the information age. Recombinant architecture has at its heart issues of retribution of the functions of buildings, transportation systems and computer networks [18]. The recombinant city results in a redistribution of the senses and this fundamentally defines our relationship and obligation to the physical city. Unlike the recombinant city with its reorganization of human activity into new and mediated forms guided by a novel architecture and infrastructure, the *tertium quid* city infers and requires the preservation of the old with the new and the rediscovery of the physical environment experiences through all the senses.

7 Sustainability and the Digital City

There is a literature that looks at sustainable media environments – an orientation primarily found outside the United States and inextricably linked with the "MacBride, Third World, Developing Nations, Digital Divide," and "The People's Communication Charter" critique based upon the inequitable distribution of communication wealth [11]. Sustainable media environments have been the topic of concern to organizations concerned with media development. In the 21st century, the community related themes of sustainable development are now, or potentially will be, intertwined with media development. Community building is facilitated and altered by (if not relegated to) media space. The resultant *tertium quid city* raises unique questions of sustainable development.

Where does the "digital city" exist in the scheme of things? By this time, all cities, whether by design or by accident, whether in a deteriorating or renaissance state are, to some degree, "digital." (As we found out recently in New York, you cannot have a city without electricity.) Digitalization promotes a sense of transparency, this permeability of function and medium, is linked to an illusion of transparency that characterizes the digital city. Psychological presence shifting seamlessly from online environment to home, from text messaging on a mobile phone to the commuter train in which one is traveling raises questions as to the degree to which the introduction of digital communication technology shifts and alters the equilibrium of social interaction.

For the first time in human civilization there is a choice. Leaving the digital city for the virtual city? "Theoretically, a virtual world is perfectly sustainable placing the individual in a position of total media dependency in regard to social relationships and community construction. In a virtual world the individual functions in multiple non-place based communities. It is, however, not possible to exist in a totally virtual world. The reality of 21st century daily life involves more individuals beginning to migrate into more controllable [16], less physically threatening realms of cyberspace and surveillance camera filled streets. [6]. Unable to depart from the physical city completely, the physical environment and the media environment have come to shape and redefine each other.

Sustainable development in the physical environment elevates strength of community, self-sufficiency, economic opportunity, equal access to resources and conservation as essential. Local conditions, including natural resources, politics, and quality of life are essential matters. Today, is it possible for a community to be sustained in the 21st century without dependency upon global media connections? Has media dependency been integrated into a contemporary vision of community? The challenge for the digital city is found in the question: How much can a community depend upon external connection and remain an identifiable community.

The digital revolution challenges traditional forms of social cohesion associated with traditional cities. Given the fixed features of digital media it comes as no surprise that "t[T]he technology of communication, while extending our ability to transcend locality also accepts and demands control of the environment" [8]. Media technology provides individuals with the ability to insulate oneself by controlling connection and exposure. Unpredictability or serendipity is reduced in an environment in which content and connection "on demand" is available. By nature, cities offer a precarious balance predictability and unpredictability, of recognized contact and the choice of some anonymity. Cities offer opportunities to engage or evade interaction. But cities are threatened with unwanted sensory stimulation: undesired noise, unpleasant sounds, smells and unwelcome physical contact. The control and choices offered by digital media are not generally available in the physical realm of the digital city. Gone is sensory selectivity, contact and content by choice, and safety in personal preference. City life has a downside.

8 The Paradigm of the "Tertium Quid City"

The real challenge is to design the digital city, that is to say, the *tertium quid* city, to encompass the values of traditional cities. How can the technology be used to generate a sense of place needed for sustainable community development? The people who inhabit digital cities are of a new media generation. They are people with a digital consciousness and expectations. They are not the same as those who inhabited the traditional city yet sustainable communities and social cohesion remain positive goals of development. The social and political institutions structuring and governing the lives of the digital generation are shaped by and in turn shape the digital city.

One simple exemplar of the new city is the integration of wireless data technology, Wi-fi, in which hot spots are transforming the use of airport waiting lounges, college campuses and even coffee shops. By providing immediate high-speed wireless electronic connection for a mobile data generation, the physical environment provides a transparent interface between traditional and virtual cities. A recent Gartner report said the number of North Americans who access the Internet from public Wi-Fi hot spots jumped to 4.7 million this year from 1.6 million last year, and will reach 17.5 million in 2005. There will be approximately 29,000 public hot spots available by the end of the year in North America, a vast increase in just one year [25]. From McDonald's to Starbucks, marketers see a value in offering Wi-Fi. From New York and to smaller cities like Long Beach, California, Wi-Fi is being integrated into the infrastructure of the city, if not the psyche of the public [15]. Experiments in Paris could make that city of light and public life, a leader in Wi-Fi. In May, 2003, in a trial, a dozen antennas were erected outside Metro stations lining a major north-south bus route providing internet access to anyone with the proper equipment. In July 2003 Webgazon was launched by a group of organizations including France Telecom as an experiment to study the integration of free hot spots throughout Parc LaVillette [1]. In response to the quandary of designing a profitable business plan for Wi-Fi, a free Wi-Fi movement has been launched. While accommodating the digital generation, societal impact can be anticipated. What effect will Wi-Fi have on "physical presence," that is to say, a sense of physical space? What effect could "a sense of being there" have on civility or social cohesion in cities if surfing the web while café sitting results in "perceptual immersion?" [13].

The technological infrastructure required for such a wireless environment is beginning to receive the attention of planners and urban developers who view Wi-Fi as a device to attract commerce and individual users back to the city – that such an innovation might serve as a tool for urban renewal in which cities offer free wireless access to downtown areas and provide some a means of reconciling community and 21st century urban/technological developments. There is a sense of paradox in these developments in which a renaissance in the physical is contingent upon access to the digital.

Because communication technology is not reversible, one cannot undiscover the technology or eradicate the awareness of that invention from human consciousness, digital cities must be understood and considered as a force with potential transformational influence. Digital media individuals and institutions cannot merely be superimposed on traditional cities but the fixed features of digital media must be integrated into the bricks and mortar of the digital city.

References

1. Aquiton, C.: Interview, Paris, Parc LaVillette. (Aug. 2, 2003)
2. Barnes, S.B.: Online Connections: Internet Interpersonal Relationships. Cresskill, N.J. : Hampton Press (2001)
3. Collins English Dictionary, Site visited Aug. 15, 2003
   http://www.wordreference.com/english/definition.asp?en=tertium+quid.
4. Duany, A., Plater-Zyberk, E., Speck, J.: Suburban Nation, The Rise of Sprawl and the Decline of the American Dream. New York: North Point Press (2000)
5. Eger, J.: Interview Grid, Site visited Aug. 7, 2003
   www.govtech.net/publications/gt/1998/dec/grid/question1.phtml.
6. Gumpert, G. & Drucker, S.: Ubiquitous Technology in the Media Age and the Ideal of Sustainability. Explorations in Media Ecology 2 (2003) 1-14
7. Gumpert, G. & Drucker, S.: Privacy, Predictability or Serendipity and Digital Cities. In: Tanabe, M., Van den Besselaar, P., Ishida, T. (Eds.): Digital Cities II. Springer-Verlag, Berlin etc. (2002) 26-40
8. Gumpert, G. & Drucker, S.: A Plea for Chaos. Qualitative Research Reports in Communication 2 (2001) 25-32
9. Gumpert, G. Communications and Our Sense of Community: a Planning Agenda, Inter/Media 24 No.4. August/September (1996) pp.41-44.
10. Gumpert, G., Cathcart, R.: Media Grammars, Generations, and Media Gaps. Critical Studies in Mass Communication. 2 (1985) 23-35
11. Hamelink, C.: The People's Communication Charter, An Introduction. Transnational Broadcasting Studies 2 (1999) http://www.tbsjournal.com/Archives/Spring99/spr99.html.
12. Horan, T., Mitchell, W.J.: Digital Places: Building Our City of Bits. Urban Land Institute. (2000)
13. International Society for Presence Research, Site visited, Aug. 9, 2003
    http://www.temple.edu/ispr/explicat.htm.
14. Jacobs, A. B.: Great Streets. Cambridge, MA, MIT Press (1993)
15. Markoff, J.: More Cities Set up Wireless Networks, The New York Times (January 6, 2003)
16. McKenzie, E.: Privatopia - Homeowner Associations and the Rise of Residential Private Government. New Haven, CT, Yale University Press (1996)
17. Meyrowitz, Joshua. "Medium Theory." Communication Theory Today. Eds. David Crowley and David Mitchell. Stanford, California: Stanford University Press, (1994) 50-77.

18. Mitchell, William J.: Me ++; The Cyborg Self and the Networked City. Cambridge, MA, Massachusetts Institute of Technology Press (2003)
19. Paris Becoming World Wireless Leader. The New York Times (May 14, 2003)
20. Rheingold, H.: The Virtual Community - Homesteading on the Electronic Frontier. Reading, MA, Addison-Wesley Pub Co. (1993)
21. Rosen, J.: The Unwanted Gaze - The Destruction of Privacy in America. New York, Random House (2000)
22. Schuler, D. & Stone, T. (Editors): New Community Networks - Wired for Change. Reading, MA, Addison-Wesley Pub Co. (1996)
23. Solnit, Rebecca: River of Shadows - Eadward Muybridge and the Technological Wild West. Viking (2003)
24. Strate, L. "Cybertime" in Communication and Cyberspace: Social Interaction in an Electronic Environment. Cresskill, New Jersey, Hampton Press, Inc. (1996)
25. Tedeschi, B. Eating Out and Logging On. The New York Times (July 14, 2003)
26. Webber, M. N.: The Urban Place and the Nonplace Urban Realm; Explorations into Urban Structure. Philadelphia, University of Pennsylvania Press.(1964)

The Promises and Perils of Integrated Community Learning Environments

Stefan Welling, Andreas Breiter

Institute for Information Management, Bremen
welling@ifib.de, abreiter@ifib.de

Abstract. Bridging the digital divide is a major endeavour in many cities, especially offering learning opportunities for underserved groups. As a major target group, teenagers are addressed. While the first stage was to provide access to technology, empirical research has shown that support is necessary to develop the necessary digital literacy. But as we will show, only full integration into the life world of teenagers will really support their learning process. Using examples from our fieldwork in a regional learning environment, we focus on schools and youth centres as being very important locations for the personal development teenagers. Through a careful analysis of strengths and weaknesses especially of the so-called Web.Punkte projects, we will suggest further activities to reach the next stage of life world integration.

1 The Need for Improved Learning Environments

Despite all variances, there is a common understanding among researchers, politicians and businesses that learning is a crucial condition for societal participation in its different shapes. This is especially true for living in the so-called information society where the ongoing diffusion of information and communication technologies (ICT) puts new demands and challenges on learning and learners. Additionally, ICT is becoming an integral component of the learning process itself (e.g. using instructional software to achieve certain learning goals). Since technological changes are continuous, an understanding and the capability for learning are needed to follow the developments.

Accordingly, many countries have started initiatives aimed at keeping up with the increasing impact of ICT on learning. But, as studies on the so-called 'digital divide' have shown, the effective and efficient use of digital media technologies and the necessary cultural capital for dealing with information and knowledge are unequally distributed. It seems that the less formal education one has the less likely it is that he or she will make use of digital media. Overall, especially so-called underprivileged groups have not been making the utilisation of the digital media part of their everyday life [10, 11, 25]. The lack of digital literacy, i.e. the competences needed for a meaningful utilization of new media, correlates with general literacy deficits. Sufficient reading skills, for instance, are an indispensable pre-condition for Internet utilisation. It is striking that apparently many underserved youths do not meet these

P. van den Besselaar and S. Koizumi (Eds.): Digital Cities 2003, LNCS 3081, pp. 380–390, 2005.

demands [17]. This can become a vicious circle because traditional cultural skills as literacy and numeracy are a prerequisite for using digital information and communication technologies effectively and efficiently for work, everyday activities and learning.

We argue that learning occurs in different ways and that the formal, mainly curriculum-based learning in school is only one facet of the learning environment that surrounds young people. Alternative learning opportunities, like in youth centres, can be more appropriate for those who fail in school and may also include ICT. Imagine, for instance, a group of young girls who often play tenant from school but meet regularly at a youth centre to practice hip-hop dancing. With the help of a youth worker, they take some pictures and together with some info text put it all together on a web-site to promote their activities. In this informal environment the girls gain new skills and self-confidence that may foster the achievement of additional biographical orientations.

In an integrated community learning network such activities may be the result of cooperation between schools and youth centres in a certain neighbourhood. Schools may open their computer labs in the afternoon for project-oriented media work with youth centres. Both institutions could use the same network infrastructure, bringing the idea of synergy into practice. Youth centre staff may call the same technical support service as schools and thereby profit from a joint user help desk as a single point of contact. Eventually, the cooperation takes off the ground when youth workers and teachers start to cut-off their biased opinions, attend joint-trainings and closely work together to serve the youths of their catchment area.

We will explore the possible benefits and challenges of an integrated community learning network for the improvement of learning in its different shapes especially for underserved youth. Building on the idea of the social proximate space as a major point of reference for the socialisation of children and youth we will first discuss the importance of cultural and social capital for learning. Underserved youth regularly only find limited opportunities to accumulate cultural and social capital. We argue that the conditions of learning and the acquisition of social and cultural capital could be improved significantly within a regional learning network. Public schools and the entities of youth work, which are, above all, youth centres, are two major players in such a network. Against the background of these two institutions we discuss the perils and the possible benefits of a community learning network. With regard to the age range of the visitors or users of these institutions we focus on teenagers.

For this purpose we build on our experience from working with both entities for a considerable time in different contexts. With Web.Punkte (http://www.webpunkte-bremen.de) we ran a project that provided schools with an additional computer lab that should also serve the surrounding community. An extensive evaluation report provides valuable data for this paper [6, 7]. With PowerUP Bremen Neustadt we integrated a computer lab into a low-income neighbourhood and learned a lot about the challenges of computer-supported youth work [23]. Extensive work on IT planning and management in schools, a research project about the conditions of a milieu-sensitive computer-supported youth work [24] and the ongoing attempt to set up a regional learning network for the Bremen area provide us with further knowledge we build on for the purpose of this paper.

2 Community Learning Cooperation for Underserved Youth

Community learning can be conceptualised as any learning activity undertaken on an ongoing basis inside or outside educational institutions with the aim of improving individuals' literacy. The manifold notions of literacy, the confoundedness of the term with other variables as well as its covariance with other social factors as schooling, complicate the investigation of the term. Regularly, literacy is thought of as the ability to make "full sense and productive use of the opportunities of written language in the particular culture in which one lives" [21, p143]. Thereby, literacy is not "a neutral denoting of skills, it is always literacy for something – for professional competence in a technological world, for civic responsibility and the preservation of heritage, for personal growth and self-fulfilment, for social and political change" [13, p75-76]. From this understanding, literacy goes beyond a narrow cognitive skill but is rather a set of social practices. Its acquisition is therefore "a matter not only of cognition, or even of culture, but also of power and politics" [22, p45]. Many of these practices are enacted within the so-called social proximate space (see figure 1).

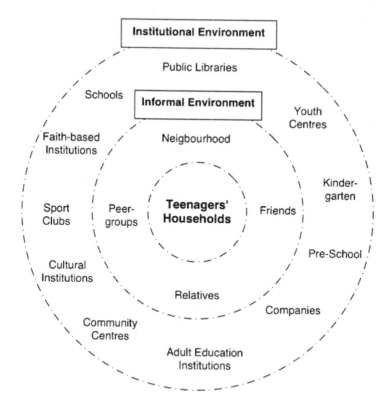

Fig. 1. Learning environment within the social proximate space

The household is the core unit of the social proximate space. Most household's teenagers live in still consist of the traditional two-parent family even if the shapes of households have been becoming increasingly diverse. Different networks within the informal environment put teens in relation to relatives, friends and acquaintances and, what is especially important to peer-group members. Due to the timely expansion and intensification of the youth period, adolescents spend more time in peer-groups than ever before. Apparently, youth has become it's own and most important reference group that shapes personality development and accomplishment of life [12]. For many youths, the peer-group is also the central location in the search for life orientations as a basis for the development of biographical perspectives [4, 19, 14]. The informal environment is surrounded by several institutions, which also offer learning opportunities for individuals as well as for families. This institutional environment provides the basis for additional relations between staff members of these institutions and teenagers.

The different relations and interdependencies within and between these two environments can also be thought of as a network. Such a network of more or less institutionalised settings of mutual awareness and acknowledgement, which embodies the entirety of current and potential resources, can also be referred to as social capital. These resources are based on the affiliation with groups like family, as well as relatives or groups mostly living in close proximity and they own shared norms, values and understandings [18, p18-25], [17]. Within the household, social capital is especially important for the accumulation of cultural capital by the adolescent generation [5, 9]. Bourdieu differentiates between incorporated and institutionalised cultural capital. Whereas the first includes all kinds of knowledge somebody owns, the latter appears in the shape of advanced graduation certificates, apprenticeship certificates or academic certificates. The ability to acquire cultural capital is strongly influenced by the family of decent, so that this form of capital is heavily shaped by the circumstances of its first acquisition. Thus, the family provides the basic ground for the symbolic effectiveness of cultural capital.

Apparently, certain societal groups lack social capital to foster the development of cultural capital of their children. This is especially true for youth with migration background. In Germany, about forty percent (in 1998) of the native adolescents attended high school ('Gymnasium'), compared to only ten percent of the youths of non-German decent. More than two thirds of this group visited lower secondary schools (up to 9th/10th grade), compared to 20 percent of the German adolescents [8, p122]. Another indicator for a strong social exclusion from cultural capital of youth from non-German decent is the reading competence level. The recent study of the OECD Programme for International Student Assessment (PISA) among 15 years old revealed huge disparities. From almost half of the teenagers from migrant families who achieved not even reading competence level 1 more than 70 percent went through the complete German school system, which requires a compulsory education of at least nine to ten years [3, p379]. Germany is the country with the highest correlation between social descent and educational success.

If we assume that digital media might support learning in and outside school, it is crucial to offer underserved youth opportunities to access and use these technologies. As empirical studies show, the intensity and quality of media use by these groups as well as the development of limited media practices may further increase this situation of disadvantage. On the other hand, digital media could provide new opportunities and chances for underserved youth. The most important precondition for such a strategy to be successful is the integration of these technologies into the every day life of the people. Yet, this has been achieved only in few projects.

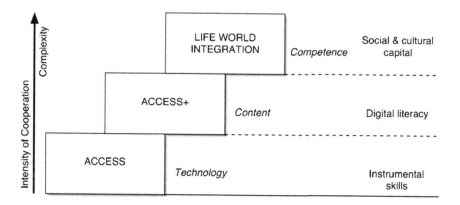

Fig. 2. Stages of ICT integration for underserved youth

First attempts to provide opportunities to engage with new media for underserved groups were mainly focused on *access* to technology (stage 1). Early studies on the digital divide were mainly concerned about this unequal access. Accordingly, the first step was to equip educational institutions with computers and Internet connections where instrumental skills like keyboarding, word processing or basic Internet use could be learnt. Enormous amounts of money have been invested in hardware, software and networks. By the end of the decade, it became clear, that the digital divide is more than just an issue of equal access [15, 16].

Stage 2 was to provide supported access (*Access+*) for specific user groups. This approach is mainly related to the necessary skills for effective use, about access to training and digital content (e.g. [20]). This is the basic concept of digital literacy [2]. But, as the work of Ba et al. illustrates, the concept of *"Access+"* still does not include the user's perspective in a sufficient matter.

Following the definition of the American Library Association (ALA), the concept of digital divide has to be redefined as it characterizes differences in access to information through the Internet and other information and communication technologies and services, and in the knowledge, skills, and abilities to use information, due to geography, race, economical status, gender and physical ability [1]. Based on empirical evidence, we suggest a broader view on digital divide as well as necessary skills for underserved youth (stage 3). Hence, both human and social systems must also change and ICT must be *integrated into the life world* of teenagers.

"Access to ICT is embedded in a complex array of factors encompassing physical, digital, human and social resources and relationships. Content and language, literacy and education, and community and institutional structures must all be taken into account if meaningful access to new technology is to be provided" [22, p6]. Given that, a stronger cooperation between the various institutions that surround the life world of teenagers is needed. While during the first two stages mainly bilateral agreements were necessary, especially between the 'parent organisations' of the learning institutions, the next step requires mutual understanding and support in a larger regional learning network (see figure 3).

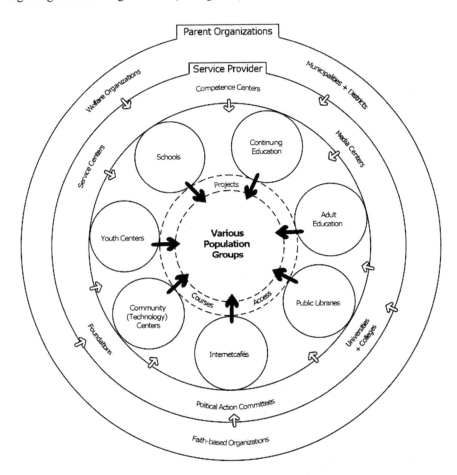

Fig. 3. The Regional Learning Network

In order to sketch the complexity of cooperation and coordination, we will focus on two institutions that play the most important role for teenagers: schools and youth centres. Establishing cooperation between these two institutions is an ambitious venture. There is ongoing competition about resources, as both institutions are mainly financed by taxpayers' money but administered by different agencies. In Germany, faith-based institutions, charities and other non-profit organisations also sponsor youth centres but not schools. As schools are a constitutional task of the state, their financial support is more sustainable. For both institutions, the political action space is limited as they belong to hierarchical organisations but they report to different agencies which themselves tend not to cooperate. Due to their size, schools are key players within the community and play an important role for the majority of families with children. Youth centres are smaller, less visible and rather serve minority groups.

Additionally, education of teachers and youth workers is different which results in different income and social status. Youth workers usually spent 3 years at a University of Applied Sciences ('Fachhochschule') and another year as apprentices. In most youth centres additional (often part time) employees do not necessarily hold a professional pedagogical degree. Turn over rate for these people are also often relatively high. This may effect the development of pedagogical strategies. Teachers have 4 years of university education, specialise in two or more subjects and gain practical experience during 2 years compulsory training in schools. During their education and even more during their work, they have developed different pedagogical philosophies and didactical approaches. Youth workers tend to favour informal learning in project-based environments with voluntary members while teachers work in institutionalised settings with compulsory members within a stronger curricular framework.

Regarding the pedagogical work with digital media, the gap is even larger. While teachers usually work in whole-class settings in computers labs – only few have PCs in their classrooms – using the computer as a tool, digital media are used flexibly and autonomously by participants in youth centres. The organisational environment and the individual action space are also different. From the schools' perspective, expanding school-community cooperation must be seen as an innovative process in connection with other reform efforts (such as accountability, autonomy, new curricula) that are loaded onto schools and their administrators. In most German state constitutions, opening the school for the community is a key goal and part of school development planning. From the youth centres' perspective, cooperating with schools requires a lot of effort to cross the boundaries between the pedagogical and professional visions.

3 Web.Punkte as Nodes of a Regional Learning Network

In order to move one step beyond access to information and communication technologies, the State of Bremen (Germany) has set up a unique project as a public-private partnership with Deutsche Telekom AG. The idea was combining access to ICT with support (*access+*). Schools build the core from which content-driven activities with students as well as with members of the local community should take place in computer classrooms. As German schools are mainly part-time schools, other institutions such as youth centres, community centres or public libraries should also use the resources. The vision of the 'Web.Punkte' project was driven by five main goals:
1. Improving the schools' resources for access and use of digital media
2. Broader use of IT resources in schools outside school hours
3. Increasing community involvement
4. Help to bridge the digital divide through providing the community with supported internet access
5. Increasing student's competencies by intensive training to work as 'Web.Scouts' to support visitors

Schools had to go through an application process before they were accepted. The project application had to be approved first by the school board, which is the ultimate decision-making committee at the school level, consisting of principal, teachers, parents and students. The applications were ranked according to the following criteria: quality of the concept for community integration, regional distribution, plan for opening hours, selection and support of Web.Scouts (especially addressing gender issues and social background), and cooperation with parents' association. The implementation was divided into a 6 months pilot phase with six pre-selected schools. After that, the review committee received 30 applications (out of 60 eligible schools) and selected 19 sites with which a contract was negotiated. The schools received a refurbished and renovated room, a high value technical infrastructure (15 PCs, a laptop, peripherals, a fast T1-line for the Internet connection and a complete local area network) and the parents' association received funding to pay the Web.Scouts and for meeting ongoing costs.

During the formative evaluation with quantitative and qualitative methods (for details see [6]), it became obvious, that school-community cooperation was only established in a few school sites and could only be achieved through an intensive coordination by the project management. Getting the local community involved was very ambitious and worked only in parts. The activities of the school to draw attention to use the Web.Punkt were very much dependent on the sites, the local project coordinator and the principal. Furthermore, schools with prior experience in working with the local community had an advantage although some new links could be established.

In many of the Web.Punkte, the initial external user group were senior citizens who took the opportunity to learn how to use the Internet with the help of the Web.Scouts. The effects of increased intergenerational communication between the different age groups are difficult to measure, but the reports, site visits and qualitative interviews showed impressive results. Hence, the group of Web.Scouts profited the most. Their motivation to come to school increased significantly and their teamwork with peers helped to support external users. Additionally, the students identified with their schools, regarding the Web.Punkt as their room, which they had to protect and to keep running. In most schools, the Web.Scouts were carefully selected according to gender and their social background. One school worked only with female Web.Scouts, another only with Web.Scouts with migration backgrounds. According to group interviews with Web.Scouts in selected locations, the students were very satisfied with the offered preparation courses that were especially designed for the project. The reward in the form of a certificate for participation was highly regarded.

Dual use of the equipment by youth centres, adult education centres and schools could only be achieved in a few sites. By far the majority of users [(80 per cent) were students of the same school who used the equipment instead of their home PCs and valued the engagement with the peer group. Unexpectedly, most teenagers also had PCs at home, which implied that the Web.Punkt was a social room rather that a place to offer access to computer and Internet for "nonliners". During after-school hours most locations are dominated by students of the school and from other schools unless there were dedicated courses for teachers or other groups.

The problems of school-community integration and joint projects with youth centres can be analysed along the framework described above. There is a need of top-down initiatives in order to change culture and attitude – pressure of change. This is a necessary but not sufficient condition. At the same time bottom-up activities are crucial in order to keep on working. Wherever schools already had strong links to community centres and youth centres, the cooperation worked easily. Only in few examples, the envisioned move to life world integration has already been begun. One school works closely together with the youth centre, offering specific courses for single mothers with a migration background. The courses are taught employees of the youth centre. The female Web.Scouts (mostly themselves from migrant families) taught them how to use the Internet while volunteers looked after their younger children in the school. In another school, the initiative was started by a group of Turkish mothers who were interested in using the Web.Punkt for their specific training needs. With the help of a social worker, they offered courses for the neighbourhood, which were attracting other families.

The intensity of cooperation between the different agencies depends on the area and the problems to be solved. On the bottom end, cooperation to save scarce resources is much easier to establish than developing pedagogical content and working intensively with teenagers within their families and peer-groups. From the perspective of the governing agencies for both schools and youth centres, due to limited public funding, the future lies in joint projects and a commonly used infrastructure. Economies of scale and increasing standardisation of hardware may foster the development of a common strategy. This includes central IT procurement processes and a shared network infrastructure (Internet access and value-added services) for all educational institutions. The cost of broadband access (which is becoming more and more important for high-quality digital material) is too high for youth centres. Attaching them to the schools' backbone will save resources and, additionally, facilitates joint Internet projects. Within the project Web.Punkte, the implementation of a user help desk was started. Currently, technical support for most schools is provided by a non-profit organisation, which has already been in charge of maintenance and service in schools for two years. Students from different faculties have helped schools with their technical problems. They have set up a user help desk with a call centre and a web-based FAQ-list. Additionally, they work on-site in schools. The support centre is working in more than 50 per cent of the schools in Bremen and might be extended to youth centres.

4 Perspectives

From our work in both youth centres and schools as well as on a project, which aimed to bring the two institutions together, we can derive the following results. There are small-scale impacts in some schools and some youth centres, which closely work together to support the development of their clients. Closer cooperation helps to build a better and mutual understanding about the basic orientations, attitudes, dispositions as well as interests and wants of teenagers as an important basis to serve their educational needs. Probably the most important large-scale impact is the popularization of the idea to work with teenagers as Web.Scouts for peer-to-peer support. This approach is highly valued by educators in both institutions as well as among students. It was already copied by other institutions which offer supported access and would like extend this concept.

Our empirical research supports the fact, that digital divide is much more than a question of access to ICT infrastructure. There is a shared understanding among researchers that access to computers and Internet is a necessary but not a sufficient condition to allow all groups to participate in the so-called information society. Using digital media as tools to achieve individual goals require skills, which are unequally distributed. Hence, underserved youth need learning opportunities that go beyond digital literacy. Supporting underserved youth today is giving them the opportunity to participate in formal and informal learning activities as adults tomorrow. More and more courses and learning content are delivered online. As most studies have shown, non-participation in education appears to be caused mainly by long-term socio-economic background characteristics rather than access to ICT. There is yet no evidence that digital information and communication technologies are doing anything other than appealing to those who are already likely to be participants in formal learning processes.

School-community cooperation can help to fill the gap but needs investment in coordination. There is empirical evidence from the Web.Punkte that school-community cooperation can work if there is a long-term engagement from both sides and a common pedagogical understanding of the clients (teenagers). In order to establish such links, coordination is necessary which needs to combine actors from all institutions as well as from the administration. Going beyond the question of access, the next step is to produce, disseminate and share valuable digital material and pedagogical concepts. In special modules, key actors in both youth centres and schools could be trained in how to use digital media in formal and informal education processes. The courses might be created in a blended learning environment in order to combine methods of educating at a distance with digital media and traditional on-site education. Even more difficult is integrating digital media to support acquiring cultural capital into the life world of teenagers. This requires intensive cooperation and a common understanding between various social agencies and the readiness of families and teenagers to participate.

References

1. ALA: Digital Divide. American Library Association. Office for Library Technology Policy. (200) http://www.ala.org [14.03.2003]
2. Ba, H., Tally, W., Tsikalas, K.: Investigating children's emerging digital literacies. Journal of Technology, Learning and Assessment 1(2002) 4. http://www.jtla.org.
3. Baumert, J., Schümer, G.: Familiäre Lebensverhältnisse, Bildungsbeteiligung und Kompetenzerwerb. In: Deutsches PISA-Konsortium (ed.): PISA 2000. Basiskompetenzen von Schülerinnen und Schülern im internationalen Vergleich. Opladen, Leske + Budrich (2001) pp. 323-397
4. Bohnsack, R., Loos, P. (et al.): Die Suche nach Gemeinsamkeit und die Gewalt in der Gruppe - Hooligans, Musikgruppen und andere Jugendcliquen. Opladen: Leske + Budrich (1995)
5. Bourdieu, P.: The Forms of Capital. In: Richardson, J. G. (ed.): Handbook of Theory for the Sociology of Education. Westport, CON: Greenwood Press (1986) 241-258
6. Breiter, A.: Public Internet Usage Points in Schools for the Local Community. Concept, Implementation and Evaluation of a Project in Bremen, Germany. Education and Information Technologies 8 (2003) 109-125

7. Breiter, A.: Regional Learning Networks - Building Bridges Between Schools, University and Community. In: T. van Weert & B. Munro (eds.): Informatics and the Digital Society. Social, Ethical and Cognitive Issues. Boston, MA: Kluwer (2003) 207-214
8. Bundesregierung: Lebenslagen in Deutschland. Der erste Armuts- und Reichtumsbericht der Bundesregierung. Berlin (2001)
9. Coleman, J.: Social Capital in the Creation of Human Capital. American Journal of Sociology 94 (1988) 95-120
10. Cooper, M.: Disconnected, Disadvantaged and Disenfranchised, Explorations in the Digital Age. Consumer Federation of America, Consumer Union (2000) http://www.consumerfed.org/digitaldivide/ disconnected102000.pdf [23.03.2001]
11. EOS Gallup Europe: Flash Eurobarometer 125. European Commission, Directorate General Information Society (2002) http://europa.eu.int/information_society/eeurope/benchmarking /list/source_data_pdf/report_eb125_en.pdf [07.01.2003].
12. Ferchhoff, W.: Aufwachsen heute: Veränderte Erziehungs- und Sozialisationsbedingungen in Familie, Schule, Beruf, Freizeit und Gleichaltrigengruppe. In: Schell, F., Stolzenberg, E. and H. Theunert (eds.): Medienkompetenz. Grundlagen und pädagogisches Handeln München, KoPäd (1999) 200-220
13. Knoblauch, C. H.: Literacy and the Politics of Education. In: Lumsford, A.A., Moglen, H. and J. Slevinn (eds.): The Right to Literacy. New York: Modern Language Association (1990) 74-78
14. Nohl, A.-M.: Migration und Differenzerfahrung. Junge Einheimische und Migranten im rekonstruktiven Milieuvergleich. Opladen: Leske + Budrich (2001)
15. NTIA: Falling Through the Net: Defining the Digital Divide. National Telecommunications & Information Administration, U.S. Department of Commerce, Washington, DC (1999)
16. NTIA: Falling Through the Net: Toward Digital Inclusion. National Telecommunications & Information Administration, U.S. Department of Commerce, Washington, DC (2000)
17. OECD: The Well-Being of Nation, the Role of Human and Social Capital. Centre for Educational Research and Innovation, Paris: OECD (2001)
18. Putnam, R. D.: Bowling Alone, the Collapse and Revival of American Community. New York: Simon & Schuster (2000)
19. Schäffer, B.: Die Band - Stil und ästhetische Praxis im Jugendalter. Opladen: Leske + Budrich (1996)
20. Servon, L.J.: Bridging the Digital Divide; Technology, Community, and Public Policy. Malden, MA: Blackwell (2002)
21. Smith, F.: The Creative Achievement of Literacy; Awakening to Literacy. In: Goellman, H. Oberg, A.A., Smith, F. (eds.): The University of Victoria Symposium on Children's Response to a Literate Environment; Literacy Before Schooling. Exeter: Heinemann Educational Book. (1987) 143-153
22. Warschauer, M.: Technology and Social Inclusion: Rethinking the Digital Divide. Cambridge, MA: MIT Press (2003)
23. Welling, S.: PowerUP Bremen Neustadt and the Engagement of the Telecommunications Research Group in the Field of Computer-Supported Youth Work. (2002) http://www.fgtk.informatik.uni-bremen.de [10.01.2003].
24. Welling, S.: Youth and New Media, Framing the Conditions of a Milieu-Sensitive Computer-Supported Youth Work. (2003) http://www.emtelconference.org [27.04.2003]
25. Wilhelm, T. (et al.): Connecting Kids to Technology; Challenges and Opportunities. (2002) http://www.aecf.org/publications/pdfs/ snapshot_june2002.pdf [09.07.02].

Effects of ICT on Social Cohesion: The Cyburg Case

Dennis Beckers[1], Wouter van Gent[1], Jurjen Iedema[2], Jos de Haan[2]

[1]University of Amsterdam, The Netherlands
D.Beckers@os.amsterdam.nl
[2] Sociaal en Cultureel Planbureau, Den Haag, The Netherlands

Abstract. We study the effects of local community networks on social capital and participation in a heterogeneous urban neighborhood. We found that the effects of ICT use on social capital are dependent on education and income, and that the use of neighborhood infrastructures is low, as the systems were very much a top-down initiative. We discuss the implications for designing and organizing systems that aim a social cohesion and supporting social capital.

1 Social Cohesion Under Pressure

The cohesion of our society has changed during the last decades. Traditional social relationships made way for new ones. The roles of institutions as the family, school, unions, church, and associations have also changed. People started to think differently about norms, values, religion and politics. The traditional family is no longer the standard and cultures from all over the world interweave. There is growing consensus that these changes in urban-industrial society have seriously effected social cohesion [5], but the opinions differ on whether this cohesion has improved or deteriorated.

Municipalities and local welfare organizations fear a decline of social cohesion in urban neighborhoods because it would lead to feelings of isolation and insecurity of inhabitants and a slow integration of foreigners. In various places, experiments are conducted with the application of information and communication technology (ICT) aimed at the local level, to contribute towards the increase of social cohesion between the residents of urban neighborhoods and to reinforce local communities. The Internet provides new possibilities for interaction between inhabitants of neighborhoods (e.g. by e-mail, chat boxes and discussion lists) in addition to already existing means of interaction. The growing use of these extra possibilities means an increase in electronically mediated social contacts. Since the time devoted to direct (face-to-face) contacts has been declining for some time now, it may be asked whether social interaction via the Internet does indeed constitute a replacement of unmediated contacts or whether other factors are (also) at work. The Internet not only provides opportunities for the maintenance of social contacts but also for entering into new ones.

In this chapter, we will contribute to the discussion on the effects of ICT on social cohesion in urban neighborhoods on the basis of empirical data. The main research question concern the relationship between social cohesion and the use of ICT in a heterogeneous, multi-cultural community, namely Zeeburg in Amsterdam, the Netherlands. Does new technology contribute to the improvement of social cohesion?

P. van den Besselaar and S. Koizumi (Eds.): Digital Cities 2003, LNCS 3081, pp. 391-406, 2005.
© Springer-Verlag Berlin Heidelberg 2005

We will answer this question on the basis of the case of the 'Cyburg' initiative in Amsterdam. Section 2 gives a brief review of literature on the concepts of social cohesion and social capital. Next, the most important findings of previous research on effects of ICT on social cohesion are presented (section 3). Section 4 describes the city area of Zeeburg, Amsterdam and the Cyburg project within the framework of this research. The research methodology and collected data are described in section 5. In section 6 the results is presented. The chapter concludes with recommendations for governmental institutions and organizations for the foundation of web sites for increasing social cohesion in city neighborhoods (section 7).

2 Social Cohesion, Social Capital, and ICT: A Literature Review

Social cohesion is a diffuse notion of which many different definitions are in use. However, all these definition have some elements in common as the notion points always towards the coherence of a social system, the bonds between people and their mutual commitment and solidarity.

The operationalization of social cohesion in this chapter is mainly based on the work of Robert Putnam. In his book *Bowling Alone*, Putnam presents an impressive amount of data and shows in this way how, during the last decades the social structure of U.S. society started to unravel. He defines social capital as the "social networks and the norms of reciprocity and trustworthiness that arise from them" [15]. Putnam thus sees social capital as the expectation of an individual that other citizens will follow norms of reciprocity and trust. In this chapter the notion of social capital will be used as an equivalent of the term 'social cohesion'.

According to Putnam, social capital, or the absence thereof, affects the well-being of individuals in every aspect of their lives. According to him, individuals with high social capital are more productive and less prone to depression. Social capital improves both their mental and physical welfare. For communities, social capital is also important as research suggest it reduces crime, juvenile delinquency, teenage pregnancy, child abuse, welfare dependency and substance abuse [15].

From the literature it appears that the degree of social cohesion an individual experiences depends both on individual characteristics as well as characteristics of groups, neighborhoods and cities. Positive influences in the amount of social cohesion of the individual level are income, education, employment and having children. On the level of the neighborhood, it appears that when large social inequality exists between groups of residents, distrust can begin and individuals will be less inclined to do one's best for each other. Ethnic diversity plays also a part. Finally, high geographic mobility would be less favorable for the social cohesion in the neighborhood; after all, one who will move soon will invest less time in social relations in a neighborhood.

Decline of Social Cohesion
The idea that social ties between residents are weakening was mentioned over 100 years ago by authors as De Tocqueville, Tönnies, Simmel and Durkheim [4]. They assumed that the transition towards modern industrial civilization would go hand in

hand with the 'uprooting' of people from their social environment, caused by among others reasons the movement of workers from the countryside to factories in cities.

With the transition towards the information society, the discussion about the decline of social cohesions has become current again. According to Putnam, the most important cause of the decline of social capital is a demographic shift. Older generations are replaced by younger generations who are far less civic-minded. Other social changes have magnified this trend. Television has become a primary source of leisure, decreasing more sociable leisure-time activities. Women have poured into the formal labor force, opening new possibilities for them, but at the same time the neighborhood and voluntary organizations have lost unpaid workers. Working professionals face increasing pressure to work long hours and weekends, forcing them to skip school meetings and family dinners. Last, the proliferation of suburbs, with their car-focused culture and absence of community spaces, has distanced neighbors from each other [15].

3 Effects of ICT on Social Cohesion

During the last decade much research has been conducted on the effects of ICT on social cohesion. However, these led to many different conclusions. Three groups of conclusions can be distinguished in order to categorize the research on the effects of ICT on social cohesion.

Internet improves social cohesion: Research in this category is positive about the effects of the Internet, particularly about the possibility for social relations without distinction by age, race, religion, gender or location [2, 6] These researchers provide empirical evidence that the Internet contributes to participation and has positive effects for finding and maintaining social relations [7, 10].

Internet reduces social cohesion: Contrary to the previous results are those authors who point to the temptations of online environments, that would cause users to spend less time with their families and friends. Also, new possibilities for global communication would alienate users from their local environments and decrease their interests in local politics. This would all lead to isolation and atomization of Internet users [19] and therefore contribute to the further disintegration of communities, the loss of social ties and decrease of wellbeing [9, 12].

Internet changes social cohesion: The third group departs from the idea that the effects of the use of the Internet are embedded in the social complexity of daily life. Internet has become part of daily life and is now a new means of communication, alongside older media. Internet is mainly used for maintaining existing social relations, for hobbies and political interests. This suggests that the Internet helps to strengthen existing patterns of social contacts and civic participation [24]. Wellman claims that contemporary communities consist of networks. These networks can be locally based, but could also be mediated, for example by telephone or the Internet and interlink with other networks. Personal social networks thus consist of various communities as family members, co-workers, members of interest groups and neighbors. Based on this line of thought, Wellman concludes that social cohesion does not decrease, but that the composition of personal social networks changes. The

Internet stimulates commitment but also exposes people to more contacts and more information, what may reduce commitment to their local community [24, p.22].

How can these differences between studies be explained? First large differences exist between the definitions and operationalization of the terms used. These differences make the results of the research difficult to compare. A second possible cause is that some studies only distinguish between those who use the Internet, and those who do not, without correcting for social demographic factors as education, age, income, work and number of people in the household. Such a simple distinction does not provide insight in the question whether Internet users have more social contacts because of the Internet, or because they are on average higher educated *and* use the Internet more often than lower educated people [13]. Studies also show the location of Internet use (at home or work), time and goal are important for the social effects of Internet use [11]. A last possibility is the difference between locations where studies took place. The majority of results comes from the U.S., but many circumstances as costs of telecommunication and cultural meaning of terms as 'individualism' and 'community' and geographical distances differ from for example European countries. Therefore the findings of these studies can not be applied to other countries without taking local circumstances into account [23]. In the Netherlands, communication via digital networks appears to be supplementing face-to-face contacts rather than undermining them, as was also the case previously with the telephone. The Internet is more likely to be integrated into existing behavioral and communication patterns than to change them [3].

4 ICT as a Neighborhood Platform

The idea to use ICT to reinforce social ties in local communities can be traced back to the beginning of the personal computer. After Arpanet fostered the growing awareness of the potential of the computer as a communication tool, the potential for supporting local communities was soon recognized. When, in the late 1970s personal computers and modems started to proliferate, bulletin board systems were founded and the first community networks came into existence. The 1980s were a pioneering age as the technology was still too complicated and expensive for widespread use. These first generation community networks were mainly the product of the desire to bring the possibilities of online communities to a broader public.

As more cities and communities drafted innovative projects and received funding, the term 'community networking' broadened to include many different systems. As computers and modems became mainstream and equipment and software became cheaper and easier to set up and use, all over the world communities came online. Many success stories can be found in the literature about various initiatives (The Well [16], Blacksburg [26]) in the US that 'brought people together to make good things happen' [16]. Also in the Netherlands successful initiatives started as the 'Digital city of Amsterdam' [20, 21].

In Europe, these initiatives got a boost in 1994, when Bangemann published his report. This report stimulated debate on the impact of new ICTs on the economy and society in general. The main message was that the information society had the potential to improve the quality of life of Europe's citizens, the efficiency of our social and economical organizations and could reinforce cohesion [1]. One of the recommendations of this report was that local initiatives should be stimulated without delay, since otherwise business opportunities and jobs would be lost.

Nowadays, nearly every town in Europe has its own web site. The reasons for building such a site are various: to inform residents, to provide a 'portal' to the city or a platform for discussion on local issues, or to give local communities an online place for communication. Especially after publications such as Putnam's book, the application of ICT for increasing social capital in local neighborhoods in cities has become a goal for experiments. Cyburg is an example of such a project aiming to help residents of a city neighborhood to organize themselves and reconnect social ties.

Cyburg

In 1999 the foundation 'Nederland Kennisland' ('The Netherlands Knowledge Society') developed the idea to give a large group of households the opportunity to experiment with new ICT applications. Secretary of State ms. Verstand called for a contest between cities for becoming the 'Knowledge Neighborhood' of the Netherlands. She made 450 million Euro available for the project, under the condition that businesses would invest the same amount. Fifteen cities competed and eventually the region of Eindhoven/Helmond won the award and the grant.

In June 2001, the other cities decided to persevere in their plans to build their own 'knowledge neighborhood'. In Amsterdam, this project is called *Cyburg*, partly funded with European money. With the cooperation of the European Union, the province of North Holland and the Amsterdam municipality founded the program 'The Transparent Region'. Besides this program, Amsterdam, like other cities such as The Hague, Deventer and Eindhoven, received the status of 'digital breeding ground', and funding for this initiative came from the national government.

The goal of Cyburg was to serve as an experimental area for research on the development and application of ICT for individuals, companies and local authorities in urban districts. In the long run, those applications and concepts that proved their worth should become available for other city districts. Within the Cyburg project a number of focus areas were formulated, including the social environment of citizens. For this focus area, the term social cohesion is central. The mobility of Amsterdam residents is high: on average, they move every two to three years, so there is little time to invest in social contacts in the neighborhood. ICT could help citizens to find each other through the Internet. One goal of the project was to improve quality of life by stimulating social contacts between citizens by means of ICT. Other priority areas of the Cyburg project were to bring politics closer to citizens, to stimulate local companies and to improve municipality services.

The location of the Cyburg project was the city area 'Zeeburg' in Amsterdam. This area consists of three neighborhoods. The first, the 'Oostelijk Havengebied' (OH) with 14,652 residents, consists of mainly newly built and more expensive houses, and a higher than average educated mainly indigenous Dutch population. In contrast, the 'Indische Buurt' (IB) with 23,573 inhabitants, is characterized by old houses, the lowest average income of Amsterdam and a high percentage of ethnic minorities [22]. The third area, 'IJburg', is still being constructed and it had a very low number of inhabitants. Therefore, this area was excluded from the research.

The most visible part of Cyburg is the website, consisting among others of a portal for the neighborhood. Cyburg hired professional journalists who edited the news bulletins on events in Zeeburg. Besides them, residents of Zeeburg can put their messages on the website, add their comments to already placed bulletins, or react to the comments of others. The website is only in Dutch, there is no content in other languages (http://www.cyburg.nl).

Another important part of Cyburg.nl is the 'email book'. This is a tool that allows users of Cyburg.nl to contact their neighbors and form interactive groups. The email book can be used anonymously and users get a Cyburg email address so their own email address remains invisible, but users can also put their personal information online, such as their email address, name, address, occupation and hobbies. Cyburg also offers mailing lists, the functionality for sharing documents and pictures and a forum for group discussions. Finally, users can place small ads.

In addition to the website, the Cyburg organization supported tens of projects for groups of citizens and companies. The focus of these projects was on social surroundings, stimulating economical innovations and experiments for improving municipality and non-profit services for citizens. Cyburg also tried to be actively involved in the discussion on the application of broadband Internet. The Cyburg project terminated at the end of 2003, but some projects continued for some time.

5 Research in the Neighborhood

5.1 Methodology

To measure the effect of ICT on social cohesion in Zeeburg, a telephone survey and an online survey was used, the log files of Cyburg.nl were analyzed and interviews were held with residents who are involved with other websites in the neighborhood.

The telephone survey was based on the 'Social Capital Community Benchmark Survey' developed at the University of Harvard [17]. The survey was translated and adapted to the Dutch context and some questions were added. The survey contained questions on social cohesion, the use of ICT and characteristics of the respondents. The survey was conducted in April 2003 among 502 respondents, half of them living in the IB, the other half in the OH. The selection of respondents was based on a random sample of telephone numbers. In spite of the random selection, the results of the survey have to be treated with care. Compared to the population statistics of both areas, ethnic minorities are underrepresented, because of language problems and because ethnic minorities are less likely to have a telephone connections. Also lower educated inhabitants are underrepresented, as this group has a different attitude towards telephonic surveys than higher educated inhabitants.

To obtain more information about use and users of Cyburg.nl an online survey was conducted. The results provide insight into the social demographic characteristics of the users, social cohesion and the use of Cyburg.nl and the Internet in general. The method of an online survey was chosen because it was expected that the target group could be reached through this medium and that they would have the necessary means and knowledge to fill in the survey. Another reason was that it is an effective and cheap way to distribute a questionnaire. The survey was available online for a month and could be reached through a banner on the first page of the portal and via a link in an article published in Cyburg.nl. Also a mailing was sent to the members of the mailing lists. The survey was completed by 102 respondents, over ten percent of the member of the email book. The respondents were not representative for all users of Cyburg.nl, but are regarded as the group of most involved and enthusiast users.

Before Cyburg.nl went online other neighborhood oriented websites already existed. To learn from their experience, interviews were held with people involved.

5.2 Empirical Findings

Table 1 shows some demographic statistics about the population of the OH and IB. These data are important because, according to the literature, the amount of social cohesion in a neighborhood depends at least partly on the characteristics of the population. For measuring the effects of ICT on social cohesion these data should therefore be taken into consideration. The data characterize the OH as a neighborhood with highly educated, often two income families with children. The average education and income in the IB is far lower and the number of foreigners is higher. The large differences in average income between the two neighborhoods are remarkable. As table 1 shows, the number of foreigners is vastly underrepresented in the sample.

Table 1. Respondents in the Indische Buurt (IB) and the Oostelijk Havengebied (OH).

	Telephonic survey		Registration of population	
	IB	OH	IB	OH
Average age	43	42	33	
Men	42%	46%	52%	
Women	58%	54%	48%	
Single	52%	25%	44%	46%
Households with children	36%	57%		
Average nr. of children per household	1.6	1.6		
Household incomes > 3.200 euro	8%	42%		
Higher educated (VWO, HBO, University)	50%	75%		
Ethnic minorities[1]	24%	15%	69%	36%

Internet Use
The results of the telephone survey show there are differences between the two neigh-borhoods in the use of the Internet. In the IB the percentage of Internet connections in households and daily Internet use is lower compared to the OH (table 2). In 2002 61% of the households in the Netherlands had Internet access at home. The use of the Internet is related to social demographic characteristics, especially to education and income. Also younger people tend to be online more often then older inhabitants[2].
About half of the respondents is aware of Cyburg, but there is a large difference between the residents of the OH (where 70% knows about Cyburg.nl) and the IB (38%). This is probably to do with the higher number of residents who do not speak

---

[1] Defined as people of who at least one parent is born in the Netherlands.
[2] The frequency of Internet use is positively related with income (Gamma=.396, p=0), level of education (Gamma=0.386, p=0) and negative related to age (Gamma=-.031, p=0).

Dutch in the latter neighborhood. The survey shows Cyburg.nl is hardly used by the residents. Of those respondents who know about Cyburg.nl, 4% used the news portal, 3% the email book and 4% other services. Among the respondents, communication and searching for information are the most popular activities, while virtual entertainment and online shopping are far less popular. 73% of the respondents did use online municipality services.

According to the log files, Cyburg.nl received 6,000[3] unique visitors per month during spring 2003. This number is higher than could be expected from the results of the telephone survey. Apparently many visitors come from outside Zeeburg. This is plausible since, apart from information about the neighborhood, Cyburg.nl also contains much general information such as ICT, open source software and national politics.

Table 2. Use of Internet and the Cyburg website in Zeeburg

	IB	OH
Uses Internet daily	57%	66%
Has Internet connection at home	79%	94%
Uses the Internet at least once a week for:		
- Communication	58%	80%
- Searching for information	50%	61%
- Providing information	7%	10%
- Leisure	15%	6%
- On line shopping	0%	1%
- E-government services	4%	2%
Aware of Cyburg.nl	38%	70%
Uses Cyburg.nl	3%	4%

Source: telephone survey 2003

Table 3. Age of respondents

age	all	respond.
0-20	22	0
20-30	17	16
30-40	25	35
40-50	18	32
50-60	9	14
60-70	5	2
70-80	3	2
80-90	2	0

All residents of Zeeburg versus respondents of the on-line survey. [14]

The respondents of the online survey represent the most enthusiast and frequent users of Cyburg.nl. 52% of them live in the OH, 27% in the IB, 1% in IJburg and 20% elsewhere. The results of the online survey show that this group is quite homogeneous, and mainly consists of men (69%) between 30 and 50 years old (73%) with a Dutch cultural background (87%). Remarkable is the high average level of education. The respondents are mainly experienced and intensive Internet users: 96% use it daily and most of them have a fast connection. This population is quite similar to the one found in other studies of a comparable web site (the digital city of Amsterdam DDS) conducted in 1994 [18], 1996 and 1998 [20, 21]. A difference between the populations of both websites is that in Cyburg.nl the group of youngsters under 20 is not present at all (table 3), while this was a large group in DDS. Some 69% of the respondents have a login-name for the email book, but only 34% is a member of an email group. This low participation among even the frequent users concurs with the results of the log files. They show that 88% of the visitors only look at the first page and do not 'click through' to other pages on the web site.

The respondents found the topics of ICT, the Internet and Cyburg, living, culture and (local) politics the most interesting of the portal and the email-book. The topics health care, education, children and religion are least favorite.

---

[3] The web site got 40,000 visitors per month, but after log files were filtered for searchbots, copyscripts and Cyburg employees, 6,000 unique visitors were left.

Cyburg as a Facilitating Organization

Besides providing the website, another goal of the Cyburg project was to facilitate initiatives from the neighborhood. Although at the start there were some contacts with inhabitants, in the end there was little cooperation between Cyburg and local initiatives. During interviews with people involved with these local web sites, they said they had the feeling Cyburg was a cumbersome and slow organization. It often took a long time before decisions were made. Also, for the respondents it was sometimes unclear who in the organization should be contacted, or they had the feeling to be sent from pillar to post. Respondents were also surprised about the redundant work Cyburg did. For example, there were already various web sites that provided news about the neighborhood before Cyburg started to do the same. Finally, Cyburg was experienced as 'top-down', instead of being part of the neighborhood. Halfway the experiment, this was also realized by the Cyburg organization. The new slogan became 'high interaction, low tech' to indicate that interaction with the neighborhood had became more important than technology.

6 Social Cohesion

In this section, we return to the main question: what is the effect of the use of Internet on social cohesion in Zeeburg?[4] In the confirmatory factor analysis, seven latent variables were distinguished. Table 4 shows an overview of the relationships between latent variables and observed variables. Within the three aspects Putnam (2000) distinguishes, trust, social contacts and participation, six factors were identified. Trust was further divided into the factors 'trust in neighbors' and 'trust in politics'. Initially there was only one path from the latent variable 'trust in neighbors' to the indicator variable 'trust in police'. Another path from the latent variable 'trust in politics' to the indicator 'trust in police' significantly improved the fit of the model, $\chi^2 (1) = 21.92, p < .0005$. The aspect 'social contacts' remained one factor. The aspect 'participation' was divided into participation in 'local politics', in 'religion' and 'local involvement', such as volunteering or being involved in local organizations.

As shown in figure 1, a number of significant correlations were found between latent variables. Interestingly, a substantial correlation was found between ICT and 'social contacts'. The most reliable indicator for 'social contacts' is the frequency of

---

[4] To be able to interpret the results of the telephone survey, the answers to the questions regarding social cohesion were analyzed by using the structural equation modeling package AMOS1. Structural equation modeling was used to, on the one hand, discern latent variables (or factors) by means of confirmatory factor analyses and, on the other hand, to estimate the relationships between these latent variables. In this way disattenuated relationships between latent variables are obtained because the effect of measurement error in the observed variables is eliminated (Jöreskog and Sörbom 1993). An additional advantage of the AMOS package is that covariances between variables with missing values can be estimated optimally by full information maximum likelihood (FIML). Amos' FIML estimation uses all information of the observed data. The likelihood is computed for the observed portion of each respondent's data and then accumulated and maximized. As about 60% of our data had at least one missing value, using FIML is far superior to using listwise or pairwise deletion of cases (see Wothke (1998) for a convincing demonstration).

visits to friends outside of the neighborhood. One might expect that the substantial correlation between ICT and 'social contacts' is mainly due to frequent e-mail contact with far-away friends. But, surprisingly, the most reliable indicator variable for ICT is

Table 4. Confirmatory factor analysis of indicator variables for social cohesion

(standardized regression weights)	ICT	Social contacts	Trust neighbors	Trust in politics	Local politics	Local involvement	Religion
Frequency Internet use	0.96						
Freq. Internet use for: Communication	0.88						
Freq. Internet use for: Searching information	0.85						
Attitude towards ICT	0.65						
Freq. Internet use for: E-government services	0.54						
Internet at home	0.53						
Freq. Internet use for: Online shopping	0.52						
Freq. Internet use for: Providing information	0.40						
Freq. Internet use for: Leisure	0.40						
Freq. visits friend outside the neighborhood		0.61					
Freq. visit friends living in the neighborhood		0.42					
Freq. visit friends, other cultural background		0.39					
Trust indigenous Dutch			0.89				
Trust ethnic minorities			0.88				
Trust neighbors			0.77				
Trust personnel in local shops			0.59				
Trust in people in general			0.44				
Trust in police			0.37	0.28			
Trust local politics				0.75			
Trust national politics				0.48			
Cooperation to improve the neighborhood					0.66		
Participation in neighborhood affairs					0.45		
Participation in political meetings					0.27		
Frequency of volunteering						0.59	
Membership organizations						0.56	
Attendance meetings clubs/organizations						0.53	
Attendance of religion							0.99

- The fit statistics for the confirmatory factor analysis are satisfactory: $\chi2$ (314) = 514.49, p < .0005, Normalized Fit Index (NFI) = .98, Relative Fit Index (RFI) = .97, Root Mean Square Error of Approximation (RMSEA) = .036.
- Adequate fit statistics are: a non-significant $\chi2$ (holds only for samples sizes up to 200), NFI and RFI values above .90 (above .95 is good fit), and an RMSEA of .05 or less (models whose RMSEA is more than .08 have a poor fit). Source: telephonic survey 2003.

frequency of Internet use and not frequency of Internet use for communication[5]. In the description of the communication variable, chatting and discussion is also included. A separate question about the frequency of using e-mail might have shed more light on

[5] A simple Pearson correlation between, on the one hand, frequency of visits to far-away friends and, on the other hand, frequency of Internet use and frequency of Internet use for communication are 0.35 and 0.13, respectively.

this relationship between 'social contacts' and ICT. The next highest correlation between latent variables is between 'trust in politics' and 'trust in neighbors' which seems (when looking at the highest indicators again) indeed mostly due to trust in local people (whether indigenous Dutch or ethnic minorities) and trust in local politics. The correlation between 'local involvement' and 'local politics' seems also straightforward as there is not that much difference between indicator variables such as 'cooperation to improve the neighborhood' and 'participation in neighborhood affairs'. There is a negative correlation between 'religion' and ICT. Furthermore, somewhat surprising, there is no correlation between 'trust in politics' and 'local politics'. But trust in, especially, local politics does not seem to be related much to one's cooperation to improve the neighborhood.

In a second structural equation model, the relationships between latent variables were controlled for a number of background variables: gender, ethnicity, education, age, income, having a job, number of household members, and area (area did not have any significant effect and was therefore excluded). The results are shown in table 5.

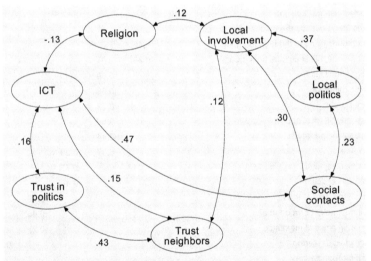

Fig. 1. Significant correlations ($p < .05$) between latent variables, confirmative factor analysis

Table 5. Relationships between background variables and latent variables

standardized coefficients, only significant values, p < .05)	ICT	Social contacts	Local particip ation	Local politics	Religion	Trust neigh bors	Trust politics
Gender (1 = male)	0.07		-0.12				0.11
Level of education	0.29				-0.15		0.23
Age	-0.31	-0.42	0.16		0.12		
Income	0.18						
Having a job (1 = yes)	0.16						
Household size			0.16	0.14		0.16	
Ethnicity (1 = minority)				0.16	0.16	-0.21	
Squared multiple correlation	0.50	0.17	0.06	0.05	0.08	0.07	0.07

Fit statistics: $\chi 2$ (457) = 883.93, p < .0005, NFI = .97, RFI = .96, RMSEA = .043 (note table 4).

Table 5 shows the relationships between the background variables and the latent variables. For ICT use, half of the variance is explained, which is much more than for the other latent variables. Older people do not use ICT as much as younger people. A higher education leads to more ICT use which also holds for a higher income, having a job and being male. Older people have fewer social contacts. Local participation is higher for females, older people, and larger households. Local politics is carried out more by larger households and ethnic minorities. Religion is practiced more by lower educated respondents, older people and ethnic minorities. Members from larger households trust their neighbors more, whereas ethnic minorities noticeably show less trust in their neighbors. Trust in politics is higher for males and higher educated respondents.

Figure 2 shows the correlations between latent variables after controlling for the back-ground variables. All correlations with ICT have become smaller and often non-significant, probably due to the large amount of ICTs variance explained by background variables. The correlation between 'local involvement' and 'trust in neighbors' has also become non-significant. All other correlations have increased somewhat.

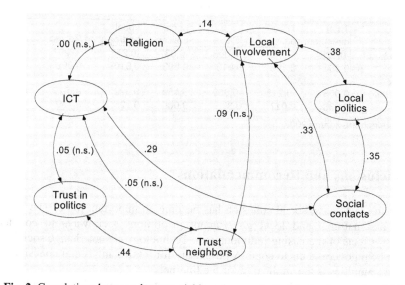

Fig. 2. Correlations between latent variables when controlled for background variables

The observed relationship between ICT on the one side and participation in religion and trust in politics and trust neighbors on the other side in figure 1 can thus be attributed to the characteristics of the participants who are both technology prone and socially active.

After statistical controls for background characteristics one significant and positive correlation remains: frequent ICT users have more social contacts. The available data do not allow causal interpretation. We cannot decide whether ICT use increases the social contacts of users or whether high sociability favors the use of ICT. Yet, a deterioration of social contacts by Internet seems very unlikely. Given the frequent non significant correlations between ICT and social cohesion indicators after statistical controls also an improvement of social cohesion seems improbable. An integration of new technology into existing communication patterns is far more likely.

Geographical Mobility and Social Cohesion

A popular hypothesis is that in an area where residents move often, social cohesion would be lower compared to other areas where residents move less frequently. To test this hypothesis, the relationship between the various aspects of social cohesion and how long residents live in the neighborhood was analyzed. A distinction was made between the two areas since many houses in the OH were built quite recently. Table 6 shows there are for the IB weak but significant (p<.05) negative relationships between how long a respondent lives in an area and local participation and participation in religion. In the OH there is only a negative relationship with trust in politics.

The data in table 6 is corrected for age, because it is plausible that older respondents life longer in the neighborhood compared to younger respondents. To be able to compare the time a respondent lives in an area it should be corrected for age. Most houses in the OH were build recently, therefore the two areas were separated.

Table 6. Relationship between how long a respondent lives in an neighborhood and various aspects of social cohesion, controlled for all background variables

	Trust neighbors	Trust politics	ICT	Local politics	Local participation	Religion	Social contacts
Indische buurt	-0,125	-0,119	-0,006	-0,032	-0,275	-0,207	-0,020
p=	0,064	0,128	0,913	0,693	0,010	0,006	0,853
Oostelijk havengebied	0,005	-0,213	-0,059	0,159	0,029	-0,022	0,146
p=	0,938	0,017	0,303	0,060	0,725	0,739	0,124

Source: telephone survey 2003

7 Conclusions and Recommendations

During the last years, social cohesion has become an important topic. The European Union and national and local government institutions seek ways to counter the negative effects of increasing individualism. Technology cannot change social trends, but can help governments to cope. A possibility for reinforcing social cohesion within local communities is the application of the Internet.

The results of this study support neither a pessimistic view of the crumbling social cohesion through the application of new technology, nor Utopian visions of the possibilities of ICT for increasing social cohesion. Based on the empirical results, the question of whether the use of the Internet results in an increase of social cohesion among residents can not be answered with a simple yes or no. After controlling for social background characteristics, the use of the Internet is related only to maintaining social contact. No significant relationships were found between ICT and trust in neighbors, trust in politics, participation in local politics, participation in religion and local involvement. The influence of social/demographic characteristics on both ICT and these indicators of social cohesion is far stronger than the relationships between ICT and social cohesion indicators itself. The observed relationship between ICT and social cohesion largely depends on contextual aspects, such as (ethnic) background of the residents, age, level of education, having a job, level of income and the number of members of the household. Thus, an integration of new technology into existing communication patterns seems to be the most plausible conclusion.

The experience of Cyburg.nl shows it is not easy to get residents involved with a website aimed at the neighborhood. Only a very small percentage of the residents in Zeeburg use the website Cyburg.nl. Reasons for this low participation are the unclear goals of the website, the complicated structure and technological problems. The survey among users shows the web site is mainly used by highly educated Dutch males with a lot of online experience. Other groups, who could benefit more from the websites compared to those who already have a head start because of their background, hardly use the web site.

The cooperation between Cyburg and other initiatives in the neighborhood progressed smoothly. Cyburg was seen as an unwieldy organization and in the end residents try to reach their goals in other ways. It seems that using a top-down approach to stimulate bottom-up initiatives does not work.

Based on the results of this study, some recommendations could be formulated for building web sites aimed at increasing social cohesion in neighborhoods.

- One should be realistic about the expectations of the effects of ICT on social cohesion. ICT is only one of the ways to stimulate social cohesion, besides other initiatives by organizations as welfare organizations, hobby clubs and places if worship.

- If the goal of a website is to contribute to social cohesion in a neighborhood, it will have to cooperate with already existing initiatives. By cooperating instead of competing, synergy can be generated between organizations with the same interests.

- Access to the Internet seems to become a less important issue, but the skills to use it in a meaningful way still are. Especially for vulnerable groups in society providing extra support such as courses or self-help groups is very important.

- Facilities for communication are the prime necessity for supporting social cohesion. The web site should support various forms of online communication, asynchronous (e-mail, mailing lists, fora) as well as synchronous (chat).

- Let the web site become the 'memory' of the neighborhood by storing the sent messages and make those accessible, for example in a forum. Make clear rules in advance about storing and moderating messages.

- Give users the possibility to be responsible for building and administering parts of the website. In this way functionality can be added by users themselves and commitment to the web site will increase. Bottom-up approach works better than top-down approach.

- When an organization has the goal to facilitate initiatives in the neighborhood, it should react very swiftly to proposals. When a resident has an idea but has to wait for a month before a decision is taken, the momentum is gone. Have a clear focal point for the organization to prevent people with valuable ideas being sent from pillar to post.

- Be very aware of the level of community the website has to serve. When the size is too big, such as the city as a whole, or the province, users will not identify with it. By focusing the website on a single street or a neighborhood, residents will feel more commitment and will be more inclined to participate.

- Identify key persons in the neighborhood and try to get them involved with the website.
- Make the goal of the website as clear as possible. Especially during the first phase, it is impossible to let a web site be a portal to the neighborhood, the business card of a project, a communication platform for the residents, a signboard for local shops, an online flea market and the gathering place of all kinds of local projects. It is nearly impossible to fulfill all these roles at once in a meaningful way and (potential) users will be confused about the goals of the web site. Keep it simple: more functionality can always be added later.
- Technical imperfections lead to irritations and drop out of users. Keep technology simple: a simple site that works well is better than a complex site with problems.
- Many visitors of Cyburg.nl did not bother to react to bulletins because they first had to register themselves, which was seen as cumbersome. Make a distinction between functionalities or parts of the website that can be used anonymously and parts for which users have to register.

Acknowledgments

We would like to thank Bob Wielinga (SWI, University of Amsterdam), Peter van den Besselaar (NIWI, Royal Netherlands Academy of Arts and Sciences), and Sally Wyatt (ASCOR, University of Amsterdam). The research was made possible by the European Fund for Regional Development, the Province of Noord Holland and the Municipality of Amsterdam.

Literature

1. Bangemann, M.: Europe and the Global Information Society; Recommendations to the European Council Report of the High-Level Group on the Information Society. European Council (1994)
2. Beamish, A. Communities On-line. Community-Based Computer Networks. (dissertation), Massachusetts: MIT (1995)
3. de Haan, J., Huysmans, F.: Revolution or eVolution; an Empirical Approach to eCulture, In: D. Dodd, eCulture: the European Perspective; cultural policy - knowledge industries - information lag, Conference reader, Circle round table Zagreb, (2003) 5-17. http://www.culturelink.org/conf/ecult/ecultread.html
4. de Hart, J. (ed.): Zekere banden: Sociale Cohesie, Leefbaarheid en Veiligheid. Den Haag: SCP (2002)
5. Ferlander, S., Timms, D.: Computer-Supported Community Networks and Social Cohesion. Paper 1st Regional Telematics Conference (1999). Consulted June 5, 2003 via http://www.stir.ac.uk/schema/conf/Tanum/tanumpaper.doc
6. Jöreskog, K.G., Sörbom, D: Lisrel 8, Structural Equation Modeling with the Simplis Command Language. Hillsdale: Lawrence Erlbaum Associates, Inc. (1993)
7. Kazmer, M.M., Haythornthwaite, C.: Judging Multiple Social Worlds, Distance Students Online and Offline. American Behavioral Scientist, 45 (2001) 510-529
8. Kline, R.B.: Principles and Practice of Structural Equation Modeling, New York: Guilford Press (1998)

9. Kraut, R., Kiesler, S., Boneva, B., Cummings, J., Helgeson, V., Crawford, A.: Internet Paradox Revisited. In: Journal of Social Issues 58 (2002) 49-74
10. LaRose, R., Eastin. M., Gregg, J.: Reformulating the Internet Paradox: Social Cognitive Explanations of Internet Use and Depression. Journal of Online Behavior, 1 (2001) 2
11. Nie, N.: Sociability, Interpersonal Relations and the Internet, Reconciling Conflicting Findings. American Behavorial Scientist 45 (2001) 420-435
12. Nie, N., Ebring, L.: Siqss Internet study. (2000) Consulted on September 10, 2003 via http://www.stanford.edu/group/siqss
13. Nie, N.H., Hillygus, D.S.: The impact of Internet Use on Sociability; Time-Diary Findings. IT and Society 1 (2002) 1-20
14. O+S: De Amsterdamse Bevolking (2003). Consulted September 10, 2003 via http://www.onstat.amsterdam.nl/index.php?onderwerp=de_amsterdamse_bevolking
15. Putnam, R.D.: Bowling Alone; the Collapse and Revival of American Community. Touchstone (2000)
16. Rheingold, H.: The Virtual Community: Homesteading on the Electronic Frontier. Secker and Warburg (1993)
17. The Saguaro Seminar: The Social Capital Community Benchmark Survey. (2003) Consulted 10-9-03: http://www.ksg.harvard.edu/saguaro/communitysurvey/index.html.
18. Schalken, K., Flint, J.: Handboek Digitale Steden. Amsterdam: DDS (1995)
19. Stoll, C. Silicon Snake Oil: Second Thoughts on the Information Highway. New York: Doubleday (1995)
20. Van den Besselaar, P., Beckers, D.: Demographics and Sociographics of the Digital City. In: T. Ishida (ed), Community Computing and Support Systems. Lecture Notes in Computer Science, Vol. 1529. Springer-Verlag, Berlin Heidelberg New York (1998) 109-125
21. Van den Besselaar, P., Beckers, D.: The life and death of the great Amsterdam Digital City. In: P. van den Besselaar, S. Koizumi (eds), Digital Cities 3. Lecture Notes in Computer Science, Vol. 3081. Springer-Verlag, Berlin Heidelberg New York (2005) pp. 64-93.
22. Van Zee, W., Hylkema, C.: Stadsdeling en Buurtcombinaties in Cijfers. Het Amsterdamse Bureau voor Onderzoek en Statistiek (2002)
23. Van Zoonen, L., Walczuch, R., Aalberts,C., Fjelsten, A.: Effects of Internet Use on Social Cohesion. Unpublished manuscript (2003)
24. Wellman, B., Haase, A.Q., Witte, J., Hampton, K.: Does the Internet Increase, Decrease, or Supplement Social Capital? Social Networks, Participation, and Community Commitment. American Behavioral Scientist 45 (2001) 437-456
25. Wothke, W.: Longitudinal and Multi-Group Modeling with Missing Data. In: T.D. Little, K.U. Schnabel, J. Baumert (eds.) Modeling Longitudinal and Multiple Group Data; Practical Issues, Applied Approaches and Specific Examples. Mahwah, NJ: Lawrence Erlbaum Associates
26. Carroll, J.M.: The Blacksburg Electronic village, a Study in Community Computing. In: P. van den Besselaar, S. Koizumi (eds,), Digital Cities 3. Lecture Notes in Computer Science, Vol. 3081. Springer-Verlag, Berlin Heidelberg New York (2005) pp. 42-63.

Citizenship and Digital Media Management

Mariana Reis Balboni & Gilson Schwartz

School of Communication and Arts, University of São Paulo
City of Knowledge, Institute of Advanced Studies, (IEA/USP), Brazil.
mbalboni@usp.br & schwartz@usp.br

Abstract. This paper describes the *Digital Media Management* program (GMD, in Portuguese), offered by the City of Knowledge[1] for staff working at public internet access points in the city of São Paulo, Brazil, since August 2002 (www.cidade.usp.br/gmd). The mission of the program is to network these professionals with the university's knowledge production centers for the profit both of 'digital inclusion agents' (advanced training and consulting with the academic community) and academicians doing research on new forms of knowledge production leveraged by information and communication technologies (ICTs). Network development is moderated by Brazil's largest public university focusing on project design and knowledge management. Networked projects must be oriented to problem-solving in underserved communities, mostly in the periphery of the city of São Paulo. The main goal of the program is to forge lifelong learning communities through networking that leverage development and social projects, putting information and communication technologies to a collaborative use.

1 Introduction

The development and deployment of digital media have become a strategic element of public policies in the realm known as 'digital inclusion'. After a fast and debatable privatization process of the telecom sector in Brazil and following the global enthusiasm towards the internet and the digital divide agenda, the Brazilian government has stimulated universal access through the installation of public internet points in schools, libraries, 'tele-centers' and 'info-centers' in various public or semi-public places (see Table 1 for internet access in the State of São Paulo). In São Paulo alone, the largest city in Brazil, there are more than 200 tele-centers and info-centers operating in poor neighborhoods and managed by the state (in partnership with NGOs) and by municipal governments (see Table 2).

---

[1] The City of Knowledge is a research project created in 1999 at the Institute of Advanced Studies of the University of São Paulo (IEA-USP), Brazil. Envisioned as a living network, it can also be described as a digital city' built by 'communities of practice' that develop new space-time frameworks for the production of cultural identities and collective intelligence. Its mission is to promote research, development and applications that foster public, community or cooperative use of new digital information and communication technologies in Brazil. More information in [16], and at www.cidade.usp.br/english/

P. van den Besselaar and S. Koizumi (Eds.): Digital Cities 2003, LNCS 3081, pp. 407-416, 2005.
© Springer-Verlag Berlin Heidelberg 2005

Table 1. Internet Access, Metropolitan Region, São Paulo, 2001

Classification	Population	Internet Access	%
Total	14.242.040	2.915.573	20,5
Male	6.760.522	1.561.686	23,1
Female	7.481.518	1.353.887	18,1
Income Class A/B > US$ 1,000	5.170.705	2.345.843	45,4
Income Class C	5.066.105	483.213	9,5
Income Class D/E < US$ 100	4.005.230	86.517	2,2
Age 10 to 14	1.647.468	376.274	22,8
15 to 19	1.809.616	565.462	31,2
20 to 24	1.562.757	417.414	26,7
25 to 29	1.372.371	355.800	25,9
30 to 39	2.761.820	584.916	21,2
40 to 49	2.259.502	447.829	19,8
50 or more	2.828.506	167.879	5,9

Source: Ibope, 2001.

The expansion of this infrastructure and its growing potential for numerous public policies (e-government is just the tip of the iceberg) makes it urgent to invest in the skills of the public servants and other professionals involved in the management of this infrastructure. Among other complex issues, there is a democratic quandary concerning the nature of the population's access to information, services and economic opportunities through the internet. The democratic challenge is to stimulate new patterns of job creation, as well as to create new identities and cultures, fostering a digital democracy.

This is the challenge of the Digital Media Management (GMD) program, which has a long term goal of incubating communities of practice among professionals in public service and thereafter creating network opportunities also with other professionals in numerous communities, thus weaving a social network of problem-solving agents in the public and private sectors, as well as among NGOs and research centers.

Table 2. Digital Inclusion Programs, City and State of São Paulo, 2004

Description	Telecenters*	Infocenters**
Number of public facilities	105	139***
Registered Users	317,143	324,022

* Governo Eletrônico, Prefeitura Municipal de São Paulo (www.telecentros.sp.gov.br).
** Programa Acessa São Paulo, Governo do Estado de São Paulo (www.acessasaopaulo.sp.gov.br).
*** 71 in the hinterland of São Paulo.
Source: Acessa São Paulo, 2004, Governo Eletônico, 2004

The GMD was conceived based on the same epistemological and philosophical concepts Gilson Schwartz [16] used to create the City of Knowledge, a new public network with decentralized and even libertarian dynamics of digital networks, defining the digital space-time as *knowware* [17]. Stressing the knowledge management capabilities of digital networks, the City of Knowledge was launched in March, 2001, with a network formation program for public and private schools.

The same network formation through 'permanent learning by problem-solving-projects' approach applied to the educational community was later, in 2002, applied to the community of workers in infocenters and telecenters, with the purpose of helping these professionals articulate social demands and explore the opportunities offered by the new digital information and communication technologies (ICTs).

The purpose of this paper is to describe the Digital Media Management program and its initial results: the elaborated proposals for social projects, and the impacts of the created network on its participants, on the university, and on the administration of municipal and state digital inclusion programs in São Paulo. It is important to notice that the *implementation* of these projects was not expected during the GMD process but we managed to help a few groups in obtaining the necessary financial support. Since the program was considered a success, we are expecting new funds to start its second phase soon. Possibly then we will be able to implement the projects that are described in this paper.

2 Methodology

The GMD program is an entrance or connection point to the university for those involved with the management of public infrastructure that stimulates network formation and continuous search for the innovative design of local development projects that reflect the needs and opportunities of communities. Initially thought of as a regular specialization course, the GMD evolved into network building among workers in digital inclusion programs at the State and Municipal levels. The program was created only after 3 months of planning (5 meetings) with research fellows from different academic areas of the University of São Paulo (sociology, economy, management, psychology, communication, among others) to discuss and elaborate the GMD agenda.

It soon became clear that it should not be a course as such, but rather a program focused on projects and problem-solving. It was also necessary to level expectations, preparing a first, basic module with the main goal of turning the staff into protagonists in the process of project creation and development, as well as enabling appropriation of the relevant technologies and production of local content on the internet. People already working in tele-centers and info-centers as well as the public servants in charge of digital inclusion programs also participated in these debates. This collaborative approach to the design of the course/network also impacted different areas of the University of São Paulo which were not used to cooperate in these matters.

For 8 months (August, 2002 - March, 2003), the GMD program trained 280 staff workers from tele-centers, info-centers and NGOs such as the CDI (Committee for the Democratization of Informatics) with the objective of designing local development projects – with cultural, social and economical focus - leveraged by information and communication technologies.

Besides skills building, the program formed a community of practice inspired by the ideal of a public space and of a social movement engaged in the discussion, research, collaboration and collective construction of "digital inclusion". It is important to remember that these professionals, mainly locals from the underserved neighborhoods where these Public Internet Access Centers are installed, are seen as leaders of a grassroots implementation of communication strategies by marginalized populations, acting as spokespersons for their communities.

Table 3. Calendar of Activities

Sessions	Activities
1, 2 and 3	Awareness and Sensitization Stage
4	Seminar – History of ICTs
5	Seminar – Digital Culture
6	Seminar – Technology and Citizenship
7	Seminar – Initiative and Creativity
8	Seminar – Communication Skills
9	Seminar – Project Management
10 to 17	Laboratories and Project Development
18	Projects: Final Presentations

Influenced by the pedagogic needs and socio-cultural demands made explicit by the participants during the 3 preparatory sessions (termed as an "Awareness and Sensitization Stage"), the collaborative and participatory model of the program included the following activities (see Table 3):

- Seminars on Technology and Citizenship, History of Information and Communication Technologies, Initiative and Creativity, Communication Skills, Digital Culture and Project Management – 6 sessions;
- Group meetings (laboratories) to work on projects related to cultural, social and economic issues – 8 sessions;
- Collaborative work through an internet forum, were participants discussed their ideas and contributed from their workplaces to the development of specific projects.

Fig. 1. Group of participants discussing its comprehension of Net

Fig. 2. Sensitization session at the University of São Paulo

During the awareness and sensitization sessions, participants formed small groups to discuss and share perceptions of social, cultural and economic challenges in their communities (see figures 1 and 2). These lively exchanges resulted in the formation of 5 so-called 'theme coalitions', that is, working groups structured by subject convergences, each with a coordinator who acted also as a moderator in a virtual forum:

- community (illiteracy, unemployment, drugs, violence, homelessness) – 58 participants
- communication (videomaking, community journalism, webstreaming) – 23 participants
- culture (hip-hop, local groups, identity and festivals) – 63 participants
- infrastructure (access and quality of service) – 34 participants
- lifelong learning (on the job training, communities of practice) – 14 participants

3 Initial Results

The more general results of the program were:
- emergence of a networked, bottom-up community more eager and capable of voicing their own concerns with respect to the future of "digital inclusion" programs in the public sphere,
- clear identification of a demand for lifelong learning as a specific thematic coalition concerned with debate, research, collaboration and collective creation of projects leveraged by digital media,
- recognition of a bias in favor of cultural production projects, a thematic coalition that attracted about 60% of the group after the awareness and sensitization sessions, a clear sign of demand for identity and expression,
- evolution of public 'digital inclusion' programs both at state and at municipality levels into a new focus that targets projects (creation and management) rather than pure "internet access" as the main public good whose supply is expected to rise with the intelligent and self-critical use of ICTs.

These results are in line with the overall perspective that guides the development of the City of Knowledge: the promotion of networks as tools in the struggle for solidarity and support among students and young adults that work or use ICTs in underserved areas in order to stimulate the digital and social empowerment of citizens who lead processes of continuous improvement of socio-economic conditions.

As a matter of fact, ICTs are only the tip of a civic iceberg: they come to life insofar as they support the weaving of networks of basic civic formation, centered on the sharing of knowledge on how to use the new technologies as well as of strategies on how to find other opportunities - through the networks of the City of Knowledge's various learning communities associated to social, cultural and economic projects sponsored among others by the University of São Paulo.

Project group members co-authored content and problem-solving ideas with Brazil's most prolific scientific producers in all areas of knowledge. The results are published in the City of Knowledge's portal, which itself gradually evolves as a digital city built on networked projects. Virtual laboratories and collaboration environments are thus gradually designed to meet each community's priorities and learning strategies in the virtual sphere.

The slow pace of access to new technologies in several cities in the country has stressed the exclusion of large parts of the population, worsening the lack of employment opportunities and further increasing the difficulties of access to benefits from citizenship services and other public policies offered through the new digital media.

The exchange of cultural and content production initiatives, evolving self-knowledge and diversity enhancing practices are inspiring ideals in the organization of the City of Knowledge initiatives, thus connecting the university not only to those who have been left behind in the recent drive to promote the so-called 'digital inclusion' but also those that are banned from certified knowledge producing processes. The resulting network also responds to the City of Knowledge's commitment to the promotion of research, development and socio-informatics applications that foster public, community or cooperative use of digital information and communication technologies in Brazil.

Table 4. Projects in GMD

Project	Objective
Communities portal Comunidades.org	To develop, build and give support to a web portal with social and communitarian information and content for the: • Exchange of information in communities served by digital inclusion programs; • Use of information technologies for participation and social inclusion; • Promotion of potentialities of marginalized populations; • Development of written and communicational skills.
News agency	Foster the democratization of communication through local information production and debate on issues related to the communities. Supply news for the Comunidades.org website and lists.
Cultural Survey	Promote a wide field survey on cultural activities of local communities (handcrafts, workshops, courses on dance, drama, music, etc.) and make it available on the Comunidades.org website.
Cultural Portal	Build a portal to serve as: • Calendar for cultural activities in the community; • Hub for citizenship as development of networks; • Investment showcase for local projects; • Public space for knowledge sharing.
São Paulo Express Festival	Rescue of local culture and artistic expressions. Cultural event with shows, local gastronomy, crafts, cultural debates and sporting championships.
Infrastructure	Network of staff experienced in the identification and solution of infrastructure problems in public internet access centers, including research on sustainability models for these centers. Main problems are: slow access to the internet, public tariffs (light, telephone, rentals), office supplies (paper, ink, cables, etc.) and physical maintenance.
Income Generation	Public internet access centers as hubs for job locating support programs and entrepreneurship skills building. The resulting data and models would then be made available on the Comunidades.org portal.
Lifelong Learning	Use of ICTs to continuously upgrade professionals working in digital inclusion programs by creating an online area for the continuous education on the www.comunidades.org.br portal as well as organizing regular face-to-face seminars.
Digital Inclusion Videomaking	Production of a video on the reality of digital inclusion programs.
Digital Music	Production of digital music and digital studio for community use.

It is important to mention that GMD participants came from digital inclusion programs that have different methodological and ideological orientations (they are sustained by the municipal and state governments, from opposing political parties). At first, in many occasions they saw each other as competitors, but at last they came to share an ideal of fighting the same social challenges, perceived as if through the lens of the 'digital divide' perspective.

Community Projects There were 10 projects developed during the GMD, as we can see in table 4. A complete description of the projects is available in Portuguese language only (www.cidade.usp.br/gmd). It is important to notice that the objective of the program was to help the participants working out a plan for these projects, and not to implement them. However, the experience they have acquired helped a few groups to achieve funds to implement similar projects in their communities.

Virtual Community During the GMD program virtual communities were created for each one of the working groups. The intense information exchange and collective construction of the projects through the Internet fostered the use of the ICTs among the group and also gave them a strong sense of community (see table 5). Besides being used as a tool for collaborative work and communication, the virtual forums and discussion lists were an important space for individual expression of the participants. The messages exchanged were mainly personal opinions about digital inclusion issues and about the difference technology was making – or not – in their lives. But the participants also posted a great deal of poetry and motivation letters. Finally, the participants exchanged information relevant for the development of the projects and for the related tasks.

Table 5. Virtual Communities in GMD

Group	Messages Exchanged	URL
Community Issues	206	Http://inforum.insite.com.br/3537/
Infrastructure	85	Http://inforum.insite.com.br/3538/
Communication	126	Http://inforum.insite.com.br/3541/
Culture	189	Http://inforum.insite.com.br/3539/
Lifelong Learning	159	Http://inforum.insite.com.br/3540/

The Newsletter *Impressão Digital* (Digital Impression) is a great achievement of the GMD community. It originated from the participants' need to communicate, be heard, and keep discussing issues related to the digital inclusion and universal access to information, also after the program was concluded (figure 3). Besides that, it is a digital medium entirely produced and managed by the community, with technical support from the Knowledge City. From February until August 2003, seven monthly issues were published on the internet – and sent to its 400 subscribers. All texts were written by the participants and by the coordinator of each working group. The issues are still available at www.cidade.usp.br/impressaodigital.

Permanent Forum on Digital Inclusion Another important initiative from the GMD community was the transformation of the program into a Permanent Forum on Digital Inclusion, that, starting April 2003, met once a month to discuss concepts, democratic practices, public politics, and the functioning of these programs. It was also supporting the implementation of the projects elaborated during the GMD. It has a virtual discussion list available at: inforum.insite.com.br/5629.

In this virtual forum, 810 messages have been posted on various issues from news on digital inclusion programs to personal chats on individual projects. In mid-March 2004, 75 messages were related to information on the continuation of the GMD program, to be publicly announced in April, 2004 with important renewal in form and content of the GMD program, such as the creation of special public areas focused on project selection, management and evaluation, as well as a new collection of technical courses. From an original group of about 250 people, 216 have subscribed to the virtual forum (while the other 34 were not program fellows). However, about 20 people are responsible for most of the messages, and they have regular board meetings of the Digital Inclusion Permanent Forum. These meetings took place between April and September, 2003 and sum up to this date 15 sessions held at the University of São Paulo (6), at one of the telecenters (Parque do Carmo, 2) and at the City's Cultural Center (7). It is important to note that not all sessions were held at the University of São Paulo. Given the fact that most of the participants are low-income, it is critical for the university fellows to move and meet wherever it is more convenient to the participants, rather than stay in campus and wait for the community to come and reach a "central" knowledge hub.

Fig. 3. Front page of the newsletter Impressão Digital (first issue)

Digital Generation A very important initiative was the 'Digital Generation Show' organized by the City of Knowledge, as part of the activities of the Comdex Fair in São Paulo. The show was organized in August 2003, with the help of the digital inclusion workers and sponsored by IBM and SUCESU, the main IT professionals association in Brazil. The show included guided tours to the trade fair, roundtable discussions on digital inclusion issues, workshops on themes that were deemed important by the workers, such as open source software development, multimedia production, community radio, content production techniques like screenwriting, and accessibility issues.

4 Concluding Remarks

The effective and democratic participation of citizens in the construction of a new digital citizenship infrastructure requires not only access to information, but mainly the possibility of creating content and new forms of locally relevant knowledge. The creation, exchange and distribution of knowledge in the cyberspace may be an efficient way of fighting not only the digital divide but also other forms of social and economic exclusion. Collaboration with the largest public university in Brazil made the technology available but also served as an anchor for the credibility of the program.

Both the state government (Acessa São Paulo) and the Prefecture of São Paulo (Governo Eletrônico – Telecentros) are now extending their digital inclusion programs, following the project-based approach that was the focus of the GMD program. Both are contracting the City of Knowledge for a second cycle of community development.

It is also important to stress the influence of the GMD approach on other projects in the City of Knowledge. The *bottom-up, community-driven* and *project-based* architecture of digital social networks is now being used to set up new 'cities of knowledge' in other parts of Brazil, especially in the poorest areas of the Northeast. This is made possible by contract with the National Institute of Information Technology (ITI) at Brazil´s Presidential Office. These new and evolving programs look very much like 'nation-wide GMDs'.

Conceived as an incubator for networked social initiatives, the City of Knowledge is in its early phase of development. The creation of inter-institutional channels linking the university, public policy-makers and community leaders is in itself a major outcome. However, it is unclear whether the program will reach a phase of sustainable evolution, as it depends on government funds that stopped to become available when a recession in 2003 created fiscal constraints.

As an incubator, the GMD succeeded insofar the designed projects obtained funds from the government and from other sources. Some of the projects also made it to the final stage in a national prize for excellence in public informatics (Conip Congress).

The permanent Digital Inclusion Virtual Forum is still active, and the Impressão Digital Newsletter will be issued again in 2004 (written by workers and users of the tele-centers and info-centers). Similar experiences under supervision of the City of Knowledge are underway elsewhere in Brazil, but it is still too early to draw final conclusions about the results and effectiveness of the GMD program. Research is now being designed to investigate the impacts of this emerging socio-technical development process on individuals and organizations that took part in it.

5 Bibliography

1. Afonso, Carlos: A Internet no Brasil: O acesso para todos é possível? Policy Paper, n.26, São Paulo, Friedrich Ebert Stfitung (2000) <http://www.fes.org.br/publicacoes.htm>
2. Assumpção, Rodrigo Ortiz: Além da Inclusão Digital: O Projeto sampa.org. São Paulo, USP, fev. 2002. Dissertação (Mestrado em Ciências da Comunicação), Escola de Comunicações e Artes, Universidade de São Paulo (2001) <http://www.sampa.org>
3. Assumpção, Rodrigo Ortiz (et al): Relatório da 1ª Oficina de Inclusão digital. Brasília, Ministério do Planejamento (2001) <http://www.sampa.org>
4. Balboni, Mariana Reis: Les politiques de télécommunications brésiliennes vers l'accès universel. Montreal, Universidade de Montreal. Dissertação (Mestrado em Ciências da Comunicação), Faculdade de Artes e de Ciências, Universidade de Montreal (1999)
5. Castells, Manuel: The Rise of Network Society. (Vol. 1). Cambridge (Mass), Blackwell (1996)
6. Compaine, Benjamin: The Digital Divide: Facing a crisis or creating a myth?. Cambridge (Mass), MIT Press (2001)
7. Costa, Rogério da: A cultura digital. São Paulo, Publifolha (2002)
8. Dowbor, Ladislau (ed.): Desafios da Comunicação. Petrópolis, Vozes (2001)
9. Lévy, Pierre: As tecnologias da inteligência: o futuro do pensamento na era da informática. São Paulo, Editora 34 (1993)
10. Lévy, Pierre: Cibercultura. 2.ed. São Paulo, Editora 34 (2000)
11. Morin, Edgar (et al): Educação e Complexidade: Os sete saberes e outros ensaios. São Paulo, Cortez (2002)
12. Morin, Edgar: A Cabeça bem feita: repensar a reforma e reformar o pensamento. 6. ed. Rio de Janeiro, Bertrand Brasil (2002)
13. Neri, Marcelo Côrtes (Ed.): Mapa da exclusão digital. Rio de Janeiro, CPS/FGV/IBRE (2003)
14. Reinhard, Nicolau, Macadar, Marie Anne: Telecentros Comunitários possibilitando a Inclusão Digital: um estudo de caso comparativo de iniciativas brasileiras. Salvador, Publicado nos anais do 26. Enanpad (2002)
15. Rheingold, Howard: The virtual community. Cambridge (Mass), MIT Press (2000)
16. Schwartz, Gilson. Vida e política na Cidade do Conhecimento. In: Torquato, Cid (ed.): E-dicas: Desvirtualizando a nova economia. São Paulo, Usina do Livro (2002) 203-212
17. Schwartz, Gilson: Knowledge City, a digital knowware. As PDF file obtainable from: http://www.thinkcycle.org/tc-filesystem/file?file_id=13067
18. Silveira, Sérgio Amadeu de: Exclusão Digital: a miséria na era da informação. São Paulo. Fundação Perseu Abramo (2001)
19. Setzer, Valdemar: Dado, informação, conhecimento e competência. DataGramaZero - Revista de Ciência da Informação (1999) <http://www.dgz.org.br/dez99/Art_01.htm>
20. Takahashi, Tadao (ed): Sociedade a Informação no Brasil: livro verde. Brasília, Ministério da Ciência e Tecnologia (2000) <http://www.socinfo.org.br>

Digital Cities and the Opportunities for Mobilizing the Information Society: Case Studies from Portugal

José L. Moutinho, Manuel Heitor

Center for Innovation, Technology and Policy Research,
Technical University of Lisbon, Av. Rovisco Pais, 1049-001 Lisbon, Portugal
{jmoutinho, mheitor}@ist.utl.pt

Abstract. The development of case studies in selected Portuguese cities and regions which have been engaged in "digital city" projects is considered in this paper in a way to discuss main challenges and opportunities for mobilizing the information society in Europe, with emphasis for the conditions affecting less favourable zones. It is argued that value-based networks have the potential to make both public administration and markets more effective, which helps promoting learning trajectories for the inclusive development of society, but require effective infrastructures, incentives and adequate institutional frameworks.

1 Introduction

In view of the current socio-economic context, in which innovation is a key driving force for the sustainable development, which challenges are facing the diffusion and adoption of information and communication technologies at regional level, in a way to contribute for regional policies that could mobilize the information society in less favoured regions in Europe?

This broad question has motivated the work behind the present paper, which considers the development of case studies in selected Portuguese cities and regions, which have been engaged in building digital networks. It is argued that value-based digital networks have the potential to make both public administration and markets more effective, which helps promoting learning trajectories for the inclusive development of society, but require effective infrastructures, incentives and adequate institutional frameworks promoted over time and across space [1]. Early-stage developments are shown to be particularly dependent on public funding and the necessary institutional framework, including the development of knowledge-integrated communities. The analysis builds on the need to continually adapt trajectories and foster the necessary learning capacity of increasingly diversified communities, which refers to social capital as a relational infrastructure for collective action [2], in a context much influenced by a dynamic of change and a necessary balance between the creation and diffusion of knowledge.

In this context, the paper discusses a *knowledge-based view of the territory* to foster institutionally organized metropolitan *systems of innovation* [3] *and competence*

P. van den Besselaar and S. Koizumi (Eds.): Digital Cities 2003, LNCS 3081, pp. 417-436, 2005.

building [2], which derives from observations in different Portuguese metropolitan areas with the ultimate goal of increasing regional competitiveness, by promoting public awareness and participation in decision-making processes. It is argued that the territory is a basic infrastructure that justifies and invites for the construction of several layers of information about cities and regions were people live, visit or do business. Digital city schemes should also encourage the global legibility of the information architecture of the territory and promote broad and informed participation in the decision-making process of the future of its entire influence area and not only within city limits [4].

Although we are still in a very early and limited stage of what Mitchell [5] called 'cities of bits', it is clear that it has become a "commonplace" to discuss the diffusion of knowledge, and the "knowledge-driven economy" in general, in close association with the introduction and use of information and communication technologies [6,7]. In this context, several national initiatives for the Information Society aim to achieve four broad objectives: to create a more open state, to link and make available to all the available knowledge, to promote Internet usage in education, and to support and develop digital technologies usage by firms [8]. The evidence calls for our attention for the critical role of public funding and the dynamic adaptation and development of the context necessary to facilitate digital cities.

The work follows current discussion in Europe aiming to: (a) ensure widespread broadband access and a secure information infrastructure; and (b) services, applications and content, covering online public services and e-business [9], but argues for the need to plan systematic actions of competence building with the ultimate goal of attracting new communities of users and to build the necessary capacity for connectivity. Community building and demand creation for digital services became the critical factor for implementing digital cities, requiring proper incentives and institutional settings.

The remainder of this paper attempts to frame these aspects from the perspective of the challenges facing *digital cities* in Portugal. We begin by bringing empirical evidence on the Portuguese situation, as a specific case study within EU. Clearly, Portugal has significant quantitative shortcomings, but, at the same time, the country has been making good progress, in a catching-up dynamics that is well known. This combination of rapid catch up but persistent shortcomings make the Portuguese case useful to illustrate the main point of the paper: network societies occur across time and space and require the dynamic adaptation of infrastructures, incentives and institutions, in a way that calls our attention for the need to foster learning societies. The third section, informed by the empirical evidence associated with the analysis of the Portuguese situation, discusses current evidence from specific case studies, based on specific digital city projects. Finally, we conclude by briefly presenting policy implications, the necessary conditions for the establishment of knowledge driven activities and a summary of our most important conclusions.

2 Building the Diverse Network Society: Portugal in Europe

Focusing our attention to information and communication technologies (ICT), Figure 1 presents the intensity of ICT expenditure in 1997 against the growth rate of this intensity from 1992 to 1997. Following recent analysis for knowledge-based industries [10], the results show that Portugal was the leading OECD country in the growth rate of ICT expenditure from 1992 to 1997, with a growth rate of more than 10%, and mainly accounted for by increases in expenditures in telecommunications (about 9%). Expenditures in IT services and software are particularly low, below 1%, and only Turkey, Greece and Poland have shares of expenditure on IT software and services below the Portuguese value. The growth in this category has been equally dismal, below 2% a year.

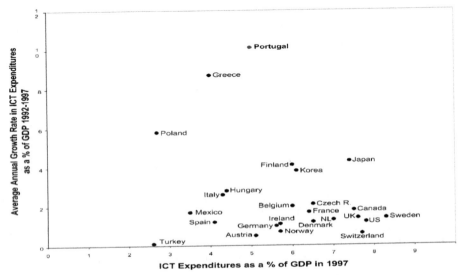

Fig. 1. ICT expenditures: level and growth (1992-97); *Source* [13]

In terms of our analysis, we would like to argue that the figure shows large variations associated with countries characterized by small absolute values, exhibiting patterns typical of latecomer industrialization for Portugal. In addition, the results may represent indications of the process through which latecomer countries become engaged in the new techno economic paradigm [11]. Most countries are clustered in the bottom of the figure, with growth rates below 4%. The levels, as indicated by the horizontal distribution of countries, confirm the perception that the US is a leading country. The expenditures on ICT as a percentage of GDP in the US are about 2% above the European average. Individual countries, such as Sweden, outperform the US, but most countries lag behind.

The evidence of still low absolute investments on ICT in Portugal is clearly illustrated in Table 1, which shows values per capita for sample European regions in the census whose programming documents indicate information society actions and that provide the necessary financial information [8]. It is clear that the table refers, above all, to regions that have attracted European structural funds and, on this basis, it is important to mention the wide diversity of situations and framework conditions for attracting these funds, which clearly influence any analysis to be considered. But for the purposes of our analysis, it is interesting to attempt defining the extent to which the performance of digital networks and cities would depend exclusively on the limitations of funds, as well as from the capacity to attract them.

Table 1. Expected ICT expenditure per capita, EU selected regions, 2000-06; Source: [8]

Border Midland & Western Region	357.8 €	Alentejo	44.5 €
La Rioja	357.8 €	Peloponese	43.1 €
South Aegean	269.4 €	Continental Greece	42.8 €
Ionian Islands	241.4 €	Algarve	42.5 €
Baleares Islands	238.2 €	Centro	29.9 €
Western Greece	151.1 €	Norte	13.3 €
Açores	117.9 €	Southern Scotland	9.2 €
Highlands & Islands	98.4 €	Lisboa e Vale do Tejo	6.8 €
Epirus	83.4 €	Liguria	2.2 €

Besides large growth rates in ICT investments, the extent to which the Portuguese society is engaged in the knowledge economy comparatively to other nations can be analysed making use of the recently established systematic assessment by the World Economic Forum in collaboration with INSEAD and the World Bank's *info*Dev programme through the "networked readiness" [12]. This indicator offers an aggregated idea of "the degree of preparation of a nation to participate in and benefit from ICT developments" and illustrates the still weak position of Portugal in the European context, only above Greece. The main point to note is that the results for Portugal and for most of the OECD countries appears to be dependent from other than the country's overall wealth (as measured in terms of GDP per capita). Portugal is in fact entering the cluster of countries where the effect of increasing GDP on network readiness is less pronounced and other factors, namely at institutional and contextual level, have been shown to particularly influence country's competitiveness [10].

The pattern of small absolute values regarding the mobilization of information society, but large variations, can be further analysed making use of a number of typical indicators to characterize the penetration of ICTs in a country. For example, Portugal had the highest Internet penetration rates in southern Europe for 2002 (Portugal 42%, Spain 42%, Italy 40%, Greece 18%, with an EU average of 51%), although far away from typical north European penetration rates [14]. A similar pattern can be observed in the use of Internet access in the household, with Portuguese rates of 31%, as compared with 29% for Spain and 9% for Greece, while 40% for the EU average and 74% for the USA, although Portugal exhibits growth rates between 2000 and 2002 considerably larger than the European average (namely 72% for Portugal, with 81% for Spain and 89% for France, as compared with 43% for EU average) [15]. Turning to the type of telecom infrastructure, the country follows typical average EU trends, with standard telephone lines as the most frequent connection to the Internet access at home (Portugal 74%, EU average 72%), followed by cable modem (Portugal 12%, EU average 7%). ISDN, ADSL and Wireless connections are still relatively low.

But the values presented above should be further explored in terms of the main point of this paper, in that we are aimed to improve our understating of the conditions necessary for digital networks to succeed. Learning from the conceptualization of knowledge-based economies [6], it can be said that, fundamentally, the performance in knowledge-rich competitive environments in terms of innovative performance depend on the quality of human resources (their skills, competencies, education level, learning capability) and on the activities and incentives that are oriented towards the generation and diffusion of knowledge. But beyond human capital, which corresponds to the aggregation of an individual capacity for knowledge accumulation, developing a collective capacity for learning—as suggested by Wright [16] in the context of the US—is as, if not more important, than individual learning. Instead of individual or even aggregated human capital, a further important concept for learning seems to be social capital, as analysed by Conceição et al. [17], among others.

Before further exploring social capabilities and related issues associated with the development of digital networks, we present below further evidence on the penetration of ICTs in Portugal through the analysis of specific projects aimed to build digital cities, namely making use of European structural funds.

3 Institutionalizing Digital Cities: Evidence from Portugal

The evidence presented in this section is built on the analysis of sample projects for digital cities and regions in Portugal, which have been structured around the electronic provisioning of local government administrative services complemented by some pilot projects in areas such as e-business and telemedicine.

The first experiences in Portugal with digital cities started in 1998 through a program jointly funded by the Portuguese Government (who contributed with 25% of the total investment through the national Science and Technology Foundation) and the European Union (75% of the total investments through the European Regional Development Fund). Private investments were insignificant. The program involved 5 small and mid-sized cities (Aveiro, Bragança, Guarda, Marinha Grande, Castelo Branco) and 2 rural regions (Trás-os-montes and Alentejo), as identified in Figure 2. The main objectives of the program were to (a) improve the quality of life in cities; (b) contribute to development of peripheral areas; (c) improve local economy and employment; and (d) fight info-exclusion and help citizens with special needs [18]. The project sites were chosen for reasons which are out of the scope of this paper and we concentrate our analysis on issues associated with their effective implementation.

Alentejo and Trás-os-montes are remote agricultural regions, among the least developed in Portugal and Europe, sparsely inhabited by an aging population. Both projects were designed to create new opportunities for the local population, mitigate social and economic disparities, promote regional networking and provide public administration electronic services to peripheral local parishes.

Aveiro is developing a true innovative and entrepreneurial image, in particular connection with the local university and the local branch of Portugal Telecom, which includes important research and development activities. On the other hand, Marinha Grande is particularly engaged in traditional, labour-intensive industries and the digital city project has been particularly promoted through the industrial network associated with the local moulds industry. Both these two projects invested mainly on local competitiveness and competence building.

Bragança, Guarda and Castelo Branco are peripheral cities with relative regional significance. Their approach was to support the adoption of information and communication technologies by individuals, firms, associations and local government and other public organizations.

Fig. 2. Main projects for the specific development of digital cities and regions, established over the period 1998-2001, making use of European structural funds. Adapted from [18]

3.1 The Overall Picture

In terms of regional penetration, Table 2 shows that the projects listed above covered about 11.30 % of the total Portuguese population (10.44% of the population under 15 years of age) and about 42% of the total surface of Portugal. All projects involved a broad range of relevant actors and change agents within each one of the territories being nonetheless always leaded by local municipalities. Local higher education institutions were particularly involved only in a limited number of projects (Aveiro, Bragança, Trás-os-Montes).

It should be noted that, at least for the initial projects analysed here, the institutional framework established by the central government was quite flexible and fostering local voluntary initiatives. It was based on the simple provision of guidelines focused on providing content and services related to local public administration and to specific activities with social implications (e.g., healthcare), economic impact (e.g, business-driven corporate networks for regional competitiveness), and aimed to promote cultural contents [19-22]. Initiatives to mobilize and promote the adoption of the Information Society were part of various applications, although not always considered at the required level, at least beyond that given to the implementation of infrastructures [21].

Table 2. Characterization of digital city projects (population and area) Source: INE, 2001

Municipality	Population	% total	Pop. < 15	% total	Km²	% total
Aveiro	69,560	0.67	12,160	0.73	208	0.23
Bragança	32,440	0.31	4,760	0.29	1,138	1.23
Castelo Branco	54,260	0.52	7,440	0.45	1,440	1.56
Guarda	38,560	0.37	6,230	0.38	709	0.77
Marinha Grande	33,370	0.32	5,050	0.30	186	0.20
Alentejo	510,690	4.93	71,930	4.34	27,227	29.55
Trás-os-Montes	431,540	4,17	65,450	3.95	11,122	12.07
Total	1,170,420	11.30	173,020	10.44	42,030	45.61

Table 3 show sample data in terms of public funds made available to the seven projects mentioned above, illustrating diversified situations, with levels of funds per capita raging from low to moderate when compared with those considered within the overall usage of European structural funds [8].

Within the broad range of digital city projects considered at international level [4], *Aveiro Digital* represents an interesting case study in that it has comprised diversified initiatives promoted and coordinated by an autonomous organization formed among the local government, the local University and the incumbent Telecommunication operator, PT Telecom. It represented the result of a long preparation effort and provided the opportunity to evaluate concepts and dynamically testing ideas, involving a limited but well informed group of people [21].

Bragança Digital focused on creating basic ICT infrastructures and wireless networking environment for local government buildings, health institutions, educational institutions, and local employment agency to provide information and services to local citizens. Other initiatives included the provision of local products (www.rural.net), health, educational and e-business activities [22].

Guarda Digital was promoted by and organization formed by the municipality, local educational institutes, associations" and the incumbent telecommunication operator. It included pilot projects in healthcare e-business, tele-working and educational initiatives [23].

Table 3. Public funds expenditure per capita, first phase of digital cities program, 1998-2000.

Project	Pop. (a)	investment	per capita
Aveiro	69,560	€ 5,590,000 (b)	€ 80.39
Marinha Grande	33,370	€ 1,200,000 (c)	€ 35.96
Bragança	32,440	€ 1,044,000 (d)	€ 32.18
Castelo Branco	54,260	€ 1,082,000 (e)	€ 19.94
Guarda	38,560	€ 350,000 (f)	€ 9.08
Trás-os-Montes	431,540	€ 1,735,000 (g)	€ 4.02
Alentejo	510,690	€ 1,500,000 (h)	€ 2.94

Sources: (a) INE, 2001; (b) PACD, Final Evaluation Report, 2001; (c) ; (d) Associação para o Desenvolvimento de Bragança, Final Evaluation Report, February 2001; (e) http://www.dpp.pt/pdf/info52.pdf; (f) http://www.freipedro.pt/tb/110698/guarda3.htm; (g) Final Evaluation Report, 2001; (h) http://home.telepac.pt/telepac/net/13/regionalismo_2.html.

Castelo Branco Digital aimed to connect all public institutions (municipality, social security and health institutions) and local associations (sports, culture and business) to provide an integrated information network to citizens and tourists. For example, it has included the provision in rich media of old Portuguese theatre contents [24].

Marinha Grande Digital, as managed by the local municipality and the Technological Centre associated with the moulds and plastic injection industries, focused on creating an Extranet to provide business-related (mould, plastics and glass) content and services and on facilitating communication among companies and clients. Other initiatives included a centre of advanced telecommunications to promote the use of the Internet [25].

Trás-os-Montes Digital included regionally-based web contents (i.e., www.espigueiro.pt), managed by the local University, that aggregates content and services of 31 municipalities. The portal is still managed by the local university and includes business and employment opportunities, geo-referenced information, healthcare facilities and technologies to coordinate medical services in rural areas [26]. An important feature of this project is the support network constituted by 84 service centers scattered throughout the region that provide public Internet access, as well as human support to help citizens' interactions with new technologies.

Alentejo Digital brought together 47 municipalities and 3 regional agencies to create a regional information network to provide services and territory-related content to citizens and local firms through regional web-based contents. The main objective was to enable local government teams to learn, use and promote new technologies, namely computer network management and digital content production and publishing. An Intranet was set up linking all municipalities and regional agencies to enable the necessary collaborative work environment. About 50 people were recruited, mostly from local unemployment lists, to work on the project that lasted until July 2001 [27].

Most of those people worked as local agents, based on each one of the town hall facilities of all the 47 municipalities involved, who proactively produced, collected or published relevant local content in the portal. Although they did not work directly with the general public, they were a very important factor of Internet diffusion in the territory covered by the project.

3.2 Building Competencies for Mobilizing the Information Society: Aveiro

Aveiro is a seaport, located at the Vouga estuary, with a population of 69,560. The city's innovative and active character, although recent, draws from the singular institutional framework established in close collaboration between the local university and the local business environment, mainly driven by the national telecommunication operator. Following the launch of the first Digital Cities public funding program in Portugal (1998-2000), the municipality, the university and the incumbent operator set up a public-private partnership to develop the idea of Aveiro Digital City focusing on (a) quality of life in the city; (b) democratic participation; (c) extensive access to public and private digital information and services; (d) local public administration modernization; (e) inclusive development and sustainable growth; and (f) job creation and lifelong learning [19-21]. The complete funding life cycle was expected to be 8 years, with the first phase of the project starting in February 1998 and lasting until December 2000, totalling an investment of 5,590,000 Euros. The second phase, originally planned to start in January 2001, has only begun on June 2003 and is planned to last until December 2006. The new round of public funding is expected to be some four times larger than the previous investment.

After a troubling start – budget allocation negotiations and bureaucracy caused lengthy delays, mostly for over than one year, in both the formal approval procedures and the technical implementation schedule – the first phase included 37 projects covering several different aspects of the use of information and communication technologies, as illustrated in Figure 3. Emphasis was given to infrastructures and digital contents, including local e-government, e-health, e-business and entertainment, as listed in Table 4.

a) Aveiro Digital City Centre
http://digipraca.aveiro-digital.net/)

b) Interactive learning website for kids
(http://www.cidadedamalta.pt/)

Fig. 3. Sample infrastructures and contents provided through *Aveiro Digital*.

E-business and education related activities accounted for 35.1% of the total number of approved projects and 40.7% of the budget allocated. E-government used up to 20.4% of the available funds. University-based and e-health projects included only two projects and utilized less than 9% of the total budget. On the other hand, entertainment, culture and arts accounted for about 30% of the total number of approved projects, but only received about 8% of the total budget available. In general, ICT infrastructure – computers, applications, Internet access and basic ICT training – was the most important component of all projects, while investments in activities oriented towards the mobilization of the population for the information society were practically inexistent.[1] Consequently, the evaluation of many activities claims for reduced levels of public participation, with some of the initiatives falling short from their original objectives [21]. E-government and other projects involving basic and secondary schools had more permanent effects, while e-commerce and e-health performed poorly. Budget cuts and uneven financing flows during the implementation phase posed extra difficulties and increased risk unnecessarily. Nonetheless, Aveiro is considered a paradigm to be followed in the development of digital cities in Portugal. The relative success of the project is argued to be dependent on three conditions: (a)

---

[1] The projects in Table 4 were chosen from 70 applications in a 'call for ideas' competition held in June 1998. 42 were approved, predominantly from public institutions or not-for-profit organizations and 37 projects were actually implemented.

Table 4. Main digital contents included in the first phase of the Aveiro Digital City Project. (source: http://www.aveiro-digital.pt/)

Intervention Areas	Main Activities	Main Related Websites
Communitiy Building (5 activities 1,040,000 €)	Internet access points in 13 public buildings and 5 cultural organizations	digipraca.aveiro-digital.net digibairros.aveiro-digital.net
e-Government (4 activities 1,139,000 €)	Municipality geographical and administrative information systems	n.a
	Water and sewage municipal services one-stop shop	www.smaveiro.pt
	Water quality sensing and monitoring system	www.simoqua.pt
	Justice Court Intranet	n.a
Education (7 activities 904,000 €)	Computers, Internet access and ICT training in local basic and secondary schools for teachers, parents and students	veraria.aveiro-digital.net cspveracruz.aveiro-digital.net membros.aveiro-digital.net/esvir
	Cybergames and interactive leaning applications	tictac.aveiro-digital.net www.cpj.ua.pt www.cidadedamalta.pt
Environment (1 activity 201,000 €)	Biology knowledge network	www.biorede.pt
Health (1 activity 267,550 €)	Computers, Internet access and ICT training for health professionals	saudenet.aveiro-digital.net
Social Cohesion (4 activities 216,618 €)	Computers, Internet access and ICT training for low income families and people with special needs.	Resea.aveiro-digital.net portal.ua.pt/projectos/meu bancoalimentar.aveiro-digital.net
	Teleworking	portal.ua.pt/projectos/ist
eBusiness (6 activities 1,372,088 €)	Computers, Internet access, services and ICT training for 20 SMEs.	n.a.
	Port authority telecommunication and management infrastructure.	n.a.
	eCommerce service centre	n.a.
	On-line shopping mall	http://www.aveiromegastore.com
	Livestock information network	n.a.
	eLearning and interactive training	www.ibjc.pt
Entertainment, Culture and Arts (10 activities 450,125 €)	Interactive TV pilot project	n.a.
	On-line news	www.netpaginas.pt
	Digital arts workshops	Oadgv.aveiro-digital.net
	Interactive listening music CD Rom	www.orquital.ua.pt
	12 public access information Kiosks	n.a.
	History, culture, art and nature from Aveiro	aveirana.doc.ua.pt camarinha.aveiro-digital.net www.net-moliceiro.inovanet.pt ciadanca.aveiro-digital.net

ICT skills locally available or capacity to learn; (b) existing ability to work within multidisciplinary teams; and (c) social responsibility [28].

Nonetheless, during 1999-2000, Aveiro Digital City made available 446 personal computers to diverse public and private organizations, published 8 CD ROMs and 32 websites, supplied 73 interactive services, and trained 529 people, as listed in Table 5. The number of Intranets and Extranets users exceeded 3,000 people in different public and private organizations and the Aveiro Digital City Website (www.aveiro-digital.pt) accounted for a monthly average of 4,700 visitors in 2000.

Table 5. Number of trainees and users, first phase Aveiro Digital City. Adapted from [19]

Trainees	Technical	28
	Teachers	108
	Students	47
	IS promoters	51
	Project Managers	38
	Public servants	257
	Total	529
Users	Internal	3,020
	External	4,700 unique visitors/month (year 2000)

The main question raised by local people involved in the project has been consistently associated with the structure of public financing and the conditions for long term sustainability, mainly due to the fact that when the limited public funds dried up some of the projects came to a close, while others kept their presence in the Internet although rarely updated. Moreover, the funding concentrated mostly on the inputs of a long change process, namely infrastructures, information systems and ephemeral content, giving little consideration to the improved understanding of forms of mobilizing the population at large.

The time frame of the project and the extent to which public funds were continuously available at the early stage appear to be critical conditions, namely to guarantee the evolution of a process of gradual competence building. This is a major issue learnt form the Aveiro project and here we refer to competence as skills and capacities, both individual and collective. It is important to stress that new skills are part of the competence foundation, but we are not necessarily arguing that technological change is skill-biased [2].

3.3 Fostering the Provision of Local Contents from Peripheral Zones, but Looking for Communities of Practices: The Case of Bragança

Bragança Digital City project, leaded by the local government and the local Technical Institute, promoted several initiatives that included basic ICT infrastructure, local e-government one-stop shop, Internet access in public schools, telemedicine and a very successful e-commerce website for local products (i.e., *RuralNet*). Several public service buildings were connected (local government, health institutions, schools and local employment agency) through a Wireless MAN [29], as partially shown in Fig. 4. The municipality implemented a management information system and a geographical information system that supported the provisioning of digital services by the Internet.

Other projects included an agricultural information network for the local irrigation perimeter and activities to attempt mobilizing young people.

a) *RuralNet* (source: http://www.ruralnet.pt/)   b) Wireless MAN (source: http://rdc.bcd.pt//)

Fig. 4. Sample digital contents and infrastructures provided trough *Bragrança Digital*

RuralNet (www.ruralnet.pt) was aimed to improve the competitiveness of rural SMEs by providing local firms with (a) innovative marketing ideas supported by digital technologies; (b) knowledge sharing environments and (c) new opportunities and new markets for their products and services. It mobilized several local manufacturers of high quality traditional goods – wine, olive oil, sausages, cheese and handcraft among others (total of 46 firms) – to sell their products and services through the Internet. The digital contents were developed at the local Polytechnic Institute in 1998 and were integrated in the *Bragança Digital City* project in 2000. The period of incubation of the project can de derived from the statistical information of Figure 5, which shows a lengthy, but significant process of market penetration although very low in comparison with traditional sales and orders. Although it involved about 40 providers of local products, 5 firms of smoked sausages, cutlery and cheese, had more than 50% of the total 1999 sales. Local clients accounted for only 25.6% of total number of orders, while orders from Lisbon (25.7%) and Porto (9.0%) together summed up almost the same number of orders as those from the rest of Portugal (34.4%). International sales totalled 5.3%.

Usually, local traditional manufacturers are very focused on production and lack the necessary competences and resources to address the needs of a global market. *RuralNet* makes available to local firms a new sales channel and a new marketing tool to expand local markets. It also provides training for all the partners and follows-up closely the information and communication technologies adoption process. Although net sales weren't very high, the mobilization effect among local firms was very strong and not only all of the companies that have participated in the first phase of the project continue to use and sell through the Internet.

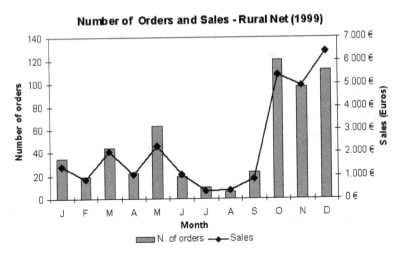

Fig. 5. Monthly evolution of orders and sales during the first year of operation of *"RuralNet"* (adapted from: www.ruralnet.pt).

4 Discussion and Conclusions

The evidence provided shows that mobilizing the information society at regional level may provide the necessary form of knowledge for the inclusive development of society at large, but it requires effective infrastructures, incentives and adequate institutional frameworks promoted over time and across space. Our discussion is framed within three main levels of analysis, namely infrastructures, contents and context, which are comparable with those schemes that consider five mains aspects, namely: infrastructure, access, applications and services, digital content development, and ICT skills development. In fact, the evidence provided by Lena Tsipouri throughout Europe [8] leaves us to jointly consider the first two levels under infrastructure, as well as to join applications and services and digital content developments into a single level of analysis. In addition, we broaden the scope of the so-called ICT skills development to include other contextual issues and local characteristics of communities of practice.

Turning to incentives, current understanding of knowledge-driven activities based on endogenous growth theories are based on the existence of dynamic externalities and imperfect markets, and require a careful understanding of the structure of competition. On the one hand, because of the nature of knowledge, investment of private agents often fails to acknowledge spill-over effects, or may not be able to anticipate the full extent to which there is further learning potential in a new technology. On the other hand, incentives to invest in new knowledge depend on the existence of some degree of monopolistic rents. These rents may not exist in latecomer countries exposed to international competition, if they are solely adopting foreign technology.

As a result, Conceição et al [1] call our attention that private investment levels (which result from the incentive structure provided by the market to economic agents) in activities with learning or spill-over potential tend to be lower than the social optimum, and may even generate what is known in the literature as 'low-level equilibrium traps' [30, 31]. In principle, these shortcomings of the market mechanism call for some sort of government intervention. Governments are concerned with making sure that societal costs and benefits are endogenized in the decisions of private firms. In a learning environment this may mean subsidizing specific activities, investing in education, or protecting infant industries [32, 33, 34]. But government intervention must balance the potential distortions on competition that may come from intervention with the needs to 'correct market failures'.

Against the background of the conditions described above, it is clear that digital cities cannot be promoted independently of an innovation policy fostering capacity and connectivity and that in turn innovation determines and is determined by the market. However, it is also clear that it will require an effective mix of public support mechanisms that take a relatively long-term perspective, taking into consideration specific regional and thematic aspects, thus promoting a diversified environment.

But still focusing on the issues of incentives and looking at their relation with the operational effectiveness of digital infrastructures, applications and services, figure 6 shows that the most important web contents associated with the digital city projects discussed before were available to the public domain only for the time public support was also available. Besides the notable exception of the Aveiro Digital Project, this result may be obvious for the local promoters of those projects, but should be acknowledge as a major issue for public policies fostering the information society. We will argue that early stage developments, as those we are considering throughout this paper, do require continuous support, together with adequate monitoring and evaluation procedures, in order to acquire the necessary strength for their sustainable development. The evidence is that market mechanisms do not necessarily work at the level of the issues associated with digital cities, namely in less favourable zones, where incentives structures should de effectively designed and adapt over time.

Although incentives and infrastructure greatly inform our understanding of economic development, they do not tell the whole story about the differences across the various projects discussed in section 3, or even across the countries briefly discussed in section 2 above. This is because both incentives and infrastructure do not operate in a vacuum, being shaped by and shaping the particular context where they operate. In the scope of our analysis, the city or region must have embedded a set of social capabilities that define the context under which digital cities evolve. Consideration of contextual issues in building-up network societies have not always been considered in many different situation throughout the world, as acknowledge by Castells [7], among others, and evidence shows that specific measures to promote adequate contexts in the projects considered in this paper have also been scarce.

If one considers the broad social and economic context under which digital cities may be facilitated, we must consider the conditions for integrated learning processes. This has led Conceição, Heitor and Lundvall [2] to build on Lundvall and Johnson's learning economy [35] and to discuss the learning society in terms of innovation and competence building with social cohesion. They view innovation as the key process that characterizes a knowledge economy understood from a dynamic

Table 6. Main initiatives (Aveiro and Bragança Digital Cities Programs 1998-2000)

Levels of Analysis		Projects	
		Aveiro	Bragança
Physical Infrastructures	Networking and Connectivity (a)	Local health institutions communication network; Internet at public schools; People with special needs	Municipality communication network; Internet access in public schools
	Information Systems (b)	Local public administration management information systems; Justice court Intranet; GIS	Municipality management information systems; GIS
Content (non-physical infrastructures)	Information Services (c)	City guide; Entertainment, Arts & culture initiatives; Local government website	City guide; Local government website
	Interactive Services (d)	e-business, Agriculture; Job opportunities; Environment; Teleworking	e-business; Telemedicine; Agriculture
Context (e)		Community building based on city metaphors	

Sources: (a) Networking and connectivity includes communication networks and Internet access; (b) Information Systems includes technological components that store and process data like data bases, electronic mail, ERPs, management information systems, content management, application serves and business intelligence software; (c) On-line presence or downloadable forms; (d) Electronic form submission or interaction through the web; (e) Mobilization and context building initiatives.

perspective, while competence is the foundation from which innovation emerges, and which allows many innovations to be enjoyed. In other words, it contributes both to the "generation" of innovations (on the supply side of the knowledge economy) and to the "utilization" of innovations (on the consumptions side of the knowledge economy). Conceptually, the foundations for the relationship between learning and economic growth have been addressed in the recent literature [36], with learning being reflected in improved skills in people and in the generation, diffusion, and usage of new ideas [37, 38, 39].

Learning can occur in many shapes and forms, some of which are informal, some formal. As described before, the institutional framework that comprise the national and regional systems of innovation formalize the technological infrastructure critical to generate the learning processes for individuals, firms, and nations, that ultimately lead to long-term development. Thus, looking at a particular set of organizations, their capabilities and related institutions, provides important lessons for development. This is the reason we argue for the need to combine adequate infrastructures and incentives with institutions, to foster the necessary context for digital cities to succeed.

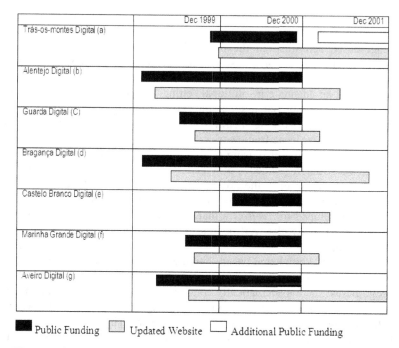

Fig. 6. Public funding of projects by the availability of updated web-contents.[2]

The analysis above is broad in scope and considers network societies as wide social and economic processes, which we argue occur across time and space and require the dynamic adaptation of infrastructures, incentives and institutions, in a way that calls our attention for the need to foster learning societies. However, the evidence of the projects discussed in this paper show that we must extend our analysis to other aspects of the learning society. This is because the experience of projects such as those developed in the cities of *Marinha Grande* and *Aveiro* clearly shows the important mutual relationships that specific project-based communities have on the facilitation of network societies, but also the fact that the implementation of digital cities may significantly improve the efficiency of those communities. In the following paragraphs, we extend this evidence and argue that the success of digital cities rely on the specific development of knowledge-integrated communities, KICs.

---

[2] (a) 10 Municipalities; 20 "Juntas de Freguesia"; Regional Agricultural Agency; Hospitals of Vila Real, Chaves e Macedo de Cavaleiros; 80 basic and secondary schools; Trás-os-Montes and Alto Douro University (UTAD). The second phase started January 2001 and it will end October 2003 (source: SCETAD, Trás-os-Montes Digital Presentaion, Vidago, November 20-21, 2002); (b) Only 8 out 47 municipalities were connected during the first half of 1999 (source: http://www.alentejodigtal.pt); (c) A very limited pilot project of Telemedicine started April 1999 (source: http://www.ipg.pt/adsi/); (d) Most of the projects started in February 1999. RuralNet Started on January 2000 (source: Associação para o Desenvolvimento de Bragança, Final Evaluation Report, February 2001); (e) Website still available but there is no updated information since April 2001; (f) Website still available but no updated information since March 2001; (g) Projects submission and evaluation started in July 1998, but only started implementation in May 1999 (source: PACD, Final Evaluation Report, 2001).

We refer to project-based communities, oriented to specific social and economic goals, that will benefit, and gain from, digital networks if particularly challenges by knowledge-based activities. In the case of *Marinha Grande* the evidence is that economically-oriented networks based on mould-forming companies has particularly launch business networks, which still require long-term processes and continuous funding, as well an adequate institutional setting. In this case, it should be noted the role of the related industrial association and technology centre in promoting the necessary links and networking facilities, which again support our previous analysis of the need to consider basic framework conditions.

In a different scale, but also using relatively reduced level of incentives, namely at an international scale, the evidence provided by the *RuralNet Project* developed in the city of *Bragança* also shows the critical importance of project-based mechanism to support and sustain digital cities. But of specific interest in our context, are some of the activities developed in *Aveiro*, in that knowledge-based activities could promote and sustain digital networks well beyond the period under which public incentives were made available.

The reason why knowledge-based activities are particularly prone to foster and sustain digital networks is because they will increasingly rely on "distributed knowledge bases", as a systematically coherent set of knowledge, maintained across an economically and/or socially integrated set of agents and institutions, as discussed by Smith [40] and Conceição et al [1], among others. The relevance of considering distributed knowledge bases across economically and/or socially integrated set of agents and institutions leads us to the concept of social capital. In the broadest sense, social capital is associated with the "social capabilities" [41] that allow a country or region to move forward in the process of development. In a more sophisticated treatment, Coleman states that social capital is "a variety of different entities, with two elements in common: they all consist of some aspect of social infrastructure, and they facilitate certain actions of actors—whether personal or corporate actors—within the structure." The relationship of social capital for the economic performance of nations was recognized by Olson [42] and North [43], in broad descriptions of the process of development.

In Portugal, most of the complex social, economic and political advances towards the Information Society are governed by public decisions. The evidence provided in this paper shows that investments in ICT infrastructures, although very necessary, haven't been sufficient to create a sustainable knowledge-based living and working environment. Consistent public policies, innovative regulatory frameworks and strong incentives are thus needed to create over time the conditions to catch up with more developed societies and mitigate the uncertainty associated with the adjustment process [6].

Within this perspective, our analysis calls for policies that consider long-term approaches of dynamic environments, which require continuous monitoring and evaluation. Specific incentives for infrastructures should continue, but articulated with the need to foster knowledge integrated communities as drivers of larger communities of users. This requires a continuous pubic effort, but also a better understanding of the effectiveness of the mix of public support mechanisms and private incentives for the development of digital cities.

The analysis is based on observations in different Portuguese metropolitan areas and regions with the ultimate goal of increasing regional competitiveness, by promoting public awareness and participation in decision-making processes. It is argued that the territory is a basic infrastructure that justifies and invites for the construction of several layers of information, but above all for communication infrastructures and digital contents, but well arranged with local contexts. It is suggested that knowledge driven communities, KICs, are important drivers of larger communities of users and different types of KICs are identified. Particular attention is suggested for those established among basic and secondary schools with university and research groups and evidence is provided from sample case studies in Portugal.

Our analysis led us to suggest that while the role of institutions needs to be re-examined, the variety of demands and the continuously changing social and economic environment is calling for diversified systems able to cope with the need to produce policies that nurture and enhance the learning society. We refer to the need for individuals, firms and organizations to operate in dynamic environments, where markets and technology are changing fast and in unpredictable ways. This calls for the need to combine adequate infrastructures and incentives with institutions, to foster the necessary context for digital cities to succeed. The institutional framework should be dynamically considered in order to foster local conditions over time, and this does not necessarily mean less government, but rather continuous public support and monitoring.

References

1. Conceição, P., Heitor, M.V., Veloso, F.: Infrastructures, Incentives and Institutions: Fostering Distributed Knowledge Bases for the Learning Society. In: Technological Forecasting and Social Change 70 (2003) 2
2. Conceição, P., Heitor, M.V., Lundvall, B.-A. (eds.): Innovation, Competence Building, and Social Cohesion in Europe - Towards a Learning Society, London: Edward Elgar, 2003
3. Fischer, M., Dietz, J., Snickars, F.: Metropolitan Innovation Systems: Theory and Evidence from Three Metropolitan Regions in Europe, Springer-Verlag, Berlin, 2001
4. Tanabe, M., Van den Besselaar, P., Ishida, T.: Digital Cities II – Computational and Sociological approaches. Berlin, Springer Verlag 2002
5. Mitchell, W.: City of Bits. MIT Press, 1995
6. Mansell, R., Steinmueller, W.E.: Mobilizing the Information Society. Oxford University Press, 2000
7. Castells, M.: The Internet Galaxy, Reflections on the Internet, Business and Society. Oxford University Press, 2001
8. Tsipouris, L.: Final Report for the Thematic Evaluation of the Information Society. Technopolis, 2002
9. European Commission: e-Europe 2005, an Information Society for All. COM(2002)263. Brussels, 2002
10. Conceição, P., Heitor, M.V.: Innovation and Competence Building: Learning from the Portuguese Path in the European Context. Connecticut, Praeger, Greenwood Publ. 2003
11. Freeman, C., Louçã, F.: As Time goes By, Oxford Univ. Press, 2002
12. Dutta, S., Jain, A.: The Networked Readiness of Nations, The Global Information Technology Report 2002-2003. World Bank's InfoDev Programme 2003
13. OECD: Information Technology Outlook. Paris: OECD 2002
14. Eurobarometer 2003, http://europa.eu.int/comm/research/press/2003/pdf/cc-report_en.pdf
15. EOS Gallup Europe: Flash EB N°125 - Internet and the Public at Large. European Commission (Directorate General «Information Society») (2002)

16. Wright, G.: Can a Nation Learn? American Technology as a Network Phenomenon. In: N. Lamoreaux, D.M.G. Raff, P. Temin (eds): Learning by Doing in Markets, Firms, and Countries. University of Chicago Press, Chicago and London (1999)
17. Conceição, P., Gibson, D.V., Heitor, M.V., Sirilli, G.: Knowledge for Inclusive Development: the Challenge of Globally Integrated learning and Implications for Science and Technology Policy. Technological Forecasting and Social Change 66 (2000) 1- 29
18. MCT: Iniciativa Internet. Portuguese Ministry of Science and Technology, Lisbon (1997) (in Portuguese)
19. Aveiro Digital City Coordination Team: Relatório de Avaliação do PACD_1998-2000. (2001) Available from http://www.aveiro-digital.pt/
20. Municipality of Aveiro, University of Aveiro, Portugal Telecom, S.A: Programa Aveiro — Cidade Digital. (1998) Available from http://www.aveiro-digital.pt/
21. Aveiro Digital City Coordination Team: Relatório Global da 1ª Fase do Programa Aveiro Cidade Digital 1998 – 2000. (2001) Available from http://www.aveiro-digital.pt/
22. Associação para o Desenvolvimento de Bragança Cidade Digital: Relatório Final Bragança, Cidade Digital". (2001) Available from http://www.braganca-digital.pt/
23. http://www.ipg.pt/adsi/; Guarda Digital
24. http://www.cm-castelobranco.pt/cb_digital/; Castelo Branco Digital
25. http://www.marinhagrandedigital.com/; Marinha Grande Digital
26. http://www.espigueiro.pt/; Trás-os-Montes Digital
27. http://www.alentejodigital.pt/; Alentejo Digital
28. Rocha, N: A Digital Town. In: W. McIver Jr., A. Elmagarmid (eds.): Advances in Digital Government, Technology, Human Factors and Policy. Kluwer Academic Publishers, Boston (2002)
29. Amaro, J., Lopes, R.: A Wireless MAN in Bragança – Digital City. Instituto Politécnico de Bragança, Bragança (2001)
30. Tsipouri, Lena: Europe and the Information Society: Problems and Challenges for Supranational Intervention. In: Journal of Comparative Policy Analysis: Research and Practice 2 (2000) 301–319
31. Azariadis, C., Drazen, A: Threshold Externalities in Economic Development. In: Quarterly Journal of Economics 105 (1990) 501-526
32. Aghion, P., Howitt, P.: Endogenous Growth Theory. Cambridge, MA; MIT Press (1998)
33. Shapiro, H., Taylor, L.: The State and Industrial Strategy. In: World Development 18 (1990) 861-875
34. Chandler, A., Hikino, T.: The Large Industrial Enterprise and the Dynamics of Modern Economic Growth. In: A. Chandler, F. Amatori, T. Hikino (eds), Big Business and the Wealth of the Nations, New York: Cambridge University Press (1996)
35. Lundvall, B.-A., Johnson, B.: The Learning Economy. Journal of Industry Studies 1 (1994) 23-42
36. Bruton, H.J.: A Reconsideration of Import Substitution. Journal of Economic Literature 27 (1998) 903-936
37. Conceição, P., Heitor, M.V.: Knowledge Interaction towards Inclusive Learning, Promoting Systems of Innovation and Competence Building. Technological Forecasting and Social Change 69 (2002) 641-651
38. Lamoreaux, N., Raff, D.M.G., Temin, P. (eds.): Learning by Doing in Markets, Firms, and Countries. Chicago, University of Chicago Press (1999)
39. Arrow, K.: The Economic Implications of Learning by Doing. In: Review of Economic Studies 28 (1962) 155-73
40. Smith, K.: What is the Knowledge Economy? Knowledge-Intensive Industries and Distributed Knowledge Bases. UNU-INTECH Discussion Paper 2002-6; also available from http://www.intech.unu.edu/publications/index.htm (2002)
41. Coleman, J.: Social Capital in the Creation of Human Capital. In: American Journal of Sociology 94 (1988) S95-S120

42. Olson, M.: The Rise and Decline of Nations—Economic Growth, Stagflation, and Social Rigidities, New Haven, CT; Yale University Press (1982)
43. North, D.C.: Institutions, Institutional Change and Economic Performance. Cambridge, Cambridge University Press (1990)

Author Index